THE LAWS

OF

PLATO

Translated, with NOTES
and an INTERPRETIVE ESSAY, *by*

THOMAS L. PANGLE

The University of Chicago Press

CHICAGO AND LONDON

The University of Chicago Press, Chicago 60637
The University of Chicago Press, Ltd., London

08 07 06 05 04   6 7 8 9 10

Reprinted by arrangement with Basic Books, Inc.

Library of Congress Cataloging in Publication Data

Plato.
  The laws of Plato.

  Reprint. Originally published: New York : Basic
Books, c1980.
  Bibliography: p.
  Includes index.
  1. State, The—early works to 1800. 2. Political
science—Early works to 1800.   I. Pangle, Thomas L.
II. Title.
JC71.P2633 1988   321'.07   87-25563
ISBN 0-226-67110-0 (pbk.)

To Allan Bloom

Contents

Translator's Preface

This translation aims at the greatest literalness attainable within the confines of sound and comprehensible English. It has been my aspiration to come as close as a translator can to providing direct and undistorted access to Plato's thought, exactly as Plato expressed it. Underlying this effort is the conviction that we can no longer remain satisfied with the loose, if polished and graceful, translations of Plato executed under the influence of traditional classical scholarship. We live in an age when reading knowledge of Greek cannot be presumed to be part of the intellectual equipment of thoughtful citizens, students, and scholars; yet at the same time we find ourselves in the grip of increasingly serious doubts about the meaning and validity of the fundamental political principles we have inherited from the Enlightenment, principles that have gone largely unchallenged for generations. These doubts, if thought through, urgently impel us to recover a detailed and unbiased understanding of the alternative, classical conception of man and political life. In this unprecedented situation the precise translation of Greek philosophic texts takes on an importance, and the responsibility of the translator assumes a gravity, that has rarely before been equaled. The time is past when the translator could look upon himself as an elegant paraphraser, offering popularized and lively versions of classical culture to readers who are too young or too disadvantaged to have acquired a gentleman's education. What is more, the translator alive to his responsibilities ought no longer to feel confident that he is contributing to a "clarification" of Platonic thought when he employs easily assimilated modern categories and terminology to rephrase Plato's baffling oddities, obscurities, and apparent confusions or contradictions; for our distrust of the certainty of all modern philosophic categories, our willingness to question once-unquestionable givens of our modern Western culture, has opened us to the suspicion that it is precisely the most peculiar-sounding Platonic passages that have the potential of revealing to us the limitations of our own intellectual horizon.

It is in this spirit, and with this conception of my task, that I have undertaken the present translation. I have not had in view the reader who wishes to get a hasty, easy, and superficial impression of Plato;

instead, I have tried to respond to the needs of the reader who is intent on encountering in its entirety the thought-provoking strangeness and complexity of Plato's way of thinking about politics. In bending all my efforts to reproducing exactly the thought and content of the speeches in the *Laws*, I have necessarily had to assign a lesser priority to the goal of creating an echo of their style. To gain a fuller taste of that style (which captures perfectly the tone of a conversation between old statesmen who meet one another for the first time, and subsequently become engaged in the solemn task of lawgiving), the reader should perhaps supplement my translation with others. But if he wishes truly to savor the style, he must, I am afraid, learn to read the Greek.

I have been fortunate in being able to base my translation on Des Places's and Diès's recent edition of the Greek text.[1] By carrying out a far more extensive and painstaking collation of the manuscripts than has ever before been achieved, they have produced a text that surpasses in reliability all previous versions, and, in addition, have provided us with a new and rich awareness of almost all the important variant readings. The only other English translation based on this first truly critical edition is that of Trevor Saunders.[2] Since the principles that inform what Saunders calls his "Penguinification" are diametrically opposed to those that inform my translation, a brief consideration of what Saunders has to say will delineate more sharply the character of the present translation.

Saunders is convinced that "modern readers" are incapable of appreciating—or even reading through—the *Laws* without the help of numerous "aids" invented by the translator: "The translator must perforce go to some trouble to *present* and *interpret* his text to his modern readership. He must, to put it crudely, be something of a showman" (Saunders's italics). Plato's work must be broken up into sections and subsections, "attractively labeled and listed so as to give the prospective reader an idea of the contents, and short enough to encourage him to dip his finger into the pie." "But these appetite-whetters are not enough." In order to sugarcoat Plato, Saunders has resorted to what he calls "overtranslations," creating "versions louder than the originals." Saunders does not hesitate to confess that

1. *Les Lois,* in Platon, *Oeuvres Complètes,* vols. 11–12 (Paris: Société d'Édition "Les Belles Lettres," 1951–56).

2. Plato, *The Laws* (Harmondsworth, England: Penguin Books, 1970). The quotations that follow are taken from pages 39–40 of the "Introduction" to this translation, and from Saunders's more extensive discussion in "The Penguinification of Plato," *Greece and Rome,* 2nd series, 22, no. 1 (April, 1975), pp. 19–28.

"a number of colloquialisms have been admitted as spice." Still, "overtranslation is one thing; mistranslation is another. Should one ever dare to cultivate inaccuracy?" Saunders answers his question strongly in the affirmative: "deliberate technical inaccuracy" is justified by the need to infuse Plato's "rather wooden" writing with "idiom and colour." "The style of a version must, it is true, be determined partly by the nature and purpose of the original text" (Saunders generously concedes), but "it must be determined also by the current status of the text and the characteristics of the intended readership of the translation." Saunders aims at the casual reader, who while "skimming through" will be encouraged to "pick out rapidly those parts of the text likely to be relevant to him." Saunders takes no account of the obstacles that are thus placed in the way of the serious reader, who does not approach the *Laws* to quarry what fits his preconceived notions of "relevance" but rather seeks to engage Plato's work as a *whole,* as part of an open-minded and unfinished quest for the true standards of relevance.

Given Saunders's attitude of condescension toward both the reader and what he characterizes as Plato's "careless" Greek, it is perhaps no surprise to find that he disdains to preserve consistency in his translation of important political, psychological, and philosophical terms in Plato's vocabulary. As a result, the reader using Saunders's translation is unable to follow the evolution of terms like virtue, justice, citizenship, the soul, and nature; moreover, any attempt to undertake a systematic comparison between two different speeches dealing with a similar theme is bound to be hamstrung.

But what is most amazing about Saunders's approach is that in his rather clumsy attempt to import an alien liveliness into the *Laws* he is almost oblivious to the subtle details by which Plato portrays the characters of the old interlocutors and their appropriately subdued, though intense, interplay. The *Laws* is far more than a set of speeches about law; through the interaction of the characters Plato intends to show how a philosopher might win the confidence of powerful old political leaders and guide them towards a revolutionary refounding. The drama reveals the rare conditions and special rhetoric which would be needed to carry out this delicate project: what is at issue is nothing less than the question of the degree to which theory, and the human type that embodies the life of reason, can guide political practice. To understand the meaning of any speech in the *Laws,* then, one must be keenly aware of its place in the dramatic context. And this context—the changing moods and crucial junctures of the dramatic interchange—is revealed by such features as the interlocutors' oaths, hesitations, and repetitions, their interruptions of one another, and the diversity in the ways they address each other. Far from allowing the reader to see such things, Saunders consistently smooths out, deadens, and even removes what he apparently regards as these cumbersome or jarring trifles of Plato's artistry.

The translations made by Taylor and Bury early in this century,[3] though based on inferior Greek texts, are considerably more reliable than Saunders's. This is especially true in the case of Bury, who only occasionally lapses into paraphrase. Indeed, by employing a somewhat archaic English, replete with antique connective words and constructions, Bury manages to reproduce the lengthy and elaborate sentence structure of the original better than I. Unfortunately, neither Bury nor Taylor is at much pains to maintain consistency in translating key terms, and both take a rather cavalier attitude toward the dramatic details of the dialogue. The only previous translation that has attempted to be strictly literal, that of George Burges,[4] is marred by the translator's uncertain grasp of Greek and by his willingness to carry literalness to the point of unintelligibility.

The criticisms I have leveled against earlier translators should not be taken to mean that I do not feel obliged to my classicist colleagues for the important advances that have been made in our understanding of the textual difficulties in the Greek manuscripts of the *Laws*. Testimony to this indebtedness will be found in my notes, where I have tried to indicate all important variant readings or textual ambiguities, and have referred the reader to fuller scholarly discussions of these obscurities.[5] The notes are also meant to shed light on the historical, mythological, and poetic references that abound in the *Laws*, and whose original contexts—when they can be determined—always illuminate the significance of what is being said by the speaker. In addition, I have frequently noted the first appearance of important words, so as to give the reader an appreciation of their broad meaning.

In the notes, as in the translation, I have striven to avoid as

3. Plato, *The Laws*, trans. A. E. Taylor (London: Everyman's Library, 1934); Plato, *The Laws*, 2 vols., trans. R. G. Bury (Cambridge, Mass.: The Loeb Classical Library, 1926).

4. *The Laws*, trans. George Burges, in *The Works of Plato*, 6 vols., vol. 5 (London: George Bell and Sons, 1880).

5. As will be evident, I have had constant recourse to E. B. England's masterful and authoritative philological commentary, *The Laws of Plato*, 2 vols. (Manchester: University Press, 1921).

much as possible the imposition of any interpretation. My interpretive reflections are reserved for the essay that is appended to the translation. The essay is written in such a way as to be of most value to those readers who turn to it after they have immersed themselves in the *Laws* and have arrived at some interpretive hypotheses of their own. For such readers, the confrontation between their views and the distillation of my own study of the dialogue will, I hope, stimulate a continuous rereading and reconsideration of Plato's text.

In attempting to unravel Plato's substantive teaching in the *Laws*, I have not derived much assistance from the scholarly literature. Almost without exception, that literature approaches Plato in the light of modern preconceptions which prevent one's taking Plato seriously, as a thinker who may have liberated himself from his historical culture in all important respects and who claims to have uncovered the permanent nature of political life. I have, however, benefited from the two extant philosophical treatments—Farabi's *Summary of Plato's Laws* 6 and, above all, Leo Strauss's *The Argument and the Action of Plato's Laws.* 7 Each of these books is a work of philosophy in its own right, characterized by amazing concision, and making enormous demands upon the reader. Farabi's *Summary* is in fact a re-working and re-presentation of Plato's teaching, in a new form that is only rather loosely connected to the *Laws* and that is adapted primarily for an audience of Islamic readers; in my essay I have occasionally indicated passages in the *Summary* which illuminate a particular passage or point in the *Laws*, but I have not pretended to discuss thematically Farabi's overall interpretation. Strauss's work is to a far greater degree a commentary on Plato's dialogue, and I have accordingly found it much more accessible and helpful. I am sure I have not begun to profit from many of the treasures Strauss's dense and obscure book contains, but I believe I have progressed far enough in understanding it to be able to appreciate something of the didactic achievement it represents. Strauss has constructed a commentary that remains almost impenetrable until one has gained an intimate and long-meditated familiarity with the *Laws;* but when one turns to Strauss after having begun to secure such familiarity, one realizes that Strauss intends to indicate what he regards as the

6. A portion of Farabi's *Summary* has been translated and printed in R. Lerner and M. Mahdi, eds., *Medieval Political Philosophy: A Sourcebook* (Ithaca: Cornell University Press, 1972). I have made use of an unpublished working translation of the entire *Summary* made by Muhsin Mahdi.

7. Leo Strauss, *The Argument and the Action of Plato's Laws* (Chicago: University of Chicago Press, 1975).

most important observations that must be made in studying the *Laws*, and the order in which these pieces of evidence must be considered. Much of the full thinking-through of the import of these ordered observations is left to the reader. Strauss thus performs the function of the highest sort of guide or teacher, focusing his readers' gaze and drawing them back from wandering confusion, but leaving to them the challenge, and the satisfaction, of completing the interpretive thought. If and when that thought is completed, one sees with perfect clarity the reasons for Strauss's choice of emphasis; until then, one is engaged in a kind of fascinating argument or dialogue with Strauss about the *Laws*—wondering why Strauss stresses what he does, in the order that he does. Sometimes, one is also led to disagree, however tentatively and cautiously. My own essay is the fruit of such a dialogue with Strauss, and with Plato. I must leave it to others to judge the extent to which the differences between my commentary and Strauss's are due to divergences in understanding as opposed to divergences in purpose—for I, of course, have intended to address a less rare or restricted audience, and as a result have provided a much more expansive commentary.

I am indebted to the National Endowment for the Humanities for supporting me during one of the years which I devoted to this project, and to the American Academy in Rome for allowing me to make use of its excellent library during that year. The A. Whitney Griswold Fund at Yale University paid for much of the typing of the final manuscript. A number of persons gave generously of their time to read early drafts of portions of the translation and offer suggestions: I extend my thanks to David Bolotin, Christopher Bruell, Ralph Lerner, Carnes Lord, Diane Rennell, and Arlene Saxenhouse. Certain sections of the interpretive essay have benefited from criticisms offered by Laurie Fendrich Danford, Lorraine Smith, and members of the Boston Area Political Theory Group.

THOMAS L. PANGLE
April, 1979

THE LAWS

THE LAWS[1]

[or *On Lawgiving*]

DRAMATIS PERSONAE

An Athenian Stranger[2]
Kleinias
Megillus

BOOK I

Ath.   Is it a god or some human being,[3] strangers, who is given the   624a
credit for laying down your laws?

Kl.   A god, stranger, a god—to say what is at any rate the most just
thing. Among us Zeus, and among the Lacedaimonians, from
whence this man here comes, I think they declare that it's
Apollo. Isn't that so?

Meg.   Yes.

Ath.   Don't you people follow Homer,[4] and say that Minos got   624b
together with his father every ninth year and was guided by
his oracles in establishing the laws for your cities?[5]

Kl.   So it is said among us. And also that his brother Rhadamanthus,[6] at least—you've both heard the name—became   625a
very just. We Cretans, at any rate, would assert that he won
this praise because he regulated judicial affairs correctly in
those times.

Ath.   His fame is splendid[7] at least, and very appropriate for a son
of Zeus. But since you and this man here were reared in such
conventions and habits, I expect it would not be unpleasant
for you to pass the present time[8] discussing the political
regime[9] and laws, talking and listening as we go on our way.   625b
The road from Knossos to the cave and temple of Zeus[10] is altogether long enough, as we hear, and there are resting places
along the way, appropriate for this stifling heat; there are
shady spots under tall trees, where it would be fitting for men
of our age to pause often. Encouraging one another with
speeches, we would thus complete the whole journey in ease.

Kl.   And as one goes along this route, stranger, there are groves   625c

[3]

with cypresses [11] of amazing height and beauty, and meadows in which we could rest and pass the time.

Ath. What you say is correct.

Kl. Yes indeed. And when we see them we'll assert it even more emphatically. But let's proceed, accompanied by good fortune.

Ath. So be it. Tell me this, now. For what reason has your law ordained the common meals, and also the gymnastic training and the weapons you employ?

Kl. I think, stranger, that it's easy for anyone to understand our ways. As you can both see, the nature [12] of the entire Cretan

625d countryside is not flat like the Thessalian, [13] and hence, while they use horses more, we depend on running. The unevenness of the terrain here is more fitted to the practice of running on foot. In such country light arms, not heavy arms, are necessary if one is to be able to run, and the lightness of bows and arrows seems to harmonize with this. [14] So all these practices of

625e ours exist with a view to war, and to me at least it appears that our lawgiver had this in view in everything he did. Thus with the common meals: it's very likely he set them up after seeing that all men, when on a military campaign, are compelled by the business to eat together during this time in order to keep up their guard. I believe he condemned the mindlessness of the many, who do not realize that for everyone throughout the whole of life an endless war exists against all cities. And if, when a state of war exists, defense requires common meals

626a and orderly relays of rulers and ruled among the guards, then this same thing should be done in peacetime. For what most humans call peace he held to be only a name; in fact, for everyone there always exists by nature an undeclared war among all cities. If you look at it this way, you are pretty sure to find that the lawgiver of the Cretans established all our customs, public

626b and private, with a view to war, and that he handed down the laws to be guarded according to these principles. For according to him nothing is really beneficial, neither possessions nor customs, unless one triumphs in war. For then all the good things of the defeated belong to the victors.

Ath. You appear to me, stranger, to have had a fine gymnastic training [15] in understanding the legal customs of the Cretans. But explain this to me more clearly: the definition you seem to

626c me to have given for a well-governed city is that it must be ordered in such a way as to defeat the other cities in war. Isn't that so?

Kl. By all means. And I think that's how it seems to this man here.

Meg. How else would any Lacedaimonian answer, you divine man? [16]

Ath. Well, is it the case that this definition is correct for cities, in relation to cities, but that another would be correct for a neighborhood, in relation to another neighborhood? [17]

Kl. In no way.

Ath. The same applies?

Kl. Yes.

Ath. What then? For a household in relation to another household in the neighborhood, and for one man in relation to another man, the same still?

Kl. The same.

Ath. For a person in relation to himself, should the relationship be understood to be one of enemy to enemy? Or how then should we speak of this? 626d

Kl. O Athenian stranger—I would rather not address you as merely "Attic," for you seem to me worthy of being called rather by the name of the goddess—you have correctly followed the argument up to its source and have thus made it clearer, so that you will the more easily discover that we were correct just now in saying that all are enemies of all in public, and in private each is an enemy of himself.

Ath. What are you saying, you amazing man? 626e

Kl. Why, right here, stranger, is the first and best of all victories, the victory of oneself over oneself; and being defeated by oneself is the most shameful and at the same time the worst of all defeats. These things indicate that there is a war going on in us, ourselves against ourselves.

Ath. Let's turn the argument back in the reverse direction. Given that each one of us is superior [18] to himself or inferior to himself, should we also assert that a house and a neighborhood and a city all have this same thing within them? Or should we not assert it? 627a

Kl. You mean that one is superior to itself and another inferior?

Ath. Yes.

Kl. You're correct in asking this. Now such a situation certainly does exist, and not least in cities. For in those where the better men are victors over the majority, and the worse, the city would correctly be said to be superior to itself, and would very justly be praised for such a victory. But the opposite would hold where the opposite things happen.

627b Ath. Let's set aside the question whether the worse can ever somehow be superior to the better (that would require a longer discussion). Here is how I now understand what you are saying:
sometimes citizens of a common stock and of the same city
become unjust and numerous, and combine to enslave by
force the just who are less numerous. When they do prove superior, the city itself would correctly be said to be inferior to
itself and at the same time bad; but where they prove inferior,
stronger and good.

627c Kl. What is now being said is very odd, stranger; yet it is very
necessary to agree to it.

Ath. Just a moment—let's also consider this once again: where
there were many brothers, the sons of one man and one
woman, it wouldn't be at all surprising if more of them turned
out unjust and fewer of them just.

Kl. No, it wouldn't.

Ath. Now it wouldn't be fitting for me and the two of you to go
hunting after whether the whole household or family should
itself be called "inferior to itself" when the wicked are vic-

627d torious, and "superior" when they are inferior; we aren't now
investigating the speech employed by the many with a view to
the question of the seemliness or unseemliness of words, but
rather with a view to laws, seeking whatever in them constitutes correctness and faultiness according to nature.

Kl. What you say is very true, stranger.

Meg. I agree that what you've said so far, at least, is certainly fine.

Ath. Then let's look at this: presumably there would be some judge
for these brothers just mentioned?

Kl. By all means.

627e Ath. Which would be better: the one who destroyed the wicked
among them and set the better to ruling themselves, or the one
who made the worthy men rule and allowed the worse to live
while making them willing to be ruled? But I suppose we
should also mention the judge who is third in respect to virtue[19]—if there should ever be such a judge—one capable of

628a taking over a single divided family and destroying no one, but
rather reconciling them by laying down laws for them for the
rest of time and thus securing their friendship for one another.

Kl. Such a judge and lawgiver would be better by far.

Ath. And surely he would be enacting laws for them with a view
not to war but to its opposite.

[6]

Kl.   That is true.

Ath. Now what about someone who brings harmony to the city?
      Would he order its way of life with a view more to external
      war or more to that internal war called "civil war," which   628b
      occurs from time to time and which everyone would wish
      never to come to pass in his city and, if it does, would wish to
      end as soon as possible?

Kl.   Clearly, with a view to this latter.

Ath. Which of these sets of circumstances would someone prefer:
      civil peace brought about by the destruction of some and the
      victory of others, or friendship as well as peace brought about
      through reconciliation—supposing it were necessary to pay
      attention to external enemies?

Kl.   Everyone would prefer the latter rather than the former for his   628c
      own city.

Ath. Then wouldn't the lawgiver also?

Kl.   How could he not?

Ath. And doesn't everyone set up all his lawful customs for the sake
      of what is best?

Kl.   How could he not?

Ath. The best, however, is neither war nor civil war—the necessity
      for these things is to be regretted—but rather peace and at the
      same time goodwill towards one another. Moreover, it is
      likely that even that victory of the city over itself belonged not   628d
      to the best things but to the necessary things. To think other-
      wise is as if someone held that a sick body, after it had re-
      ceived a medical purgation, were in the best active condition,
      and never turned his mind to a body which had no need of
      such remedies at all. Likewise, with regard to the happiness of
      a city or of a private person, anyone who thought this way
      would never become a correct statesman, if he looked first and
      only to external wars, and would never become a lawgiver in
      the strict sense, if he didn't legislate the things of war for the
      sake of peace rather than the things of peace for the sake of   628e
      what pertains to war.

Kl.   This argument appears somehow to be stated correctly,
      stranger; but I would be amazed if our customs and those of
      Lacedaimon were not directed, in all seriousness, to what per-
      tains to war.

Ath. Perhaps so. Still, *we* should not fight harshly with one an-   629a
      other, but should rather make a calm inquiry about the

present matters, since we, as well as they, are very serious about these things. So follow the argument along with me. Let us appeal to Tyrtaeus,[20] who was by birth an Athenian but who became a naturalized[21] citizen of this fellow's people, and who was the most serious of human beings about these matters. He says: "I would not memorialize nor set down in speech a man," even if someone were the wealthiest of human beings, he declares, even if he possessed many good things (and then he mentions just about all of them), unless that man always were best in war. Presumably you too have heard these poetic lines; and this fellow, I believe, is surfeited with them.

629b

Meg.   Yes, indeed.

Kl.   They've been brought to us from Lacedaimon.

Ath.   Come now, let's question this poet in common, roughly as follows: "Tyrtaeus, most divine poet! You seem to us to be wise and also good, because you have praised in so distinguished a manner those who are distinguished in war. Now I, and this fellow here, and this other fellow, Kleinias the Knossian, happen to be very much in agreement with you regarding this matter, we believe. But we want to know clearly whether we are referring to the same men or not. So tell us: do you clearly hold, as we do, that there are two forms[22] of war? Or what?" To these things I think even a much less respectable figure than Tyrtaeus would respond with the truth, namely that these are two, one of which we all call civil war—the harshest of all wars, as we just now declared. The other I believe we would all set down as the kind that is waged against outsiders and members of other tribes, and this is much milder than the former.

629c

629d

Kl.   How could it not be?

Ath.   "Well, then, which sort of men in which sort of war were you praising when you gave such strong praise to some and such blame to others? That waged against outsiders, it appears. For you have said in your verses, at any rate, that you cannot at all abide men who do not dare

629e

> . . . to look on bloody death,
> And staying near assail the foe."[23]

So after these things we would say, "It appears, Tyrtaeus, that you praise especially those who become conspicuous in foreign and external war." Presumably he would affirm that this is so, and would agree?

Kl.   But of course.

Ath. But we, at any rate, would assert that while these men are   630a
good, better by far are those who reveal themselves to be best
in the greatest war. And we have a poet as witness—Theognis, a citizen of Sicilian Megara,[24] who declares:

> Cyrnus, in harsh civil strife a trustworthy
> Man is equal in value to gold and silver.

This man in the harsher war, we assert, is altogether better
than that other man, in almost the same degree as justice and   630b
moderation and prudence, existing in a man along with
courage, are better than courage itself alone. For a man would
never become trustworthy and sound in the midst of civil
wars if he didn't have the whole of virtue. There are very
many mercenaries who are willing to take a stand and fight to
the death in the war Tyrtaeus mentions, and most of them are
rash, unjust, insolent, and very imprudent, with only a very
few who are not.

Where has this argument of ours wound up now, and what   630c
does it want to make clear when it says these things? Isn't it
obvious that it wanted to show us that above all others the
lawgiver of this place, who came from Zeus, as well as any
other lawgiver worth much of anything, will never set down
laws with a view to anything but the greatest virtue? And this
is, as Theognis asserts, trustworthiness in the midst of
dangers—that quality which someone would call perfect justice. As for what Tyrtaeus praised especially, it is something
noble, and the poet has adorned it in a fitting way; yet one
would speak most correctly if one said it was fourth in number
and in claim to honor.   630d

Kl.   Stranger, we are consigning our lawgiver to a pretty low rank
among lawgivers!

Ath. No, it's ourselves that we're consigning to a low rank, O best
of men, when we show that we think Lycurgus and Minos arranged all the customs at Lacedaimon and here chiefly with a
view to war!

Kl.   But what should we have been saying?

Ath. What is true, I think, and just, since we were carrying on a dialogue on behalf of a divine man.[25] We should have said that   630e
he had in view not just some part of virtue—and that the
lowest—but that he looked to the whole of virtue, and that in
seeking his laws he arranged them in forms that are different

631a

from the forms used by those who now seek to put forward laws. Nowadays, each seeks merely to add on that form which he needs. So one concerns himself with inheritances and heiresses, another with assaults, and others with myriad other such things. But we assert that the search for laws belongs to those who seek well, as we have now begun to do. For I wholly admire the way you started out interpreting the laws; it is correct to begin from virtue and say that he laid down the laws for the sake of this. But when you claimed that he legislated by referring everything to a part of virtue—and that the smallest—I was sure you were no longer correct, and that is why all this last part of the argument has been put forward

631b

now. How then would I have liked to hear you proceeding in your talk? Do you want me to show you?

Kl. By all means.

Ath. "O stranger," it should have been said, "not in vain are the laws of Crete in especially high repute among all the Greeks. They are correct laws, laws that make those who use them happy. For they provide all the good things. Now the good things are two fold, some human, some divine. The former depend on the divine goods, and if a city receives the greater

631c

it will also acquire the lesser. If not, it will lack both. Health leads the lesser goods; in the second place is beauty; third is strength, both in running and in all the other motions of the body; and fourth is Wealth[26]—not blind but sharp-sighted, insofar as it follows prudence. Prudence, in turn, is first and leader among the divine goods. Second after intelligence[27] comes a moderate disposition of the soul, and from these two

631d

mixed with courage comes justice, in third place. Courage is fourth. All of these last goods are by nature placed prior in rank to the first, and this is the rank they should be placed in by the legislator.

After these things, the citizens should be told that the other orders are given to them with a view to these goods, of which the human look to the divine and the divine all look to the leader, intelligence. It is necessary to care for the citizens by apportioning honor and dishonor correctly among them, in

631e

their marriage associations, and then later in the birth and rearing of the children, male and female, while they are young and also as they get older, until they reach old age. In all their mingling with one another one must keep a guard, watching

632a

their pains and pleasures, their desires and the ardors of all

their erotic longings, blaming and praising correctly by means of the laws themselves. Moreover, in fits of anger, in fears, in the disturbances that come over souls in bad fortune and the release from such things that comes with good fortune, in the experiences brought by diseases and wars and poverty, and the experiences brought upon human beings by the opposite circumstances—in all such situations what is noble and what   632b
is ignoble in each case must be taught and defined.

After these matters necessity demands that the lawgiver guard the citizens' acquisitions and expenditures, in whatever way these take place, and also that he watch over the formation and dissolution of their associations with one another for all these purposes, both voluntary and involuntary, keeping an eye on how they behave towards one another in each of these sorts of activity, and observing which sorts are just and which are lacking in justice. For those citizens who obey the laws he should ordain honor, and for those who disobey he should ordain penalties. When he comes to what is the end[28]   632c
of the whole political regime, he should consider how each of those who has died should be buried and what honors should be allocated to them.

Looking back over all these things, the one who frames the laws will set up guards—some grounded in prudence, others in true opinion—so that intelligence will knit together all these things and may declare that they follow moderation and justice but not wealth or love of honor."

Thus, O strangers, I at least would have wished and still do   632d
wish that you would speak: explaining how all this is to be found in the laws that are said to be from Zeus and the Pythian Apollo, the laws laid down by Minos and Lycurgus. And then I would like to be shown why it is that their order is so clear to anyone with experience in laws, either because of technical skill[29] or because of certain habits, while it remains quite unapparent to the rest of us.

Kl.   What should be said after these things, stranger?

Ath.   In my opinion, it's necessary to start over again from the   632e
beginning, commencing just as we did, by first discussing the practices that contribute to courage and then proceeding through another and then yet another form of virtue—if you wish to do so. As soon as we've been through the first, we will try to use it as a pattern for the others and thus have a comforting discussion[30] about them as we go along our route. Later, if

god is willing, we'll show how what we just went through is aimed at virtue as a whole.

633a Meg. What you're saying is fine. How about trying first to test our praiser of Zeus here?

Ath. I will, but I'll also try to test you and me as well. For the discussion is common to us all. So both of you tell me now: didn't we assert that the common meals and the gymnastics were devised by the legislator with a view to war?

Meg. Yes.

Ath. And what would come third, and fourth? For one probably ought to count in this way as regards the things that constitute the rest of virtue too (whether one calls them "parts" or speaks of them by themselves, so long as it's clear what one means to say).

633b Meg. Thirdly, I and any Lacedaimonian would say, he devised hunting.

Ath. Let's try to give a fourth, or a fifth if we can.

Meg. In the fourth place I at least would try to put the great attention that we pay to endurance of suffering, in the fistfights we hold with one another and in certain practices of theft we have, which always involve many blows. Then too, there is a prac-
633c tice called the "secret service,"[31] which is amazingly full of the sort of toils that instill endurance; they go barefoot and sleep without blankets in winter, and they have to take care of themselves without any servants as they wander by night as well as by day through the whole territory. And then there is the festival of naked games,[32] where we undergo terrible suffering, combatting the stifling heat of summer. There are many other such practices—so many that one would almost never stop if he tried to enumerate them all.

Ath. You've spoken well indeed, Lacedaimonian stranger. But look, as to courage, how shall we define it? Shall we leave it at
633d saying that it's a combat against fears and pains only, or also against longings and pleasures, and certain terrible cajoling flatteries that can turn to wax the spiritedness[33] even of those who think themselves solemn?

Meg. I agree; it fights against all these.

Ath. If we recall the earlier arguments, this fellow here said that a certain sort of city is inferior to itself, and also a certain sort of man; isn't that so, Knossian stranger?

Kl. It certainly is.

Ath.   Are we now saying that the man inferior to pains is bad, or do   633e
       we mean the man inferior to pleasures also?

Kl.   More the one inferior to pleasures, in my opinion at least. Pre-
       sumably we all mean the one overcome by pleasures rather
       than the one overcome by pains when we refer to one who is
       blamably inferior to himself.

Ath.   Surely the lawgiver of Zeus or of the Pythian hasn't instituted   634a
       a crippled courage, able to resist only on the left side but un-
       able to resist on the right, the side of cunning and flattery?
       Isn't his resistant on both sides?

Kl.   On both, I at least would maintain.

Ath.   All right then, let's go back and say what these practices are in
       both your cities that constrain men to taste pleasures and not
       flee them—just as they were constrained not to flee pains, but
       were dragged right into the midst of them and, by the use of
       force and by persuasion through honors, were made to con-   634b
       quer them. Where in the laws is this same thing set up with
       regard to pleasures? Let it be said what this practice of yours is
       that makes the same men equally courageous before sufferings
       and pleasures, triumphing over what they should and in no
       way proving inferior to their own nearest and harshest
       enemies.

Meg.   Although I was able to list for you many laws ordained with a
       view to sufferings, stranger, I couldn't with equal ease pro-   634c
       duce major and conspicuous examples with regard to plea-
       sures. I would probably have no trouble in finding some
       minor examples.

Kl.   Nor could I myself, in regard to the Cretan laws, show this as
       clearly as I could the other.

Ath.   Best of strangers, this is not surprising. But if one of us should
       blame some feature in the laws belonging to each of the oth-
       ers, being led to this out of a wish to see what is true and, at
       the same time, what is best, let's accept such behavior from
       one another not in a harsh way, but gently.

Kl.   What you've said is correct, Athenian stranger, and it should
       be heeded.

Ath.   For of course, Kleinias, that kind of thing wouldn't be fitting   634d
       for men of our age.

Kl.   Indeed it wouldn't.

Ath.   Whether or not someone can correctly blame the Laconian and
       the Cretan regime is another question. But I am probably in a

better position than either of you to tell what things are said by the many. Because, given that what pertains to your laws has been put together in a measured way, one of the finest is the law that does not allow any of the young to inquire which 634e   laws are finely made and which are not, but that commands all to say in harmony, with one voice from one mouth, that all the laws are finely made by gods; if someone says otherwise, there is to be no heed paid to him at all. And yet if some old man has been thinking over something in your laws, he is to make such arguments before a magistrate and someone his own age, with no young person present.

635a   Kl.   Most correctly spoken, stranger, and like a diviner! Even though you're far away in time from the thought of him who laid down these strictures, I think you've fairly hit upon it. What you say is very true.

Ath.   Well, there are no youngsters around us now; and on account of our old age the lawgiver allows us a dispensation—carrying on a conversation about these matters alone by ourselves, we'll be doing nothing wrong, will we?

Kl.   That's so, and don't hold yourself back from laying blame on our laws. It's not dishonorable simply to find out about something that is ignoble; in fact, if the one who hears is not re-635b   sentful, but well disposed, the outcome may be a remedy of the ill.

Ath.   Nobly spoken. What I have to say will not really be a blame of the laws—not, at least, until I am on firm ground after inquiring as closely as I can—but will be rather an expression of perplexity. For you are the only peoples of whom we know, among Greeks as well as barbarians, whose lawgiver has given orders to keep away from and not taste the greatest sorts of pleasure and play; while as to pains and fears, as we just 635c   remarked, he held that if someone flees them, from childhood until the end of life, the result will be that when he gets into unavoidable toils and fears and pains, he will flee before those who have had gymnastic training in such things and will be enslaved by them. I think the same legislator should have thought the same thing about pleasures. He should have said to himself, "If our citizens grow up from youth lacking experience in the greatest pleasures, if they aren't practiced in enduring pleasures and in never being compelled to do anything 635d   shameful, their softness of spirit before pleasures will lead them to suffer the same thing as those who are overcome by fears. They will be enslaved in another and more shameful fashion to those who are capable of enduring pleasures, who know about pleasures, and who are sometimes human beings vicious in every way. They'll have souls that are part slave and part free, and will not be worthy of being called courageous and free men without qualification." Consider now whether you think any of this that's just been said is to the point.

Kl. Offhand, the argument seems to us, at least, to make sense. 635e But to be quickly and easily persuaded about matters of such gravity might well betoken youth and mindlessness.

Ath. Well, Kleinias, and Lacedaimonian stranger, suppose we turn to the next matter we proposed to deal with. Let's discuss moderation after courage. What will we find in these regimes that is different from what is, in regimes arranged at random, parallel to the features we just discovered pertaining to war? 636a

Meg. It's not too easy to say, but it's likely that the common meals and the gymnastics have been devised so as to be fine for both.

Ath. It's likely indeed, strangers, that it is difficult for regimes to become as uncontroversial in deed as they are in speech. It's the same as with bodies: it's almost impossible to prescribe one exercise for any one body that would not appear in some respects harmful as well as in some respects beneficial to our 636b bodies. So it is with these gymnastics and common meals: in many other ways they now benefit cities, but in the event of civil strife they are harmful (as is shown by the examples of the Miletian, Boeotian, and Thurian boys).[34] What's more, there is an ancient law concerning sexual[35] pleasures not only of humans but of beasts, a law laid down even in nature, which this practice seems to have corrupted.[36] For these offenses your cities might be the first to be accused by someone, 636c along with other cities that zealously pursue gymnastics. However such things are to be considered, in a playful or a serious mood, it should be understood that the pleasure is given according to nature, it seems, when the female unites with the nature of males for procreation. Males coming together with males, and females with females, seems against nature; and the daring of those who first did it seems to have arisen from a lack of self-restraint with regard to pleasure. But the fact is, we all accuse the Cretans of being the originators of 636d

the myth of Ganymede:[37] since their laws were believed to have come from Zeus, they added this myth about Zeus so that they could be following the god as they continued to reap the enjoyments of this pleasure. About the myth no more need be said; but about human beings who inquire into laws almost their entire inquiry concerns pleasures and pains, in cities and in private dispositions. These two springs flow forth by nature, and he who draws from the right one, at the right
636e   time, and in the right amount, is happy; the same holds for a city and for a private individual and for every animate thing. But he who does so without knowledge and at the wrong time lives a life that is just the opposite.

Meg.   What's been said, stranger, is in some ways fine, and we have trouble finding words in response to these things, but to me at least, the lawgiver in Lacedaimon seems to have done what's correct when he ordered fleeing from pleasures. As for the
637a   laws in Knossos, this fellow here, if he wishes, will take the field in their support. But the ways of Sparta[38] with regard to pleasures are in my opinion the finest to be found among humankind. For our law proscribed from the entire country that practice which leads humans to fall into the greatest pleasures and the greatest sorts of insolence and total mindlessness. Never would you see in fields or towns under Spartan supervision any drinking parties[39] or any of the stuff that goes with them, which has such power to incite men to every sort
637b   of pleasure. There isn't a one of us who wouldn't immediately inflict the gravest punishment when he encountered one of those drunken revellers, and the Dionysia[40] wouldn't afford an excuse that would protect him,[41] if he were doing the sorts of things I saw them do in the carts once among your people. Why, in Tarentum[42] among our colonists I witnessed the whole city drunk at a Dionysia! That kind of thing just doesn't exist among us.

Ath.   O Lacedaimonian stranger, all such things are praiseworthy,
637c   where there is endurance; where that is loosened, they do become pretty stupid. Perhaps someone from our side might defend himself by taking you up, and pointing to the looseness of your women.[43] But whether in Tarentum or among my people or among yours, there is one response that seems to acquit all such things of evil and make them correct. To a stranger amazed at seeing what he is not used to seeing

among his own people, everyone answers this way: "Don't be amazed, stranger. This is the law among us—among your people perhaps there is a different law pertaining to these same things." Yet our present discussion is not about the rest of mankind, my dear sirs, but about the vice and virtue of the 637d lawgivers themselves. So let's speak at greater length about the whole subject of intoxication. It is not a practice of minor significance, and to understand it is not the part of any paltry lawgiver. I'm speaking now, not about the drinking or non-drinking of wine in general, but about getting drunk, and whether it should be employed as the Scythians and Persians do, and also the Carthaginians, the Celts, the Iberians, and the 637e Thracians (all these being warlike races),[44] or whether it should be employed as you do. You people, as you say, wholly abstain from it, while the Scythians and Thracians drink wine completely undiluted, women as well as men, and pour it over their cloaks, believing that they're engaging in a fine and happy practice. The Persians also use it a great deal, along with other luxuries you abstain from, but they preserve more orderliness than those others.

Meg. But, O best of men, we do put all these peoples to flight when 638a we take up our arms.

Ath. Best of men, don't talk that way. Many routs and pursuits have occurred, and will occur again, without a clear cause. So we should always set down victory or defeat in battle not as a clear but as a controversial criterion for whether practices are noble or not. The fact is, bigger cities defeat smaller ones in 638b battle: the Syracusans enslave the Locrians, who seem the best-governed of the people in that area; the Athenians enslave the Ceians;[45] and we could find ten thousand other such examples. So with regard to each practice we discuss, let's now leave aside the talk about victories and defeats and try to persuade ourselves with arguments, showing how one sort of thing is noble and how another sort is not noble. But first hear me out as I explain how one should inquire into what is advantageous and what is not in these matters.

Meg. How do you say it should be done? 638c

Ath. It seems to me that all those who take up a practice for discussion and propose to blame or praise it as soon as it's mentioned proceed in a manner that is not at all proper. They do the same as someone who, when he hears another strongly praising a kind of cheese[46] as a good food, immediately blames it, without learning either its effect or the way it is administered—in what manner, by whom, along with what, in what condition, and to persons in what condition. This is the

638d

very thing, it seems to me, we're now doing in our arguments. Having heard only this much about the subject of drunkenness, some of us are immediately blaming it and others are praising it—both absurdly. On both sides we present our praise by using witnesses and praisers: one side claims that what they say is decisive because they bring forward so many, while the other side replies that their claim is decisive because we see that those who don't use the practice are victorious in battle. And then this has become a subject of controversy be-

638e

tween us. I really don't think it makes sense for us to go through each of the other legal customs this way. Instead, I am willing to go through this very custom, drunkenness, in another way, which to me appears the required way. In so doing I will try, if I can, to demonstrate what is the correct method for our inquiry into all such things. For thousands upon thousands of nations would disagree with your two cities and fight with them in speech over these things.

Meg. Well, if in fact we have some correct method of inquiry into

639a

such things, there should be no hesitation to hear about it.

Ath. Let's carry out the inquiry, then, in roughly the following way: come, suppose someone were to praise the raising of goats, and the animal itself as a fine possession. Suppose someone else, who had seen goats grazing without a goatherd and doing damage to cultivated fields, were to denounce the animal and blame, in the same way, every animal he had ever seen without a ruler or with bad rulers over it. Would we consider such a man's denunciation—whatever he might denounce—to be sound?

Meg. How could we?

639b Ath. Do we suppose someone is a worthy ruler in ships if he possesses only the knowledge of navigation, regardless of whether he is subject to seasickness or not? Or what would we say?

Meg. Not at all, if in addition to possessing the art, he suffers from the defect you mention.

Ath. And what of a ruler over an army? Is it sufficient qualification that he possess the knowledge of war even if he's cowardly in the midst of dangers, even if he's seasick with the drunkenness of terror?

Meg. How could it be?

Ath. And what if in addition to being a coward he lacked the art?

Meg. Now you're speaking of someone who is a complete wretch—a ruler of certain womanish women but not at all of men.

Ath. Take any community for which there is by nature a ruler, and   639c
which is beneficial when that ruler is present: what would we say about someone who praised it or blamed it without ever having seen it operating in a correct communal way under its ruler, but had always seen such social intercourse without a ruler or under bad rulers? Do we believe onlookers like these will ever have any worthwhile praise or blame for such communities?

Meg. How could they, when they've never seen or taken part in a   639d
correct version of any of the communities?

Ath. Hold on a moment. Should we set down drinking parties and drinking gatherings as one sort of social intercourse, among the many sorts of communities?

Meg. Very much so.

Ath. Well, has anyone ever yet seen one of these proceed correctly? For you two it's easy to reply, "Never yet at all," because among you this practice is neither customary nor legal; but I have encountered many drinking parties in many places, and what's more I have studied all of them, so to speak. I have   639e
hardly seen or heard of a single one being run correctly in its entirety—if a few small aspects of some were correct, the vast majority were, so to speak, entirely faulty.

Kl. What do you mean by that, stranger? Speak still more clearly. For, as you've said, we lack experience of such gatherings, and if we happened upon them we probably wouldn't know   640a
straight off what was correct or not in the way they were proceeding.

Ath. That's likely. Try to learn from my explanation. You do understand, don't you, that in every gathering, in every community formed for any kind of action, there is always a correct ruler in each case?

Kl. How could there not be?

Ath. And we said just now that for fighting men a courageous ruler is needed.

Kl. But of course.

Ath.   Now a courageous man is less disturbed by fears than are cowardly men.

640b   Kl.   That, too, is so.

Ath.   So if there had been some device for putting a general who wasn't at all fearful or disturbed at the head of an army, shouldn't we have exerted every effort to do so?

Kl.   Most certainly.

Ath.   At the moment, though, we're speaking not of a ruler of an army in gatherings of men who are fighting enemies in war, but rather of friends communing with friends in peace and with goodwill.

Kl.   That's correct.

640c   Ath.   And such intercourse, if accompanied by drunkenness, is not without disturbance, is it?

Kl.   How could it be? Entirely the opposite, I think!

Ath.   First, then, these also need a ruler.

Kl.   How could they not? More than in any other action!

Ath.   Should a ruler be provided who is undisturbed, if possible?

Kl.   But of course.

Ath.   And it's likely that he should be someone who is prudent in regard to social intercourse, at any rate. For he becomes both
640d   the guardian of their present friendship and the one who sees to it that the friendship will increase through the intercourse they will have.

Kl.   Very true.

Ath.   So shouldn't a sober and wise ruler be set over the drunkards, and not the opposite? For if the ruler of drunken men were a young drunk who wasn't wise, he'd need a lot of good fortune to avoid doing some great evil.

Kl.   A lot indeed.

Ath.   Now if someone were to blame this kind of intercourse even
640e   in cities where it proceeds in the most correct way possible—if he objected to the activity itself—he might perhaps be correct in his blame. But if someone reviles the practice when he has only seen it proceeding under the most mistaken conditions, he shows first that he doesn't know that this is an example of an incorrect version, and then in addition shows that he is ignorant of the fact that any activity proceeding thus—without a sober despot and ruler—appears wicked. Or don't you agree
641a   that a drunken pilot, and indeed any drunken ruler of anything, will upset all—whether ship, or chariot, or army, or whatever might be governed by him?

Kl. What you've said here, stranger, is in every respect true. But tell us this next: suppose this custom regarding drinking were to proceed correctly—what good would it then do us? Just as, to refer back to what we said a moment ago, if an army were led correctly, then victory in war would accrue to the followers (and that's no small benefit), and so on with the rest; so from a correctly instructed[47] drinking party what great thing accrues to private individuals or to the city?

641b

Ath. Well, from one child or one chorus[48] correctly instructed, what great thing would we claim accrues to the city? If we were asked the question in this way, wouldn't we reply as follows? "From one, only a little good comes to the city, but if you ask about the education in general of all who are educated, what great benefit it gives the city, the answer is not difficult: those who are well educated become good men, and becoming such, they act nobly in other respects, as well as in winning victories when they fight their enemies. Education brings victory, although victory sometimes brings a loss of education; for many have grown more insolent because of victories in war, and through their insolence have been filled with ten thousand other vices. And education has never become 'Cadmean,'[49] although many such victories have happened and will happen again to human beings."

641c

Kl. You seem to us to be saying, friend, that spending time drinking together is a great contribution to education, if it is done correctly!

641d

Ath. Why not?

Kl. Well, could you explain next how what's just been said is true?

Ath. Stranger, to be sure of the truth in these matters, when so many disagree, would belong to a god. But I don't begrudge giving my own view, if that's what's required, since we have now embarked on the discussion of laws and a regime.

Kl. That is precisely what we should try to understand, your view on these now-disputed matters.

641e

Ath. All right then, that's what we must do: you two must strive somehow or other to understand the argument and I must strive somehow or other to make it clear. First, however, hear me out on this: all the Greeks regard our city as one that loves to talk and that talks a great deal; but as for Lacedaimon and Crete, the former is considered to be pithy in speech and the latter to be clever rather than talkative. Now I'm anxious not to give you the opinion that I'm long-winded about small mat-

642a

ters, as I go ahead to elaborate what is a very lengthy argument about the small activity of getting drunk. Because it would never be possible to regulate this according to nature without giving a clear and sufficient account of what is correct in music;[50] and it would never be possible to give an account of music without going into the whole subject matter of education. All this means very long speeches. So consider what we should do. How would it be if we leave off the discussion of these things for now and turn to a different discussion about laws?

642b

Meg. Athenian stranger, you probably are not aware of the fact that our hearth happens to be the consulate[51] for your city. And in all us children who hear that we are the "consuls" for some city there probably sinks in, from the time we are young, a friendly disposition towards that city, as if it were a second fatherland after one's own city. Now this is just what has happened to me. For whenever the Lacedaimonians were blaming or praising the Athenians for something, I would immediately hear the children crying, "That's your city, Megillus, that's dealing with us ignobly or nobly." Hearing these things, and always fighting over them on your behalf against those who blamed your city, I became entirely well disposed; even now your dialect is a friendly sound to me, and I believe that what is said by many is very true, namely, that those Athenians who are good are good in a different way. They alone are good by their own nature without compulsion, by a divine dispensation: they are truly, and not artificially, good. So with regard to me at any rate, you should take heart and talk as long as you like.

642c

642d

Kl. Once you've heard and accepted what I too have to say, stranger, you may surely take heart and talk as much as you wish. As you may have heard, Epimenides,[52] that divine man, was born around here and is, as a matter of fact, related to my family. In obedience to a god's oracle he journeyed to you people ten years before the Persian Wars and made some sacrifices that had been demanded by the god. He told the Athenians, who were at that time living in dread of a Persian expedition, that "the Persians won't come for another ten years and when they do come, they'll go away having accomplished nothing of what they hoped, and having suffered more evil than they've inflicted." At that time, then, our an-

642e

cestors formed a bond with yours, and from that day to this, I   643a
and my family have felt well disposed towards your people.

Ath.   It's likely, then, that you're ready to take your part and listen.
I'm willing to take my part, but it's not a part that's very easy
to carry out. Still, it must be tried. First, for the purposes of the
argument, let's define education—saying what it is and what
power it has. That's the way we assert the argument we have
now taken in hand should go, until it arrives at the god.

Kl.   By all means let's do just that, if it pleases you.

Ath.   Now as I say what one ought to assert education is, you think   643b
over whether what is said is acceptable.

Kl.   Say on.

Ath.   I will, and what I assert is this: whatever a man intends to
become good at, this he must practice from childhood;
whether he's playing or being serious, he should spend his
time with each of the things that pertain to the activity. Thus,
in the case of someone intending to become a good farmer or a
good housebuilder of some sort, the housebuilder should play
at games that educate in housebuilding, and the farmer simi-   643c
larly, and the person who raises each child should provide
each with miniature tools that are imitations of the true ones.
Moreover, the child should learn any knowledge that is a necessary preliminary: a carpenter, for example, should learn to
measure and gauge things, and a soldier should play at horseback riding or some other such things. The attempt should be
made to use the games to direct the pleasures and desires of
children toward those activities in which they must become
perfect. The core of education, we say, is a correct nurture, one   643d
which, as much as possible, draws the soul of the child at play
toward an erotic attachment to what he must do when he
becomes a man who is perfect as regards the virtue of his
occupation.

    Now, as I said, see if what has been said up to this point is
acceptable to us.

Kl.   Why shouldn't it be?

Ath.   Because what we mean by education is not yet defined! When
we at present blame or praise the upbringing of different persons, we say that one of us is "educated" and another is "un-   643e
educated," sometimes applying the latter characterization to
human beings who are very well educated in trade or merchant shipping or some other such things. So it's appropriate

644a that in our present discussion we do not consider these sorts of training to be education; we mean rather the education from childhood in virtue, that makes one desire and love to become a perfect citizen who knows how to rule and be ruled with justice. It is this upbringing alone, it appears to me, that this discussion would wish to isolate and to proclaim as education. As for an upbringing that aims at money, or some sort of strength, or some other sort of wisdom without intelligence and justice, the argument proclaims it to be vulgar, illiberal, and wholly unworthy to be called education. But let's not get into a dispute with each other over the name. Let's simply hold fast to the argument now being agreed to by us, the argument that states: "Those who are correctly educated usually become good, and nowhere should education be dishonored, as it is first among the noblest things for the best men. If it ever goes astray, and if it is possible to set it right, everyone ought always to do so as much as he can, throughout the whole of life."

Kl. That is correct, and we agree with what you're saying.

Ath. Now long ago, at least, we agreed that the good are those able to rule themselves, and the bad are those who cannot.

Kl. What you say is very correct.

644c Ath. Let's consider again in a clearer way what we mean by that. Allow me to clarify it for you, if I can, by means of an image.

Kl. Just speak on.

Ath. May we then assume that each of us is one person?

Kl. Yes.

Ath. But possessing within himself two opposed and imprudent counselors, which we call pleasure and pain?

Kl. That is so.

Ath. Connected to these two there are opinions about the future, common to both of which there is the name "expectation," but each of which also has its own peculiar name: "fear" is the ex-

644d pectation of pain, and "boldness" the expectation of the opposite. Over all these there is calculation as to which of them is better and which worse—and when this calculation becomes the common opinion of the city, it is called law.

Kl. I follow this only with great difficulty; but say what comes next as if I were following.

Meg. I'm experiencing similar difficulties.

Ath. Let's think about these things in this way: let's consider each

644b

of us living beings to be a divine puppet, put together either for their play or for some serious purpose—which, we don't know. What we do know is that these passions work within us 644e like tendons or cords, drawing us and pulling against one another in opposite directions toward opposing deeds, struggling in the region where virtue and vice lie separated from one another. Now the argument[53] asserts that each person should always follow one of the cords, never letting go of it and pulling with it against the others; this cord is the golden 645a and sacred pull of calculation, and is called the common law of the city; the other cords are hard and iron, while this one is soft, inasmuch as it is golden; the others resemble a multitude of different forms. It is necessary always to assist this most noble pull of law because calculation, while noble, is gentle rather than violent, and its pull is in need of helpers if the race of gold is to be victorious for us over the other races. 645b

Thus, the myth of virtue, the myth about us being puppets, would be saved,[54] and what was intended by the notion of being superior to oneself or inferior would be somewhat clearer. Moreover, as regards a city and a private individual, it'll be clearer that the latter should acquire within himself true reasoning about these cords and live according to it, while a city should take over a reasoning either from one of the gods or from this knower of these things, and then set up the reasoning as the law for itself and for its relations with 645c other cities. Thus, certainly, vice and virtue would be more clearly distinguished for us. With this distinction sharpened, education and other practices will perhaps be clarified, and the practice of spending time drinking together, which might be considered too trivial to be worth so many words, may well appear not unworthy of such lengthy speech.

Kl. You speak well; let's complete whatever may be demanded by our present pastime.

Ath. Then tell me: if we introduce drunkenness into this puppet 645d what effect shall we produce?

Kl. What do you have in view in asking this?

Ath. Nothing in particular as yet, but just what happens, in general, when the two come together. But I'll try to explain what I want more clearly. What I'm asking is this: doesn't the drinking of wine make pleasures, pains, the spirited emotions, and the erotic emotions, more intense?

Kl.   Very much so.

645e   Ath.   What about sensations, memories, opinions, and prudent thoughts? Do they become more intense in the same way? Or don't they abandon anyone who becomes thoroughly soused?

Kl.   Yes, they completely abandon him.

Ath.   So he arrives at a disposition of the soul that is the same as the one he had when he was a young child?

Kl.   But of course.

Ath.   At such a time he would be least the master of himself.

646a   Kl.   Least.

Ath.   Don't we assert that such a man is most wicked?

Kl.   Very much so.

Ath.   It's likely, then, that it's not only the old man who becomes a child for a second time, but also the man who is drunk.

Kl.   Very well put, stranger.

Ath.   Is there really any argument that will try to persuade us that we must taste such a practice and not flee from it with all the strength we have?

Kl.   It's likely that there is. You, at any rate, assert that there is, and were ready just now to state it.

646b   Ath.   What you two remember is true. And I am indeed ready, now that you two have asserted that you would listen in a spirit of eagerness.

Kl.   How could we not listen—if for no other reason than the wonder, the strangeness, of the notion that a human being should ever voluntarily cast himself into a state of complete degradation.

Ath.   . . . of soul, you mean? Or don't you?

Kl.   Yes.

Ath.   Well, what about badness in the body, comrade: would we be
646c   amazed if someone ever voluntarily got into a state that was emaciated, ugly, and weak?

Kl.   How could we not be?

Ath.   Well, but what about those who go voluntarily to a dispensary to drink medicine: do we think they are ignorant of the fact that a little while later and for many days thereafter they may be in a bodily state such that if they had to live thus until the end of their lives they would refuse to go on living? And don't we know that those who go to gymnasiums for exercise become exhausted right afterwards?

Kl. We know all this.

Ath. And that it's for the subsequent benefit that they go
voluntarily?

Kl. That's a very noble way of putting it. 646d

Ath. Shouldn't one think about other practices in the same way?

Kl. Certainly.

Ath. Then this is the way one should think about the pastime of
drinking wine—if it can correctly be thought of as among
these other practices.

Kl. Why not?

Ath. Now if it's evident that this practice procures for us a benefit
no less than that which accrues to the body, it will gain the
victory over the bodily practices at the outset, because they involve suffering while this doesn't.

Kl. What you say is correct, but I would be amazed if we were 646e
able to discover such a thing in it.

Ath. Then it's likely that this is what we must now try to explain.
Tell me this: can we distinguish in our minds two forms of
fear that are nearly opposite?

Kl. Which?

Ath. These: on the one hand we presumably fear evils, when we
expect them to come to pass.

Kl. Yes.

Ath. And on the other hand we often fear opinion, when we think
we will be considered evil if we say or do something that is
not noble. This is the sort of fear that we at least, and I believe 647a
everyone, calls "shame."

Kl. What else?

Ath. These are the two fears I spoke of. The latter opposes sufferings and other fears, but also opposes the most frequent and
greatest pleasures.

Kl. What you say is very correct.

Ath. Now won't the lawgiver, and indeed anyone worth much of
anything, revere with the greatest honors this sort of fear,
calling it "awe" [55] and the boldness opposed to it "lack of
awe"? Won't he consider lack of awe to be the greatest evil for 647b
everyone both in private and in public life?

Kl. You speak correctly.

Ath. Doesn't this fear save us from many great evils, and in particular doesn't it play a greater role than anything else in procur-
ing for us victory and safety in war? For there are two things

that procure victory: boldness with enemies and with friends fear of shame on account of vileness.

Kl.   That is so.

Ath. Each of us then must be at the same time fearless and fearful: in respect to what, in each case, we have just indicated.

647c

Kl.   Indeed.

Ath. Now, when we wish to make each man immune to many fears, we accomplish this by dragging him into the midst of fear in a manner that is consistent with the law.

Kl.   It appears that we do.

Ath. What about when we try to make him fearful, in a manner that is consistent with justice? Shouldn't we throw him against shamelessness, and by thus giving him gymnastic training in combatting it, make him a victorious fighter against his own pleasures? A man becomes perfect in courage by fighting against and conquering the cowardice within him; surely no man who lacks experience and gymnastic training in these struggles would ever attain half his potential in virtue. Can a man then become perfect in moderation if he has not fought triumphantly against the many pleasures and desires that try to seduce him into shamelessness and injustice, using the help of speech, deed, and art, in games and in serious pursuits? Can he remain inexperienced in all such things?

647d

Kl.   That wouldn't make sense.

647e Ath. Well, now, is there a fear drug, handed down to human beings by some god, which has the effect that the more one is willing to drink, the more unfortunate one conceives oneself to be with each drink, fearing for oneself everything in the present and in the future, until finally the most courageous human being experiences total terror, and yet when he has slept it off and the drink has been sloughed off he becomes himself again each time?

648a

Kl.   What drink of this sort could we claim human beings possess, stranger?

Ath. There is none. But if one had appeared from somewhere, could the lawgiver have used it in any way to promote courage? We might well carry on a dialogue with him about it as follows: "Come, lawgiver—whether you are the lawgiver for the Cretans or whoever—would you like to be able, first, to test the citizens for courage and cowardice?"

648b

Kl.   Obviously, every one of them would say he would.

Ath. "Well then, would you prefer a test that was safe, without great risks, or the opposite?"

Kl. All would also agree on a test that was safe.

Ath. "And would you use it to drag them into fears and test them in their sufferings, so as to force them to become fearless—encouraging, exhorting, and honoring them, but dishonoring anyone who refused to obey you and become in every respect the type of person you ordered him to be? The man who had performed well and courageously in this gymnastic you would dismiss without penalty, wouldn't you? And the man who did badly you would penalize? Or would you refuse to use the drug at all, even though you had no other objection to it?"

648c

Kl. But why wouldn't he use it, stranger?

Ath. At any rate, friend, compared to our present gymnastics this gymnastic would certainly be amazingly easy—for one person, for a few, or for as many as one might want to apply it to on each occasion. Then too, if someone went off alone to a deserted place, excusing himself out of a sense of shame at being seen before he was in what he considered good condition, and engaged in gymnastic exercise against fear by merely drinking, instead of performing tens of thousands of other activities, he would be acting in a correct manner. On the other hand, a man would act just as correctly if, trusting in himself on account of the fine preparation given by nature and by training, he did not hesitate to perform such gymnastic exercise in the company of many fellow drinkers, making a display of his capacity to outstrip and overcome the power of the necessary transformation effected by the drink. Thus would he show that because of his virtue he was not made to fall into a single major disgraceful act nor to act like a different person, but that he could go away before taking that last drink, because he was afraid of the weakness all human beings have in the face of the drink.

648d

648e

Kl. Yes. For he too would be moderate, stranger—the man who acted in this way.

Ath. Let's speak to the lawgiver again: "Well, lawgiver, it's likely that no god has bestowed such a fear drug on human beings, and we have not devised one for ourselves—I'm not including magicians in the banquet. But what about a drink that induces fearlessness, boldness that is too great, at the wrong time, and

649a

toward the wrong things—does one exist or how shall we say?"

Kl. "One does," he will presumably assert, naming wine.

Ath. Isn't it just the opposite of the one now mentioned? Doesn't it first make a human being who drinks it immediately more cheerful than he was before, and to the degree to which he tastes more, doesn't he become more puffed up with good hopes and an opinion of his own power? Then, finally, doesn't he wind up being filled with complete license of speech, believing himself wise; isn't he filled with freedom and total fearlessness, so that he doesn't hesitate to say or even to do anything? Everyone would agree with us on this description, I think.

Kl. How could they not?

Ath. Let's recollect how we asserted that there are two things in our souls that need to be cultivated: on the one hand that we be as bold as possible, and on the other hand the opposite, that we be as fearful as possible.

Kl. Which you said belonged to awe, we suppose.

Ath. You two remember in a fine way. But given that courage and fearlessness in the midst of fears should be practiced, one should consider whether the opposite quality in the midst of the opposite things should also be cultivated.

Kl. That seems likely, anyway.

Ath. Then it's likely that those experiences in which we are naturally inclined to be especially rash and bold are the ones in which we should practice becoming as little filled with shamelessness and boldness as possible, and instead be afraid to say or suffer or do anything shameful on each occasion.

Kl. That's likely.

Ath. Aren't all the experiences where we're like that these: spirited anger, erotic desire, insolence, lack of learning, love of gain, cowardice, and, in addition, wealth, beauty, strength, and everything which drives a person out of his wits with the intoxication of pleasure? Now is there any one of these that is as inexpensive or comparatively harmless, first for testing and then for practicing, than the test and play associated with wine? What pleasure can we say is more measured, if indulged in with any kind of care? Let's just consider it. To test a harsh and savage soul from which tens of thousands of injustices come, is it safer to run the risks involved in making con-

649b

649c

649d

649e

tracts or to get together with it at the festival sights of Diony- 650a
sus? Or take the example of a soul dominated by sexual
desires: is it safer to test it by turning over one's own daughters, sons, and wives, and risk those who are dearest, in order
to see the soul's disposition? One could give ten thousand
such examples without ever showing fully how different the
method is which observes people through play, and involves
no other payoff or penalty. Indeed, in this respect we believe
that neither the Cretans nor any other human beings would 650b
disagree that this is a decent way of testing one another—one
which in cheapness, safety, and speed differs from the other
tests.

Kl. That, at least, is true.

Ath. This then—the knowledge of the natures and the habits of
souls—is one of the things that is of the greatest use for the art
whose business it is to care for souls. And we assert (I think)
that that art is politics. Or what?

Kl. It certainly is.

BOOK II

652a   Ath.   In the next place, what probably ought to be investigated is whether the insight into our natures is the only good to be derived from correctly managed wine parties, or whether there is not a great benefit, worthy of much serious consideration. What do we say, then? The argument seems to want to indicate that there is such a great benefit. Let's listen to hear in

652b   what sense and how, doing so with attentive minds, lest the argument ensnare us.

       Kl.   Say on.

653a   Ath.   I have a desire to recollect again what we say correct education is, in our view. Because it's now my guess that a safeguard for this education is to be found in this institution, when it's nobly directed.

       Kl.   That's a big claim you make!

       Ath.   Well, I say that the first infantile sensation in children is the sensation of pleasure and pain, and that it is in these that virtue and vice first come into being in the soul; as for prudence, and true opinions that are firmly held, he is a fortunate person to whom it comes even in old age. He who does possess them,

653b   and all the good things that go with them, is a perfect human being. Education, I say, is the virtue that first comes into being in children. Pleasure and liking, pain and hatred, become correctly arranged in the souls of those who are not yet able to reason, and then, when the souls do become capable of reasoning, these passions can in consonance[1] with reason affirm that they have been correctly habituated in the appropriate habits. This consonance in its entirety is virtue;[2] that part

[32]

of virtue which consists in being correctly trained as regards pleasures and pains so as to hate what one should hate from the very beginning until the end, and also to love what one should love—if you separate this off in speech and assert that this is education, you will, in my view, be making a correct assertion.

653c

Kl. Stranger, what you said earlier about education and what you have said now both seem correct to us.

Ath. Fine. Now, this education which consists in correctly trained pleasures and pains tends to slacken in human beings, and in the course of a lifetime becomes corrupted to a great extent. So, taking pity on this suffering that is natural to the human race, the gods have ordained the change of holidays[3] as times of rest from labor. They have given as fellow celebrants the Muses,[4] with their leader Apollo, and Dionysus—in order that these divinities might set humans right again. Thus men are sustained by their holidays in the company of gods.

653d

It is necessary to see whether or not the things the argument is singing to us now are true according to nature. The argument asserts that every young thing, so to speak, is incapable of remaining calm in body or in voice, but always seeks to move and cry: young things leap and jump as if they were dancing with pleasure and playing together, and emit all sorts of cries. The other animals, the argument goes, lack perception of orders and disorders in motions (the orders which have received the names of "rhythm" and "harmony"); we, in contrast, have been given the aforementioned gods as fellow-dancers, and they have given us the pleasant perception of rhythm and harmony. Using this[5] they move us, and lead us in choruses, joining us together with songs and dances; and that is why they bestowed the name "choruses"—from the "joy" [charā] which is natural to these activities.

653e

654a

First, then, do we accept this? Do we proclaim that the first education comes through the Muses and Apollo, or what?

Kl. So be it.

Ath. So the uneducated man will in our view be the one untrained in choral performances, and the educated ought to be set down as the one sufficiently trained in choral performances?

654b

Kl. But of course.

Ath. Now a chorus is the combination of dance and song taken together as a whole.

[33]

Kl. Necessarily.

Ath. He who is finely educated will be able then to sing and dance in a fine way.

Kl. That's likely.

Ath. Let's see exactly what it is that has just been said.

Kl. Which part of what was just said?

Ath. "He sings in a fine way," we declared, "and he dances in a fine way": should we add, "if he also sings fine songs and dances fine dances," or not?

654c

Kl. We should add that.

Ath. What about someone who regards as fine the things that are fine and regards as ugly the things that are ugly, and uses them this way? Which version of such a man shall we hold to be better educated in the choral art and in music: the one who is able to give adequate devotion with his body and voice to what is understood to be fine each time, while neither delighting in the fine things nor hating the ignoble; or the one who is not fully able to express correctly with voice and body what he understands,[6] yet feels pleasure and pain correctly—welcoming what is fine and being disgusted by what is ignoble?

654d

Kl. You're speaking of a vast difference as regards education, stranger.

Ath. Then, if we three know what is fine in song and dance, we will also know who has been correctly educated and who is uneducated. But if we don't know the former we will never be able to know if, and where, a safeguard exists for education. Isn't this so?

654e

Kl. Yes, that's so.

Ath. Then the next thing for us to do is to track down, like dogs sniffing out prey, what is fine in posture, tune, song, and dance. If these elude us and get away, our discussion that should come after—about correct education, whether Greek or barbarian—would be in vain.

Kl. Yes.

Ath. Well, what should we declare constitutes beauty in posture or tune? Consider this: if a courageous and then a cowardly soul undergo identical and equal sufferings, do the same postures and utterances result?

655a

Kl. How could they, when not even the pallor or color is the same?

Ath. What you say is fine, comrade. It should be noted, though, that music includes postures and tunes, since music involves

rhythm and harmony; now one can speak of "good rhythm" and "good harmony," but one cannot correctly apply to either tune or posture and image "good color"—as the chorus teachers, speaking in images, do. On the other hand, with regard to the posture or tune of the coward and the courageous man, it is correct to call what pertains to courageous men "fine," and what pertains to cowards "ugly." To avoid our   655b
getting involved in a very lengthy discussion of all these things, let's simply let all the postures and tunes that belong to virtue of the soul or of the body (whether they belong to virtue itself or to an image of it) be beautiful, and those belonging to vice be entirely the opposite.

Kl. Your proposal is a correct one, and for now let us respond by saying that's the way things are.

Ath. Here's another question: do we all feel a similar joy in every choral performance, or is this far from being the case?   655c

Kl. It's not at all the case.

Ath. What shall we say is the reason for our wavering? Shall we say that the beautiful things are not the same for all of us? Or that they are the same but don't seem to be the same? Surely no one will say, at least, that choral performances of vice are ever more beautiful than those of virtue, nor again that he himself delights in the postures appropriate to depravity, while the rest like an opposite Muse. Most people do say, at least, that the criterion for correct music is its power to provide pleasure   655d
to the souls. But that is not acceptable, nor is it at all pious[7] to utter such a thing.

The source of our wavering is in all likelihood rather the following—

Kl. What?

Ath. Choral performances are imitations of characters, in all sorts of action and fortune, and each brings to bear both his habitual dispositions and his capacity to imitate. Now those whose character is in accord with what is said and sung and in any way performed—because of nature or habit or both—are   655e
necessarily delighted by the things, and led to praise them and pronounce them fine. Those, on the other hand, who find that the things go against nature, character, or a certain habituation, are unable to delight in them or to praise them, and must necessarily pronounce them ugly. Then there are some whose nature is correct but whose habituation is opposed,

656a   and others whose habituation is correct but whose nature is opposed, and these make pronouncements of praise that are opposed to their feelings of pleasure. They call each performance pleasant, but wicked; in the presence of others whom they think prudent, they are ashamed to move their bodies in such ways and ashamed to sing, because they will show that they treat them as fine things, and take them seriously. Nevertheless, they do delight in them when they're all by themselves.

Kl.   What you say is very correct.

Ath.   Isn't a person who delights in wicked postures or songs harmed in some way, and aren't those who take pleasure in the opposite things benefited in some way?

Kl.   That's likely, anyway.

656b   Ath.   Is it only a matter of likelihood or is it not a necessity that such a person be in the same position as one who comes into contact with the wicked habits of evil human beings and doesn't hate them, but instead accepts them with delight—blaming them only in a playful way, on those occasions when he sees as in a dream their vileness? Surely it is necessary that one who takes delight in things becomes then similar to the things he takes delight in, even when he is ashamed to praise them; and what greater good or evil could we declare there is for us than such completely necessary assimilation?

Kl.   I believe there is none greater.

656c   Ath.   Where there are or will some day be fine laws laid down regarding the education and play which concerns the Muses, do we suppose that poets will be allowed to teach the children of those who live under good laws, and the young men in the choruses, whatever the poet himself finds pleasing in the rhythm or tune or words of poetry, so that he makes them similar to whatever he happens to be as regards virtue or wickedness?

Kl.   That at least wouldn't make sense. How could it?

656d   Ath.   Yet this is just what can be done nowadays, at any rate, in all cities, so to speak, except Egypt.

Kl.   What sort of legislation on this matter do you claim they have in Egypt?

Ath.   It's astounding to hear. Long ago, as is likely, this argument which we are now enunciating was known to them—the argument which says that it's necessary for the young in the cities to practice fine postures and fine songs. They made a list of these, indicating which they were and what kind they were, and published it in their temples. Painters and others who represented postures and that sort of thing were not allowed to make innovations or think up things different from the ancestral. And they are still not allowed to—not in these things or in music altogether. If you look into this you will find that for ten thousand years—not "so to speak" but really ten thousand years—the paintings and sculptures have been in no way more beautiful or more ugly than those that are being made, with the very same skill, by their craftsmen now.[8]

656e

657a

Kl.   What you say is astounding!

Ath. An extreme in the lawgiving and political art. There are other features in their law that you would find pretty poor. But this much about the music is true and worthy of thought: it was possible to be firm about such things, and mandate in law songs which are by nature correct.[9] This would have to be the work of a god or someone divine[10]—even as they claim there that the songs which have been preserved for this long time were the poetry of Isis.[11] So, as I said, if someone could grasp in any way what is correct in these things, he ought boldly to order it in law. The search, dictated by pleasure and pain, for a music that is continually new brands the sanctified chorus "old-fashioned"; but this will not have a very corrupting effect on a chorus that has been made sacred. In that land, at any rate, it has probably had no corrupting power; entirely the contrary.

657b

Kl.   So it appears from what you say now.

657c

Ath. So won't we take heart and elaborate the correct use of music and the correct play associated with the choric art, in something like the following way? Don't we feel delight when we think we are doing well? Isn't this so?

Kl.   Yes, that is so.

Ath. And when we are in such a mood, a mood of delight, we aren't able to remain still?

Kl.   Such is the case.

Ath. Isn't it also the case that while our young men are ready by themselves to perform in the chorus, we elders hold that it is fitting for us to look on at their performance, delighting in their play and festivity? Isn't it because we are now no longer very lively, and yet miss and welcome liveliness, that we es-

657d

tablish contests for those who can as much as possible restore us, through memory, to youthfulness?

Kl. Very true.

657e Ath. Then do we think that the account the many give about cele-brators of holidays is completely vacuous, when they say that the person who as much as possible gives us joy and delight is the one who should be considered wisest and judged victorious? For since we give ourselves over to play on such occasions, the one who makes the most people enjoy themselves the most should be the one who is most honored and, as I just
658a now said, given the victory prizes. Isn't this correctly spoken, and wouldn't things be done correctly, if they were done in this way?

Kl. Maybe.

Ath. But let's not judge such a thing quickly, blessed one. Instead, let's analyze it part by part and consider it in something like the following way: suppose someone once set up a contest simply—without specifying whether it was for gymnastic or for music or for horseback riding. Suppose he gathered together everyone in the city and proclaimed a victory prize, open to anyone who wanted to compete regarding pleasure
658b alone, the prize to go to that person who had pleased the spectators the most. No restrictions on the means; the winner to be simply he who had done this the most and who was judged to be the most pleasant of all the contestants. What do we think would ever result from this proclamation?

Kl. In which respect do you mean?

Ath. Well, I suppose it's likely that one, like Homer, would present a rhapsody, and another a recital on the kithara,[12] and another a tragedy, and another, again, a comedy; and it wouldn't be
658c surprising if someone thought he could best win by present-ing puppets. If performers such as these came forward and tens of thousands of others as well, can we say which justly wins?

Kl. Your question is strange. Who could ever answer you as if he knew, before he had heard and had himself been part of the audience for each contestant?

Ath. What then? Do you want me to give the two of you the strange reply?

Kl. Why not?

Ath. If the very little children are the judges they'll choose the man who presents puppets. Isn't that so?

Kl.　How could they not?　　　　　　　　　　　　　　　　　658d

Ath.　If the bigger boys, the one who presents the comedies. Trag-
　　　edy will be the choice of the educated among the women, the
　　　younger men, and probably almost the majority of the whole.

Kl.　Most probably.

Ath.　But the rhapsode, who gave a beautiful recital of the *Iliad* or
　　　the *Odyssey* or something from Hesiod, would probably
　　　please us old men listeners most and be proclaimed the win-
　　　ner by far. Now who would have correctly been winner?
　　　That's the next question, isn't it?

Kl.　Yes.

Ath.　Clearly, for me at least and the two of you, it's necessary to　658e
　　　declare that the ones chosen by men of our age are the ones
　　　who are the correct winners. For our kind of habituation
　　　seems to be the best by far of the sorts of habituation nowa-
　　　days found in all the cities and everywhere.[13]

Kl.　But of course.

Ath.　For my part I go along with the many to this extent, at least,
　　　that music must be judged by pleasure, but not by the plea-
　　　sure of any chance listeners. Almost the finest Muse is she
　　　who pleases the best men and the adequately educated men,
　　　and especially finest is she who pleases the one man who is　659a
　　　distinguished in virtue and education.

　　　　The reason why we assert that the judges of these matters
　　　should have virtue is that they must partake of the rest of
　　　prudence and especially of courage. The true judge should not
　　　learn from the audience how to judge, swept away by the
　　　noise of the many and his own lack of education. Nor, again,
　　　should lack of manliness and cowardice make him contra-
　　　dict what he knows, and pronounce a soft-spirited judg-
　　　ment, lying through the very same lips that just finished
　　　swearing an oath to gods. If justice prevails, it's not as a stu-　659b
　　　dent but as a teacher that the judge will sit before the audi-
　　　ence, and he will oppose himself to those who provide the
　　　spectators with pleasure in a way that is not appropriate or
　　　correct. That's the way it used to be, under the ancient Greek
　　　law—just the opposite[14] of what the law commands today in
　　　Sicily and Italy. There it has given way to the majority of the
　　　spectators, and decides the winner by a show of hands. Thus
　　　it has corrupted the poets themselves, who now create with a
　　　view to the lowly pleasure of the judges; as a result, the spec-　659c
　　　tators educate the poets! In addition, it has corrupted the plea-

sures of the theater itself: an audience should be continually hearing about characters better than their own, and hence continually experiencing better pleasure; but now they make it so that entirely the opposite takes place among them.

What is it that the things now gone through again in the argument wish to indicate to us? Consider if it's the following—

Kl.   What?

659d Ath.   It seems to me that the argument has come around again for the third or fourth time to the same thing, namely, that education is the drawing and pulling of children toward the argument that is said to be correct by the law and is also believed, on account of experience, to be really correct by those who are most decent and oldest. So, to prevent the child's soul from becoming habituated to feeling delight and pain in a way opposed to the law and to those who are persuaded by the law, to make the child's soul follow and feel the same joys and

659e   pains as an old man, the things we call songs, but which are really incantations for souls, have now come into being. These have as their serious goal the consonance we are speaking about. But since the souls of the young cannot sustain seriousness, these incantations are called "games" and "songs," and are treated as such. It's just like when people are sick and their bodies are weak; those in charge try to give them the needed

660a   nourishment mixed with other pleasant tasting foods and drinks, and offer them the bad things mixed with unpleasant stuff, so that they will welcome one and become correctly habituated in hating the other. This is the same thing the correct lawgiver will persuade—or, if he cannot persuade, compel— the poet to do in his beautiful and praiseworthy phrases: to create poetry correctly by depicting in rhythms and harmonies the postures and songs of moderate, courageous, and wholly good men.

660b Kl.   In the name of Zeus, stranger! Do they seem to you to create poetry this way nowadays, in other cities? As far as I observe, I know of no place except among us and the Lacedaimonians where things are done as you now say. There is continual innovation in dances and in all the rest of music, and the changes are not ordained by the laws but by certain disorderly pleasures, which, far from remaining the same and being con-

660c   cerned with the same things (as in the Egyptian system you have interpreted) never stay the same.

Ath. Excellent, Kleinias! If I seemed to you to say that the things you refer to exist now, I wouldn't be surprised if I did so by not expressing clearly what I was thinking. What I was describing was what I wish would come to pass in regard to music, but perhaps I did speak in such a way as to seem to you to say that this is the way things are. For it is not at all pleasant to rail at incurable practices and errors that are far developed, though sometimes it is necessary.   660d

But come, since you also are in agreement with these standards: are you claiming that they are followed among your people and among his people more than among the rest of the Greeks?

Kl. Why not?

Ath. And what if the rest were to adopt them? Would we then claim things were in a finer condition than they are now?

Kl. Presumably it would be a big change if things were done as they are among his people and my people, and also as you just now said things should be done.

Ath. Look, let's come to an agreement regarding the matters under discussion now. Among your peoples, in all education and   660e music is anything said other than the following? You compel the poets to say that the good man, being moderate and just, is happy and blessed, whether he be great and strong or small and weak, whether he be rich or not. Even if someone is richer "than Cinyras or Midas," [15] if he is unjust, he is a wretch and lives a life of misery. And "I would not memorialize," declares your poet—if, that is, he speaks correctly—"nor set down in speech a man" who without justice performed and acquired all the things said to be noble; not even if such a man were to   661a "stand near and assail the enemy"; if he were unjust, I would not want such a man to remain bold after "seeing bloody death," or win a victory in running against "the Northwind of Thrace," or ever to obtain any of the things said to be good. For the things said to be good by the many are not correctly so described. It is said that the best thing is health, and second is beauty, and third is wealth—and then there are said to be ten thousand other goods: sharp sight, hearing, and good percep-   661b tion of all the objects of the senses; and then, by becoming a tyrant, to do whatever one desires; and finally the perfection of complete blessedness, which is to possess all these things and then to become immortal, as quickly as possible. But you two and I, presumably, speak as follows: we say that these

[41]

661c things, beginning with health, are all very good when possessed by just and pious men, but all very bad when possessed by unjust men. To see, to hear, to perceive, and, in general, to live as an immortal for the whole of time, while possessing all the things said to be good except for justice and the whole of virtue, is the greatest of evil. The evil gets less as the time such a man continues to live gets shorter.

661d Now you two are going to persuade and compel your poets to say just the things I've been saying, I suppose; in addition, they must furnish rhythms and harmonies that go along with this, and thus educate your young. Or isn't this so? See what you think. To speak plainly, I say that the things said to be "bad" are good for unjust men and bad for just men, while the good things are really good for good men but bad for bad men.

Well, I ask again, are we in consonance, I and you two, or what?

Kl.   Well, in some respects we appear to me, at least, to be, but in other respects not at all.

Ath. Given a man who possesses in a lasting way health, wealth, and tyrannical power—and for you two, I add exceptional
661e strength and courage along with immortality—but who has nothing else of the things said to be bad, and who has within himself only injustice and insolence—given a man who lives such an existence, perhaps I don't persuade you when I say he is unhappy and indeed manifestly miserable?

Kl.   That is very true, you don't.

Ath. Well, what should we say after this? Doesn't it seem to you two that a man who is courageous, strong, beautiful, and rich,
662a and who does whatever he might desire throughout his whole life will, if he should also be unjust and insolent, necessarily live in a shameful way? This perhaps you would agree to, that he would live in a shameful way, at any rate?

Kl.   By all means.

Ath. What then? Also in a bad way?

Kl.   No, there is no longer the same agreement.

Ath. What then? That he would live also in an unpleasant way and in a way that was not to his benefit?

Kl.   Now how could we agree to these things in addition?

662b Ath. How? It would be likely, my friends, if some god were to give us consonance—for now, at any rate, we sing pretty much at variance with one another. For to me, dear Kleinias, these things appear more necessary than the proposition that Crete is manifestly an island; and if I were a legislator I would try to compel the poets and everyone in the city to speak in this way: I would lay down almost the gravest penalty for anyone in the territory who should say that there are some human beings who were once wicked but live in a pleasant way, or who said that some things are profitable and gainful while others are more just. I would persuade my citizens to say things that are different from the things that are now said, it appears, by Cretans and Lacedaimonians—and by the rest of mankind too, doubtless.

662c

Come now, best of men, in the name of Zeus and Apollo! Suppose we could question these very gods who were your lawgivers and ask: "Then is the most just way of life the most pleasant? Or are there two ways of life, of which the most pleasant happens to be one, and the most just another?" If they were to declare that there are two, we would probably ask them again, if we were questioning correctly: "Then which men must be called the happier—those who live the most just life or those who live the most pleasant?" If they were to reply, "those who live the most pleasant," their answer would be a strange one.

662d

But I don't want such a thing to be put by me in the mouth of the gods; rather, in the mouths of fathers and lawgivers. Let the questions I asked just now be asked of a father and lawgiver, and let him say that the one who lives the most pleasant life is most blessed. Then, after these things I at least would declare: "O father, didn't you want me to live as happily as possible? Yet you never ceased bidding me to live always as justly as possible." Now the lawgiver or father who laid things down in this way would appear strange, I think, and unable to speak in consonance with himself. And if, on the other hand, he had proclaimed the most just life to be the happiest, I think everyone who heard him would ask whatever this was that the law was praising, what good and noble thing, superior to pleasure, was possessed by this life. For what indeed would be this good, separate from pleasure, that accrues to the just man?

662e

663a

Come now, is fame, and the praise that comes from human beings and gods, something good and noble, but unpleasant? Is ignominy the opposite? "Far from it, dear lawgiver," we will declare. But is it unpleasant, though good or noble, neither to do someone injustice nor to be done an injustice by someone? Are the opposites pleasant, though shameful and bad?

Kl.   How could they be?

663b Ath.   So then the argument which does not split the pleasant from the just, and the good from the noble, is (if nothing else) persuasive in making some willing to live the pious and just life. And this means that for a lawgiver, at least, the most shameful and most opposed of arguments is the one that fails to declare that these things are so. For no one would voluntarily be willing to be persuaded to do that which does not bring him more joy than pain.

Looking at things from a distance produces a dizzying obscurity in everyone, so to speak, and especially in children; but our lawgiver will do the opposite to opinion by taking
663c   away the obscurity, and will somehow or other persuade, with habits and praises and arguments, that the just and unjust things are shadow-figures. From the perspective of the unjust and evil man himself, the unjust things appear pleasant, the opposite of the way they appear to the just man, while the just things appear very unpleasant. But from the perspective of the just everything appears entirely the opposite.

Kl.   So it appears.

Ath.   Which shall we claim is the better authority for judging the truth: that of the worse soul or that of the better?

663d Kl.   Necessarily, I suppose, that of the better.

Ath.   Necessarily then, the unjust way of life is not only more shameful and more wicked, but is also truly more unpleasant than the just and pious way of life.

Kl.   That's pretty much the way it is according to the argument being presented now, at any rate, my friends.

Ath.   Even if what the argument has now established were not the case, could a lawgiver of any worth ever tell a lie more profitable than this (if, that is, he ever has the daring to lie to the
663e   young for the sake of a good cause), or more effective in making everybody do all the just things willingly, and not out of compulsion?

Kl.   Truth is a noble and a lasting thing, stranger; but it is likely that it's not easy to persuade people of it.

Ath.   So be it. Now didn't it prove easy to persuade people of that myth told by the Sidonian,[16] though it was incredible, and doesn't the same hold for tens of thousands of other myths?

Kl. What myths?

Ath. About the teeth that were once sown in the ground, from which grew [17] heavily-armed men. Indeed, this myth is a great example for the lawgiver of how it is possible to persuade the souls of the young of just about anything, if one tries. It follows from this that the lawgiver should seek only the convictions which would do the greatest good for the city, and he should discover every device of any sort that will tend to make the whole community speak about these things with one and the same voice, as much as possible, at every moment throughout the whole of life, in songs and myths and arguments.

664a

Now if anyone thinks things are otherwise, let him not hesitate to carry on the controversy through argument.

Kl. It seems to me that with regard to what you've now said, at least, neither of us would ever be able to dispute you.

664b

Ath. What follows after this, then, would belong to me. So I assert that the choruses, three in number, must all sing incantations for the tender young souls of the children, repeating to them all the noble things we have been saying and will say later on, the sum of which is this: when we claim that the gods say that the most pleasant life and the best life are the same, we will be saying what is most true, and also persuading those who must be persuaded, more effectively than if we spoke in some other way.

664c

Kl. What you say must be agreed to.

Ath. First, it would be most correct for the children's chorus dedicated to the Muses to lead off, singing such things in complete seriousness before the whole city. Second should come the chorus for those up to thirty years of age, invoking Paean [18] as witness to the truth of what is said and praying that he be gracious and make the young believers. Then it is necessary that a third group sing, the men between the ages of thirty and sixty; the ones who come after these, since they aren't able anymore to bear the toil of singing, should use their divinely inspired voices to present mythical speeches about the same kinds of characters.

664d

Kl. Who do you say is to make up this third chorus, stranger? We didn't follow very clearly what you intended to explain about them.

Ath. Yet most of the arguments that have been uttered up until now have been pretty much for the sake of these men!

664e Kl. We haven't understood; try to explain more clearly.

Ath. We said, if we remember, at the beginning of our discussion, that the nature of all young things is fiery, and unable to remain calm either in body or in voice, but is always crying and leaping in a disorderly way. We said that none of the other animals attains perception of order in either of these,

665a but that human nature alone has this. The name for order in movement is "rhythm," and for order in voice, the mixture of sharp and deep, the name is "harmony"; the two things together are called "a chorus." The gods, we asserted, have taken pity on us and given us as fellow members or leaders of our choruses Apollo and the Muses; then, if we remember, we spoke of a third, Dionysus.

Kl. How could we not remember?

Ath. Now the chorus of Apollo, and that of the Muses have been

665b described; the third and last, the chorus of Dionysus, must necessarily be described.

Kl. What? Explain. For it sounds very strange, at first hearing, a Dionysian chorus of elders—if, that is, men over thirty or even fifty, men as old as sixty, are to dance in his honor.

Ath. What you say is certainly very true. This does require an argument, I think, showing how this would be reasonable.

Kl. But of course.

Ath. So then, are we in agreement on what went before?

665c Kl. In what respect?

Ath. That every man and child, free and slave, female and male—indeed, the whole city—must never cease singing, as an incantation to itself, these things we've described, which must in one way or another be continually changing, presenting variety in every way, so that the singers will take unsatiated pleasure in their hymns.

Kl. How could it not be agreed that this is how things must be done?

665d Ath. Where would our best part of the city—the part that is most persuasive of those in the city because of its age and also its prudence—do its singing of the most beautiful things, so as to effect the most good things? Or will we foolishly neglect this part which would wield authority over the most beautiful and beneficial songs?

Kl. But it's impossible to neglect them, at least according to what's being said now.

Ath. So what would be fitting for this part? See if it's the following—

Kl. Which?

Ath. Everyone as he gets more elderly is presumably full of reluctance to sing songs; he gets less delight from doing this and would become rather ashamed if compelled to do it. The more elderly and more moderate he becomes, the more this increases. Isn't that so? 665e

Kl. That is so.

Ath. Then he would be still more ashamed to sing at the theater, standing up before all sorts of human beings. Especially if such men were compelled to sing under the same conditions as the choruses that train their voices for competitions, lean and without having eaten, they would presumably do so entirely without pleasure, ashamed, and without any eagerness of spirit.

Kl. What you say would be inevitable. 666a

Ath. How then will we encourage them so as to make their spirits eager to sing the songs? Won't we legislate as follows? First, children until the age of eighteen are not to taste wine at all. We will teach that one shouldn't pour fire into the fire that is already in the body and the soul until they've taken up their tasks, and that they must be on their guard against the madness that is habitual in youth. After this, up until the age of thirty it will be permitted to taste wine with due measure; but drunkenness and copious wine drinking will be totally 666b forbidden to the young man. As a man approaches forty he is to share in the enjoyment of the common meals, invoking the presence of the other gods, and especially Dionysus, at this mystery-rite [19] and play of older men, which he has bestowed on human beings as a drug that heals the austerity of old age. Its effect is that we are rejuvenated, and the soul, by forgetting its despondency of spirit, has its disposition turned from 666c harder to softer, so that it becomes more malleable, like iron when it is plunged into fire.

First, then, if each man were so disposed, wouldn't he become more eager in spirit and less ashamed to sing and (as we've often put it) to chant incantations—not before many, but only before a measured number; and not in the presence of strangers, but only among his own intimates?

Kl. Very much so!

Ath. So this method wouldn't be entirely unseemly as a device for inducing them to partake of our singing.

666d Kl. Not at all.

Ath. In what sort of voice will the men sing? Or isn't it obvious that they must have some Muse that is fitting for them?[20]

Kl. What else?

Ath. So which would be fitting for divine men? Would it be that of the choruses?

Kl. My people at any rate, stranger, and this fellow's as well, wouldn't be able to sing any song other than the ones we learned to sing when we were habituated in the choruses.

666e Ath. Of course not. For you have really never attained to the most beautiful song. Your regime is that of an armed camp and not of men settled in cities. You keep your young in a flock, like a bunch of colts grazing in a herd. None of you takes his own youngster apart, drawing him, all wild and complaining, away from his fellow grazers.[21] None of you gives him a private groom and educates him by currying and soothing him, giving him all that is appropriate for child rearing. If you did,

667a he would become not only a good soldier but someone capable of managing a city and towns, someone who, as we said at the beginning, was more of a warrior than those warriors in Tyrtaeus. He would always and everywhere honor the possession of courage as the fourth, not the first, part of virtue, for private individuals and the whole city.

Kl. Somehow or other, stranger, you are once again belittling our lawgivers.

Ath. No!—but if I am, I'm not doing so intentionally, my good man. Let's follow wherever the argument carries us, if you will.

667b Now if we possess a Muse that is more beautiful than that of the choruses and that in the common theaters, let's try to give her to these men whom we assert are ashamed of that one and seek to share in this one that is most beautiful.

Kl. By all means.

Ath. First, then, isn't it the case that in all things which are accompanied by some charm,[22] the most important or serious feature is either this charm itself, alone, or a certain correctness, or, third, the benefit? I mean, for example, that food, drink, and nourishment in general are accompanied by a charm, which we would call pleasure. As for the correctness and the benefit, the healthiness which we say is in each meal is also the most correct aspect. 667c

Kl. Yes indeed.

Ath. Then again, accompanying the experience of learning there is something of charm, the pleasure; but the correctness and the benefit, the goodness and the beauty, come from its truth.

Kl. That is so.

Ath. What about the image-making arts which produce resemblances? Isn't it the case that when these arts produce this, the accompanying pleasure in them—if there is pleasure—would be very justly pronounced "charm"? 667d

Kl. Yes.

Ath. Presumably the correctness in such things is, generally speaking, produced primarily by equality in quantity and quality, not by pleasure.

Kl. Nobly put.

Ath. So then pleasure would be a correct criterion only for something which wasn't produced to provide some benefit, or truth, or similarity, nor of course harm, but was produced only for the sake of what accompanies these, the charm. And when it is accompanied by none of the other things, it would be very noble for someone to call the charm "pleasure." 667e

Kl. You are speaking now of harmless pleasure only.

Ath. Yes, and this is what I call "play"—when something doesn't do any harm or any benefit worthy of serious consideration.

Kl. What you are saying is very true.

Ath. Well then, wouldn't we assert that it follows from the things that have just been said that pleasure and untrue opinion are the least appropriate criteria for judging any imitation—or, for that matter, any equality? Surely it's not just because of somebody's opinion, or because somebody doesn't feel charmed, that the equal would be equal or the proportionate wholly proportionate; wouldn't it be because of the truth, most of all, and least of all anything else? 668a

Kl. Entirely so.

Ath. Now don't we assert that all music, at least, is imagery and imitation?

Kl. But of course.

Ath. So the argument that is least acceptable is when someone asserts that music should be judged by pleasure. If there should
668b exist somewhere such a music, it should be sought as the least serious; what should be sought as serious is music that contains a resemblance to the imitation of the beautiful.

Kl. Very true.

Ath. And these who seek the most beautiful song and Muse should seek, it is likely, not she who is pleasant, but she who is correct. For correctness of imitation, we have asserted, exists when there is complete reproduction both in quantity and quality of the thing imitated.

Kl. How could it be otherwise?

Ath. And in the case of music everyone would agree to this at least,
668c that all its creation is imitation and image-making; wouldn't everybody—poets, audience, actors—agree to this at least?

Kl. Very much so.

Ath. Then it's likely that in the case of each creation one must know what it is, in order to avoid making mistakes about it. If one doesn't know the being—what is intended and what the image is really of—one will scarcely know whether it is correct in its intention or mistaken.

Kl. Scarcely. How could it be otherwise?

668d Ath. He who does not know what is done correctly would never be able to know what is done well or badly, would he? But I have not put this very clearly. Perhaps it would be clearer if put this way—

Kl. How?

Ath. There are of course myriad images which are visible to our eye.

Kl. Yes.

Ath. What then, if someone doesn't know what each of the bodies of the things imitated is? Would he ever know what is correctly executed in them? What I mean is something like this: doesn't he have to know whether the imitation captures the
668e number and the arrangement of each of the parts, how many there are and how they fit next to one another in the appropriate order, and also the colors and shapes, or whether all these things have been put together in a confused way? Do you think someone can ever know these things if he is completely ignorant of what the living thing is that has been imitated?

Kl.   How could he?

Ath.   What if we were to know that the thing that has been painted
       or sculpted is a human being, and that all his own parts, col-   669a
       ors, and shapes have been captured by the art? Does it follow
       necessarily that whoever knows about these things also read-
       ily knows whether the work is beautiful or just where it is
       deficient in beauty?

Kl.   That would mean, stranger, that all of us, so to speak, know
       what is beautiful in any paintings of living things.

Ath.   What you say is very correct. Isn't it the case, then, that with
       regard to each image, in painting and in music and in all the
       rest, the person who is going to be a prudent judge must have
       three kinds of knowledge? He must know first what the thing
       is, and then know how correctly, and then—the third thing—   669b
       how well, any of the images of it in words, tunes, and rhythms
       are produced.

Kl.   That's likely, anyway.

Ath.   Now we mustn't fail to indicate the way in which music
       presents a difficulty. Since people sing on about music more
       than about the other sorts of images, music requires the most
       careful treatment of all the images. For if someone makes a
       mistake in regard to music, he becomes well disposed toward   669c
       wicked characters and he suffers the greatest harm. Yet it is
       very difficult to perceive that one has made a mistake, because
       the poets are so inferior, as poets, to the Muses themselves.
       The latter would never make a mistake like setting a man's
       words to a woman's color and tune, or like harmonizing the
       tune and postures of free men with the rhythms of slaves and
       men who are not free, or, again, giving to free rhythms and
       postures they've constructed a tune or speech that contradicts
       the rhythms. Nor, again, would they mix together the sounds
       of beasts, humans, instruments, and every sort of noise, pre-   669d
       tending to imitate some one thing. But the human poets do
       indeed weave and jumble together such things, creating a
       senseless mishmash such as would be laughable to the
       humans who, in the words of Orpheus,[23] "are at the age when
       pleasure blooms." For they see that all these are jumbled con-
       coctions, and moreover, that the poets are guilty of separating
       rhythm and postures from melodies—that they write bare
       words in meter without any accompaniment, and create mel-
       ody and rhythm without words, to be played on kithara or   669e

[51]

670a

aulos[24] all alone, and thus make it very difficult to know what is intended and which of the worthwhile imitations are being imitated by this rhythm and harmony presented without words. But all those creations which depend on speed, dexterity, and beast-like cries, which lead to the employment of aulos or kithara without dance and song, must be considered completely uncouth. The use of aulos or kithara all alone must be regarded as unmusical virtuosity.

670b

Enough said about such things. Our task, after all, is to consider what use our thirty-year-olds and men over fifty should make of the Muses, not what use they should not make. Now from what has been said our argument seems to me to be indicating the following: those fifty-year-olds for whom the singing is appropriate must have an education superior to that given by the chorus Muse. For they must necessarily be sensitive themselves to and knowledgeable about rhythms and harmoniae.[25] Otherwise how will any of them know what is correct in melodies—whether a given melody is or is not suitable for the Dorian and whether or not the poet has set the melody to a correct rhythm?

Kl. Obviously, they won't know at all.

Ath. It's laughable that the great mob considers itself capable of knowing what is good harmony and good rhythm, and what is not, as many of them as have been drilled to sing to an aulos

670c

and dance in rhythm; they don't realize that they practice these things without understanding each of them. The fact remains, every melody when accompanied by the appropriate things is presumably correct, and when accompanied by inappropriate things erroneous.

Kl. Most necessarily.

Ath. What then? Will someone who doesn't know this ever know what we're speaking of—that is, whether the melody has been performed correctly?

Kl. How could he possibly?

Ath. Once again now, it seems, we have discovered that our

670d

singers, whom we have now invited and in a way compelled to sing willingly, must, almost of necessity, be educated to this point: each of them must be able to follow the steps of the rhythms and the notes of the melodies, so that by keeping an eye on the harmoniae and rhythms, they may choose what is appropriate, what is fitting for men of their age and condition

to sing; then they will sing in this way what is chosen, and by
singing, they will themselves enjoy harmless pleasures at the
moment and will lead the younger men to take the proper   670e
enjoyment in worthy characters.

Now in becoming educated to this extent, they would handle an education which is more exacting than both the education of the majority and the education of the poets themselves.
For there is no necessity that a poet know the third thing—that
is, whether the imitation is noble or ignoble; but it is almost a
necessity that the poet know about the harmonia and rhythm.
The former, however, must know all three things, in order to
choose which music is most noble as well as which is second.
Otherwise the young will never hear an adequate incantation
on behalf of virtue.   671a

The argument has done its best to present what it wished to
demonstrate in the beginning, namely, that it is noble to
speak out in favor of the Dionysian chorus; let us consider
then whether this is the case.

Presumably, such a meeting will always become, of necessity, more boisterous as more drinking goes on—from the
beginning we laid this down as a necessary hypothesis
regarding the things that are taking place [26] now.   671b

Kl.   Necessarily.

Ath.   Everyone becomes lighter than he really is, rejoices, becomes
filled with license of speech, and fails to listen to his neighbors; each considers himself capable of ruling the others as
well as himself.

Kl.   How could it be otherwise?

Ath.   Didn't we assert that when these things come to pass, the
souls of the drinkers, like some iron, become fiery, softened,
and youthful, so that they can easily be led—as they were
when they were young—by someone who possesses the ability and the knowledge required to educate and mold souls?   671c
Didn't we say that the one who did the molding is the same as
he who molded them earlier, the good lawgiver, whose laws
must be fellow drinkers at the banquet? They must be able to
make whoever becomes sanguine, bold, and more shameless
than he should be, whoever refuses to take his orderly turn in
being silent and in speaking, in drinking and in music, willing to act just the opposite. When ignoble boldness appears,
these laws will be able to send in as a combatant the noblest   671d

sort of fear accompanied by justice, the divine fear to which we gave the name "awe" and "shame."

Kl. So we did.

Ath. And as guardians of these laws, and fellow craftsmen, we will appoint steady and sober men as generals to command those who are unsober. Without them, it would be more dangerous to fight against the effects of drunkenness than it is to fight against enemies in war when one's commanders are unsteady. Anyone who is incapable of willing obedience to these and to the Dionysian leaders (who will be men over sixty years of age) will bear shame equal to or surpassing that of the man who is disobedient to Ares's[27] commanders.

671e

Kl. Correctly spoken.

Ath. Suppose, then, such drunkenness, and such play, were to be instituted; suppose the fellow drinkers were to carry on all their intercourse in accordance with the laws, obeying whenever the sober men gave orders to the unsober: wouldn't those who drank together benefit? Instead of becoming enemies as happens now, wouldn't they part from one another closer friends than they had been before?

672a

Kl. Correct—if, that is, it were to take place as you now say.

Ath. Let us not then simply blame any more the gift of Dionysus, as if it were evil and unacceptable in a city. Indeed, someone might say still more on its behalf, but one must be wary of speaking in the presence of the many about the greatest good it brings; human beings misinterpret it, and don't understand what is said.

672b

Kl. What are you referring to?

Ath. There is an argument and oracle spread about somehow, telling how this god had his soul deprived of its wits through the agency of his stepmother Hera.[28] In revenge, it is said, he inflicts Bacchic frenzies with all their mad choruses; and this is the cause of the gift of wine. I'll leave it to those who think it's safe to say such things about gods to say them; but this much I do know: every living being, to the degree to which it is appropriate for it to possess intelligence when fully developed, to this same degree it lacks intelligence when it first is born.[29] During the time in which it lacks the prudence that is proper to it, every being is completely mad and cries out in a disorderly way; as soon as it can stand by itself, it jumps in a disorderly way. Let us recollect that we asserted that these

672c

motions and cries were the source of music and gymnastic.

Kl. We remember; how could we not?

Ath. We also asserted that this source gave us humans the percep- 672d
tion of rhythm and harmony, and that Apollo, the Muses, and
Dionysus are the gods responsible?

Kl. But of course.

Ath. The argument put forward by the others seems to claim that
wine was given to human beings out of revenge and was intended to drive us mad; the argument we are putting forth, in
contrast, claims that it is a medicine given with just the opposite intention—to put awe in the soul and health as well as
strength in the body.

Kl. You have recalled the argument in a very fine way, stranger.

Ath. And half of the discussion about the choral art has been com- 672e
pleted. Shall we complete the other half in whatever way may
seem well, or shall we skip it?

Kl. What are you talking about, and how are you making this
division?

Ath. Presumably the choral art as a whole is for us the same as education as a whole, and the vocal aspect of this is rhythms and
harmoniae.

Kl. Yes.

Ath. Now the aspect that pertains to bodily movement has rhythm,
which is shared by the movement of the voice, and posture,
which is peculiar to it alone; while peculiar to the movement 673a
of the voice is melody.[30]

Kl. Very true.

Ath. The vocal aspect, reaching to the soul, we regarded as education in virtue and we named it—how I don't know—"music."

Kl. And correctly so.

Ath. Now with regard to the bodily aspect, which we referred to as
"dance" in the case of persons at play, if this sort of movement
becomes effective in instilling the virtue of the body we would
give the name "gymnastic" to the art of training involved in
the process.

Kl. That is very correct.

Ath. With regard to music, we said a moment ago—and let it be 673b
said again now—that almost half of the choral art has been
gone through and completed; shall we talk about the other
half, or what shall we do, and how?

Kl. Best of men, you are carrying on a dialogue with Cretans and

Lacedaimonians, and we have gone through music but have omitted to speak of gymnastic: now how do you think either of us is going to answer you this question?

Ath. I at least would assert that you have with your question given
673c   a pretty clear answer; I understand your present question to be an answer, as I say, and in fact a command to complete the discussion of gymnastic.

Kl.   You have understood very well: so do it.

Ath. It must be done; of course, it's not very difficult to talk to you about what you both know. You have much more experience in this art than you had in the other.

Kl.   What you say is pretty much true.

Ath. Well, the source of this play is once again the fact that every
673d   living being is by nature accustomed to jumping, and that humankind, as we asserted, obtained a perception of rhythm and thus engendered and gave birth to dance. When song recalled and awakened rhythm, the two in common gave birth to the chorus and to play.

Kl.   Very true.

Ath. Now the one, as we said, we've already gone over; next we will try to go through the other.

Kl.   Yes indeed.

Ath. First, though, if it's all right with you two, let's put the cap-
673e   stone on our discussion of the use of drunkenness.

Kl.   What capstone and what sort do you mean?

Ath. If a city will consider the practice that has now been discussed as something serious, and will make use of it, in conformity with laws and order, for the sake of moderation, and will not refrain from other pleasures but will arrange them with a view to mastering them according to the same argument, then all these things should be employed, in this manner.

On the other hand, if this is treated as something playful, if anyone who wishes will be allowed to drink whenever he
674a   wishes, with whomever he wishes, along with all sorts of other similar practices, I would not vote for the use of drunkenness at any time by this city or this man. Indeed, I would go beyond the Cretan and the Lacedaimonian usage, and advocate the Carthaginian[31] law which forbids anyone to taste this drink while out on campaign and requires that only water be drunk for all that time. I would add to that law, and forbid drinking within the city too, among female and male slaves,

and among magistrates during the year in which they serve; 674b
pilots and judges would not be allowed to taste wine at all
while they were performing their services, and the same
would apply to anyone who was about to give advice in an important council meeting. Moreover, no one would be allowed
to drink at all during the day except for purposes of physical
training or illness, nor at night would any man or woman who
was intending to create children. And someone might list
many other circumstances in which those who possess intelligence and a correct law should not drink wine.

So according to this argument no city would need many 674c
vines, and while the other farm products and the diet as a
whole would be regulated, the wine production would be almost the most measured and modest of all. Let this, strangers,
if you agree, be our capstone to the argument about wine.

Kl. Beautifully spoken, and we agree.

BOOK III

676a   Ath.   So then that's how these things should be done. But what shall we assert was the original source of the political regime? Wouldn't one see it in the easiest and finest way by looking from this viewpoint . . . ?

Kl.   From which?

Ath.   From the same viewpoint one should always choose in order to see the progression of cities as they change towards virtue and at the same time towards vice.

Kl.   What viewpoint are you speaking of?

676b   Ath.   I suppose I mean one that embraces an infinite length of time and the changes during that time.

Kl.   How do you mean?

Ath.   Come, do you think you could ever conceive how long a time there have been cities, and human beings engaged in politics?

Kl.   It's not at all easy, at least.

Ath.   You do see, though, that it would be an immense and immeasurable time?

Kl.   Yes, that at least, indeed.

Ath.   Don't we suppose that tens upon tens of thousands of cities

676c   have come into being during that time, and that just as many, in the same proportions, have been destroyed? And hasn't each place been governed often by every kind of regime? And haven't they at one time gotten bigger from being smaller, and then smaller from being bigger, and haven't they gone from better to worse and from worse to better?

Kl.   Necessarily.

Ath.   Let us grasp, if we can, the cause of this change. For this might perhaps show us the first origin and transformation of political regimes.

Kl. You speak well, and we should proceed with eager spirits—you to show what you think about these things, and we to follow.

Ath. Well, then, do both of you believe that there's some truth in   677a
the ancient sayings?

Kl. Which sayings?

Ath. The ones that tell of many disasters—floods and plagues and many other things—which have destroyed human beings and left only a tiny remnant of the human race.

Kl. This sort of thing seems entirely credible to everyone.

Ath. Come, of the many disasters let's focus our minds on one that occurred once on account of a flood.

Kl. What shall we think about in regard to it?

Ath. How those who then escaped the destruction would almost all   677b
be mountain herdsmen—little sparks of the human race saved on the peaks somewhere.

Kl. Clearly.

Ath. Presumably men such as these, at least, necessarily lack experience in the arts, and especially in the contrivances that city dwellers use against one another, motivated by the desire to have more, the love of victory, and all the other mischief they think up against each other.

Kl. That's likely, anyway.

Ath. Shall we assume that the cities settled in the plains and along   677c
the sea were utterly destroyed at that time?

Kl. So we shall assume.

Ath. Won't we assert that all tools were destroyed, and that if some serious and important part of an art—whether politics or some other sort of wisdom—had been discovered, all these things would have perished at that time? For otherwise, best of men, if these things had remained through all time as thoroughly ordered as they are today, how could anything new ever have been discovered?[1]

Kl. In other words, for tens upon tens of thousands of years these   677d
things were unknown to the men at that time, and only within the past one or two thousand years have they been brought to light, some by Daedalus, others by Orpheus, and others by Palamedes; the things that pertain to music by Marsyas and Olympos, the things that pertain to the lyre by Amphion; and

very many other arts by other men—just yesterday or the day before, so to speak.[2]

Ath. Is there any reason, Kleinias, why you omitted your friend, who really was around only yesterday?[3]

Kl. You don't mean Epimenides?

677e Ath. Yes, him. He far surpassed all others among your people in inventiveness, my friend; what Hesiod had divined in speech long ago, he actually brought to completion in deed—as you people claim.[4]

Kl. So we claim.

Ath. So what shall we say human affairs were like after the destruction? Wasn't there a vast and frightening desolation, but a great mass of abundant land? Won't we say the other animals were destroyed, while the cattle, and the remnant of the stock of goats that might have happened to remain somewhere, 678a barely supported the life of the herdsmen at the beginning?

Kl. How else could it have been?

Ath. With regard to the city and the political regime and law-giving—the subjects with which our discussion is now concerned—do we suppose that there was, so to speak, any memory at all?

Kl. None at all.

Ath. So from those men, in that situation, have developed all the things we possess now: cities and political regimes and arts and laws, and much wickedness—but much virtue as well.

Kl. How do you mean?

678b Ath. Do we suppose, you amazing man, that men at that time—inexperienced in the many beautiful things that go with urban life, and inexperienced in the opposite sorts of things as well—ever became either perfectly virtuous or perfectly vicious?

Kl. You've stated it beautifully, and we understand what you mean.

Ath. Then as time went on, and as our race multiplied, everything arrived at the state it's in now?

Kl. That's very correct.

Ath. Not straightaway though, it's likely, but rather little by little over a very long period of time.

678c Kl. This seems most appropriate.

Ath. For I suppose that the fear of descending from the heights into the valleys was ringing in everyone's ears.

Kl. How could it be otherwise?

Ath. Weren't they glad whenever they saw each other, because there were so few of them during that time, although the means of transportation by land and by sea were almost all destroyed, so to speak, along with the arts? I don't think, therefore, that it was very easy to mix with one another. For iron and copper and all metals had disappeared under the mud, 678d and they were at a complete loss as to how to extract such things; as a result they had very little cut timber. If some tool had survived somewhere up in the mountains, it was soon worn out with use and disappeared, and there weren't others to replace it until the art of metals had appeared among human beings.

Kl. How could there have been?

Ath. And how many generations later do we suppose this happened?

Kl. Very many, obviously. 678e

Ath. Doesn't it follow that the arts which depend on iron and copper and all such things would have disappeared for an equal or even longer time?

Kl. How could they not?

Ath. For a variety of reasons, then, civil war and war were destroyed during that time.

Kl. How so?

Ath. First because they were delighted with one another and full of goodwill on account of the desolation. Then again, food was not something they fought over. At that time most lived from herding, and there was no lack of pasture land—except perhaps for some people at the start. So they didn't lack milk and 679a meat. Besides, by hunting they provided themselves with food that was neither poor in quality nor scanty in amount. They were well off in cloaks, bedding, houses, and equipment for use over the fires and also for tasks that don't call for fire. For not one of the molding and weaving arts requires iron; and a god has given these two arts to provide all these things for 679b human beings, so that whenever the human race finds itself in such straits it may be able to grow and progress. Hence they weren't terribly poor, and weren't compelled by poverty to differ with one another. On the other hand, since they lacked gold and silver they didn't ever become rich, either—and such was their situation then. Now the most well bred dispositions usually spring up in a home when neither wealth nor poverty

679c dwell there. For neither insolence nor injustice, nor again jealousies and ill will, come into being there.

They were good on account of these things and also because of what is called naive simplicity. For whenever they heard something was noble or something was shameful, in their simplicity they considered what had been said to be the very truth, and believed it. No one had the wisdom, as they do nowadays, to know how to be on the lookout for lies. They believed that what they heard about gods as well as about human beings was true, and lived according to these things. That is why they were in every way as we have just described them.

679d Kl. To me at least, and to him too, it seems this is the way things were.

Ath. Shouldn't we go on to say that the many generations who passed their lives this way were less practiced and less knowledgeable in the arts generally than those who lived before the flood or those who live now, and especially as regards the arts of war? They didn't know all the present-day arts of war on land or on sea, or in a city all by itself, which are called lawsuits and civil wars, and in which every sort of contrivance of
679e words and deeds is devised in order to do mutual mischief and injustice. So, for the reason we already have explained, shouldn't we say that they were simpler and more courageous and also more moderate and in every way more just?

Kl. What you say is correct.

Ath. Now what we've been saying, and all that is still to follow from it, has been said as a means to our coming to understand
680a what need the men of that time had for laws, and who was lawgiver for them.

Kl. You've stated it in a fine way.

Ath. Isn't it the case, though, that they didn't yet need lawgivers, and that such a thing wasn't yet likely to occur in those times? For writing doesn't yet exist among those born in that part of the cycle, and their lives are guided by habits and by what are called ancestral laws.

Kl. That's likely, anyway.

Ath. But even this is already a kind of political regime.

Kl. Which kind?

680b Ath. I think everyone calls the regime of that epoch "dynasty,"⁵ and even now it still exists in many places, among Greeks as well as barbarians. This is presumably the regime Homer[6] speaks of in connection with the household of the Cyclopes, when he says

>Among these people are neither deliberative
>   assemblies nor clan-rules,[7]
>But they dwell on crests of lofty mountains
>In hollow caves, and each gives the rule to
>His own children and wives, and they don't
>   trouble themselves about one another.

680c

Kl. This poet of yours seems to have been quite charming. We've gone through other verses of his and found them very urbane. But we're not familiar with much of what he says because we Cretans don't make much use of foreign poetry.

Meg. We, however, do; and he is probably the chief of such poets, although he portrays in each case a way of life that is not Laconian but rather sort of Ionian. He certainly seems to be a good witness now to your argument, since through his myth he attributes their ancient ways to savagery.

680d

Ath. Yes, he is a witness, so let's take his word for it that such regimes do sometimes arise.

Kl. Fine.

Ath. Aren't they found among those who have been scattered in single households or clans in the confusion caused by the destructive disasters? The eldest rules with an authority handed down from the father and mother, whom the others follow, like birds[8] forming one flock. Thus aren't they ruled by paternal laws and by a monarchy that is the most just of all monarchies?

680e

Kl. Most certainly.

Ath. After this, larger numbers come together in bigger communities, making cities. Those who live in the foothills are the first to turn to farming; and they create one common, large dwelling by erecting defensive walls of stone around themselves, on account of wild beasts.

681a

Kl. It seems likely, at any rate, that it happened this way.

Ath. Then what? Isn't the following likely . . . ?

Kl. What?

Ath. As these dwellings are growing bigger out of the smaller original ones, each of the small family groups arrives clan by clan, possessing both its own eldest who rules, and its own particular customs because it has lived apart. The variety of their dif-

681b

[63]

ferent customs pertaining to the gods and to themselves derives from the variety in their parents and in those who reared them; the rather orderly have rather orderly customs and the manly have rather manly customs. Since they each thus imprint their own conceptions on their own children and on their children's children, they come, as we say, to the larger common dwelling bringing their own particular laws.

Kl. Of course, how could they not?

681c Ath. Moreover, presumably the laws of each are necessarily pleasing to them, while the others' are less so.

Kl. So it is.

Ath. It's likely that we've stumbled unawares, as it were, upon the origin of legislation.

Kl. Indeed it is.

Ath. Surely, after this, those who have come together are compelled to choose certain men common to them who look over the customs of all the clans and, having picked out the ones they find especially agreeable for the community, display them clearly

681d and present them for the approval of the leaders and chiefs, the monarchs as it were, of the populace. The men who do this will be called lawgivers; but although they have appointed the ruling officials, thus fashioning a sort of aristocracy or even monarchy out of the dynasties, during the period when the regime is undergoing the transformation they themselves will rule.

Kl. Things would turn out just this way, though step by step.

Ath. Now let's say that yet a third pattern of regime emerges, in which all forms and experiences of political regimes and of cities come together.

681e Kl. Which is this?

Ath. The one that comes after the second, as Homer[9] reveals when he says the third emerged in this way: ". . . and he founded Dardania," he asserts somewhere,

since sacred Ilium had not yet been
Founded on the plain, a city of human beings endowed
with speech,
But instead they still dwelled among the foothills of Ida
with the many springs.

682a When he speaks these words, and those others that he spoke about the Cyclopes, he speaks somehow according to god, as well as according to nature. For the race of poets is divine, and becomes inspired when it sings: each time, singing in the company of certain Graces and Muses, they hit upon many things that truly happened.

Kl. They surely do.

Ath. Let's proceed still further into this myth which has now come upon us, since it may reveal something about the object of our inquiry. Shouldn't we?

Kl. Certainly. 682b

Ath. Ilium was settled, we assert, when they left the heights for the wide and beautiful plain and settled on a low hill with many rivers that rushed down from Ida.

Kl. So they say, anyway.

Ath. Don't we suppose that this came to pass many ages after the flood?

Kl. It had to be many ages.

Ath. It's likely that they were possessed by an amazing degree of forgetfulness regarding the disaster just now discussed, when 682c they thus set up a city close to a lot of rivers flowing down from the heights, putting their trust in some hills that were not very high.

Kl. This makes it completely clear that they were separated by a great interval of time from such suffering.

Ath. I suppose that already, at that time, there were many other cities being settled down below, since human beings were multiplying.

Kl. But of course.

Ath. And presumably these others undertook a military expedition against this one, and probably came by sea, since now everyone was making use of the sea without fear. 682d

Kl. So it appears.

Ath. After remaining about ten years, presumably, the Achaeans [10] sacked Troy.

Kl. They certainly did.

Ath. And so during this time, a ten-year period, while Ilium was being besieged many evils befell each of the besiegers at home, through the revolts of the young men. [11] When the soldiers returned to their cities and homes they were not nobly received by these, nor with justice, but instead in such a 682e way as to produce many deaths and slaughters and exiles. The ones who were driven into exile came back again though, having changed their name from Achaeans to Dorians because

[65]

Dorieus was the one who gathered the exiles together at that time.[12] And surely it is you, O Lacedaimonians, who tell the myth and complete the account of all the things that happened after this.

Meg. But of course.

Ath. We have come now once again, as if according to a god, to the point at the beginning of our dialogue about laws where we digressed and fell into the topics of music and drunken carousals. The argument is, as it were, letting us get a good hold[13] on it again, for it has arrived at the very settling of Lacedaimon, which you both were asserting to have been correctly settled (along with Crete, as if by codes of law that were brothers). Now we've gained this much by the meanderings of the argument, by going through certain regimes and settlements: we have seen the first, the second, and the third city, settled one after the other, as we believe, over immense stretches of time. And here this fourth city—or nation, if you wish—comes before us, having been settled in an earlier time and now being settled once again. If from all of this we are able to learn what has and has not been nobly settled, which laws preserve the things that are preserved and which destroy the things that are destroyed, and what sort of changes would make a city happy, then, Megillus and Kleinias, we ought to discuss all these things again, from the beginning as it were— unless we have some objection to what has been said so far.

Meg. If, stranger, some god would promise us that if we make a second attempt at an investigation into lawgiving we will hear arguments no worse and no shorter than what were said just now, I at least would be willing to have a long walk, and for me this day would seem to become short—even though we are close to the day when the god turns from summer toward winter.[14]

Ath. So it's likely that these things must be investigated.

Meg. By all means.

Ath. Let's put ourselves in thought back into that time when not only Lacedaimon but also Argos and Messene and their dependencies were sufficiently under the control of your ancestors, Megillus. According to what is said in myth[15] at least, they decided next to divide the army into three parts and found three cities—Argos, Messene and Lacedaimon.

Meg. Indeed they did.

683a

683b

683c

683d

Ath. Temenos became king of Argos, Kresphontes of Messene, and
Procles and Eurusthenes of Lacedaimon.

Meg. But of course.

Ath. And everyone at that time swore that they would come to their
aid if anyone subverted their monarchies. 683e

Meg. Of course.

Ath. In the name of Zeus! Is a monarchy dissolved, or has any rule
ever been dissolved, by anybody other than the rulers themselves? Or have we now forgotten that we established this just
a little while ago now, in the speeches we chanced to make?

Meg. How could we?

Ath. Then we shall now have made such a thesis even firmer. For
it's likely that the deeds we've chanced upon lead us to the
same argument, so we won't be investigating the same argument on the basis of some empty figment, but on the basis of 684a
something that really happened and possesses truth.

What happened was this: the three kings and the three cities that were to be governed monarchically all swore mutual
oaths, in accordance with the common laws they set up for
ruling and being ruled. The former swore not to make their
rule harsher as time went on and the line continued, while the
latter swore that if the rulers kept their oaths, they in return
would never dissolve the monarchies or allow others to try to 684b
do so. They also promised that the kings would help the other
kings or the populaces if they were treated unjustly, and that
the populaces would help the other populaces or kings if they
were treated unjustly. Isn't that the way it was?

Meg. That's the way it was.

Ath. Now, whether the kings or certain others did the legislating,
wasn't this a very great advantage in the three regime-
establishments that were legislated in the three cities . . . ?

Meg. What?

Ath. The fact that there were always two cities ready to take the
field against any one of the cities that disobeyed the established laws.

Meg. Clearly.

Ath. Of course, the many command their lawgivers to establish 684c
such laws as the populaces and the majorities will accept voluntarily, just as if someone were to command gymnasts or
doctors to do what is pleasant as they care for and cure the
bodies they care for.

Meg. Entirely so.

Ath. Yet in fact it is often the case that one must be contented if someone can make bodies strong and healthy with only modest pain.

Meg. But of course.

684d Ath. At that time, they were provided with yet this other advantage that had no small role in making the laying down of the laws easy.

Meg. What?

Ath. When the lawgivers were arranging for them some sort of equality in property they were not subjected to that very great reproach raised in many other cities during the time of the establishment of laws, whenever someone seeks to change land tenure and dissolve debts because he sees that otherwise a sufficient degree of equality will never be possible. When a

684e lawgiver tries to change any of such things, everyone raises against him the cry, "Do not move the immovable!"[16] and curses him for introducing redivision of the land and dissolution of debts, and thus putting every man at his wit's end. But for the Dorians there was this further advantage, that the process went along in a fine way and was free from blame,[17] because they could divide up the land without disputes and, in addition, there were no large, ancient debts.

Meg. True.

Ath. So then how, you two best of men, did the settlement and legislation ever turn out so badly for them?

685a Meg. What do you mean, and what do you blame in them?

Ath. The fact that of the three existing dwelling places, two of them swiftly corrupted their regime and laws, while only one held fast—your city.

Meg. That's not a very easy question you're asking.

Ath. But this is what we must now investigate and inquire into, playing at this moderate old man's game concerning laws, and proceeding on our way without discomfort, as we asserted we

685b would do when we began our walk.

Meg. Why not? It must be done as you say.

Ath. And what more beautiful inquiry into laws could we make than an inquiry into the laws which have brought order to these cities? Could we inquire into the settlement of cities more famous and greater than these?

Meg. You wouldn't easily find substitutes for these!

Ath. Now it's pretty clear that at that time they at least intended their arrangement to be a sufficient defense not only of the Peloponnese but of all the Greeks, in case any of the barbar-   685c ians might do them injustice, as happened when the people who once lived in the area around Ilium relied on the support of the Assyrian Empire of Ninos and rashly stirred up the Trojan War.[18] For what was left of the grandeur of that empire was not insignificant: just as we nowadays fear the Great King,[19] so they at that time trembled at that combined system; and in fact, since Troy was a part of that empire, its second[20]   685d capture was a grave charge against them. In the face of all this, the unified arrangement whereby the army was then divided up into three cities seemed to be a fine discovery on the part of the brother kings, the sons of Heracles,[21] and a mode of organization superior to that of the expedition against Troy. For in the first place, the sons of Heracles were considered to be better rulers than the descendants of Pelops; then again, this army of theirs was considered to be superior in virtue to the   685e army that went against Troy. After all, these bore the victory, and the others were defeated by them: the Achaeans were defeated by the Dorians. Don't we suppose that the men of those days organized themselves this way and with this intention?

Meg. Certainly.

Ath. Isn't it also likely that they supposed these things would remain stable, and last a long time, since they had shared   686a together many toils and risks, and had been organized by brother kings belonging to a single family? Moreover, hadn't they employed many diviners, including the Delphic Apollo?

Meg. That is indeed likely.

Ath. It's likely, however, that these great expectations flew away soon after—except, as we just said, what pertained to the small part in your area, and even that part has never to this   686b day ceased fighting with the other two parts. For if the original intention had been carried through, and unified consonance had been established, it would have possessed an irresistible power in war.

Meg. How could it not have?

Ath. So how and in what way was it destroyed? Isn't it worthwhile to investigate what sort of chance it was that ever destroyed so great a system of this kind?

Meg. If one were to disregard this investigation, one would seek in

686c   vain to see other laws or regimes that preserve or, on the contrary, utterly destroy the fine and great matters.

Ath.   Then it looks as though we have somehow been fortunate enough to come across an adequate investigation.

Meg.   It surely does.

Ath.   But look here, you amazing man, haven't we now fallen into the same error that affects all us human beings? We are always supposing, whenever we see some fine object, that it would
686d   achieve amazing things if only someone knew the way to put it to a fine use. But maybe we aren't yet thinking about this particular matter correctly, or according to nature—and maybe this is true of everything that everyone thinks of in this way.

Meg.   What are you talking about? What are we to declare you're referring to when you make this argument?

Ath.   My good man, I just had a laugh at my own expense. For when I gazed at this armed force we're discussing, it appeared to me to be a wholly fine and amazing possession that had fallen to the Greeks—if, as I said, someone had used it in a fine way at that time.

686e   Meg.   And wasn't all that you said—and we praised—spoken well and sensibly?

Ath.   Maybe. I do think that everyone who sees something big, with a lot of power and strength, immediately feels that if only the possessor knew how to use a thing of such quality and magnitude, he would perform many amazing deeds and thus become happy.

687a   Meg.   Well isn't that correct? Or what do you say?

Ath.   Consider for a moment what a person has in view in each case when he correctly gives this sort of praise to something. Consider first the very case under discussion. If those who arranged affairs in those days had known how to order the army properly, what would they have done to make the best of their opportunity? Wouldn't they have kept the army firmly together and preserved it for the rest of time, in order to maintain their own freedom while they ruled over anyone else they wished, and in order to enable themselves and their descen-
687b   dants to do whatever they wanted with the whole human race, Greeks as well as barbarians? Wouldn't it be on account of these things that men gave them praise?

Meg.   Certainly.

Ath.   Furthermore, isn't it the case that when someone speaks this way after having seen great wealth, or an especially honorable family, or any such thing, he does so with a view to the fact that through this thing one might gain all, or most—and the worthiest part—of what one desires?

Meg. That's likely, anyway.

Ath. Well then, do all human beings have one desire in common, the one revealed by the present argument—as the argument itself claims?

687c

Meg. Which desire?

Ath. To have things happen in accordance with the commands of one's own soul—preferably all things, but if not that, then at least the human things.

Meg. But of course.

Ath. Then since all of us wish such a thing always, when we're children, when we're men, and when we're elderly, wouldn't it necessarily follow that we pray for this throughout?

Meg. How could it not?

Ath. And presumably we would also join with our friends, at any rate, in praying that they might have the things they wish for themselves.

687d

Meg. But of course.

Ath. A son is a friend of a father though one is a child and the other is a man.

Meg. How could it be otherwise?

Ath. Yet many of the things a child prays he will get, a father would pray the gods never to allow in accordance with the son's prayers.

Meg. You mean when the son who prays lacks intelligence and is still young?

Ath. And also when the father, either because he is an old man or all-too-much a youth, knows nothing of what is noble and just, and, experiencing passions akin to those of Theseus against Hippolytus (who died so unfortunately),[22] prays with a vehement spirit, do you suppose that the son—the son who knows—will ever join in the father's prayers?

687e

Meg. I understand what you mean. You mean, I think, that one shouldn't pray or be eager to have everything follow his own wish, but rather to have his wish follow his prudence.[23] This is what a city and each one of us should pray and strive for—to possess intelligence.

Ath. Yes, and also that the man who is a statesman-lawgiver must

688a

always look to this in setting up the orderings of the laws; and I'm reminded here, and I'd like to recollect for you two as well, what was said at the beginning of the discussion, if you remember: you two maintained that the good lawgiver should lay down all his enactments for the sake of war; I on the other hand maintained that this would constitute an exhortation to set up laws for the sake of only one virtue out of four, whereas

688b

what should be done was to look to the whole of virtue, and especially at the first part, the leader of all virtue, which would be prudence, and intelligence, and opinion—with eros and desire following upon these. The argument has arrived again at the same place, and I, the speaker, now say again what I said back then—playfully, if you wish, or seriously, but this is what I assert: it is dangerous for one who lacks intelligence to

688c

pray, and the opposite of what he wishes comes to pass. If you want to take me seriously here, you may.

I do certainly expect that you two will now find, if you follow the argument we set forth a little earlier, that the cause of the destruction of the kings and of the whole plan was not cowardice, nor a lack of knowledge of war on the part of the rulers or those for whom it was fitting to be ruled. The corruption was caused by all the rest of vice, and especially ignorance regarding the greatest of human affairs. That this is how

688d

things happened then, and still can happen now in similar circumstances, and will happen again in times to come, I will try my best—since we're friends—to discover and show you, if you're willing, by proceeding along the course of the argument.

Kl. It would be rather tasteless for us to praise you in speech, stranger, but we will enthusiastically praise you in deed. We will follow what is said with attentive spirits, and it's in this way that a free man makes clear what he finds praiseworthy and what he does not.

688e Meg. Excellent, Kleinias! Let's do as you say.

Kl. So be it, if god is willing. Go ahead and speak.

Ath. We are now asserting, as we follow the rest of the path of the argument, that the greatest sort of ignorance is what destroyed that earlier power and that it is natural for it to do the same in the present as well. If this is so, then the lawgiver at least should try to instill as much prudence as possible in the cities and to drive out lack of intelligence as much as possible.

Kl.   Clearly.

Ath.   What then would justly be called the greatest sort of igno-   689a
rance? See if you both agree with what is going to be said. I
now set it down to be something like the following—

Kl.   What?

Ath.   When someone doesn't like, but rather hates, what in his
opinion is noble or good, and likes and welcomes what in his
opinion is wicked and unjust. This dissonance between pleasure and pain on the one hand, and the opinion that is according to reason on the other, I assert to be the ultimate and greatest ignorance, because it belongs to the major part of the soul.
In the soul, you see, the part that feels pain and pleasure is like   689b
the populace and the majority in the city. So when the soul opposes knowledge, or opinions, or reason—the natural rulers—
this I call lack of intelligence: in a city, when the majority refuses to obey the rulers and the laws, and in one man, when
the noble arguments in the soul achieve nothing, but indeed
go contrary to these things. All these, I at any rate, would set
down as the sorts of ignorance that are most discordant, both   689c
in the city and in each one of the citizens, and not the sorts of
ignorance belonging to craftsmen—if you understand what I
mean, strangers.

Kl.   We understand, friend, and we agree with the things you're
saying.

Ath.   This, then, can be set down as something resolved and declared: nothing that pertains to ruling is to be given to citizens
who are ignorant in the above respects; and they are to be
blamed for their ignorance, even if they are shrewd at calculating and have been trained in all the elegant niceties whose   689d
natural effect is to make the soul agile. It is just the opposite
sort who are to be proclaimed wise—even if, as in the proverb, they "know neither how to read nor swim"—and the
ruling offices are to be handed over to them on the grounds
that they are the prudent ones. For without consonance, my
friends, how can prudence—even in its smallest form—come
about? It isn't possible. But the finest and greatest of conso-
nances would most justly be called the greatest wisdom, and
whoever partakes of this evidently lives according to reason,
while he who doesn't partake of it evidently brings ruin to his
home and is in no way a savior of his city, but is instead just
the opposite, as a result of his ignorance in these matters. So,   689e

as we just said, let these things stand as the declaration in this matter.

Kl. Let them stand indeed.

Ath. Now I suppose there must necessarily be rulers and ruled in cities.

Kl. But of course.

690a Ath. Well then, which and how many are the worthy titles to rule and to be ruled, in large and small cities and in households as well? Wouldn't one be that of the father and mother, and in general, wouldn't it be everywhere correct for parents to have title to rule over their descendants?

Kl. Emphatically so.

Ath. And, following upon this, for the well born to rule over those who are not well born. Thirdly, following these, the elderly ought to rule and the younger ought to be ruled.

Kl. But of course.

690b Ath. Fourthly, then, that slaves be ruled and masters rule.

Kl. How could it be otherwise?

Ath. Fifth at any rate, I think, that the stronger rule and the weaker be ruled.

Kl. Now you've mentioned a kind of rule that is compellingly necessary.

Ath. And the one most widely spread among all living things, and according to nature, as the Theban Pindar [24] once asserted. But it's likely that the greatest title would be the sixth, the one bidding the ignorant to follow and the prudent to lead and

690c rule. Indeed it is this title, O most wise Pindar, that I at least would hardly assert is against nature, but rather according to nature: the natural rule exercised by the law over willing subjects, without violence.

Kl. What you say is very correct.

Ath. "Dear to the gods" at any rate, and "lucky," is what we call the seventh sort of rule—where we bring forward someone for a drawing of lots and assert that it is very just for the one who draws a winning lot to rule and for the one who draws a losing lot to give way and be ruled.

Kl. What you say is very true.

690d Ath. "Do you see then," we would say, "O lawgiver," (joking with one of those who undertakes lightly the task of laying down laws) "how many worthy titles to rule there are, and that they are by nature opposed to one another? Here, indeed, we have discovered a source of civil strife, which you must treat.

"But first investigate with us how and why the kings of Argos and Messene managed to go wrong in respect to these matters, and destroy both themselves and the power of the Greeks, which was so amazing at that time. Didn't their mistake consist in the fact that they were ignorant of what Hesiod has stated very correctly—that 'the half is often more than the whole'?[25] When it is harmful to take the whole, but the half is a measured amount, then the measured amount should be considered more than the amount that is unmeasured—for the one is better and the other is worse."

690e

Kl. That is very correct, at least.

Ath. Do we suppose that this occurs and causes corruption each time among the kings first, or the populaces?

Kl. It's likely that most of the time this is a disease of kings who live in an arrogant manner because of luxury.

691a

Ath. Then isn't it clear that it was the kings of that time who were first seized by this—the desire to have more than the established laws allowed—and that they weren't in consonance with themselves as regards what they praised in speech and in their oath? The dissonance—which we have asserted to be the greatest ignorance but which seems to be wisdom—corrupted everything, through discord and a shrill lack of music.[26]

Kl. That's likely, anyway.

Ath. All right then: what should the legislator have set up at that time in order to forestall the emergence of this affliction? In the name of the gods! It doesn't take any wisdom to understand now, does it, nor is it difficult to say; but if it had been possible to foresee it back then, the foreseer would have been wiser than we are, wouldn't he?

691b

Meg. What are you referring to?

Ath. By looking at what has happened to your people, Megillus, it is now possible to know and, knowing, easy to say what should have happened back in that time.

Meg. Speak still more clearly.

Ath. The clearest way of putting it would be about as follows—

Meg. How?

Ath. If someone goes against due measure and gives more power to those who are inferior—whether it involves giving sails to ships or food to bodies or ruling offices to souls—he will presumably overturn everything; filled with insolence, some things will run to sickness, others to the injustice that is born from insolence. So what then is our point? Isn't it something

691c

like this? There does not exist, dear sirs, a mortal soul whose nature, so long as it is still young and irresponsible, will ever

691d   bear the greatest sort of rule among human beings. The result is always that its thought becomes filled with the greatest sickness, namely lack of intelligence, and hence comes to be hated by its closest friends; and this, when it occurs, swiftly destroys it and obliterates all its power. Knowing how to preserve due measure in this respect is the sign of great lawgivers. So a very well measured guess to make now is that such a thing did occur in those days. It seems likely that there was—

Meg.   What?

Ath.   —that there was some god taking care of you, who foresaw the

691e   future, and by bringing about the birth[27] of twin kings from a single line made things more measured for you.[28]

Then after this some human nature, having been mixed with some divine power, saw that your system of rule was still

692a   feverish and proceeded to mix the moderate power of old age with the willful strength of family lineage: the council of the twenty-eight old men was given, in the greatest matters, a vote equal to the power of the kings.[29]

Your third savior,[30] seeing that your system of rule was still swollen and irritated with spiritedness, put a sort of bridle on it through the power of the Ephors, and drew near to the power based on a lottery.[31]

So according to this account your monarchy, having become a mixture of the proper things and having attained due measure, preserved itself and was the cause of the preservation of

692b   the rest. If it had been left to Temenos and Kresphontes and the lawgivers of that time—whoever those lawgivers might have been—even the portion of Aristodemus[32] wouldn't have been saved. For they were not sufficiently experienced in lawgiving; otherwise they would hardly ever have thought they could keep a young soul within measured bounds by means of oaths, once the soul had obtained a rule which might become tyrannical. Now, however, the god has shown what had to be done and what should still be done to bring about an

692c   especially stable rule. And as I said at the beginning, it isn't any mark of wisdom for us to figure out these things now, because it isn't difficult to see them by looking at the model that has emerged; but if someone had foreseen these things then, and had been able to arrange the ruling offices in due measure—creating one out of three—he would have saved all the fine plans of that time, and there would never have been an expedition by the Persians or by anybody else against Greece, caused by their looking down on us as people who count for little.

Kl.   What you say is true.

Ath. Anyway, it was shameful the way they repulsed them, Klein-   692d
ias. When I say it was shameful I don't mean to deny that the men of that time were victorious and won noble victories on land and sea; what I assert was shameful at that time was the following: first, that of these cities, being three in number, only one defended Greece, while the other two were so far gone in corruption that one of them prevented Lacedaimon from assisting in the defense [33]—fighting against her with might and main—and the other, the one in Argos (which had the primacy, in those days of the original division), refused to   692e
pay heed or help defend when called upon to repulse the bar-barian. [34] There are many things that went on during the war at that time that would be the occasion for someone's making unseemly accusations against Greece. And if one were to say that Greece defended itself, he would not be speaking cor-rectly; had not the common resolution of the Athenians and the Lacedaimonians warded off the approaching slavery, the   693a
Greek races would by this time probably be all mixed together, and there would be barbarians among Greeks and Greeks among barbarians, like the peoples the Persians now tyrannize over, who live scattered in a miserable fashion after having been dispersed and herded together.

These are the things, Kleinias and Megillus, for which we can blame the so-called statesmen and lawgivers of old—and also the ones now. And the reason we engage in such blame is to investigate the causes and to find out what should have   693b
been done differently. As we said with regard to the present case, they shouldn't have legislated great ruling offices, or unmixed authority; they should have considered something like the following: that a city should be free and prudent and a friend to itself, and that the lawgiver should give his laws with a view to these things.

By the way, let's not be surprised to find that we have often before laid down goals which we've asserted the lawgiver

693c   should look to when he lays down his laws, but that the goals don't appear to be the same for us each time. One should reason as follows: when we asserted one should look toward moderation, or toward prudence, or friendship, these goals are not different but the same. Even if many other words of this sort crop up, let's not let it disturb us.

Kl.   We'll make an attempt to proceed in this way when we go back over the arguments. But for now, tell us what you intended to say—just what is it the lawgiver should aim at with regard to friendship and prudence and freedom?

693d   Ath.   Listen, then. There are, as it were, two mothers of regimes. It would be correct for someone to say that the others spring from these, and correct to call one monarchy and the other democracy, and to say that the Persian type is the full development of the former, while my people's country is the full development of the latter. Almost all other regimes, as I said, are woven from these. Both of them should and must necessarily

693e   be present if there is to be freedom and friendship, together with prudence: this is what the argument wishes to set before us when it says that no city will ever have a fine political life if it lacks a share in either of these.

Kl.   Of course not, how could it?

Ath.   Now one of these two nations delighted exclusively and more than was necessary in monarchy, the other in freedom, and neither possessed due measure in these matters. Your regimes, on the other hand—the Laconian and the Cretan—have more measure. The Athenians and Persians of old were also

694a   once somewhat well measured, but now are less so. Let's go through the causes, shall we?

Kl.   By all means, if, at any rate, we're going to complete the task we laid out.

Ath.   Let's listen then: the Persians under Cyrus, possessing the proper amount of slavery and freedom, began by becoming free and then became despots over many others. For the rulers shared their freedom with the ruled and drew toward equality; as a result the soldiers felt more friendly toward their generals and faced danger with eager spirits. Moreover, if some-

694b   one among them was prudent and capable of giving counsel, the king wasn't jealous but allowed freedom of speech and honored those capable of giving counsel; hence, a man was willing to share his capacity, in their midst, as something

common. Everything prospered for them in those days because of freedom and friendship and a common sharing in intelligence.[35]

Kl. It's likely, at any rate, that things happened somewhat in the
way they've been described.

Ath. How then was this ever destroyed under Cambyses and then   694c
almost saved again under Darius? Do you want us to figure it
out, as if we were using divination?

Kl. That at least would help us in the investigation we've embarked upon.

Ath. Now I divine that Cyrus, though in other respects a good general and a friend to his city, failed completely to grasp what is
a correct education, and didn't direct his mind at all to household management.

Kl. What makes us assert such a thing?

Ath. It's likely that he spent his whole life, from youth on, preoc-   694d
cupied with military matters, and turned his children over to
the women to be brought up. They brought the children up as
though they were happy from the time they were babies, and
blessed from the moment they were born, lacking nothing.
The women allowed no one to oppose them in anything, on
the grounds that they were endowed with happiness, and
compelled everyone else to praise whatever the children said
or did: that was the sort of children they raised.

Kl. It sounds lovely, this upbringing you've described!

Ath. A feminine upbringing—the children were brought up by   694e
royal, newly-rich women, and in the absence of the men, who
were unable to find leisure because of wars and many other
dangers.

Kl. That stands to reason.

Ath. Their father, meanwhile, kept acquiring flocks and herds, including many droves of men along with many other animals,
on their behalf; but he didn't know that they to whom he was   695a
going to give all this were not being educated in their father's
art, which was Persian (for the Persians are shepherds because
of the rough country from which they originate). This art is a
tough one, sufficient to make men very strong herdsmen, capable of living outdoors, able to keep watch without sleep,
and ready to serve as soldiers whenever they have to. Anyway, he failed to see that women and eunuchs had given his
sons an education which had been corrupted by the so-called

695b   happiness of the Medes, and the sons turned out as one would expect, after having been brought up without any restraint. When his children took over from Cyrus after his death, they were bursting with luxury and lack of restraint. First one killed the other because he couldn't bear to share equally; after this the one who remained, maddened by drunkenness and lack of education, had his rule destroyed by the Medes and by the fellow they, at that time, called "the Eunuch," who had nothing but contempt for the silliness of Cambyses.[36]

695c   Kl.   These things are said to have happened, anyway, and it is likely that they happened more or less this way.

Ath.   And presumably it is said that the rule passed back into the hands of the Persians because of Darius and the Seven.

Kl.   But of course.

Ath.   Let's observe as we follow the argument. For Darius[37] was not the son of a king, and was not brought up under a luxurious education. He came into the rule and seized it as the seventh member of a group, and divided it into seven parts (traces of this division still remain now). He saw fit to govern by es-
695d   tablishing laws, through which he introduced a sort of general equality and regulated by law the tribute promised to the Persians by Cyrus; thus he brought about friendship and a sense of community among all the Persians, and won over the Persian populace with money and gifts. That's why his army was well disposed to him and gave him additional territories, no less than those left by Cyrus. But then after Darius Xerxes was once again educated in a royal and luxurious education:[38]
695e   "O Darius!" it's perhaps very just to say, "you have failed to learn from the vice of Cyrus and have brought up Xerxes in the same habits as Cyrus did Cambyses!" Anyway, as he was an offspring of the same sorts of education, so he wound up suffering just about the same things as Cambyses. And since that time there has arisen among the Persians hardly a single truly "great" king, except in name. The cause of this is not chance, my argument goes, but rather the
696a   evil life led for the most part by children of exceptionally rich and tyrannical men. No child or man or old man will ever become outstanding in virtue if he has been brought up in such a way. And these, we assert, are matters a lawgiver ought to look into, and that we ought to look into right now.

As for your city, Lacedaimonians, it is just to give it this at least: in the distribution of honor, and training, you draw no distinctions between poverty and wealth, private individual and king—except for distinctions laid down by the divine ora- 696b cle given you by some god at the beginning. And as far as the city is concerned at least, there shouldn't be preeminent honors bestowed on someone because he is especially rich— any more than if he is swift or beautiful or strong—unless he has some virtue. And not if he has virtue, unless it includes moderation.

Meg. How do you mean this, stranger?

Ath. Presumably courage is one part of virtue?

Meg. How could it not be?

Ath. You yourself be the judge, after you've heard the argument: would you be willing to have as a member of your household or as a neighbor someone who was very courageous, but was lacking in restraint, rather than moderate?

Meg. Hush! 696c

Ath. What about an artisan, wise in these matters but unjust?

Meg. In no way!

Ath. What is just, at least, does not by nature grow apart from moderation.

Meg. How could it?

Ath. Nor does the man we've just now set down as wise, the one who possesses pleasures and pains that are in consonance with and follow the correct reasonings.

Meg. No indeed.

Ath. Now we should also consider the following with regard to the question of which honors are correctly or incorrectly bestowed 696d on each occasion in the city.

Meg. What?

Ath. Suppose moderation exists alone in some soul, without any of the rest of virtue: would it be just to honor it or dishonor it?

Meg. I can't say.

Ath. What you have said, at least, is measured. For if you had given either of the answers I suggested, you would have seemed, to me at least, to be speaking out of tune.

Meg. So the answer turned out to be fine.

Ath. Indeed. After all, an adjunct to the things that qualify for honors or dishonors would be worthy not of talk, but of some 696e silent sign.

Meg. You appear to me to be speaking of moderation.

Ath. Yes. As for the rest, the most correct way to apportion honors is to honor preeminently the thing which, when combined with this adjunct, gives us the greatest benefit, then to honor second the thing which gives the second-greatest benefit. If the rest were honored in succession according to this principle, then each would get its correct share.

697a Meg. That's so.

Ath. What then? Won't we assert again that this apportionment is the lawgiver's responsibility?

Meg. Emphatically.

Ath. Do you want us to leave it to him to apportion everything for every deed in detail, and shall we try to make a threefold distinction—distinguishing the greatest things, and the second, and the third? For we ourselves are somehow desirous of laws.

Meg. By all means.

697b Ath. We say, then, that the likelihood is that if a city is to be preserved and is to become happy within the limits of human power, it must necessarily apportion honors and dishonors correctly. The correct apportionment is one which honors most the good things pertaining to the soul (provided it has moderation), second, the beautiful and good things pertaining to the body, and third, the things said to accrue from property and money. If some lawgiver or city steps outside

697c this ranking either by promoting money to a position of honor or by raising one of the lesser things to a more honorable status, he will do a deed that is neither pious nor statesmanlike. Shall these things be declared by us, or what?

Meg. Let this be declared by all means, and clearly.

Ath. We've been led to speak about these things at greater length because of the investigation into the regime of the Persians. We find that they got worse year by year, and we claim the cause is this: by going too far in depriving the populace of freedom, and by bringing in more despotism than is appro-

697d priate, they destroyed the friendship and community within the city. Once this is corrupted, the policy of the rulers is no longer made for the sake of the ruled and the populace, but instead for the sake of their own rule; if they suppose just a little more will accrue to themselves each time, the rulers are willing to overturn cities and overturn and destroy with fire friendly nations, and as a result, they give and receive bitter, pitiless hatred. When they come to need the assistance of their populaces to fight in their defense, they discover that there no longer exists a community with a spirit eager to run risks and fight. They have countless myriads of subjects in number, but all of them are useless in war; so they have to hire helpers as if they lacked human subjects: they think they can then protect themselves by relying on mercenaries and foreign human beings. In addition to these things, they're compelled to become so stupid as to proclaim by their deeds that the things regularly said to be honorable and noble in the city are worthless each time compared to gold and silver. 697e

698a

Meg. That is certainly so.

Ath. Then let this be the end of the discussion of what pertains to the Persians, and of how their affairs are at present incorrectly managed because of an excess of slavery and despotism.

Meg. By all means.

Ath. Next we should go through the discussion of what pertains to the Attic regime in the same way, showing how total freedom from all rule is to no small extent inferior to a measured degree of rule by others. 698b

For at that time, when the Persian expedition came against the Greeks, and probably against all the settlements of Europe, there was an ancient regime with certain rulers based on a division into four classes.[39] In it was a certain despotic mistress—Awe—on account of whom we were willing to live as slaves of the laws that then existed. In addition, the magnitude of the invading force, on land and sea, struck us with a helpless feeling of fear: this made us even more the slaves of the rulers and the laws, and all these things created a very strong sense of friendship among us. 698c

For you see, almost ten years before the naval battle of Salamis,[40] Datis came, bringing a Persian expedition, sent by Darius expressly against the Athenians and Eretrians with orders to bring them back enslaved, and under the threat of death if he failed in this. In a brief space of time Datis with his myriad hordes completely subdued the Eretrians by force and then sent a frightening message to our city, to the effect that not a single Eretrian had escaped him: Datis's soldiers had actually joined hands to form a dragnet around the whole of Eretria. This report, whether true or not, and wherever it came from, terrified all the Greeks and especially the Athenians. But when they sent embassies everywhere for help, no one was 698d

698e

[83]

willing to come except the Lacedaimonians.⁴¹ However, they were held up by a war they were waging at that time with Messene and maybe by some other impediment (we don't know what was alleged) and arrived one day too late for the battle of Marathon.

After that, reports came in of vast preparations and myriad threats on the part of the king. As time went on, it was reported that Darius had died but that a robust young son of his had taken over the rule and was in no way abating the assault preparations. The Athenians supposed that all these preparations were aimed at them on account of what had happened at Marathon. When they heard that a canal was being dug across the peninsula at Athos and that the Hellespont was being bridged, and how many ships there were, they came to believe that there was no way of saving themselves, by land or by sea. For they expected no one would help them—remembering how on the earlier occasion, when Eretria had fallen, no one had come to help or had dared to fight on their side. They expected the same thing to happen this time, on land at least; on the sea they felt they were completely at a loss because more than a thousand ships were coming against them. They figured out one means of survival. It was a slender and desperate recourse, but the only one available. Besides, they looked back at what had happened before, when victory had appeared to come when they were fighting in a situation that was desperate. Embarking on this hope they found their refuge in themselves alone, and in the gods.⁴²

So all these things instilled in them a friendship for one another: fear, both that which came at the time and that which sprang from the laws they already had—the fear which they possessed as a result of their enslavement to those previous laws, which we have often in the arguments before called "awe," and which we claimed those who are going to be good must be enslaved to. The coward is free from this and is fearless in respect to it. But if our populace had not at that time been seized by this sort of fear,⁴³ they would never have banded together as they then did to defend themselves, nor would they have defended the temples, the graves, the fatherland, and their relatives, as well as their friends. Instead, each of us would have been scattered from the rest at that time and little by little dispersed here and there.

699a

699b

699c

699d

[84]

Meg. You have spoken altogether correctly, stranger, and in a manner befitting both you and your fatherland.

Ath. That is so, Megillus. And it's just to speak about what happened in that time with you, surely, who share the nature of your forefathers.

But consider now, you and Kleinias, if what we're speaking of is pertinent to lawgiving. After all, that's why I'm going 699e through all this, I'm not doing it for the sake of the myths. See how this sounds to you: my people have in a way suffered the same thing the Persians suffered—they by leading their populace into complete slavery and we by leading the majority in the opposite direction, into complete freedom. Given this, the arguments we laid down earlier are in a way fine for showing us what we should say here and how we should say it.

Meg. You speak well: but try to give us a clearer indication of what 700a is being said now.

Ath. All right. Under the ancient laws, my friends, our populace was not sovereign over certain matters but was rather voluntarily enslaved, in a certain sense, to the laws.

Meg. Which laws are you speaking of?

Ath. First those regulating the music of that time—if we are to start from the origin of the excessive development of the free way of life. Our music in those days was divided according to its own forms and postures. There was a form of song comprising 700b prayers sung to the gods, called "hymns"; opposite to this was another form of song which someone might well call "dirges." "Paeans" were another. Then there was yet another called the "dithyramb," which was about the birth of Dionysus, I believe. They gave the name "laws" [*nomoi*] to another form of song—this sort was for the kithara, they used also to say. Once these, and certain others, had been arranged, it was not allowed to misuse one form of song for another. The authority 700c that knew about these things and used its knowledge to judge them, penalizing anyone who disobeyed, was not, as is the case today, whistling, nor the majority, with its unmusical shouts, nor the clapping that bestows praise. Instead it was accepted practice for the educated to listen in silence until the end, while the children and their attendants and the general mob were kept in order by the threat of a beating.

So the majority of the citizens were willing to be ruled in an 700d orderly fashion in these respects, and did not dare to render

700e

701a

701b

701c

judgment by their noise. But later, with the passage of time, the poets became rulers and held sway over unmusical lawlessness. Although by nature poetic, the poets were ignorant about what is just and lawful for the Muse. In a sort of Bacchic frenzy, more overwhelmed by pleasure than they should have been, they jumbled together dirges with hymns and paeans with dithyrambs; they used kithara sounds to imitate the sounds of the aulos—they confounded everything. In their mindlessness they involuntarily falsified music itself when they asserted that there was no such thing as correct music, and that it was quite correct to judge music by the standard of the pleasure it gives to whoever enjoys it, whether he be better or worse. By creating works of this kind, and then by adding these sorts of arguments, they instilled in the many a lawlessness as regards music, and made them dare to suppose that they were adequate judges. The outcome was that the theaters have become noisy instead of quiet, claiming to understand what is beautiful in the Muses and what is not; and in place of an aristocracy in music, a wretched theatocracy has emerged.

If only there had emerged a democracy of free men, in music, what has happened wouldn't be so terrible. But as it was, the opinion that everyone is wise in everything, together with lawlessness, originated in our music, and freedom followed. People became fearless, as if they were knowers, and the absence of fear engendered shamelessness. For to be so bold as not to fear the opinion of someone who is better, this is almost the same as vile shamelessness, and springs from an excessively brazen freedom.

Meg. What you say is very true.

Ath. Next after this freedom would come the sort that involves the loss of the willingness to be enslaved to the rulers; following upon this is the rejection of the enslavement to and guidance by one's father and mother and elders; the next to the last stage involves seeking not to have to obey laws; after this comes the ultimate freedom when they cease to give any more thought to oaths and pledges and everything pertaining to the gods, but instead display and imitate what is called the ancient Titanic [44] nature—arriving back again at those same conditions, and introducing a harsh epoch in which there is never a cessation of evils.

[86]

Why, again, have these things been said by us? In my view at least, it's clearly necessary to pull up the argument like a horse, every now and then, and not allow oneself to be carried along by force as if the argument had no bridle in its mouth. To avoid the proverbial[45] fall from the ass, one needs to insist on the question just asked—for the sake of what have these things been said?

Meg. Fine question.

Ath. Well, they have been said for the sake of the earlier things.

Meg. Which?

Ath. We said that the lawgiver must in laying down his laws aim at three things, namely that the city for which he legislates be free, that it be a friend to itself, and that it possess intelligence. Those were the goals—weren't they?

Meg. Certainly.

Ath. For the sake of these things we chose the most despotic regime and the freest, and are now investigating which of these is correctly governed. We have seen that when either—the despotic or the free—was limited within measure, affairs went outstandingly well; but when either marched on to its extreme—the one to slavery and the other to the opposite—there was no advantage in either case.

Meg. What you say is very true.

Ath. It was also for the sake of these things that we looked at the establishment of the Dorian armed camp, the hill dwellings of Dardanos and the establishment on the sea, the first people, who were the survivors of the catastrophe, the arguments about music and drunkenness that emerged earlier than these, and the things that came even before that. All these things have been discussed for the sake of understanding how a city might best be established sometime, and how, in private, someone might best lead his own life.

But what sort of a test in conversation might we ever set for ourselves in speech, Megillus and Kleinias, to reveal whether we have been making something that is useful?

Kl. I, stranger, think that I can conceive one. It's likely that some stroke of luck has brought before us the subjects of all these arguments we've gone through, for I at any rate have now come almost to the point of needing them, and you, and also Megillus here, have come along at an opportune time. For I won't hide from you two my present situation but will treat

701d

701e

702a

702b

702c

[87]

this as a good omen. The greater part of Crete, you see, is attempting to found a certain colony and has put the Knossians in charge of the affair. The city of the Knossians has in turn delegated it to me and nine others. We have been commissioned to establish the same laws as the ones there, if we find some satisfactory; but if we discover some laws from elsewhere that appear to be better, we are not to hesitate about their being foreign. So now let's do ourselves—me and you two as well—this favor: making a selection from the things that have been said, let's construct a city in speech, just as if we were founding it from the very beginning. That way there will be an examination of the subject we are inquiring into, while at the same time I may perhaps make use of this construction, in the city that is going to exist.

702d

Ath.   You're not declaring war, at any rate,[46] Kleinias! Unless it would be somehow irksome to Megillus, you may consider that I for my part will do all in my power to accommodate your intention.

Kl.   Well spoken!

Meg.   For my part, I'll do the same.

702e   Kl.   The two of you have spoken very nobly! So let's try now, first in speech, to found the city.

BOOK IV

Ath. Come then, what must one think the city is going to be? In saying this, I'm not asking what name it has at present or what it will be necessary to call it in time to come, because that will probably depend on the circumstances of its settlement, or on the locale—a name taken from some river or spring, or from one of the local gods. One of these will give its august name to the new city. What I mean to ask about it now is rather this: whether it will be on the sea or inland. 704a 704b

Kl. The city we're now discussing, stranger, is roughly eighty stades[1] from the sea.

Ath. What then? Does it have harbors along the near coast, or is it entirely without harbors?

Kl. It has the best possible harbor there, stranger.

Ath. Alas, what are you saying! But what about the land around it? Is it productive in all respects or lacking in some things? 704c

Kl. It lacks practically nothing.

Ath. And will there be any nearby neighbor city?

Kl. None at all, that's why it's being settled. For an ancient migration from the place has left the land deserted for an incalculably long time.

Ath. What about plains and mountains and forests? What portion of each do we have?

Kl. It resembles the nature, as a whole, of the rest of Crete. 704d

Ath. You'd say the land is quite rough rather than quite flat.

Kl. Very much so.

Ath. Then it would not be incurable, at least, as regards the acquisition of virtue. For if it was to be right on the sea, with a good harbor, and not productive in all respects but lacking many things, why, with such a nature it would have required some great savior, and some lawgivers who were divine, to prevent it from coming to have many diverse and low habits. As it is, there is comfort in the eighty stades. It is indeed nearer to the

705a

sea than it should be, the more so since you declare it has good harbors, but this has to be made the best of. For although a land's proximity to the sea affords daily pleasure, the sea really is a "briny and bitter neighbor."[2] It infects a place with commerce and the money-making that comes with retail trade, and engenders shifty and untrustworthy dispositions in souls; it thereby takes away the trust and friendship a city feels for itself and for the rest of humanity. In this regard there's comfort in the fact that the city will be productive in

705b

every way, while the roughness of the terrain obviously prevents it from being *both* productive of great quantities *and,* at the same time, fertile in all respects. If it were, that would mean large exports and a resulting infection of silver and gold money. And on balance there is nothing that does more harm, so to speak, to a city's acquisition of well-born and just dispositions—as we asserted, if you remember, in our earlier discussions.

Kl. But we do remember, and we agree that we spoke correctly then, as well as now.

705c Ath. Next, then: how is the land in our place as regards timber for shipbuilding?

Kl. There's no fir worth mentioning, nor pine, and not much cypress. One wouldn't find much pitch pine and plane, either— the trees shipbuilders must always use for the inner parts of ships.

Ath. These natural features would also not be bad for the land.

Kl. How's that?

705d Ath. It's good that a city cannot easily imitate its enemies when it comes to wicked imitations.

Kl. Which of the things mentioned do you have in view, in saying what you've said?

Ath. Be on your guard with me, you demonic man! Keep in view what was said back at the beginning, about how the Cretan laws looked to one goal. You two said this goal was what pertains to war. I then interrupted, saying it was fine that such legal institutions looked somehow to virtue, but that I could

not at all go along with them when they looked only to a part
and not to almost the whole. Now you two in your turn, as   705e
you follow the present legislation, must guard against my
legislating something that doesn't aim at virtue, or that aims
at a part of virtue. For I assert that the only law correctly laid
down is this: one which, just like an archer, aims each time at   706a
what alone is constantly accompanied by something noble,
one which leaves all the rest aside, even if there is a chance of
producing some wealth and some other such things by ignoring the things just mentioned.

Now the evil imitation of enemies I was referring to is the
sort that occurs when someone dwells near the sea and is
vexed by enemies—as in the days when (I say this not intending to remind you of ills) Minos imposed a certain harsh trib-   706b
ute on the inhabitants of Attica. He wielded great power on
the sea, while they did not possess ships, as they do now, for
war, nor a territory well stocked with shipbuilding timber that
allows for the easy creation of naval power. As a result they
were not able, through nautical imitation, to become seafarers
immediately and defend themselves, at that time, against
their enemies. For it would have been in their interest to have
had many times seven youths destroyed, if by doing so they   706c
could have remained steady, heavily-armed infantrymen instead of adopting the habits of marines. Marines are quick to
jump forward, then to retreat at a run back into their ships;
they see nothing shameful in not daring to stand and die in
the face of attacking enemies. Excuses are readily made for
them, and they're quite prepared to throw away their
weapons and flee, in certain routs they claim are not shameful!
Such are the sentiments armed marines are apt to express—
and these sentiments merit not myriad and frequent praises,   706d
but just the opposite.[3] There should never be habituation in
wicked ways, especially among the best part of the citizenry.

This at least could presumably be gathered from Homer, too
(that is, that such a practice isn't noble). For his Odysseus reviles Agamemnon on the occasion when the Achaeans are
being hard pressed in battle by the Trojans and he has ordered
the ships to be dragged down to the sea. Taking him to task,
Odysseus says[4]

> . . . you who bid us, while war and shouting still rages   706e
> 'round,

> Draw our well-benched ships down to the sea, so that yet more
>
> The prayers of the Trojans may be fulfilled—even though they have long wished for this—
>
> And we be overtaken by utter destruction. For the Achaeans will not
>
> Maintain the war once the ships are drawn seaward;
>
> They'll be always looking behind, and will draw off from the battle.

707a

> That will be the evident outcome of the counsel you're proclaiming!

So that man also knew these things and realized that it's bad to support the combat of heavy infantry with triremes at sea. By using customs of this sort one would habituate lions to flee deer!

Besides, cities that rest their power on their navies, after being saved, don't give honors to the noblest of their warriors, since the deliverance is brought about by the art of the pilot and the boatswain and the rower—in fact, by all sorts of

707b human beings who aren't very serious—and one wouldn't be able to apportion honors correctly to each. Yet how would a regime become correct if it lacked this?

Kl. It's almost impossible. But look, stranger: we Cretans at least assert that it was the naval battle of the Greeks against the barbarians at Salamis that saved Greece.

Ath. The many, both Greek and barbarian, do indeed say these
707c things. But we, my friend, myself and Megillus here, assert that it was the land battles at Marathon and Plataea: the former began the deliverance of the Greeks and the latter completed it. Moreover, we assert that these battles made the Greeks better, while those other battles made them no better—if it's all right for us to speak in such a way about the battles that contributed to our salvation in those days. For I would add the sea battle of Artemisium to your mention of that at Salamis.[5]

707d But anyway, in our consideration of the nature of the land and the order of the laws, we're looking now to the virtue of the regime. We do not hold, as the many do, that preservation and mere existence are what is most honorable for human beings; what is most honorable is for them to become as excellent as possible and to remain so for as long a time as they may exist. This too, I think, was said already, in our earlier discussions.

Kl. Why, of course.

Ath. Then let's consider this alone: whether or not we are continuing to proceed along the path that is best as regards the establishing of, and legislating for, cities.

Kl. By all means.

Ath. Now tell about what comes next after these things. Who are 707e the people who will be your colonists? Will they be made up of anyone who wishes to come from all of Crete, because a sort of overflow mob, outstripping the earth's food supply, has come into being in each city? I'm assuming you people aren't collecting every Greek, at any rate, who wants to come (although I notice that you already have some colonists in your territory from Argos and Aegina and elsewhere in Greece). But come, 708a tell us where you claim this armed camp of citizens will now come from.

Kl. It's likely that they'll come from all over Crete; as for the rest of Greece, it's clear to me that fellow colonists from the Peloponnese will be especially welcome. For what you just now said, about the people from Argos, is true: they make up the most famous of the tribes here now, the Gortynian. You see, they happen to be colonists from the Peloponnesian Gortyn.[6]

Ath. Colonization wouldn't be as easy a thing for cities when it 708b doesn't take place in the manner of bee-swarms, where one tribe from one land undertakes the new settlement, a friend coming from friends, because it was hemmed in by a shortage of land or compelled by other such sufferings. There is also the occasion when a part of a city may be compelled to move to some foreign place because of civil strife. There have even been times when a whole city went into exile, completely 708c overpowered by an irresistible attack. In all these situations it is in one sense easier to settle and lay down laws, but in another sense more difficult. The tribal unity, the similarity of language and of laws, since they imply a sharing of the sacred things and all such matters, create a certain friendship; but then again, they do not easily accept laws and regimes different from their own. Sometimes, even when they have suffered from civil strife as a result of the wickedness of their laws they still prefer, out of habit, to live with the same habitual customs that corrupted them before. So they give trouble to

708d the founder and lawgiver and become disobedient. In contrast, the tribe that has been collected from all over would probably be more willing to obey certain new laws; but for it to breathe together and grow[7] to be constantly united—like a team of horses, as they say—would require much time and trouble.

Yes, it is really the case that lawgiving and the founding of cities is the most perfect of all tests of manly virtue.

Kl. That's likely; but explain more clearly what you have in view in saying this.

708e Ath. My good man, when I go back over and consider lawgivers again, I'll probably say something belittling about them. Still, if we say something that is opportune, it shouldn't cause trouble. And after all, why should I ever be upset about it? It's likely that almost all the human things are in a similar condition.

Kl. What are you talking about?

709a Ath. I was about to say that no human being ever legislates anything, but that chances and accidents of every sort, occurring in all kinds of ways, legislate everything for us. Either it's some war that violently overturns regimes and transforms laws, or it's the baffling impasse of harsh poverty that does it. Diseases, too, make many innovations necessary, when epidemics occur or bad weather comes and frequently lasts many years. If he looked ahead to all these things, someone might be

709b eager to say what I just said—that no mortal ever legislates anything, but that almost all human affairs are matters of chance. With regard to the sailing art, the pilot's art, the art of medicine, and the art of the general it seems good to say all this; but it seems equally good to speak about these same affairs in the following way.

Kl. In what way?

Ath. To the effect that in all things god—and together with god, chance and opportunity—pilots all the human things. One

709c must, indeed, concede that these are accompanied by yet a third thing, a gentler thing: art. For I at least would declare that the pilot's art is a great advantage when it comes to co-operating with the opportune moment in the midst of a gale. Isn't that so?

Kl. That is so.

Ath. So the same argument would hold in the same way for the other cases, and in particular this very thing must be granted in the case of lawgiving. Along with the rest of the good luck a land needs to have befall it if it would ever dwell in happiness, there must always happen along, for such a city, a lawgiver who possesses the truth.

Kl. What you say is very true.

Ath. Now in each of the cases mentioned the one who possesses 709d the art would presumably be able to pray in the correct way for that which, being available to him through chance, would make nothing lacking except the art?

Kl. By all means.

Ath. All the others who were mentioned just now, if asked to pronounce their prayer, would speak up. Isn't that so?

Kl. Sure—why not?

Ath. And the lawgiver would do the same, I think.

Kl. I think so.

Ath. "Come, then, lawgiver!" let's say to him, "what city shall we 709e give you and in what condition, so as to enable you to take it and proceed henceforth by yourself to arrange the city satisfactorily?" So what is the correct thing to say next after this? Shall we explain, on behalf of the lawgiver? Or what?

Kl. Yes.

Ath. Here it is: "Give me a tyrannized city," he will declare, "and let the tyrant be young, possessed of an able memory, a good learner, courageous, and magnificent by nature. And what we earlier said must accompany all the parts of virtue must now 710a attend the tyrannized soul, if its other qualities are to prove beneficial."

Kl. It seems to me that the stranger is referring to moderation, Megillus, when he speaks of the necessary accompaniment. Isn't that so?

Ath. The popular sort, that is, Kleinias—not the sort one would speak of in a solemn way, compelling prudence to be moderation, but rather the sort that blooms naturally, from the beginning, in children and beasts, and by which some lack self-restraint with regard to pleasures while others possess self-restraint. We asserted that when this quality is separated 710b from the many other things said to be good it is not worthy of mention. You get what I'm saying, I suppose.

Kl. Certainly.

Ath. So our tyrant should possess this nature in addition to those other natural qualities, if the city is to gain, in the shortest possible time and in the best possible manner, the political regime whose possession will make it most happy. For there is not now nor would there ever be a speedier and better process of founding a regime.

710c   Kl.   How, and by what argument, stranger, could someone say this and persuade himself that what he is saying is correct?

Ath.   Presumably, Kleinias, it is easy to think this at least, that such a thing is according to nature.

Kl.   What are you saying? If there were to be a tyrant, you claim, who was young, moderate, a good learner, with an able memory, courageous, and magnificent?

Ath.   Add "with good luck"—not in other respects, but in this: that in his epoch there should arise a praiseworthy lawgiver, and
710d   that some chance should bring the two of them together. For if this should happen, then the god has done almost all the things that he does when he wants some city to fare especially well. Second is the situation where two such rulers arise; then comes the third situation, and so on in proportion, the situation becoming progressively more difficult the more there are, and the opposite as it moves in the opposite direction.

Kl.   You're asserting, it appears, that the best city emerges out of tyranny, with an eminent lawgiver and an orderly tyrant, and that the city would be transformed most easily and most
710e   swiftly from such a situation; second would be a transformation from oligarchy—is that what you mean?—and third from democracy.

Ath.   No, not at all; in first place would be the transformation from tyranny, second would be from a monarchic regime, and third would be from some sort of democracy. Oligarchy would be in fourth place, since it would with the greatest difficulty allow such a thing to come into being, because it has the largest number of all-powerful rulers.[8]

We say that these things come to pass when there comes into being by nature a true lawgiver, who coincidentally shares some of the strength of those who are the most power-
711a   ful in the city. If this should occur where the powerful are the smallest in number, but the strongest, as in tyranny, then the change is apt to take place there swiftly and easily.

Kl.   How? The fact is, we don't understand.

Ath.   Yet we've said it, at least, not once but many times now, I think! But you two have probably never witnessed a city being tyrannized.

Kl. Nor am I, at least, desirous of witnessing it!

Ath. But you'd see in it what's been spoken of now. 711b

Kl. Namely?

Ath. You'd see that if a tyrant wishes to change a city's habitual ways, he doesn't need to exert great efforts or spend an enormous amount of time. What he has to do is first proceed himself, along the route he'd like the citizens to turn toward, whether it be toward the practices of virtue or the opposite. He need only first trace out a model in his own conduct of all that is to be done, praising and honoring some things while 711c assigning blame to others, and casting dishonor on anyone who disobeys in each of the activities.

Kl. And why do we suppose that the other citizens will swiftly follow someone who has adopted such a combination of persuasion and violence?

Ath. Let no one persuade us, friends, that there will ever be a quicker or easier way for a city to change its laws than through the hegemony of all-powerful rulers. This is the case now and it will always be so. And for us this is not impossible or even 711d difficult to bring about. What is difficult is the following, which seldom comes to pass even in a great span of time, but which, when it does happen in a city, brings to that city myriads of all that is good.

Kl. What are you talking about?

Ath. The possibility that a divine erotic passion for moderate and just practices should arise in some of the great and all-powerful rulers—whether they derive their power from monarchy, or from outstanding superiority in wealth or birth, or from the 711e fact that some day one of them possesses the nature of Nestor,[9] who they claim surpassed all human beings in moderation to an even greater degree than he surpassed them in the power of speaking.[10] This man lived in the time of Troy, as they claim, though never among us; but if such a man has ever existed, or will exist some day, or is now among us, then he himself lives a blessed life, and blessed are those who join in paying heed to the words that flow from his moderate mouth.

The very same argument applies to every sort of power: when the greatest power coincides in a human being with 712a prudence and moderation,[11] then occurs the natural genesis of the best regime, and laws to match; but otherwise it will never come to pass.

Let these remarks be like a myth pronounced in oracular fashion, revealing, on the one hand, that it would be difficult for a city with good laws to come into being, but, on the other hand, that if what we discussed did occur, such a city's origin would be the quickest and by far the easiest of all.

Kl.   How?

712b Ath.   Let's try to harmonize this with your city, and like elderly children, let's try to fashion the laws in speech.

Kl.   Yes, let's get on with it and not delay anymore.

Ath.   Let us invoke a god in the setting up of the city. Let him hear us, and having heard, let him graciously and propitiously come to us and take part with us in the ordering of the city and the laws.

Kl.   Let him come indeed!

712c Ath.   Now what sort of regime do we have in mind to arrange for the city?

Kl.   Just what do you mean by this question? State it yet more clearly: do you mean what sort of democracy, or oligarchy, or aristocracy, or monarchy? Surely you wouldn't be referring to tyranny—at any rate, we would assume not.

Ath.   Come now: which of you two is more willing to answer first, by saying which of these fits his own regime?

Meg.   Since I am the elder, wouldn't it be more just for me to speak first?

712d Kl.   Perhaps.

Meg.   Well, if I reflect on it, stranger, I can't explain to you which of these names ought to be given to the regime in Lacedaimon. It seems to me that the regime does resemble tyranny—for the institution of the Ephors in it is surprisingly tyrannical; but then again, it sometimes appears to me that ours, of all cities, resembles most closely a democracy. Yet it would be altogether strange if I were not to assert that it was an aristoc-

712e racy. Then too, there is a monarchy in it with a king for life: in fact, this is the most ancient of all monarchies, according to what is said by all human beings, including us. So when I'm now asked to reply on the spur of the moment I really can't, as I said, separate it off and say which of these regimes it is.

Kl.   I find myself undergoing the same difficulty as you, Megillus. For I am altogether at a loss to say definitely which of these characterizes the regime in Knossos.

Ath. That's because you two really belong to *regimes*, best of men. The other things we just named, they aren't regimes, but city administrations where the city is under the sway of despots, 713a with some parts enslaved to other parts of itself. Each takes its name from the authority that is the despot. If one ought to name the city in this way, then one must use the name of the god who truly rules as despot over those who possess intellect.

Kl. Who is this god?

Ath. Should a little more use be made of myth, if it will allow us somehow to clarify, in a harmonious way, the answer to the present question?

Kl. Is that, then, the way one has to proceed?[12]

Ath. By all means. Now long before the cities whose formation we 713b described earlier, there is said to have come into being a certain very happy rule and arrangement under Kronos.[13] The best of arrangements at the present time is in fact an imitation of this.

Kl. Then it seems one certainly ought to hear about it.

Ath. So it appears to me at least; that's why I introduced it into the midst of the discussion.

Kl. And you acted in a most correct way. So you'd be quite correct in going on to complete the rest of the myth, if in fact it's 713c relevant.

Ath. One must do as you two say. Now we have received an oracular report of the blessed way of life of those who lived in that time, how it had everything without stint and spontaneously. And the cause of these things is said to have been something like the following: Kronos understood that, as we have explained, human nature is not at all capable of regulating the human things, when it possesses autocratic authority over everything, without becoming swollen with insolence and injustice. So, reflecting on these things, he set up at that time kings and rulers within our cities—not human beings, but demons, 713d members of a more divine and better species. He did just what we do now with sheep and the other tame herd animals. We don't make cattle themselves rulers of cattle, or goats rulers of goats; instead, we exercise despotic dominion over them, because our species is better than theirs. The same was done by the god, who was a friend of humanity: he set over us the better species of demons, who supervised us in a way that provided much ease both for them and for us. They provided peace and awe and good laws and justice without stint. Thus 713e they made it so that the races of men were without civil strife, and happy.

What this present argument is saying, making use of the truth, is that there can be no rest from evils and toils for those cities in which some mortal rules rather than a god. The argument thinks that we should imitate by every device the way of life that is said to have existed under Kronos; in public life and in private life—in the arrangement of our households and our cities—we should obey whatever within us partakes of immortality, giving the name "law" to the distribution ordained by intelligence. But if there is one human being, or some oligarchy, or a democracy, whose soul is directed to pleasures and desires, and needs to be filled with these, and retains nothing, but is sick with endless and insatiable evil—if such a one rules a city or some private individual, trampling underfoot the laws, there is, as we just now said, no device of salvation.

714a

714b
We must think over this argument, Kleinias, and decide whether we will obey it, or just how we will behave.

Kl. Presumably it is necessary to obey it.

Ath. Do you understand, now, that some assert there are as many forms of laws as there are regimes, and that the forms of regimes spoken of by the many are those we have just enumerated? And do not suppose that this present disagreement is about something paltry: it concerns something very great. For once again we are involved in the dispute over the aim of the just and the unjust. They are claiming that laws ought not look to war or to virtue as a whole, but ought to look to what is in the interest of the established regime, to whatever will allow that regime to rule forever and avoid dissolution. They claim that the finest way to formulate the definition of justice that is according to nature is this—

714c

Kl. How?

Ath. That it is the interest of the stronger.

Kl. Speak still more clearly.

Ath. It is as follows: "Presumably," they assert, "it is the strong authority who lays down the laws on each occasion in the city. Isn't that so?"

Kl. What you say is true.

714d Ath. "Well do you think," they assert, "that when the populace is victorious, or some other regime, or even a tyrant, that it will voluntarily set up laws aimed primarily at something other than what is in the interest of the maintenance of its own rule?"

Kl. How could it be otherwise?

Ath. And if someone violates these things that are set down, won't the one who established them punish this person as someone who does injustice, naming the things set down "the just things"?

Kl. That's indeed likely.

Ath. So these things would at every moment, thus and in this manner, be what is just.

Kl. So this argument asserts, at any rate.

Ath. For this is one of those worthy titles to rule.

Kl. What titles?   714e

Ath. The ones we investigated earlier, to see who should rule over whom. It emerged that parents should rule over offspring, that the younger should be ruled by the elder, that the well born should rule over those not well born; and then there were several others, if we remember, and they were obstacles to one another. One of them was this very thing. We asserted, I suppose, that "according to nature" Pindar "pushes through and   715a
makes just what is most violent," [14] as he asserts.

Kl. Yes, these were the things that were said then.

Ath. Consider, then, to which men our city is to be turned over. For this sort of thing has already happened tens of thousands of times in some cities.

Kl. What sort of thing?

Ath. The ruling offices become matters for battle, and those who are victorious take over the city's affairs to such an extent that they refuse to share any of the rule with those who lost out— with either them or their descendants—and the two sides live keeping watch on one another lest someone ever get into of-   715b
fice who might remember the old wrongs and start a revolt. These we presumably declare now not to be regimes, nor do we declare any laws correct that are not laid down for the sake of what is common to the whole city. Where the laws exist for the sake of some, we declare the inhabitants to be "partisans" rather than citizens, and declare that when they assert their ordinances to be the just things they have spoken in vain.

We have said these things because of the following: we will not apportion the offices in your city on the basis of someone's

715c wealth or any such possession, be it physical strength or size or descent. Whoever is most obedient to the established laws and wins this victory in the city must, we assert, be given the service dedicated to the gods: the greatest service to the one who is first, the second-greatest to the one who is ranked second in mastery, and so on in the same proportion for each rank of service after these.

715d I have now applied the term "servants of the laws" to the men usually said to be rulers, not for the sake of an innovation in names but because I hold that it is this above all that determines whether the city survives or undergoes the opposite. Where the law is itself ruled over and lacks sovereign authority, I see destruction at hand for such a place. But where it is despot over the rulers and the rulers are slaves of the law, there I foresee safety and all the good things which the gods have given to cities.

Kl. Yes by Zeus, stranger! For you see with the sharpness of age!

Ath That is because every young human being sees such things indistinctly, when he looks by himself, but when old sees them with great sharpness.

715e

Kl. Very true.

Ath. So what's next after these matters? Shouldn't we assume that the colonists have arrived and are present, and that the rest of the argument ought to be completed before them?

Kl. Why not?

Ath. "Sirs," let us address them, "the god, just as the ancient saying has it, holding the beginning and the end and the middle of all the beings,[15] completes his straight course by revolving, according to nature. Following him always is Justice, avenger of those who forsake the divine law. He who is going to become happy follows Her, in humility and orderliness. But anyone who is puffed up with boastfulness, or who feels exalted because of riches or honors or good bodily form accompanied by youth and mindlessness, anyone whose soul burns with insolence and hence regards himself as needing neither ruler nor any leader but rather considers himself capable of leading others, is left behind, abandoned by the god. Once left behind, he takes up with others like himself and leaps around overturning everything; to many, he seems to be somebody, but after no long while he undergoes the blameless vengeance of Justice, bringing complete ruin to himself and his household and city as well.

716a

716b

"Now if things are ordered in this way, what should and should not the prudent man do and think about in regard to them?"

Kl.   Well, this at least is clear: every man must think about how he may become one of the followers of the god.

Ath.   "What then is the activity that is dear to and follows god?   716c
There is one, and it is expressed in a single ancient saying: [16]
'like is dear to like, if it is measured'; things that lack measure are dear neither to one another nor to things that possess measure. For us, the god would be the measure of all things in the highest degree, and far more so than some 'human being,' as they assert. [17] He who is to become dear to such a being must   716d
necessarily do all in his power to become like him; and according to this argument the moderate man among us is dear to god, because similar, while the man who is not moderate is dissimilar and different and unjust—and the other things follow thus, according to the same argument. [18]

"Let us understand that from these observations there follows a principle of the following sort (the noblest and truest of all principles, I believe): for the good man it is very noble, very good, and most efficacious for a happy life, as well as pre- 716e
eminently fitting, if he sacrifices to and always communes with the gods—through prayers, votive offerings, and every sort of service to the gods. But for the bad man just the opposite of these things holds by nature. For the wicked man is impure in his soul, while his opposite is pure, and it is never correct for either a good man or a god to receive gifts from   717a
someone who is polluted. The great effort spent by the impious on the gods is therefore spent in vain—though such effort is very opportune for all the pious.

"This, then, is the target at which we must aim. What is the most correct way to characterize the missiles one should shoot and their trajectory? First, we assert, one would most correctly hit the target of pious reverence if one honored the gods of the underworld after the Olympians and the gods who possess the city, assigning to them the even-numbered, the second place, and the left side. The higher things—the odd-numbered and   717b
the other opposites—should be assigned to those just now mentioned. After these gods, the prudent man at least would worship the demons, and then next after these, the heroes. Following close upon them would be the private shrines of ancestral gods, worshipped as the law directs, and then after these

the honors that are due to living parents.[19] For it is just that one in debt pay back his first and greatest debts, the eldest of all his obligations, and that he consider all his acquisitions and possessions as belonging to those who engendered and nourished him; he should strive with all his power to devote these things to their service—starting with property, then secondly the things of the body, and thirdly the things of the soul. Thus he will pay back the ancient loans that were bestowed on the young—the cares and laborious pains suffered—and will be returning help to the ancient ones when they especially need it, in their old age. Beyond all this, it is essential that one maintain throughout life a tone of special respect in one's speech to parents, because there is a very heavy penalty for flippant or winged words. Nemesis,[20] the messenger of Justice, has been set to keep watch over everyone in this regard. So when parents become enraged it is necessary to bear with them and appease their spiritedness, whether they vent it in words or in deeds; one must keep in mind that it is very likely that a father feel an especially spirited anger at a son who he believes is doing him an injustice. And when parents die, the most moderate burial ceremony is the most beautiful, one not more elaborate than is customary and yet not falling short of those which the forefathers held for their parents. The yearly ritual services in honor of those who have reached their end should preserve a similar orderliness. One should reverence them especially by never ceasing to remember them and by continuing to allot to those who have passed away a well-measured portion of the wealth fortune bestows.

"If we do these things and live according to these precepts, each of us will on each occasion reap what we deserve from the gods and from those who are stronger than we are, and we will pass most of life in good hopes."

As for what pertains to offspring, relatives, friends, and citizens, as well as whatever services the gods require toward strangers, and how one is to commune with all these, the sequence of the laws themselves will show how one adorns and lawfully orders his own life by fulfilling his duties. Sometimes the law will persuade, and sometimes—when dispositions are recalcitrant—it will persuade by punishing, with vi-

717c

717d

717e

718a

718b

olence and justice. Thus, if the gods are willing, the laws will succeed in making our city blessed and happy.

There are also some things which a lawgiver who thinks as I do should and must necessarily say, but which cannot be presented harmoniously in the shape of law; it seems to me that the lawgiver should present an example of these things for himself and for those he will give laws to. After he has done 718c this, and has proceeded through everything else to the best of his ability, he should begin to establish the laws.

Kl. What shape should such things preferably take?[21]

Ath. It is not too easy to embrace them by speaking of a single model, as it were; but let's conceive of them in something like the following way and see if we can get a firm grasp on them.

Kl. Say what sort of way you mean.

Ath. I would wish that the people would be as persuadable as possible with regard to virtue; and it's clear that the lawgiver will also strive to achieve this, in every facet of his legislation.

Kl. How could it be otherwise? 718d

Ath. Now it seemed to me that the things that were just said, if they took hold of a soul that was not entirely savage, would contribute something to making the hearer listen in a more tame and agreeable mood to the advice. So even if these words have no great effect, but only a small one, still, insofar as they make the one who listens to what was said more agreeable and a better learner, that is in every way desirable. For there is no great plenty or abundance of persons who are eager in spirit to become as good as possible in the shortest possible time; in- 718e deed, the many show that Hesiod is wise when he says that the road to vice is smooth to travel and without sweat, since it is very short, but "before virtue," he asserts,[22]

> the immortal gods have put sweat,
> And a path to it that is long and steep,
> And rough at first. When you arrive at the top, 719a
> Then it's easy to endure; but the ascent is hard.

Kl. He sounds like someone who speaks nobly, at any rate.

Ath. He certainly does. Now I want to set directly before you two the effect produced on me by the preceding speech.

Kl. Do so.

Ath. Let's engage then in the following dialogue with the lawgiver: "Tell us, O lawgiver: If in fact you knew what we should do 719b and say, isn't it obvious that you would state it?"

Kl.   Necessarily.

Ath. "Well, didn't we hear you saying just a little while ago that a lawgiver should not allow the poets to create whatever they like? For they would not know what in any of their speeches was opposed to the laws and hence harmful to the city."

Kl.   What you say is indeed true.

Ath. Now if we were to reply to him on behalf of the poets, would the following remarks be well measured?

Kl.   Which?

719c Ath. The following. "There is an ancient myth, O lawgiver, which we ourselves always repeat and which is also the accepted opinion of all the others, to the effect that the poet, when seated on the tripod of the Muses,[23] is not at that time in possession of his senses, but is like some spring that readily lets flow whatever comes up from within. Since his art consists of imitation, he is compelled to contradict himself often, by creating human beings who are opposed to one another; and he doesn't know if either of the diverse things said is true. For

719d the lawgiver, however, it isn't possible to create this in a law—to make two speeches about one subject—but he must always exhibit one speech about one subject. Take a look at something from the speeches you pronounced just now. Burial ceremonies can be either overly elaborate, or skimpy, or of measured size. You chose one of these, the medium size, and enjoined and praised this one without any qualifications. But as for me, if in my poetry some especially wealthy woman

719e were to give orders for her funeral, I'd praise the overly elaborate funeral; or again, if some thrifty and poor man were involved, he'd praise the skimpy funeral; if he were someone possessing a measured amount of property, and were himself a person of measure, he'd praise the same funeral as you. Now, in your case it isn't sufficient to leave it at what you just now said, about a well-measured size; one must tell what and how much constitutes well measured. Until that is done you shouldn't think that such a speech has become a law."

Kl.   What you say is very true.

Ath. So, then, is the one who is to have charge of our laws going to pronounce no such preface at the beginning of the laws? Is he

720a just going to explain straightaway what must and must not be done, add the threat of a penalty, and turn to another law, without adding a single encouragement[24] or bit of persuasion to his legislative edicts? There is one sort of doctor who used to proceed in this way, and another sort who used to proceed in the other way each time he took care of us. Let's recollect each of those different modes of procedure, so that we may beseech the lawgiver the same way children beseech a doctor, asking him to care for them in the most gentle way. Now just what sort of thing are we referring to? Presumably we assert that there are certain persons who are doctors; and then, that there are in addition doctor's servants, whom we also, I suppose, call "doctors."

Kl.   Certainly.   720b

Ath. Whether they be free men or slaves, they acquire the art by following their masters' command, by observing, and by experience, but not by following nature, as the free doctors do, who have themselves learned in this way and who teach their disciples in this way. Would you set these down as the two species of what are called doctors?

Kl.   But of course.

Ath. Then you also understand that sick people in the cities, slaves and free, are treated differently. The slaves are for the most   720c part treated by slaves, who either go on rounds or remain at the dispensaries. None of these latter doctors gives or receives any account of each malady afflicting each domestic slave. Instead, he gives him orders on the basis of the opinions he has derived from experience. Claiming to know with precision, he gives his comands just like a headstrong tyrant and hurries off to some other sick domestic slave. In this way he relieves his   720d master of the trouble of caring for the sick.

The free doctor mostly cares for and looks after the maladies of free men. He investigates these from their beginning and according to nature, communing with the patient himself and his friends, and he both learns something himself from the invalids and, as much as he can, teaches the one who is sick. He doesn't give orders until he has in some sense persuaded; when he has on each occasion tamed the sick person with persuasion, he attempts to succeed in leading him back to health.   720e

Which of the two procedures is better, whether for a doctor who is curing or for a gymnast who is exercising people? Should the practitioner execute his single power in a split way or in only one way, employing only the worse and more savage of the two?

Kl.   The double method would presumably make a great difference, stranger.

Ath. Do you want us to observe this double method, and then the simple, in the very acts of lawgiving?

Kl.   How could I not want to!

Ath. Come, then, in the name of the gods, what would be the first law the lawgiver would lay down? Won't he proceed according to nature, and with his regulations bring order to what is the first cause of childbirth in cities?

721a Kl.   But of course.

Ath. Isn't intercourse and partnership between married spouses the original cause of childbirths in all cities?

Kl.   How could it be otherwise?

Ath. Then it's likely that in every city it's fine, with a view to what is correct, if the marriage laws are the first laid down.

Kl.   In every way, surely.

Ath. Let's pronounce first the simple version, which would perhaps be something like this:

721b   Everyone is to marry after he reaches the age of thirty and before the age of thirty-five. If not, there is to be a penalty of fines and dishonor, the fines to be of such-and-such an amount, the dishonor to be of such-and-such a character.

         Let something like that be the simple formula regarding marriage. Here's the double formula:

         Everyone is to marry after he reaches the age of thirty and before he reaches thirty-five, bearing in mind that there is a sense in which the human species has by a certain nature a
721c   share in immortality, and that it is the nature of everyone to desire immortality in every way. For the desire to become famous and not to lie nameless after one has died is a desire for such a thing. Thus the species of human beings has something in its nature that is bound together with all of time, which it accompanies and will always accompany to the end. In this way the species is immortal; by leaving behind the children of children and remaining one and the same for always, it partakes of immortality by means of coming-into-being. For anyone voluntarily to deprive himself of this is never pious, and whoever does not care for children and a wife does so intentionally deprive himself.

721d   Now let him who obeys the law depart without penalty; but he who disobeys, he who at the age of thirty-five does not marry, is to pay a fine of such-and-such an amount every year—so that he won't be of the opinion that the bachelor's life is a source of gain and ease for him—and further let him be excluded from the honors the younger men in the city pay to their own elders on each occasion.

After listening to this law next to the other it's possible to decide in every single case whether they should become at the very least double in length by embodying persuasion as well as threats, or whether by employing threats alone they should remain simple in length.   721e

Meg. The Laconic way, stranger, is to give more honor always to the shorter. Yet if someone were to ask me to be the judge who decides which of these writings I would want used in the written statutes of my city, I would choose the lengthier; in fact, in   722a
the case of every law I would make this same choice—if, as in this example, both possibilities were present. Of course, presumably the present legislation must also be satisfying to Kleinias here. After all, the city that is thinking of using such laws is his.

Kl. You've spoken nobly, at any rate, Megillus.

Ath. It's extremely simple-minded to argue over whether writings should be long or short; for what should be honored, I think, are the best writings, not the shortest or the lengthy. Besides,   722b
in the laws just mentioned, not only does the one version differ by double the amount of practical virtue, but, as was said just a moment ago, the comparison with the dual species of doctors is a very correct comparison.

In this regard, it's likely that none of the lawgivers has ever reflected on the fact that it is possible to use two means of giving laws, persuasion and violence (insofar as the uneducated condition of the mob permits). They have used only the latter;   722c
failing to mix compulsion [25] with persuasion in their lawgiving, they have employed unmitigated violence alone. But I, O blessed ones, see the need for yet a third way of handling laws, one not at all in use nowadays.

Kl. What are you referring to?

Ath. Something which has emerged, by the aid of some god, out of the very things about which we're now carrying on a dialogue! We began to discuss laws about dawn, and it has become high noon and we've paused in this altogether lovely resting place. In all this time we've been having a dialogue

722d   about nothing except laws. Nevertheless, it seems to me that we have only just begun to enunciate laws, and that everything said before consisted of our preludes to laws.

        Why have I said these things? What I wish to say is this: all speeches, and whatever pertains to the voice, are preceded by preludes—almost like warming-up exercises—which artfully attempt to promote what is to come. It is the case, I suppose, that of the songs sung to the kithara, the so-called "laws" or

722e   *nomoi*, [26] like all music, are preceded by preludes composed with amazing seriousness. Yet with regard to things that are really "laws," the laws we assert to be political, no one has ever either uttered a prelude or become a composer and brought one to light—just as if it were a thing that did not exist in nature. But the way we've been spending our time has shown us, it seems to me, that such a thing really does exist; and the laws which were talked of as double seemed to me just now to be not simply double but rather composed of two different parts, a law and a prelude to the law. What was called a

723a   tyrannical command, and likened to the image of the commands of the doctors we said were unfree, seemed to be unmixed law; what was spoken of before this, and was said to be persuasive on behalf of this, really did seem to be persuasion, but seemed to have the power that a prelude has in speeches. For it became clear to me that this whole speech, which the speaker gives in order to persuade, is delivered with just this end in view: so that he who receives the law uttered by the legislator might receive the command—that is, the law—in a frame of mind more favorably disposed and therefore more

723b   apt to learn something. That's why, according to my argument at least, this would correctly be called a "prelude" rather than an "argument" of the law.

        Having said these things, what would I wish myself to say next? Just this: the lawgiver must always provide that all the laws, and each of them, will not lack preludes, so that the laws will differ from themselves to as great a degree as the two that were spoken of just now differed from one another.

Kl.   For my part at least, I think that we should bid the one who knows about these things to legislate in no other way.

723c   Ath.   To me what you say seems fine to this extent, Kleinias—insofar as you say that *all* laws have preludes, and that at the beginning of every legislation as well as at the beginning of every speech one should pronounce the prelude which is by nature appropriate to each.[27] For what is going to be said after this is of no small significance, and it makes no small difference whether or not the things are remembered clearly or unclearly. Yet if we should ordain that every one of the aforementioned laws, great or small, is to have a prelude, we would not be speaking correctly. Such a thing isn't necessary in the case of every song and every speech: even though there does exist by nature a prelude for all of them, it ought not be employed in all cases. In this regard one must leave a certain latitude to the particular orator, singer, or legislator in each case.

Kl.   What you say seems very true to me. But look, stranger, let's not use up any more time in delay; let's retrace the steps of our discussion and begin, if it's all right with you, with the things you said a little while ago when you were not pronouncing a prelude. Let's repeat, with a second and better start, as they declare in playing games, but this time with the intention of completing a prelude and not just any chance sort of speech, as we were doing; let's take it as agreed that the beginning of them was a prelude. As regards honoring the gods and caring for ancestors, the things said just now are sufficient. Let's try to say what comes next, until the whole prelude seems to you to be sufficiently set forth. Then after this you will go ahead with the pronouncement of the laws themselves.

Ath.   So we are now saying that earlier we pronounced a sufficient prelude as regards the gods, those who come after the gods, and the living and dead ancestors. And you appear to me to be asking now that I bring to light, as it were, whatever has been left unsaid.

Kl.   Entirely so.

Ath.   Well, next after such things it is fitting and very much in the common interest for the speaker and the listeners to deal with how they should be serious and how they should relax as regards their own souls, their bodies, and their property; by pondering these matters, they'll attain education—insofar as they are able. These, then, are for us the very matters that really should be spoken of and hearkened to next, after those others.

Kl.   What you say is very correct.

723d

723e

724a

724b

BOOK V

726a   Ath.   "Listen, then, each of you who has heard what was said just now about the gods and the cherished forefathers.

"Of all the things that belong to one, the most divine—after the gods—is the soul, the thing that is most one's own. It is the case with everybody that all one's possessions fall into two classes. The superior and better sort are masterful, while the inferior and worse are slavish. Hence one's masterful possessions should always be honored above one's slave possessions. So I speak correctly when I urge that one honor one's

727a   soul second after the gods, who are masters, and those who follow after the gods. There is no one among us, so to speak, who assigns honor correctly, though we are of the opinion that we do. For honor is presumably a divine good, and cannot be bestowed through what is bad: he who thinks that he is making his soul greater with words or gifts or certain indulgences, yet fails to change its condition from worse to better, seems to honor it, but in fact is not doing so at all.

"Every boy who has barely become an adult human being right away considers himself capable of understanding every-

727b   thing, thinks that he honors his soul by praising it, and with an eager spirit encourages it to do whatever it might wish; whereas, according to what is now being said, this sort of behavior harms rather than honors it. And yet, we assert, it should be honored second after the gods. And when a human being refuses to consider himself responsible on each occasion for his errors and most of his gravest evils, but assigns responsibility to others and always excuses himself, he is seeming to

accord honor to his soul while falling far short of doing as he   727c
should. For he is doing harm. And when he delights in pleasures contrary to the advice and praise given by the lawgiver,
then he does not honor it at all and instead dishonors it by filling it with evils and remorse. And when, in the opposite situation, he fails to endure firmly the hardships, fears, pains, and
sufferings that are praised, and instead gives in to them, then
he does not honor it, by giving in. Through all such actions he
brings dishonor upon it. And when he considers survival to be   727d
always good, then too does he dishonor rather than honor it.
For in this case he has given in and allowed the soul to go on
supposing that everything done in Hades is bad; he has failed
to struggle as he should, teaching and attempting to refute it
in order to show that one doesn't know whether things aren't
just the opposite—it may be that among the gods below are to
be found the things that are by nature the greatest goods of all
for us. And when someone honors beauty more than virtue,
this constitutes nothing other than a real and thorough
dishonoring of the soul. For this argument falsely claims that
the body is more honorable than the soul. Yet nothing earth-   727e
born is more honorable than the Olympians, and he who has a
different opinion when it comes to the soul fails to compre-
hend what a marvelous possession he is neglecting. And
when someone has an erotic passion for ignoble gain, or fails   728a
to be troubled when he makes such gain, he then honors his
own soul by giving it gifts—entirely missing the point. For he
is selling what is honorable and beautiful in it for a small bit of
gold; whereas all the gold on earth or beneath the earth is not
equal in value to virtue.

"In short, with regard to the things the lawgiver enumerates
and sets down as shameful and bad, and the opposite, good
and noble, whoever is unwilling to use every means to avoid
the former and employ all his capacities in the practice of the
latter—every such human being—is ignorant of the fact that in   728b
all these matters he is treating his soul, a most divine thing, in
a most dishonorable and unseemly way. No one, so to speak,
takes into account the gravest of the so-called 'judicial penalties' for wrongdoing: what is gravest is to become similar to
men who are wicked, and, in becoming similar, to avoid good
men and be cut off from good conversation, and instead to attach oneself to the bad by seeking intercourse with them. He

[113]

728c who grows similar in nature to such people must necessarily do and suffer what such men by their natures do and say to one another. To suffer in this way is not, indeed, a 'judicial penalty,' since what is just—including penalty—is noble. It is retribution, a suffering that is a consequence of injustice. Both he who undergoes this and he who escapes it are miserable: one because he does not get cured, the other because he is destroyed in order that many others may be saved. To speak generally, 'honor' means for us following the better things and, in the case of the worse things that allow for improvement, bringing them as close as possible to the same end. And

728d hence no human possession is more naturally well-suited than the soul for fleeing the bad or for tracking down and capturing what is best of all, and, after capturing it, dwelling in common with it for the rest of one's life. That's why it was assigned the second rank of honor.

"The third rank of honor belongs by nature to the body (everyone would understand this at least). Here too it is necessary to look into the various sorts of honor to see which are true and how many are false, and this is the responsibility of the lawgiver. It appears to me that he would announce and distinguish them as follows: the honorable body is not the one

728e that is beautiful, or strong, or swift, or large, or even healthy—though many would believe this, indeed, to be rather honorable—nor, of course, a body that has the opposite characteristics. Instead, those attributes which occupy the middle ground, in between all these, are the most moderate and steady by far. For the former extremes make souls boastful and rash, while the latter make them humble and unfree.

"The same holds true for the possession of money and property; honor should be bestowed on this according to the same

729a scheme.[1] Excesses of each of these create enmities and civil strife both in cities and in private life, while deficiencies lead, for the most part, to slavery.

"And let no one be a lover of money for the sake of his children, so that he may leave them as wealthy as possible: this is better neither for them nor for the city. A portion that will not attract flatterers around the young but will avoid neediness is the most musical and the best of all; for this brings us consonance, and through harmony makes life painless in all

729b respects. Children should be left an abundance of awe rather than gold. Now we think that we bestow this legacy on the young by rebuking them whenever they behave shamelessly. Yet this is not the result produced if the young are exhorted the way they are nowadays, when they are urged to be ashamed before everyone. The prudent lawgiver would instead urge the elderly to be ashamed before the young, and to take care above all lest any young person ever see or hear them doing or saying anything shameful; for where the old are lacking in a sense of shame, there the young necessarily lack modest awe. What really makes a difference in education—not only of the young but of ourselves—is not so much the precepts one gives others, as the way one exemplifies the precepts one would give to another, in one's conduct throughout life.

729c

"If a man honors and reverences family ties and his entire natural blood-community that shares in the family gods, he may expect the gods who watch over births to be proportionately well disposed towards his own begetting of children.

"Moreover, as for friends and comrades, one will make them favorably disposed in the interminglings of life if one thinks more highly than they do of the worth and importance of their services to oneself, and assigns to one's own favors to friends a lesser value than that assigned by the friends and comrades themselves.

729d

"With regard to the city and its citizens, the best person by far is the one who prefers, above any Olympic victories or any victories in contests of war or peace, the victorious reputation of having served his own laws—a reputation as the one who throughout his life served the laws more nobly than any other human being.

729e

"Again, as regards strangers, one must consider contracts made with them to be the most hallowed.[2] For almost all the wrongs committed among strangers or against strangers are linked more closely to an avenging god than are the wrongs committed among citizens. This is because the stranger, being bereft of comrades and relatives, evokes more pity on the part of both human beings and gods; therefore he who has the power to avenge him has a spirit that is more eager to come to his aid. And especially powerful, in each case, are the demon and the god of strangers, who follow Zeus, god of strangers. Thus anyone with even a little foresight will take great care to complete his life's journey without having done any wrong to

730a

strangers. The gravest of these wrongs done to strangers, and native inhabitants as well, is in every case that done to suppliants; for the god who bore witness to the agreement the suppliant happened to obtain becomes a special guardian of the one who suffers, so that whatever he happens to suffer never goes unavenged."

730b We have now just about covered the relations with parents, with oneself, and with what belongs to one, as well as with the city, friends, and family, and also strangers and the natives; what should come next after this is an explanation of what sort of person one should be oneself if one is to lead the most noble sort of life. In turning to these next matters we must speak not of law, but rather of how praise and blame can educate each of them so that they become more obedient and well disposed to the laws that are going to be laid down.

730c "Truth is the leader of all good things for gods, and of all things for human beings. Whoever is to become blessed and happy should partake of it from the very beginning, so that he may live as a truthful man for as long a time as possible. Such a man is trustworthy. The untrustworthy man is one who finds the voluntary lie congenial; he who finds the involuntary lie congenial is without intelligence. Neither of these is enviable, because every man who is untrustworthy, certainly, and ignorant, is also friendless. As time goes on such a man is discovered, and in the hard time of old age, near the end of life, he makes himself completely deserted, so that whether his comrades and children are living or not he lives almost as if he were an orphan.

730d "He who does not do injustice is indeed honorable; but he who does not allow unjust men to work their injustice is more than twice as honorable. The former has a value of one, but the latter, by reporting the injustice of the others to the magistrates, is equal in value to many others. Yet the great man in the city, the man who is to be proclaimed perfect and the bearer of victory in virtue, is the one who does what he can to assist the magistrates in inflicting punishment.

730e "This same praise should of course be bestowed on moderation and prudence, and on any other good possessions which can be given to others as well as possessed by oneself. The one who does the giving should be honored most highly; in the second rank should be put the one who is willing to give, but unable; as for the one who begrudges certain good things and does not, out of friendship, voluntarily share them in common with anyone, he should be blamed—though the possession itself should not be dishonored on account of the possessor, and one should still strive to acquire it, as much as one can.

731a

"Let all of us be lovers of victory when it comes to virtue, but without envy. The man of this sort—always competing himself but never thwarting others with slander—makes cities great. But the envious man, who fancies he must gain superiority by slandering the others, both lessens his own efforts to attain true virtue and makes his competitors dispirited by getting them unjustly blamed. Thus he makes the whole city a flaccid³ competitor in the contest for virtue and does what he can to diminish its fame.

731b

"Every real man should be of the spirited type,⁴ but yet also as gentle as possible. For there is no way to avoid those injustices done by others that are both dangerous and difficult, or even impossible, to cure, except to fight and defend oneself victoriously, in no way easing up on punishment. This, every soul is unable to do, if it lacks a high-born spiritedness. On the other hand, in regard to the curable injustices men commit, one must first understand that no unjust man is ever voluntarily unjust. For no one anywhere would ever voluntarily acquire any of the greatest evils—least of all when the evil afflicts his most honored possessions. Now the soul, as we asserted, is truly the most honorable thing for everyone; therefore no one would ever voluntarily take the greatest evil into his most honorable possession and keep it for the rest of his life. So the unjust man, like the man who possesses bad things, is pitiable in every way, and it is permissible to pity such a man when his illness is curable; in this case one can become gentle, by restraining one's spiritedness and not keeping up that bitter, woman's raging. But against the purely evil, perverted man who cannot be corrected, one must let one's anger have free rein. This is why we declare that it is fitting for the good man to be of the spirited type and also gentle, as each occasion arises.

731c

731d

"The greatest of all evils for the mass of human beings is something which grows naturally in the soul, and everyone,

731e by excusing it in himself, fails to devise any way to escape it. This is shown by the way people talk, when they say that every human being is by nature a friend to himself and that it is correct that he should be so. The truth is that the excessive friendship for oneself is the cause of all of each man's wrongdoings on every occasion. Everyone who cares for something is blind when it comes to the thing cared for, and hence is a

732a poor judge of what is just and good and noble, because he believes he should always honor his own more than the truth. Yet a man who is to attain greatness must be devoted not to himself or to what belongs to him, but to what is just— whether it happens to be done by himself or by someone else. This same failing is the source of everyone's supposing that his lack of learning is wisdom. As a result, we think we know everything when in fact we know, so to speak, nothing:

732b and when we refuse to turn over to others what we don't know how to do, we necessarily go wrong, by trying to do them ourselves. So every human being should flee excessive self-love, and should instead always pursue someone who is better than himself, without putting any feeling of shame in the way.

"There are some matters that are often talked about which are smaller, but no less useful, than these things; each person should repeat them to himself and keep recollecting them. For just as where there is a constant flow outward, there must be the opposite, constant replenishment, so recollection is the

732c inflow that replenishes the supply of prudence. Thus excessive laughter or weeping should be restrained, and every man should remind everyone else to that effect. On the whole, one should try to keep all great joy or great pain hidden under a seemly veil, whether each person's demon remains in good condition or whether in some enterprises chance brings high, steep slopes for the demons to climb. With regard to the troubles that fall upon men, they should hope that for good men at

732d least the god will always diminish them, and change their present lot for the better, by means of the gifts he bestows;[5] with regard to the good things, they should hope that, with the help of good luck, the opposite sort of change will always take place for them. It's in these hopes that each should live and with recollections of all such admonitions, never flagging, but always recollecting them clearly, for another and for oneself, playfully and seriously."

Now thus far, what has been said describing the practices that are to be followed and the sort of person each should be himself, concerns mainly the divine things; we have not yet discussed the human things, though we must—for we are carrying on a dialogue with human beings, not gods.

732e

"By nature, the human consists above all in pleasures and pains and desires. To these every mortal animal is, as it were, inextricably attached and bound in the most serious ways. The noblest life should be praised not only because it is superior as regards the splendor of its reputation, but also because, if someone is willing to taste it and not become a fugitive from it because of his youth, it will prove superior in respect to that which we all seek—namely, having more delight and less pain throughout the whole of one's life. That this will be clear, if one tastes in the correct way, will be very obvious. But what is 'the correct way'? This is what must now be investigated, under the guidance of the argument: one way of life must be compared with another, the more pleasant with the more painful, to see whether the life grows for us according to nature or whether it grows otherwise, against nature.

733a

"Now we want pleasure for ourselves, while we neither choose nor want pain; we don't want what is neither pleasant nor painful instead of what is pleasant, but we do want it in exchange for pain; we want less pain with more pleasure but we don't want less pleasure with more pain; where the pleasant things and the painful things are equal in each of two situations, we could not say clearly which situation we choose. As each choice is exercised, all these do or do not make a difference to him who is wishing, depending on their number, size, intensity, and equality, or the opposites. This being the way these things are necessarily ordered, in the case of a life that has many great and intense pleasures and pains, we want the life in which the pleasures predominate and don't want the life in which the opposite predominate. Again, in the case of a life that has a few small and calm pleasures and pains, we don't wish the life in which the painful things predominate but we do wish the life in which the opposite predominate. Further, the life whose intensity is balanced we have to understand in the same way: we wish the balanced life that has more of the things we like, but if it has more of the things we find repugnant, we do not wish it.[6] One must understand that

733b

733c

733d

all ways of life open to us are naturally limited by this range of alternatives, and on this basis one must decide which ways of life we wish for by nature. If we claim we wish something beyond these alternatives, we are speaking from a certain ignorance and lack of experience of what the ways of life really are.

"So then what and how many are the ways of life among which one must distinguish the wished-for and voluntary

733e
from the unwished and involuntary—looking to a law that one gives to oneself, and choosing what is dear and also pleasant and best and most noble, and thus living as blessed a life as is humanly possible? One of these lives, let us say, is the moderate life; one is the prudent; and one is the courageous; in addition, let us set down the healthy life as one. Opposed to these, being four, are four others—the imprudent, the cowardly, the unrestrained, and the sickly. Now he who knows will set down the life of moderation as a life that is mild in every way,

734a
with gentle pains and gentle pleasures, a life characterized by desires that are mild and loves that are not mad. The unrestrained life he will set down as intense in every way, with strong pains and strong pleasures, a life characterized by desires that are vehement and frenzied, and loves that are as mad as possible. In the moderate life, he will say, the pleasures predominate over the griefs, while in the unrestrained life the pains are greater and more numerous and more frequent than the pleasures. From this it falls out, necessarily

734b
and according to nature, that the one life is more pleasant for us and the other more painful; and he at least who wants to live pleasantly will no longer, voluntarily at any rate, permit himself to live in an unrestrained way. Indeed, it is now obvious—if what is being said now is correct—that every unrestrained man must necessarily be living this way involuntarily. The whole mob of humanity lives with a lack of moderation because of their ignorance or their lack of self-mastery or a combination of both. One must understand the sickly and healthy ways of life in the very same way. Both have their pleasures and pains, but in a healthy life the plea-

734c
sures predominate over the pains, while sick men have more pains than pleasures. In choosing among ways of life we do not wish that the painful should predominate, and the life where pain is subordinate is the life we have judged to be

more pleasant. Now in comparing the moderate life with the unrestrained, the prudent with the imprudent, and even the life of courage with that of cowardice, we would assert that in the former lives both pleasures and pains are fewer, smaller, and rarer, and the one life surpasses the other in pleasures, while the latter lives surpass the others in pain. The coura- 734d geous man defeats the coward, the prudent man defeats the imprudent, and so their lives are more pleasant than the lives of the others: the moderate, courageous, prudent, and healthy lives compared to the cowardly, imprudent, unrestrained, and sickly. In sum, we would assert that the life that possesses virtue, of body or also of soul, is more pleasant than the life possessing vice, and that in the other respects—beauty, correctness, virtue, and fame—it is far superior to the life of vice. Thus it makes the one who possesses it live more happily than 734e his opposite, in every way and on the whole."

Let the speeches that constitute the prelude to the laws come to an end here. After the "prelude" it is presumably necessary that a "law" follow[7]—or rather, in truth, the outline of the laws of a political regime. Now just as in some web or any other woven article the woof and the warp[8] can't be made of the same materials, and the warp must necessarily be different in regard to virtue (for it should be strong, with a certain 735a firmness in its ways, while the other should be softer, with a certain just, yielding quality), so with respect to those who are to fill the ruling offices in cities one must in each case discriminate, in some reasonable way, between them and the others who have been tested and hardened by only a small education. For a political regime has two fundamental parts:[9] on the one hand, the appointment of men to fill each ruling office, and on the other hand, the laws that are given to the ruling offices.

But before all these matters, it is necessary to think through such matters as the following. With regard to every herd, one 735b who takes up the task of a shepherd or cowherd or horse breeder or any other such things will never attempt to care for his charges otherwise than by first instituting the purge appropriate to each group. Picking out the healthy from those who are not, and the well born from those not well born, he will send the latter away to other herds and direct his care to

735c the former. He understands that his labor would be vain and endless, as regards both the body and the souls, if someone didn't carry out a purification by the appropriate means. For in the case of each animal he owns, the souls that have been ruined by nature and by a corrupt upbringing will ruin the stock that has healthy and undefiled habits and bodies. With the other animals it is a less serious matter, and deserves mention in the argument only to serve as an example; but in the case of human beings it is a task of the greatest seriousness for the lawgiver to discover and give an account of what is appropriate for each group, as regards the purge and all other activi-

735d ties. So, without further ado, the account of the purges of the city would go as follows. There are many sorts of purification, some gentler and some harsher. If the same man were a tyrant as well as a lawgiver he could employ the purges that are harsh and best; if a lawgiver who lacks tyranny is setting up a new regime with laws, he should be glad if he can purify using even the gentlest of purges. The best method is painful, like

735e medicines of this kind, since it involves punishing with justice and retribution, and completes the retribution by means of death and exile. That is how the greatest offenders, those who are incurable and who represent the greatest harm to the city, are usually gotten rid of. But our method of purification is one of the gentler—something like this: those who, because they lack food, show themselves ready to follow men who lead

736a the have-nots in an attack on the property of the haves will be looked upon as a disease growing [10] within the city; they will be sent away in as gentle a manner as possible, in an expulsion that bears the euphemistic name "colonization." Every lawgiver must somehow or other accomplish this at the beginning, but for us now the problem happens to be rather unusual. There isn't any need to devise a colonizing expedition or some purgative selection at present; instead, just as in the case of a single reservoir formed by the flowing together of

736b many springs and mountain torrents, we are compelled to turn our minds to insuring that the water flowing in will be as pure as possible, partly by drawing off some and partly by diverting some in side-channels. But it's likely that toil and danger are present in every political project. Since things are being done now in speech but not in deed, let's assume that our selection has been carried out and that the purification has happened according to our manner of thinking. By thorough testing—with every sort of persuasion over a sufficient period of time—we will discover those who are bad among the people trying to become citizens of the present city and prevent them from entering; to those who are good we will extend as gentle and as gracious an invitation as we can. 736c

Let us not, by the way, overlook the good fortune that has befallen us, the same luck that we said befell the colony founded by the descendants of Heracles: they avoided the terrible, dangerous strife occasioned by redivision of land, cancelling of debts, and redistribution. When a city with ancient 736d roots is compelled to legislate about this, it finds that it cannot leave things as they are, unchanged, nor is it able to change them in any way; the only thing left, so to speak, is prayer, and small, careful transformation that gradually produces a small result over a long period of time. For this to happen there must be a continual supply of reformers from among those who possess an abundance of land and many debtors. These reformers must be willing, out of a sense of fairness, to share in some way what they have with any of their debtors who are in distress, forgiving some of the debts and parcelling 736e out some of their land. Thus they bring about a kind of measure and show that they believe poverty consists not in a lessening of one's property but in an increase of one's avarice. This is the most important source of a city's preservation, and provides a sort of sturdy foundation upon which someone can later build whatever political order befits such an arrangement. But if this foundation is rotten, political activity would 737a always encounter difficulties in the city.[11] This danger, as we assert, we're avoiding; nevertheless, it is more correct to discuss it, at any rate, and show how we might find a way out if we were not escaping it. It's been said that what would be needed is an absence of the money-loving that goes with justice: there is no other way of escape, broad or narrow, besides this device. So let this stand now as a kind of buttress for our city. Somehow or other things must be arranged so that they 737b don't have disputes over their property, because those who have even a little intelligence won't voluntarily go ahead with the rest of the arrangements as long as ancient property disputes remain unsettled among themselves. But for men in a situation like ours now, where a god has given a new city to found, and where there are as yet no hatreds against one another; no human ignorance, even if combined with complete evil, would lead men to set up a division of land and houses that would introduce these hatreds among themselves.

737c

What then would be the method of a correct distribution? First the numerical mass has to be decided—how many of them there ought to be. After that there must be agreement on the distribution of the citizens—how many divisions there should be, and how big they should be. Among these divisions the land and houses should be distributed as equally as possible. Now the only correct way to determine the adequate size of the population is by consideration of the land and the neighboring cities. The land should be large enough to support a certain number[12] of people living moderately, and no more. This number should be large enough to enable them both to defend themselves, if they suffer an injustice from their neighbors, and to be in a position to give at least some aid to their neighbors if someone else does them an injustice. When we have looked over the territory and the neighbors we will decide on these things in deed as well as in speech. At the moment, for the sake of giving a sketch in outline, let the argument proceed to the giving of the laws, so that it can be completed.

737d

737e

As a suitable number, let there be five thousand forty landholders and defenders of the distribution; and let there be the same division of the land and the households, each man paired with an allotment. First let the whole number be divided by two, and then the same number by three—for its nature is to be divisible also by four, and five, and so on up to ten. Any man who is a lawgiver must understand at least this much about numbers: which number and what kind of number would be the most useful for all cities. Let's choose the number that has the most numerous and most nearly consecutive divisors within itself. The entire number series is divisible by every number for every purpose. Five thousand forty has no more than sixty, minus one, divisors, including all the numbers from one to ten, consecutively.[13] And these divisions are useful in war and in peace—in all contracts and associations, in revenue-gathering, and in disbursements. These matters must be studied at leisure and firmly understood by those who are given this duty by the law; at any rate,

738a

738b

this is the way it is, and the person who is going to set up a city should proclaim these things with a view to the following. The same applies whether someone is making a new city from the beginning or refounding an old city that has become corrupted: as regards gods and temples—which things are to be constructed in the city for each of them, and which gods or demons they are to be named after—no one of intelligence will try to change what has been laid down by Delphi or Dodona or Ammon,[14] or what has been ordained by the ancient sayings, however they may have become manifest—whether they issue from apparitions or from an inspiration said to come from gods. Through such advice men have established sacrifices, mixed with mystery-rites, some of which have local origins and some of which are borrowed from Etruria, or Cyprus,[15] or somewhere else. Such sayings have led them to sanctify oracles, statues, alters, and shrines, and to lay out sanctuaries for each of these things. Now a lawgiver should not change any of these things in the least. He should give to each group a god or demon or some hero, and before he makes any other land distribution he should set aside choice places for sanctuaries and everything that goes with them. In this way, when the various parts of the population gather together at the regularly established intervals, they'll be amply supplied with whatever they need; they'll become more friendly to one another, at the sacrifices, will feel they belong together, and will get to know one another. There is no greater good for a city than that its inhabitants be well known to one another; for where men's characters are obscured from one another by the dark instead of being visible in the light, no one ever obtains in a correct way the honor he deserves, either in terms of office or justice. Above everything else, every man in every city must strive to avoid deceit on every occasion and to appear always in simple fashion, as he truly is—and, at the same time, to prevent any other such man from deceiving him.

The next move in the process of establishing laws is analogous to the move made by someone playing draughts,[16] who abandons his "sacred line," and because it's unexpected, it may seem amazing to the hearer at first. Nevertheless, anyone who uses his reason and experience will recognize that a second-best city is to be constructed. Perhaps someone would not accept this because he is unfamiliar with a lawgiver who is

738c

738d

738e

739a

739b

not a tyrant. But the most correct procedure is to state what the best regime is, and the second and the third, and after stating this to give the choice among them to whoever is to be in charge of the founding in each case. Let us, too, follow this procedure now: let's state what regime is first as regards virtue, what is second, and what is third. Then let's give the choice to Kleinias, in the present circumstances, and to anyone else who might be willing, at any time, to proceed to choose among such things—taking over from his own fatherland whatever his particular character leads him to cherish in it.

739c

That city and that regime are first, and the laws are best, where the old proverb holds as much as possible throughout the whole city: it is said that the things of friends really are common.[17] If this situation exists somewhere now, or if it should ever exist someday—if women are common, and children are common, and every sort of property is common; if every device has been employed to exclude all of what is called the "private" from all aspects of life; if, insofar as possible, a way has been devised to make common somehow the things that are by nature private, such as the eyes and the ears and

739d

the hands, so that they seem to see and hear and act in common; if, again, everyone praises and blames in unison, as much as possible delighting in the same things and feeling pain at the same things, if with all their might they delight in laws that aim at making the city come as close as possible to unity—then no one will ever set down a more correct or better definition than this of what constitutes the extreme as regards virtue. Such a city is inhabited, presumably, by gods or chil-

739e

dren of gods (more than one), and they dwell in gladness, leading such a life. Therefore one should not look elsewhere for the model, at any rate, of a political regime, but should hold on to this and seek with all one's might the regime that comes as close as possible to such a regime. If the regime we've been dealing with now came into being, it would be, in a way, the nearest to immortality and second in point of unity.[18] The third we will elaborate next after these, if the god is willing.

Now then what do we say this regime is and how do we say it comes to be such? First, let them divide up the land and the

740a

households, and not farm in common, since such a thing

would be too demanding for the birth, nurture, and education that have now been specified. However, the division of lands is to be understood in something like the following way: each shareholder must consider his share to be at the same time the common property of the whole city, and must cherish his land, as a part of the fatherland, more than children cherish their mother; he must consider the land as a goddess who is mistress of mortals. And he should have the same understanding of the native gods and demons.

In order that these arrangements remain fixed for all the rest of time, the following must also be understood: the number of hearths we establish now is never to be altered, never to become greater or smaller. To maintain this arrangement firmly through the whole city, let each allotment holder always leave behind only one heir to his household from among his children. The child who is especially dear to him shall become his successor in ministering to the gods of the family and of the city, looking after both the living gods and those who may have reached their end by that time. As for the other children, in families where there are more than one, the females should be given in marriage according to the law that will be ordained, and the males should be distributed as sons to those citizens who lack sons. Personal likes and dislikes should be followed as closely as possible. If there are some who can find no one who pleases them, or if a surplus of females or males occurs, or on the contrary a deficiency because of a lack of childbirths, there will be a magistracy which we will designate—the greatest and most honored, in fact—which should, after looking into all these things, devise means of assisting those who have too many offspring and those who are lacking, so as to maintain the five thousand forty households always intact insofar as is possible. There are many devices, including ways of preventing birth in those who conceive too many offspring, and, on the contrary, various ways of encouraging and stimulating a greater number of conceptions. The use of honors and dishonors, as well as the encouraging words of elders addressed to young people, can accomplish what we're talking about. Finally, if we're at a complete loss as to how to deal with the inequalities among the five thousand forty households, if we have an overflow of citizens because of the warmth of feeling among those who live together in house-

740b

740c

740d

740e

holds, and can't devise any other way out, there is presumably the old device we've often spoken of: the dispatch of colonists from among those who seem suitable—colonists who will depart as friends leaving friends. If, on the other hand, the opposite dilemma ever occurs, if a floodwave of disease washes over them, or destructive wars, and through bereavements their number becomes much smaller than the number ordained, then, though they should never voluntarily admit citizens educated in a bastard education, against necessity it is said that even a god is unable to use force.[19]

741a

Let us next assert that our present argument itself is speaking and giving counsel in the following way: "O you best of all men, never cease to follow nature in honoring similarity and equality and sameness and what has been agreed upon—in number and in every sort of capacity that pertains to noble and good practices. First, guard throughout your whole lives the number that has been stated just now. Moreover, do not dishonor the well-measured height and magnitude of property that you were allotted at the beginning, by buying and selling it among yourselves. If you do, neither the Lot itself—which made the distribution, and is a god—nor the lawgiver will remain allied with you." He who disobeys this injunction will find first the law set against him, having warned him that he himself chose either to accept the allotment on these conditions or not; that he accepted it, in the first place, on the condition that Earth is sacred to all the gods, and, in addition, that he saw priests and priestesses praying at the first, the second, and the third sacrifices. The law will go on to warn that whoever sells or buys an allotted house or land will suffer penalties appropriate to these circumstances which have been enumerated: to wit, they will engrave the story of the offender on cypress tablets stored in temples, there to be read and remembered for the rest of time. They will give responsibility for guarding and executing these provisions to that one of the magistrates who is believed to see the sharpest, so that the transgressions on any occasion will never escape their notice and they will be able to punish anyone who disobeys the law and the god.

741b

741c

741d

The amount of good that the system now being laid down will do for all the cities that follow it (given, in addition, the appropriate arrangements) is, as the ancient proverb has it, forever unknown to the evil man and knowable only by him who has become experienced and decent through habituation. For under such a system great money-making is impossible, and the consequence is that there should not and cannot be anyone who makes money in any way from illiberal pursuits. No one need seek in any way to accumulate money from the sort of occupation that receives the contemptible epithet "gross vulgarity" and that can distort the character of a free man. 741e

There is another law that is closely linked to all these matters: no one is to be allowed to possess any gold or silver in any private capacity. There is a need for currency in daily exchange—the money that can scarcely be avoided when dealing with craftsmen, and that is required by all who pay hired help—slaves and foreigners—their wages. For these purposes, we assert that they should possess a kind of coin that carries value among themselves but is valueless among other human beings. The city itself, however, must necessarily possess some money of the sort that is common to the Greeks, for use by army expeditions and by travelers who go abroad among other human beings—ambassadors, for instance, and any other necessary messengers whom the city must send out. For the sake of these things, the city must, on each occasion, possess Greek money. If a private individual is ever compelled to go abroad, let him go, if the magistrates allow it, but if he has any extra foreign money on his return home, let him deposit it with the city and receive back an amount of native currency equal in value. If anyone is caught keeping the illicit currency on his own, let the money be confiscated for the public, and let anyone else who knew of it, but failed to inform, share equally in the curse and blame and additional fine, which is to be an amount not less than the foreign currency that was brought back. 742a 742b 742c

When someone marries or gives away a daughter in marriage, there is to be no dowry whatsoever given or received; moreover, no one should give money to someone he can't trust, and no money should be lent at interest. Anyone who has received a loan will be permitted to refuse to pay it back, both interest and principal.

That these are the best practices for a city to follow will be seen by anyone who looks into the matter correctly, always re- 742d ferring back and judging according to the first principle and intention. The intention of the intelligent statesman, we assert, is not that which the many would assert a good legislator should have. They claim he should intend to make the city for which he is benevolently legislating very big and as rich as possible, possessing gold and silver, and ruling over as many people as possible, on land and sea. And they would add that he who legislates correctly, at any rate, should also wish the

742e city to be the best and happiest possible. But of these things some can be achieved and others cannot. The one who orders things should aim at what is possible, and not waste his wishes or his efforts on what is in vain. Now it is almost a necessity that those who become happy also become good—and this he should wish for—but it is impossible that those who become very rich become also good, at least if by "rich" is meant the same thing the many mean. They mean those few human beings who possess the property that is worth the most money—the sort of possessions even some wicked man

743a might have. If this is so, I at least would never agree with them that a rich man becomes truly happy, if he is not also good. But it is impossible for someone to be both unusually good and unusually rich.

"But why?" someone might perhaps ask.

"Because," we would reply, "the gain derived from both just and unjust means is more than twice that derived from just means alone; and he who is willing to spend money neither nobly nor shamefully spends less than half as much as they who are noble and are willing to spend money on noble

743b objects. They who get twice as much and spend twice as little will never be exceeded in wealth by the one who does the opposite. Now of these men, one is good; the other is not bad so long as he is a miser, but utterly bad otherwise, and never good—as was said just now. The man who makes money both justly and unjustly and who spends it neither justly nor unjustly is rich—so long as he's a miser; but the utterly bad man, since he's mostly not a saver, is very poor. The man who

743c spends on noble things and makes money only from just enterprises would never easily become either unusually rich or very poor. Thus our argument is correct: the very rich are not good, and if they're not good then they're not happy."

The hypothesis that underlies our laws aims at making the

people as happy and as friendly to one another as possible. Now citizens don't ever become friends where they have many lawsuits among themselves, and where there are many injustices, but rather where such affairs are as minor and rare as possible. Indeed, we say there should be no gold and silver in the city, nor again big profits made through vulgar occupations, or usury, or other sorts of shameful breeding.[20] There should be just the things that farming gives and yields, and only as much of that as will not compel one because of money-making to neglect those things which money is by nature intended to serve—namely, the soul and the body (and even these, when they lack gymnastics and the rest of education, would never become worthy of mention). That, indeed, is why we have said more than once that the pursuit of money ranks last in the scale of honor. Of the total of three things that every human being is serious about, the serious and correct caring for money ranks last and third, for the body somewhere in the middle, and for the soul first. And in the case of the regime we are now elaborating, the legislation has been correct if honors are assigned according to this scale. But if one of the laws that will be laid down in the future there should show greater honor to health than to moderation, in the city, or should honor wealth above health and being moderate, it will reveal that it has not been correctly formulated. This, then, is what the lawgiver must repeatedly ask himself: "What is it that I want?" and, "Am I obtaining this or am I straying from the goal?" If he does this he may perhaps get through with his legislation, and relieve others of the task as well—but there is not a single other way that he ever will.

743d

743e

744a

Now the man who receives one of the land allotments is to keep it, we declare, on the conditions that we've described. It would surely have been a fine thing if each one could have entered the colony possessing an equal amount of everything else as well; but since that is impossible, and one will arrive with more money and another with less, it follows that for many reasons, and for the sake of equality of opportunities in the city, there must be unequal classes, so that when it comes to offices, revenues, and distributions, the honor that is due to each person will depend not only on the virtue of his ancestors and himself, and the strength and handsomeness of bodies,

744b

744c but also on the way one uses money or poverty. Quarrels will be avoided because honors and offices will be distributed as equally as possible on the basis of proportional inequality. For these reasons, four classes should be created, according to the amount of property: a First, a Second, a Third, and a Fourth—or they may be known by some other names, both when indi-

744d viduals stay in the same class and when they pass over each other into the appropriate class, by becoming richer from being poor or by becoming poor from being rich.

Following upon these things, I at least would set down a law whose outline is as follows. We assert that if (as we presume) the city must avoid the greatest illness, which has been more correctly termed "civil war" than "faction," then neither harsh poverty nor wealth should exist among any of the citizens. For both these conditions breed both civil war and faction. It follows, therefore, that the lawgiver must announce a limit for

744e both conditions. So let the limit of poverty be the value of the allotment, which must be maintained, and which no magistrate, and none of the others who desires to be honored for virtue, should ever allow to be diminished in the case of anyone. Taking this as the measure, the lawgiver will allow citizens to acquire twice again, and three times again, and up to four times again this amount. But if anyone acquires more than four times this amount—by finding something or by being given something, or by money-making, or some other

745a such stroke of luck—let him dedicate the surplus to the city and to the gods who possess the city. Thus he would attain a good name and avoid all penalty. If, however, someone disobeys this law, then anyone who wishes can denounce him and take half the surplus, while the guilty party will pay an equal amount from his own property, and give the other half to the gods. Everything that anyone possesses apart from the original allotment must be clearly recorded in books kept by guardian-officials whom the law will designate, so that all

745b lawsuits over property may proceed easily and with matters made very clear.

After this the first thing to be done is to build the city as close to the center of the territory as possible, having chosen a spot which has also those other advantages for the city that can without difficulty be understood and enumerated. Then after these things there should be a division into twelve parts. First a sanctuary should be set up to Hestia,[21] Zeus, and Athena, called the "acropolis," and surrounded with a circular wall. From there the twelve parts should radiate, dividing the 745c city itself as well as the whole territory. The twelve parts should be equal, in the sense that the ones where the earth is good should be smaller and the ones where it is worse larger. There should be a division into five thousand forty allotments, but each of these should be divided in two, and the two parts put together to constitute an allotment, one part nearer and one part farther away. The part closest to the city should be paired with the part closest to the borders to make one allotment, and the second-closest to the city paired with the 745d second-closest to the borders, and so on with all the rest. They should mingle the sterility and virtue of the soil in these double plots, using the device just mentioned: by assigning plots of larger and smaller size, the shares should be made equal. The men should also be distributed into twelve parts, in such a manner as to make the twelve parts as equal as possible with respect to the rest of their property—all having been duly recorded. And then, after this, they should give the twelve parts to the twelve gods as allotments, naming and sanctifying each after the god to whom it has been allotted, and calling the part a "tribe." The twelve parts of the city are to be divided just as 745e the rest of the country was. Each individual is to have two houses, one near the center and the other near the border. Thus the settlement will be completed.

Yet we must by all means keep in mind something like the following: the things that have just been described may never all coincide with such opportune circumstances as would allow all of them to come to pass exactly the way the argument has indicated. There may not be found men who will live 746a together in such a fashion without complaint, who will tolerate the stated and fixed limits on money throughout their whole lives, and the childbirth policies we've ordained for each person, or who will live deprived of gold and the other things the lawgiver must clearly proscribe according to what's been said now. They may not accept a territory and city such as he's described, with dwellings located at the center and all around; in fact, he's been talking in every respect almost as if

746b he were telling dreams, or as if he were molding a city and citizens from wax. In one way it wasn't bad to talk that way, but he has to remind himself of things such as the following. Once again, then, the lawgiver expresses to us the following:

"Friends, you shouldn't suppose that in the course of this discussion I have overlooked the fact that what has just been said is in a way true. But I think that when future courses of action are being considered, the most just thing to do in each case is this: he who presents the model of what should be attempted should depart in no way from what is most noble and

746c most true; but, when some aspect of these things turns out to be impossible for a fellow, he should steer away and not do it. Instead, he should contrive to bring about whatever is the closest to this from among the things that remain, and by nature the most akin from among the things that are appropriate to do. He should allow the lawgiver to complete things according to his wish; then, when that is done, he should investigate in common with him to see which part of what he has described is expedient and which part of the legislation he has described is too difficult. For a craftsman of even the meanest

746d thing, who's going to be worth anything, must be everywhere consistent in his activity, I suppose."

Now, after the division into twelve parts has become accepted opinion, one should with an eager spirit look to see in what way each of the twelve parts (which will contain within themselves very many possible subdivisions) may be clearly subdivided, and then how those subdivisions may be further subdivided in successive stages until a division into five thousand forty parts is reached. In this way clans and districts and

746e villages will be created, as well as military units and marching arrangements, and also currency units, dry and liquid measures, and weights: all of these should be so ordained by law as to be convertible and consonant with one another. In addition, the fear of appearing to speak in a petty way should not frighten one from ordering that all the tools they possess be of standard sizes; the general principle one should hold to

747a is that the divisions and variations of numbers are useful for everything—both the variations that exist within numbers themselves and also those that exist in plane and solid figures, in sounds, and in motions (both straight up-and-down and circular revolution). With a view to all these things, the lawgiver must order all the citizens to do all in their power to avoid abandoning this sort of coherence. For in household management, and in the political regime, and in all the arts, there is no single part of education that has as much power as the study of numbers. Most important of all, it awakens him who is by nature sleepy and unlearned, giving him ease of learning, memory, and sharpness, and thus making him surpass his own nature by a divine art. All these branches of education would be fine and fitting then—so long as one employs other laws and practices to take illiberality and the love of money away from the souls of those who are going to be competent in, and benefit from, the studies. Otherwise, before one knows it, one will have created a capacity for what is called mischief-making rather than wisdom, similar to what can now be seen among the Egyptians, the Phoenicians, and many other nations, who are formed by a lack of freedom in their other practices and possessions—either because they had a miserable lawgiver who gave them such ways, or because harsh luck befell them, or because of some other such natural thing.

747b

747c

747d

For, Megillus and Kleinias, we mustn't overlook the fact that some places differ from one another in their tendency to breed better and worse human beings, and such factors shouldn't be defied when one makes laws. All sorts of winds and different exposures to the sun can presumably make places unfavorable or favorable, as can the local waters, and the type of plants in the earth. The latter can provide better or worse nourishment not only for the bodies but also for the souls—to no less degree and in all the similar respects. But of all these places, those territories which would differ the most would be those that have some divine presence in the winds and are under the care of demons, and hence receive those who come to settle each time either graciously or in the opposite way. An intelligent lawgiver, at least, will inquire about these places as closely as a human being can in such matters, in order to try to formulate laws that are appropriate. That's what you must do as well, Kleinias: when you're about to settle the territory, you must first turn your attention to such matters.

747e

Kl.   What you say is in every way fine, Athenian stranger, and that's what I must do.

BOOK VI

751a	Ath.	At this point—after, that is, all the things that have just been discussed—almost your next task would be the establishment of offices[1] for the city.
	Kl.	Yes, that is surely so.
	Ath.	There happen to be these two fundamental parts[2] to the ordering of a political regime: first, there's the establishment of ruling offices and officeholders, including the decision as to how many there should be and how they should be selected;
751b		then, the laws must be given to each of the offices, and this, again, includes the decision as to what kind of laws there'll be, how many, and which ones would be fitting for each office.
		But let's pause a bit before we make the choice, because there's something pertinent that we should say about it.
	Kl.	What's that?
	Ath.	The following. Presumably it's clear to everyone that although the giving of laws is a grand deed, still, even where a city is well equipped, if the magistrates established to look after the well-formulated laws were unfit, then not only would the laws no longer be well founded, and the situation most ridiculous,
751c		but those very laws would be likely to bring the greatest harm and ruin to cities.
	Kl.	How could it be otherwise?
	Ath.	Well, let's recognize this very possibility in the case of your present regime and city, my friend. For you see that, in the first place, if the powers of office are to go to the correct persons, they and their families must each have been given a sufficient test—from the time they were children until the time

they are selected. Then again, those who are to do the selecting should be reared in lawful habits, and well educated in the   751d
capacity of distinguishing correctly between the candidates,
accepting or rejecting them as they deserve.³ Now how could
people who are newly gotten together, and unknown to one
another, and also uneducated, ever be able to make a blameless selection of officials?

Kl.   It's unlikely that they ever could.

Ath. Nevertheless, a contest, as they claim, doesn't tolerate excuses
at all; you, and I too, must now accomplish this task. For, as   751e
you've asserted just now, the ten of you have made a promise
to the Cretan nation that you will, with a firm spirit, carry out
a founding; and I have promised to help you, with the mythic   752a
discourse we're now involved in. And surely when I'm telling
a myth I wouldn't voluntarily leave it unfinished.⁴ Because if it
wandered around like that, without a head, it would appear
shapeless!

Kl.   You've made your point very well, stranger.

Ath. Not only have I made it, but I'll act on it, as far as I'm able.

Kl.   Let's by all means do as we say.

Ath. So be it, if the god is willing and if we can overcome old age
sufficiently.

Kl.   Well, it's likely that he's willing.   752b

Ath. That is likely. Following him, let's start with this observation.

Kl.   Which?

Ath. Observe how much courage and willingness to take risks will
be needed, to found our city in the present circumstances.

Kl.   Why? What exactly do you have in view in making this remark
now?

Ath. The fact that we are confidently legislating for men who lack
experience, without any fears as to how they'll ever accept the
laws that are now being laid down. After all, Kleinias, this
much at least is obvious to almost everyone, even to someone
who isn't very wise: they won't easily, at any rate, accept any   752c
of them at the beginning. What is needed is for us to survive,
somehow, for a long enough time so that the children who
have grown up tasting the laws from an early age, having been
reared under them and having become sufficiently accustomed to them, have taken part in the selection of magistrates
for the whole city. If in some way, by some device, what we're
now describing could come to pass correctly, I at least think

that the city that had been given such a childhood training would, after this period of time, remain very stable.

752d Kl. That's a reasonable supposition, certainly.

Ath. Let's see now if we couldn't devise some adequate way of dealing with this problem, along the following lines:

For I assert, Kleinias, that the Knossians must, more than any of the other Cretans, not only remove any obstacles to the profanation of the territory that is being settled, but also strain with all their might to insure that the first rulers are the safest

752e and best possible. The other magistrates present a less difficult task, but it is very necessary that your first Guardians of the Laws be chosen with total seriousness.

Kl. So what procedure and plan can we find for this task?

Ath. The following:

"I assert, O children of the Cretans, that the Knossians must, because they take precedence of age among the many cities, join with those who are arriving at this settlement in selecting, from among themselves and those, a total of thirty-seven men, nineteen of whom are to be chosen from the colo-

753a nists and the rest from Knossos itself."

The Knossians should give these men to your city, and should make you yourself a citizen of this colony and one of the eighteen—either by persuading you or compelling you, with a measured amount of force.

Kl. And why then don't you and Megillus take part in our regime, stranger?

Ath. Kleinias, Athens thinks big—as does Sparta. And both are far away, while for you it is convenient, in every way. The same holds for the other founders, to whom what was just now said about you also applies.

753b Let this be the description of the most equitable solution, given our present conditions; after a certain time has passed, if the regime lasts, let the method of selecting them be some such thing as the following:

Eligibility to share in the selection of the magistrates is to be extended to all who possess heavy weapons,[5] cavalry or infantry, as well as to those who have taken part in war as long as the capacity of their age allowed. The selection is to be carried

753c out in the temple which the city considers most honorable. Each is to carry to the altar of the god a little tablet on which he has written the name of the candidate, his father's name, his

tribe's name, and the name of the district where the candidate
resides. Adjacent, each is to write his own name in the same
way. Then, during a period of not less than thirty days, anyone who wishes may remove and set out in the marketplace
any of the written tablets that doesn't please him. From the
tablets that have thus been judged suitable, the magistrates
are to take the first three hundred and display them for the   753d
whole city to see; from these the city is to select again, in the
same way, each carrying up whomever he prefers. After this
second round they are to display to everybody again the one
hundred preferred names. In the third round, anyone who
wishes should carry up his preference from among the hundred, by walking between the parts of a sacrificial animal. The
thirty-seven who receive the most votes, after being scrutinized, are to be appointed to office.

    Now who is there, Kleinias and Megillus, who will set up all   753e
these things concerning the offices and their scrutinies [6] in our
city? Don't we recognize that there must necessarily be such
persons in cities that are being thus yoked together for the
first time? And yet who would it be, before there are any magistrates? In one way or another, they must be there, and they
can't be men of little capacity, but of the highest possible. For
as the proverbs have it, "the beginning [7] is half the whole
deed," and we all praise a noble beginning, at least, on every
occasion; in fact, in my view, the beginning is more than half,   754a
and no one has bestowed enough praise on the beginning that
is noble.

Kl.   What you say is very correct.

Ath.   Let's not, then, knowingly pass by the problem without discussion, leaving completely unclarified the manner in which
we ourselves will deal with it. Now I for my part can see no
way of dealing with it at all, except to make one statement that
in the present situation is both necessary and useful.

Kl.   What is that?

Ath.   I assert that this city we are about to found has no "father" or
"mother" except the very city that is doing the founding. I say   754b
this without ignoring the fact that many colonies have had
and will have differences, sometimes frequent, with those
who colonized them. But at present it is just like a child: even
if someday in the future a difference arises with its parents, in
the present, at least, while it lacks education, it cherishes and

is cherished by the parents, and always flees to its own people to find those who alone are allies by necessity. These are the ties that I assert will now readily bind the Knossians to the young city (because they care for it) and the young city to Knossos. So I repeat what I said just a moment ago (it doesn't hurt to repeat the noble, at least, a second time): the Knossians should share in supervising all these things, by choosing not less than one hundred men from those who have arrived at the colony, selecting the oldest and the best men they can. Then there should be another one hundred from the Knossians themselves. These are the men I assert should go to the new city and together see to it that the magistrates are installed according to the laws, and, after being installed, scrutinized. Once these things are accomplished, the Knossians should go dwell in Knossos and the young city should try by itself to find its own safety and good fortune.

The thirty-seven who are elected, now and in all the rest of time, are to be chosen by us to do the following: first they are to stand as guards over the laws; then in addition, they are to be the guards of the written records in which each individual has written down for the rulers the amount of his property (except each person of the highest class may omit up to four minas,[8] the second class three minas, the third class two minas, and the fourth class a mina). If it becomes evident that someone possesses something other than this and what has been written, then the whole such amount is to be turned over to the public; in addition, anyone who wishes may bring a judicial action against the culprit, and if he is convicted of holding the laws in contempt for the sake of gain, the judicial procedure shall be neither noble nor illustrious, but shameful. So let anyone who wishes accuse him of shameful gain and take him to trial before the Guardians of the Laws. If the defendant loses, he is to have no share in common property, and whenever some division is made by the city, he is to go without a share—save for his original allotment. Moreover, as long as he lives his guilt is to be written down where anyone who wishes may read about it.

Let a Guardian of the Laws rule for no more than twenty years, and let the minimum age for election be fifty years. If a man is sixty when elected, let him rule only ten years, and so

754c

754d

754e

755a

on, according to this principle; if someone lives beyond sev- 755b
enty he is not to think that he can remain among these magistrates, ruling in such a high office.

Let these then be stated as the three duties of the Guardians
of the Laws. As the laws unfold further, each law will enlarge
upon the responsibilities that have now been assigned to
these men.

At this point we may move on to discuss the selection of the
other magistrates. Next after these, the Generals should be
chosen, as well as those who are like assistants to them during 755c
wartime—Cavalry Commanders, Tribe Commanders, and
those officers who supervise the marching order of the infantry tribes, whom it would be fitting to call by the very same
name the many apply to them, "Rank Commanders."

Of these, as regards the Generals, let the Guardians of the
Laws make up a list of nominees drawn from this city itself,
and from these nominees let all who took a share in war when
they were of the proper age, or who are now ready to do so,
choose. (If someone thinks there is someone who hasn't been 755d
nominated who is better than someone who was nominated,
let him name his nominee and the one he thinks should be replaced, and, swearing an oath, let him nominate the rival candidate. Then let whichever of the two wins in a vote by show
of hands be placed on the election list.) The three who win the
most votes by show of hands are to be made Generals and
supervisors of the affairs of war—after having undergone the
same scrutiny as the Guardians of the Laws. Let the elected
Generals nominate their own twelve Rank Commanders, a 755e
Rank Commander for each tribe, and let there be the same
procedure for counter-proposals in the case of the Rank Commanders as there was for the Generals, the same vote by show
of hands, and the same scrutiny.

For the present, since Presidents and Council are not yet
selected, it will be the Guardians of the Laws who will call
together this public meeting, convening it in a place that is as
sacred and spacious as possible, and separating off the heavily-
armed infantry, ʻhe cavalry, and, in a third section next to
these, the whole auxiliary military force. Let everyone participate in the show of hands by which the Generals and the Cavalry Commanders are elected, but let those who bear shields 756a

elect the Rank Commanders, while the entire cavalry should choose the subordinate Tribe Commanders. The leaders of the lightly-armed troops, or archers, or any other auxiliaries, the Generals should themselves appoint.

We have remaining the appointment of the Cavalry Commanders. Let these be nominated by the same people who nominated the Generals, and let the election and the procedure for counter-proposals also be the same as it was for the

756b   Generals, but the cavalry should elect by show of hands while the infantry look on, and the two who receive the most votes by show of hands should become leaders of all the cavalry.

Two recounts after disputed votes by show of hands are allowed; if somebody challenges the count on the third showing of hands the decision will rest with those who are responsible for making the count of hands on each occasion.

The Council is to number thirty twelves, for three hundred sixty would be an appropriate number for the subdivisions.

756c   By dividing the number into four parts of ninety each, there will be ninety councilmen elected from each of the classes. The first vote will be for men from the highest class, and all are to be compelled to vote: he who doesn't obey must pay the appointed fine. When the voting is completed, the names voted for are to be recorded. Then, on the next day, they are to vote for men from the second class according to the same procedures as on the day before. On the third day anyone who wishes may vote for men from the third class; while the upper three classes are to be compelled to vote, anyone who belongs

756d   to the fourth and lowest class and doesn't wish to vote is to be let off free of any fine. On the fourth day everyone is to vote for men from the fourth and lowest class, but there is to be no fine for anyone from the third or fourth class who doesn't wish to vote, while anyone belonging to the second and first classes who fails to vote must pay a fine. In the case of someone from

756e   the second class, it will be triple the first fine and, in the case of someone from the first class, quadruple. On the fifth day the magistrates will display the recorded names for all the citizens to see, and every man must vote on this list or pay the first fine. One hundred eighty are to be elected from each class;

half of these are then to be chosen by lot, and, after being scrutinized, these are to be the Councilmen for the year.

This selection procedure would strike a mean between a monarchic and a democratic regime, which is the mean the regime should always aim for. For slaves and masters would 757a never become friends, nor would lowly types and serious gentlemen, if they were both held equal when it comes to honors. Both these situations fill regimes with civil strife; equal rewards would become unequal if they were distributed to men who are unequal, unless the distribution struck a proper measure. The ancient pronouncement is true, that "equality produces friendship": the saying is both very correct and graceful. But just whatever is the equality that has this effect? Because this is not very clear, we get into a lot of trouble.

For there are two equalities, the same in name, but in many 757b respects almost diametrically opposed in deed. Every city and every lawgiver is competent to assign honors according to the other sort—the equality that consists in measure and weight and number—and by the use of the lot applies it in distributions. But it's not so easy for everyone to discern the truest and best equality. For it is the judgment that belongs to Zeus, and it assists human beings only to a small degree, on each occasion; still, every bit of assistance it does give to cities or private individuals brings all the good things. By distributing 757c more to what is greater and smaller amounts to what is lesser, it gives due measure to each according to their nature: this includes greater honors always to those who are greater as regards virtue, and what is fitting—in due proportion—to those who are just the opposite as regards virtue and education. Presumably this is just what constitutes for us political justice. It is for this that we should now strive, and to this equality that we should now look, Kleinias, to found the city 757d that is now growing.[9] The same holds in the case of another city someone might found sometime: it is to this that one should look while giving laws, not to the tyranny of a few, or of one, or some rule by the populace, but always to justice. And this is what has just been described—the natural equality given on each occasion to unequal men.

Nonetheless, necessity compels every city to blur sometimes the distinction between these two, if it is to avoid par-

757e taking of civil war in some of its parts. For equity and forgiveness, whenever they are applied, are always enfeeblements of the perfection and exactness that belong to strict justice. Because of the discontent of the many they are compelled to make use of the equality of the lot, but when they do, they should pray both to the god and to good luck to correct the lot in the direction of what is most just. Thus, of necessity, both

758a equalities ought to be employed, though the type that depends on chance as rarely as possible. A city that is going to last is compelled, for these reasons, to do things this way, my friends.

Now just as a ship sailing at sea must have a watch at all times both day and night, so a city, driven by the waves of other cities and dwelling in danger of being taken over by all sorts of conspiracies, needs magistrates who rule in uninterrupted succession through the day until nightfall and through

758b the night until daybreak, guards who always pass the watch on to guards without a break. It can never be the business of a large number to keep a sharp watch in this way; most of the time all but a few of the Councilmen must of necessity be allowed to stay at their own private business and attend to their own domestic affairs. But by dividing the Council into

758c twelve parts corresponding to the twelve months, each single part can stand guard for one month, always ready to meet with someone coming from abroad or from within the city itself, who wants to give information or make inquiries about the replies it is fitting for a city to make other cities and about the answers it is fitting for it to receive when it asks others. They will also be ready to contend at any time with the innovations that are constantly wont to occur in cities everywhere: if possi-

758d ble they'll forestall them, but if they can't, they will at least see to it that the city knows about them as soon as possible, and can cure the sickness. That is why this presiding part of the city must always have the authority to convoke and dissolve the public meetings—both those that meet regularly according to the laws and those the city needs on sudden notice. Each twelfth part of the Council is to have charge of ordering all these things, and is to be at rest during eleven parts of the year; at all times this part of the Council is to share with the other officials in maintaining this guard over these matters throughout the city.

Thus the things of the city would be arranged in due measure; but what supervision and what order is there to be in all the rest of the territory? Now that the whole city and the whole land have been divided into twelve parts, shouldn't some supervisors be appointed for the streets of the city itself, the houses, the buildings, the harbors, the marketplaces, and the fountains—as well as the sanctuaries, temples, and all such things? 758e

Kl. How else?

Ath. For the temples, let's say that there should be Temple Custodians as well as Priests and Priestesses. For the roads and buildings, and the maintenance of order around such places— to prevent the humans from committing injustices and to make the rest of the beasts behave, in the city itself and in the suburbs, in a manner that befits cities—three forms of officials must be selected: one, that will be called "City Regulators," to take care of the things just mentioned; another, the "Market Regulators," to keep order in the markets; then, if there are Priests and Priestesses who hold hereditary priesthoods, they shouldn't be changed, but if, as is likely in such matters with people who are being settled together for the first time, there are none or only a few set up, then Priests and Priestesses should be established to be the Temple Custodians for the gods who do not already have some. 759a 759b

Of all these officials, some should be elected and others chosen by lot, and for the sake of friendship we should mix individuals who belong to the populace with those who are not of the populace in each land and city, so that the place would be as much as possible of the same mind.

What pertains to the Priests should be turned over to the god himself so that what pleases him comes to pass: their choice should be given to the divine chance of the lottery, with the proviso that he who obtains the lot each time is to be scrutinized to make sure first that he is sound [10] and of legitimate birth, and then that he comes from households that are as nearly unpolluted as possible—that he and his father and mother have lived without any pollution from homicide or any of the other crimes that offend in such ways against the divine. They should get their laws regulating all the divine things from Delphi, and establish Interpreters of them who will explain how to use them. Each Priesthood should be held for one year and no longer, and no one who is less than sixty 759c 759d years of age should be considered qualified to administer the divine things for us, in accordance with the sacred laws. Let these same legal customs apply to the Priestesses.

For the Interpreters: thrice the four tribes are to elect four, each of whom is to come from among themselves; the three who receive the most votes are to be scrutinized; then the nine are to be sent to Delphi, where one is to be chosen from each triad.[11] The scrutiny and the age limit are to be the same in their case as for the Priests. These Interpreters are to serve for life, and when one passes away a replacement will be elected by the four tribes to whom the vacancy belongs.

759e

The Treasurers in charge of the sacred funds in each of the temples, as well as of the sanctuaries and their harvests and revenues, are to be elected from the highest property class—three for the largest temples, two for the smaller, and one for the most elegant little ones. The election and scrutiny of these officials are to be the same as they were for the Generals. So let these be the arrangements for the sacred things.

760a

To the extent of our power, nothing is to be unguarded. There are these guards for the city: the supervisory Generals, the Rank Commanders, the Cavalry Commanders, the Tribe Commanders, and the Presidents, as well as the City Regulators and the Market Regulators (once we have them adequately elected and installed). All the rest of the land should be guarded in the following ways:

760b

Since our entire territory has been divided into twelve sections that are as close to being equal as they can be, let one tribe be assigned by lot to each section for the period of a year. The tribe is to supply five men who will be like Field Regulators or Officers of the Guard, and each [of the] five is to choose from their tribe twelve young men not less than twenty-five nor more than thirty years of age.[12] These contingents should be given by lot the parts of the land, one part to each month, so that all will become experienced and knowledgeable about the whole country. The term of the office and guard duty will be two years for both guards and officers. Starting from the parts they are allotted first—the districts of the land, that is—the Officers of the Guard should always lead them each month to the next district on the right in a circle (on the right meaning toward the dawn). When one year's circuit has been

760c

760d

completed and they are to begin the second year, in order to make as many of the guards as possible experienced with the land during more than one season of the year, in order that as many as possible not only know the land but also what goes on in each area in each season, the leaders should then lead them back around, always changing to the district on the left, 760e until they have completed the second year. In the third year other Field Regulators or Officers of the Guard should be chosen, sets of five to supervise the sets of twelve.

During their periods of service they are to look after each district in something like the following way. First, to make the land as well defended as possible against enemies, they'll dig ditches wherever they're needed, and trenches, and do all they can with fortifications to check those who would try in any way to do harm to the land and property. They can employ the beasts of burden and domestic servants in each dis- 761a trict in these tasks, using the former and supervising the latter, though insofar as they can, they should requisition them when they are not being used in their domestic tasks. They should make every place difficult of access for enemies but as easily accessible as possible for friends—for humans, and for beasts of burden and herds as well—by taking care that each of the roads be kept as smooth as possible. To prevent the water Zeus sends from doing evil to the land, and instead to make it beneficial, as it flows down from the heights into the 761b hollow-like gulleys in the mountains, they can prevent the runoff with fortifications and ditches, thus containing and absorbing the water from Zeus, and thereby providing streams and springs for the lower fields and all the other areas. Thus they'll furnish the driest areas with plenty of water and good water. They should adorn the watering holes in a more becoming way, whether they be rivers or springs, with shrubbery [13] and buildings, and by collecting the streams in pipes 761c make sure there is an abundant supply; and if any sacred grove or sanctuary is located nearby they should adorn it with water in every season, introducing streams into the very temples of the gods. Everywhere in such places the young men should maintain gymnasia for themselves and for the old men as well, providing hot baths for the old and maintaining an abundant supply of seasoned, dry wood; thus they should 761d give a cheerful welcome to those worn out with sicknesses and those whose bodies are weary from the farmer's toils. Surely this does more good than a welcome from some doctor who isn't very wise. These and all such activities would bring adornment and benefit to the areas while providing a kind of play that is not at all lacking in grace.

Their serious business in these matters is to be the following. Each group of sixty is to guard its district not only against enemies but also against those who profess to be friends. If a slave or a free man does an injustice to a neighbor or any of the rest of the citizens, they should be judges for the man who claims to have been done the injustice. For small matters the five officers themselves should sit in judgment; for greater matters (up to three minas in damages claimed by one man against another), they should sit together with the twelve, and the seventeen should be judges.

But no judge or magistrate shall sit in judgment and perform his ruling functions without being subject to an audit; the only exceptions are those quasi-regal judges of last appeal. In particular, if these Field Regulators are in some way insolent in their treatment of those they supervise—if they levy unequal assessments, if they try to take and carry something from the farms without getting permission, if they accept something given as a bribe, if they assign unjust penalties—then, for being susceptible to flatterers, they are to be held in ill repute throughout the entire city, and for the other sorts of injustice they commit against those in the district, if the damage claimed is one mina or less, they should voluntarily submit to be tried by a jury of the villagers and neighbors; if the damages claimed for the injustices on any occasion are more, or if, where the damages are less, the accused are unwilling to submit (because they trust they'll flee prosecution by means of the monthly rotation that always takes them out of a district), then the party done the injustice is to bring charges concerning these matters in the common courts: if he wins, let him exact double from the one who fled and was unwilling to undergo retribution voluntarily.

During their two years' service the Officers and Field Regulators will live in some such way as follows. First, there will be common meals in each of the districts, where all must dine together. If anyone is absent from a common meal on any day, or if anyone spends a night sleeping somewhere else, without

761e

762a

762b

762c

being ordered to do so by the Officers or compelled by some dire necessity that befalls him, and if the five decide to take notice of this lapse and post his name in writing in the marketplace as a deserter from the guard, then he is to be held in ill repute, as one who betrayed his share in the regime. Moreover, let anyone whom he encounters and who wishes punish him with blows, without retribution. If someone among the 762d Officers themselves does such a thing, he must come under the purview of all sixty; if one of these perceives and learns of such delinquency but fails to prosecute, let him be punished under the same laws that apply to the young—only more. He is to lose all eligibility to serve in any office that pertains to the young. The Guardians of the Laws are to keep a precise watch over these matters, to prevent his obtaining such office, or, if he should obtain one, to see to it that he gets the punishment 762e he deserves.

Indeed, every real man must understand that no human being would ever become a praiseworthy master unless he has been a slave, and that one should be more attentive to the adornment that comes from a noble enslavement than that which comes from a noble rule. The first enslavement is to the laws (for this is really an enslavement to the gods), and the next is that of the young to their elders at all times, and also to those who have lived honorable lives.

In the next place, someone who has served his two years among the Field Regulators should have developed a taste for a daily ration of humble and uncooked food. For once the sets of twelve have been chosen and put together with the sets of five, they must resolve that since they themselves are like do- 763a mestic servants they will not have their own domestic servants and slaves; they won't use the servants belonging to the other farmers and villagers for private tasks, but only for public tasks. When it comes to the rest, they must resolve that they are going to live by their own efforts and as their own servants. In addition, they are to scout over the whole country with their heavy weapons, summer and winter, so as constantly to guard and get to know all the districts. It's likely that 763b no learning they pursue is more important than that which gives all of them accurate knowledge of their own country. It's for this reason, as much as for the rest of the pleasure and benefit such activities bring to everyone, that a young man should go in for hunting with hounds and the rest of hunting. Now these men—they and their functions—can be called the Secret Service, or the Field Regulators, or whatever one likes:

763c

whatever it's called, this is the service that every real man, everyone who's going to defend his city adequately, should serve in, with an eager spirit and to the best of his ability.

Next in order in our selection of rulers was to be the selection of the Market Regulators and City Regulators. Following the sixty Field Regulators would be three City Regulators, who will divide the twelve parts of the city three ways. Imitating those others, they should attend to the city roads and to the thoroughfares coming into the city at each point from the

763d

country, as well as to the buildings, watching to see that all are constructed and maintained according to law. They should also attend to the water, seeing to it that the well-tended waters sent in and turned over to them by the Guards are conducted in sufficient amounts and in a pure condition to the fountains, so as to adorn and benefit the city.

These too should have the capacity and the leisure to look after the common things. That is why, for City Regulator, every man may nominate anyone he wishes from the highest

763e

class: then they are to vote by a show of hands and determine the six who have the most votes. Those who are responsible for drawings should select three of the six by lot; when these three have passed the scrutiny they are to rule according to the laws that have been assigned to them.

Next after these come the Market Regulators, five of whom are to be chosen from the second and first classes; in other respects the election procedure is to be the same as it was for the City Regulators. When the nominees are reduced to ten by voting with a show of hands, five are to be chosen by lot; when these have passed the scrutiny they are to be proclaimed magistrates.

Everyone must participate in the vote by show of hands, and this applies to every office. Anyone unwilling to do so, if

764a

he is reported to the magistrates, should be fined fifty drachmas—besides getting the reputation of being a bad fellow. Anyone who wishes may attend the assembly and the public meetings, but it should be compulsory for the second and first classes. If any of them is absent from the meetings he is to be fined ten drachmas. Attendance will not be compulsory for the third and fourth classes; unless some necessity should compel the magistrates to announce that all must attend, a member of these classes who is absent will incur no penalty.

As for the Market Regulators, they are to keep order in the marketplace as the laws direct and look after the temples and fountains in the vicinity of the marketplace, seeing to it that no one does any injustice. They are to punish anyone committing injustice—with blows and bondage if he is a slave or stranger, while if it is one of the native inhabitants who is disorderly concerning such things, they should themselves wield the judging authority where the monetary fine involved is one hundred drachmas or less; for fines up to an amount twice this much, they should pass judgment and penalize the unjust offender together with the City Regulators. Let the City Regulators employ the same penalties and punishments in their own official jurisdiction: where the fine is one mina or less, let them inflict the penalty themselves, and where it is up to twice this amount, let them act together with the Market Regulators. 764b

764c

After this it would be fitting to establish magistrates for music and gymnastics. There should be two sets of each kind of official: some for education and some for contests. By "education" the law means to say those officials charged with looking after the gymnasia and schools, supervising their orderliness and the education given in them, and also the attendance and housing of the male and female youths. By "contests" the law means those who award prizes to athletes [14] in gymnastic events and concerning music. These should again be divided into two sets: some for music and others for contests. In contests the same men can be judges, whether the competition be among human beings or horses. But in music it would be fitting that those who award prizes to solo singing and imitation—such as rhapsodes, kitharists, aulists, and all such—should be different from those who award prizes to choral singing. 764d

764e

[151]

First, I suppose, magistrates should be chosen to judge the play of the choruses of children, men, and young women, which consists of dances and the whole ordered arrangement that is music. One magistrate is enough for these things; he should be not less than forty years of age. And one magistrate not less than thirty years of age will suffice for solo singing: he will perform the function of Director and will judge adequately among the competitors. The magistrate who presides over and arranges the choruses should be selected in some such manner as the following. Those who are devoted to such pursuits should go to a public meeting. If they don't go, they are to be penalized: the Guardians of the Laws will be judges of this. The rest will not be required to attend this meeting if they do not wish to. The elector should nominate from among those who have experience, and in the scrutiny, the one issue about which there should be favorable and unfavorable statements is whether the one who has won the draw lacks or possesses experience. Of the ten who receive the most votes by show of hands, one is to be selected by lot, and after being scrutinized, is to rule for a year over the choruses, according to law. With the same procedures, and in the same way as these, let one who wins the draw rule for that year over those who enter competitions in solo singing and singing to aulos accompaniment, after handing over to the other judges the decision as to the fitness for office of he who wins the draw.

765a

765b

Next, those who award the prizes at gymnastic contests of horses and human beings should be chosen from the third and second classes. The top three classes are to be required to participate in the election, but the lowest class may absent itself without penalty. Let three be chosen by lot from twenty who have been selected by a show of hands, and let the three out of twenty who win the draw be installed after having received a ratifying vote from those who conduct the scrutiny.

765c

765d

If anyone fails to pass the scrutiny in any appointment to, or examination for office, let others be selected instead, by repeating the same procedures and the same scrutiny.

There remains, for the affairs we mentioned, another office—that of Supervisor of Education in general for females and males. Let there be for these one official under the laws, a

man not less than fifty years of age, who is a father of legitimate children—of sons and daughters both, if possible, but if
not, of either. He who is judged preeminent, and the person   765e
who so judges him, must bear in mind that this office is by far
the greatest of the highest offices in the city. For in everything
that grows [15] the initial sprouting, if nobly directed, has a sovereign influence in bringing about the perfection in virtue that
befits the thing's own nature. This holds for the other growing
things, and for animals—tame, wild, and human. The human
being, we assert, is tame; nevertheless, though when it hap-   766a
pens upon a correct education and lucky nature, it is wont to
become the most divine and tamest animal, still, when its upbringing is inadequate or ignoble, it is the most savage of the
things that the earth makes grow. This is why the lawgiver
must not allow the upbringing of children to become something secondary or incidental, and since the one who is going
to supervise them should begin by being chosen in a fine way,   766b
the lawgiver should do all he possibly can to insure that he
provides them with a supervisor to direct them who is the best
person in the city, in every respect. So all magistrates except
the Council and the Presidents are to go to the temple of
Apollo, there to vote by secret ballot for that man among the
Guardians of the Laws who each believes would most nobly
rule over educational affairs. Whoever receives the most votes
is to be scrutinized by the other magistrates who elected him,
with the exception of the Guardians of the Laws. He is to rule   766c
for five years, and at the sixth year another is to be chosen for
this office in the same way.

If someone who rules in a public office should die with more
than thirty days remaining in his term of office, another
should be appointed to the office, according to the same procedures and by the individuals to whom this responsibility is
appropriate. And if someone who is a guardian of orphans
should die, the appropriate individuals who happen to be at
home (the relatives on both the father's and the mother's sides
extending as far as the children of first cousins) must appoint
another within ten days, or pay a fine of one drachma a day   766d
each until they have appointed a guardian for the children.

Now doubtless every city would cease to exist as a city if it
were not to have duly established courts of justice. Moreover,

if our judge couldn't speak, if he could say no more than what is said by the opposing parties at a preliminary inquiry, as in arbitration proceedings, he would never make an adequate judgment about what is just. For this reason it isn't easy for many, or even a few, if they lack capacity, to judge well. The dispute must always be made clear on each side, and time is required, as well as slow and frequent questioning, in the interest of illuminating the dispute. To achieve this the litigants should go first before their neighbors, who are their friends and are as familiar as possible with the disputed actions. If someone fails to get an adequate judgment from these, let him go on to another court. Then there will be a third court, which must terminate the judicial contest if the other two courts could not settle it.

In a way, the establishment of courts is a selection of ruling officers. For every ruling officer is necessarily a judge of some affairs, and, though a judge is not a ruler, on the day when he makes his decision and concludes a judicial trial, a judge is in some sense a ruler—and no very petty one, at that. Treating judges as if they were rulers, then, let's say who would be fitting judges, what affairs they should judge, and how many of them should preside at each sort of hearing.

The court which the litigants put together themselves, by choosing judges together, should be most authoritative. The other courts should be resorted to for two reasons: either because a private individual accuses a private individual of doing him some injustice, and takes him to court wishing to get a judgment, or because someone wishes to defend the community when he thinks one of the citizens has done an injustice to the public. And it must be said how many and who the judges should be.

So first we should have a common court for all those private parties who are going through the third round of their disputes with one another. It should be constituted in something like the following way. On the day before the new year begins, with the new moon which follows the summer solstice, all officials whose term lasts a year, and those whose term lasts longer, should get together in one temple. After swearing an oath to the god they should, as it were, dedicate to him one judge chosen from each category of official—in each magistracy, the one who seems the best and who gives

766e

767a

767b

767c

767d

promise of rendering the best and most pious verdicts to his fellow citizens in the coming year. Those who have been elected should undergo scrutiny at the hands of the electors themselves; if any of them fails to pass scrutiny, another should replace him according to the same procedures. Those who pass the scrutiny will sit in judgment over all who have fled from the other courts, rendering their vote openly. The 767e Councilmen as well as the other magistrates, who elected these judges, should be compelled to attend and witness the proceedings of this court, along with anyone else who wishes to attend. If someone accuses one of the judges of having voluntarily rendered an unjust verdict, he should go and lay his accusation before the Guardians of the Laws. Anyone convicted of rendering such a verdict must pay to the individual who was hurt half the damages suffered; if the convicted judge seems to merit a stiffer penalty, the judges in the case should decide what additional penalty he should suffer or pay to the community and to the one who brought him to trial.

In regard to crimes against the public, it is necessary, first, that the majority have a share in the decision. For when some- 768a one does an injustice to the city everyone suffers the injustice, and they would justly be vexed if they had no share in such trials. Still, while the beginning of such a trial and its final conclusion ought to be in the hands of the populace, the investigation should be the responsibility of three of the highest magistrates, chosen with the consent of the accused and the accuser. If they are unable to agree, then the Council should decide between their respective candidates.

Even in private suits it is necessary that everyone take part 768b as much as possible. For anyone who does not share in the right of judging considers himself not at all a sharer in the city itself. That is why there should also be tribal courts, with judges selected by lot and as each occasion arises, and not judging corruptly in response to special pleading. But the final sentence in all such affairs belongs to the court which we claim has been so devised as to be as uncorruptible as human power, at least, can make it. It is to this court that appeal must 768c be made by those who have been unable to reconcile their differences in the neighborhood courts or the tribal courts.

Now with regard to our courts—which, we assert, cannot easily be discussed either as ruling offices or as not, without difficulties arising—a sort of exterior outline has been presented, with certain things pretty much left out. For it would be most correct if the precise establishment and delineation of the laws concerning judicial matters were presented at length 768d   near the end of the lawgiving. Let these subjects, then, be asked to wait for us at the end. Most of the legislation concerning the installation of the other ruling offices has, on the other hand, been just about completed. Of course, the complete and precise account of each and every arrangement of the city and of the political art in general cannot be made clear until the exposition has proceeded from the beginning, to the second things, then to the middle, and thus through every part of itself until it arrives at the conclusion. But the point now 768e   reached, the selection of the magistrates, would be an adequate conclusion to what has preceded, and the laying down of the laws can begin without any further hesitations or delays.

Kl.   The things you've said up until now have been entirely agreeable to me, stranger; but what you've just said—linking the beginning of what is going to be said with the end of what's been said—is still more pleasing than those things.

769a   Ath.   Then our prudent game of the elderly would have been played in noble fashion thus far.

Kl.   It's likely that what you're setting forth is a noble and serious pursuit for real men.

Ath.   It's likely, at least. But let's see if the following appears to you as it appears to me.

Kl.   What do you mean, and whom does it concern?

Ath.   You know how the painter's activity, for example, never seems to finish working on each of the figures, but keeps 769b   touching up or highlighting—or whatever it is painters' disciples call such activity? It seems never to cease its adorning, and hence never to reach a point where there can be no further improvement of the paintings as regards beauty and clarity.

Kl.   I too know pretty well these things you're talking about, by hearsay—for I am not at all practiced, at least, in such an art.

Ath.   That's no hindrance for you. We'll still make use of this allusion to it that's cropped up in our discussion now, in some769c   thing like the following way: suppose someone once took it into his head to paint the most beautiful figure possible, one that would never get worse but would always improve as time went by. Don't you see that since he's mortal, he'll have to leave behind a successor, able to make it right if the painting suffers some decay at the hands of time, as well as to make future touch-ups that improve on deficiencies left by his own artistic weaknesses? Otherwise, won't his very great labor last but a brief time?

Kl. That's true.

Ath. Well, then, don't you think the lawgiver has such a purpose? 769d He first writes[16] his laws with as nearly adequate a precision as he can muster. Then, with the passage of time, as his opinions are tried out in deed, do you suppose there's any lawgiver who is so imprudent as to be ignorant of the fact that he must necessarily have left very many such things that require being set right by some follower, if the regime and order of the 769e city he has founded are always to become in no way worse but instead better?

Kl. It's likely—how could it be otherwise?—that everyone wants such a thing.

Ath. So if someone had some device indicating the way in which, by deed or by words, he might teach another to understand, more or less, how he ought to guard and set right the laws, would he ever give up explaining such a thing before he had achieved his end?

Kl. How could he? 770a

Ath. So now, in the present circumstances, is this what I and you two should do?

Kl. Just what do you mean?

Ath. We are about to give laws, but certain Guardians of the Laws have been chosen for us; since we are in the twilight of life,[17] while they are young, relative to us, we shouldn't only give laws ourselves—as we claim—but should at the same time try our best to make these same men lawgivers as well as Guardians of the Laws.

Kl. Why not?—if, that is, we are up to it. 770b

Ath. But it ought at least to be attempted, and with an eager spirit.

Kl. Indeed, why shouldn't it?

Ath. Then let's speak to them:

"Dear Saviors of the laws, we will leave out many things as regards each of the matters for which we have established laws. This is inevitable. Still, in all but the small points, at least, and on the whole, we will do all we can not to leave the

770c outline sketch, as it were, unfinished. Your task will be to help fill in the outline. You must hear now where you should look when you carry out this task. Megillus here, and I and Kleinias, have said the same things to one another not infrequently, and we are in agreement that they are nobly spoken. We want your agreement and your attention as our pupils, so that you will look to the things we have agreed together should be looked to by a Guardian of the Laws and a giver of the laws.

"In brief, this was the substance of the agreement: in whatever way a member of the community, whether his nature be male or female, young or old, might ever become a good man,[18] possessing the virtue of soul that befits a human 770d being—whether this be as a result of some practice, or some habituation, or some possession, or desire, or opinion, or certain things learned at some time—toward this, which we are describing, every serious effort will be made throughout the whole of life; no one of any sort is to be seen giving prece-dence in honor to any of the other things that are impedi-770e ments, not even, finally, to the city, if it appears necessary that the alternative to its destruction is either willingly tolerating the slavish yoke of being ruled by worse men or departing from the city in exile.[19] All such things must be borne, and suf-fered, rather than allowing the regime to be changed into one whose nature is to make human beings worse.

"These are the things we agreed to in our previous discus-sions, and now you must look to both these goals of ours as 771a you pass our laws in review.[20] You should blame those that aren't capable of effecting these goals, but those that are ca-pable, you should welcome and, gladly adopting them, live under them. As for other pursuits that aim at other things among those that are said to be good, you must proclaim good-bye to them."

Now the beginning of our laws that come after these things should be as follows, starting with the sacred things: first we should consider again the number five thousand forty and the 771b many convenient divisions it had and has, both as a whole and within its tribal subdivisions—each of which we set down as a twelfth part of the whole, and each of which is by nature exactly twenty taken twenty-one times. Our number as a whole has twelve divisions, and the number contained in each tribe also has twelve. Each part must be understood as a sacred entity, a gift of the god, corresponding to the months and to the revolution of the whole. That is why every city is naturally led to sanctify these divisions, though some people probably have made a more correct distribution and have been more fortunate in making the division divine than others have. We for our part now assert that the most correct number to choose is five thousand forty, which has as its divisors all the numbers from one to twelve—except for eleven, and for this there is a very minor remedy: one way the number becomes whole again is if two hearths are set aside.[21] To show how these things truly are would not require a long tale, if one had leisure. But for now let's take the present oracle and argument on trust, and proceed to make this division, solemnly assigning a god or the child of gods to each part, along with altars and the appropriate accoutrements. Let's make sacrificial processions to two of these altars each month, twelve for the divisions within the tribe and twelve for the divisions of the city.[22] We should do this first for the sake of pleasing the gods and the things connected with the gods, and second, we would assert, for the sake of our own kinship and familiarity with one another, and for the sake of every sort of intercourse.

For indeed, with regard to the community and commingling of those who are married, it is necessary to dispel the ignorance concerning the bride's people, the bride herself, and the people to whom they are giving her. Everything possible must be done, to the best of one's ability, to prevent any mistakes at all being made in such affairs. To achieve such a serious goal, play must be devised that consists of choral dancing by the boys and girls, where they can see and be seen, in a reasonable way and at an occasion that offers suitable pretexts. Both sexes should be naked, within the limits a moderate sense of shame sets for each. The supervisors and regulators of all these matters ought to be those who rule over and give laws to the choruses; in cooperation with the Guardians of the Laws they can arrange whatever we have left out.

For it's inevitable, as we've said, that in the case of all such matters the lawgiver will leave out the small and numerous details; and those who constantly gain experience in them, learning from yearly practice, must make yearly arrangements and corrective changes until what seems to be a satisfactory

771c

771d

771e

772a

772b

772c

definition of such customs and practices has been reached. Ten years of sacrificing and dances would be a measured and sufficient period of time to assign for gaining experience in each and every aspect. If the lawgiver is still alive, they can share the task in common with him, but if he has died, each of the magistrates should bring to the attention of the Guardians of the Laws whatever omissions need correcting within their own jurisdictional spheres, and continue to do so until each feature seems to be perfected in noble fashion; then the customs are to be made unchangeable, and adhered to along with the rest of the laws the lawgiver laid down for them at the beginning. They are never voluntarily to change a single one

772d

of them. But if some necessity should ever seem to overtake them, they must consult with all the magistrates and the whole populace and all the oracles of the gods. If all these are in consonant agreement, then the change can be made, but otherwise never in any way. If there is any opposition, the law will be that it always prevails.

So when anyone anywhere has passed twenty-five years of age, has observed and been observed by others, and trusts that he has found someone who pleases him and is appropriate for sharing and procreating children, let him marry. And

772e

everyone is to do so by the age of thirty-five. First, however, let him hearken to an account of how he should seek what is fitting and harmonious. For it is necessary, as Kleinias asserts, to preface each law with its own prelude.

Kl.   You've reminded us in a very splendid way, stranger, by choosing what seems to me to be an opportune and especially well-measured moment in the argument.

Ath.   Well spoken. "My lad" (let's address someone who has

773a

grown[23] from good parents), "one should make a marriage of the kind that is held in good repute by prudent men, who would counsel you not to avoid someone of poor parents nor to pursue especially someone of rich parents, but, other things being equal, always to give precedence in honor to the less highly placed of your prospective partners. For this would be in the interest of the city, and also of the hearths that are being united; for the even-keeled and the commensurable are distinguished ten thousandfold from the unrestrained when it

773b

comes to virtue. A man who knows himself to be too impatient and hasty in all his affairs should be eager to become related by marriage to orderly parents, and one whose natural disposition is the opposite should proceed to ally himself with the opposite sort of in-laws. In general, let there be one myth regarding marriage: in each marriage what must be wooed is not what is most pleasant for oneself, but what is in the interest of the city. It is according to nature that everyone always be somehow attracted to what is most similar to himself, and because of this the city as a whole becomes uneven as regards 773c wealth and the dispositions of characters. The consequences of this, which we wish to avoid for ourselves, are very prevalent in most cities."

To enact by law, through discourse, that a rich man is not to marry from the rich, and a man capable of doing many things is not to marry someone similar to himself—and to compel those of hasty dispositions to join in marriage with those who are more phlegmatic, and the more phlegmatic with the hasty—besides being laughable, would stir up the spiritedness of many. For it's not easily understood that a city should be mixed, just like the drinker's bowl: the 773d wine, when poured in, is throbbing with madness, but under the chastening of another, sober god, it forms a noble partnership that creates a good and measured drink. No one, so to speak, can perceive that this also holds for the commingling that produces children. That is why it is necessary to leave such things out of the law, and instead try to use enchanting song to persuade them that each should value more the similarity of their children than the equality in marriage which is 773e insatiable for money. One must also use blame to dissuade anyone who is seriously bent on getting money through marriage; but one shouldn't apply force through written law.

So let these be the things said[24] to encourage marriage, in addition to what was said a while ago, to the effect that one must partake of the eternal coming-into-being of nature by always leaving behind children of children, whom one leaves 774a as one's successors in serving the god. So someone would say all these things and yet more about marriage, about how it is necessary to marry, if one were giving a prelude in the correct way.

If, despite this, someone voluntarily disobeys, estranging himself and not sharing in the city, but persisting in an unmarried state at the age of thirty-five, let him pay a penalty

774b

each year: one hundred drachmas if he belongs to the class with most property, seventy if to the second, sixty if to the third, and thirty if to the fourth. Let this be sacred to Hera.[25] Anyone who fails to make the yearly payment will have to pay ten times the penalty. It will be up to the Treasurer of the goddess to collect the fine; if he fails to do so he himself will incur the obligation to pay it, and everyone must give an accounting of such things at the audits. As far as money goes, then, these are the penalties everyone unwilling to marry must pay; in addition, let him be excluded from every honor paid by those who are younger, and let none of the young voluntarily pay him any heed. If he raises his hand to punish

774c

someone, everyone should come to the aid of and defend the one who is being treated unjustly, and if any bystander fails to come to his aid, let the law call him a coward and also a bad citizen.

The subject of dowries has already been discussed, but let it be repeated that there is no reason why the poor should reach old age having been unable, because of a lack of money, to take a wife or give away a daughter. For in this city everyone is to possess the necessities. Thus there would be less inso-

774d

lence on the part of wives and less humble and illiberal slavery because of money on the part of husbands.

He who obeys will have done one of the noble things. He who disobeys and gives or receives for the trousseau an amount worth more than fifty drachmas, or one mina, or one and one-half minas, or two minas for someone in the class possessing the most property, must pay to the public an amount equal to whatever excess he spent, and the sum given or received is to be consecrated to Hera and Zeus. The trea-

774e

surers of these two gods are to take care of things in this case just as the treasurers of Hera were said to take care of things each time in the case of those who don't marry, and if they fail to do so, each of them is to pay the fine out of their own funds.

The authority to make the marriage pledge should belong first to the father, second to the grandfather, and third to brothers sprung from the same father. If one of these is not available, then the authority should pass to the same line of relatives on the mother's side. If some unusual mischance should intervene, then the authority should pass to the nearest relatives in each case, together with the guardians.

In regard to rites preliminary to marriage, or any other such sacred ceremonies that are appropriate to celebrate before, during, and after the marriage, a person should make inquiries with the Interpreters and, by obeying whatever they say, everyone may believe that he has done everything in a well-measured way.

775a

As for the marriage feasts, no more than five male and five female friends should be invited on each side, and a similar number from each family and household. The expenditure should in no case be more than the property will bear—a mina for the class with the most money, half that much for the next, and so on, in proportion, as the property of each class is less. He who obeys the law should be praised by everyone, but he who disobeys should be punished by the Guardians of the Laws as one who lacks experience in things beautiful and who is uneducated in the laws[26] of the Muses of marriage.

775b

Drinking to the point of drunkenness presumably befits no other occasion except the festivals of the god who has given wine, nor is such behavior safe, above all for someone who takes getting married seriously. Prudence is especially fitting in this time for the bride and groom, who are making no small transformation in their lives, and, at the same time, it's needed for the sake of the child to be engendered, to insure that it is conceived by parents who are as much as possible in possession of their senses at all times. For it's quite hard to tell just what night or day, with the god's help, the child will be conceived. Moreover, children shouldn't be made in bodies saturated with drunkenness. What is growing[27] in the mother[28] should be compact, well attached, and calm, but someone who's been drinking carries himself and is carried every which way, raging with frenzy in body and soul; as a result, a drunk is a clumsy and bad sower of seed, and is likely to beget at such a time offspring who are irregular, untrustworthy, and not at all straight in character or body. That's why one should strive throughout the whole year and all one's life, but especially at the time when one is engendering children, to be careful and to avoid doing anything that voluntarily brings on sickness or involves insolence or injustice. Otherwise, one will necessarily stamp these effects on the souls and bodies of the embryos, and create children who are in every way inferior. One must especially avoid such things that day and night. For the beginning, which among human

775c

775d

775e

beings is established as god, is the savior of all things—if She receives the proper honor from each of those who make use of Her.

776a

Considering the other of the two allotted households as a sort of nest[29] where the young will be born and raised, the bridegroom must separate from his father and mother and go there to make the marriage and a new home and nursery for himself and the children. For in the case of endearing attachments, a certain amount of longing cements and binds together all the dispositions, while excessive intercourse, without the longing that time produces, makes people drift apart through satiety. On this account they should leave

776b

mother and father and the wife's family in their own homes and, like colonists who have gone abroad, see them only on visits or when receiving them as visitors at home, where they are bearing and raising children, as if passing the lamp of life on from one generation to the next, always devoted to the lawful gods.

After this comes the question of property: what sort would one possess if one's belongings were to be most harmonious? There are many things that are not difficult either to understand or to acquire; but with regard to domestic servants there

776c

is every sort of harsh difficulty. The cause of this is the fact that we speak of them in ways that are somehow incorrect and yet in a certain manner correct. For our speech about slaves sometimes contradicts the ways we use them, while at other times our speech is consistent with the ways we use them.

Meg. What's this again that we're saying? We certainly do not understand, stranger, what things you're pointing out now.

Ath. That's surely not surprising, Megillus. For among almost all the Greeks the Helot system of the Lacedaimonians provokes the most perplexity and strife—some holding that it is good, others that it is not good. There would be less strife about the

776d

enslavement of the Mariandynoi to the Heracleans, or again about the serf nation of the Thessalians.[30] But considering these and all such systems, what ought we to do about the possession of domestic servants? You quite reasonably asked whatever I meant to indicate by the remark I happened to make as I proceeded through the argument, and it was this: presumably we're aware that we all would say that one should own slaves who are as well disposed and good as possible. Indeed, there have been many slaves superior in every virtue to their owner's brothers and sons, slaves who have saved their masters' lives, their property, and their entire households. These things, we presumably know, are said about slaves. 776e

Meg. Doubtless.

Ath. But also the opposite—how no slave's soul is healthy, how no one who has intelligence should ever trust any of their race? In fact, our wisest of the poets[31] has made the following pronouncement, referring to Zeus: "half of one's intelligence," he declares, 777a

> far-seeing Zeus takes away
> From men, whom the day of slavery seizes.

Everyone chooses between these ways of thinking. Some decide they will trust no one who belongs to the race of domestic servants, and, treating them as if they had the nature of wild animals, they use goads and whips to reduce the souls of domestic servants to a threefold and much more than threefold state of slavery. Others, again, do entirely the opposite of these things.

Meg. Doubtless.

Kl. So then given these different policies, what should we do in our land about possession and punishment of slaves, stranger? 777b

Ath. What, indeed, Kleinias? It's obvious that the human animal is a difficult possession; for it is stiff-necked, and evidently not willing at all to be or become easily managed in terms of the inevitable distinction in deed between slave, free man, and master. It has often been demonstrated in deed how many evils result—by the regular and frequent revolts of the Messenians, by the cities which possess many domestic servants who speak one language, and also by the robberies and other ills suffered at the hands of the so-called Peridinoi around Italy.[32] Looking at all this, one would find oneself at a loss as to what should be done about all such things. The fact is, there are only two devices that remain: those will more easily serve as slaves who aren't compatriots and whose languages are as discordant as possible; and one should train slaves correctly by treating them with dignity—not only for their sakes but even more for our own. The training of people in such a condition avoids a certain sort of insolence, and does domestic ser- 777c

777d

777e

778a

vants even less injustice, if that is possible, than is done to equals. For a man shows clearly that he reverences justice naturally, and not artificially, and that he really hates injustice, when he does so in his dealings with human beings whom he might easily treat unjustly; he who in his disposition and actions toward slaves remains undefiled by what is impious or unjust, would be a man who is fully capable of sowing the natural seed of virtue. The same thing can be said, and correctly said, about a master and a tyrant, and about one who exercises any sort of absolute rule[33] over someone weaker than himself. Of course, it is necessary to punish slaves, in a just way, and not spoil them by mere chiding, as if they were free men. And in speaking to a domestic servant one should almost always use a straightforward command; one should never joke with domestic servants in any way, whether they be females or males, and the many who are very thoughtlessly fond of this playfulness with slaves spoil them—thereby making life more difficult both for those who are ruled and for themselves who do the ruling.

Kl. What you say is correct.

Ath. Now when every effort has been made to provide a mass of domestic servants adequately trained in every way to assist in action, shouldn't what comes next, in speech, be the housing plans?

778b Kl. By all means.

Ath. It's likely that in the new and hitherto uninhabited city there must be supervision of the way in which everything, so to speak, is constructed—including the temples and walls. These things come before marriage, Kleinias; but since now the thing is coming into being in speech, it's quite all right if it proceeds in this order, for now. When it comes into being in deed we can put these things prior to marriage, if the god is willing, and can at last complete the latter business after all the architectural details. For now let's just go through a brief sketch of them.

778c

Kl. By all means.

Ath. The temples should be constructed all around the marketplace and in a circle around the city, on the highest ground—for the sake of both defense and cleanliness. Near them should be buildings for the magistrates and for the courts. Thus cases will be accepted and judgments dispensed on the most sacred soil, reflecting not only the questions of piety involved in the cases but also the fact that the buildings belong to such gods. In the same buildings will be housed those courts in which it would be fitting to hear homicide trials and all charges of injustice involving the death penalty.

As for walls, Megillus, for my part I would go along with Sparta, and leave the walls sleeping in the earth, and not set them up. The reasons are these. It's a fine poetic argument that people sing about them, to the effect that walls should be made of bronze and iron rather than earth.[34] What is more, our plan would justly incur much ridicule—the plan to send the young out into the countryside in yearly relays, making trenches and ditches and certain buildings to thwart enemies, as if they weren't going to let them cross the borders—if we were still to put up a wall, when a wall is, first, not at all beneficial to cities from the point of view of health, and, in addition, usually instills a certain habit of softness in the souls of those who dwell within it. The wall tempts men to flee within it instead of standing against the enemies, and makes them think they needn't always keep up a guard, night and day, in order thus to obtain safety, but can have the means for real security by going to sleep fenced in behind walls and gates. They think they were born not to toil, not knowing that ease really comes as the result of toils. And the fact is, I believe, that toils naturally reappear as a result of shameful ease and softness of spirit.

But, if some wall is necessary for humans, then it ought to be created by constructing the private homes at the beginning so as to form the whole city into one wall, with the evenness and uniformity of all the houses as they face the street providing good defense. In presenting the appearance of one house it would not be unpleasant to look at, and would on the whole make a difference in every way as regards the ease of guarding and providing security.

It would be fitting that the responsibility for maintaining the buildings in accordance with the original plan lie mainly with the inhabitants, but the City Regulators ought to exercise supervision, using penalties to compel anyone who becomes careless. They should see to it that everything in the city is kept clean, and should insure that no private individual encroaches in any way on what belongs to the city when con-

778d

778e

779a

779b

779c

[167]

779d structing buildings or ditches. These same officials should see to it that there is good drainage for the water that comes from Zeus, and should oversee any construction pertaining to the water that would be fitting within the city or outside. The Guardians of the Laws should take cognizance of all these matters and make additional laws as needs arise—and the same goes for anything else the law might, in its perplexity, omit.

Now that these buildings, the buildings of the marketplace, the buildings of the gymnasia, and all the school buildings, stand ready for those who will frequent them, now that the theater stands ready for the spectators, let's proceed to the matters that come after marriage, following the order of lawgiving.

Kl. By all means.

779e Ath. Let's suppose then that our marriages have been made, Kleinias. After this, a length of time of not less than a year would elapse before children were born. What way of life the groom and the bride ought to pursue during this time, in a city which will differ so greatly from the many, is the subject that comes next after the things just now discussed. But it is not exactly the easiest thing to say. In fact, although there have been more than a few things of this kind already, this is even less acceptable to the majority than all of them. Nevertheless, whatever seems correct and true should be spoken in its entirety, Kleinias.

Kl. By all means.

780a Ath. Whoever intends to promulgate laws for cities, and regulate how men should act in regard to public and common actions, but supposes he need not apply a degree of compulsion to the private things, supposing that each can live his daily life as he wishes, that it's not necessary for everything to be ordered—whoever leaves the private things unregulated by law and believes the people will be willing to live with the common and public things regulated by the laws—is incorrect in his thinking.

780b Why have these things been said? For the following reason: we are going to assert that our grooms must participate in the common meals no differently, and no less, than in the time before marriage. This institution aroused amazement at the beginning when it was first introduced in your territories—

when some war, as is likely, or some other affair of equal power legislated it because of the great difficulty created by a scarcity of human beings—but once you had tasted and had been compelled to use the common meals, the custom seemed to you to make a great contribution to security. In some such way the practice of common meals was instituted among you. 780c

Kl. That's likely, at any rate.

Ath. What I said about it, that this practice was once an amazing, and for some a frightening, thing to institute, would no longer hold in the same way now, or present the same difficulty for the one undertaking to legislate it. But there is another practice that follows from this one, and which would be correct according to nature if it came into being. Because it exists nowhere now, the lawgiver effects little and finds himself in the situation they tell of in the joke: he cards his wool into a fire and engages in ten thousand other such fruitless efforts. Yet 780d the practice is not an easy thing to talk about nor, having been discussed, to carry into execution.

Kl. What is this, stranger, that makes you seem to hesitate so, as you try to explain it?

Ath. You shall hear, to prevent a great deal of discussion being wasted on it. Everything that partakes of order and law in the city has entirely good effects, while most things that lack order or are badly ordered weaken the other things that are well ordered. This principle applies directly to the subject under discussion. For among your peoples, Kleinias and Megillus, the 780e common meals for men were established in a fine and, as I said, amazing way by some divine necessity; but women's af- 781a fairs were in an altogether incorrect way left without legislative regulation, and the practice of common meals for them never saw the light. That race of us humans that is by nature more secretive and cunning because of its weakness—the female—was incorrectly left in disorder by the legislator's failure to be firm. On account of this neglect there are many things that have gotten out of hand among you that would have fared better than they do now, if they had happened to be regulated by laws. When one overlooks the disorderliness of women's affairs, what is affected is not only, as one might 781b suppose, a half; in fact, to the degree that our female nature is inferior to that of the males as regards virtue, by so much would the harm approach being more than double. So, if this were revised and corrected, if it were ordained that every practice is to be shared in common by women as well as men, it would be better for the happiness of the city.

As things stand, the human race has so failed to be fortunate in this respect that in other places and cities, where common meals are not at all officially accepted customs in the city, it's not possible for someone of intelligence even to mention it. How then, without being laughed at, will someone attempt in deed to force women to take their food and drink in the open, where they can be clearly seen? There is nothing that would be harder for this race of women to bear, for it is habituated in a retired, indoor way of life; it'll use every means to resist being dragged by force into the light, and will prove much superior to the legislator. Thus, anywhere else, as I said, they wouldn't tolerate the utterance of the correct argument without much screaming, but perhaps they would here. If it doesn't seem unlucky for the discussion of the whole regime to unfold—for the sake of the argument, anyway—I am willing to state how this practice is both good and fitting, if you two agree to listen. But if not, let's just let it go.

Kl.   But stranger, the two of us are amazingly and in every way agreeable to hearing about it, at any rate!

Ath.   Let's indeed hear it. But don't be amazed if I seem to you to undertake the subject by going way back. After all, we're enjoying leisure, and there's nothing pressing that prevents us from making a complete inquiry into every aspect of the laws.

Kl.   What you've said is correct.

Ath.   Let's go back again to the first things that were discussed. Every man ought to have a good understanding of this much at least: either the coming into being of humans had no beginning at all and will never have an end, but existed always and will exist always, in every respect, or an immeasurable time would have elapsed since the beginning, when it came into being.

Kl.   But of course.

Ath.   What then? Don't we think that every part of the earth, in every sort of way, has had foundings and destructions of cities, every kind of practice orderly and disorderly, and every sort of desire for food, both liquid and solid? And don't we think that there have been climatic revolutions of all types, in which it is likely that the animals underwent very many transformations?

781c

781d

781e

782a

Kl. How could this not be so? 782b

Ath. What then? Presumably we believe that the vines appeared at a certain time, when they had not existed before? Doesn't the same hold for olive trees, and the gifts of Demeter and Korē? Wasn't a certain Triptolemus the one who brought such things?[35] During the time when these things didn't exist, don't we think that animals used one another for food, as they do now?

Kl. But of course.

Ath. In fact, we see that even now the practice of human beings 782c sacrificing one another still persists among many peoples. And we hear just the opposite about other peoples: how there was once a time when we did not dare to taste cattle, and sacrificed to the gods no animals, but instead gruel and fruits soaked in honey and other such hallowed sacrifices. They abstained from flesh on the grounds that it wasn't pious to eat it or to pollute the altars of the gods with blood. Those of us who existed then had ways of life that were what is called "Orphic": we partook of everything that lacked soul but abstained 782d from the opposite, from everything possessed of soul.

Kl. What you've described is certainly what people say, and can be trusted.

Ath. "But," someone would ask, "with a view to what, have all these things been said by you now?"

Kl. You are correct in supposing that, stranger.

Ath. And now then, if I can, I'll try to explain what follows after these things, Kleinias.

Kl. Say on.

Ath. I observe that for human beings everything depends on a threefold need or desire, and that if they are guided correctly by these, virtue results, while if they are guided badly, the op- 782e posite. Of these, the need for food and the need for drink are present as soon as they're born. In all this regard, every animal has a natural erotic longing, is full of frenzy, and refuses to listen if someone says it ought to do anything except satisfy the pleasures and desires connected with all these things, and always avoid for itself all the pain connected with them. Our 783a third and greatest need or erotic longing is that which urges most sharply and comes latest, the one which makes human beings burn with complete madness: that most insolent flame involved in the engendering of offspring. What is needed is to turn the three illnesses toward what is best and away from

783b

what is said to be most pleasant, attempting to restrain them with the three greatest checks—fear, law, and true reason. These must be reinforced, of course, by the Muses and the gods of contests, in order to quench the growth and spread of the illnesses.

Let's put the procreation of children after the subject of marriages, and, after procreation, upbringing and education. Perhaps if the discussion proceeded thus, each of our laws that pertain to the common meals would be completed later on, so that when we arrive at such occasions of fellowship and partake of them, we will be in a position to look closely and perhaps see whether they should be common to women too, or should be only for men. The preliminaries to these common meals still remain unlegislated for now, but later we will bring them into order and set them up. At that time, as was just said, we will see them more distinctly, and would lay down the laws that are appropriate and fitting for them.[36]

783c

Kl. What you say is very correct.

Ath. Let's guard in our memories the things that have been said just now; for perhaps we'll have need of all of them sometime.

Kl. Which in particular do you bid us to remember?

Ath. The things we distinguished by three terms. We spoke of food, did we not, and second of drink, and third of a certain fluttering excitement of sex.

783d

Kl. We will doubtless remember all the things you now bid us to, stranger.

Ath. Fine. Let's proceed then to the newlyweds and teach them how and in what way they should procreate the children; if we can't persuade them, then we'll threaten them by means of certain laws.

Kl. How?

Ath. The bride, and the groom as well, must think about how they may do all they can to provide the city with the noblest and best children possible. All human beings who take a common share in any action perform everything nobly and well if they reflect intelligently upon themselves and upon the deed itself; but if they don't apply their intelligence to it, or if they lack intelligence, they do just the opposite. So the groom should reflect intelligently on the bride and the making of children, and the bride should do likewise—especially during the time when they don't yet have children. To supervise them, there

783e

784a

are to be the women we have chosen, whose number, greater or less, and time of appointment will be left to the rulers to fix; each day they will meet together for up to a third of an hour at the temple of Eileithuia,[37] and at their meetings they'll bring to one another's attention any man or woman among those engaged in the procreation of children whom someone has observed preoccupied with something other than what was enjoined upon them at the marriage sacrifices and the sacred rites.

784b

If the flow of conception is strong, let the parents procreate children and keep a watch over themselves for ten years, but no longer. If some remain childless after this period of time, let them be divorced, after consulting with their families and the women magistrates about the terms that would be for the benefit of both parties. If some quarrel arises over what terms would be fitting and beneficial to both, they should choose ten of the Guardians of the Laws to whom they should turn the matter over, and abide by their ruling.

784c

The women should go into the houses of the young people, and by exhortations and threats prevent them from doing anything wrong or foolish. If they are unable to do so, let them go and make a report to the Guardians of the Laws, who will proceed to prevent them. But if they also can't do it, let them report it to the public at large, by putting the matter in writing and swearing an oath to the effect that they have been unable to reform so-and-so. He who is written up, and fails to get a judgment against his accusers, must suffer dishonor in the following ways: he is not to attend weddings or the thanksgiving rites after a child has been born, and if he should attend them, let anyone who wishes punish him with blows and suffer no retaliation. Let the same customs apply to the wife: if her disorderliness leads to her being written up and she fails to get a court judgment, she is not to participate in the processions and honors of the women, nor attend weddings and the celebrations at the time of the birth of children.

784d

When they have finished procreating children according to the laws, if someone has relations of this sort with another woman, or if a wife has them with another man, and if the other persons involved are still at the child-procreating age, they must suffer the same penalties that have been described for those who are still procreating children. But thereafter, the

784e

785a

man or woman who behaves moderately in all such respects should be accorded an entirely good reputation; he who behaves in the opposite fashion should be honored in the opposite way—or rather dishonored. If most people live well-measured lives in such respects, let the subject be passed over in silence, without legislation; but if they get disorderly, let legislation be put into effect in this way, according to laws that'll be laid down at that time.

The first year is the beginning of each person's whole life, and each boy and girl should have it written down in the ancestral temples: "his or her life began on . . ." Written next to this, on the whitewashed wall for every clan, should be the number of the rulers, who are numbered according to the years. Nearby, the names of those in each clan who are alive at any given time should be written; the names of those who depart from life should be erased.

785b

A girl should marry between the ages of sixteen and twenty, to state the longest time period, and a boy between thirty and thirty-five. A woman can enter office at forty, a man at thirty. A man is subject to service in war from the age of twenty until the age of sixty; in whatever military services it seems women should be employed, each will be ordered to do what is possible and fitting for her, after she has borne children and until she is fifty years old.

BOOK VII

Ath.   Now that the male and female children have been born, pre-   788a
sumably the most correct procedure would be for us to turn
next to a discussion of their upbringing and education. To
avoid speaking about this is completely impossible; yet it
would appear to us more reasonable to utter a kind of instruction and admonition rather than laws. For there are many little
things, not visible to everyone, that take place in private and
in the home, which, because of each person's pain, pleasure,   788b
and desire, go against the advice of the lawgiver, and would
easily make the dispositions of the citizens diverse and dissimilar. This is bad for cities. For while the pettiness and
frequency of these practices render it unfitting and unseemly
to make laws imposing penalties, it nevertheless corrupts
even the written laws to have human beings become accustomed to act against the law in petty, frequent ways. The re-   788c
sult is that there's perplexity as to what to legislate about these
things, and yet it's impossible to remain silent.

But I should try to clarify what it is I'm saying by sort of
bringing to light examples; so far what's been said is pretty
dark.

Kl.   What you say is very true.
Ath.   Presumably it was correct[1] to say that an upbringing that is
correct in every way must manifest the power to make bodies
and souls the most beautiful and the best possible.
Kl.   But of course.
Ath.   And if they are to have the most beautiful bodies I suppose the   788d
simplest requirement, at least, is that the children grow[2] with
the straightest possible posture from youngest infancy.
Kl.   Most certainly.

Ath.   What then? Isn't this our understanding, that the first sprouting of every animal involves by far the greatest and most substantial growth, so that many people would strongly contend
that humans, at least, fail to attain, in the twenty years after
the age of five, a size that is double the size attained in the first
five years?

Kl.   True.

Ath.   What then? Aren't we aware that a great deal of growth, occur-
789a   ring without much well-measured exercise, produces myriad
evils in the bodies?

Kl.   Certainly.

Ath.   Therefore it's when bodies are getting the most nourishment
that they need the most exercise.

Kl.   What's that, stranger? Are we going to assign the most exercise to the newborn and youngest?

Ath.   Not at all, but to those even younger, those being nourished
inside their mothers!

Kl.   Best of men, what are you talking about? You mean the fetuses?

789b   Ath.   Yes. It's not surprising that you two are ignorant of the gymnastic art pertaining to that time of life; and although it's
something strange, I'd like to explain it to you.

Kl.   By all means.

Ath.   My people can understand this sort of thing better because
among us some play games more than they should. Some of
us—and not only boys but certain elderly men as well—raise
young birds for battles against one another. Those who raise
789c   beasts for such purposes are far from thinking that the creatures get sufficient exercise when they are stimulated to struggle with one another in gymnastic competition. In addition to
these exercises, they each take their birds under their cloaks,
smaller birds in the hands and bigger ones under the arm, and
proceed to walk very many stades—not for the well-being of
their own bodies, but for that of these young creatures. By
such a practice they show, to anyone capable of under-
789d   standing, that all bodies benefit from the invigorating stir produced by all sorts of shaking and motions, whether the bodies
be moved by themselves, or in litters, or on the sea, or by
being carried on horses or on any other body. These motions
allow the bodies to digest the foods and drinks that nourish
them, and make them capable of providing us with health,
beauty, and the other sorts of strength.

If these things are so, what would we claim we ought to do next? Do you wish us to go ahead despite the laughter and set 789e forth laws to the effect that a pregnant woman must go for walks, and that when the child is born she must mold it like wax so long as it remains moist, wrapping it in swaddling clothes until it is two years old? Shall we compel nurses, by legal penalties, to somehow carry the children about continually, to the fields, or the temples, or to relatives, until the babies have become capable of standing, and even then to be very careful lest the children, being still young, should distort their limbs by somehow putting too much weight on them? Shall we command the nurses to keep carrying the children until they've reached the age of three? Ought the nurses to be as strong as possible, and ought there be more than one? And 790a shall we set down a written penalty accompanying each of these laws, applicable to those who fail to carry them out?

Or would this be far off the mark? After all, it would produce a very great deal of what was just mentioned.

Kl. What's that?

Ath. The great laughter we'd incur, in addition to the unwillingness to obey on the part of the nurses' womanly as well as slavish dispositions.

Kl. But then why have we claimed that these principles ought to be announced?

Ath. The reason is this: the dispositions of the masters and free men in the cities may perhaps listen, and if so, they would 790b come to the correct understanding that unless private homes within cities are correctly regulated it is vain for someone to suppose the common things will stand on a firm legal footing. Once someone understood these things, he would adopt for himself the laws mentioned just now, and, by using them to make his own home and city well run, would become happy.

Kl. What you've said is very likely.

Ath. For this reason, we shouldn't leave such legislation until 790c we've described which pursuits are appropriate to the souls of the very young children, proceeding in the very same way as when we began to go through the myths that were told about the bodies.

Kl. That is altogether correct.

Ath. Let's take this as a sort of fundamental principle that applies to both body and soul: in the very young, nursing and motion should be as continuous as possible, the whole night and day,

790d because it is beneficial for all, and not least for the very youngest, to dwell—if it were possible—as if they were always on a ship at sea. As it is, what is needed in the case of new-born nursling creatures is to approach as close as one can to achieving this state.

Evidence for this principle is found in the facts that it has been adopted, and is known to be useful from experience, by the women who nurse little ones and by the women who per-form the mystery-rite cures of the Corybantes. For presumably when mothers want to lull their restless children to sleep they don't provide stillness but just the opposite, motion; they rock

790e them constantly in their arms, and not with silence but with some melody. It's exactly as if they were charming the chil-dren with aulos-playing, even as is done for the maddened Bacchic revelers, to whom they administer this same cure, which consists of the motion that is dance and music.[3]

Kl. What are we to suppose is the principal cause of these things, stranger?

Ath. It's not very hard to understand.

Kl. How so?

Ath. In both cases the passion being experienced is presumably terror, and the terror is due to some poor habit of the soul.

791a When someone brings a rocking motion from the outside to such passions, the motion brought from without overpowers the fear and the mad motion within, and, having over-powered it, makes a calm stillness appear in the soul that replaces the harsh fluttering of the heart in each case. This has wholly desirable effects. In the one case it makes them go to sleep; in the other case, with the help of the gods to whom each sacrifices and from whom each receives good omens, the process incites to dancing, and influences the dancers through

791b the aulos music: it thereby replaces our mad dispositions with prudent habits. For a brief discussion, at least, these remarks convey an account that is plausible.

Kl. Indeed they do.

Ath. If, then, these procedures do thus have some such power, one is also led, by the example of these people, to understand the following: every soul that dwells with terror from the time of childhood would be especially likely to become accustomed to feeling fear; and presumably everyone would assert that this is practice in cowardice rather than courage.

Kl. How could it be otherwise?

Ath. And we would assert that the opposite, the practice in courage   791c
from earliest youth onward, consists in triumphing over the
terrors and fears that come upon us.

Kl. Correct.

Ath. Then with regard to this one part of the virtue of the soul, let
us assert that the use of the gymnastic of motions among the
little children is of great assistance to us.

Kl. By all means.

Ath. Moreover, the absence or presence of ill-humor in the soul is
no small factor in determining whether stoutness[4] of soul or
weakness of soul would result.

Kl. How could it not be?

Ath. Then in what way might we have naturally implanted in the   791d
newborn, at the outset, either of these dispositions we might
want? We ought to try to explain how and to what extent
someone would successfully handle this.[5]

Kl. How could we not do so?

Ath. I say that this is the dogma accepted among us: luxury makes
the dispositions of the young ill humored, irascible, and easily
moved by minor matters, while the opposite—extreme, savage enslavement—by making them humble, illiberal, and
misanthropic, renders them unsuited for living with others.

Kl. How then ought the city as a whole bring up those who cannot   791e
yet speak or partake of the rest of education?

Ath. Roughly as follows. Presumably every newborn animal customarily gives forth cries from the moment it's born, and this
applies not least to humankind. Indeed, it is more given to
tears as well as cries than the others.

Kl. That is certainly so.

Ath. In fact, nurses judge by these very signs when they bring
things and thus see what it desires; when they see it falls   792a
silent when something is brought, they think they've done
fine in bringing the thing, and when instead it weeps and
cries they think what they've done isn't fine. Babies make
manifest what they love and hate through their tears and
cries—a way of communicating that is not at all fortunate. And
yet this goes on for at least three years' time (no small portion
of life to spend in a condition that is either bad or not bad).

Kl. What you say is correct.

Ath. Doesn't it seem to you two that the man who is ill humored

792b

Kl.

Ath.

Kl.

792c

Ath.

Kl.

Ath.

792d

792e

793a Kl.

and not at all gracious is more glum and, for the most part, more filled with complaints than a good man ought to be?

It seems that way to me, anyway.

What then? If someone were to apply every device in an attempt to make the three year period for our nursling contain the least possible of suffering and fears and every sort of pain, don't we suppose that he would give the soul of the one brought up this way a better spirit, and make it more gracious?

Clearly; and it would be especially the case, stranger, if someone should provide many pleasures for it.

In this I would no longer go along with Kleinias, you amazing man! That kind of behavior is for us the greatest of all corruptions. For it starts each time at the very beginning of the upbringing. But let's see if what we're saying holds up.

Say what you're asserting.

Our argument now is not about a matter of small importance; so you too, Megillus, must consider this and help us judge. My argument asserts that the correct way of life should neither pursue pleasures nor entirely flee pains. Instead, it enjoys the middle course, for which I just now used the name "gracious." Guided by some saying of an oracle, this is how we all characterize precisely the situation of god. And I assert that this is the habit that should be pursued by any one of us who is to be divine: one should not allow oneself to pursue pleasures headlong, thinking one can in this way avoid the experience of pain, nor allow anyone else among us—old or young, male or female—to suffer this. Least of all the newborn, if one can help it, for that is the age when, through habituation, the most decisive growth[6] in the entire character occurs for everyone. Moreover, I at least would assert (if I could avoid the appearance of joking) that of all women the most special attention should be paid to those who are carrying children inside their stomachs, during that year, so as to prevent the pregnant woman's having many or violent pleasures—or pains—and to provide that she lives through the period honoring what is gracious, even, and gentle.

You don't have to ask Megillus which of us has spoken more correctly, stranger: I myself grant you that everybody should avoid a life of unrestrained pain and pleasure, and should always cut it somewhere in the middle. So now both what you have said and what you have heard are noble.

Ath. Both are indeed very correct, Kleinias. But let us, being three, turn our thoughts next, after these things, to the following.

Kl. To what?

Ath. To the fact that all these things we're now going through are what the many call "unwritten customs." Indeed, what they 793b name "ancestral laws" are nothing other than all such things as these. What is more, the argument that has been poured over us now, to the effect that one shouldn't ordain these in law, and yet also shouldn't leave them unmentioned, has been nobly put. For these are the bonds of every regime, linking all the things established in writing, and laid down, with the things that will be set forth in the future, exactly like ancestral and in every way ancient customs; if nobly established and made habitual, they provide a cloak of complete safety for the 793c later written laws, but when they perversely stray from the noble they are like props of the walls of houses which buckle in the middle and cause the whole edifice to fall, one part under another, the parts that were later constructed in a fine way collapsing after the props themselves, the ancient things, have collapsed. Keeping these things in mind, Kleinias, we must bind your new city together in every way, neglecting, so far as is in our power, neither the great nor small aspects of 793d what are called "laws," "habits," or "practices." For a city is bound together by all such things, and in the absence of either of them the other ceases to be stable. So it should not be surprising to find that the laws are made lengthier by an overflow of customs or even habits that seem numerous and minor to us.

Kl. But what you're saying is correct, and we will keep it in mind.

Ath. With regard, then, to the first three years of life (whether for a 793e boy or a girl), if someone would carry out these things punctiliously, and not treat what's been said as peripheral, the benefit that would accrue to the young who are being raised would not be inconsiderable.

As for three-year-olds, and four-year-olds, and five-year-olds, and even six-year-olds, the character of their souls would require games, while punishment must be employed to detach them from luxury. The punishment should not be dishonorable, but should resemble the sort we just said was to be used on the slaves; they should punish in a way which is not insolent and hence does not instill anger in those who are punished, yet which doesn't permit luxury by leaving them 794a

[181]

unpunished. This same approach should be used on those who are free. The games for children of this age spring up naturally, mostly discovered by the children themselves when they get together. And all the children of this age, three to six, should gather together in the district temples, the children of each district coming together in the same common place. The nurses should keep watch over the orderliness or lack of restraint of those who are still at this age, while supervision over the nurses themselves and over the whole herd should be the responsibility of one of the previously selected twelve women: the Guardians of the Laws should assign a woman to each herd, to keep order for a period of a year. The selection of these women is to be the responsibility of the women who are in charge of overseeing marriages, who will select one woman, of the same age as themselves, from each tribe. The one who is selected should pay an official visit to the temple each day and punish anyone she finds acting unjustly on each occasion. She can use some of the servants belonging to the city to punish, on her own authority, male or female slaves and male or female strangers, but if the accused is a citizen, and disputes the punishment, she must take him to court before the City Regulators. If he doesn't dispute her claim, let her punish even the citizen on her own authority.

The sexes should be separated after they reach the age of six—boys spending their time with boys, and, similarly, the virgins spending their time with one another. Both should turn to studies, the males going to teachers of horseback riding, archery, javelin throwing, and the sling. Females too, if somehow they will agree, should at least know about these things—and especially about the use of heavy arms.[7] For almost everyone fails to recognize the prejudice that prevails about such matters at the present time.

Kl. What is that?

Ath. I refer to the belief that nature makes our right and left sides differ with respect to the way they are used in each of the actions done by our hands, whereas with respect to chores done by the feet and the lower limbs no difference is apparent. On account of the mindlessness of our nurses and mothers we have each become like cripples as regards our hands. For by nature the limbs on both sides are almost equally balanced; *we* have made them differ through habituation, by not using them correctly. In some activities where it doesn't make much difference—such as in playing the lyre, where the instrument is held in the left hand and the plectrum in the right, and in other such activities—no harm is done. But to use these activities as models for other activities, where such usage isn't necessary, is practically mindless. The Scythians have a convention that makes this evident: instead of holding the bow in the left hand and pulling the arrow back only with the right, they use either hand to the same extent for both. There are very many other such models—in chariot driving and other activities—from which one could learn that those who contrive to make the left weaker than the right do so against nature. As we said, when this affects plectrums made of horn and other such tools, it doesn't make a big difference; but in war, when one must employ tools made of iron, it does make a big difference, not only as regards bows and javelins, but especially when heavy arms must be used against heavy arms. At that point, there is a very great difference between one who has learned and one who hasn't, and between one who has been trained in gymnastic and one who hasn't been trained in gymnastic. Just as someone perfectly trained for the pankration,[8] or for boxing, or for wrestling, is never unable to fight with his left side, and thus is not a cripple or a clumsy bumbler whenever someone, by switching over, compels him to fight on that side; in the very same way, I think, one should correctly expect that for fighting in heavy armor and all the rest, whoever possesses two limbs with which to defend himself and attack others should do all he can not to allow either to be idle or untrained. And if someone should grow[9] up with the nature of even a Geryon or a Briareus, he ought to be able to throw a hundred javelins with his hundred hands.[10] All these things should be supervised by the female rulers and the male rulers—the former keeping a watch over the games and the nurses, the latter over the studies—so that all the boys and all the girls will have feet and hands that are ambidextrous, and so that insofar as possible they won't harm their natures through habits.

It would presumably be useful if the studies were twofold, so to speak: the gymnastic would be those that pertain to the body, and the musical would be for the sake of stoutness of soul.[11] The gymnastic, in turn, would be divided in two, into

795a

795b

795c

795d

[183]

795e dancing and wrestling. One kind of dancing involves their imitating the speech of the Muse, while preserving a magnificent and free demeanor; the other kind, which is for the sake of health, agility and beauty, involves the proper bending and stretching of the limbs and parts of the body, and produces rhythmic motion in each of them as they adequately extend and retract themselves in every sort of dance.

796a As for the sort of wrestling techniques Antaeus or Cercyon developed in their arts, out of their useless love of victories, or the boxing techniques developed by Epeius or Amycus,[12] since they're useless in the encounters[13] of war, they're not worthy of being adorned by a discussion. But the things that fall under straight wrestling, including releases for the necks, hands, and sides, when practiced with a love of victory, when one is tough and graceful, and for the sake of strength and health, should not be neglected, since they are useful in every way. When we get to that stage in the laws we should, how-

796b ever, require the teachers to give all such lessons gently and the students to take them with a good grace.

Nor should one neglect whatever is appropriate in choral imitations, such as the armed games of the Kuretes that are held in this area, or those of the Dioscuri in Lacedaimon.[14] And presumably our virgin mistress,[15] who delights in the play of the chorus, doesn't think it proper to dance with empty

796c hands; so she decks herself out with a complete set of armor and performs the entire dance that way. These are the sorts of things that would be entirely fitting for the boys and also the girls to imitate, as they honor the graciousness of the goddess,[16] for the sake of their use both in war and in festivals. Presumably, it would be required that from the very beginning of their lives, and throughout all the time that passes until they go to war, the children always be arrayed with weapons and accompanied by horses as they make processions and ceremonial marches in honor of each of the gods. Thus with quick and slower steps, in the dances and processions, they will make their supplications to the gods and the children of the gods.

796d It is for no other ends—if for any—that contests and preparatory contests ought to be waged. For these are useful in peace and war, in the political regime and in private households; but the other sorts of playful and serious bodily exercises are not for free men,[17] Megillus and Kleinias.

I have now given a pretty full elaboration of the gymnastic art that I said, in the first parts of the conversation, had to be elaborated: this is it, complete in every way. But if you two have something better than this to suggest, speak up, and set it before us in common. 796e

Kl. It isn't easy, stranger, to set aside these things and proceed to tell of other things that are better than these as regards both the gymnastic art and contests.

Ath. What follows next in order, then, is a discussion of the gifts of the Muses and Apollo. Earlier, indeed, we thought we had discussed all this, and had left only what pertains to the gymnastic art. Now, however, it is clear what things were omitted and that those things should be the first things one tells everyone. So let's proceed to discuss these very matters next in order.

Kl. This ought to be discussed, by all means.

Ath. Listen to me, then; even though you've listened before, still, 797a care must be taken now too, as something very strange and uncustomary is spoken and heard. For I'm going to present an argument that is somewhat frightening to utter; yet by becoming bold, somehow, I will not flinch.

Kl. What is this, stranger, that you're talking about?

Ath. I assert that in all the cities, everyone is unaware that the character of the games played is decisive for the establishment of the laws, since it determines whether or not the established laws will persist. Where this is arranged, and provides that 797b the same persons always play at the same things, with the same things, and in the same way, and have their spirits gladdened by the same toys, there the serious customs are also allowed to remain undisturbed; but where the games change, and are always infected with innovation and other sorts of transformations, where the young never call the same things dear, where good form and bad form—in the postures of their own bodies or in other things they use—are not always agreed upon, where instead they honor especially the man who con- 797c tinually innovates with something new and carries in[18] shapes and colors and all such things that are different from the usual, we would be speaking in an entirely correct way if we were to assert this of such a man: there is no greater ruin than this that can come to a city. For, escaping notice, this man transforms the characters of the young, and makes them dishonor what is ancient and honor what is new. Of this man and his talk and dogma I say once again: there is no greater punishment for all cities. Hear how much evil I assert this is.

797d Kl. Are you referring now to the blame laid on the ancient things in the cities?

Ath. Yes, indeed.

Kl. Well, then, you'd find that we're by no means inattentive listeners to this part of your speech; nay, we'll be as receptive as we can.

Ath. That's to be expected.

Kl. So just say on.

Ath. Come then, let us surpass ourselves both in listening to the argument and enunciating it to one another.

Change, we shall find, is much the most dangerous thing in everything except what is bad—in all the seasons, in the 797e winds, in bodily habits, and in the characters of souls. It isn't the case that change is, so to speak, safe in some things and dangerous in others, except, as I just now said, in bad things.

Thus, if one were to look at bodies, one would see how they become accustomed to all foods and all drinks and exercises, even if at first they are upset by them; one would see how, with the passage of time, they grow,[19] out of these very mate798a rials, flesh that is akin to these things, and come to like, be accustomed to and familiar with, a whole regimen—thriving on it in the best way from the point of view of both pleasure and health; one would see that if someone is ever compelled to change back to one of the reputable diets, he is at first upset with sickness, but then once again with difficulty recovers, by regaining a habituation in the food. Now one must hold that this very same thing applies to the thoughts of human beings and the natures of their souls. If they're brought up under 798b laws which by some divine good fortune have remained unchanged for a great length of time, if they neither remember nor have heard that things were ever otherwise than they are at present, then the entire soul reverences and fears changing any of the things that are already laid down. Somehow or other the lawgiver must think up a device by which this situation will prevail in the city. The following is what I at least have discovered: as we said before, everyone thinks that very great and serious harm can't follow from changes in the games 798c of the young, on the grounds that these are really just games. As a result, they don't prevent such changes but give in to and follow them, not taking into account the fact that these boys who practice innovations in their games must necessarily grow up to be men who are different from those the earlier children grew into; being different, they seek a different way of life, and in seeking it they desire different practices and laws; from this it follows that none of them fears the arrival of what was now said to be the greatest evil for cities. There are, indeed, other changes—those affecting outward appearance—that would do less damage; but whatever brings about frequent change in the praise and blame accorded to dispositions is the greatest of all changes, I believe, and would require the most attentive watching. 798d

Kl. How could it not?

Ath. What then? Do we trust the earlier arguments, where we said that things pertaining to rhythms and music as a whole are imitations of the characters of better and worse human beings? Or what? 798e

Kl. Among us at least there would be no change in opinion whatsoever.

Ath. Do we assert, then, that every sort of contrivance should be contrived to prevent our boys from desiring to partake of other imitations, in dances or songs, and to prevent anyone from using all sorts of pleasures to persuade them?

Kl. What you say is very correct.

Ath. With regard to these matters, does any of us have an art better than that of the Egyptians? 799a

Kl. What things are you referring to?

Ath. The sanctification of all dance and all songs. First comes the arranging of the holidays in a yearly calendar, showing what they are, when they occur, and to whom among the gods, the gods' children, or the demons they should be dedicated. After this, certain persons should first arrange which song is appropriately sung at each of the sacrifices to the gods, and which choruses should celebrate the sacrifice on each occasion; then 799b all the citizens in common, by making sacrifices to the Fates [20] and all the rest of the gods, and by pouring out libations, should sanctify each of the songs ordained for each of the gods and the others.

  If anyone dedicates to one of the gods other hymns, or presents choruses, contrary to these, the Priests and Priestesses together with the Guardians of the Laws will be acting piously and lawfully if they exclude that person. If the one excluded refuses, voluntarily, to abide by the exclusion, he will for the rest of his life be subject to indictment for impiety by anyone who wishes to bring the charge.

Kl. Correctly spoken.

799c Ath. Now that we've entered into this discussion, let's undergo what is fitting for men like us.

Kl. What are you talking about?

Ath. Presumably every young man, not to speak of an elderly man, when he sees or hears something strange and utterly unaccustomed, would never, I suppose, rush to agree right away with whatever is puzzling in such things; instead he'd stand there, like someone confronted with the triple fork at a crossroads and not knowing the road very well. Whether he were alone or

799d should happen to be travelling with others, he'd ask himself or the others about what is puzzling, and wouldn't hurry on before he'd somehow placed on firm ground the inquiry into which way the path leads. The same should certainly be done by us at the present juncture: it is necessary, presumably, to make a complete inquiry into the strange argument about laws that has now cropped up. At our age, and about such matters, we shouldn't make a facile claim to be able to say something clear at a moment's notice.

Kl. What you say is very true.

799e Ath. So we'll devote some time to this, and when we've investigated it sufficiently, we'll then put it on firm ground. But in order to avoid the possibility that we might be uselessly prevented from completing the sequence of regulations that goes with the laws we have before us now, let's proceed to the end of them. And maybe, if the god would be willing, the way itself as a whole, taken to its end, would reveal sufficiently the answer to what now is puzzling.

Kl. An excellent suggestion, stranger—let's do as you've said.

Ath. So, we assert, this strange dogma has been accepted: our songs have become "laws." [21] This is in agreement with the name the ancients, as is likely, somehow gave to songs accom-

800a panied by the kithara, and so they probably wouldn't have disagreed entirely with what's being said now: someone prophesied it vaguely in a dream, either while asleep or while in a state of waking vision. At any rate, this is to be the dogma about it: let no one voice anything or make any dance movement contrary to the public and sacred songs, or the whole choral exercise of the young, any more than he would go against any of the other "laws." He who goes along may depart unpunished. He who disobeys will be punished, as was just now said, by the Guardians of the Laws, the Priestesses, 800b and the Priests. Shall these things be laid down in speech by us now?

Kl. Let them be laid down.

Ath. Now in what way would someone legislating these things avoid becoming totally ridiculous? Let's consider something like the following additional point in regard to these matters: the safest thing to do is first to shape some molds for them in speech. I say one of the molds is something like this: suppose a sacrifice is taking place and the sacred meats are being burned as the law dictates, and let's say someone in a private capacity, a son or a brother, while standing near the altars and sacred things, breaks out in a total blasphemy. Wouldn't we 800c assert that his utterance would fill his father and his other kinsmen with despondency,[22] and a sense of bad omen and prophetic warning of evil?

Kl. How could it not?

Ath. Well, in our part of the world this happens in almost every city, so to speak. For whenever some official carries out some sacrifice in public, a chorus comes along afterwards—in fact not just one, but a mass of choruses—and standing not far 800d from the altars, indeed sometimes right beside the altars, pours total blasphemy on the sacred things! They use words, rhythms, and very mournful harmoniae to get the souls of the hearers all worked up, and whoever can straightaway make the city that is engaged in sacrificing weep the most is the fellow who wins the victory prize! Won't we vote down this "law"?[23] If it is sometimes necessary for the citizen to hear such wailings, on certain impure and ill-omened days,[24] then there should rather be certain choruses of singers who come, 800e hired from abroad, of the sort that are paid to walk before funeral processions, inspired by some Carian[25] Muse. Presumably such would be the fitting occasion for songs of that kind. And presumably it wouldn't be fitting for the garb that goes with the funeral songs to be crowns or golden ornaments, but entirely the opposite—so as to leave off discussing these matters as quickly as I possibly can.

With regard to such a thing, I ask us ourselves once again: should we lay down this first instance as one satisfactory mold for songs?

Kl.   Which?

801a   Ath.   Auspicious speech. Shouldn't our species of song be wholly auspicious in speech, on every occasion? Or shall I not ask, but shall I just ordain it this way?

Kl.   Ordain it by all means; for this law wins by unanimous vote.

Ath.   What would be the second law of music after auspicious speech? Is it not that there are to be prayers to the gods to whom we are sacrificing on each occasion?

Kl.   What else, except this?

Ath.   The third law, I believe, should be that the poets must realize that prayers are requests to the gods, and they must apply 801b   their intelligence to the utmost in order to avoid ever mistakenly requesting evil in place of good. For the situation becomes laughable indeed, I think, when such a prayer is made.

Kl.   But of course.

Ath.   Now weren't we convinced a little earlier by the argument that neither the Silver nor the Golden Pluto[26] was to have an established dwelling place in the city?

Kl.   Certainly.

Ath.   What, then, shall we claim this argument illustrates? Isn't it 801c   this, that the race of poets is not entirely capable of understanding well what things are good and what things are not? Presumably, if some poet creates, through words or melody, a work that is erroneous in this respect—if he creates prayers that are incorrect—he will make the citizens pray in a way opposed to what we ordain, in respect to the greatest matters. And as we said, we won't find many mistakes that are graver than this. So shall we set this down as one of the laws and outlines concerning the Muse?

Kl.   Set down what? Tell us more clearly what you mean.

Ath.   The poet is to create nothing that differs from the city's con-801d   ventional and just version of the beautiful or good things; he may show none of his creations to any of the nonexperts before he has shown them to the judges appointed in these matters as well as to the Guardians of the Laws, and met with their approval. (We've practically selected these judges already, since we've chosen both those who are to legislate in musical affairs and the one who is to be Supervisor of Education.) What then? I ask again what I've often asked: shall we ordain this as the third law, outline, and mold? Or how does it seem?

Kl. Let it be ordained—why should it not be?

Ath. Next, after these things at any rate, it would be quite correct to sing to the gods hymns and encomia mixed with prayers. After the gods would come, in the same way, prayers, with encomia, to the demons and the heroes, whatever is fitting to every one of these.

Kl. How could it be otherwise?

Ath. Now after these things, at any rate, this law could immediately follow, without hesitation: it would be fitting for any citizens who have reached life's end, who have performed noble and laborious deeds with either their bodies or their souls, and who have been obedient to the laws, to obtain encomia.

Kl. How else?

Ath. But it isn't safe to honor through encomia and hymns those still living (before a person has run through the entire course of his life and arrived at a noble end). Among us let all these matters be applied to men and women in common, to all those of either sex who become conspicuous for their goodness.

The songs and dances should be ordained thus. From the ancients have come many ancient and beautiful creations in music, and also for the bodies, dances of the same quality. There should be no hesitation to pick out from these what is fitting and harmonious for the political regime that is being set up. To make the choice among these, examiners should be selected who are not younger than fifty years of age. They should decide what seems adequate among the ancient creations and what is either deficient or wholly unsuitable. In the latter case they should cast it entirely away, while in the former case they should take it up again and rework it, seeking the aid of the poetic and musical men. They should use the poetic powers of these men, but they shouldn't be guided by their pleasures and desires, except in the case of a few of them; instead, by interpreting the intentions of the lawgiver, they should put together dance and song and choral performance as a whole in a way that comes as close as possible to the intentions in his mind. Every disorderly pursuit involving the Muse becomes better ten thousandfold when it attains order, even if it doesn't partake of the sweet Muse. Pleasure, after all,

801e

802a

802b

802c

is common to all the Muses. If someone passes the time from childhood until the age of adulthood and prudence hearing a moderate and orderly Muse, then every time he hears the opposite he will hate Her and proclaim Her to be lacking in freedom; but if he's brought up with the common and sweet Muse, he'll assert the opposite to this is cold and unpleasant. So, as was just now said, from the point of view of pleasure or lack of pleasure, at least, neither side gets more; the big difference lies in the fact that one makes those brought up with Her better while the other always makes them worse.

Kl. You've spoken beautifully.

Ath. In addition, it would presumably be necessary to distinguish, in an outline, the songs fitting for females from those fitting for males, and it's necessary to harmonize them with the harmoniae and rhythms. For it's terrible to sing something discordant with the harmonia as a whole, or to use a meter that's unsuitable to the rhythm, by failing to assign to the songs what is appropriate in each of these respects. So it's necessary to legislate at least the outlines of these matters. Now both kinds of song must be assigned certain necessary accompaniments; and since what belongs to females is determined by the very way they differ in nature, one must make use of this difference in order to make clear the difference in the songs. Magnificence, then, and whatever inclines to courage, ought to be declared to be masculine looking; whatever leans rather toward the orderly and the moderate should be proclaimed, in legal convention and in speech, as belonging more to the feminine. This will be the arrangement.

What needs to be discussed next after this is the teaching and handing down of these very things—in what way, to whom, and when each of the subjects should be practiced.

It's evident to me that what I'm doing here myself is much the same as what a shipwright does in beginning to build ships, when he sketches the shape of ships in outline by laying down the keels. I'm trying to distinguish the outline of ways of life as they accord with characteristics of souls, and thus really "laying down their keels"[27]—investigating, in the correct way, what device we should use and what characteristics we should at any time incorporate if we are going to be carried through this voyage of existence on the best way of life. Of course, the affairs of human beings are not worthy of

802d

802e

803a

803b

great seriousness; yet it is necessary to be serious about them. And this is not a fortunate thing. But since we're here, if somehow we would carry out the business in some appropriate way it would perhaps be a well-measured thing for us to do. But whatever am I saying? Someone would perhaps be correct to take me up in this very way.

Kl.   Indeed!   803c

Ath. I assert that what is serious should be treated seriously, and what is not serious should not, and that by nature god is worthy of a complete, blessed seriousness, but that what is human, as we said earlier, has been devised as a certain plaything of god, and that this is really the best thing about it. Every man and woman should spend life in this way, playing the noblest possible games, and thinking about them in a way that is the opposite of the way they're now thought about.

Kl.   How's that?   803d

Ath. Nowadays, presumably, they suppose the serious things are for the sake of the playful things: for it is held that the affairs pertaining to war, being serious matters, should be run well for the sake of peace. But the fact is that in war there is not and will not be by nature either play or, again, an education that is at any time worthy of our discussion; yet this is what we assert is for us, at least, the most serious thing. Each person should spend the greatest and best part of his life in peace. What then is the correct way? One should live out one's days   803e playing at certain games—sacrificing, singing, and dancing— with the result that one can make the gods propitious to oneself and can defend oneself against enemies and be victorious over them in battle. The sort of things one should sing and dance in order to accomplish both these things have been described in outlines, and the trails, as it were, have been blazed along which one should go, expecting that the poet speaks well when he says: [28]

Telemachus, some things you yourself will think of in   804a
    your own thoughts,
And some things a demon will suggest; for I do not
    think
That you were born and raised against the will of the
    gods.

This is the way our nurslings should consider things: they should believe that what's been said has been adequately spo-

804b ken, but that the demon and god will suggest things to them regarding sacrifices and choral performances, thus indicating those whom they should offer games and propitiate, and when they should play each game for each, so as to live out their lives in accordance with the way of nature, being puppets, for the most part, but sharing in small portions of truth.

Meg. Stranger, you are belittling our human race in every respect!

Ath. Don't be amazed, Megillus, but forgive me! For I was looking away toward the god and speaking under the influence of that experience, when I said what I did just now. So let our race be something that is not lowly then, if that is what you 804c cherish, but worthy of a certain seriousness.

With regard to what follows these things, it has already been said that buildings for gymnastics and for common instruction should be located at three places in the center of the city, and that outside, at three places again around the city, there should be gymnasia and open spaces arranged for horses as well as for archery and the other long-range weapons, where the young can learn and practice. If these things weren't described adequately before, let them be described now, in speech and also in laws. In all these buildings there 804d should dwell teachers of each subject, strangers persuaded by pay to teach those who attend all the things they should learn, with a view to war and with a view to music. And it will not be left up to the father's wish to decide who shall attend and whose education shall be neglected, but rather, as the saying goes, "every man and child insofar as he is able" must of necessity become educated, on the grounds that they belong more to the city than to those who generated them. Indeed, my law would say all the very same things about females that 804e it says about males, including that females should be trained on an equal basis. I would speak without being at all afraid of the argument that horseback riding and gymnastics are fitting for men but not fitting for women. For I am persuaded by the ancient myths I've heard, and at this very moment, so to speak, I know there are countless myriads of women around the Black Sea—the women called Sarmatians [29]—who are en- 805a joined to handle not only horses, but the bow and the other weapons as well, in equality with the men, and who practice them equally. Besides this, I make some such calculation as the following, in regard to these matters: I assert that if, indeed, it is possible for these things to turn out this way, then the way they're now arranged in our lands—where it's not the case that all the men with their entire strength, and united in spirit, practice the same things as the women—is the most mindless of all. For this way, almost every city is just about half of what it might be, when with the same expenditures and efforts it could double itself. And this would be an amazing mistake on the part of the lawgiver.   805b

Kl. That's likely, anyway. Still, there are very many aspects of what we're now saying, stranger, that run counter to what is usual in political regimes.

But you spoke very reasonably when you said that the argument should be allowed to unfold, and that once it had unfolded well, one should then choose what one approved. As a matter of fact, what you said makes me rebuke myself now, for   805c the things I just said. So say next after these things whatever you find pleasing.

Ath. What would please me, at least, Kleinias, is the following (something I've said before): if the possibility of what we're discussing hadn't been sufficiently demonstrated by deeds, one might perhaps say something against the argument, but now, presumably, he who cannot in any way accept this law will have to seek some other way of opposing it. He won't extinguish our insistence that one should say that our female race must, as much as possible, have a common share in edu-   805d cation and in the other things along with the race of males. For that's about the way one should think about these matters. Look, if women don't share their entire lives in common with men, won't it be necessary to have some different regimen for them?

Kl. That will indeed be necessary.

Ath. So which of the regimens now in evidence would we set up, instead of this common regimen we are now establishing for them? Would it be that of the Thracians and many other   805e tribes, who use their women to farm, tend cattle, herd sheep, and to serve no differently than slaves? Or our own practice and that of everyone in our area? For nowadays, among us, these things are done as follows: "bringing all our goods together in some one house," as the saying goes, we give to the women the responsibility of acting as stewards, setting them to rule over the shuttles and everything having to do

806a with spinning. Or shall we, Megillus, prescribe the practice that is midway between these, the Laconic? Should the girls live partaking of gymnastics and music, while the women, without having to work at spinning, weave a rather laborious way of life that is neither mean nor cheap, and arrives at a middle ground between taking care of people, acting as steward again, and bringing up the children? But then they'd take no part in the things of war, so even if someday some chance should compel them to fight for their city and their children,

806b they wouldn't be able to shoot arrows, like certain Amazons, nor ever be capable of partaking in the artful use of any other missile, nor be able to take up shield and spear in imitation of the goddess,[30] and thus nobly oppose the sack of their own fatherland—being able to strike fear at least, if nothing more, in the enemy, by being seen in some battle order. Living this way of life, they wouldn't at all dare to imitate the Sarmatians,

806c whose women would appear to be men in comparison with them.

With regard to these things, let whoever wishes to do so praise your lawgivers. For my part, I can only stand by what's been said: a lawgiver must be complete, and not half a lawgiver; to let the female live in luxury, spend money, and follow disorderly pursuits, while supervising the male, is to leave the city with only about half of a completely happy life instead of double that.

Meg. What are we going to do, Kleinias? Are we going to let the stranger run down Sparta in front of us this way?

806d Kl. Yes. Freedom of speech has been granted him, and we have to let him go on until we've gone through the laws in a way that is entirely sufficient.

Meg. What you say is correct.

Ath. Then probably I may try to explain the things that come next after these?

Kl. Why not?

Ath. What then would be the way of life of human beings for whom the necessities were taken care of in due measure, for whom matters pertaining to the arts were handed over to others, and

806e whose farms, assigned to slaves, provided sufficient produce from the things of the land to allow human beings to live in an orderly way? Suppose there were separate common meals arranged for the men, and nearby common meals for the members of their families, including female children and their mothers; at all of these common tables there would be male and female rulers assigned to dismiss each of them, having observed and watched over the conduct of the common meals each day; then, after the ruler and the others had poured a 807a libation to whichever gods the particular night and day might happen to be consecrated, they would thus make their way home. To lives ordered in this way, is there no necessary and wholly appropriate activity left, but is each of them to live out his life getting fattened up, like a cow? It isn't just, we assert, nor noble, nor is it possible for one who lives that way to avoid the appropriate fortune: for it's appropriate that an idle, soft-spirited, and fattened animal usually is ravaged by one of 807b those other animals who have been worn very hard with courage and labors.

Of course, these things we're now seeking probably wouldn't ever be realized with adequate precision so long as women and children and homes are private, and all such things are arranged privately by each of us. But if the second-best arrangements after those would come into being for us as they've now been described, things would achieve due measure.

And for men who lived this way the activity that would be 807c left is neither the smallest nor the humblest, we assert, but is in fact the greatest of all the tasks that can be assigned by a just law. For just as the life of a man who aims at victory in the Pythian or Olympian games wholly lacks leisure for all the other activities, so doubly or much more than doubly lacking in leisure is the life that's most correctly called a "life"—that of a man who is devoted to cultivating his body in all respects and his soul as regards virtue. Not even a small part of any of 807d the other activities should be allowed to pose an obstacle to his giving the body its appropriate exercises and food, and the soul teachings and habits; the whole night and day are scarcely sufficient time for the man who's doing this to get the complete and adequate benefit from these things.

Given that this is the way things are by nature, it follows that there should be a schedule regulating how all the free men 807e spend all their time, beginning almost at dawn and extending to the next dawn and rising of the sun. Of course, there are many little and frequent details regarding the management of a household that it would be unseemly for a lawgiver to speak of—including the provisions for curtailing sleep at night that would be needed by men who intend to keep a complete and accurate guard over the whole city. If any of the citizens spends the whole of any night slumbering, and fails to show

808a

himself always the first to be up and around, before any of his domestic servants, his behavior must be regarded by everyone as shameful and unworthy of a free man, whether such a provision be called a law or a practice. Indeed, if the mistress of a house is awakened by some of her maids and fails to get up first herself and wake the others, it should be talked of as something shameful among the slaves—male, female, and children—and, if somehow it were possible, by the whole

808b

house itself in its entirety. Moreover, everyone should be up during the night performing a good part of the business of politics as well as of the households—the magistrates acting in the city and the masters and mistresses in the private homes. A great deal of sleep does not by nature harmonize with our bodies or souls, or with the activities pertaining to all these things. For while a person sleeps he is worth nothing—no more than one who isn't living. But whoever among us cares

808c

for living and thinking to a special degree stays up the longest time, reserving only so much time as is useful for his health, and that isn't much, once a fine habit has been established. Again, where the magistrates are awake at night in cities they strike more fear in the wicked, both enemies and citizens, and are more prized and honored by the just and moderate men because they are beneficial both to themselves and to the city as a whole. Now a night spent in such a way would, in addition to everything else that's been said, instill a certain

808d

courage in the souls of each of those in the cities.

As for the day, when dawn arrives and people are up, the children should presumably be turned over to their teachers; but just as sheep and every other herd animal shouldn't live without a herder, so children shouldn't live without certain tutors, nor slaves without masters. And the child is the hardest to handle of all beasts, because insofar as it has within it, to a high degree, a not yet disciplined source of thought, it becomes treacherous, sharp, and the most insolent of beasts.

808e

That's why it's necessary to fetter it with many sorts of bridles, as it were: at first, when it has just been separated from its nurses and mothers, one needs to use tutors for its playfulness and childishness; later one needs to use teachers and subject matters of all sorts, as befits a free man. But it's as befits a slave that the boy himself, and his tutor and his teacher should be punished, if any of them does wrong, by any of the free men who happen along. If someone should happen upon such wrongdoing and fail to give it a just punishment, let him first bear the greatest sort of blame, and then let the Guardian of the Laws who has been chosen to fill the office of the children watch this fellow, who happened upon what we're describing, but failed to punish one who needed punishment or carried out the punishment in an improper way. This same magistrate of ours should keep a sharp watch and exercise an especially careful supervision over the upbringing of the children, so as to keep their natures on a straight path, by always turning them toward what is good according to the laws.

Yet how would this man himself be educated adequately by our law? Up to this point it has mentioned some things, and omitted others, but has said nothing yet that is clear or sufficient. As nearly as possible, it should omit nothing that concerns this magistrate; the whole argument should be interpreted for him, so that he can become the interpreter and protector of the others.

"Now while chorus matters—the songs and dancing, and which kinds should be chosen, corrected, and consecrated—have been discussed, we haven't talked about the writings that are not in meter, showing what sort they should be and how they should be handled by those whom you are bringing up, O best Supervisor of Children. You do of course have an account of what they should learn and practice for war, but you lack an account as regards first, the written things; second, the lyre; and then, arithmetical calculations—about which we declared everyone must grasp as much as is necessary for war, household management, and the management of the city. Moreover, they should learn whatever is useful, for these same purposes, of what pertains to the revolutions of the divine things, the stars and the sun and the moon: they should learn about the arrangements every city needs to make in respect to these things. But just what are we referring to? What we mean is the ordering of the days into the revolutions of the months, and the months in each year, so that each of the

809a

809b

809c

809d

809e

seasons, sacrifices, and festivals will receive its due for itself according to the sequence of nature, will keep the city alive and awake, will render honors to the gods, and will make the humans more prudent in these matters. All these things, my friend, have not yet been explained to you sufficiently by the lawgiver; so turn your mind to what is going to be said next after these things.

"We just said that, in the first place, you don't have a sufficient explanation of the written things. Now just what were we finding fault with when we said this? The following: it hasn't yet been explained to you whether someone who's going to become a well-measured citizen should pursue the subject to the point of precision or whether he should not pursue it at all. The same goes for the lyre. So at this point we do indeed assert that these subjects should be pursued. In the case of the written things, for about three years, commencing at the age of ten; in the case of lyre-playing, another three years, commencing at thirteen, would be a due measure of

810a

time. Neither for the father nor for the child himself, whether he be a lover of learning or a hater, will it be permissible to prolong or shorten, with more or less time, this lawful period of study. Anyone who disobeys will be excluded from the educational honors that will be mentioned a little later. What the children are to learn in these years, and what the teachers are

810b

to teach, you must first learn yourself. They should practice the written things until they are able to write and read; but it isn't required that some, whom nature doesn't urge during the appointed years, develop a precise capacity for speed and beauty. As regards lessons in poets' writings that are not accompanied by the lyre, some of which are in meter and some of which are without rhythmical parts (writings that follow speech alone, and lack rhythm and harmony), there are harm-

810c

ful writings left among us by some of the many human beings who have composed such things. So what are you[31] going to do about them, you best of all Guardians of Laws? Or rather, what, indeed, would be the correct regulations for the legislator to give you to use? I expect he's going to be very much at a loss."

Kl.   What is this, stranger, that you're evidently speaking with yourself about in real perplexity?

Ath.   You're correct in your surmise, Kleinias; and since you two are sharers in the laws, it's necessary to indicate when the path appears clear and when not.

Kl. What, then? What are you referring to in the present subjects, and what is it you're experiencing? 810d

Ath. I'll tell you: it is not at all easy to take the path of speaking against what has been said often, by myriads of mouths.

Kl. Come now, you think what we've said before about laws is opposed to what the many say in a small way, or in a few matters?

Ath. This at least that you say is very true. You're urging me, I think, since the very path that is hateful to the many is cherished by others who are perhaps no fewer—or, if fewer, 810e not inferior at least—you're urging me to go ahead in the company of these latter, to risk and dare the path of legislation now opened up by the present arguments, and not to hang back.

Kl. What else?

Ath. All right, I won't hang back. I say, then, that we have very many poets, composing verses in hexameters, trimeters, and all the other meters that are spoken about, some of whom aim at what is serious and others at what is laughable; now tens of thousands of people often assert that the young who are educated correctly must be brought up and steeped in these poets, that they should learn whole poets by heart, and gain vast ex- 811a perience of hearing, and much learning, through their readings. Others, again, make a collection of excerpts from all the poets, including some complete poems, and assert that the collection must be learned by heart and stored in the memory, if any of our students is to become good and wise through much experience and much learning. Now isn't it the case that you're urging on me a freedom of speech that will permit me to show these people which part of what they say is fine and which is not?

Kl. What else but that?

Ath. What could I ever say in brief that would characterize all these men adequately? I think something like the following will 811b about suffice: everyone would agree with me that each of these men has uttered many things in a noble fashion, but also many things in the opposite fashion. If that is so, then I assert that there is a danger in imbuing the children with much learning.

Kl.   Then how and what would you recommend to the Guardian of the Laws?

Ath.   About what, do you mean?

Kl.   About what model he should look to, at any time, to decide
811c   what he would allow all the young to learn and what he would prevent them from learning. Speak up; don't hesitate to say it.

Ath.   Good Kleinias, in a way I may well have been rather lucky.

Kl.   In what respect?

Ath.   Inasmuch as I'm not altogether at a loss for a model. As I looked now to the speeches we've been going through since dawn until the present—and it appears to me that we have not been speaking without some inspiration from gods—they seemed to me to have been spoken in a way that resembles in
811d   every respect a kind of poetry. It's probably not surprising for me to have had such a feeling, to have been very pleased at the sight of my own speeches, brought together, as it were; for compared to most of the speeches that I have learned or heard, in poems, or poured out in prose like what's been said, these appeared to me to be both the most well-measured, at any rate, of all, and especially appropriate for the young to hear. I don't think I would have a better model than this to describe
811e   for the Guardian of the Laws and Educator, or anything that would be better for him to bid the teachers to teach the children, other than these things and things that are connected to them and similar. He should work through the poems of poets, as well as prose writings and things that are simply recited without being written down, and if, as can be presumed, he comes across speeches that are the brothers of these, he should on no account let them pass by but should write them down. Then, in the first place, he should compel the teachers themselves to learn and to praise these writings; if there are any teachers who find the writings unpleasing, he should not employ them as his assistants, but should instead use those who vote with him in their praise. It is to these men
812a   that he should give the young, to be taught and educated.

Here and in this way let there be a conclusion to this myth of mine, that has told about instructors in the written things, and also about writings.

Kl.   We don't appear, to me at least, to have gone outside the bounds of the speeches proposed by the fundamental hypothesis, stranger; yet perhaps it is difficult to be sure whether or not our discussion is correct as a whole.

Ath. It's likely, Kleinias, that this at least will itself be more evident
when, as we've often said, we've arrived at the end of the
whole discourse on laws.

Kl. That is correct. 812b

Ath. Well, after the grammarian shouldn't we address the kitharist?

Kl. Why not?

Ath. It seems to me that we should recollect the earlier arguments,
as we allocate to the kitharists what is appropriate as regards
their teaching and the education as a whole in such matters.

Kl. You're referring to the arguments about what things?

Ath. We asserted, I believe, that the sixty-year-old Dionysian
singers had to become especially perceptive about rhythms
and the schemes of the harmoniae, in order that there would be 812c
someone who could pick out, as regards the imitation in songs
that makes the soul feel passions (whether the imitation be
well done or badly done), the resemblances to the good and
the resemblances to the opposite; the one he was to cast away,
while the other he was to produce in their midst, singing to
and enchanting the souls of the young and calling upon each
of them to join in pursuing the acquisition of virtue, by means
of the imitations.

Kl. What you say is very true.

Ath. These, then, are the ends for which the kitharist and the per- 812d
son being educated should use the sounds of the lyre, because
of the clarity of its strings: they should present notes that are
like the notes sung by voices. But as for heterophony or variety in the lyre, with the strings emitting a tune different from
that of the composer of the melody, either by presenting a consonance of notes close together in contrast to notes sung further apart, or by swift tempo in contrast to slow, or by sharp
notes in contrast to flat, or as for using the sounds of the lyre to 812e
present all sorts of similar variations in rhythm—all such
things will be inappropriate for those who are supposed to
grasp quickly, in three years, what is useful in music. Things
that contradict one another are disturbing, and produce difficulty in learning. But the young need to be as good at learning as possible, since they have before them necessary subjects of study that are neither minor nor few in number (and
what these are the argument will show as it proceeds, with the
passage of time). So that is the way our Educator should supervise these things concerning music.

As for the songs themselves and the words, which sort and

813a   which of them the chorus teachers should teach, that has all been elaborated by us before: we declared that the songs had to be sanctified, and each harmonized with the festivals, so as to benefit the cities by providing lucky pleasure.

Kl.   Here again what you've explained is true.

Ath.   It's indeed very true. Let the magistrate who is elected to be concerned with the Muse take these things from us and supervise them with the help of kindly luck; for our part, let us give additional guidance, beyond the things said before, as regards

813b   dancing and the whole gymnastic that has to do with the body. Just as we supplied what was left in regard to the teaching of music, so let us do the same for gymnastic. For surely the boys and girls must learn to dance, and to exercise in the nude. Isn't that so?

Kl.   Yes.

Ath.   With a view to their exercising, it would not be too unsuitable if the boys had male dancing teachers and the girls female.

Kl.   Let it be arranged this way.

Ath.   Once again let's call upon the man who'll have the most busi-
813c   ness to take care of, the Supervisor of the Children, who, with his supervision of the things pertaining to both music and gymnastics, won't have much leisure.

Kl.   How will a rather old man like that be able to supervise so many things?

Ath.   Easily, my friend. The law has given and will give to him the power to take as his assistants in this supervision any men or women citizens he chooses. He'll know whom to choose, and he won't want to go astray in the choice, because he'll feel a
813d   prudent awe for, and understand, the greatness of the office; he'll keep in mind the calculation that when the young have been, and are being, brought up well, all sails correctly for us, but if not—well, it's not worthwhile describing the consequences, and we won't do it here in the presence of this novel city, out of our reverent respect for those who are especially attached to prophecy.

     Now we've already said a great deal about these matters as well, about dances and the whole of gymnastic motion. For we're setting up gymnasia and all the bodily exercises for
813e   war—for archery, for every sort of throwing, for skirmishing with the sling, for the whole of heavily-armed fighting, for tactical maneuvers, for all the movements of armies, including

pitching camps, and for whatever one should learn that pertains to horseback riding. There should be common teachers for all these things, hired for pay by the city, and the boys and men in the city must become pupils of these subjects, while the girls and women must become knowers of all these subjects. So long as they're still girls, they should practice all the dancing and fighting that goes with heavy armor; when they 814a get to be women, they should have grasped maneuvers, battle orders, and how to put down and take up weapons. They should do this if for no other reason than for the sake of being fit to do this much at least: to take the responsibility of guarding the children and the rest of the city if the whole mass of the army with all its power should ever have to leave the city and fight outside. Or then again the opposite could happen (something that no one can swear is impossible): some enemies from abroad, whether barbarians or Greeks, might fall upon them with enormous strength and violence, compelling them to make a fight for the city itself. It would presumably 814b show much evil in the political regime if the women had been so shamefully reared that they didn't do as the birds do (who are willing to run every risk, and even to die, fighting on behalf of their babies against even the strongest beasts), but instead rushed immediately to the temples and crowded around all the altars and inner shrines, bringing down on the race of humans the reputation of being by nature the most cowardly of all the beasts.

Kl. By Zeus, stranger, wherever this should happen in a city it would not look good at all, apart from the harm that would be 814c done!

Ath. Well then, won't we establish this as a law, that the women must not neglect the business of war, to this extent, at least, and that it must be a concern of all male citizens and female citizens?

Kl. I, at least, go along with this.

Ath. With regard to wrestling we've talked about some things, but what I would declare the most important part we have not discussed, nor is it easy to do so without using bodily demonstrations to accompany one's explanation in speech. So let's pronounce our judgment on this later on, when speech can 814d accompany deed and make clear other things that have been said, and especially that the wrestling we have in mind is really, of all motions, the most akin by far to fighting in war, and that the former is to be practiced for the sake of the latter, and the latter is not to be learned for the sake of the former.

Kl. In this respect, at least, you speak nobly.

Ath. So let this much be said by us for now about the power of the wrestling school.

814e   As for the rest of the motion of the body as a whole, one would be speaking correctly if one called the greatest part of this a kind of "dance." It should be held to comprise two forms: one is the imitation of noble bodies in solemn movement, the other is the imitation of shameful bodies in low movement. Then again there are two forms of the low sort and two other forms of the serious sort. One of the serious forms is the imitation of noble bodies entangled in violent exertions during war, where the soul is manly; the other is the imitation where the soul is moderate, in prosperous settings and well-measured pleasures. If someone called such a dance "The

815a   Peaceful" he would speak according to nature. The warlike of these, whose essence is different from the peaceful, one would correctly call "The Pyrrhic."[32] It consists in imitating, on the one hand, movements that evade all kinds of blows and missiles—by dodging, giving way completely, jumping up, humble crouching—and then again striving to imitate the opposites to these, aggressive postures involved in striking with missiles—arrows and javelins—and with all sorts of blows.[33]

815b   In dances of this kind, when imitation of good bodies and souls takes place, correctness and vigor are achieved for the most part by keeping the limbs of the bodies straight; such a posture is correct, and the opposite sorts of postures are not considered right.[34]

With regard to the Peaceful dance, one should in each case observe the following—whether in the choral dances a person succeeds in correctly keeping to the noble dance, in a manner that befits men of good conventions, or whether he does not succeed in doing so according to nature. Now first it is neces-

815c   sary to separate off the controversial dancing from the uncontroversial. What then is this, and how should it be separated off from the other? Whatever dances are Bacchic, and everything that goes with these—the dances in which, as they claim, they imitate as drunks the so-called "Nymphs," "Pans," "Silenuses," and "Satyrs," and thereby celebrate certain purifications and mystery-rites—this entire class of dance is not easily defined either as peaceful or as warlike, or indeed as to just what it intends at any time. To me it seems that just about the most correct way to define it is this: it must be dis- 815d tinguished from the warlike, and distinguished from the peaceful, and one must say that this class of dancing is not political. Let it be, lying in that region, while we return now to the warlike and peaceful dances, since there is no controversy as to whether they are our business.

With regard, then, to what belongs to the unwarlike Muse who is manifested in the dances where men honor the gods and the children of the gods, one whole kind of dance would be that which portrays an opinion of prosperity. This in its 815e turn we would subdivide: one sort, involving more pleasures, would represent people fleeing from certain toils and risks, into good things; the other sort would represent the preservation and augmentation of the aforementioned good things, involving pleasures gentler than those of the others. In such circumstances every human being presumably moves his 816a body more when the pleasures are greater, and less when they are lesser; moreover, the human being who is more orderly and who has a better gymnastic training in courage moves his body less, while the coward and the one who lacks gymnastic training in moderation presents greater and more violent changes in his motion. In general, no one who is using his voice—whether in songs or in speeches—can remain very calm in his body. That is why, as the imitation through gestures of what is being said came into being, it gave rise to the whole art of dancing. With regard to all these gestures, one of us moves harmoniously, while another moves in ways that are 816b not in harmony. Now we should understand that many of the ancient names are well assigned and according to nature, and therefore deserve our praise: one of these is the name given to the dances of men in prosperity who are themselves handling pleasures in a well-measured way. Whoever it was at that time who named the dances, he spoke correctly, musically, and reasonably, when he gave them all the name "Harmonies," and established two forms of noble dances—the warlike or "Pyrrhic" and the peaceful or "Harmony." In each case he assigned a name that is fitting and harmonious. The lawgiver 816c should go through these dances in outline, while the Guard-

816d

816e

817a

817b

ian of the Laws should seek them out, and, once he has discovered them, should put the dances together with the rest of the music and distribute them among all the holidays, assigning what is suitable to each of the sacrifices. When he has thus sanctified all these things in an ordered arrangement, he should no longer make any change in what pertains to either dance or song. Thus the same city, with citizens that are as similar to one another as possible, should experience the same pleasures, and live well and happily.

This brings to a conclusion the discussion of how beautiful bodies and well-born souls behave in the choral performances that have been prescribed; but it is necessary to look at and get to know what pertains to shameful bodies and thoughts, as well as those who turn themselves to laughter-provoking comedies—through speech and song, dance, and the comic imitations all these contain. For someone who is going to become prudent can't learn the serious things without learning the laughable, or, for that matter, anything without its opposite. Yet one can't create in both ways if one is to partake of even a small portion of virtue, and indeed one should learn about the ridiculous things just for this reason—so that he may never do or say, through ignorance, anything that is ridiculous, if he doesn't have to. The imitation of such things should be assigned to slaves and to strangers who work for hire. There should never be any seriousness whatsoever about these things, nor should any free person, woman or man, be observed learning these things; in fact, these imitations should always manifest something new. Let the play that provokes laughter, the play we all call "comedy," be thus ordained in law and in argument.

As for what they call the "serious" poets, our tragic poets, suppose some of them should at some time come to us and ask something like this: "Strangers, shall we frequent your city and territory or not? And shall we carry and bring along our poetry, or what have you decided to do about such matters?" What kind of a reply regarding these matters would we correctly give to the divine men? For my part, I think it should be as follows: "Best of strangers," we should say, "we ourselves are poets, who have to the best of our ability created a tragedy that is the most beautiful and the best; at any rate, our whole political regime is constructed as the imitation of the most beautiful and best way of life, which we at least assert to be really the truest tragedy. Now you are poets, and we too are poets of the same things; we are your rivals as artists and performers of the most beautiful drama, which true law alone can by nature bring to perfection—as we hope. So don't suppose that we'll ever easily, at any rate, allow you to come among us, set up your stage in the marketplace, and introduce actors whose beautiful voices speak louder than ours. Don't suppose we'll easily let you make public speeches to the children and the women and the whole mob, speaking of the same pursuits that we speak of, but saying things that are in great part the most opposite to what we say. For we'd be almost completely mad—we and every city, if it allowed you to do what's just been described, before its rulers had passed a judgment on whether or not the words and practices you had created were to be spoken in its midst or not. Now then, you children descended from the soft Muses, we will first display to the rulers your songs alongside ours; if the things said by you are evidently the same, at least, or better, we will give you a chorus. But if not, friends, we could never do it." 817c 817d

Let these be the lawfully ordained customs as regards the entire choral art and the learning connected with it, the things appropriate for the slaves being kept separate from the things appropriate for the masters—if this is acceptable. 817e

Kl. At this point, at any rate, how could it not be acceptable?

Ath. For the free men there are in addition three subjects to be learned. One subject is calculation and what pertains to numbers; second is measurement of length, surface, and volume, considered as one subject; third is the way the stars revolve, in their natural relation to one another as they move. The many need not labor at all these things to the point of precise accuracy; that will be required of a certain few (who they are we will explain when we get to the end, for that would be fitting). But as for the majority, though it's shameful for the many not to know as many of these things as are in a sense very correctly called "necessary," it isn't easy, in fact it isn't at all possible, for everyone to pursue these studies to the point of precise accuracy. Of course, the necessity that inheres in these subjects can't be dispensed with, and it's likely that whoever first formulated the proverb about god was looking to these when he said that "even a god is never seen to fight against neces- 818a 818b sity"[35]—meaning, I believe, whatever necessities are divine. But as applied to human necessities, which the many look to when they utter such a thing, this is by far the most naive of all sayings.

Kl. What are the necessities in these subjects, stranger, that are not of this sort, but are instead divine?

Ath. In my opinion, they are those which one cannot avoid acting
818c according to and knowing something about if one would ever become, among human beings, a god or a demon or a hero capable of exercising serious supervision over humans. A human being, at any rate, would fall far short of becoming divine if he couldn't learn about one and two and three and in general the even and odd things, or if he didn't know anything about counting, or if he couldn't number the nights and the days, and lacked familiarity with the orbits of the moon and the sun and the other stars. It is a great stupidity to think
818d that all these aren't necessary subjects of learning for anyone who is going to know almost any of the noblest subjects of learning. What parts of each of these should be learned, and how much, and when, and which should be learned in conjunction with which, and which apart from the others, and in general the way of mixing them all—these are things that should first be grasped correctly, before going on to learn the other subjects to which these subjects lead. For thus has it been established according to natural necessity, which we assert none of the gods fights against now, nor will ever fight against.

818e Kl. It's likely at least, stranger, that what's just now been said has been said correctly somehow, and that what you say is in accordance with nature.

Ath. That is indeed the case, Kleinias—though it is difficult to legislate about these matters in this way beforehand; if it is all right with you, let's legislate in a more precise way at some other time.

Kl. You seem to us, stranger, to be frightened off by our habitual lack of familiarity with such things. But you are incorrect in this fear; try to speak up, and hide nothing on this account.

819a Ath. I do indeed fear what you're now describing, though I fear even more those who have had some contact with these studies but in a bad way. After all, extreme lack of experience in everything is not at all a terrible thing, nor is it the greatest evil; a far greater penalty is incurred by much experience, and much learning, acquired under a bad course of study.

Kl. What you say is true.

Ath. So one should declare that the free men must learn, in each of   819b
these subjects, as much as the whole mob of children in Egypt learns along with their reading lessons. In the first place, as regards calculations, lessons have been invented even for little children that involve them in play and pleasure as they learn: distributions of certain fruits and garlands so that the same numbers harmonize with more and with less, or distributions of boxers and wrestlers into byes and pairs, in turn and in sequence according to the natural order. Also, in play, they mix together flat bowls of gold, bronze, silver, and other such   819c
materials, and then divide them into wholes in various ways.[36] Thus, as I said, by harmonizing the play with the use of numerical necessities they help their students in the ordering of army camps, in marches, and in military campaigns, as well as in their households, and in general make them both more useful to themselves and more alert human beings. Then after these things they go on to measurements in length and   819d
surface and volume, dispelling a certain ridiculous and shameful ignorance which exists by nature in all human beings, as regards all these subjects.

Kl. What sort of ignorance is this you're referring to?

Ath. Kleinias my friend, when I myself heard about this at a rather late date, I too was utterly amazed to find what our situation is, in respect to these matters; it seemed to me it was one that belonged not to humanity but to the offspring of certain pigs. I was ashamed not only for myself but for all the Greeks.   819e

Kl. About what? Say what it is you're claiming, stranger.

Ath. I'm doing so. Or rather I'll show by questioning you. Answer me a small question: presumably you know about length?

Kl. How not?

Ath. What then? About surface?

Kl. In every way.

Ath. And that these are two things, and that there is a third thing besides these, namely volume?

Kl. How could there not be?

Ath. Now don't all these seem to you to be commensurable[37] with one another?

Kl. Yes.

	Ath.	Length, I believe, seems commensurable with length, and sur-
820a		face with surface, and volume, in the same way, seems by na-
		ture capable of commensurability.

Ath. Length, I believe, seems commensurable with length, and surface with surface, and volume, in the same way, seems by nature capable of commensurability.

Kl. Very much so.

Ath. But if some are not capable of it at all—neither "very much so" nor even a little bit—and some are commensurable and some are not, while you hold that all are, what do you think of your situation in respect to these things?

Kl. It's clear that it's wretched.

Ath. And what then? What about length and surface in relation to volume, or surface and length in relation to one another? Don't all we Greeks think about these things this way, as though they are somehow or other commensurable one with another?

820b Kl. Completely.

Ath. But if, again, they are not at all, in any way, and yet, as I said, all we Greeks think they are, wouldn't it be proper to feel ashamed of us all, and say to us "O best of the Greeks, isn't this one of those things which we declared it shameful not to know, although knowing such necessities is not very noble?"

Kl. How could it not be?

820c Ath. And there are, in addition, other matters akin to these, which again involve us in many errors that are the brothers of those errors.

Kl. Which matters?

Ath. The relations commensurables and incommensurables have to one another because of a certain nature. For it is necessary to investigate and get to know the difference between these, if one is not to be utterly wretched. By constantly proposing problems of this kind to one another, they should pass their time in a manner much more graceful for old men than playing at draughts, and thus indulge their love of victory in leisure pursuits that are worthy of them.

820d Kl. Perhaps. It is likely, anyway, that draughts and these subjects of learning are not very widely separated from one another.

Ath. For my part, Kleinias, I assert that the young should learn these things. For they aren't harmful or difficult, and if they're learned during play they'll bring benefit, while in no way harming our city. But if someone says otherwise, he should be heard.

Kl. How else?

[212]

Ath. Well then, if these activities evidently proceed thus, it's clear that we'll judge them acceptable; but if it should appear that they don't proceed in this way, they'll be judged unacceptable.

Kl. Clearly, how else? 820e

Ath. So now, stranger, shall these things be laid down as belonging to the required subjects of study, so that there won't be gaps in our laws? Let them be laid down like deposits, outside the rest of the political regime, redeemable in case either we, the depositors, or you, the holders, find the pledge in no way welcome.

Kl. You are describing a just deposit.

Ath. Next after these things see if what the young are to learn about the stars suits us, as it's stated, or the opposite.

Kl. Just state it.

Ath. Well, there's something very amazing involved in these things, something that's simply intolerable in every way.

Kl. What's that? 821a

Ath. With regard to the greatest god, and the cosmos as a whole, we assert that one should not conduct investigations nor busy oneself with trying to discover the causes—for it is not pious to do so. Yet it's likely that if entirely the opposite of this took place it would be correct.

Kl. What do you mean?

Ath. The thing being said is paradoxical, and one may think it unfitting for older men. But when someone thinks there's a subject of learning that is noble, true, beneficial to the city, and dear in every way to the god, it is in no way possible for him 821b to refrain from telling about it.

Kl. What you say is likely; but what subject of this sort will we find in what pertains to the stars?

Ath. Good sirs, all of us Greeks, so to speak, nowadays tell a falsehood about the great gods, Sun and also Moon.

Kl. What falsehood?

Ath. We claim they never keep to the same path, and we say there are other stars that also don't, which we name "wanderers."[38]

Kl. By Zeus, stranger! This is true, what you say! For in my life- 821c time I myself have often seen the Morning Star and the Evening Star, and certain others, never going along the same course, but wandering all over the place; and I suppose we all know that the sun and the moon do these things all the time.[39]

[213]

Ath.   These are the things, Megillus and Kleinias, I now assert that
821d   our citizens and our young people, at least, ought to learn
         about the heavenly gods; they should learn enough about all
         of these things so that they won't utter blasphemies about
         them, but will always speak of them auspiciously, while sacri-
         ficing or engaged in reverent prayer.

Kl.   That is correct—if, that is, it is first possible to learn about
         what you refer to. If so, and if we now say something about
         them that is incorrect, and through learning will speak cor-
         rectly, then I too agree that to this extent, at least, this kind of
         thing should be learned. These things being so, you try to
         explain fully what you mean, and we'll try to learn by follow-
         ing you.

821e   Ath.   But it isn't easy to learn what I'm speaking of. On the other
         hand, it isn't totally difficult, nor does it require a great deal of
         time. The proof is that I, who heard about this when I was no
         longer young—in fact not so long ago—could make it clear to
         you two without taking up much time. If the subject were a
         difficult one, I would never be able, at my age, to make it clear
         to men of your age.

Kl.   What you say is true. But what do you claim this subject mat-
822a   ter is, that you say is amazing, and appropriate for the young
         to learn, but that we are ignorant of? Try to explain this much
         about it, at least, as clearly as possible.

Ath.   It ought to be attempted. Best of men, that dogma is incorrect
         which holds that the moon, the sun, and other stars some-
         times wander. The case is entirely the opposite to this: each of
         them always moves in the same circular path, which is one
         and not many—though each appears to move in many. More-
         over, the swiftest of them is incorrectly opined to be the
822b   slowest, and vice versa. If this is the way these things are by
         nature, but our opinion holds things to be otherwise—well, if
         in the races of horses or long-distance runners at Olympia we
         considered things in this way, announcing the fastest as the
         slowest and the slowest as the fastest, and creating encomia in
         which we sang of the defeated as though he were victor, I
         think we would be singing encomia that were both incorrect
         and not pleasing to the runners, who would be human. But
         now, when it's the gods that we're making the same mistakes
822c   about, don't we suppose that what was laughable and incor-
         rect in the earlier case will be not at all laughable in the present

[214]

case, and as applied to these—for surely it is not at all pleasing to the gods for us to be singing hymns about gods that contain a false report?

Kl.   That is very true, if indeed this is the way these things are.

Ath.   So if we do demonstrate that this is the way these things are, then all such things should be learned, to this extent at least, but if the demonstration fails, these things ought to be left alone? Shall we agree in this way about these matters?

Kl.   By all means.   822d

Ath.   At this point one should declare that the legal customs regarding the subjects of learning that pertain to education have reached their end.[40] But about hunting and all things of that sort one should think in the very same way. For there is a risk that the task of the legislator involves yet more than just the laying down of laws and thus being finished, and that there is something else in addition to laws, something that by nature lies in the middle between admonition and laws. We have come across this often in our discussions, as in those concern-   822e ing the rearing of very young children. We assert that these things shouldn't be left unmentioned, but that to suppose, in speaking about them, that they are being laid down as laws would be great folly. Indeed, even when the laws and the whole political regime have been thus written down, the praise accorded to the citizen distinguished as regards virtue is not complete when someone declares that he serves the laws best and is especially obedient to them, and that this constitutes a good man. A more perfect sort of praise is that which speaks of a man who has passed his life in unbroken obedience to those writings in which the lawgiver legislates,   823a praises, and blames. This is the speech that is most correct as regards praise of a citizen. And what is really required of a lawgiver is that he write not only laws, but, in addition to laws, things interwoven with the laws, writings that reveal what seems noble and ignoble to him. The highest citizen is limited by these things no less than by the things sanctioned by legal penalties. We would make clearer what we mean if we brought forward as a sort of witness the present subject matter.

For hunting is a very widely extended activity even though   823b it is now comprehended, for the most part, in a single name. There is much hunting of things in water, and much of winged things, and very much of beasts who move on their feet, which includes not only wild beasts but also a hunting of human beings which is worth reflection. One sort occurs in warfare, but there is also a great deal of hunting—sometimes praiseworthy, sometimes blameable—that occurs through friendship. The assaults of robbers and of armies against armies are hunts. Now the lawgiver who is laying down the laws about hunting can't avoid clarifying these things, and yet he can't establish threatening legal customs that give orders and penalties to every sort of hunting. So what should be done about such matters? The one party, the lawgiver, ought to praise and blame what pertains to hunting with a view to the exercises and practices of the young; the other party, the young man, should obey what he hears, without allowing himself to be deflected either by pleasure or by toil. At the same time, he should honor more, and carry out more fully, the orders uttered in praises than either the threats accompanied by penalties or the things legislated.

Having said these things as a preliminary, what would come next is a measured praise and blame as regards hunting; there should be praise for the sort that makes the souls of the young better and blame for the opposite sorts. So let's say what comes next in order, addressing the young through prayer:

"O friends, may you never be seized by a desire or an erotic love for hunting on the sea, for angling, or in general for hunting of the animals that dwell in water, or for those basket-traps that perform the toil of a lazy hunt, whether the hunters are awake or asleep! May there never come over you a longing for the catching of humans by sea, and piracy, and may you never thus be made cruel and lawless hunters! May it never enter your minds in the least to engage in theft, in the countryside or in the city! May a seductive, erotic love of bird-hunting, which is hardly a liberal pursuit, never come over any of the young!

"What is left for our athletes is only the hunting and catching of animals that move on their feet. One branch of this, practiced by men who take turns sleeping, is called night-hunting; it belongs to idle men and is not worthy of praise. The same holds for the sort of hunting that provides periods of rest from toils because the hunters depend on nets and snares, instead of on the victory of a soul that likes struggle, to handle the fierce strength of the wild beasts. What alone remains and is best for everyone is the hunting of four-footed prey that employs horses, dogs, and the bodies of the hunters themselves. In this type the hunters use running, blows, and missiles thrown by their own hands to prevail over all their prey, and this is the type that should be practiced by whoever cultivates the courage that is divine."

Let the speech just uttered constitute the praise and blame pertaining to all these things; the law is as follows:

No one is to prevent these hunters, who are really sacred, from hunting with dogs whenever and however they please, but no one is ever to allow the night-hunter, who trusts in nets and traps, to hunt anywhere. The bird-hunter is not to be hindered on land that is not in use or on mountainsides, but anyone who happens along should put a stop to it on cultivated or sacred land. The water-hunter is not to be hindered, except in harbors, sacred streams, ponds, and reservoirs. Elsewhere he is permitted to hunt, so long as he doesn't muddy the waters with juices.

So now at this point one should declare that all the legal customs that pertain to education have reached their end.[41]

Kl.   And nobly would you say it.

BOOK VIII

828a   Ath.   Following on these things, the festivals need to be arranged and legislated. Delphic oracles will help indicate which sacrifices, to which of the gods, it would be better and more agreeable [1] for the city to perform; but as for when they should take place, and what their number should be, that legislation is probably up to us—at least in the case of some of the festivals.

    Kl.   Probably as regards the number.

    Ath.   The number, then, is what we should speak of first. Let there
828b   be three hundred sixty-five without any omissions, so that there will always be at least one magistrate performing a sacrifice to some god or demon, on behalf of the city, the people, and their possessions. The Interpreters, Priests and Priestesses, and Diviners should get together with the appointed Guardians of the Laws to arrange whatever the lawgiver is forced to leave incomplete in regard to these matters. These same persons are the ones who must determine just what he
828c   has left incomplete. The law itself will proclaim twelve festivals for the twelve gods, each of whom has a tribe named after him. They'll make sacred monthly sacrifices to each of these, along with choruses, musical contests, and gymnastic contests, distributing them in a way that befits both the gods themselves and each of the seasons. They'll also distribute women's festivals, both those that are appropriately celebrated apart from the men and those that are not. Furthermore, what pertains to the underworld gods should not be mixed with what pertains to the gods whom we ought to call

"heavenly" or with what belongs to them; these underworld rites they should keep separate and assign, according to law, to Pluto's month, the twelfth month.[2] Nor should warlike human beings abhor such a god; they should rather honor him as being always the best for the human race, because, I would seriously affirm, for soul and body, community is not superior to dissolution. 828d

In addition to these things, those who are going to make adequate distinctions in these affairs should keep in mind some such things as the following: one wouldn't find, nowadays, another city the equal of ours in its provision of leisure time or of the necessities, but it is nonetheless necessary for this city, just as for a single human being, to live well. Now those who live happily must first avoid doing injustice to others and suffering injustice themselves at the hands of others. Of these two, the former is not very difficult, but what is very difficult is acquiring the power that prevents being done injustice—this cannot be completely achieved unless one becomes completely good. This very same thing applies to a city: if it becomes good it lives a life of peace, but it lives a life of external and internal war if it is evil. Since this is just about the way things are, no one should wait until wartime to exercise the gymnastic of war, but all should do so while living at peace. So any city that possesses intelligence should engage in army maneuvers not less than one day every month, and even more if the rulers think it advisable. They should exercise paying no heed to cold or hot weather—themselves and their women and children as well—whenever the rulers think it fitting to lead the whole populace out; then at other times they'll be led out in sections. They should always be devising noble games to accompany the sacrifices, so that there'll be certain festival battles that imitate as clearly as possible the battles of war. On every such occasion prizes should be distributed for victory or prowess, and they should compose for one another poems of praise and blame that reflect what sort of person each is becoming both in the contests and in life as a whole, adorning the one who seems to be best and blaming the one who does not. And the poet who composes such things shouldn't be just anyone. First of all, he must be at least fifty years of age; then again, he can't be one of those who possess poetry and the Muse within themselves in an adequate way, but have never 829a 829b 829c 829d performed a noble and conspicuous deed. What should be sung are the poems of those who are good and honored in the city, those who are artists of noble deeds, even if their compositions are not by nature musical. The selection of these men will belong to the Educator and the other Guardians of the Laws. They will give to these men the prize of being the only ones who may have freedom of speech in musical compositions, while all the others will lack this privilege. Let no one dare to sing a Muse judged unseemly by the Guardians of

829e the Laws, not even if She is sweeter than the hymns of Thamyrus or Orpheus;[3] instead, let them sing the poems that have been judged sound and consecrated to the gods, as well as the songs of blame or praise composed by good men who are judged to have spoken in a well-measured way. As regards both the military and the freedom of speech in poetry, I say that the same regulations should apply equally to women and to men.

Now there are some other considerations the lawgiver ought to alert himself to, by reasoning with himself: "Come now, what sort of people am I rearing by putting together this

830a entire city? Aren't they athletes in the greatest of contests, in which they are confronted with tens of thousands of competitors?"—"Certainly," someone who spoke correctly would reply.—"What then? If we had been rearing boxers, or pankratists,[4] or athletes in some other of such contests, would we have entered the competition without having spent the time before in daily fighting practice against someone? If we were boxers, at any rate, wouldn't we for very many days

830b before the contest have been learning to fight and practicing, imitating all those things we intended to use later on when we fought for victory, and coming as close as we could to resemblance, putting on padded gloves instead of thongs in order to do what we could to practice in an adequate way the striking and eluding of blows? And if we ran short of gymnastic sparring partners would we fear the laughter of mindless people, and not dare to hang up a dummy lacking any soul, and carry out our gymnastic against that? And if we then ran short

830c of both all the opponents with souls and opponents without souls, in the absence of gymnastic partners wouldn't we dare to literally shadowbox against ourselves? Or what else would someone ever call the sort of practice where one just gesticulates?"

Kl.   Probably nothing other than what you've just said, stranger.

Ath.   What then? Will the fighting force of our city dare to enter the greatest of contests, each time, with a preparation inferior to that of the contests just mentioned? Is this the way it would enter the contest where what is at stake is the soul, children,   830d
property, and the whole city? Will their lawgiver, because he fears that the way they carry on these gymnastic exercises with one another might appear ridiculous to some, fail to legislate military exercises of a minor sort, without heavy arms, for nearly every day? Will he fail to aim at this in setting up choruses and the whole gymnastic art? Won't he order that certain major gymnastic exercises with heavy arms be held no   830e
less than once a month, where they must struggle with one another over every point of the territory, competing to capture positions and set ambushes? Won't he have them imitate the whole art of war so that they are actually "fighting with padded practice gloves," using missiles that come as near as possible to true ones, though with less risky weapons? That way, the play they engage in with one another will not be altogether lacking in fear, and through the fear it will in a certain way make apparent who has a stout soul and who does not; as a result, couldn't he correctly assign honors to the former and   831a
dishonor to the latter, thereby equipping the whole city to be serviceable in the true contest it must wage throughout life? And moreover, if someone should die as a result of these exercises, wouldn't the murder be considered involuntary, and wouldn't the lawgiver decree that the killer's hands are clean once he's undergone the lawful purification, figuring that not many human beings will die this way, and that others no worse will grow[5] to take their place, but that if fear should, as it were, die, then he could not find another way of testing, in all such exercises, who is better and who is worse, and that for the city this would be a much greater evil?   831b

Kl.   We at least would go along in declaring, stranger, that such things should be legislated and practiced by the whole city.

Ath.   Do we all know the reason why in cities nowadays such choral activity and contests are almost in no way practiced, except perhaps to a very small degree? Shall we assert that the situation is due to the ignorance of the many and of those who give them their laws?

Kl.   Probably.

831c   Ath.   Not at all, O blessed Kleinias! One should assert there are two quite sufficient causes of these things.

       Kl.   What are they?

       Ath.   One is the erotic love of wealth, that prevents a person from having leisure to look after anything except his private possessions; hanging on these, the entire soul of every citizen would never be capable of caring for anything other than daily gain. Whatever learning or practice conduces to this, everyone in

831d   private is most eager to learn or pursue—but the rest he laughs at. This single thing, then, is one reason that should be stated to explain why a city is unwilling to undertake in a serious way this or any other noble and good activity, but, on account of an insatiable greed for gold and silver, every man is willing to put up with every art and contrivance, whether it be more noble or more unseemly, if it will make him wealthy, and is willing to perform without disgust any action, whether pious, or impious, or utterly shameful, if only it gives him, like a

831e   beast, the power to eat and drink all sorts of things and provides him with total gratification of every sexual lust.

       Kl.   That is correct.

       Ath.   Let this, then—which I'm stating—be set down as one cause that prevents cities from practicing everything else noble and in particular the adequate preparations for war; it turns those human beings who are orderly by nature into merchants, commercial ship traders, and complete servants, and makes

832a   those who are courageous into pirates, housebreakers, temple robbers, warriors, and tyrannical types—and sometimes they aren't deficient in nature, but only in luck.

       Kl.   What do you mean?

       Ath.   How could I not speak of them as totally unlucky—those, at any rate, who are compelled to live out their lives with their own souls always hungry?

       Kl.   So this is one—now what do you say the second cause is, stranger?

       Ath.   It's fine of you to remind me . . .

832b   Kl.[6]   This is one, you're saying—a lifelong, insatiable quest that leaves each man without leisure, and becomes an obstacle to each man's noble preparation for war. So be it. Now say what the second cause is.

       Ath.   Do I give the impression that I'm failing to speak and taking up time because I'm at a loss?

Kl.   No, but you do give us the impression that you're so filled with hatred that you chastise this sort of disposition more than is required by the present argument.

Ath.   You have rebuked me in a very fine way, strangers. And it's likely that you would like to hear what comes next.

Kl.   So speak!

Ath.   I at least affirm that the causes are the nonregimes which I've often mentioned in the earlier arguments—democracy and oligarchy and tyranny. None of these is a regime, but all would most correctly be termed "factions." For none of them constitutes a voluntary rule over voluntary subjects, but instead a voluntary rule, always with some violence, over involuntary subjects. Since he is afraid, the one ruling will never voluntarily allow the one ruled to become noble, or wealthy, or strong, or courageous, or in any way warlike. These, then, are the two principal causes of nearly everything, and certainly of the things just mentioned. Now the present regime, which we are legislating, has escaped both of the causes we've described. For it presumably dwells in the greatest leisure, and they are free as regards one another, and because of these laws they would be the least likely, I think, to become lovers of money. So it's likely and reasonable that the establishing of such a regime would, alone of all existing regimes, allow for the warrior education and play that has been elaborated, once the elaboration has been correctly completed in speech.

832c

832d

Kl.   Nobly spoken.

Ath.   Following on these things, shouldn't it be borne in mind, in regard to all the gymnastic contests, that any which are for the sake of war are to be practiced and to have victory prizes, but any which are not are to be passed over? But it would be better if their character were described and legislated from the beginning. First of all, shouldn't one set up the contests in running and in speed generally?

832e

Kl.   Yes, that's what should be set up.

Ath.   Surely the most important thing for war is total bodily keenness, one part of which pertains to the feet and the other to the hands. Keenness of the feet allows one to flee and to effect captures, while the other is for the close, stand-up fighting that requires sturdiness and strength.

833a

Kl.   But of course.

Ath.   Neither is of very great use, however, without weapons.

Kl. How could it be?

Ath. First, then, our herald will call the stade[7] runner to the contests, just as is done nowadays, but the runner will come forth fully armed: we won't establish prizes for an unarmed contestant. So first will come the contestant who runs the stade with
833b heavy weapons, second the double-stade runner, third the horse-length[8] runner, fourth the long-distance runner, and fifth will be a race in which the first, armed, runner is called "heavily-armed" because of the weight of arms he carries, and whom we'll require to run a length of sixty stades over more level ground to some temple of Ares and back, while his competitor, an archer fully equipped in archer's gear, is required to run one hundred stades over hills and all sorts of ground to
833c some temple of Apollo and Artemis, and then back. Having set up the contest we'll await their return and then give the victory prizes to each of the winners.

Kl. Correctly spoken.

Ath. We should think of these contests as divided into three categories, one for children, one for the beardless boys, and one for the men. For the beardless boys we should set races of two-thirds length and for the children races of half-length, whether they contend as archers or in full armor. As for the women, girls who have not reached puberty should compete naked in
833d the stade, double-stade, horse-length, and long-distance run, within the racing stadium itself; unmarried girls over thirteen should continue to take part at least until they are eighteen, but not after they have reached twenty, and they should come down to compete in these races clothed in suitable garments. Let these be the arrangements for races, for men and women.

With regard to contests of strength, instead of the wrestling
833e matches and all those other sorts of difficult contests held nowadays, there'll be combat in heavy armor—one against one, and two against two, and so on up to ten against ten competing with one another. What it is one needs to avoid or to inflict in order to win, and how much of this one must succeed in doing, is something that should be determined just as is done now in wrestling, where those who are involved in wrestling have themselves established laws regulating what action belongs to fine wrestling and what to wrestling that isn't fine: in the same way, those who are the top fighters in heavy armor should be called in and asked to help lay down

laws determining who is justly the victor in these battles and what it is such a victor should avoid or inflict, and similarly what rules decide who is defeated. The same things should be legislated for the females who are not yet married. 834a

The fighting part of the pankration[9] should be replaced by the whole art of lightly-armed combat, with bows and arrows, light shields, javelins, and stones thrown by hand or by slings. There should be laws regulating these competitors also, distributing prizes and victories to the one who most nobly fulfills the conventions.

Next in order after these things would come legislation about contests with horses. But we don't have much use for horses in any great number, inasmuch as we're in Crete, so it's inevitable that there's not much serious attention paid either to their rearing or to contests for them. No one at all maintains a chariot among us, nor would there be any appreciable love of honor connected with these matters, so that to set up contests of this sort, not native to the land, would both seem and be mindless. But if we were to establish prizes for single horsemen—riding on colts who have not yet shed their foal teeth, horses whose age is between full-grown horses and such colts, and full-grown horses—we would be establishing a sport for horses that is suitable to the nature of the land. So let there be lawful contests and competitions for victory among such riders, and let the Tribe Commanders and Cavalry Commanders share in judging both all the races themselves and the dismounting armed competitors. We would legislate incorrectly if we were to establish contests for those without weapons either in gymnastics or in the present case; and since the mounted Cretan archer or javelin thrower is not without value, let there be strife and contests, for the sake of play, in these categories too. It isn't worth the trouble to compel females, by laws and commands, to take a common share in these contests, but if from a habitual disposition developed in the earlier games their nature permits such activity and does not take it ill, then girls and virgins should be allowed to participate without incurring blame. 834b 834c 834d

Now at this point contests, and the learning of the gymnastic art—both what pertains to contests and what we must work at each day in school—are subjects that have been entirely completed. Most of the subject of music has also been simi- 834e larly completed, although the arrangements for rhapsodes, their retinue, and the necessary choral contests during the festivals will be made after the months and days and years have been assigned to the gods and those who accompany the gods;

835a at that point it can be determined whether the festivals are to be held every third year or every fifth year, or how and in what way they are to be distributed, in accordance with the indications the gods may give of their preferences as to the order. On the same occasions it is to be expected that the musical contests will be held, each in turn. They will have been arranged by the Regulators of the Games, the Educator of the Young, and the Guardians of the Laws, who will have met together and become themselves legislators in these matters. They will decide, with respect to all choruses and choral contests, when they are to be held, who is to perform, and who is to accompany the performers. The first lawgiver has often explained what ought to be established for each contest as

835b regards the words, the songs, and the harmoniae mixed with rhythms and dances; the lawgivers who come second should follow these guidelines as they take up the task, arranging, at appropriate times, contests that befit each sacrifice, and thus giving the city its festivals to celebrate.

It isn't difficult to know how these and other such matters should be put in lawful order, and if they are altered here and

835c there the city would neither gain much nor suffer much of a penalty. But there are other matters which make no small difference, about which it is difficult to be persuasive, and which are in fact the task of the god, if it were somehow possible to get the orders themselves from him; as things stand now, what is required, in all probability, is some daring human being, who by giving unusual honor to outspokenness will say what in his opinion is best for the city and the citizens. Speaking before an audience of corrupt souls, he will order what is fitting and becoming to the whole political regime; opposing the greatest desires, and having no human ally, all alone he will follow reason alone.

835d Kl. Just what argument is it again that we're now pronouncing, stranger? For we don't yet understand.

Ath. That's not surprising; I'll try to explain it to you yet more clearly. When I arrived, in the course of the argument, at edu-

cation, I saw young men and young women mixing together affectionately. As might be expected, a fear came over me as I reflected on the problem of how someone will manage a city like this, in which young men and women are well reared, and released from the severe and illiberal tasks that do the most to   835e
quench wantonness; and where sacrifices, festivals, and choruses are the preoccupations of everyone throughout their whole lives. How, in this city, will they ever avoid the desires that frequently cast many down into the depths, the desires that reason, striving to become law, orders them to avoid? It won't be surprising if the legal customs ordained earlier should predominate over the mass of desires: the fact that it's   836a
impossible to get terrifically rich is no small benefit to moderation; the education as a whole has well-measured laws that promote such things; and in addition, there is the trained eye of the rulers which never looks elsewhere but is always watching things, including the young themselves, so as to limit the other desires as much, at least, as is humanly possible. But with regard to the erotic love of and for children—both male and female—and the erotic love of women for men and of men   836b
for women, whence tens of thousands of things have happened to human beings in private and to whole cities, how could one take proper precautions? And what sort of medicine will one apply, in each of these cases, so as to find an escape from the danger? It is in no way easy, Kleinias. For although in quite a few other matters Crete as a whole and Lacedaimon have been decent enough to give us considerable aid as we establish laws that differ from the ways of many, in regard to erotic things—speaking now among ourselves—they are to-   836c
tally opposed to us. If someone were to follow nature and lay down the law that prevailed before Laius,[10] if he were to say that it was correct to avoid, with males and youths, sexual relations like those one has with females, bringing as a witness the nature of the beasts and demonstrating that males don't touch males with a view to such things because it is not according to nature to do so, his argument would probably be unpersuasive, and not at all in consonance with your cities.[11]

But in addition, these practices do not agree with what we   836d
assert should always be the object of the lawgiver's care. For we are always seeking which establishments are conducive to virtue and which are not. Come, suppose we were to agree

that the present legislation says this sort of activity is noble or at least in no way shameful, to what extent would this help us promote virtue? Will a courageous disposition be nourished [12] in the soul of the seduced, or will the offspring of the *idea* of a moderate man be nourished in the soul of the seducer? Or isn't it the case that nobody would ever be seduced by such

836e

claims, but rather everyone expects just the opposite, blaming the softness of the one who gives in to the pleasures and is incapable of mastering them, and reproving the resemblance in image presented by the one who undertakes the imitation of the female? What human being will ever legislate such a practice as this? Hardly anyone, at least if he has true law in his mind. But how then do we affirm that this is true? If someone is going to think these things through in a correct manner, he

837a

must necessarily examine the nature of friendship, of desire, and of what are called "the erotic desires." For there are two entities here, and from their combination comes yet a third form, but because they are all given just one name, total confusion and obscurity is created.

Kl.　How so?

Ath.　Well, presumably we use the term "friend" to characterize the relationship between similars in point of virtue, and also the relationship between equals; then again, the term "friend" also characterizes the needy in its relationship to the wealthy, where they are opposite in kind. And when either of these becomes vehement, we name it "erotic love."

837b Kl.　That is correct.

Ath.　Now the friendship between opposites is terrible and savage, and is seldom mutual among us, while the friendship between those who are similar is gentle and mutual throughout life. As for the friendship that is a mixture of these, it is in the first place not easy to learn what the one who has this third erotic attraction might ever want to obtain for himself. Moreover, because he's drawn in opposite directions by the two loves, he finds himself at a loss, with one bidding him to pick the bloom

837c

of youth and the other telling him not to. For the man who loves the body, hungering for the bloom as for ripe fruit, bids himself take his fill without honoring the disposition of soul of the beloved. The other sort of lover holds the desire for the body to be secondary; looking at it rather than loving it, with his soul he really desires the soul of the other and considers the gratification of body by body to be wantonness. He holds in awe and reverence what is moderate, courageous, magnificent, and prudent, and would wish to remain always chaste with a beloved who is chaste. This love mixed from these two is the one we characterized a moment ago as the "third."   837d

Since this is how many categories there are, should the law exclude all of them and prevent them from arising among us, or isn't it obvious that we would want to have in our city the type which belongs to virtue and desires that the youth become as excellent as possible, while we would forbid the other two, if we could? What shall we say, Megillus, my friend?

Meg. What you have said now about these particular matters is in   837e
every way fine, stranger.

Ath. It looks like—as I guessed—I've obtained your harmonious assent, dear friend. I don't need to inquire what the law among your people thinks about such things—it's sufficient to accept your agreement to the argument. Later on I'll come back to these same matters and try to use incantations to persuade Kleinias. For now let's let it stand that you've both granted assent to me, and so proceed through all the laws.

Meg. Very correctly spoken.

Ath. In order to establish this law, I have now a certain art, which   838a
will be in one respect easy to employ but in another respect extremely difficult in every way.

Meg. What do you mean?

Ath. Presumably, we know that even at the present time most human beings, however lawless they may be, nevertheless punctiliously refrain from intercourse with beautiful persons, and do so not involuntarily, but with the greatest possible willingness.

Meg. When do you mean?

Ath. When the beautiful person is one's brother or sister. More-   838b
over, with regard to a son or daughter, the same unwritten law guards in a very effective way, as it were, against touching them—by open or secret sleeping together, or by any other sort of embracing. In fact, among the many there isn't the slightest desire for this sort of intercourse.

Meg. What you're saying is true.

Ath. And isn't it just a little phrase that quenches all such pleasures?

Meg. What phrase are you referring to?

838c   **Ath.**   The phrase that declares these things are not at all pious, but are hateful to the gods and the most shameful of shameful things. Isn't the cause the fact that no one ever says anything else, but from the moment of birth each of us hears people saying these things, always and everywhere? In jokes and in every serious tragedy isn't it frequently said, and when they bring on Thyestes-figures or certain Oedipuses, or certain Macareuses, who secretly have intercourse with their sisters, isn't it seen that they promptly inflict upon themselves the just punishment of death for their crime? [13]

838d   **Meg.**   You are quite correct to this extent: when no one ever even tries to breathe against the law in any way, then the pronouncement has an amazing power.

      Ath.   So what was said a moment ago is correct: when a lawgiver wishes to enslave a certain desire which especially enslaves human beings, it's easy to know, at least, how he should handle it. By having everyone—slaves, free men, children, women, the whole city in agreement together—hold this pronouncement to be something sacred, he will have succeeded in making this law very firm.

838e

      Meg.   That's certainly so. But now how it will ever be possible to arrange things so that everyone is willing to say such a thing—

      Ath.   —It's fine of you to take me up this way. For this was the very thing I said, that in regard to this law I had an art that would promote the natural use of sexual intercourse for the production of children—by abstaining on the one hand from intercourse with males, the deliberate killing of the human race, as

839a   well as from the wasting of sperm on rocks or stones where it will never take root and generate a natural offspring, and on the other hand by abstaining from any female field in which you wouldn't wish your sperm to grow. [14] If this law becomes permanent and holds sway (if it were justly victorious in the other cases, as it is now in regard to intercourse on the part of parents), tens of thousands of good things would result. For in the first place, it is laid down according to nature; then too, it will prevent erotic frenzy and madness, as well as all adul-

839b   teries, and all excessive drinking and eating, and will make men familiar with and dear to their own wives. Indeed, there are very many other good things that would come to pass, if someone had enough control to pass this law. But if there were standing here some vehement young man full of a lot of sperm who had been listening to the laying down of the law, he would probably revile us for setting up mindless and impossible customs, and would fill the air with his clamor. It was with a view to such that I made my pronouncement, about a certain art I possessed, in one respect the easiest of all things to apply 839c and in another respect the most difficult, which would promote the permanent establishment of this law. It's very easy to understand that it's possible and in what way: we assert that if this custom is sufficiently sanctified, it will enslave every soul and instill it with a fear that will insure its total obedience to the established laws. But a point has now been reached where it doesn't seem that this law would take hold even under those conditions. The same sort of thing occurs in the case of the practice of common meals—it's not believed that an entire city 839d can live practicing this throughout its life. Yet the disbelief was refuted by the deed, by the fact that it actually came to pass among your people—although with regard to women it still doesn't seem natural to your cities. It's because of this, because of the strength such disbelief possesses, that I have described both these practices as things that are very difficult to make permanent in the law.

Meg. What you say is correct, at any rate.

Ath. But do you want me to try to present to you two a somewhat persuasive argument to the effect that it is not beyond human ability, but is in fact possible?

Kl. Sure, why not?

Ath. Would someone more easily refrain from sexual things, and be 839e more willing to follow in a measured way the relevant ordinance, if his body were in good shape and not lacking in training, or if it were in poor shape?

Kl. Much more easily, I suppose, if he's not lacking in training.

Ath. Well, then, don't we know by hearsay about Iccus of Tarentum, because he competed in the Olympian and other con- 840a tests? He was so filled with love of victory, and possessed in his soul such art, and such courage mixed with moderation, that he never touched a woman—or a boy, for that matter— during the entire time of his intensive training. So the account goes. The same account is presumably given of Crison, and Astylus, and Diopompus, and very many others.¹⁵ And their souls were much less well educated than the citizens that belong to me and you, Kleinias, while their bodies were much 840b more full blooded.

Kl. It's true, as you say, that the ancient stories confidently report these things as really having happened with regard to these athletes.

Ath. What then? Those fellows, for the sake of victory in wrestling and running and that sort of thing, had the heart to refrain from an activity that the many say is happy; now will our children be unable to restrain themselves for the sake of a much nobler victory, whose great beauty we will have, it is likely, enchanted them with from the time they were babies,

840c   using spellbinding myths, speeches, and songs?

Kl. Which victory?

Ath. The victory over pleasures. If they master pleasures they will live happily, but if they're defeated by them they'll experience entirely the opposite. And besides, can't we expect that their fear that the thing is in no way pious will give us the capacity to master what people inferior to these have shown the capacity to master?

Kl. That's likely, anyway.

Ath. Since we've come to such a pass with regard to this custom,

840d   having fallen into perplexity because of the depravity of the many, I assert that the only thing left for our custom to do is to plunge on, saying that our citizens must not be inferior to the birds and many of the other beasts, who are born amid great flocks and live celibate, pure, and chaste, until the time of child-rearing; then when they arrive at this age they pair off, male with female according to preference, and female with male, and live out the rest of their lives in pious and just fash-

840e   ion, remaining steadfast to the first agreements of friendship. Now surely they ought to be superior to the beasts, at least! But, if they become corrupted by the other Greeks and most of the barbarians, by seeing among themselves and hearing about the very great power of the so-called "disorderly Aphrodite," and so are incapable of mastering it, then the Guardians of the Laws, becoming lawgivers, will have to devise for them a second law.

841a Kl. What law would you advise them to establish, if the one being laid down now escapes them?

Ath. Obviously the one that comes right after this one would be the second law, Kleinias.

Kl. Which do you refer to?

Ath. The strength of the pleasures should, as much as possible, be deprived of gymnastic exercise by using other exercises to turn its flow and growth elsewhere in the body. This would be the case if the indulgence in sexual things never occurred without a sense of awe. For if shame made their indulgence 841b rare, the infrequency would weaken the sway over them of this mistress. So let it be the custom laid down in habit and unwritten law, that among them it is noble to engage in these activities if one escapes notice, but shameful if one doesn't escape notice—though they are not to abstain entirely. Thus our law would come to possess a second-rank standard of the shameful and the noble, a second-rank correctness, and those whose natures have been corrupted—whom we proclaim to be 841c "weaker than themselves"—being one tribe, would be surrounded and forcibly prevented from disobeying the law by three tribes.

Kl. Which are these?

Ath. Reverence for the gods, and also love of honor, and being desirous not of bodies but of the beautiful characteristics of souls. These things that have now been said, perhaps as if in a myth, are prayers; if they should come to pass they would bring about by far the best effects in all cities. But maybe, if a god would be willing, we could enforce one of two ordinances 841d regarding erotic matters:

Either no one is to dare to touch any well-born and free person except the woman who is his wife, and no one is to sow unhallowed, bastard sperm in concubines or go against nature and sow sterile seed in males; *or* we should abolish erotic activity between males altogether, and in the case of women, if anyone should have sexual intercourse with a woman other than those who enter his house with the sanction of the gods and the sacred marriage ceremonies, whether they be purchased or secured in any other way, and fails to escape the no- 841e tice of all men and women, we would probably seem to be legislating correctly if we legislated that he should be barred from all honors in the city on the grounds that he is really a stranger.

Let this law, whether it ought to be called one law or two, be laid down concerning sexual matters and all the erotic things: 842a it regulates our mingling with one another caused by such desires, both when we act correctly and when we act incorrectly.

Meg. Stranger, *I* would readily accept this law from you, but

Kleinias ought to express for himself what he thinks of these
matters.

Kl. That will be done, Megillus, when I think an opportune time
has arrived. For now, let's allow the stranger to go ahead still
further with the laws.

Meg. Correctly spoken.

842b Ath. Well, if we go ahead we find that we're now just about at the
point where the common meals have been set up. We assert
that elsewhere this would create difficulty, but that in Crete
nobody would suppose there ought to be any other arrangement. As to the way they are to be organized—whether as
they are here or as they are in Lacedaimon,[16] or whether there
is yet some third form of common meals better than both of
these two—I don't think it's a very difficult matter to figure
out, and no great advantage is to be had by figuring it out:
they're well arranged now.

842c   Following upon these things is the arranging of the means
of livelihood, and the way in which these meals are to be
supplied. In other cities there would be many kinds of food
from many sources, and they would have at least twice the
resources of these people, since most Greeks get what pertains
to nourishment from both the land and the sea, while these
people get it from the land alone. For the lawgiver this makes

842d   things easier. They'll need only half as many laws, or even far
less than half, and the laws are more fitting for free human beings. The lawgiver for this city can just say good-bye to most
of what pertains to shipowning, wholesale trading, retail mer-
chandising, innkeeping, customs duties, mining, loans, com-
pound interest, and tens of thousands of other such things,
and proceed to give laws regulating farmers, herdsmen, bee-

842e   keepers, and those who guard such things and take care of the
tools. The most important things have already been taken care
of in legislation—marriage, the generation and rearing of children, and then also education and the institution of ruling
officers in the city. Now he is compelled to turn to the legislation concerning food and those who work to provide it.

In the first place, there should be laws named "The Farming
Laws." The first, belonging to Zeus the god of boundaries,
should run as follows:

No one is to move the boundary markers of the earth,
neither when they belong to a neighbor who is one of his

fellowcitizens nor when he possesses a boundary at the edge, adjoining another foreigner; one should hold that the saying about moving the immovable [17] truly applies to this. Everyone should prefer to try to move an enormous rock that is not a boundary marker rather than move a little stone that marks the boundary—protected by an oath to the gods—between friendly and enemy land. In the former case, Zeus the god of tribal kinship is the witness, while in the latter case it is Zeus the god of strangers; when either is aroused, most hateful wars follow.

843a

He who obeys the law would not experience the evils that attend it, but he who shows contempt for the law would become liable to two penalties—one, and the first, from the gods and the second from the law:

843b

Let no one voluntarily move the boundary markers of his neighbors' land. If someone should move them, let anyone who wishes report him to the farmers involved, and they shall take him to court. If someone is convicted of such an offense, it will be up to the court to estimate what the loser should suffer or pay, as one convicted of attempting to redistribute the land in secret and by force.

Next after this are the many petty injuries neighbors do to one another which, because of repetition, instill immense hatred and bring about a harsh and very bitter relationship among neighbors. On this account every care must be taken by a neighbor to refrain from doing anything inimical to his neighbor, in other respects and especially as regards any encroachment; for it's not difficult but is in fact in the power of any human being to do harm, while it's by no means everyone who can do a benefit.

843c

Anyone who oversteps boundaries and encroaches on a neighbor must pay for the damages and, in order to be cured of lack of awe and illiberality, must pay the injured party an additional amount equal to twice the damages. Field Regulators are to take cognizance of these and all such things and are to act as judges and assessors; in the case of graver offenses, as was said earlier, the entire twelfth part is to preside, while in the case of lesser offenses just the Commanders. If anyone lets his cattle graze on someone else's land, they are to inspect the damage and then arrive at a judgment and assessment. If any-

843d

843e one appropriates someone else's bee swarms, working on the
pleasure bees take in certain noises and thus getting them to
like him, he is to pay for the damages. If someone while burn-
ing wood is negligent of his neighbor's wood, he is to pay
whatever penalty the magistrates think appropriate. If someone plants[18] trees but fails to leave between them and his
neighbor's land an adequate gap . . . such as has been adequately stated by many lawgivers—whose laws one ought to
make use of, and not demand that the great orderer of the city
legislate about everything, including all the numerous petty
affairs that can be handled by any run-of-the-mill lawgiver.[19]

844a For instance, with regard to the water supply for farms,
there are some ancient and fine laws laid down that aren't
worthy of irrigating the discussion; but still, anyone who
wishes to draw water to his land may go ahead and do so,
starting from the common streams; he must not tap the above
ground springs of any private individual, but he can lead the
water along any course he wants so long as he avoids houses,
certain temples, and memorial markers, and does no damage
except the actual digging of the channel. If there are some nat-

844b urally dry districts where Zeus's water just runs off the land in
streams and the necessary drinking water is lacking, one
should dig down in his own land until he reaches clay earth,
and if at that level he still fails to strike any water, he is to obtain from his neighbors the necessary drinking water for each
member of his household. If the neighbors have only just
enough for themselves, the Field Regulators should fix a ration
of the water and he must go and get this each day, thus shar-

844c ing water with his neighbors. When Zeus's water comes pouring down, if someone who lives below another or shares a
boundary line with him does damage by not allowing excess
water to flow off the farm of the one above, or if the opposite
happens, if the one above is careless about the runoff and does
damage to the one below, and on account of this they aren't
willing to come to some common agreement between themselves about these matters, anybody who wishes can call in a
City Regulator (in the city) or a Field Regulator (in the country); he is to arrange what each of the parties ought to do. If

844d someone fails to abide by the arrangement, he is indictable for
having an envious and ill-humored soul; if convicted he must
pay double the damages to the injured party for not having
been willing to obey the magistrates.

The Harvest should be shared by all in some such way as the following. This goddess in Her graciousness has given us two gifts, the plaything of Dionysus which is not stored, and the fruit which by nature is put away and kept. [20] So this is the law that should be ordained regarding the Harvest:

Whoever tastes of field fruits, grapes or figs, before the vintage season that coincides with the rising of Arcturus—whether it be from his own lands or from that of others—must, if he plucked the fruit from his own fields, pay fifty drachmas sacred to Dionysus; if from the neighbors', a mina; if from others' two-thirds of a mina. 844e

Whoever wishes to harvest what are now called "well-born" grapes or what are named "well-born" figs may do so in whatever way he wishes and whenever he wants, if he takes them from his own crop; but if he harvests without permission from other persons' he must always fall under the penalty of the law that says "one shouldn't move what one didn't set down." If a slave touches any such things without getting the permission of the master of the lands, he is to be whipped with a number of strokes equal to the grapes in the bunch or the figs in the fig tree. A resident alien who has purchased it may harvest the well-born fruit if he wishes. If a stranger who is visiting should desire some fruit to eat as he goes along the roads he may without penalty pick the well-born fruit if he wishes, enough for himself and for one attendant, and thus receive the hospitality accorded to strangers; but the law should prevent us from sharing the so-called "field" fruits and the like with strangers. If someone out of ignorance, or his slave, should pick this fruit, the slave is to be punished with blows and the free man is to be sent away after having been advised and instructed to pick the other fruit which is not suitable for storing, to make raisins for wine and dried figs. 845a 845b

With regard to pears, apples, pomegranates, and all such, there should be no shame if one takes them in stealth, but if someone under thirty is caught at it he is to be driven off by being struck, though without any wounding, and it will not be permissible for a free man to seek any judicial redress for such blows. A stranger may partake of such fruits just as he could partake of the harvest. If an elderly man picks such fruits to eat on the spot, and doesn't carry any away, he should be allowed in all such things the same share the stranger has; but if he disobeys this law, he will risk losing the right to be a 845c 845d competitor in the contest for virtue, if on a later occasion someone recollects such conduct on his part and at that time brings it to the attention of the judges.

Water is the most nourishing of all the things that contribute to gardening, but it is easily polluted. In the case of the earth, sun, and winds, which together with water nourish the things that grow up from the earth, it isn't easy to do harm by means of poisons or diversions or thefts—but the nature of

845e water is such that all these things are possible. Therefore it needs the help of a law, which should run as follows:

If anyone should voluntarily pollute someone else's water, whether it be a spring or a cistern, using poisons or excavations or thefts, let the injured party file charges with the City Regulators, including a written estimate of damages; if someone should be convicted of doing such damage through the use of poisons, he must not only pay the penalty but also purify the water in the springs or reservoir, according to whatever rites of purification are prescribed, for each occasion and each person, by the Interpreters' laws.

846a As regards the bringing home of all the harvest fruits: Anyone who wishes may bring home what belongs to him by any route whatsoever, provided that he penalizes no one else in any way, or that he himself profits in an amount that is three times that of the penalty inflicted on the neighbor. The magistrates are to be the assessors of these matters, and of all other cases where someone voluntarily uses his own property to harm—violently or stealthily—the person or property of another who is unwilling that the harm be done. In all such cases the injured party should show the damage to the magistrates and receive reparation, so long as the harm done amounts to three minas or less. But if someone accuses someone else of

846b having done greater damage, he should take the case to the common courts and there exact judicial retribution from the unjust party. If one of the magistrates is thought to have rendered an assessment of penalty with unjust purpose, he is to be held liable for double the damages to the party he harmed. Anyone who wishes may bring the injustices of the magistrates, in the case of each particular complaint, before the common courts.

There are tens of thousands of these petty legal customs that regulate the imposing of retributions, and that pertain to written complaints, judicial summonses, the witnesses to a summons (whether there should be two, or how many there should be) and all such things. They can't be left unlegislated, and yet aren't worth the trouble of a legislator who is old; so the young men should take care of these aspects of the legislation, imitating what their predecessors have already laid down in law and patterning the petty matters after the great. They should profit from the experience they gain in the cases where it's necessary to use such arrangements, until they arrive at a point where all the details seem to have been satisfactorily laid down; then they should make the customs unchangeable, and live using these procedures that have attained the proper measure.

846c

The rest of the craftsmen should be regulated as follows: First, no native inhabitant, nor any domestic servant of a man who is a native, is to labor at the craftsmen's arts. For the man who is a citizen possesses already a sufficient art, requiring much practice and many branches of learning: preserving and holding the common order of the city, which must not be a part-time pursuit. There's almost no human nature that is capable of laboring with precision at two pursuits or two arts, or even of practicing one adequately himself while overseeing someone else who is practicing another. This, then, is the first rule that should prevail in the city:

846d

846e

No one is to be a metal worker and at the same time a carpenter, nor again is a carpenter to supervise others who are working in metal instead of his own art, advancing the excuse that if he supervised many domestic servant artisans working for him, he could reasonably be expected to oversee them better, in order to get a bigger income than he would get from just his own art. Each single individual in the city is to have one art and make his living from that. The City Regulators must labor to maintain this law, and if one of the native inhabitants inclines to some art instead of cultivating virtue, they are to punish him with blame and dishonors until they have succeeded in putting him back on his own straight track. If a stranger practices two arts, they are to punish him with bondage, monetary penalties, and expulsions from the city and thus force him to be only one person and not many.

847a

847b

With regard to their pay, and refusals to take delivery of their work, and injustices done to them by another or done by them to another, the City Regulators are to judge in cases involving fifty drachmas or less, and the common courts are to have legal jurisdiction where the amount is more than this.

847c
No one is to pay any duty on either exported or imported goods in the city. No one is to import frankincense or any other such foreign incenses that pertain to the gods, nor purple dye or any other dyeing ingredients that aren't produced in this country, nor substances from foreign lands that are needed for an unnecessary purpose in any other art. On the other hand, no one is to export anything in the country that needs to remain.

All these matters are to be under the cognizance and supervision of the twelve Guardians of the Laws who are next eldest after the five eldest are subtracted.

847d
With regard to heavy arms and all the implements of war, if for such a purpose the importation of some art, or plant,[21] or metal object, or binding material, or certain animals, becomes necessary, the Cavalry Commanders and Generals are to be in charge of the import and export of these things. The city itself should carry on such giving and taking, and these things will be regulated by fitting and adequate laws laid down by the Guardians of the Laws. But retail trade for the sake of money

847e
in this or any other merchandise will never be allowed in any part of the entire territory or city.

As regards the food supply and the distribution of the country's produce, it's likely that a method close to that of the Cretan law would possess some correctness:

Everybody must make a division of all the country's produce into twelve parts, according to the order in which it is to

848a
be consumed. Each of the twelve parts, such as of wheat and barley (and all the other harvests should be distributed following the same procedure, as well as all the animals which may be for sale in each district), is to be divided proportionally into three parts, one of which is for the free men and one of which is for their domestic servants. The third share is to go to the artisans and the strangers in general: some of them will be in need of necessary foodstuffs because they are living here

together as resident aliens, and others will be visiting because of some need a city or a private individual has. Once all the necessities have been divided, they will be required to sell only this third part, and no one is to be compelled to sell any of the two parts. 848b

But just what would be the most correct way to make these divisions? In the first place, it's obvious that our division is in one sense equal but in another sense unequal.

Kl. How do you mean?

Ath. Presumably it's necessary that for each of these things that grow²² and are nourished from the earth, some turn out worse, and some better.

Kl. How could this not be the case?

Ath. In this respect, then, none of the three parts ought to be greater, neither what is distributed to the masters and the slaves nor again what goes to the strangers; the distribution should assign to everyone the same—an equality in similarity. Each citizen, taking his two parts, is to be in charge of the dis- 848c tribution to slaves and free persons, and is to distribute as much and of whatever sort he sees fit. Any surplus should be distributed according to a measure and number arrived at in the following way: taking the number of all the animals that must be fed from the land, they are to make the distribution on this basis.

After this there must be the arrangement of their separate houses. The appropriate ordering of such houses is as follows: There ought to be twelve villages, each one located in the middle of one of the twelve districts. In each village there 848d should first be a site for the temples and marketplace belonging to the gods, and to the demons who follow after the gods. If there are any local Magnesian deities, or shrines of some other ancients who have been preserved in memory, they should pay them the honors that were paid by humans in ancient times; but temples should be set up everywhere to Hestia, Zeus, and Athena, and to whichever of the other gods is the primary patron of each twelfth part. First, there should be buildings around these temples, on the highest ground, thus 848e providing the guards with the best-defended barricades possible. Then all the rest of the land should be furnished with craftsmen, who are to be divided into thirteen groups. One of these groups will be settled in the city; it will in turn be divided into twelve parts, one for every section of the city, and will be settled in a circle outside. And in each village the farmers are to have the appropriate kinds of craftsmen living next to them. The Commanders of the Field Regulators are to be the supervisors of all these matters, deciding how many and what sort each place needs, and where they should be settled so as to be the least painful and the most beneficial to the farmers. Similarly, in the city the magistracy of the City Regulators is to take in hand and supervise these matters.

849a

The Market Regulators presumably have the job of looking after each of the things that pertains to the market. Besides watching to see that no one does any injustice to the temples around the marketplace, they should, in the second place, watch over the human affairs, keeping an eye out for moderation and insolence, and punishing anyone who needs punishment. With regard to commodities, they must first see that each of the articles city dwellers are supposed to sell to strangers is sold according to law. Let there be one law:

849b

On the first day of every month the portion that is to be sold to strangers should be brought forth by the selling agents (either strangers or slaves, who will act for the city dwellers). The first commodity is the twelfth-part of grain. Each stranger should at the first market buy the grain that he will need for the whole month, along with whatever else goes with grain. Then on the tenth day of the month the one party should sell, and the other buy, enough liquid goods to last the whole month. The third market, for livestock, should take place on the twentieth of each month.[23] At that time there should be whatever selling and buying of animals is necessary for each, as well as the sale on behalf of the farmers of any equipment or other goods the strangers must acquire by purchase from others (such as animal skins and all sorts of clothing, woven goods, wool felt, and some other such things).

849c

But as regards retail trade in any of these things, including barley, wheat turned into flour, and every other sort of food, no one is ever supposed to sell to or buy from the city dwellers or their slaves; it should be in the strangers' marketplaces that a stranger does his selling to craftsmen and their slaves, and performs those dealings in wine and grain that are termed "retail trade" by most people. Once animals have been slaugh-

849d

tered and cut up, the butchers should distribute them to strangers and craftsmen, or their domestic servants. And any stranger who wants to, can on any day buy any sort of firewood in bulk from agents out in the country, and then sell it himself to other strangers—in whatever amount and whenever he wishes.

All the other sorts of goods and equipment each needs should be brought to the common marketplace and sold in a location for each, where the Guardians of the Laws and the Market Regulators, along with the City Regulators, should mark out appropriate boundaries for stalls for the goods to be bought. In these allotted spaces they should exchange money for goods and goods for money, not allowing each other to get anything without gaining something in return. He who gives something on trust must be content whether or not he receives the thing, since there'll no longer be a just cause of action in such transactions.

If what's purchased or sold creates an excess or a deficiency contrary to the law that has said there must not be an increase or a decrease beyond a certain sum, then, in the former case, the excess should be recorded with the Guardians of the Laws and, in the opposite case, the shortfall should be cancelled. The same ordinances concerning registration of property apply to resident aliens.

Anyone who wishes may become a resident alien upon the following explicit conditions:

There is a place for strangers to live in, and anyone who is willing and able can settle there; he must possess an art; he can prolong his visit no longer than twenty years after the time of his enrollment; he will pay no resident alien tax, not even a small one, except for the requirement that he be moderate; he will pay no other tax on any purchases or sales. When the time has elapsed, he is to take his property and depart. But if in these years he has attained noteworthiness because of some sufficiently good deed done for the city, and he trusts he can persuade the Council and the Assembly to respond to his request by granting a sovereign delay of his departure, or even permission to stay for life, he should go ahead and make his case to the city, and whatever he succeeds in persuading it to agree to, should be fully carried out. The resident aliens'

849e

850a

850b

850c

children, if they are craftsmen and have attained the age of fifteen, should begin the period of their residency when they reach the age of fifteen. Each may remain twenty years on these conditions and then must depart for wherever he likes. If one of them wishes to remain he can do so if he persuades as has just been described. He who departs should go after having erased the written records which he previously wrote down and left with the magistrates.

BOOK IX

Ath. The judicial penalties that are consequent to all the earlier ac-   853a
tivities would come next after these things, according to the
nature of the ordering of the laws. Some of the matters that
require judicial actions have been discussed—those that pertain to farming and whichever follow them—but with regard
to the greatest matters there has been as yet no discussion,
showing in each single case what retribution should be attached and who the judges should be at the time. These are   853b
the things that should be stated next, after those others.

Kl. Correct.

Ath. It is indeed in a certain way shameful even to legislate all the
things we are now about to lay down, in a city such as this,
which we claim will be well administered and correctly
equipped in every way for the practice of virtue. Even to assume that in such a city someone may grow up[1] who shares in
the wickedness of the greatest other places, so that it's necessary to have legislation that anticipates and threatens such   853c
a man, if he comes into being—to lay down laws to deter
these men and punish them when they do arise, as if they are
going to arise—is, as I said, in a certain way shameful. But we
aren't in the same position as were the ancient lawgivers who
gave their laws to heroes, the children of gods (as the present
account has it, they were themselves sprung from gods and
legislated for others who had such an origin); we're humans,
and legislating now for the seed of humans. Therefore, there is
no blame[2] incurred by our fearing lest one of our citizens   853d
become, as it were, "hornstruck"[3]—so tough by nature that

[245]

he wouldn't melt. Just as those seeds are unmelted by fire, so these men are unmelted by strong laws.

Thanks to these men I would first state an unpleasing law about temple robberies, in case someone should dare to do this. We wouldn't wish, and there isn't any great expectation, that one of the correctly brought up citizens will ever contract this disease, but their domestic servants, as well as the strangers and the slaves of strangers, would try many such things. Especially on account of them, but also as a precaution against the general weakness of human nature, I will pronounce the law about temple robberies and all other such things that are difficult to cure or incurable. According to the argument agreed on earlier, preludes (the briefest possible) should preface all these laws. Someone would say the following, by way of a dialogue and an encouragement[4] to that man who is urged during the day and awakened at night by an evil desire to despoil something of the sacred things:

854a

854b

"You amazing man, the evil that now moves and turns you to temple robbery is neither human nor divine, but a certain gadfly[5] that grows naturally in human beings as a result of ancient and unexpiated injustices. It is an accursed thing that revolves around, which one must take precaution against with all one's strength. Learn now what the precaution is: When any of such opinions seize upon you, go partake of exorcisms; go as a suppliant to the temples of the gods who ward off evil; go and frequent the company of the men said to be good among you; hear, and try yourself to say, that every man must honor the noble and the just things. Flee, without turning back, the company of bad men. If by your doing these things the disease abates somewhat, well and good; but if not, look to death as something nobler, and depart from life."

854c

These are the preludes we sing to those who are considering all these deeds that are impious and destructive of the city. For him who obeys, the law should be left silent; but for him who disobeys, it sings in a loud voice, after the prelude:

854d

"Whoever is caught robbing a temple, if a slave or a stranger, is to have the misfortune written on his face and hands and, after having been whipped as much as the judges decide, is to be thrown naked out beyond the borders of the country."

Perhaps by paying this penalty he would become better, by

becoming moderate. For no judicial punishment that takes place according to law aims at what is bad, but for the most part accomplishes one of two other aims: it makes the one who receives the judicial punishment either better or less wicked. 854e

If some citizen is ever detected doing such a thing, committing one of the grave and unspeakable injustices against gods or parents or city, the judge should think of this man as already incurable, considering that even though he happened to get such an education and upbringing from childhood, he didn't refrain from the gravest evils. The judicial penalty for this man is to be death, the least of evils, and by which he'll present an example that will benefit the others, once he's dis- 855a appeared, without fame, beyond the borders of the country. But let his children and family, if they avoid the paternal disposition, receive fame and be spoken of with honor, as persons who well and courageously fled from evil to good. It wouldn't be fitting, for the regime in which the allotments are to remain always the same and equal, if the property of any such men were forfeited to the public. So when someone seems to commit an injustice that merits a monetary penalty, let him pay as much as he has in excess of an equipped allot- 855b ment—let him pay so much, but no more. The Guardians of the Laws are to inspect the written records to get precise figures in this regard, and are to announce them clearly to the judges on each occasion, so that none of the allotments ever becomes idle because of a lack of funds. If someone seems to merit a greater penalty, and if some of his friends aren't willing to pledge security for him and give him his freedom by helping to pay, he is to be punished with conspicuous, lengthy imprisonment and with certain humiliations. But no 855c one is ever to be completely dishonored for a single fault, not even if he is in exile beyond the borders. Let the punishments be death, or prison, or beating, or sitting or standing in certain disgraceful ways, or standing at temples on the frontiers of the country, or money paid in the way we earlier said this judicial penalty should be paid.

For a capital offense, the judges are to be the Guardians of the Laws and the court composed of those magistrates from the previous year who were selected because they were best.[6] The younger lawgivers should attend to the indictments, sum- 855d monses, and such matters in these cases, and how they should take place; but it's our task to legislate about the voting. Let the vote be taken openly, but before this let our judges sit down in a row right next to one another, in order of age, directly facing the accuser and the defendant, and let all the citizens, as many as are at leisure, stand as serious listeners to

855e

such trials. First one speech is to be spoken by the accuser, and then a second speech by the defendant. After these speeches, the oldest should begin his judging, making an adequate inquiry into the things that have been said; after the eldest, they should all one by one go through whatever someone finds wanting in some way in what was said or not said by either of the litigants. He who finds nothing wanting should turn the judging over to another. Whatever seems to them to

856a

be to the point in what was said should be ratified, by affixing the written signatures of all the judges, and deposited on the altar of Hestia. The next day they should assemble again in the same place, to go through a judicial inquiry into the case in the same way and to affix signatures again to the things said. When they've done this a third time, and have paid sufficient heed to the evidence and witnesses, each should give a sacred vote, swearing before Hestia to judge what is just and true to the best of his ability, and thus such a trial should be brought to its end.

856b

After matters pertaining to gods come matters pertaining to the dissolution of the regime. Whoever enslaves the laws by bringing them under the rule of human beings, whoever makes the city subject to a faction, and does all this through violence and the stirring up of civil strife against the law, this man must be regarded as the greatest enemy of all to the whole city. And he who doesn't take part in any such things, but, holding one of the highest offices in the city, lets these things

856c

escape his notice—or, not because they escape his notice, but because of cowardice, fails to wreak retribution on behalf of his own fatherland—such a citizen must be held to be second in evil. Every man who's capable of even a little good should inform the magistrates by bringing any plotter to trial, on a charge of violent and also illegal overthrow of the regime. The judges for these men are to be those who judge temple robbers, and the whole trial for these men is to proceed just as it did for the latter. The victory by a majority of votes shall bring death.

To put it in one word, the blame and retribution exacted 856d
from a father is to fall on none of the children, except in the
case of someone whose father, grandfather, and grandfather's
father have one after the other been condemned to death.
These the city is to send away to their ancient fatherland and
city, along with their property, except for what is part of the
fully equipped allotment. Then, of the sons of citizens who
have more than one son not less than ten years of age, ten are
to be chosen by lot from among those nominated by their father or their grandfather on their father's or mother's side. The 856e
names of those who draw lots shall be sent to Delphi, and the
one whom the god selects shall be set up, with better luck, in
the household of those who departed.

Kl. Fine.

Ath. Let the law concerning which judges are to preside and the
procedure of the trials be common to yet a third case, that of
the man whom someone brings to trial on a charge of treason.
Likewise, as to whether the offspring are to remain or to leave
the fatherland, let this one law regulate these matters in the 857a
three cases of the traitor, the temple robber, and the man who
destroys the laws of the city through violence.

As to stealing, whether someone steals something great or
something small, again let there be one law and one judicial
retribution in all cases. First, double the value of the item
stolen should be paid as a fine, if someone is convicted of such
an offense and possesses enough other property, over and
above the allotment, to pay; but if not, let him be imprisoned
until he does pay or persuades the successful prosecutor. If 857b
someone is convicted of stealing from the public, if he persuades the city or pays double the value of the theft, let him be
let out of prison.

Kl. How comes it, stranger, that we're saying it makes no difference to the thief whether he's convicted of stealing something great or something small, whether from sacred or profane places,[7] or whatever other respects in which a theft can be
entirely dissimilar? For crimes that are thus various, is the
lawgiver in no way to follow with penalties of a similar
variety?

Ath. Excellent, Kleinias! As I was being all but borne along you've 857c
collided with me and woken me up, reminding me of what I
was thinking about earlier—namely, that what pertains to the

laying down of laws has never been worked out correctly in any way, as in fact can be said on the basis of what has cropped up now. What, again, do we mean by this? We didn't make a bad image, when we compared all those living under legislation that exists now, to slaves being doctored by slaves. For it's necessary to know well some such thing as the following: if one of those doctors who practices medicine on the basis of experiences rather than reason should ever encounter 857d a free doctor carrying on a dialogue with a free man who was sick—using arguments that come close to philosophizing, grasping the disease from its source, and going back up to the whole nature of bodies—he would swiftly burst out laughing and would say nothing other than what is always said about such things by most of the so-called doctors. For he would declare, "Idiot! You're not doctoring the sick man, you're practically educating him, as if what he needed were to be- 857e come a doctor, rather than healthy!"

Kl. Well, wouldn't he be speaking correctly when he said such things?

Ath. Maybe—if, at any rate, he went on to reflect that this man who goes through laws in the way we're doing now, is educating the citizens but not legislating. Would he not appear to be saying this too in the right way?

Kl. Perhaps.

Ath. The present situation is fortunate for us.

Kl. In what way?

Ath. In that there is no necessity to legislate, but just that we our-
858a selves, by becoming engaged in an inquiry about the whole regime,[8] try to discern in what way the best and also the most necessary would each come into being. Indeed, it's likely that we can now, if we wish, inquire into what is best, or, if we wish, into what is most necessary, as regards the laws. So let's choose which it seems we'll do.

Kl. We're proposing a ridiculous choice, stranger, and we'd be-
858b come exactly the same as lawgivers constrained by some great necessity to legislate immediately, because tomorrow it'll no longer be possible. But the fact is that for us—if god is in ac- cord with what I say—it's possible, just as it is for masons or those beginning some other construction, to accumulate in- discriminately the materials from which we'll select what's to be used in the structure that is about to come into being, and

indeed to make the selection at leisure. So let's assume that we are now housebuilders who aren't working under constraint, but are in a leisurely way still accumulating some things and incorporating others. Thus it is correct to speak of some things pertaining to the laws as being established, and others as being accumulated.

Ath. That way, Kleinias, our synoptic review of the laws would be more in accordance with nature, at any rate. So then let's look—in the name of the gods!—at some such thing as the following, pertaining to legislators.

Kl. What's that?

Ath. Presumably there exist in the cities writings and written arguments of many others, and also the writings and arguments of the lawgiver.

Kl. How could there not?

Ath. Should we turn our minds to the writings of the others, of poets and of those who without meter or with meter have left a written record of their advice about life, but not pay attention to those of the lawgivers? Or should we pay attention to the latter most of all?

Kl. The latter, by far!

Ath. But is the lawgiver alone, among the writers, not supposed to give advice about the noble, good, and just things, teaching what sorts of things they are and how they must be practiced by those who are going to become happy?

Kl. How could that be?

Ath. But is it then more shameful for Homer, and Tyrtaeus, and the other poets to make bad written pronouncements about life and practices, and less so for Lycurgus, and Solon, and whoever has become a lawgiver and written down things? Or isn't it correct, at any rate, that of all the writings in the cities, the things written about the laws appear, when opened up, by far the noblest and best, and that the writings of the others either follow those or, if they speak in dissonance, be laughed at? How do we conceive writing about laws in the cities should be: should the writings appear in the shapes of a father and mother, caring dearly and possessing intelligence, or, like a tyrant and despot, should they command and threaten, post writings on the walls and go away? Let's consider now, ourselves, whether we're going to try to speak with this conception concerning laws—evincing an eager spirit at least,

858c

858d

858e

859a

859b

whether or not we have the capacity. And if by going this route we have to suffer something, let's suffer it! May it be a good thing, and, if god is willing, so it shall be.

Kl. You've spoken nobly, and let's do as you say.

Ath. First then, there must be a precise inquiry, such as we have undertaken, into what pertains to temple robbers, and stealing in general, and all injustices; and we mustn't take it ill if in the midst of giving laws, we've established some things and are inquiring further into others. For we're becoming lawgivers but we aren't yet lawgivers, though probably we may be. If it seems as though we should inquire into the things I've mentioned, and in the way I've mentioned, let's carry out the inquiry.

Kl. By all means.

Ath. Then with regard to the noble things and all the just things, let's try to see something like the following: to what extent we now agree, and to what extent we disagree with ourselves— we who would claim to be eager in spirit, if nothing else, to differ from most people—and then again to what extent the many agree and disagree among themselves.

Kl. What differences of ours do you have in mind when you say this?

Ath. I shall try to explain. With respect to justice as a whole and just human beings, deeds, and actions, we all somehow agree that all these are noble; so if someone would maintain that just human beings, even if they happen to be ugly⁹ in their bodies, were nevertheless entirely beautiful people in respect to their very just disposition considered by itself, in almost no case would the one who speaks thus seem to speak off key.

Kl. Isn't that correct?

Ath. Maybe. But let's observe how, if all things are noble which partake of justice, then the "all" includes the things we undergo, almost as much as the things we do.

Kl. So what then?

Ath. In the case of an action that is just, it partakes of the noble to about the extent to which it shares in the just.

Kl. But of course.

Ath. Then in the case of something one undergoes that shares in the just, to agree that it becomes noble, to the same extent, would not be to present a dissonant speech?

Kl. That is true.

859c

859d

859e

860a

Ath.   But if, at any rate, we agree that something one undergoes is just, but shameful, the just and the noble will be in dissonance since the just things will be said to be most shameful.

Kl.   What do you mean by this?

Ath.   Nothing difficult to understand. For the laws established by us a little earlier would seem to pronounce things totally opposed to the things now being said.

Kl.   To what things?

Ath.   Presumably we established that the temple robber should   860b die—justly—and the same for the enemy of well-made laws; and when we were about to establish very many such legal customs we stopped, seeing that these sufferings were limitless in number and severity, and that while they were the most just of all sufferings, they were also the most shameful. So don't the just things and the noble things appear to us at one time to be all the same, and then at another time very opposed?

Kl.   I'm afraid so.

Ath.   It's with regard to such things that the many proclaim, without   860c consonance, that the noble things and the just things are separate.

Kl.   So it appears anyway, stranger.

Ath.   Let's look again, Kleinias, to see how we have a harmony about these same matters.

Kl.   What harmony, and in what respect?

Ath.   In the earlier discussions I believe I said expressly somehow, or if I didn't earlier, set me down now as saying . . .

Kl.   What?

Ath.   That the bad are all bad involuntarily in every respect. Since   860d this is so, it is presumably necessary that the next argument follows upon this.

Kl.   What do you mean?

Ath.   That the unjust man is presumably bad, but the bad man is involuntarily so. Now it never makes sense that the voluntary is done involuntarily. Hence the man who does injustice appears involuntarily unjust to the one who sets down injustice as something involuntary. This is what I must agree to now. For I agree that everyone does injustice involuntarily. And if someone, out of love of victory or love of honor, asserts that   860e the unjust are indeed involuntarily so, but that many voluntarily do injustice, my argument, at any rate, remains the former and not the latter. So then in what way would I, at least, speak in consonance with my own arguments? Suppose, Kleinias and Megillus, you were to ask me:

"If these things are so, stranger, what advice do you have for us concerning the legislation for the city of the Magnesians? Should we legislate or not?"

"Why not?" I'll declare.

861a
"Are you going to distinguish for them the involuntary from the voluntary injustices, and will we establish greater penalties for the voluntary faults and injustices, and lesser for the former? Or equal penalties for all, on the grounds that there aren't any voluntary injustices at all?"

Kl. Correctly spoken, stranger. What use, indeed, shall we make of these things that are now being said?

Ath. A noble question. First, let's use them for the following.

Kl. What?

Ath. Let's recollect that just now we made a noble remark to the effect that concerning the just things we were in a very great deal of confusion and disharmony. Seizing upon this, let's question

861b
ourselves again: "Well, we haven't found our way clear of the difficulty in these matters, nor defined what the difference is between these things, which in all the cities, by all the legislators who have ever existed, have been held to be two forms of injustices, voluntary and involuntary, and have been so legislated. Is the argument now being uttered by us going to say only this much and depart, as if it were being spoken by a god, giving no argument as to why it has spoken correctly,

861c
and just legislating in defiance of the difficulty in some way?"—that's impossible. Before legislating, it's necessary to make clear somehow that these things are two, and what the other difference is, so that whenever someone imposes the judicial penalty on either of them, everyone may follow the things that are being said and may be able to judge, somehow or other, what is fittingly laid down and what is not.

Kl. You appear to us to be speaking in a noble way, stranger. For we ought to do one of two things—either refrain from saying that injustices are all involuntary, or make clear how this is the correct thing to say, by first making a distinction.

861d Ath. Well, of these two alternatives presumably one is wholly unacceptable to me—refraining from saying it, when I believe it to be the truth. For that would be neither according to legal custom [10] nor pious. But in what way are they two, if they don't differ from one another by being involuntary and voluntary? Somehow or other then, one must try to make it clear on the basis of some other distinction.

Kl. There's simply no other way we can think about this, at least, stranger.

Ath. So it shall be. Come, then: it's likely that many injuries are   861e
done by the citizens to one another in their associations and minglings, and that these involve an abundance of the voluntary, as well as the involuntary.

Kl. How could it be otherwise?

Ath. Let not someone set down all the injuries as injustices, thus supposing that the injustices in them become, in this way, double—some voluntary and some involuntary. For of all injuries, the involuntary are not less in number or severity than the voluntary. But consider whether I'm saying anything in   862a
saying what I'm about to say, or whether I'm saying nothing at all: for I at least do not assert, Kleinias and Megillus, that if someone injures somebody in some way, not intending to do so, but involuntarily, that he does injustice involuntarily. And I won't legislate in this fashion, legislating to the effect that this is an involuntary injustice; I'll set such an injury down as being not an injustice at all, whether it be greater or smaller. Indeed, if my view, at least, is victorious, we'll often assert that when a benefit comes to pass that is not correct, the one responsible for the benefit is committing an injustice. Gener-   862b
ally speaking, friends, if someone gives something to somebody, or, on the contrary, takes something away, such a thing shouldn't thus be called simply just or unjust, but what the lawgiver should observe is whether someone employs a just disposition and character in doing some benefit or injury to somebody. The lawgiver should look to these two things, injustice and injury; he should do what he can through the laws to redress the injury—by preserving what may be destroyed, setting upright again what has fallen, and making sound what   862c
has been killed or wounded—and once compensations have made atonement for each of the injuries, he should always try through the laws to create friendship in place of discord between the doers and sufferers.

Kl. In doing these things, at least, he'd be acting nobly.

Ath. On the other hand, in the case of unjust injuries, and gains as well—when someone makes somebody gain by doing him an injustice—as many of these as are curable, being regarded as diseases in the soul, should be cured. And it should be declared that our cure for injustice proceeds in the following direction.

Kl. In which?

862d Ath. Toward making it so that whatever injustice, great or small, someone might commit, the law will teach and compel him in every way either never again to dare voluntarily to do such a thing or to do it very much less; this is in addition to paying compensation for the injury. To accomplish these things by deeds or words—with pleasures or pains, by honors or dishonors, even by monetary penalties or gifts, and in general by whatever procedure someone may use to bring about hatred of injustice and desire, or lack of hatred, for the nature of the

862e just—it is this that is the task of the noblest laws. But what about the one whom the lawgiver perceives to be incurable in these respects: what judicial penalty and law will he lay down for these people? Because he knows, presumably, that in the case of all such men it isn't better for them if they go on living, and that by departing life they would confer a double benefit on the others (becoming examples to the others of why not to

863a do injustice, and emptying the city of bad men), the lawgiver must necessarily assign to such men the punishment of death for their faults, though this must not be done in any other case.

Kl. It's likely that the things you're saying are in some way very well measured, but nevertheless we'd be more pleased to hear these things put still more clearly, indicating how it is that the difference between injustice and injury has gotten mixed up with the difference between the voluntary and the involuntary in these matters.

863b Ath. One must try to do and say what you ask. Now it's clear that you say and hear from one another at least this much about the soul: that one thing in its nature, either a passion or a part, is spiritedness—a possession that is by nature quarrelsome and pugnacious, overturning many things with uncalculating violence.

Kl. But of course.

Ath. And pleasure, we proclaim, is not the same as spiritedness, but, we assert, holds absolute rule[11] through a strength opposite to it: through persuasion and forceful trickery [12] she does whatever her intention wishes.

Kl. Very much so.

Ath. Someone wouldn't speak falsely if he said that ignorance is the 863c third cause of faults. It would be better for the lawgiver, however, to divide this in two, holding the simple version of it to be responsible for light faults. The double version occurs when someone lacks understanding because he partakes not only of ignorance but also of the opinion that he is wise, and believes he knows completely things about which he knows nothing; if this is accompanied by strength and force, the lawgiver sets such things down as the causes of great and unmusical faults, while if this is accompanied by weakness, 863d leading to the faults of children and the elderly, he'll set such things down as faults indeed, and will establish laws, as for those who are at fault, but the laws will be the gentlest, at any rate, of all and the most forgiving.

Kl. What you say is reasonable.

Ath. Now with regard to pleasure and spiritedness, we almost all say that one of us is "stronger," while another is "weaker"; and this is the way it is.

Kl. Entirely so.

Ath. But with regard to ignorance, at least, we've never heard that one of us is "stronger," while another is "weaker."

Kl. Very true. 863e

Ath. And we assert that all these things, at least, often turn each man in directions opposite to that toward which his intention at the same time draws him.

Kl. Very often indeed.

Ath. Now at this point I would clearly define for you what I say is the just and the unjust, without complication. The tyranny in the soul of spiritedness, fear, pleasure, pain, feelings of envy, and desires, whether it does some injury or not, I proclaim to 864a be in every way injustice. When, on the other hand, the opinion about what is best (however a city or certain private individuals may believe this will be) [13] holds sway in souls and brings order to every man, then, even if it is in some way mistaken, what is done through this, and the part of each man that becomes obedient to such a rule, must be declared to be entirely just and best for the whole of human life—even though many are of the opinion that such injury constitutes

864b involuntary injustice. We aren't now involved in a quarrelsome argument about names, but since the three forms of
faults have been made clear, these ought first to be still more
firmly fixed in the memory. So, then, one of our forms is that
of pain, which we name "spiritedness" and "fear."

Kl. By all means.

Ath. A second, again, is that of pleasure and desires; third and distinct is the striving for expectations and true opinion concerning what is best.[14] When this last is divided into three by
being cut twice, there come to be five forms, as we now assert,
and for these five forms there should be laws established that
864c differ from one another, and that are of two kinds.

Kl. What are these?

Ath. One concerns what is done through violence and open deeds
on each occasion, the other concerns what takes place secretly,
with darkness and trickery; then sometimes what is done
combines both of these, and the laws dealing with this case
would be the harshest, if it is to receive its appropriate share.

Kl. That makes sense.

Ath. After these things let's go back to the point from which we
digressed to get here, and complete the laying down of the
864d laws. I believe we had set down what pertains to those who
plunder the gods and what pertains to traitors, and also what
pertains to those who corrupt the laws with a view to the
dissolution of the existing regime. Now someone might perhaps do one of these things while insane, or while so afflicted
with diseases or extreme old age or while still such a child as
to be no different from such men. If, on the plea of the doer or
of the doer's advocate, it should become evident to the judges
chosen for the occasion that one of these circumstances ob-
864e tains, and he should be judged to have broken the law while
in such a condition, let him pay to the full exact compensation
for the injury he has done someone, but let him be released
from the other judicial sentences, unless he has killed someone and has hands that are not unpolluted by murder. In the
latter case, he is to go away into another country and place,
and dwell away from home for a year; if he comes back prior to
the time which the law has ordained, or sets foot at all in his
own country, he is to be incarcerated in the public prison by
the Guardians of the Laws for two years, and then released
from prison.

Let's not hesitate to proceed just as we began, and lay down   865a
laws that cover completely every form of murder. Let's speak
first about violent, involuntary murders.

If someone in a contest and in the public games has involuntarily killed somebody dear to him, whether it happens immediately or at a later time as a result of the blows, or if this
happens during war or during the preparation for war—when
they practice the javelin without using body armor, or imitate   865b
the activity of war with certain heavy arms—let him be free
from pollution once he has been purified according to the law
brought from Delphi for these purposes.

In the case of all doctors, if the person being cared for by
them should die against their intention, they are to be held
unpolluted according to law.

If with his own hands, but involuntarily, one man should
kill another, whether it be with his own unarmed body, or
with an instrument, or missile, or by giving some drink or
food, or by applying fire or cold, or by deprivation of air—   865c
whether he acts with his own body or through other bodies—
in all cases let it be as if by his own hands, and let him pay
something like the following judicial penalties. If he should
kill a slave, he must render the master of the dead slave free of
injury and penalty by reckoning what it would cost him to be
deprived of a slave of his own, or else sustain a judicial penalty equal to twice the value of the deceased—the value to be
assessed by the judges. He is to employ purifications that are
greater and more numerous than those employed by persons
who kill during the games, and the Interpreters whom the god   865d
selects are to be sovereign in these matters. If it's his own
slave, he is to be released under law from the murder once he's
undergone purification. If someone should involuntarily kill a
free man, let him purify himself by the same purifications as
in the case of one who kills a slave, and let him not underestimate a certain old saying of the ancient myths. It is said that
he who dies a violent death after having lived with the outlook
of a free man feels, when freshly dead, spirited rage against
the perpetrator. Filled with fear and horror on account of his   865e
violent experience, and seeing his own murderer going about
in his own accustomed haunts, he feels horror; being himself
disturbed, he does all he can, having Memory as an ally, to
disturb the perpetrator and his doings. That is why the perpe-

trator must go away from the sufferer during all the seasons of a year, and desert all his accustomed places throughout the entire fatherland.[15] And if the one who has died should be a stranger, the perpetrator must also keep away from the stranger's country for the same amount of time. If someone voluntarily obeys this law, the nearest of kin to the one who has died, who is the one who watches to see that all these things have come to pass, should be forgiving—and it would be entirely well measured for him to have peaceful dealings with the man. But if someone is disobedient—if, first, he dares to frequent the sacred places and sacrifice while being unpurified, and then if he isn't willing to go away as a stranger and fulfill the stated time period, the nearest of kin to the one who has died should prosecute the killer for murder, and all the retributions are to be doubled for the man who is convicted. And if the nearest kinsman doesn't prosecute for what has been suffered, it shall be as if the curse has gone on to him because he who has suffered makes supplication in the name of what he has suffered; anyone who wishes should prosecute this man and compel him under law to stay away from his own fatherland for five years. If a stranger involuntarily kills one of the strangers who are in the city, let anyone who wishes prosecute under the same laws: if he's a resident alien, let him go away for a year; if he's a total stranger, in addition to the purification, whether he's killed a stranger or a resident alien or a member of the city, he must spend all the rest of his life away from the country that is sovereign over these laws. If he comes back illegally, the Guardians of the Laws are to penalize him with death, and, if he has some property, are to give it to the nearest of kin of the one who suffered. If he comes back involuntarily, if he's shipwrecked at sea near the country, he must camp where his feet will be moistened by the sea and watch for a sailing opportunity; if certain persons violently drag him in by land, the first of the city's magistrates who happens along should release him and give him safe-conduct across the border.

If someone kills a free man with his own hands, but the deed was done out of spirited anger, it is necessary first to distinguish between two versions of such an act. For sometimes it is done out of spirited anger by those who act on a sudden

impulse, who all at once and without intending to kill before-   866e
hand destroy someone with blows or some such thing, and
feel regret immediately after the deed is done. On the other
hand, killing is also done out of spirited anger by those who
have been insulted by words or dishonorable deeds, who seek
retribution, and who later kill someone, intending to kill and
feeling no regret once the deed is done. So it's likely that they
should be set down as two sorts of murder, both pretty much
done out of spiritedness, and it would be most just to say that   867a
they are somewhere in the middle between the voluntary and
the involuntary. Nevertheless, each of them is an image of one
of the other two: he who guards his spiritedness and doesn't
immediately get retribution at the moment, but does so at a
later time after deliberating, resembles the voluntary; he who
doesn't hoard his rages and immediately employs them at the
moment, without prior deliberation, is similar to the involuntary—though this man again is not wholly involuntary, but an
image of the involuntary. That's why it's difficult to define   867b
murders done out of spiritedness, to decide whether one
ought to legislate for them as voluntary or as in a sense involuntary. The best and most truthful thing to do is to set them
both down as images, and make a division between them on
the grounds of the presence or absence of prior deliberation:
one should legislate harsher retributions for those who kill
with prior deliberation and in anger, and gentler for those
who kill without prior deliberation and all of a sudden. For
one should assign greater retribution to the image of the
greater evil, and less to that of the lesser. And that's the way   867c
our laws should do.

Kl.   In every respect.

Ath.   Let's go back again, then, and say:

If, then, someone kills a free man with his own hands, and
the deed was done out of a certain anger, without prior deliberation, let the killer suffer the other things that were assigned
the one who kills without spirited anger, but let him also be
compelled to spend two years in exile, restraining his own
spiritedness. He who kills out of spirited anger, but with prior   867d
deliberation, is to suffer in other respects the same again as
the former, except that he is to spend three years in exile instead of the two years for the other. Thus he'll pay a greater
retribution of time because of his greater spiritedness. The re-

turn from exile in these cases should be as follows. (This is difficult to legislate with precision. For there would be times when the one the law defines as the harsher of the two is rather gentle, and when the "gentler" is rather harsh, having committed a more savage act of murder, or when the former would have committed a gentler. But the procedure will for the most part follow what is now being said.) The Guardians of the Laws ought to take cognizance of all these things, and when the time of exile in either case has elapsed, they should send twelve of their number out to the borders of the country as judges: during this time they should have carried out a more minute investigation of the actions of the exiles, and should be judges as regards forgiving [16] them and allowing them to come back. The exiles must abide by the verdicts of such magistrates. In either of the two cases, if, after his return, the exile ever again commits the same act because he is overcome by anger, he must go into exile and never return; if he should return, let him suffer the same thing as the stranger who returns. If it's a slave that someone has killed, and it's his own, he is to undergo rites of purification; if it's someone else's slave that he's killed out of spirited anger, he is to pay twice the value of the injury to the owner.

If any of all those who kill should disobey the law and defile the marketplace, the athletic games, and the other sacred places by frequenting them while unpurified, anyone who wishes may prosecute the dead man's kinsman who is permitting this, and the killer, compelling them to exact and pay double the money and the other actions, and taking the fine for himself according to the law.

If some slave should kill his own master out of spirited anger, the kinsmen of the dead man are to do whatever they wish to the killer and remain unpolluted, so long as under no circumstances they let him continue to live in any sense. If some other slave should kill a free man out of spirited anger, his masters are to hand the slave over to the kinsmen of the dead man, and they must necessarily kill the perpetrator, in whatever manner they wish. If a father or mother should out of spirited anger kill a son or daughter, with blows or in some violent fashion—something that does occur, though rarely—they are to undergo the same rites of purification as the others and go into banishment for three years; when the kill-

867e

868a

868b

868c

868d

ers return, the wife is to separate from the husband, and the husband from the wife, and they are never again to share in creating children, nor is the perpetrator ever to become part of the hearth or a sharer in the sacred things with those whom he has deprived of a son or brother. He who is impious about these matters and disobeys is to be subject to prosecution for impiety by anyone who wishes. If some man out of rage should kill some woman who is his wife, or if a woman should do this same thing in the same way to her husband, let them undergo the same purification rites and complete three years in banishment. When he who has done such a thing returns, he is not to share in the sacred things with his children, and is never to become part of the same dining table. If the parent or the progeny disobeys, here again he is to become subject to prosecution for impiety by anyone who wishes. If a brother should kill a brother or sister out of spirited anger, or if a sister should kill a brother or sister, let it be said that these must undergo the purification rites and banishment in the same way as was said for parents and offspring: let him never become part of the hearth or a sharer in the sacred things with those whose brothers he has deprived of brothers and whose children he has deprived of parents. If someone should disobey, he would correctly and with justice become subject to prosecution under the law that has been described regarding impiety in these matters. If someone becomes so unrestrained in his spirited anger towards his parents that he dares, in an insanity of rage, to kill one of his parents, then, if the one who has died voluntarily absolved the perpetrator of murder before he died, the perpetrator is to undergo purification of the same sort as those who carry out an involuntary murder. Once he has done whatever other things those do, he is to be free of pollution. But if he was not absolved, the one who has done such a thing is to be liable to many laws. For he would become liable to the most severe judicial penalties for assault, and, likewise, impiety and temple robbing (for having plundered the soul of his parent). So if, indeed, it were possible for the same man to die often, the parricide or matricide, who committed this deed out of spirited anger, would very justly undergo many deaths. In this case alone (where a man is about to be killed by his parents), no law will permit killing to defend oneself against death; with regard to father or mother, the

868e

869a

869b

869c

ones who brought one's nature into the light, the law will legislate that one must endure, suffering everything rather than doing such a deed. So how would it be fitting for this man to receive a judicial penalty under the law in any other way? Let the punishment be death for him who kills his father or mother out of spirited anger.

Should a brother kill a brother in a battle that takes place during civil strife or in some such fashion, defending himself with his hands against the other who started it, let him be unpolluted just as if he had killed an enemy. The same holds for a citizen who kills a citizen, or a stranger who kills a stranger. If a member of the city should kill a stranger in self-defense, or a stranger a member of the city, he is to be unpolluted in the same way. The same holds for a slave who kills a slave. But if a slave should kill a free man in self-defense, he is to be liable to the same laws as the man who kills his father. Let what was said about being absolved of murder by the father apply in the same way to every absolution in such cases: if anyone voluntarily absolves somebody of this, let it be as if the murder was involuntary, let there be purification rites for the perpetrator, and let the law impose one year of exile.

869d

869e

Now what pertains to murders that involve violence and the involuntary, and that occur because of spiritedness, has been discussed with due measure. Next after these matters we should discuss what pertains to those that are voluntary and totally unjust, as well as the plotting involved—which spring from weakness in the face of pleasures, desires, and envies.

Kl. Correctly spoken.

Ath. First let's again do our best to say how many such things there would be. The greatest is desire, that dominates a soul driven wild by longings. This occurs especially where there is the yearning that is most frequent and strongest among the many: because of the wickedness due to nature and lack of education, money has the power to engender tens of thousands of erotic desires for its insatiable and limitless acquisition. The cause of the lack of education is the wicked praise of wealth that is spread abroad by both the Greeks and barbarians. For by judging it to be first among the goods when in fact it is third, they ruin their posterity as well as themselves. The noblest and best thing of all for every city is that the truth be told about wealth, namely, that it is for the sake of the body, and

870a

870b

the body is for the sake of the soul. Since, therefore, there are goods for the sake of which wealth by nature exists, it would come third after virtue of the body and of the soul. Thus this argument would become a teacher, showing that he who is to be happy shouldn't seek to be wealthy, but to be wealthy 870c justly and moderately; and then there wouldn't occur in cities murders that require murders to purge them. But now, as we said when we began to discuss these things, this is one, and the greatest, thing that brings about the most severe judicial penalties for voluntary murder. The second is the habit of the honor-loving soul. This breeds envies, which are harsh companions, especially for the one who possesses the envy, but secondly for the best among those in the city. The third cause is the cowardly and unjust fears that stir up many murders, in 870d a situation where someone is doing or has done something that he wants no one to become or to have become knowledgeable about. They remove those who would inform about these things by killing them, when they can do so in no other way.

Let these things that have been said be the preludes for all these cases, and in addition the argument [17] many earnestly believe because they've heard it from those who are seriously involved in the mystery-rites concerning such matters, to the effect that vengeance is exacted for such things in Hades, and that when they return back here again they must necessarily 870e pay the just penalty according to nature, which is that of suffering whatever he himself inflicted on the victim and having his life brought to an end this time by the same fate at another's hands. For him who believes and is wholly fearful of such a penalty, because of the prelude itself, it isn't necessary to sing the law [18] in addition to this; but for him who doesn't 871a believe let the following law be stated in writing:

He who with forethought, unjustly, and with his own hands kills any of his fellow tribesmen [19] must, in the first place, stay away from the places conventionally proscribed: he must not pollute the temples, or the marketplace, or the harbors, or any other common place of meeting, whether or not one of the human beings has pronounced this prohibition to the perpetrator. For the law prohibits it, and is always seen prohibiting it, and will always be seen prohibiting it, on behalf of the whole city. And anyone related to the deceased as 871b closely as a cousin, on either the male or female side, who fails to prosecute as he ought, or fails to proclaim to the perpetrator his banishment, would, in the first place, have the pollution and the enmity of the gods fall on himself—for the enmity of the law urges the omen on. Then, in the second place, he is to be liable to prosecution by anyone who is willing to seek retribution on behalf of the deceased. He who is willing to seek retribution should carry out everything, in the way of attention to rites of lustration for these matters and whatever other things the god prescribes for these conventional proceedings, and, after proclaiming the warning, should proceed to compel the perpetrator to submit to the lawful execution of the judicial penalty.

871c

That these things should be accompanied by certain prayers and sacrifices, to certain gods who make such matters their concern, so that murders won't occur in cities, would be easy for the lawgiver to show. But which are the gods, and what manner of initiating such trials would be most correct with a view to the divine, are matters that will be legislated by the Guardians of the Laws, together with the Interpreters, the Diviners, and the god, and thus they shall initiate these trials.

871d

The judges in these trials are to be the same as were said to have sovereign judgment over those who plunder the temples. He who is convicted is to be given the death penalty, and he is not to be buried in the country of the one who suffered, in order to show he is not forgiven,[20] as well as with a view to the impiety. If he flees and isn't willing to stand trial, let him remain in perpetual flight. If one of these people[21] should set foot in the country of the man who was murdered, the first member of the deceased's household or the first citizen who comes across him, should kill him with impunity, or bind him and hand him over to be killed by the magistrates who judged the trial. He who is prosecuting should at once demand guarantees from the one he's prosecuting, and the latter should present guarantors who are judged substantial by the judicial magistracy in charge of these matters—he should present three substantial guarantors, who guarantee his presence at the trial. If someone is either unwilling or unable to do so, the magistracy is to take him, guard him in bonds, and present him for judgment at the trial. If someone didn't kill with his own hands, but planned death for another, and after having

871e

872a

killed by the planning and plotting is dwelling in the city as one responsible for the murder, and impure in his soul, let the same judicial proceedings be followed in these cases, except for the guarantee. If the man is convicted, he is to be allowed his own tomb, but in other aspects the same things are to happen to him as were described for the previous case. These same things are to apply to strangers in relation to strangers, and to city dwellers and strangers in relation to one another, and again to slaves in relation to slaves, whether the murder 872b be by one's own hands or by plotting—except for the guarantee. As regards this, those who kill with their own hands must give guarantees, as was said, but he who makes the public accusation of murder should in these cases at the same time demand guarantees. If a slave should voluntarily kill a free man and be convicted at a trial, whether it be with his own hands or by planning, the common executioner of the city should take him near the memorial marker of the deceased, to a spot from where he can see the tomb, and whip him as many times as the one prosecuting prescribes; if the murderer is still 872c alive after the beating, he is to put him to death. If someone should kill a slave who was doing no injustice, out of fear lest he inform about his shameful and wicked deeds, or for some other such reason, then, just as he would have submitted to judicial proceedings for murder if he had killed a citizen, so let him submit to the same things for the death of such a slave.

If there should come to pass cases about which it is terrible and is no way pleasing even to legislate, but which it is impossible not to legislate for—voluntary and wholly unjust 872d murders of kinsmen, that take place either by one's own hands or through plotting, and which occur for the most part in cities with bad organization and rearing, but which presumably would also occur in some way in a country where someone wouldn't ever expect them—the account that was uttered a little while ago should be restated again, in case someone who hears us might become better able, on account of such things, to refrain voluntarily from murders that are in every way the most impious. For indeed the myth, or argument, or whatever it ought to be called, has been stated 872e clearly, as it has come down from ancient priests:

It is to the effect that watchful Justice, the avenger of the blood of kinsmen, uses the law mentioned just now, and ordains for the perpetrator of such a deed that he must necessarily suffer the very same things he has perpetrated. If someone ever kills his father, he must endure to suffer violently this same thing at the hands of his children at some time; if he should kill his mother, it is necessary that he himself be born partaking of female nature, and having become such, must at a later time depart life at the hands of the offspring. For there is no other purification for the shared polluted blood, nor is the pollution willing to be washed away, until the soul that perpetrated the deed pays for murder with murder, like for like, and thus, by appeasing, lays to rest the spiritedness of the entire family.

873a

These things should restrain someone who fears such retributions from the gods; but if some should be overtaken by such a miserable condition that they dare voluntarily, with forethought, to take the soul from the body of father, mother, brothers, or children, the law of the mortal lawgiver will legislate about such persons as follows:

873b

The warnings about staying away from places customarily proscribed, and the guarantees, are to be the same as those stated for the earlier cases. If someone is convicted of such a murder, of having killed one of these, the magistrates who are servants of the judges shall kill him; then they are to throw him down naked at a specified crossroads outside the city and all the magistrates, on behalf of the whole city, are each to bring a stone and throw it at the head of the corpse, to remove the impiety from the whole city. After this they are to carry him to the borders of the country and cast him out unburied, according to law.

873c

But what of one who kills the person that is most of all his own, and is said to be dearest to him—what should he suffer? I'm speaking of one who kills himself, violently robbing his Fate-allotted share, when he isn't ordered to do so by the city's judicial decree, nor compelled by some terribly painful and inescapable bad luck that's befallen him, and hasn't been allotted some baffling shame that he can't live with, but out of lack of effort and unmanly cowardice inflicts an unjust judicial penalty upon himself.

873d

In other respects the god knows what the legal conventions of purifications and burials ought to be in this case, and the nearest of kin should inquire about them with the Interpreters and also with the laws concerning these matters, and then act as these prescribe. But the tombs for those destroyed in this way should, in the first place, be off by themselves without a single companion tomb; then they should be buried without any fame, in uncultivated and nameless boundary regions of the twelve districts, without tablets or name markers indicating the tombs.

If a beast of burden or any other living thing should murder someone, except in the case where it does such a thing when competing for the prizes established in a public contest, the kinsmen should prosecute the killer for murder, and the judges are to be whichever and as many of the Field Regulators as the next of kin shall ordain. The convicted party they should kill and cast out beyond the borders of the country. If some soulless thing should take away the soul from a human being, except in cases where it's a lightning bolt or some such missile coming from a god, but in the case of any of the other things that may kill someone through his falling upon it or its falling upon him—the next of kin should appoint the closest neighbor to be judge, and thus remove the impious impurity from himself and the whole family. The convicted party they should cast beyond the borders, just as was stated in the case of the class of living things. 873e

874a

If someone has evidently died, and the killer remains uncertain and undetected even after they seek him in a way that is not careless, there should be the same warnings as in the other cases, but proclaimed "for the perpetrator of the murder." After the prosecution is successful, they should announce in the marketplace to the killer of so-and-so, who has been convicted of murder, that he is not to set foot in the temples nor in the whole country of the one who has suffered, because, if he should be detected and known, he will be killed and thrown unburied outside the country of the one who has suffered. 874b

Let this then be our one law that stands sovereign in regard to murder, and what's been said until this point is what covers such things. But the cases and circumstances in which the killer would correctly be unpolluted are to be as follows:

If at night he should catch and kill a thief entering his house to steal goods, let him be unpolluted. If he should kill 874c while defending himself against a highwayman, let him be unpolluted. If someone should use violence for sexual purposes against a free woman or boy, he may be killed with impunity by the violently outraged party, or the father, or the brothers or sons. If a man should come upon his wedded wife being violently attacked, let him be unpolluted under the law if he kills the violent attacker. If someone should kill somebody while defending his father from death, when his father is doing nothing impious—or his mother, his children, his brothers, or his fellow procreator of children—let him be entirely unpolluted.

874d

Let this be the legislation concerning the living soul's nurture and education—whose presence makes life livable for it and whose absence does the opposite—and concerning the retributions that should follow violent deaths. What concerns the nurture and education of the bodies has also been discussed. Following on these things, one ought to define as well as one can the acts of violence they do to one another involuntarily and voluntarily, showing what they are, how many they are, and what retribution would be appropriate for each to obtain. It's likely that these are the things that it would be correct to legislate next.

874e

Even the lowliest of those who turn to arranging laws would treat wounds and maimings that arise from wounds second after deaths. Now wounds should be distinguished just as murders were distinguished, into those that are involuntary, those that occur because of spirited anger, those that occur because of fear, and those that occur voluntarily out of forethought.

Something like the following preliminary statement should be made about all such cases, to the effect that it's necessary for human beings to establish laws for themselves and live according to laws, or they differ in no way from the beasts that are the most savage in every way. The cause of these things is this, that there is no one among human beings whose nature grows so as to become adequate both to know what is in the interest of human beings as regards a political regime and, knowing this, to be able and willing always to do what is best. For, in the first place, it is difficult to know that the true political art must care not for the private but the

875a

common—for the common binds cities together, while the private tears them apart—and that it is in the interest of both the common and the private that the common, rather than the private, be established nobly. Secondly, even if someone should advance sufficiently in the art to know that this is the way these things are by nature, and after this should rule the city without being audited, and as an autocrat, he would never be able to adhere to this conviction and spend his life giving priority to nourishing what is common in the city, while nourishing the private as following after the common; mortal nature will always urge him toward getting more than his share and toward private business, irrationally fleeing pain and pursuing pleasure, and putting both of these before what is more just and better. Creating a darkness within itself, it will completely fill both itself and the whole city with everything bad. Of course, if ever some human being who was born adequate in nature, with a divine dispensation, were able to attain these things, he wouldn't need any laws ruling over him. For no law or order is stronger than knowledge, nor is it right²² for intelligence to be subordinate, or a slave, to anyone, but it should be ruler over everything, if indeed it is true and really free according to nature. But now, in fact, it is so nowhere or in any way, except to a small extent. That is why one must choose what comes second, order and law—which see and look to most things, but are incapable of seeing everything.

875b

875c

875d

These things have been said for the sake of what follows: we are now going to ordain what someone who wounds or does injury to someone else other than himself ought to suffer or pay.

Of course, it's available to anyone, in regard to anything, to interrupt and correctly ask, "What sort of wounding, inflicted on whom, or how, or when, are you talking about? For each of these has ten thousand varieties, which are very different from one another." Now it's impossible either to turn all of these things, or none of them, over to the judicial courts for judgment. There is indeed one thing, that applies to every case, that must necessarily be turned over to them to judge: whether each of these things happened or not. Then again, to turn over nothing about what penalty should be paid by the one who has been unjust in one of these respects, or what he

875e

876a

ought to suffer, and to legislate about everything, small and great, oneself, is almost impossible.

Kl. So what is to be said after this?

Ath. This: that some things ought to be turned over to the judicial courts and some things shouldn't be turned over, but one should legislate them oneself.

Kl. What then ought to be legislated and what things ought to be given to the judicial courts to judge?

Ath. After these things, it would be most correct to say the following things: in a city in which the judicial courts are wretched and inarticulate, keep hidden their opinions, deliver their judgments in secret, and, what is more terrible than this, when they aren't silent but are full of noise just like a theater, judging each of the orators in turn with shouts of praise and blame, then the whole city is wont to undergo a harsh experience. To be led by some necessity to legislate for such judicial courts is not a lucky thing, but nevertheless, if led by necessity, one ought to turn over to them the authority to fix the penalties in the smallest possible matters, and one should legislate most matters expressly oneself—if someone should ever legislate for such a regime. But in a city in which the judicial courts were set up correctly, insofar as possible, and where those who are going to judge have been well brought up, and tested with complete precision, there it would be correct, good, and noble to turn over to such judges the judgment of most things pertaining to what those who are convicted ought to suffer or pay. In the present situation, we'll incur no blame [23] if we don't legislate for them concerning the greatest and most frequent matters, in regard to which even rather wretchedly educated judges would be able to discern and assign to each fault the value of what is suffered and done. Since we believe those we're legislating for are not the most poorly fitted to become judges of such matters, most ought to be turned over to them. Nonetheless, what we've often said and done in legislating the earlier laws—describing an outline and sketches of retributions, to give examples to the judges of how always to avoid going beyond the bounds of justice—was very correct at that time, and indeed this same thing should be done now, as we return once again to the laws. Our writing about wounding should go as follows:

If someone should in his thought intend to kill somebody

876b

876c

876d

876e

dear—except in cases where the law directs him to do so—but
only wounds, and is unable to kill, the one who has wounded
with this thought in mind is unworthy of pity; he is not to be 877a
forgiven [24] any more than if he had killed, and is to be compelled to submit to a judicial trial for murder. Yet out of reverence for his not entirely bad luck, and for the demon, who
from pity for him and the person wounded prevented the
wound from becoming incurable for the latter, and warded off
the accursed luck and outcome for the former—to show gratitude to this demon and not oppose it—the one who did the
wounding is to be spared death, and is to be removed to some 877b
neighboring city to spend his life, continuing to reap the benefits of all his property. But as for the injury done, if he has
done some injury to the person wounded, he must pay the one
injured, the value to be set by the judicial court which judged
the trial—and the judges are to be those who would have
judged the murder case if the man had died from the blow that
inflicted the wound. If a child should thus wound his parents
from forethought, or a slave his master, death is to be the penalty. And if a brother should thus wound a brother or sister,
or a sister a brother or sister, and he be convicted of wound- 877c
ing from forethought, death is to be the penalty. If a wife
should wound her own husband with the intention of killing,
or a husband his own wife, the person is to go into perpetual
exile. If they should have sons or daughters who are still children, the guardians are to take care of the property and look
after the children as if they were orphans. If they're grown
men, it shall not [25] be necessary for the offspring to take care of
the exile, and they are to acquire the property. In the case
where someone who has no children falls into such straits, the 877d
family relations of the exile as far removed as the children of
cousins on both sides, men and women, are to meet together
and, in consultation with the Guardians of the Laws and the
Priests, are to appoint a lot holder for this five thousand forti-
eth household in the city. They should think about this in a
way and in terms of an argument that is something like the
following: none of the five thousand forty households is the
property of the occupier or of his entire family so much as it is
the property of the city, in both a public and a private sense. 877e
And it is necessary for the city, at least, that the households it
owns be as pious and as lucky as they can possibly be. So

whenever one of the households is rendered unlucky and at the same time impious, with the result that the owner leaves in it no children, dying a bachelor, or a married man without children, who has been convicted of voluntary murder or of some other fault pertaining to gods or citizens for which death is the penalty expressly stated in the law, or when someone without grown male children has gone into perpetual exile, the house must first be purified and cleansed of this, accord-

878a

ing to the law. Then, as we said just now, the relatives should meet together with the Guardians of the Laws to look for the family that has the best reputation of those in the city for both virtue and also good luck, and in which there are several children. They should take one from that family and give him to the father and family forebears of the man who has died, as their son, and should name him after them for the sake of the omen; praying that he will become a begettor of children for them, a guardian of the hearth, and a minister of the profane

878b

and sacred things with better luck than his father, they should appoint him lot holder according to law, and let the man who was at fault lie nameless and without children or estate, when such disasters overtake a man.

It is likely that not all the beings have a boundary that is contiguous with the boundary of another, but for those in which there is an area between the boundaries, this would lie in the middle of both, stretching in between the boundaries and encountering each of them. And indeed, what takes place out of spiritedness we asserted to be just such a thing, between the involuntary and the voluntary. Let the same hold for wounds that occur because of rage.

878c

If someone is convicted, he is in the first place to pay twice the value of the injury, if the wound turns out to be curable; for incurable wounds he is to pay four times the value. If it's curable, but casts some great shame and disgrace on the wounded party, he is to pay triple the value. And insofar as someone who wounds somebody injures not only the one who suffers but also the city, by rendering the victim incapable of helping the fatherland against enemies, in this case he is to pay for the injury to the city along with the other penalties.

878d

For in addition to his own military services he is to serve for the one who is incapacitated, and carry out the military duties

on behalf of that man; or if he fails to do these things let him
be subject under the law to prosecution, by anyone who
wishes, for failing to perform his military service. The value of
the injury, whether double, triple, or quadruple is to be paid,
should be determined by the judges who voted on the conviction. If one member of a family should wound another
member of the same family, in the same way as this person
just discussed, the family and kin as distant as children of
cousins on the women's and men's sides, both women and
men, should meet together and, after arriving at a judgment,
hand over to the natural parents the estimation of the injury. If
the estimation is in dispute, those on the male side are to have
sovereign authority to make the estimation; if they are unable
to do so, they must finally turn the matter over to the Guardians of the Laws. The judges for those offspring who inflict
such wounds on their parents must necessarily be men over
sixty years of age who have children—not created by adoption, but truly. If someone is convicted, they must decide if
such a person ought to die, or suffer something else greater
than this or something not much less. None of the perpetrator's family are to serve as judges, not even if one should have
lived as long a time as the law has stated. If some slave should
wound a free man out of rage, the owner should hand the
slave over to the person wounded, to use as he wishes. If he
should fail to hand him over, he himself is to cure the injury. If
someone accuses the slave and the wounded party of having
agreed to contrive what happened, he should dispute the case:
if he should fail to win, let him pay three times the value of the
injury, but if he should win he shall hold the one who artfully
colluded with the slave liable for kidnapping.

878e

879a

He who involuntarily wounds another should pay simply
for the injury—for no lawgiver is sufficient to rule over
chance—and the judges are to be those who were said to judge
in cases of offspring who wound their parents: let them estimate the value of the injury.

879b

All the sufferings we've discussed so far are violent, and the
whole class of assault is also violent. So every man, child, and
woman ought always to think about such things in the following way:

The elder is to no small degree more venerable than the

879c

younger, in the eyes of gods and of human beings who are going to be saved and become happy. It is therefore shameful, and hateful to the gods, to see in the city an assault by a younger man on an elder. And it's reasonable for every young man who is beaten by an old man to endure his rage with a soft spirit, thereby laying up for himself in old age this same honor. So let it be as follows. Every one of us is to evince awe, in deed and word, toward one elder than himself. Whoever exceeds us by twenty years in age, male or female, should be considered as a father or a mother, and care must be taken ac-

879d cordingly: one must always abstain from the entire generation that is capable of having begotten or borne one, for the sake of the gods who preside over childbirth. One should abstain in the same way from a stranger, whether he's lived here from old or is newly arrived. One shouldn't at all dare to chastise such a person with blows, whether one initiates the attack or is defending against it. If someone thinks a stranger should be punished for having licentiously and brazenly struck him, he should seize him and take him before the magistracy of the City Regulators, but should abstain from beating him, so that

879e he will be far from daring ever to strike a native inhabitant. The City Regulators should take him and judge him, paying due regard to the god of strangers; if the stranger then should seem to have struck a native inhabitant unjustly, they are to give the stranger as many blows with the whip as he himself struck, and thus put a stop to the brazenness of strangers. But if he hasn't done an injustice, they are to threaten and blame the one who brought him before them, and dismiss both. If a

880a man of a certain age should strike a man of the same age, or a man more advanced in age than himself but childless—an old man against an old man, or a young man against a young man—let the man defend himself according to nature, without a weapon and using his bare hands. But if a man over forty years of age should dare to fight, whether he initiates it or is on the defensive, he is to be spoken of as boorish, illiberal, and slavish, and it would be fitting if he incurred a degrading judicial penalty.

If someone should become obedient to such admonitions,[26] he would be a docile man. But he who obeys poorly and thinks nothing of the prelude would have a law such as the following waiting for him:

If someone should strike somebody elder than himself by 880b
twenty years or more, then, in the first place, the one who
comes upon this, if he isn't of the same age or younger than
the combatants, must try to separate them or else be a bad
man according to law. If he is of the same age or yet younger
than the man being beaten, he must defend him as if the one
being done the injustice were a brother or a father or a more
senior relative. Then, in addition, the one who, as was said,
dared to strike an elder must submit to a trial for assault, and if
he should be convicted in the trial is to be imprisoned for not 880c
less than a year. If in the judges' estimation the time should be
longer, let the time the court decides be authoritatively binding. If a stranger or one of the resident aliens should strike
someone elder than himself by twenty years or more, the same
law concerning help from bystanders is to have the same
power. He that loses such a trial, if he's a stranger and not a
resident, must pay the judicial penalty of spending two years
in prison; if he's a resident alien and has disobeyed the laws
he must spend three years in prison—unless in the court's es- 880d
timation the judicial penalty for him should be a longer period
of time. He who was a bystander in any of these cases and
failed to give help according to the law must pay a penalty: if
he's a member of the highest class, a mina, if of the second,
fifty drachmas, if of the third, thirty, and twenty if of the
fourth. The judicial court for such cases is to be constituted by
the Generals, Rank Commanders, Tribe Commanders, and
Cavalry Commanders.

The laws, it is likely, come into being partly for the sake of
the worthy human beings, in order to teach them the way in
which they might mingle with one another and dwell in 880e
friendship, and partly for the sake of those who have shunned
education, who employ a certain tough nature and have been
in no way softened so as to avoid proceeding to everything
bad. It is these who have brought about the words that are
going to be uttered. On their account the lawgiver would
legislate the laws, from necessity, wishing that the need for
them would never arise. For whoever will dare at any time to
touch in some violent assault his father or mother, or yet their
progenitors, terrified neither by the wrath of the gods above
nor by the retributions said to be beneath the earth, but hold- 881a
ing in contempt the ancient sayings repeated by everyone, as

if he knew things he doesn't know at all, and breaking the law—this man requires some ultimate deterrent. Now death is not the ultimate, and the toils said to await these people in Hades, though they're closer than this to being ultimates, and though they speak very truly, do not succeed as a deterrence for such souls. If they did, there would never be assaults on mothers or daring, impious, attacks on the other progenitors.

881b

It is necessary, then, that the punishments here for such things, inflicted on these men while they are living, be no less than those in Hades, insofar as possible. Let what is said after this be as follows:

If someone should dare to strike his father or mother, or their fathers or mothers, and should do so while not afflicted with madness, then, in the first place, one who happens along should help just as in the earlier cases. If a stranger who's a resident alien helps, he is to be invited to take a front seat at the contests, while if he hasn't helped, he is to be exiled per-

881c

petually from the country; he who is not a resident alien should receive praise if he helps, and blame if he doesn't help. A slave who has helped is to become a free man, while if he hasn't helped, he is to be beaten a hundred strokes with the whip—by the Market Regulators, if the incident occurred in the marketplace. If it occurred outside the marketplace but in the city, the resident City Regulator will inflict the punishment, while if it occurred somewhere in the fields of the country, it will be inflicted by the Officers of the Field Regulators. If the person who happens along should be some native inhabitant, whether it be child or man or even a woman, everyone

881d

must come to the defense, crying out against the impious one. He who fails to come to the defense must according to law bear the curse of Zeus who watches over kinship and fatherhood. If someone should be convicted in a judicial trial for assault on his parents, he must in the first place be perpetually exiled from the city, into the rest of the country, and must avoid all sacred places. If he doesn't avoid them, the Field Regulators are to punish him with blows and entirely as they wish, while if he comes back from exile, he is to be penalized with death. And if someone among the free men should eat

881e

with such a man, or drink with him, or partake in common with him in some other such community, or even if he should only touch him in greeting, voluntarily, when encountering him somewhere, he is not to go into any temple, nor into the marketplace, nor into the city as a whole, until he has been purified, believing that he has partaken of accursed luck. But if in disobedience to the law he should illegally pollute the temples and the city, and any of the magistrates should be aware of the fact and doesn't bring to trial such a man, then in the audits this is to be one of the gravest accusations against 882a the magistrate.

If, again, a slave should strike a free man, whether he be a stranger or a member of the city, the bystander is to help or pay a fine according to his class, as has been stated. Those who happen along, together with the one beaten, should tie up the culprit and hand him over to the one who has been done the injustice. The latter shall take him, bind him in fet- 882b ters, and whip him as much as he wishes, so long as he does no injury to the master, to whom he shall turn him over to be kept according to law. The law should be: Whoever, being a slave, should strike a free man when the magistrates haven't commanded it, should be taken in bonds by his owner from the person beaten, and shouldn't be released until the slave 882c persuades the one who was beaten that he is worthy of living released. The same legal customs are to apply to women in all such relations with one another, and to women in relation to men, and men in relation to women.

BOOK X

884a   Ath.   After assaults, let a single legal custom such as the following be pronounced concerning acts of violence in general: no one is to carry or drive away anything belonging to others, or use anything belonging to a neighbor, if he hasn't persuaded the owner. For such behavior has been, is, and will be a source of all the evils that have been mentioned.

     Of the evils that are left, the gravest are the unrestrained and insolent things done by the young. These offend the worst when they offend the sacred things, and are especially grave when they offend things that are public as well as hal-lowed—or are common to a part (being shared by members of

885a   a tribe or some other such groups). Second and second-worst is when they offend private sacred things and tombs. Third is when someone is insolent against his parents, apart from the cases discussed earlier. A fourth kind of insolence is when someone, heedless of the rulers, drives or carries away or uses something belonging to them without persuading them. A fifth would be insolence against the political right of each of the citizens, of a sort that calls for judicial penalty. A law should be given to all these in common.

     As to temple robbery, what ought to be suffered, whether the robbery takes place violently or by stealth, has been stated

885b   in summary fashion. But as regards the ways by which some-one may in speech and in deed be insolent toward the gods either by speaking or by acting, what must be suffered should be stated after the exhortation[1] has been laid down. Let the latter be the following:

No one who believes in gods according to the laws[2] has ever voluntarily done an impious deed or let slip an illegal utterance unless he is suffering one of three things: either this, which I just said, he doesn't believe; or, second, he believes they exist but that they do not think about human beings; or, third, he believes they are easily persuaded[3] if they are brought sacrifices and prayers.

Kl.   So what should we do or even say to them?   885c

Ath.   My good man, let us first hearken to what I divine they say in a joking way, out of contempt for us.

Kl.   What's that?

Ath.   These are the things they would probably say, in a jocular speech:

"O Athenian stranger, and Lacedaimonian, and Knossian, the things you say are true. For some of us don't believe in the gods at all, and others believe them to be as you say. Now we demand, just as you demanded in regard to the laws, that   885d before you direct harsh threats at us, you try to persuade and teach that there are gods, adducing adequate evidence, and that they are too good to be turned aside and beguiled from what is just by certain gifts. For as it is now, since we hear these and other such things from those who are said to be best among the poets, orators, diviners, and priests, as well as from myriads upon myriads of others, most of us don't turn to refraining from doing unjust things, but rather try to make healing amends after we've done them. From lawgivers who   885e are claiming to be not savage but gentle, we demand that persuasion be used on us first. And perhaps we would be persuaded by you, even if you didn't speak much better than the others about the existence of the gods, so long as you spoke better as regards the truth. But do try, if we're saying something well measured, to say what we're asking for."

Kl.   Well, doesn't it seem easy, stranger, to say that the gods exist and to be speaking the truth?

Ath.   How?   886a

Kl.   First, there's the earth, the sun, the stars, and all things, and this beautiful orderliness of the seasons, divided into years and months. Then there's the fact that all Greeks and barbarians believe the gods exist.[4]

Ath.   I am afraid, at least, my blessed man—for I would never say that I am in awe—lest the wicked will somehow be contemp-

886b tuous of us. For you[5] don't know about what is responsible for our difference with them, but believe that it's only because of a lack of self-restraint in the face of pleasures and desires that their souls are urged on to an impious life.

Kl. But what in addition to these things would be responsible, stranger?

Ath. Something you would hardly know of because you live entirely out of it, and which would escape your notice.

Kl. What is this you're now explaining?

Ath. A certain very harsh lack of learning, that seems to be the greatest prudence.

Kl. How do you mean?

886c Ath. Among us there are accounts found in writings, which aren't among you because of the virtue of the regime, as I understand. These are discussions about the gods, some with certain meters and others without meters. The most ancient discuss how the first nature of heaven and the other things came into being, and then, proceeding on to a point not much after the beginning, they go through how the gods came into being[6] and how they mingled with one another once they had come into being. It's not easy to pass judgment, in the case of writings so ancient, as to whether they have some other sort of noble or ignoble effect on the hearers, but as regards services

886d and honors toward parents, I at least would never speak of them in praise, either as beneficial or as spoken entirely in accordance with reality. What pertains to the ancients should be left alone and bid good-bye, and spoken of in whatever way is pleasing to the gods; but what pertains to our new and wise men must be accused, insofar as it is responsible for bad things. Now the following is what is done by the arguments of such men: when I and you adduce evidence that the gods exist, bringing forward these very things—sun and moon and stars and earth—as being gods and divine things, those who are convinced by these wise men would say that these things are earth and stones, and incapable of thinking anything

886e about human affairs, however well decked-out they may somehow be, with arguments that make them plausible.

Kl. You happen to have uttered an argument that is indeed difficult, stranger, even if it were alone and single; but now when there are very many arguments, it is still more difficult.

Ath. So what then? What do we say? What must we do? Will we

pronounce a defense[7] as if someone were accusing us before impious human beings, who say to those defending themselves in regard to the legislation that we are doing terrible things when we legislate that gods exist?[8] Or shall we let it go, bidding good-bye and turning back again to the laws, lest our prelude become longer than the laws? For the argument once unfolded would not be short, if we would use arguments of due measure and demonstrate to those desiring to be impious the things they indicated had to be discussed, and if we would convert him to fear, and then, having created a sense of repugnance, would legislate whatever was fitting after these things.

887a

Kl. But stranger, we've often—considering the short time anyway —said this very thing, that in the present circumstances there's no need to honor brevity of speech over length. For there's no one, as the saying goes, in pressing pursuit of us. Indeed, to show that we choose the shorter in preference to the best would be ridiculous and petty. Moreover, it makes no small difference, if somehow or other there is some persuasiveness in our arguments that the gods exist and are good, honoring justice differently from human beings. For this would be just about our noblest and best prelude on behalf of all the laws. So without feeling repugnance or being in a hurry, mustering whatever capability we have for making such arguments persuasive, let's go through the arguments in as adequate a way as we can, holding back nothing.

887b

887c

Ath. Prayer is what it seems to me your present speech is calling for, so zealous are you, and eager in spirit! There's no room for further delay in speaking. Come then, how would someone speak without spirited anger about the gods, and that they do exist? For it's inevitable that we be harshly disposed toward, and hate, those who have been and are now responsible for our getting involved in these arguments: they refuse to believe the myths which they heard from their nurses and mothers since the time they were still young children being nourished on milk, hearing them spoken as if in incantations, playfully and seriously. And they heard them in prayers that go with sacrifices, and saw them accompanied by spectacles, executed during the sacrifices, that are most pleasant for the young man, at least, to see and hear. They saw their own parents evincing the greatest seriousness, on behalf of themselves and them, as they carried on a dialogue in prayers and

887d

887e

supplications with gods who were assumed to exist in the highest degree. At the rising of the sun and moon, and at their settings, they heard of and saw Greeks and all the barbarians, in every sort of disaster and in prosperity, kneeling and prostrating themselves—not as if those things didn't exist, but as if they existed to the highest degree and gave no hint that they are not gods. Those who now compel us to say what we're saying are people who have contempt for all these things, and not on account of a single adequate argument—as would be affirmed by those who possess even a small amount of intelligence; how could someone use gentle arguments to admonish, and at the same time to teach, these people about gods, and first that they exist? Yet it must be dared. For it shouldn't be that both are maddened at the same time, at least—some of us by gluttony for pleasure, and others by spirited anger at such men. Let some such preliminary speech as the following proceed, without spiritedness,[9] for those who are thus corrupted in their thinking, and let's speak gently, quenching spiritedness, as if we were carrying on a dialogue with one such man:

888a

"Lad, you are young, and the passage of time will make you alter many of the opinions you now hold, and exchange them for their opposites. So wait until then to judge the greatest things—and the greatest thing, which you now consider nothing, is thinking correctly about the gods and thus living nobly or not. If I first reminded you of one great thing about them, I would never be asserting a falsehood, and it is to the following effect: neither you alone nor your friends are the first and foremost to have this opinion about gods, but there always arise people, sometimes more, sometimes less, who have this illness. And having encountered many of them, I would declare to you the following: no one has ever adopted from his youth this opinion about the gods, that they don't exist, and continued until old age remaining in this frame of mind.

888b

888c

"The other two states of mind do remain (not for many people, but they do remain for some)—that the gods exist, but think nothing of human things, and the one after this, that they do think about them, but are easily persuaded[10] by sacrifices and prayers. If you should be persuaded by me, you'll wait until you have a doctrine about these matters that has become as clear as it can be, and meanwhile you'll investigate

whether things are thus or are otherwise, and will inquire   888d
from others, and especially from the lawgiver. During this
time you would not dare to do anything impious concerning
the gods. The one who establishes the laws for you should try,
now and in the future, to teach how these very things are."

Kl.   What's been said until now at least, stranger, is very fine with
us.

Ath.   In every way, Megillus and Kleinias. But without our realizing
it, we've fallen into an amazing argument!

Kl.   Which one do you mean?

Ath.   The one that in the opinion of many is the wisest of all   888e
arguments.

Kl.   Explain yet more clearly.

Ath.   Presumably, certain people say that all affairs come into
being, have come into being, and will come into being, by nature, by art, and through chance.[11]

Kl.   Isn't that finely expressed?

Ath.   It's likely, at any rate, that men who are presumably wise
speak correctly. Let's follow them, anyway, and investigate   889a
whatever it is that those people over there happen to think.

Kl.   By all means.

Ath.   It's likely, they assert, that the greatest of them, and the finest,
are produced by nature and chance, and the smaller by art,
which, taking from nature the genesis of the greatest and first
deeds, molds and constructs all the smaller things which we
all call artificial.

Kl.   How do you mean?

Ath.   I'll express it still more clearly, as follows. Fire, water, earth,   889b
and air are all by nature and by chance, they claim, and none
of these is by art; and the bodies that come after these—of the
earth, sun, moon, and stars—came into being through these,
which are beings completely without soul. They are each carried about by the chance of the power each has; when they fall
together with things that somehow harmonize with what is
proper to them—hot things with cold things, or dry things in
relation to wet things, and soft things in relation to hard   889c
things, and all things that are mixed together, by the mixing of
opposites according to chance, that arises out of necessity—
then in this way and according to these means, the whole
heaven and all things in heaven, and also the animals and all
the plants[12] have come into being, once all the seasons had

come into being out of these things: not through intelligence, they claim, nor through some god, nor through art, but, as we're saying, by nature and chance. Art is later, coming into 889d being later from these; being itself mortal and from mortals, it later has brought into being certain playthings that don't partake much of truth, but are certain images that are akin to one another—such as the things brought into being by painting and music and whatever arts are fellow workers with these. But some of the arts do bring into being something serious, and these are the ones that have their power in common with nature—such as, again, medicine and farming and gymnastics. And indeed, as for the political art, they claim that there is a small portion of it that is in partnership with nature, but 889e that most of it is by art; and thus the whole of legislation, whose assumptions [13] are not true, is not by nature but by art.

Kl. How do you mean?

Ath. The gods, blessed one, are what these people first assert to exist by art—not by nature but by certain legal conventions, and these differ from one place to another, depending on how each group agreed among themselves when they laid down their laws. They claim that the noble things by nature are different from those by convention, and that the just things are not at all by nature, but that men are continually disputing with one another and are always changing these things, and whatever changes they've made at a given time are each at that 890a time authoritative, having come into being by art and by the legal conventions, but not, surely, by any nature.

All these things, friends, are put forward by men considered wise by young people,[14] private men who write in prose [15] and poets, who explain that what is most just is whatever allows someone to triumph by force. This is the source of the impieties the young people contract, to the effect that the gods are not such as the law commands they must be conceived; by means of these things civil strife is instigated, by those who draw people toward the way of life that is correct according to nature—which is, in truth, to live dominating the rest and not to be a slave to others according to legal convention.

890b Kl. What an argument you've gone through, stranger! And what ruin for young people,[16] in the public life of cities and in private homes!

[286]

Ath. What you say is indeed true, Kleinias. So what do you think the lawgiver ought to do, seeing how these men have been preparing in this way for a long time? Is he merely to stand up in the city and threaten all the human beings, that if they don't affirm that the gods exist and don't conform their thoughts to the opinion that they are such as the law affirms—and about noble things and just things and all the greatest matters, the same speech, and about whatever aims at virtue and vice, that it is necessary to act in these respects while thinking in the way the lawgiver has instructed in writing—is he to say that whoever does not show himself obedient to the laws must in one case die, and in another case be punished with blows and prison, and in another case with dishonors, or, in other cases, with poverty and exile? Is he to present no persuasion for the human beings, mixed in with his speeches as he gives them laws, so as to make them as tame as he can? 890c

Kl. Not at all, stranger! If there happens to be even some small bit 890d of persuasion as regards such matters, the lawgiver of even slight merit should in no way grow faint, but should lend his whole voice, as they say, in assistance to the ancient law's [17] argument to the effect that there are gods, and the rest that you just now went through; indeed, he should take the field on behalf of law itself and art, showing that they are by nature, or by something not inferior to nature, if they are offspring of intelligence—according to the correct argument, which you appear to me to be pronouncing, and on the basis of which I put my trust in you now.

Ath. O most eager-spirited Kleinias! What now? Isn't it difficult to 890e follow arguments of this kind spoken before crowds, and, in addition, aren't they of enormous length?

Kl. What, stranger? About drunkenness and music we put up with ourselves talking at such length, and we're not going to put up with it when it comes to gods and such matters? Besides, at least for legislation that is to proceed with prudence, it is presumably a very great help when the prescriptions per- 891a taining to the laws are set down in writing and are entirely stable, because they provide for all time an opportunity for questioning; as a result, if they're difficult to listen to at the beginning, there's no need to fear, so long as the slow learner can go and examine them often. Even if they're lengthy, if the arguments are beneficial, it doesn't appear to me, at least, to be at all reasonable or pious for any man to fail, on this account, to help these arguments as best he can.

Meg. What Kleinias says seems excellent to me, stranger.

891b Ath. And certainly, Megillus, one ought to do as he says. Of course, if such arguments weren't spread about among the whole of humanity, so to speak, there'd be no need for arguments in defense of the gods' existence. But now they're necessary. When the greatest laws are being undermined by bad human beings, who is a more appropriate defender than the lawgiver?

Meg. Nobody is.

891c Ath. But now you tell me again, Kleinias (for you must share in the arguments): the one saying these things ventures to hold that fire, water, earth, and air are the first of all things, and ventures to name these very things "nature," and to say that soul is something that comes later, out of these things. But it's likely that he doesn't "venture," but really makes these things manifest to us in his argument.

Kl. By all means.

Ath. Well then, in the name of Zeus! Haven't we discovered something like a source of the mindless opinion of those human beings who have at any time engaged in investigations into
891d nature? Consider and investigate the whole argument. For it would make no small difference if those who handle impious arguments, and initiate others into them, were evidently using the arguments not well, but erroneously. And such seems to me to be the case.

Kl. Well spoken, but try to explain how this is.

Ath. It's likely that rather unfamiliar arguments are going to have to be handled now.

Kl. There shouldn't be hesitation, stranger. For I understand that you think it's necessary to go outside the realm of legislation,
891e if we are to handle such arguments. But if there is no other way whatsoever, except this, by which there can be consonant agreement that what are now called gods by legal convention are correctly so called, then this is the way the discussion must proceed, you amazing man!

Ath. It's likely, then, that at this point I may present something like the following rather unfamiliar argument. The arguments which have shaped the soul of the impious have asserted that what is in fact the first cause of the coming into being and passing away of all things is not first, but has come into being later, and that what in fact comes later comes earlier. That is why they have fallen into error concerning the real existence of gods.

Kl. I don't yet understand. 892a

Ath. It is soul, comrade, that almost all of them have dared to misunderstand: what sort of thing it happens to be, what power it has, and, among other things about it, how it comes into being—how it is among the first things, how it comes into being before all bodies, and how it is, more than anything, the ruling cause of their change and of all their reordering. And if these things are so, isn't it necessarily the case that the things akin to soul would come into being before the things belong- 892b ing to body, since it is elder than body?

Kl. Necessarily.

Ath. Opinion, then, and supervision, intelligence, art, and law would be prior to hard things, soft things, heavy things, and light things. And, indeed, the great and first deeds and actions would be those of art, since they're among the first things, while the things that are by nature, and nature, which they incorrectly name in this way, would be later and would have as their ruling causes art and intelligence.

Kl. How do you mean "incorrectly"? 892c

Ath. Nature, they mean to say, is the coming into being connected with the first things. But if soul is going to appear first, and not fire or air, and it's soul that has come into being among the first things, it would be most correct, almost, to say that it is especially [18] by nature. These things are so if someone should demonstrate that soul is a being elder than body, but otherwise not at all.

Kl. What you say is very true.

Ath. So, after these things, shall we address ourselves to this very 892d task?

Kl. But of course.

Ath. Let us be on our guard against an argument that is wily in every way, lest with its youthful vigor it cajole us, who are elderly, and get away, making us laughable, and seem like people who reached for great things but failed to obtain even the smaller. Consider therefore: suppose it was necessary for us, being three, to cross a very swift flowing river, and I, happening to be the youngest of us and experienced in many cur-

892e   rents, said that I ought to try it first by myself, leaving you in safety and investigating whether it is fordable for more elderly men such as you, or just how it is. If it appeared to be, I would then call to you and help you across with my experience, while if it were unfordable for you, the risk would be mine. I would have seemed to speak in a well-measured way. Now the argument coming up is rather swift and perhaps almost unfordable

893a   for your strength. Lest it create in you a dizziness and whirling, sweep you away by asking unfamiliar questions, and engender an unpleasant unsightliness and unseemliness, it seems to me that I ought now to proceed thus: first I should question myself, while you listen in safety, and then after this I again should answer myself, and go through the entire argument this way, until what pertains to soul is completed and it has been demonstrated that soul is prior to body.

Kl.   You seem to us, stranger, to have spoken in an excellent way. Do as you suggest.

893b   Ath.   Come then, if ever we should invoke the aid of a god, it's now that this should happen—at the demonstration of their own existence let their aid be invoked in all seriousness—and holding on as if to some safe cable, let's set forth into the present argument.

     If I am examined about such matters through some such questions as the following, it appears to me to be safest to answer as follows. When someone should ask, "O stranger, do all things stand still then, and is there nothing in motion?[19] Or is the case entirely the opposite to this? Or are some of the

893c   things in motion, and some remaining still?"—"Some things are presumably in motion," I will declare, "and some things remain still."—"And then isn't it in a certain place that the standing things stand and the things in motion move?"—"How could it be otherwise?"—"And some, at least, would presumably do this in one location, but some in many."—"Are you speaking of those that obtain the power of things that stand still in the middle," we will declare, "and thus move in one place, just as the circumference turns in circles that are said to stand still?"—"Yes."—"And we learn, at any rate, that in this rotation such motion carries the largest and

893d   smallest circles around together, distributing itself proportionally to the small and the large, being less and more according to proportion. That is how it has become a source of all wonders, conveying the large and small circle at the same time, at slow and fast speeds that are in agreement, an effect that someone would expect to be impossible."—"What you say is very true."—"And in speaking of things that move in many locations, at least, you appear to me to refer to whatever moves in a course by which it always changes to another place: sometimes they possess one axis of support,[20] and sometimes more, because they roll. Each time they encounter each other, if they encounter things that stand still, they are split, and if they encounter the others, coming from opposite directions, they coalesce and become one, in the middle and in between such things."—"Now I do say that these things are this way, as you are saying."—"And when things coalesce there is growth, while when they are separated, then there is decay, so long as the established character of each thing lasts; if it doesn't last, both processes are destructive. Now the coming into being of all things takes place when what experience occurs? Clearly, when the original cause, obtaining growth, proceeds to the second transformation, and from this to the next, and, when it arrives at the third, it allows of perception by perceivers. By this transformation and change everything comes into being. And it is really in being, so long as it lasts, but when it is transformed into another character, it is completely destroyed."

893e

894a

So then haven't we enumerated in forms all motions, except, friends, for two?

894b

Kl.   Which two?

Ath.   Those two, my good man, for the sake of which just about our entire investigation is now taking place.

Kl.   Speak more clearly.

Ath.   Presumably it was for the sake of soul?

Kl.   Certainly.

Ath.   Let there be a motion that is capable of moving others, but incapable of moving itself, and that is always one; and let there be another, that is always capable of moving itself as well as others, in coalescences and separations, growths and the opposite, generations and destructions—another one motion among all the motions.

Kl.   Let it be so.

894c

Ath.   So then the one that always moves another and is transformed by another we will set down as the ninth, and the one that moves itself as well as others, in harmony with all actions and all experiences, and which is called the real transformation and motion of all the beings, this we will call just about the tenth.

Kl. By all means.

894d Ath. Which of our roughly ten motions would we most correctly judge to be the strongest of all and especially active?

Kl. Presumably it's necessary to declare that the one capable of moving itself differs ten thousandfold, and that all the others are later.

Ath. Well spoken. So then shouldn't one or even two of our statements just now that were incorrect, be changed?

Kl. Which do you claim are so?

Ath. What was said about the tenth was pretty incorrect.

Kl. How?

Ath. It is first, in generation and in strength, according to reason.
894e And the one we have after this is second to this, though it was just said, strangely, to be ninth.

Kl. What do you mean?

Ath. The following. When we always have one thing transforming another, and this another, will one of such transformations ever be first? How will that which is set in motion by another ever be first of the things that are altered? It's impossible. But when there's something that, having moved itself, alters an-
895a other, and that other another, and thus thousands upon tens of thousands of things moved come into being, what will be a ruling cause of all their motion other than the transformation of what has moved itself?

Kl. What you've said is very fine, and there ought to be agreement to these things.

Ath. Let us go on to speak in the following way, and again answer ourselves. If somehow all the things that have come into being should stand still, as most of those men dare to say, which then of the motions mentioned would necessarily come into
895b being first among them? Doubtless, the motion that moves itself. For it would never be changed by another before it, there being no prior change among them. Therefore we will assert that the motion which moves itself, since it is the ruling cause of all motions, as well as the first to have come into being among things standing still and the first to exist among things moving, is necessarily the eldest and the strongest transforma-

tion of all, while the motion that is altered by another and moves others is second.

Kl. What you say is very true.

Ath. Now that we're at this point in the argument, let's answer the following. 895c

Kl. What?

Ath. If we should see that this had come into being somewhere, in something composed of earth, or of water, or in something having the form of fire—whether separated or mixed—what then will we ever claim is the condition of such a thing?

Kl. Would you be asking me if we'll speak of it as alive, when it moves itself?

Ath. Yes.

Kl. Alive. How could it not be?

Ath. What then? When we see soul in certain things, do we say anything other than this same thing? Shouldn't it be agreed that they're alive?

Kl. Nothing else.

Ath. Hold it, in the name of Zeus! Wouldn't you be willing to think 895d
about each thing in three ways?

Kl. What do you mean?

Ath. One is the being, one is the definition of the being, and one is the name. And indeed there are two questions about every being.

Kl. How two?

Ath. Each of us sometimes presents the name itself and seeks the definition, and sometimes, again, presents the definition itself and asks for the name. So do we mean, then, something like the following here?

Kl. Which?

Ath. There is presumably a division into two in other things and 895e
also in number. The name for this in number is "even," and the definition is, "a number divisible into two equal parts."

Kl. Yes.

Ath. It's such a thing that I'm explaining.[21] Aren't we speaking of the same thing in either case, whether we are asked about the definition, and give the name, or asked about the name, and give the definition? By the name, "even," and by the defini- tion "number divisible in two," aren't we speaking of the same being?

Kl. In every way.

896a **Ath.** Now what is the definition of this thing to which the name "soul" is given? Do we have another besides what was just now said, "the motion capable of moving itself"?

Kl. Do you claim that the definition, "to move itself," belongs to the same being as that to which we all give the name "soul"?

Ath. That's what I claim, at least. And if this is so, are we yet lacking an adequate demonstration that soul is the same being as that which is the first generation and motion of the things that exist, that have come into being, and that will be, and of all

896b the opposites to these, since it has come to sight as the cause of all transformation and motion in all things?

Kl. No, but it has been very adequately demonstrated that soul is the eldest of all things, having come into being as the ruling cause of motion.

Ath. And isn't the motion that comes into being in one thing on account of another, but that never allows anything to move itself in itself, second—or as many numbers down as someone would wish to count, being really a transformation of soulless body?

Kl. Correctly spoken.

Ath. So then we would have spoken correctly, authoritatively, very

896c truly, and most perfectly, when we said that for us soul has come into being prior to body, and that body is second and later, being ruled, while soul rules, according to nature.

Kl. That is indeed very true.

Ath. Now we of course remember what we agreed to earlier, that if soul should be evidently elder than body, then the things pertaining to soul would be elder than the things pertaining to the body.

Kl. By all means.

896d **Ath.** Temperaments, then, and dispositions, wishes, calculations, true opinions, supervisions, and memories would have come into being prior to lengths of bodies, widths, depths, and strength—if, indeed, soul came into being prior to body.

Kl. Necessarily.

Ath. Well now, after this, isn't it necessary to agree that soul is the cause of things good and bad, noble and shameful, just and unjust, and of all the opposites, if indeed we are going to set it down as the cause of all things?

Kl. How could it not be?

Ath. Isn't it also necessary to assert that since soul manages and
      resides in all things that are in motion everywhere, it also   896e
      manages heaven?

Kl.   But of course.

Ath. One or several? Several; I will answer for both of you. Presum-
      ably we should assume no less than two, anyway—one that
      does good, and another capable of doing the opposite.

Kl.   What you've said is surely correct.

Ath. So be it. Soul then drives all things in heaven, on earth, and in
      the sea through its motions—which are named wishing, in-   897a
      vestigating, supervising, deliberating, opining correctly and
      falsely, rejoicing, being pained, being bold, being fearful, hat-
      ing, and desiring—and through all the motions that are akin
      to these or primary; these take over the secondary motions of
      bodies and drive all things to growth and decay, separation
      and coalescence, and to what follows these—heat, cold, heavi-
      ness, lightness, hard and soft, light and dark, bitter and
      sweet; soul makes use of all these and, every time it takes as a   897b
      helper Intelligence—god, in the correct sense, for the gods [22]—
      it guides [23] all things toward what is correct and happy, while
      when it associates with lack of intelligence it produces in all
      things just the opposite to these. Are we to set down these
      things as being so, or are we still in doubt lest it is somehow
      otherwise?

Kl.   Not at all.

Ath. Then which kind of soul are we to assert has become master of
      heaven and earth and of the whole orbit? The one full of pru-
      dence and virtue, or the one that possesses neither? Do you   897c
      wish us to answer these questions as follows?

Kl.   How?

Ath. If, you amazing man (we should declare), the entire path and
      motion of heaven and of all the beings in it has the same na-
      ture as the motion, revolution, and calculations of In-
      telligence, and proceeds in a kindred way, then it is clear that
      one ought to affirm that the best soul supervises the entire
      cosmos and drives it along such a path as that.

Kl.   Correctly spoken.

Ath. But the bad soul, if they move in a mad and disordered way.   897d

Kl.   These things are also correct.

Ath. So what nature does the motion of Intelligence possess, then?
      Now this, friends, is a question that's difficult to answer while

speaking in a prudent way. That's why it's just, at this point, for you to take me as a helper in answering.

Kl. Well spoken.

Ath. Let's not make our reply by looking straight on, and thereby, as if we were looking at the sun, create night at midday— because we supposed Intelligence were ever visible and ade-

897e quately knowable by mortal eyes. One can see in more safety by looking at an image of what is being asked about.

Kl. How do you mean?

Ath. Let's take as the image that one among those ten motions which Intelligence resembles. Recollecting it for you, I'll make our common reply.

Kl. You would say what is most beautiful.

Ath. Do we still remember this much, at least, of what was said earlier: we set it down that of all things, some are in motion and some at rest?

Kl. Yes.

Ath. And again, of the things in motion, some move in one place,

898a and some in several.

Kl. That is so.

Ath. Now of these two motions, the one that moves always in one place must necessarily move around some center, being an imitation of circular things turned on a lathe, and it must in every way have the greatest possible kinship and resemblance to the revolution of Intelligence.

Kl. How do you mean?

Ath. Surely, if we said that moving according to what is the same, in the same way, in the same place, around the same things, toward the same things, and according to one proportion and

898b order characterized both Intelligence and the motion that moves in one place—speaking of them as images of the motions of a sphere turned on a lathe—we'd never appear to be poor craftsmen of beautiful images in speech.

Kl. What you say is very correct.

Ath. On the other hand, wouldn't the motion that never moves the same, nor according to what is the same, nor in the same place, nor around the same things, nor toward the same things, nor in one place, nor in regularity, or order, or some proportion, be akin to complete lack of Intelligence?

Kl. It would, most truly.

898c Ath. Now, indeed, it's no longer difficult to say explicitly that,

since soul is what drives everything around for us, it ought to
be affirmed that the revolution of heaven is necessarily driven
around under the supervision and ordering of either the best
soul or the opposite.

Kl.   But stranger, from what has now been said at any rate, it isn't
pious to say anything other than that the soul—whether it be
one or several—that has every virtue drives things around!

Ath. Kleinias, you've attended to the arguments in a very fine way.
But attend also to this.   898d

Kl.   To what?

Ath. If indeed sun and moon and the other stars are *all* driven
around by soul, isn't *each one* of them?

Kl.   But of course.

Ath. Let's take the case of one and make the arguments, which will
then seem, to us, to apply harmoniously to all the stars.

Kl.   Which one?

Ath. In the case of the sun, every human being sees the body, but
no one the soul. And the same holds for the soul of any other
living body, either while it's alive or when it's dying. It is very
likely,²⁴ rather, that this entire class of things grows by nature
all around us, imperceivable through any of the bodily senses,
but intelligible through intelligence alone. Let us, indeed, use
intelligence and thought to grasp something of the following
sort concerning it.

Kl.   What?

Ath. If soul does drive the sun around, we will hardly be wide of
the mark if we say it does this in one of three ways.

Kl.   Which ways?

Ath. Either it resides within this spherical-appearing body and
conducts it, being such, everywhere, just as our soul carries us
around everywhere; or it provides itself with some outside   899a
body of fire or some kind of air, as the account of some people
has it, and pushes the body with bodily force; or, third, being
itself without body, it possesses certain other exceedingly amazing powers, and exercises guidance.

Kl.   Yes: this is necessary, that soul drives all things by doing
some one, at least, of these things.

Ath. Now hold it right there. This soul, whether it carries light to
all of us by being in the chariot of the sun, or by acting from
the outside, or however and in whatever way it does it, ought
to be held to be a god by every man. Or how should it be?

899b Kl.   Yes—at least, I suppose, by every man who hasn't arrived at the ultimate in lack of intelligence!

Ath. And with regard to all the stars, and the moon, the years, months, and all the seasons, what other account will we give except this same one, to the effect that since soul or souls are evidently the causes of all these things, and souls good with respect to every virtue, we will declare that they are gods—whether they order the entire heaven by existing within bodies, as living beings, or in whatever way and however they do it? Is there anyone who will agree to these things and maintain that all things are not full of gods? [25]

899c Kl.   There is no one so bereft of sense, stranger.

Ath. Then let's state terms to the one who didn't believe in gods earlier, Megillus and Kleinias, and be done with him.

Kl.   What terms?

Ath. Either to teach us how we aren't speaking correctly when we set down soul as the primal generation of all things, and whatever else we said followed from this, or, if he's not able to speak better than us, to believe us and live believing in gods
899d for the rest of his life. So let's see whether what we've said to those who don't believe in gods—showing that there are gods—is sufficient at this point, or whether it is lacking.

Kl.   It is the least lacking of all, stranger!

Ath. Then let our arguments with these people be concluded. But the one who does believe the gods exist, and that they don't think about human affairs, must be persuaded. [26]

"Best of men," let us declare, "the fact that you believe in gods probably indicates some kinship with the divine that draws you to what is of a like nature, to honor and believe in
899e its existence. But the private and public fortunes of bad and unjust human beings, not happy in truth, but very happy according to mistaken opinions, draw you toward impiety by the way in which they're sung about through incorrect Muses and in all sorts of accounts. Or perhaps you see human beings
900a approaching the end of old age, leaving behind children of children in the highest honors, and you are now disturbed when you see in all these cases—either by hearing of it or by seeing it all yourself—that there are some who have partaken of many terrible impieties and by means of these very things have risen from low positions to tyrannies and the highest stations. Then, on account of all such things, since you are ob-

viously unwilling, because of kinship, to blame the gods as being responsible for such things, you are drawn by ill reasoning and an incapacity to hold the gods in contempt to the condition you have now come to: it is your opinion that they exist, but that they despise and don't care about human affairs. In order, therefore, to prevent your present belief from impelling you toward an even graver condition of impiety, let's try, if somehow we can possibly exorcise it by arguments when it approaches, to connect the next argument to the one we went through from the beginning against the person who didn't believe in gods at all, making use of the latter in the present circumstances." But you, Kleinias and Megillus, take the part of the young man in answering, just as you did in the previous arguments; if something troubling comes up in the arguments, I'll take over from you two and ford the river as I did just now.

900b

900c

Kl. What you say is correct. You do these things, in this way, and we'll do our best to do what you say.

Ath. But there'd probably be no difficulty in demonstrating to this fellow, at least, that the gods supervise the small matters not less, but more,[27] than the especially big matters. For presumably he heard and was present at the things that were said just now, to the effect that since they are good, at least, with respect to every virtue, they possess, as very proper to them, the supervisory care of all things.

900d

Kl. He certainly heard.

Ath. After this let them[28] join in examining what virtue of the gods was referred to when we agreed they were good. Come, do we assert that being moderate and possessing Intelligence belong to virtue, and the opposites to vice?

Kl. We do assert that.

Ath. What then? That courage belongs to virtue, and cowardice to vice?

900e

Kl. By all means.

Ath. And will we assert that some of these are shameful, and some noble?

Kl. Necessarily.

Ath. And will we say that whichever of those qualities are low befit us, if anyone, but that the gods partake neither in the great nor the small aspects of such things?

Kl. Everyone would agree that these things too are so.

Ath. What then? Will we set down carelessness, idleness, and luxury as belonging to the soul's virtue, or what do you say?

Kl. How could we?

Ath. But as belonging to the opposite?

Kl. Yes.

901a Ath. Then the opposites to these as belonging to the opposite?

Kl. The opposite.

Ath. So what then? Wouldn't everyone who is luxurious, without care, and idle become for us such as the poet explains: "resembling especially stingless drones"? [29]

Kl. And he speaks very correctly, at least.

Ath. Then the god, at least, shouldn't be said to have such a disposition, which he, at least, himself hates; and he who tries to say such a thing is not to be tolerated.

Kl. Indeed not. How could he be?

901b Ath. Suppose it belongs to someone to act and exercise special supervision over something, and his intelligence supervises the great things but neglects the small: according to what argument would we in praising such a one not err in every way? Let's consider it as follows: doesn't the action of one who acts in such a way, whether god or human, take one of two forms?

Kl. Which two are we speaking of?

Ath. Either he neglects the small things, thinking it makes no dif-
901c ference to the whole, or he neglects them out of softness of spirit and luxury—if it does make a difference. Or is there some other way that neglect comes about? For surely when it's impossible, at any rate, to supervise all things, then it won't be *neglect* of small or great matters, in the case of that god or low person who fails to supervise things because he lacks the power and is incapable of supervising them.

Kl. How could it be?

901d Ath. At this point let the two of them reply to the three of us (they both agree that gods exist, and the other of them says they're appeasable, while this one says they're careless of the small things): "In the first place, do you both claim that the gods know, see, and hear all things, and that nothing of which there are perceptions and knowledge can escape their notice?" Is this the way these things are said [30] to be, or how?

Kl. Thus.

Ath. What then? Are they, again, capable of all those things that mortals and immortals are capable of?

Kl. How will they not agree that these things too are so?

Ath. And we, being five, have agreed that they are good, at least, 901e
and even the best.

Kl. Emphatically.

Ath. Well then, since they are, at any rate, such as we agree, isn't it
impossible to agree that they do anything at all out of softness
of spirit and luxuriousness? For in us, at any rate, idleness is
an offspring of cowardice, and softness of spirit of idleness
and luxury.

Kl. What you say is very true.

Ath. Then no one among the gods is careless because of idleness or
softness of spirit; for surely he doesn't share in cowardice.

Kl. What you say is very correct.

Ath. Then what is left—if indeed they do neglect the small and few 902a
things pertaining to the whole—is either that they would do
this because they know it's not at all necessary to supervise
any of such things, or, . . . what else, except the opposite of
knowledge?

Kl. Nothing else.

Ath. Well then, most excellent and best of men,³¹ are we to set you
down as saying they are ignorant, and neglect what ought to
be supervised because of ignorance, or that they know what is
necessary, and, like the lowest of human beings are said to do,
they know it is better to act otherwise than the way they're 902b
acting, but they don't do so on account of certain weaknesses
in the face of pleasures or pains?

Kl. How could that be?

Ath. Don't human affairs, at any rate, partake of the nature of what
has soul, and isn't the human being the most god-revering of
all living things?

Kl. That's likely, anyway.

Ath. Surely we assert that all mortal, living things are possessions
of gods, to whom the whole heaven belongs.

Kl. How could this not be so?

Ath. So at this point someone may assert that these are either—
small or great—to the gods: because in neither case would it 902c
be appropriate for our owners to neglect us, since they're the
most careful supervisors, at any rate, as well as the best. For
let's just consider the following, in addition to these matters.

Kl. What?

Ath. Take what pertains to perception and power: are the two not by nature opposite to one another as regards ease and difficulty?

Kl. How do you mean?

Ath. Presumably it's more difficult to see and hear the small things than the big, while it's easier for everyone to carry, master, and supervise the small and few things rather than their opposites.

902d Kl. Very much so.

Ath. If some whole is given to a doctor to care for, and he wishes and is able to supervise the big parts, but neglects the small, will the whole ever turn out in a fine way for him?

Kl. Not at all.

Ath. Nor for pilots or generals or household managers, nor even
902e certain statesmen, nor for any other such person: the many or great things won't turn out in this way without the few and small. For the stonemasons claim that the big stones don't lie well without little stones.

Kl. How could they?

Ath. Let's never judge the god, at least, to be less than mortal craftsmen, who, the better they may be, just so much the more exactly and perfectly do they use one art to carry out both the small and large aspects of the work that is appropriate to them—nor that the god, being very wise, and willing and able
903a to exercise supervision, won't in any way supervise the things that are easily supervised, being small, but just the big things, like some idle or cowardly fellow whose spirit becomes soft in toils.

Kl. Let's by no means accept such an opinion about gods, stranger; for we would be thinking a thought that is in no way pious or true.

Ath. We seem to me at this point to have carried on a very well-measured dialogue with the one who is fond of accusing the gods of neglect.

Kl. Yes.

Ath. And it was done by forcing him, through arguments, to agree
903b that he wasn't speaking correctly; but it seems to me that there are still needed, in addition, some mythic incantations.

Kl. Which, my good man?

Ath. Let's persuade the young man, through arguments, that "He who supervises everything has put all things together with a view to the safety and virtue of the whole, and each part suffers and does what befits it, insofar as it can. Rulers have been set up over the suffering and activity of each of these at any time, down to the smallest aspect, and they have achieved perfection to the last detail. And one of these is your part, stubborn one, and it constantly strives and looks toward the whole, even though it is entirely small; but it has escaped your notice, in this very regard, that all generation comes into being for the sake of this: that a happy existence might characterize the life of the whole—it hasn't come into being for your sake, but you for the sake of it. For every doctor and every artful craftsman does everything for the sake of a whole, creating a part which strives for what is best in common, for the sake of the whole, and not the whole for the sake of the part. But you complain, ignorant of how what is best in your case for the whole turns out to be best for you as well, by the power of the common generation. Now since soul is always put together with body, sometimes with one, sometimes with another, and undergoes all sorts of transformations caused by itself or by another soul, no other task is left for the draughts[32] player except that of transferring the disposition that has become better to a better place, and the worse to the worse place, according to what befits each of them, so that it obtains the appropriate fate."

903c

903d

903e

Kl. In what way do you mean?

Ath. In the way that would make sense of the gods having the greatest ease of supervision over all the things—this is what it seems to me I'm explaining. For if someone would mold and change the shape of all things without always looking to the whole, and had something like cold[33] water coming out of fire, instead of many things from one or from many, one, after the first or second or third generation there would be a limitless number of changes in the rearranged cosmos. But now it is amazingly easy for the one who supervises the whole.

904a

Kl. How do you mean this again?

Ath. As follows. "Since, indeed, our King saw that all actions are involved with souls, and that there is much virtue in them, though much vice, and that soul with body, once it has come into being, is indestructible but not eternal—just like the gods who exist according to legal convention—(for if either of these two had been destroyed there would never have been generation of living things), and since he understood that whatever

904b

is good in soul is always beneficial by nature, while the bad is harmful; since he saw all these things, he presumably contrived the situation of each part so that in the whole, virtue would very much triumph, and vice meet defeat, in the easiest and best way. For the sake of the whole he has, in fact, contrived it so that when a certain sort of thing comes into being it must always take a certain place, and then dwell in certain

904c   regions. And he has assigned to the wishes of each of us the responsibility for what sort of person comes into being: the way one desires and what one is in one's soul just about determines each time, the type and character every one of us, for the most part, becomes."

Kl.   That is likely, at any rate.

Ath.   "So all things that partake of soul are transformed, possessing within themselves the cause of the transformation, and, undergoing transformation, are moved according to the order and law of destiny: for smaller and lesser transformations of dispositions there is lateral regional movement; when the

904d   transformations are greater and more unjust, there is a fall into the depths and the places said to be below, to which in their fear people give the name 'Hades' and others connected to this, both while they're alive and dreaming, and when they've become separated from their bodies. But when a soul's own wishing and familiarity with others have become strong, and as a result it obtains a large share of vice or virtue—then, when by mingling with a divine virtue it comes to be such in an exceptional degree, it undergoes an especially great trans-

904e   formation in locale and is borne along a hallowed path to some other, better place; and when the opposite things occur, it transfers its own life to the opposite sorts of places. 'This, indeed, is the justice of the gods who hold Olympus,'[34] O lad and young man who suppose yourself neglected by the gods: he who becomes more vicious is transported among the more vicious souls, while he who becomes better is transported among the better, and in life and in every death suffers and

905a   does the things that are appropriate for similars to do to similars. Neither you nor anyone else who has become unfortunate will ever boast of having eluded this justice of the gods.[35] Those who ordained it have ordained it to be preeminent among all justices, and one ought to be careful in every way as regards it. For you will never be neglected by it—not if you should be small enough to sink into the depths of the earth, not if you should become high enough to fly up into heaven—but you will pay them the appropriate retribution, either while remaining here, or after having been transported to Hades, or after having been moved to some place still fiercer[36] 905b than these. You'll find that the same account would hold for those you observe having risen from pettiness to greatness through acts of impiety or some such thing, whom you supposed to have become happy, from being miserable, and in whose actions, as in mirrors, you believed you had seen the carelessness of all the gods—not knowing how their contribution ever assists the whole. But how can you suppose, O most 905c courageous of all men, that it isn't necessary to know this? If someone doesn't know it, he would never see an outline, nor become capable of contributing an account, of life, as regards happiness and an unhappy[37] fortune.

"Now if Kleinias here and our entire Council of Elders[38] persuade you of these things, that you don't know what you're saying about gods, god himself would aid you nobly; but if you should be still in need of some argument, hearken 905d to us as we speak to the third party—if you have any intelligence."

For that gods exist, and exercise supervision over human beings, I at least would claim has been demonstrated by us, in a not altogether paltry fashion. But that gods can be appeased by the unjust, if they get gifts, is something one ought not go along with, and that ought also to be refuted by every means in one's power.

Kl. What you've said is very fine, and let's do as you say.

Ath. Come then, in the name of the gods themselves! In what way would they become appeasable by us, if they were to become 905e so? And what, or what sort, would they be? Presumably they must necessarily be rulers, since they manage the entire heaven perpetually.[39]

Kl. That is so.

Ath. But then to which of the rulers are they similar? Or which are similar to them from among those we can compare to them, lesser to greater? Would it be certain drivers of competing teams, or pilots of ships? But perhaps they might be compared to certain rulers of armies; it might even be that they are like doctors taking care of a war against diseases in bodies, or

906a   farmers fearfully awaiting seasons that are usually difficult for the generation of plants,[40] or those set over flocks. For since we've agreed among ourselves that heaven is full of many good things, and also of the opposite, and that there are more of the latter, we assert that there is an immortal battle of this kind going on, requiring an amazing guard, and that the gods and demons are our allies, while we in turn are the property of

906b   the gods and demons. Injustice and insolence, together with lack of prudence, destroy us, while what saves us are justice and moderation, together with prudence—qualities which dwell in the soul-imbued powers of the gods, but a small portion of which someone would also discern clearly dwelling here in us. Now there dwell on earth certain souls which have acquired unjust gain and are obviously beastly in form; they fawn upon the souls of the guards—the dogs, shepherds, or those who are in every way the highest masters—persuading them, with speeches of flattery or through certain prayerful in-

906c   cantations, of what the claims of the bad men assert, that it is possible for them to get more than their share among human beings and suffer no harshness. But we presumably assert that the fault just now named, getting more than one's share, is the thing called "disease" in the flesh of bodies, "plague" in seasons and years, and, in cities and regimes, having had its name refashioned, is injustice.

Kl.   That is altogether the case.

Ath.   This, indeed, is the argument that must necessarily be made

906d   by the one who says the gods always forgive unjust human beings and those who act unjustly, so long as one distributes to them a share of the unjust gains: it's just as if wolves were to distribute to the dogs small portions of what they've pillaged, and the latter, rendered gentle by the gifts, were to go along with the pillaging of the flocks. Isn't this the argument of those who claim the gods are appeasable?

Kl.   This is it indeed.

Ath.   To which of those mentioned before could any human being whatsoever compare the gods as guards who are similar, and

906e   avoid becoming ridiculous? Could it be pilots, who are "turned aside by the libation and aroma"[41] of wine, and overturn ship and sailors?

Kl.   In no way.

Ath.   But surely not drivers lined up together for competition, persuaded by a gift to betray the victory to the other teams.

Kl.   You would describe a terrible image in uttering this speech!

Ath.   And not generals, surely, nor doctors, nor farmers, nor herds-
       men, nor yet certain dogs softened by wolves.

Kl.   Hush! How could they be?

Ath.   But isn't it our view that all the gods are the greatest of all   907a
       guards, and of the greatest thing?

Kl.   By far.

Ath.   Are we going to assert that those who guard the noblest af-
       fairs, and are themselves preeminent in the virtue of guard-
       ing, are inferior to dogs and ordinary human beings, who
       would never betray what is just in return for gifts bestowed
       impiously by unjust men?

Kl.   Not at all; this speech is intolerable, and of those involved in   907b
       every sort of impiety, every man who maintains this opinion
       risks being very justly judged the worst and most impious of
       all the impious.

Ath.   Shall we not assert, then, that the three propositions—that the
       gods exist, exercise supervisory care, and are in every way not
       to be appeased in a manner contrary to what is just—have
       been sufficiently demonstrated?

Kl.   How could we not? We vote, at least, in accordance with these
       arguments.

Ath.   Yet they were spoken, at any rate, rather vehemently some-
       how, on account of a fondness for victory over bad human be-   907c
       ings. The reason, dear Kleinias, why they were animated by a
       fondness for victory was a concern lest the bad should believe
       that if they ever were stronger in arguments, they could act in
       the ways they wish, according to the sorts of notions they have
       about gods. It's on account of these things that an eagerness of
       spirit has prompted us to speak with youthful vigor; but if
       we've made some brief contribution to persuading the men in
       some sense to hate themselves, and to desire somehow the op-
       posite dispositions, the prelude to the laws about impiety   907d
       would have been spoken by us in a noble way.

Kl.   But there is hope; and if not, the character of the argument will
       at least not discredit the lawgiver.

Ath.   After the prelude it would be correct for us to have a speech
       that is like an interpreter of the laws, proclaiming to all the im-
       pious that they should change their ways into pious ones. For
       those who don't obey, let the law concerning impiety be as
       follows:
           If someone should be impious in words or deeds, the one

907e who comes across such behavior is to help defend by reporting the occurrence to the magistrates, and the first magistrates that learn of it are to bring the accused before the judicial court designated to judge these matters according to the laws. If some magistracy hears of such a thing and should fail to do this, it shall become liable to prosecution for impiety by anyone who wishes to seek retribution on behalf of the laws. If someone should be convicted, the court is to impose one pen-

908a alty for each one of those who are impious. Imprisonment is to be imposed in every case.

And there will be three prisons in the city: one around the marketplace, the common jail for most prisoners, and the place where the bodies of the many are secured; one around the meeting place of the councilmen who meet at night, named the "Moderation-Tank";[42] and one, again, in the middle of the country, in some spot that is deserted and as wild as possible, having for its name some term of retribution. More-

908b over, since the matters involving impiety have three causes, which we've gone through, and each of such causes gives rise to two kinds, there would be six kinds of faults worth distinguishing, concerning the divine things, which do not call for equal or similar judicial penalties. For a naturally just disposition may come to characterize the man who doesn't believe the gods exist at all; such people do come to hate bad men, and out of disgust at injustice won't submit to doing such actions;

908c they flee the human beings who aren't just and seek the just. But there are those who, in addition to the opinion that all things are bereft of gods, may be afflicted by lack of restraint as regards pleasures and pains, and may also possess strong memories and sharp capacities to learn. The disbelief in gods would be a disease that inheres in both, but as regards the ruin of other human beings, the one would do less, the other more, harm. For the former would be full of frankness in his speech about gods, as well as about sacrifices and oaths, and

908d by his ridicule of the rest would perhaps make others like himself, if he didn't get a judicial penalty; the latter, on the other hand, while having the same opinion as the other, has what is called a "good nature," and is full of guile and trickery. From this type come many diviners and men equipped in all of magic, and sometimes tyrants, demagogues, and generals, and those who plot by means of private mystery-rites, and the contrivances of those called "sophists." There would be many forms of these things, but just two that are worthy of 908e establishing laws about: one, the ironic, commits faults that deserve not one nor two deaths; the other needs admonishment and imprisonment. In the same way, the belief that the gods are careless breeds two, and the belief that they can be appeased, another two.

Of these which have been distinguished in this way, the ones who have come to be such because of lack of intelligence, without evil anger or dispositon, the judge is to place, accord- 909a ing to law, in the Moderation-Tank for no less than five years. During this time no one else among the citizens is to have intercourse with them except those who share in the Nocturnal Council, who are to associate with them for the purposes of admonishment and the salvation of the soul. When the time of their imprisonment is up, if someone among them should seem to be moderate, he is to dwell among the moderate, but if not, and he should be convicted at such a trial again, let him be punished with death.

Then there are those who, in addition to not believing in the gods, or believing them to be careless, or appeasable, become like beasts: they hold human beings in contempt and entice 909b the souls of many of the living while pretending to entice the souls of the dead; they promise to persuade gods by charming them with sacrifices, prayers, and incantations; thus, for the sake of money, they try utterly to destroy private individuals and whole households and cities. He who should appear convicted of being one of these, the court is to imprison according to law, in the jail that lies in the middle of the country, and no 909c free man is ever to go to visit him; the Guardians of the Laws are to arrange for them to get their food from the domestic slaves. When he dies he is to be cast out beyond the borders unburied. And if some free man should take part in burying him, he is to be put on trial for impiety by whoever wishes. If the convict should leave behind children who are adequate to become members of the city, the supervisors of orphans are to supervise these as if they were orphans, treating them in no 909d way as inferior to the rest, from the day when their father is convicted in the trial.

There should be a law that applies in common to all these people, that would make many of them commit fewer offenses in deed or in word concerning the gods, and that would in fact render them less unintelligent, by making it impermissable to traffic in divine matters contrary to law. Let the following law deal with all of them in compendious fashion:

909e

Not a single person is to possess shrines in private dwellings. When someone is minded to sacrifice, he is to go and sacrifice at the public shrines, and hand the sacrificial offerings over to the priests and priestesses, whose responsibility it is to purify these things.

Let he himself and whomever he wants to accompany him join in the prayers. These arrangements are to be made for some such reasons as the following. It isn't easy to establish temples and gods, but to do such a thing correctly requires a certain amount of deep thought. It's a habit of all women especially, and indeed of people who are sick in any way, or in danger, or at a loss, however someone may be at a loss—and also in the opposite circumstances, when they prosper in some way—to sanctify whatever happens to be around at the

910a

time, to vow sacrifices, and to promise to establish shrines to gods, demons, and children of gods. Moreover, having been stirred awake by the fears they experience in apparitions and dreams, and, in the same way, recalling many visions, they make remedies against each of them by filling every house and every district with altars and temples, establishing them in places free of pollution and wherever someone happened to have such experiences. On account of all these things, one should act according to the law now being pronounced. In ad-

910b

dition to these considerations, one should do so because of the impious, to prevent them from committing fraud in these matters by setting up shrines and altars in private homes, supposing they can in secret make the gods propitious through sacrifices and prayers. They thus foster a limitless growth in injustice, bringing down on themselves and on those who tolerate them (and who are better than them) accusations on the part of the gods, and thus involving the whole city—justly, in a way—in the results of their impieties. The lawgiver, however, will not incur the god's blame, for this law is to hold:

910c

There is to be no possession of shrines to the gods in private homes. If someone is found possessing shrines and worshipping in rituals other than the public ones, and if the man or woman possessing them has committed none of the great and impious sorts of injustice, the one who discovers this is to report it to the Guardians of the Laws; they are to command that the private sacred things be carried away to the public shrines, and those who disobey are to be penalized until they are carried away. But if someone should be detected having committed an impiety that is not of the childish sort but of the sort that characterizes impious grown men, either by establishing private shrines, or by sacrificing at the public shrines belonging to any of the gods whatsoever, let the penalty be death, on the grounds that he sacrificed while being polluted. The Guardians of the Laws are to judge whether it be childish or not, and, introducing the accused into the judicial court accordingly, are to carry out the judicial penalty for impiety in these cases.

910d

BOOK XI

913a Ath. Next after these matters, our business transactions with one another would require an appropriate ordering. Presumably a compendious statement, at any rate, would go like this: insofar as possible, one should refrain from touching my goods, and should not move them even the shortest distance, if he has in no way persuaded me at all. And I should do likewise, according to the same principles, with things belonging to the others, if I possess a prudent intelligence.

Among such things, let us first discuss treasure which someone has laid in a hoard for himself and his people, in the
913b case where he was not among my forefathers. I should never pray to the gods that I may find it; nor, if I do find it, should I move it; nor, again, should I take counsel about it with the so-called diviners, who in one way or another will advise me to take what was deposited in the earth. Because I would never benefit as much in money by taking the property as I would increase in substance as regards virtue of the soul and what is just by not taking it, I would thereby have acquired a better possession than that possession, and in a better part of me, by honoring the acquisition of justice in the soul before that of wealth in property. Indeed, the saying "do not move the im-
913c movable" applies well to many things, and one should speak of this as one of those things. One ought to believe the myths spoken about these matters, to the effect that such behavior does not promote the generation of children. But what of he who may become indifferent to children and, heedless of the one who established the law, takes up what neither he himself

nor, again, some father of his fathers set down, without persuading the person who did set it down? He thereby corrupts
the noblest of laws—a most compendious act of legislation, by
a man who was in no way ill born, who said, "what you didn't
set down, don't take up." [1] What ought the man suffer, who   913d
holds in contempt these two lawgivers, and takes up what he
himself did not put down, when it isn't something small, but
is sometimes a very great mass of treasure?

What he is to suffer at the hands of the gods, is known to the
god. But he who is first to detect such a thing is to report it: if
it should occur in the city, to the City Regulators; if somewhere in the marketplace of the city, to the Market Regulators;
if somewhere in the rest of the country, he is to reveal it to the   914a
Field Regulators and their Officers. Once such things have
been revealed, the city is to send to Delphi: whatever the god
should ordain concerning the money and the person who
moved it, this the city, in service to the divinations, shall do
on behalf of the god. If the one who has informed should be a
free man, he is to acquire a reputation for virtue, but if he has
failed to inform, for vice; if he should be a slave, it would be
correct for the city to make him free for having informed, and
to give his price to his master; but if he failed to inform, he is
to be punished with death.

Following after this in order would come the same thing   914b
concerning small as well as great matters, so that this legal custom would follow:

If someone should voluntarily or involuntarily leave something that belongs to him somewhere, he who comes across it
must leave it lying, believing that the demoness of the roads
guards such things, as made sacred to the goddess [2] by law. If,
contrary to these injunctions, someone should disobey by taking it up and carrying it home, then, if he's a slave and the object is something of small value, he is to be whipped many
times by anyone who happens along who is not less than
thirty years of age. But if he's a free man, besides being held to   914c
be illiberal, and one who doesn't share in laws, he must pay
ten times the value of the object moved to the person who left
it. If someone accuses somebody of having some amount of
his goods, great or small, in his possession, and the accused
agrees that he has it, but not that it belongs to the other; then,
if the property be registered with the magistrates according to

914d law, he should summon the possessor before the magistracy, and the possessor must produce it. Once the object has been brought to light, if it should appear as registered in the written lists under either of the disputants, he is to have it and go away. But if it should appear under someone else (among those who aren't present), whichever of the two should present a worthy guarantor is to carry it away on behalf of the absent party, to hand it over to him in accordance with his right to take it away. And if the disputed object should not be registered with the magistrates, it is to lie, until the trial, with the three eldest among the magistrates; if the pledged object be a beast, the one who is defeated in the trial concerning it

914e shall pay the magistrates for its upkeep. The judicial decision is to be rendered by the magistrates within three days.

He who wishes, if he be of sound mind, may seize his own slave and do to him what he wants, so long as it is within the limits of what is pious. He may also seize a runaway, to keep him safe, on behalf of another who is a relative or friend. But if someone should try to remove into freedom someone being taken as a slave, the one who's taking him must give him up, while the one trying to remove him must provide three worthy guarantors, and effect the removal on these condi-

915a tions, but otherwise not. If someone should effect removal contrary to these conditions, he is to be liable for violent assault, and if convicted must pay to the party injured by the removal double the damages.

A freed man may be seized if he doesn't pay the freed man's homages or does so insufficiently. The homage is to consist in the freed man's attending the hearth of the man who freed him three times a month, offering to do whatever he ought that is just and of which he is capable, and his marrying in a way that may meet with the approval of his former master.

915b Moreover, he will not be permitted to become more wealthy than the man who freed him, and whatever he has in excess is to go to the master. The man who has been released is not to remain more than twenty years, but, just like the other strangers, is to go away, taking all his property, unless he should persuade the magistrates and the one who freed him. If a freed man or one of the other strangers should come to have property in an amount greater than that of the third class, he must depart, taking his property, within thirty days of the day

on which this comes to pass—and there is to be no request to 915c
stay put to the magistrates in this case. If someone should be
brought into court and convicted of having disobeyed these
injunctions, he is to be punished with death and his goods are
to go to the public. The trials of these matters are to take place
in the tribal courts, if they don't resolve the accusations
against one another earlier, before neighbors and chosen
judges.

If someone lays hold of anybody's animal as his own, or of
any other of his goods, the one who possesses it should return 915d
it to the warrantor or to the deliverer (if he's solvent and can
be sued), or to the person who conveyed it in some other authoritative way; if it was a citizen or resident alien in the city,
he's to do so within thirty days, while if it was a foreign delivery he's to do so within five months, of which the middle
month shall be that in which the sun turns from summer toward winter.

Whatever one man may exchange with another by way of
some purchase or sale is to be exchanged by making delivery
at the location assigned to each commodity in the marketplace
and receiving value on the spot, but nowhere else, and no one 915e
is to make a sale or purchase on credit. If one person should
exchange with another in another way or in any other places
whatsoever, trusting the one he's exchanging with, he is to do
these things on the understanding that there are no lawful
judicial suits for things that are not sold under the conditions
now being stated. As regards club contributions, he who
wishes may make collections as a friend from friends; but it
should be done on the understanding that if some difference
should arise concerning the collection, there are to be no suits
of any kind for anyone concerning these matters. Whoever has
sold something and received a price of not less than fifty
drachmas is to remain in the city for a necessary period of ten 916a
days, and the buyer is to know the house of the seller, on account of the accusations that regularly arise in such matters
and for the sake of lawful returns.

Lawful return and refusal is to be as follows. If someone
should sell a slave-captive who is sick with phthisis, or stones,
or strangury, or the so-called "sacred disease,"[3] or some other
long-lasting and hard-to-cure disease of the body or mind that
is unapparent to the many, then, if the sale is to a doctor or

916b gymnast, there is to be no right of return in such a case for this man, nor if someone made the sale to somebody after having told them the truth. But if someone who's a craftsman should make some such sale to a layman, the buyer may make a return within six months, except in the case of the "sacred" disease, and for this he may make the return within a year. The judicial decision is to rest with three doctors chosen in common by the parties. He who is convicted in the trial shall

916c pay twice the price for which he sold. If some layman sells to a layman, there is to be right of return and judgment just as in the cases mentioned before, but he who is convicted shall pay simply the selling price. If someone should knowingly sell a manslayer to someone who also knows it, there is to be no right of return for the purchase of such a slave; but if it's to someone who doesn't know about it, there's to be a right of return whenever one of the buyers finds out. The judgment is to rest with the five youngest Guardians of the Laws, and if it should be decided that the seller acted knowingly, he shall purify the households of the buyer according to the law of the In-

916d terpreters and pay triple the price to the buyer.

He who exchanges currency[4] for currency, or for anything else whatsoever, living or nonliving, must give and receive everything in an unadulterated state, in accordance with the law. But just as in the case of the other laws, let us receive a prelude concerning this vice as a whole:

Every man must understand that adulteration, lying, and deception constitute a single class, about which the many (speaking badly) are accustomed to make the pronouncement

916e that such a thing may often be correct if it occurs each time at an opportune moment; but by leaving unregulated and undefined the where and when of the opportune moment, they inflict many penalties on themselves and others through this saying. The lawgiver, however, isn't allowed to leave this undefined, but must always clarify what the boundaries are, great or small. So let this now be defined: No one who is not going to become most hateful to the gods shall commit in word or deed any lie, deception, or adulteration of something,

917a when this kind of thing is done by invoking gods; and such a man is the one who in swearing false oaths thinks nothing of the gods, or, in the second place, who lies in the face of those superior to him. Now the better are superior to the worse, and the elder, generally speaking, to the young, and therefore parents are superior to offspring, men to women and children, and rulers to the ruled. It would be fitting for everyone to feel awe before all of these superiors, in the case of every other sort of rule and especially in the case of political offices, which occasion our present discourse. For everyone who adulterates 917b something of the things in the marketplace lies and deceives, and, calling upon the gods, adds an oath in the face of the Market Regulators' laws and cautions—thereby evincing neither awe before human beings nor pious reverence before gods. Certainly it is in every way a fine practice not lightly to take the gods' names in vain, or to behave each time as most of us do in most matters concerning purity and what is hallowed in respect to the gods. But if someone would not obey, the law will be as follows:

The seller of anything whatsoever in the marketplace may never mention two prices for the things he may be selling, but 917c must utter the price simply, and if he doesn't obtain this, he would act correctly if he took the item away again; and he may not set a greater or lesser price on this day. There is to be no praise supported by an oath concerning anything that is sold. If someone should disobey these injunctions, any city dweller who happens along and is not less than thirty years of age should inflict punishment on the one who swears by beating him, with impunity; but if he doesn't pay attention, and disobeys, he is to be liable to be blamed for betraying the laws. In the case of the man who sells some adulterated article and is 917d unable to obey the present pronouncements, anyone who happens along who is among those knowledgeable and capable of proving it, and who does prove it in front of the magistrates, may, if he's a slave or a resident alien, take the adulterated article; if he's a citizen, and fails to prove it, he's to be proclaimed an evil man who robs the gods, but if he does prove it he's to dedicate the article to the gods who possess the marketplace. He who is detected selling such a thing, besides being deprived of the adulterated article, is to be beaten with 917e a whip as many blows as the number of drachmas he asked as the price of the article for sale, after the herald has proclaimed in the marketplace the reasons why he is about to be beaten.

As regards the adulterations and evildoings of sellers, the Market Regulators and the Guardians of the Laws, inquiring

918a   from those who have experience in each matter, should write down what a seller ought and ought not to do, and shall post the written laws on a tablet in front of the Market Regulators' office, so that there'll be clear guidelines for those involved in the use of the marketplace. What pertains to the City Regulators has been sufficiently discussed at earlier points; but if something additional should seem required, they should consult the Guardians of the Laws, write down what seems to be left out, and post on a tablet at the City Regulators' office the first and second sets of legal customs pertaining to their magistracy.

Following on the heels of the practices of adulteration come the practices of retail trade. Let's first give advice and argument about this entire matter, and establish a law for it later.

918b   Now all retail trade has come into being in the city not for the sake of injury—at least according to nature—but for entirely the opposite end. For how should everyone not be a doer of good deeds, who creates evenness and symmetry in the distribution of any sorts of goods that are asymmetrical and uneven in distribution? And this, we ought to declare, is achieved through the power of money; and we ought also to say that this is the task assigned to the merchant. The hireling, the innkeeper, and the rest, some of whom become more

918c   seemly, some less seemly, are all able to bring this about, to provide help for all the needs, and evenness in the distribution of property. So let us see what then has ever made this seem to be neither noble nor seemly, and what has brought it into discredit, so that we may remedy by law, if not the whole, then at least parts of it.

It's likely that the task is not a paltry one, and requires no small virtue.

Kl.   How do you mean?

Ath.   Dear Kleinias, it's a small class of human beings, few by nature and brought up with the highest upbringing, that is able

918d   to hold fast to what is measured when the need and desire for certain things comes over it, and which, when it can get a lot of money, is sober and chooses what is measured in preference to what is large. The bulk of human beings are entirely the opposite to these men: when in want, they want without measure, and when it's possible for them to gain measured amounts, they choose to gain insatiably. That is why every kind of retail trade, and wholesale trade, and innkeeping, has come to be discredited and held in shameful blame. Yet if someone—as should never take place nor ever will—were to compel (now it's laughable to utter this, but nevertheless it's 918e going to be uttered) the best men everywhere to become innkeepers for a certain period of time, or to carry on retail trade, or do one of such things, or were even to compel the women, out of some necessity of fate, to partake of such a way of life, we would know how friendly and desirable each of these things is; and, if it were to be practiced according to an uncorrupted principle, all such activities would be honored in the guise of a mother and nurse. But now, when someone has es- 919a tablished houses for the sake of retail trade in deserted spots having lengthy roads in every direction, and receives, with welcome resting places, those who have come to be at a loss, providing calm tranquillity to those driven by the violence of savage storms, and refreshment in stifling heat, he doesn't proceed after this to follow up his welcome as he would if he were receiving comrades, and give friendly guest-gifts, but instead, as if they were enemy prisoners who had fallen into his hands, he releases them on payment of very large, unjust, and impure ransoms! It is these and similar faults that have in 919b all such cases correctly discredited the provision of assistance to those at a loss. So the lawgiver must always contrive medicine for these things. Now it has been correctly said of old that "against two from opposite quarters it is difficult to fight,"[5] in the case of diseases and many other things; and indeed the present battle about and around these matters is against two, poverty and wealth, one of which corrupts the soul of human beings through luxury, and the other of which urges it to 919c shamelessness through pains. What aid would there be then for this disease, in a city that possessed intelligence? The first is to make use of the class of retail traders as little as one can; then, human beings ought to be assigned to retail trade whose corruption would least affront the city; in the third place, a 919d device should be found to prevent the dispositions of soul in those who partake of these practices from easily becoming unrestrainedly shameless and illiberal.

After the things that have now been said, let us, with good fortune, have some such law as the following for these matters: Among the Magnesians, whom the god is restoring and

919e

settling again, no one of those who hold a share of land among the five thousand forty hearths is ever voluntarily or involuntarily to become a retail trader, or a wholesale trader, or render any menial service whatsoever to private persons who do not return to him an equal service—except for his father and mother, and family members of a still earlier generation, and all those who are elder than he, who are free and whom he serves in a liberal way. It's not easy to legislate exactly what is liberal and what is illiberal, but let it be judged by those who have obtained recognition for excellence in hating the latter and embracing the former. He who should by some art partake of illiberal retail trade is to be indicted for shaming his family by anyone who wishes, before those who have been judged first in virtue, and if he should seem to be sullying his own ancestral hearth by an unworthy practice, let him be im-

920a

prisoned for a year and thus desist from such a thing; if it happens again, for two years, and each time he's caught he's not to cease doubling the length of time of the earlier imprisonment.

Now the second law: He who is going to engage in retail trade must be a resident alien or a stranger.

In the third place, the third law: In order that such a fellow resident in the city may be for us the best possible, or the least bad possible, the Guardians of the Laws are to understand that they are not only guards of those whom, because they have been well educated by birth and upbringing, it is easy

920b

for them to guard against becoming lawless and bad, but also that they should guard even more those who are not such, but are engaged in practices that have a certain strong influence in prompting men to become bad.

With this end in view, the Guardians of the Laws ought again to meet concerning these matters with those who have experience in each branch of retail trade, just as we earlier ordered them to do in the case of adulteration, which is a practice akin to this; with respect to those aspects of retail trade (which is extensive, and includes many practices of the sort just alluded to) which have seemed to be highly necessary in

920c

the city and have been allowed to remain, they should meet and see what receipt and expense balance at any time makes a well-measured gain for the retail merchant. The receipt and expense balance arrived at is to be posted in writing and guarded by the Market Regulators, City Regulators, and Field Regulators. In this way, what pertains to retail trade would be pretty beneficial to each person, and would do pretty much the smallest injury to those in the city who make use of it.

As regards cases in which someone agrees to cooperate in 920d doing something and fails to act according to what he agreed, except when laws or a decree stands in the way, or where he was forced by unjust compulsion to agree, or where he's involuntarily prevented by unforeseen chance, trials for unfulfilled agreements in the other situations are to be held in the tribal courts, if the parties weren't able to resolve their differences earlier in the courts of the arbitrators or neighbors.

Sacred to Hephaistos and Athena is the class of craftsmen, who have furnished our life with arts, and sacred to Ares and Athena are those who preserve the deeds of the craftsmen 920e through other, defensive, arts; and it is just that this class too, be sacred to these gods. Indeed, all these men continually take care of the country and the populace—the latter by ruling over the contests of war, the former by bringing into being tools and works for pay. In regard to such matters, because of their awe for the gods who are their progenitors, it wouldn't be fitting for them to lie. So if someone who is a craftsman should, 921a because of vice, fail to complete work within the specified time, and should lack a sense of awe before the god who gives him his livelihood (believing that his own god is forgiving), and should not look at the matter with his intelligence, he must first pay a judicial penalty to the god and, in the second place, a law shall await him:

He is to owe the price of the works about which he lied to the person giving the commission and produce them again from the beginning, within the stated time, for free.

And to him who undertakes work the law is a counselor, giving the same advice it gave to the one who sells: not to try 921b to take advantage by setting a greater price, but to set just simply what'it is worth. This same advice the law enjoins upon him who undertakes work; for the craftsman, at any rate, knows the worth. In cities of free men the craftsman himself ought never to use his art (which is by nature an activity that is above board and not dishonest) to try to take artful advantage of laymen, and the one who has been done an injustice in these matters may bring a lawsuit against him who does the

injustice. If, on the other hand, someone who has given a
commission to a craftsman should fail to pay him the correct
amount according to the lawful agreement, thus dishonoring
Zeus, the Protector of the City, and Athena, who share in the
regime, and out of desire for a small gain loosens great ties of
community, the law together with the gods must come to the
defense of the bond that holds the city together:

921c

He who has received work in advance and fails to give pay
within the agreed time period must pay double. If a year has
elapsed, although all other monies that someone may contribute as a loan are to be without interest, this man must pay one
obol[6] on the drachma per month; and the trials for these matters shall take place in the tribal courts.

921d

Because we reminded ourselves of craftsmen in general, it is
just to speak in passing about the craftsman of security
through war—the generals and whoever are artful in these
matters. These are like the former, but a different sort of craftsmen; and the law will never tire of praising him who gives just
honors, which are the pay for men of war, if one of these
should perform nobly a public work he has undertaken either
voluntarily or in following orders. But if he has received, in
advance, work that is part of the noble works of war, and
should fail to give payment, it will blame him. So let this law
be laid down, intermingled for us with the praise that concerns these matters, and counseling, rather than forcing, the
bulk of the citizens to honor in the second rank those good
men who are saviors of the whole city, either by acts of
courage or by warlike contrivances. For the greatest prize
should be given to those who rank first, those who are preeminently capable of doing honor to the writings of the good
lawgivers.

921e

922a

We have just about arranged the most important business
transactions human beings have with one another, except for
what pertains to orphans and the supervision of orphans by
their guardians; and, after what has now been discussed, it is
necessary that these matters be arranged, somehow or other.
The ruling beginnings in all matters of this kind are the desires on the part of those who are about to die to effect a distribution by will, and the chance accidents that leave some
without having made any wills at all. And I said it was "neces-

922b

sary," Kleinias, with a view to the trouble and difficulty that characterize these things. It's impossible to leave this unregulated; for everyone would set up many instructions that are in discord with one another as well as contrary to the laws, to the dispositions of the living, and even to their own prior dispositions in the time before they were about to make the will, if someone gives permission for that will to be unqualifiedly authoritative which someone may set up, no matter what condition he's in, as he approaches the end of life. The fact is, most of us are in some sense mindless and weak at the time when we believe we're about to die.   922c

Kl.   What do you mean by this, stranger?

Ath.   A human being who is about to die is difficult, Kleinias, and full of a speech that is for lawgivers very frightening and hard to handle.

Kl.   How so?

Ath.   Seeking to have authority over everything, he usually speaks with anger.

Kl.   Saying what?   922d

Ath.   "Gods! It is indeed a terrible thing," he declares, "if I'm not at all allowed to give my own belongings to whomever I wish or not, and more to one, less to another, of those who have proved miserable or good to me, having been adequately tested in periods of sickness and, in the case of some, in old age and all sorts of other twists of fortune!"

Kl.   Well, stranger, don't they seem to you to speak in a fine way?

Ath.   To me at least, Kleinias, those who became lawgivers of old   922e
       seem to have been soft, and to have looked at and thought about a small range of human affairs when they made laws.

Kl.   How do you mean?

Ath.   Fearing this speech, my good sir, they made a law that allowed a man to distribute his belongings by will simply and   923a
       entirely as he might wish; but I and you will reply more suitably, somehow, to those in your city who are about to die.

       "Friends," we will declare, "and really, creatures of a day,[7] it is difficult for you at the present time to know your own property and, what is more, to know yourselves, as even the Pythian writing[8] explains. I at any rate, being the lawgiver, ordain that neither yourselves nor this property belong to you, but that they belong rather to your entire family, both past and future, and that to an even higher degree the entire fam-   923b

[323]

ily, as well as the property, belong to the city. Since this is the way things are, I will never voluntarily go along if someone imposes upon you through flattery when you're sick or tottering with old age, and persuades you to make a will contrary to what is for the best; instead, I will legislate with a view to what is best for the entire city and family, and, with a view to all this, will justly assign a lower rank to what belongs to each individual. But you, being gracious and well disposed toward us, proceed along the way which you're now going, according to human nature; we'll take care of the rest of your belongings, looking after them to the very best of our powers—not looking after some but not others." Let these be the encouragements[9] and preludes for the living, Kleinias, as well as for the dying; the law shall be the following:

He who writes a will distributing his belongings, and is a father of children, must in the first place indicate in writing which of his sons he has decided is worthy to become the allotment holder, and with regard to the other children, if he should be giving one to someone else to take and adopt, he must indicate this too in writing; if there should be in addition some son of his who hasn't been adopted as heir to any allotment, and who it is hoped will be sent away to some colony according to law, the father may give this one as much of the rest of his property as he may wish, except for the ancestral allotment and the entire equipment of the allotment; if there should be more sons, the father may distribute the surplus over and above the allotment in any proportion he may wish. If one of the sons should have a house, he is not to distribute property to him, and the same for a daughter—if she should be betrothed to a man, he is not to distribute to her, but if that is not the case, he may distribute to her. If it should appear later, after the will has been made, that one of his sons or daughters owns a native allotment, the latter should leave what he received to the one who is heir to the allotment of him who made the will. If the man making the will should leave no males, but females, he is to leave as his son the husband of whichever daughter he wishes, indicating in writing the allotment heir. If the born or adopted son should have died while still a child, before he could take his place among the men, in this unfortunate circumstance also, the man writing the will should indicate in writing which of his children should come

923c

923d

923e

924a

second, with better fortune. If someone who is entirely without children should write his will, he may pick out one-tenth
of his property over and above the allotment, if he should
wish to give it to someone, and give it away. All the rest he is
to hand over to the adopted heir, whom he must adopt as his
son according to law—he being blameless and the son gracious.

In the case of a man whose children need guardians, if he
should die having indicated guardians in his written will, if
those whom he wished and as many as he wished will agree
voluntarily to serve as guardians for the children, the authori-   924b
tative choice of the guardians is to proceed according to these
written instructions. But if someone should die either without
any will at all, or having omitted a choice of guardians, then
the authoritative guardians shall be the nearest of kin on the
father's and the mother's sides, two from the father's and two
from the mother's, and one from the friends of the deceased:
these the Guardians of the Laws shall appoint for the orphan
in need. Guardianship in general and the orphans shall   924c
always be supervised by the fifteen eldest among all the
Guardians of the Laws, who shall divide themselves into
threes according to seniority: three are to serve for a year, and
then another three for another year, until the five orbits make
a circle. And this is never to cease insofar as possible. In the
case of a man who dies having made no will at all, and who
leaves children in need of a guardian, his children's need shall
share in these same laws. If someone should meet with an un-   924d
foreseen chance and leave females, he is to forgive the one laying down the law if the latter looks to just two of the three concerns he would have had, as he arranges the giving away in
marriage of the daughters: the closeness of kinship and the
preservation of the allotment. The third, which the father
would have considered—looking to see who among all the citizens would in dispositions and ways be appropriate as his
son as well as his daughter's groom, this shall be left aside   924e
because of the impossibility of carrying out the investigation.
The following law should stand, as the best that can be done
in such situations:

If a man who hasn't made a will should leave daughters after
he has died, a brother from the same father, or from the same
mother and without an allotment, is to have the daughter and
the allotment of the deceased. If there should be no brother,

but the son of a brother, the same shall hold for him, if the spouses are of an age with one another. And if there should be not one of these, but the son of a sister, the same shall hold. Fourth shall be a brother of the deceased's father; fifth, a son of this latter; sixth, a son of the father's sister. Thus let the family always proceed according to degree of kinship, if someone should leave female children: ascending through brothers

925a and the children of brothers, males coming before females in any one generation. The symmetry or lack of symmetry in the time of marriage for these shall be determined by an inspecting judge, who is to see the males naked and the females naked to the navel. If the family lacks relatives as far as grandsons of brothers, and children of a grandfather as well, then whomever of the other citizens the child may choose in con-

925b sultation with her guardians, she and he acting voluntarily, is to become heir to the deceased's allotment and groom for his daughter. Still, many things require many resources, and times occur when there would be a lack of enough such men in the city itself. So if someone who is at a loss for men on the spot should see somebody who has emigrated to a colony whom it would please her to have become heir to her father's allotment, then, if he should be kin, let him proceed to the inheritance of the allotment according to the arrangement in the law; if he should be outside the family, and there's no one in the city who is part of her family, then in accordance with the

925c choice of the guardians and the child of the deceased, he shall be authorized to come home, marry, and receive the allotment of the man who failed to make a will.

In the case of a man without any male or female children at all who should die without having made a will, what pertains to such a man in other respects should be governed by the aforementioned law, but a female as well as a male from the family shall proceed as mates to the deserted house each time,

925d and the allotment shall become legitimately theirs—a sister first, a brother's daughter second, third, the offspring of a sister, fourth, the sister of the father, fifth, the child of the father's brother, and sixth would be the child of the father's sister. These females are to dwell together with the males, according to consanguinity and justice,[10] in the way we have legislated earlier.

Let's not overlook the oppressiveness of such laws, the

harshness sometimes involved in their ordering the next of kin of the deceased to marry his kinswoman, and their apparent failure to consider the tens of thousands of impediments 925e that come into being among human beings and make one unwilling to obey such commands, and indeed make them ready to suffer anything whatsoever rather than obey, when diseases or maimings of the bodies or the mind arise in some of those they are commanded to marry or be married to. It might seem to some people that the lawgiver gives no thought to these things, but that impression would be incorrect. So let there be something spoken on behalf of the lawgiver and on behalf of the man to whom the law is given, almost as a common prelude, requesting those who are given the orders to forgive the lawgiver, because in his supervision of the common things he would never be able at the same time to manage the private calamities of each man, and on the other hand 926a requesting forgiveness for those to whom the legislation is given, because it's likely that sometimes they are unable to carry out fully the orders of the lawgiver, which he issued in ignorance.

Kl. What, stranger, would be the most well measured thing for someone to do in regard to such matters?

Ath. It's necessary to choose arbitrators, Kleinias, for such laws and for the persons who are the objects of the legislation.

Kl. How do you mean?

Ath. Sometimes a nephew whose father is wealthy would not vol- 926b untarily be willing to accept the daughter of his uncle, because he luxuriates, and has his mind set on a grander marriage; but sometimes one would be compelled to disobey the law because what the lawgiver commands involves a very great calamity—compelling them to take spouses who are mad or afflicted with some other terrible calamities of body or soul, which render life unlivable for the one who acquires them. So our present statement about these matters shall be established in law as follows:

If some people should complain about the established laws in regard to a will, either with respect to any other aspects 926c whatsoever or, with respect to marriages, to the effect that if the lawgiver himself were present and alive, he would never have compelled those who are now being compelled, to marry or to be married, to do either, while, on the other hand, some-

926d

one in the family or some guardian asserts that he would have, it must be declared that the lawgiver has left the fifteen Guardians of the Laws as arbitrators and fathers for the male and female orphans. Those who are in dispute about some such matter must appeal to these for a decision, and carry out their opinions as authoritative. But if it should seem to someone that this is a great power to confer on the Guardians of the Laws, he is to take them before the court of select judges [11] and obtain a decision about the matters in dispute. The losing party is to incur the blame and censure of the lawgiver—a more oppressive penalty than a large sum of money, for him who possesses intelligence.

926e

Now for orphan children there should be, as it were, a certain second birth. The upbringing and education for each of them after the first have been described; after the second, which has taken place through the loss of fathers, some way must be devised whereby the fortune of orphanhood for those who have become orphans will involve the least possible pity for their calamity. In the first place, legislation gives them Guardians of the Laws as fathers, instead of, and not inferior to, those who begot them; and indeed we assign them to the orphans each year, to supervise them as if they were their own, having presented a prelude about the upbringing of orphans that is attuned to these men as well as to the guardians:

927a

For opportune indeed, it appears to me, was our elaboration of the earlier speeches, to the effect that the souls of the dead have a certain power after they have died, by which they look after the affairs of human beings. These things are true, though the accounts concerning them are lengthy; one ought to trust the other pronouncements concerning such things, since they are so numerous and so very ancient, but also trust those who legislate that these things are so—if, that is, they don't appear wholly senseless. And if, in this way, these

927b

things are according to nature, then they ought to fear first the gods above, who perceive the bereavement of the orphans, then the souls of those who have passed away, for whom it is natural to care especially for their own offspring and to be well disposed toward those who honor them and ill disposed toward those who dishonor them, and then the souls of the living, who are in old age and held in the highest honors. Where [12] a city is happy under good laws, their grandchildren

live, loving them fondly and with pleasure; and they hear
sharply and see sharply what pertains to these matters, and   927c
are well disposed toward those who are just in regard to them,
but are very indignant,[13] on the other hand, toward those who
are insolent to orphans and the bereaved, holding this to be
the greatest and most sacred deposit. To all these the guardian
and the magistrate ought to turn his mind—if he should have
any—and take care with the upbringing and education of orphans: as if he were doing a favor to himself and his own, he
should do them all the good he possibly can, in every way.

He, then, who obeys[14] the myth that precedes the law, and
does nothing insolent to an orphan, will not know definitely
the lawgiver's anger in such matters; but he who disobeys,   927d
and does an injustice to someone bereft of father or mother,
shall pay double the total damages paid by someone who has
been bad to a child with both parents living.

As to the other legislation for guardians, concerning orphans, and for magistrates, concerning the supervision of the
guardians, if they didn't have examples of the upbringing of
free children through bringing up their own and supervising
their own properties, and moreover if laws pertaining to these   927e
very matters hadn't been discussed in due measure, it would
make some sense to lay down certain guardians' laws, as
being very different in their own way, and as differentiating,
by means of their peculiar practices, the life of the orphans
from the life of the nonorphans. But now, in regard to all such
matters, the status of our orphans doesn't call for anything
that's very different from a father's duty, although the task is
prone to be not at all equal in honors and dishonors, or supervisory responsibilities. That, indeed, is why the law has been   928a
serious in its exhortations[15] and threats concerning this subject—the legislation concerning orphans. Yet some such threat
as the following would be very timely:

Whoever should be the guardian of a female or male, and
whoever among the Guardians of the Laws should stand
guard over and supervise a guardian, shall prize the one
whose fortune it is to be an orphan no less than his own children, and supervise the goods of the ward no worse than his
own, or, indeed, better than his own, with a spirited zeal. Ev-   928b
eryone is to serve as guardian keeping this single law regarding orphans.

But if someone should act otherwise in such matters, contrary to this law, the magistrate shall punish the guardian, or the guardian shall bring the magistrate before the court of the select judges, and exact a fine that is twice the damages estimated by the court. And if a guardian should seem to the kinsmen or to any of the other citizens to be careless or to be

928c doing evil, they are to take him before the same court; whatever injury he should be convicted of, he is to pay four times this amount, half of which is to go to the child and half to the person who successfully prosecuted. At the time when one of the orphans comes of age, if he believes he has been treated badly by his guardian, he may bring a judicial action concerning the guardianship within five years after the guardianship has ended. If one of the guardians should be convicted, the court is to estimate what he ought to suffer or pay; if it should be one of the magistrates, if it seems he's done the evil to the

928d orphan on account of carelessness, the court is to estimate what he ought to pay to the child, but if it seems on account of injustice, then in addition to the fine he is to be removed from the magistracy of the Guardians of the Laws, and the common authority of the city is to appoint another Guardian of the Laws in this man's place, for the land and the city.

To a greater degree than they should, quarrels occur, on the part of fathers toward their own children, and children toward their parents, in which the fathers would hold that the legisla-

928e tor ought to legislate permission for them, if they wish, to have a herald proclaim in front of everyone that they henceforth disown the son according to law; and in which sons, on the other hand, hold that they should be given permission to indict their fathers for derangement when they are in a shameful condition on account of diseases or old age. These are prone to arise out of the dispositions of human beings who are really altogether bad, since if just half are bad—as where the father isn't the bad one, but the son, or the opposite—calamities that are the offspring of such a degree of enmity don't occur. Now in another political regime, a child who was proclaimed disowned would not necessarily be without a city; but in this one, for which these laws will hold, a person who lacks a father must necessarily go and dwell in another land.

929a For there is not to be a single addition to the five thousand forty households. That is why he who is to undergo these things in a trial should be disowned not just by one father, but by the entire family. And in such affairs it is necessary to proceed according to something like the following law:

He who, justly or not, is urged by a spirited anger that is in no way fortunate, to desire to remove from his own family the person he begot and brought up, is not to be allowed to do this in a paltry or hasty fashion. Rather, first he is to call 929b together his own kinsmen as distant as cousins, and the same kinsmen of the son on the mother's side, and is to present his accusation before them, teaching how the son deserves to be proclaimed by all of them expelled from the family; and he is to give the son equal time to speak and show why he doesn't deserve to suffer any of these things. If the father should persuade and obtain the votes of more than half of all the kinsmen—excluding the father, mother, and defendant from the voting, but including the rest of the adult women and 929c men—then in this way and according to these procedures it shall be permissible for a father to proclaim his son disowned, but in no other way. If one of the citizens should wish to adopt as his son the man proclaimed disowned, no law is to prevent his doing so—for the dispositions of the young naturally undergo many transformations during the lifetime of each—but if after ten years no one should have desired to adopt as his son the man proclaimed disowned, the supervisors of the 929d excess offspring who are to be sent to a colony are to take charge of these also, so that they may take a suitable share in the same colonization.

If some disease, or old age, or harshness of character, or all of these together, should unhinge someone's mind to a greater degree than is the case with the many, and it should escape the notice of the others—except those who live with him—and he should be destroying his household under the sovereign authority he has over what belongs to him, and the son should be at a loss and should shrink from bringing a written indictment for derangement, the law in his case shall be that first he 929e is to go and explain his father's calamity to those who are eldest among the Guardians of the Laws; after they've looked into the matter adequately, they are to advise whether or not he should bring the written indictment, and if they do advise it, they are to become witnesses and fellow plaintiffs for the one who brings the indictment. The man who is convicted shall for the rest of his life lack sovereign authority to dispose of his belongings in even the smallest detail, and is to be supervised for the rest of his life like a child.

If a husband and a wife should be in no way in agreement, because of their unfortunate characters, ten middle-aged men among the Guardians of the Laws should constantly supervise them, along with ten of the women who are concerned with marriages and are of a similar age. If they should be able to effect a reconciliation, these arrangements are to be authoritative; but if the souls seethe all the more with passion, then they should do their best to seek partners who will be suitable for each of the parties. It's likely that such persons are not possessed of gentle dispositions; they should try to harmonize these with mates of more phlegmatic and gentle dispositions of character. And where those without children or with just a few children should have a falling-out, the domestic union should be made for the sake of children. Where it's those who have enough children, then the separation and the joining should be made for the sake of growing old together and caring for one another.

If a woman should die leaving female and male children, the established law would counsel, but not compel, one to bring up the children without introducing a stepmother; but if there aren't children, one must necessarily marry, until one begets enough children for the household and the city. If a man should die leaving enough children, the mother of the children should stay there and bring them up. But if she should seem to be younger than she ought to be for healthy living without a man, the relatives should communicate with the women who supervise marriages and do what seems appropriate to themselves and to those women in such cases. If there should be a lack of children, they should act for the sake of children as well; and a barely sufficient number of children by law shall be a male and a female.

When it is agreed who the creators of an offspring are, but a judgment is needed as to which the offspring should follow, then, if a slave woman should mate with a slave, or free man, or freed man, the offspring is to belong entirely to the master

930a

930b

930c

930d

of the slave woman, but if some free woman should have intercourse with a slave, the offspring is to belong to the master of the slave. And if the offspring should be from a man's own slave, or a woman's own slave, and this should become evident, the women shall send the offspring of the woman, 930e together with its father, to another land, and the Guardians of the Laws shall do likewise with the offspring of the man, together with she who bore it.

No god or human being who possesses intelligence would ever advise anyone to neglect their parents; and one should have the prudence to see that it is correct to apply a prelude of the following sort, concerning the solicitude due the gods, to the honors and dishonors rendered to parents:

The ancient laws established among all men concerning the gods are twofold. Some of the gods we see clearly and honor; for others we set up images as objects of worship, which de- 931a light us even though they are without souls, and on account of which we believe those gods, having souls, feel great goodwill and gratitude. Now no one who has a father and mother, or the fathers or mothers of these, lying as treasures in the house[16] and weakened by old age, should ever think that a statue will be more authoritative than such a shrine established on the hearth of the home—if, indeed, the possessor cares for it in the correct way.

Kl. What do you explain to be the correct way? 931b

Ath. I will say. For such things are surely worth hearing, friends.

Kl. Just say on.

Ath. Oedipus, we assert, when he was dishonored, invoked upon his children those things which, according to what everyone sings, were fulfilled and heeded by the gods; and Amyntor in his spirited anger brought a curse upon his own child Phoenix, as did Theseus upon Hippolytus,[17] and myriad others upon myriad others; from which it became clear that 931c the gods pay heed to the curses of parents against children. For a parental curse against offspring is as no other curse against others, and it is most just that it be so. So let no one believe that a god by nature pays heed to the prayers of an especially dishonored father or mother toward children, but to one who is honored and has become exceedingly glad, and on account of such things generously beseeches the gods with

931d

prayers for good things for his children—will we believe that they don't listen with equal attentiveness, and thus distribute things to us? Why, in that case they would never be just in the distribution of goods, which is something we claim is least fitting for gods to be.

Kl. Very much so!

Ath. So then let us understand, as we said a little earlier, that we could not possess any statue more honorable in the eyes of the gods than a father or forefather in their old age, or mothers having the like capacity, and when one takes delight in them with honors, the god rejoices. For otherwise he would not pay heed to them. Surely, the shrine that is our ancestors' is marvelous to us, and preeminent over that of soulless figures. The former, which have souls, pray for us whenever they're cared for by us, and do the opposite when they're dishonored, whereas the latter do neither; as a result, if someone were to treat his father and forefather and all such persons correctly, he would possess the most efficacious of all statues for securing a destiny befriended by gods.

931e

Kl. You've spoken in a most noble way.

Ath. Everyone who has intelligence fears and honors prayers of parents, knowing that they have often been fulfilled for many people. Since this is the way these things are arranged by nature, for good men old progenitors are a godsend[18] while they live, up to the very last moments of their life, and if they depart while still young, they're especially missed; but for bad men they are a source of great fear. So let everyone, believing these words, honor his own parents with all lawful honors. But if word should have it that someone is deaf to such preludes,[19] to these men the following law would correctly apply:

932a

If someone in this city should be more neglectful of his parents than he ought to be, and, heedless of them, should fail to fulfill their wishes in every respect more than those of his sons, all his offspring, and himself, let the one who is suffering such treatment report it—either in person or by sending someone—to the three eldest Guardians of the Laws and to three also of the women who supervise marriages. They are to look after this, and punish with blows and imprisonment those committing injustice who are still young (that is, in the case of the men, those who are under thirty, but in the case of the women, they are to use the same punishments on those

932b

932c

who are up to ten years older). And if, when they are past these ages, they should not desist from the same sorts of neglect toward parents, but in some cases should do evil to them, they are to take them before a court composed of the one hundred and one eldest among all the citizens. If someone should be convicted, let the court determine what he ought to suffer or pay, ruling out nothing which a human being is capable of suffering or paying. If someone should be unable to 932d
report that he is being treated badly, anyone among the free men who learns of it should report it to the magistrates, or be an evil man and subject to prosecution for the injury by anyone who wishes. If a slave should report it, he is to become free: if he's the slave of one of those doing or suffering the evil, the magistracy shall let him go, while if he belongs to some other citizen, the public shall pay his price on his behalf to the owner. The magistrates are to see to it that no one does an injustice to such a man as retribution for his informing.

With regard to the ways in which one person harms another 932e
with poisons, the fatal cases have been discussed fully, but none of the other injuries which someone voluntarily and with forethought effects, either through drinks, or foods, or unguents, have yet been fully discussed. The discussion is arrested by the fact that poisons are twofold, in accordance with the character of the human race. The kind we expressly mentioned just now works its evil on bodies by bodies, according 933a
to nature. But another kind uses certain sorceries, incantations, and so-called "binding spells" to persuade those who dare to injure people that they can do such a thing, and others that they are injured worst of all by these men who can practice magic. Now it isn't easy to know how these and all such things are by nature at any time, nor, if one should know, is it easy to persuade others; it's not worth trying to persuade the 933b
souls of human beings who are suspicious of one another in regard to such things that, if they should ever see molded waxen images at doorways, or at places where three roads meet, or at the images of their own parents, they must pay little attention to all such things, and to urge them to do so because they lack a clear opinion about them. But, dividing in two the law concerning poisoning, according to whichever of the ways someone might try to poison, one ought first to be-

933c seech, exhort, and advise them that they should not try to do such a thing, nor frighten the many among human beings, who are as terrified [20] as children, nor, again, to compel the lawgiver and the judge to cure human beings of such fears; since, in the first place, he who tries to poison doesn't know what he might do—in regard to the bodies, if he doesn't happen to be a doctor and hence a knower, and in regard to sor-

933d ceries, if he doesn't happen to be a diviner or wizard. So let reason present the following law about poisoning:

A man who poisons someone so as to cause injury that is not mortal either to the man himself or to his human beings, or so as to cause a mortal or other injury to his livestock or beehives, if he should happen to be a doctor, and should be convicted in a trial for poisoning, is to be punished with death; but if he should be a layman, the court is to assess in his case what he ought to suffer or pay. If he should seem to be the same as one who injures by using binding spells, or

933e charms, or certain incantations, or any such poisons, and is a diviner or wizard, he is to die; but if someone should be convicted of the poisoning [21] without possessing the art of divining, the same thing is to happen to this man: for in the case of this man too, the court is to assess what they think he ought to suffer or pay.

With regard to the ways in which one person may harm another by theft or violence, if the harm be greater, he is to pay a greater indemnity to the one harmed, and if it be lesser, he is to pay a smaller penalty, but above all the person is to pay each time an amount sufficient to cure the injury. In addition, each must pay the judicial penalty attached to each evil

934a deed for the sake of instilling moderation: [22] he who has done evil because of another's lack of intelligence—giving way to persuasion on account of his youthfulness or some other such thing—shall pay a lighter penalty; he who has done evil because of his own lack of intelligence, on account of lack of self-restraint in the face of pleasures or pains—in cowardly fears, or certain desires, or feelings of envy, or spirited angers that are hard to cure—shall pay a heavier. He shall pay the judicial penalty not for the sake of the evildoing—for what has been

934b done will never be undone—but so that he and those who see him suffering justice will in future time either hate the injustice altogether, or refrain in large part from such a calamity. For the sake of all these things, and with a view to all such considerations, the laws should aim, just like an archer who is not bad, at the greatness and above all at the worthiness of the punishment for each of the offenses. And the judge must assist the lawgiver in performing this same task, whenever some law assigns to him the estimation of what the man judged guilty should suffer or pay; while the latter, like a painter, 934c must sketch in outline deeds which follow what has been written. That, Megillus and Kleinias, is just what we ought to do now, in the noblest and best manner possible. The proper sorts of penalties for all thefts and acts of violence ought to be described, insofar as the gods and the sons of the gods allow us to legislate.

If someone should be mad, he is not to appear openly in the city. The relatives in each case are to guard the persons in their homes, using any method they know of, or they must pay a 934d penalty: a man of the highest class one hundred drachmas, whether it be a slave or a free man that he's failing to look after; a man of the second class four-fifths of a mina; a third-class man three-fifths; and two-fifths in the case of a fourth-class man. Now many men are mad, in many ways. There are those whom we're now discussing, where it's on account of diseases, but there are some who are such because both the nature and the nurture of their spiritedness have become bad: in a minor dispute they give vent to loud-voiced, wicked slanders against one another, and no such behavior is in any 934e way or on any occasion fitting in a city with good laws. So let the following be the single law that applies to all abusive talk:

No one is to abuse anyone in speech. He who is disputing with another in certain discussions is to teach and learn and wholly abstain from abusing the disputant and the bystanders. For from words (a light affair at first), from imprecating and cursing one another, and bringing down on each other the shameful epithets of women's cries, there arises, in deed, 935a hatred and most weighty enmities. The one who speaks is gracious to a graceless thing—spiritedness—and gorges his anger with wicked feasts; making the part of his soul that was at one time tamed by education savage again he becomes a beast through living in ill humor, and receives as a gift in re-

935b turn the bitterness of his spiritedness. Moreover, it is often usual, somehow, for everyone in such situations to switch to uttering something that ridicules the opponent; and no one ever becomes accustomed to this behavior without either straying in some degree from a serious disposition, or destroying in large part his highmindedness. That is why no one is ever to utter any such thing at all in a temple, or at publicly funded sacrifices, or again in the contests, or in the marketplace, or in a court, or in any common assembly. The magistrate in charge of each of these is to carry out the punishment,

935c or else never desire to win a victory for excellence—on the ground that he neither cares for the laws nor does the things commanded by the lawgiver. And if in other places someone doesn't abstain from such words—whether he initiates the reviling or defends himself with it—any elder man who happens along is to defend the law by driving away with blows those who are kindly disposed toward spirited anger, that evil comrade, or else must undergo the prescribed penalty.

We are now saying that it is impossible for a man entangled in reviling to avoid trying to say something that evokes laugh-

935d ter, and we are reviling this practice, when it involves spirited anger. But what then? Do we accept the spirited eagerness of the comedians to say what is laughable about human beings, when they speak in such a way, trying to make comedies about our citizens, without spirited anger? Should we divide it in two, into what is playful and what is not, and allow someone to speak playfully in ridicule of another, without spirited

935e anger, but allow no one to do so seriously and, as we said, with spirited anger? This must in no way be given up, but we should legislate who may do so, and who may not.

A poet of comedy, or of some iambic lampoon, or a melody of the Muses, may not in any way make a comedy about any citizen, through speech or image, whether with spirited anger or without spirited anger. If someone should disobey,

936a those who preside over the contests must drive him completely out of the country on the very day, or else pay a penalty of three minas sacred to the god whose contest it is. Those, however, who were earlier said to have permission to do this concerning someone, may do so to one another, without spirited anger and in play, but may not do so in seriousness or in spirited anger. The judgment as to this distinction shall be left to the Supervisor of Education as a whole for the young; what this man judges approved, the poet may present in public, but what he judges disapproved, the poet may not himself show 936b to anyone nor ever be seen teaching to any other, slave or free, without being held to be a bad man and one disobedient to the laws.

What is pitiable is not the man who is hungry, or suffering some such thing, but rather the man who is moderate, or has some virtue or some part of virtue, yet in addition to these has some calamity; so it would be amazing if someone like this, whether slave or free, were totally uncared for, and as a result arrived at a condition of utter beggary, in a regime and city that is even moderately well managed. That is why it is safe 936c for the lawgiver to establish some such law as the following for such cases:

No one is to become a beggar in our city, and if someone should try to do such a thing, to earn his living through endless prayers, the Market Regulators are to drive him from the marketplace, the magistracy of the City Regulators is to drive him from the city, and the Field Regulators are to send him out of the rest of the country and across the border, so that the country may become completely purged of such a creature.

If a male or female slave should injure anything that belongs to someone else, and the one injured does not himself share 936d the responsibility, on account of inexperience or some other imprudent usage, the master of the one who did the injury must either cure the injury, omitting nothing, or hand over the one who did the injury. But if the master brings a counterclaim, alleging that the claim has arisen as a result of the common craft of injurer and injured, with the aim of robbing the slave, let him prosecute the man claiming to have been injured, on a charge of conspiracy. If he should win, let him 936e exact twice the value of the slave, which the court is to estimate; but if he should lose, let him both cure the injury and hand over the slave. And if a beast of burden, or a horse, or a dog, or some other animal, should do some harm to the belongings of a neighbor, let the injury be recompensed according to the same principles.

If someone should voluntarily refuse to testify, the man who needs him is to issue a summons, and the man summoned is to appear at the trial. If he should have knowledge and be willing to testify, let him testify; but if he should claim not to have knowledge, let him depart from the trial after having sworn in the name of the three gods Zeus, Apollo, and Themis

937a that he doesn't have knowledge. He who has been summoned to testify and fails to appear with the man who issued the summons is to be lawfully liable for the injury. If someone calls up as witness somebody who is a judge, the latter is not to vote on the case in which he has testified. It is permissible for a free woman to testify and support a pleading, if she should be over forty years of age, and to bring a judicial action, if she should be without a husband. If the husband is liv-

937b ing she may only testify. A female or male slave and a child are to be permitted to testify and support a pleading only in a murder case, provided they furnish a worthy guarantee that they will remain until the trial, if their testimony should be denounced as false. And either of the parties may denounce the testimony as a whole or in part, provided he makes the assertion that they have testified falsely before the case has been decided. The magistrates shall guard the denunciations once they've been sealed by both parties, and present them at the

937c trial for false testimonies. If someone should be convicted of false testimony twice, no law shall any longer compel this man to testify, and if he should be convicted three times, this man is no longer to be permitted to testify. If he should dare to testify after having been convicted a third time, let anyone who wishes expose him to the magistracy, and let the magistracy hand him over to the court; if he should be convicted, let him be punished with death. In the case of those whose testimony is condemned at the trial, and who seem to have testified falsely and brought about the victory for the party that won, if

937d over half the testimony of such persons should be condemned, the case that was won by these testimonies is to be annulled, and there shall be a dispute and trial as to whether the case was decided on these testimonies or not; the final outcome of the earlier trials shall depend on which way this is decided.

There are many noble things in the life of human beings, but most of them are, as it were, naturally subject to defects

which pollute and defile them. And indeed, is even justice,
which has tamed all the human things, somehow not noble   937e
for human beings? But if this is noble, how would judicial advocacy not be noble for us? These things, being such, are
discredited by a certain vice pretending to the noble name of
art. It claims, first, that there is for judicial proceedings a certain contrivance—itself—which can carry on judicial cases and
support the pleading of another, and can bring about victory,[23] whether the things done in each judicial case be just or
not; and it claims that the gift of this very art, and of the   938a
speeches that result from the art, is to be had if one gives
money in return. Now this, whether it is an art or a certain experience and practice without art, certainly ought not to
grow[24] in our city. The lawgiver requests that one obey, and
not utter what is opposed to justice, but go away to another
country; to those who obey, the law is silent, but to those who
disobey, this is the voice of the law:

If someone should seem to try to reverse the power of the   938b
just things in the souls of the judges, and to bring many suits
or support the suits of others, when they aren't called for, he is
to be prosecuted for evil judicial procedure or evil judicial advocacy by anyone who wishes, and tried in the court of select
judges. If he's convicted, the court is to decide whether he
seems to do such a thing out of fondness for money or
fondness for victory: if out of fondness for victory, the court
shall determine in his case how long a time such a man ought
not to undertake a suit against anyone or support anyone
else's suit; but if it's out of fondness for money, in the case of a   938c
stranger he's to depart from the country and never come
again, or be punished with death, while in the case of a
member of the city he's to die, because of having honored in
every way the fondness for money. And if someone should be
judged to have done such a thing twice out of fondness for victory, he is to die.

BOOK XII

941a Ath. If someone acting in the capacity of ambassador or herald should convey a false message from the city to some city, or, when he is sent, should fail to convey the matters he was sent to convey, or if it should become evident that in his capacity as ambassador or herald he has not brought back correctly what was sent from the enemies or even from friends, these actions should be prosecuted as illegal acts of impiety against

941b messages and commandments of Hermes[1] and Zeus; and if he's convicted an assessment should be made of what he ought to suffer or pay.

Theft of money is illiberal, and rapacity is shameless. None of the sons of Zeus has practiced either of these, through delighting in guile or violence. So let no one be deceived and persuaded about such matters by poets, or in some other way by some discordant tellers of myths, and think that when he steals or uses violence he does nothing shameful, but just what is done by the gods themselves. For that is neither true nor likely: whoever should do such a thing against the law is

941c never a god or the child of gods, and it is more fitting for the lawgiver to know about these things than it is for all the poets. He, therefore, who is persuaded by our argument has good fortune, and would have good fortune for all time; but he who doesn't believe must, after these remarks, enter into combat with some such law as the following:

If someone should steal some public thing, he must undergo the same judicial penalty, whether it be great or small. For he who steals something small has stolen under the influence of the same erotic passion, but with less power, while he who moves a greater thing that he didn't set down is unjust to the full extent. So the law would not decide to assign a lesser judicial punishment to either of them on account of the size of the theft, but only because one of them is perhaps still curable and the other incurable. In fact, if someone should convict in court a stranger or a slave of stealing something public, the judgment as to what the person ought to suffer, or what penalty he ought to pay, should be made on the grounds that it's likely that he's curable. But if a member of the city, brought up in the way he will have been brought up, should be convicted of pillaging or doing violence to the fatherland (whether he's caught in the act or not), he's to be punished with death, on the grounds that he's practically incurable.

Military organization appropriately calls for much consultation and many laws, but the most important thing is that no one, male or female, should ever be without a ruler, and that no one's soul should acquire the habit of doing something on its own and alone, either seriously or in play; at all times, in war and in peace, it should live constantly looking to and following the ruler, governed by that man in even the briefest matters—such as standing when someone gives the order, and walking and exercising in the nude and washing and eating and getting up at night to guard and carry messages, and in dangers, not pursuing someone or retiring before another without an indication from the rulers. In a word, one should teach one's soul by habits not to know, and not to know how to carry out, any action at all apart from the others; as much as possible everyone should in every respect live always in a group, together, and in common—for there is not nor will there ever be anything stronger, better, and more artful than this for producing security and victory in war. This ought to be practiced during peacetime, from earliest childhood: ruling the rest and being ruled by others. And anarchy ought to be removed from the entire life of all human beings and of all beasts that are subject to human beings. Indeed, all choral dances are to be danced with a view to feats of excellence in war, and good temper as a whole and fortitude are to be practiced for the sake of the same things, as is endurance with

941d

942a

942b

942c

942d

[343]

942e

943a

regard to foods, drinks, cold and the opposite, and hard beds; most important, they are not to corrupt the capacity of the head and feet by wrapping them with alien coverings, thus destroying the birth and growth[2] of their own felt and shoes. For if these extremities are preserved they maintain a very great capacity in the body as a whole, while they do the opposite if the opposite occurs; the one is the most ministerial part for the entire body, and the other is the most magisterial, since by nature it possesses all the sovereign perceptions of the body. This is the praise that it was necessary for a young man to seem to be listening to[3] concerning the military life, and the following are the laws:

He who is selected, or is commanded to take his turn, must serve in the military. But if someone out of a certain cowardice and without the Generals' permission should fail to do so, there are to be prosecutions before the war officers for failing to perform military service, when they come back from the military camp. The judges shall be each class of soldiers sitting separately—heavily-armed infantry, cavalry, and each of the other military classes in the same way. Heavily-armed infantrymen are to be brought before heavily-armed infantry, cavalrymen before cavalry, and the others, in the same way, before their own kind. If someone should be convicted, he shall never be a competitor for a prize in excellence as a whole, and shall never prosecute another for failing to perform military service, or be an accuser in these matters; in addition to these things, the court is also to estimate what he ought to suffer or pay. After this, when the trials for failing to perform military service have been decided, the officers are to call an assembly for each class again, and he who wishes shall be judged concerning the prizes for excellence, in their own tribes. The evidence he presents, and the confirmation from the speeches of witnesses, is not to be from an earlier war, but just from the expedition they've been on at that time. The crown of victory for each class shall be of olive branches, and this is to be hung up, with an inscription, in the temples of whichever gods of war the person may wish, as a witness during his entire life to the judgment concerning the prizes for excellence, or the second or third prizes. If someone should go on military service but return home prior to the time when the officers send him back, these men are to be prosecuted for

943b

943c

943d

deserting the ranks before the same persons as those who preside over cases of failure to perform military service; for those who are convicted, there are to be the same retributions as were exacted earlier.

Of course, every man who prosecutes a man on any charge must fear lest he bring about a false retribution, either volun- 943e tarily or involuntarily (insofar as is within his power). For Justice is said, and has been said really,[4] to be the virgin daughter of Awe, and falsehood is naturally hated[5] by Awe and Justice. So everyone must be careful about mistaking justice in other matters, and especially in the case of the throwing away of arms during war, lest one make an erroneous judgment about the occasions when it's necessary to throw them away, blaming these occasions as if they were shameful, and bringing unworthy judicial charges against a man who doesn't deserve them. Now it's not at all easy to define either of these situations, yet nevertheless the law must try somehow or other 944a to distinguish them from each other. Let's discuss it while making use of myth: if Patroclus[6] had been carried to the tent without his weapons and had recovered, as has happened to tens of thousands while Hector was in possession of those arms which the poet claims had been given by the gods to Peleus as a dowry in his marriage with Thetis, it would have been possible for whoever was base among the men of that time to blame the son of Menoetios for throwing away his arms. And then there are those who have lost their weapons by being thrown down cliffs, or at sea, or when a sudden flood 944b of water hits them in the toils of storms; indeed, there would be ten thousand such cases one might sing about in a comforting way, and thereby portray as noble an easily misrepresented evil. One must do what one can to separate the greater and more disgusting evil from the opposite. Now the application of these names in the course of blaming virtually contains a certain distinction; for it wouldn't be just to use the name "shield-hurler" in all cases, but rather "arms-thrower." The 944c one who is deprived of his arms by a reasonable degree of violence wouldn't be a "shield-hurler" in the same way as the one who voluntarily drops them: presumably they differ altogether, and in every way. So let it be put as follows in the law:

If someone overtaken by enemies possesses arms, and

[345]

doesn't turn to make a defense, but voluntarily drops them or hurls them away, striving to win a shameful life with coward-ice rather than a noble and happy death with courage, then for such a throwing away of arms there is to be judicial punish-ment for the arms hurled away; but the judge is not to be care-less in investigating the case described previously. Because it is always necessary to punish the bad man, so that he may become better, but not the unlucky man—for no more is to be gained. What then would be the appropriate penalty for the man who gave up such a power of defensive arms in the op-posite way? It isn't possible for a human being to do the op-posite of what they claim was once done by a god, who trans-formed Caeneus the Thessalian[7] from a woman's to a man's nature; but if the opposite change to that one, the transforma-tion from man into woman, were the retribution for the man who is a shield-hurler, it would be in a way the most fitting of all. As it is, to come as near as possible to this, because of his love of his soul, and so that he may not run risks for the rest of his life, but may live for the maximum length of time in ill repute, let the following law apply to these men:

A man who should be convicted in a trial for shamefully throwing away his weapons of war is never to be used as a male soldier or assigned to any post whatsoever by any Gen-eral or any other of the war officers. Otherwise, the Auditor shall condemn the officer at his audit, and if the one who gave the bad man an assignment should be of the highest class, he must pay a thousand drachmas, if of the second, five minas, if of the third, three minas, and if of the fourth, a mina. The one who was convicted in the trial, in addition to giving up manly risks, as befits his nature, must also pay a recompense: a thou-sand drachmas if he should be of the highest class, five minas if of the second, three if of the third, and likewise a mina, just as in the case of those discussed before, if he's of the fourth class.

What account would it be fitting for us to give concerning the audits of magistrates, some of whom obtain office by the fortune of the lot for a period of a year, and some of whom ob-tain office for several years and come from a previously se-lected group? Who would be an adequate Auditor of such men, in case one of them should do something that is some-

how crooked, because he's been bent by the weight and on account of his own lack of capacity in regard to what the office
requires?[8] It's not at all easy to find a ruler over rulers who is   945c
superior in virtue, but nevertheless an attempt must be made
to find some divine Auditors. For this is the way it is: in the
case of a regime, just as in the case of a ship or some animal,
opportunities for dissolution are afforded by many things—
stays, undergirdings, and the tendons of the sinews—which,
being of one nature, are dispersed all around, and which we
call by many names. And this provides one such opportunity,
and not the smallest, for the preservation or the dwelling in   945d
dissolution of a regime. For if the ones who audit the magistrates are better than them, and evince this by applying a
blameless justice in a blameless way, the entire country and
city flourish and are happy. But if what pertains to the audits
of the magistrates turns out otherwise, then the justice that
binds all the political activities into one is dissolved, and in
this way every office is split apart from the others: rather than
assenting to the same thing they make the one city many, fill it   945e
with factions, and swiftly destroy it. That is why the Auditors
must be in every way amazing men in regard to the whole of
virtue. Let us contrive, then, to bring them into being in some
such way as the following:

Each year, after the sun has turned from summer to winter,
the entire city must assemble in the precinct common to the
Sun and Apollo, to present to the god three men from among   946a
them. Each of them is to propose a man not less than fifty
years of age whom he considers to be the best in every way
(leaving aside himself). They are to pick out the half of the
nominees who receive the most votes—if, that is, their
number is even; if it's odd, they're to delete the one who
received the least votes, and leave half of them after rejecting
the others according to the plurality of votes. If some should
be equal in votes and make the half larger, they are to delete
the surplus by rejecting those who are younger. They are to   946b
judge among the rest by voting again, until three are left with
an unequal number of votes. But if either all or two of these
should have an equal number of votes, they are to turn the
matter over to good destiny and fortune, and use the lot to
choose the victor, the second, and the third, whom they are to
crown with olive branches. Giving the prizes for excellence to

946c all of them, they are to proclaim that the city of the Magnesians, again finding security under god, presents to the Sun her three best men, and dedicates them as a common first-offering to Apollo, according to the ancient law, and the Sun, for as long a time as they pursue their task of judging. In the first year they are to elect twelve such Auditors, until each has attained the age of seventy-five, and afterward three are to be added each year. These are to divide all the offices into twelve parts and examine them by means of every test appropriate for free men. They are to dwell, for as long a time as they should

946d conduct audits, in the precinct of Apollo and the Sun in which they were selected. When they've judged those who rule the city, some of whom each will judge in private and some of whom they'll judge in common with one another, they are to announce by written proclamations in the marketplace what must be suffered or paid by each magistracy, according to the sentence of the Auditors. Any of the magistracies that should not agree that it has been judged justly must take the Auditors before the select judges; if someone should win an acquittal from the Auditors' sentence, he is to bring an accusation

946e against the Auditors themselves, if he wishes. But if he should be convicted, then if the Auditors have assessed the death penalty, he is to die and no more, necessarily; but in the case of the other assessments, which it's possible to pay double, he's to pay double.

One must also hear what the audits of these men themselves will be, and how they will come about. While they're alive,

947a these men whom the entire city has judged worthy of prizes for excellence shall occupy the front seats at every festival. Moreover, from them are to be sent out the officers in charge of each mission to observe the common sacrifices, spectacles, and other sacred ceremonies shared in common with the Greeks. These men, alone of those in the city, are to be adorned with a crown of laurel. All are to be priests of Apollo and the Sun, but the one who is judged to be first among those

947b selected each year is to be the ruling priest that year, and the name of this man is to be inscribed each year, so that he might become the measure of the year's number as long as the city should last. When they die, they are to have laying-outs, funeral processions, and groves that are distinguished from those of the rest of the citizens: all the clothing is to be white,

and it is to take place without dirges and lamentations, and instead a chorus of fifteen girls and another of males are each to
stand around the bier and sing in turn praise, in the form of a   947c
poetic hymn, to the priests—glorifying their happiness in
song for an entire day. At dawn the next day, the bier itself is
to be carried to the burial by a hundred of the young men from
the gymnasia, chosen by the deceased's relatives. First in the
procession are to be the unmarried youths, each clothed in his
military garb—cavalry with their horses, heavily-armed infantry with their heavy armor, and the rest similarly—and
around the bier itself are to come, in front, boys singing the   947d
anthem of the fatherland, and following behind, girls and any
of the women who may happen to have passed the age of
child-bearing; after these, priests and priestesses are to follow, on the grounds that the tomb is unpolluted—even
though they avoid the tombs of the rest—if, that is, the Pythian should vote thus and in this way. Their grave is to be constructed underground, in the shape of an oblong crypt made
of stones that are porous and as lasting as possible, and it is to
have stone couches lying next to one another; when they've   947e
laid him who has become blessed there, and heaped up dirt
around in a circle, they'll plant a grove of trees around, except
at one extremity, so that the tomb may for the rest of time
increase in this direction, where dirt will be needed to cover
those placed there. Each year they'll dedicate to them a contest
in music, in gymnastics, and in horsemanship. These are the
prizes for the men who have passed their audits.

But if one of these men, trusting to the judgment passed
upon him, should display his human nature by becoming bad
after the judgment, let the law command anyone who wishes
to prosecute him; and let the contest in court take place in   948a
something like the following way:

Let this court be composed, first, of the Guardians of the
Laws, and then of the living Auditors, and, in addition to
these, the court of select judges; and let the prosecutor write
an indictment, concerning the man he's prosecuting, saying
that so-and-so is unworthy of the prizes for excellence and of
the office. If the defendant should be convicted, he's to be
deprived of the office, and the tomb, and the rest of the honors
assigned to him; but if the prosecutor should fail to obtain a
fifth of the votes, he is to pay a fine—a man of the highest class

948b   twelve minas, eight for a man of the second, a man of the third six, and of the fourth two.

Rhadamanthus is worthy of admiration as regards the way he is said to have judged judicial proceedings, because he saw that the human beings of that time believed that there were evidently gods—as was reasonable, since the many at that time, of whom he was one, were sprung from gods, according to report at least. Indeed, it's likely that he thought he shouldn't turn the business over to any human judge but rather to the gods, from whom he obtained simple and swift

948c   judgments. For by administering an oath to the disputants about each of the matters in dispute he settled things swiftly and safely. But now a certain part of humanity, we claim, doesn't believe in gods at all, while others think they don't pay attention to us, and the opinion of most—the worst—is that if the gods receive small sacrifices and flatteries they'll aid in robbing great amounts of money, and release them from many sorts of great penalties: as a result, Rhadamanthus's art would no longer be fitting for the trials of present day human

948d   beings. So since the opinions of human beings about gods have changed, it's necessary that the laws change too. For in judicial trials of complaints, laws that are laid down with intelligence must remove the oaths from each of the contending parties, and he that brings some judicial action against someone should write the charges but not swear an oath, while the defendant, in the same way, should write the denial and hand it over to the magistrates without an oath. For presumably it's a terrible thing, since there are many judicial actions in a city,

948e   to know for sure that close to half the parties have sworn falsely and yet carry on easy intercourse with one another at common meals, at the other meetings, and at the private gatherings of each.

Let the law be, then, that a judge is to swear an oath when he's about to give judgment, and that he who appoints the

949a   common magistrates is to do such a thing each time, by voting with oaths or by carrying the votes from sacred places, and again that the same sort of thing is to be done by the judge of choruses and of every musical event, and by the supervisors and umpires of gymnastic and equestrian contests, and of all contests in which swearing falsely doesn't produce gain—according to the opinion of humanity. But in any contests where a great gain seems evidently to accrue to him who denies strongly and with an oath, in these all the persons bringing charges against one another are to be judged by trials without oaths. And in general, those who preside at a trial are not to allow someone to speak with oaths, for the sake of persuasiveness, or to curse himself and his family, or to use unseemly supplication or womanly wailings, but a person is always to state fully what is just, teaching and learning with auspicious speech; otherwise, as if the speaker had digressed from the speech, the magistrates are to bring him back to a speech that constantly refers to the business at hand. As for a stranger in his relations with strangers, they are to receive and give authoritative oaths to one another, if they should wish, just as is done now—for they won't grow old or, as a rule, make nests of young in the city, and leave others like themselves who have the right to dwell in the country—and in judicial trials of complaints against one another the judging shall proceed in the same way, for all of them.

With regard to the ways in which some free man is disobedient to the city, not in matters deserving of blows, imprisonment, or death, but with respect to certain attendances at choral performances, or at processions, or at certain other such common ceremonies or public services—such as are involved in sacrifices during peacetime or contributions for war—with respect to all such instances, what is necessary first is the healing of the damage.[9] For those who fail to obey there must be a security deposit left with the men whom the city, and also the law, may appoint to exact pledges. Those who then disobey are to have their deposits sold, and the money is to go to the city. If a greater penalty is needed, the magistrates in each case shall impose the fitting penalties on the disobedient and bring them into court, until they are willing to do what has been ordered.

A city that isn't going to make money except for the money that comes from the land, and that isn't going to engage in commerce, must have deliberated about what it ought to do concerning both trips abroad, away from the country, on the part of its own people, and the reception of strangers from

949b

949c

949d

949e

elsewhere. So the lawgiver should give advice about these matters, first by being as persuasive as he can:

950a By nature the intermingling of cities with cities mixes dispositions in every way, as strangers produce innovations in one another. For the cities that are well governed by means of correct laws this would bring the greatest of all injuries. But for most cities, since they're not at all well regulated by laws, it makes no difference if they mingle by receiving strangers among themselves or go gallivanting off to other cities, whenever someone might desire a trip abroad, anywhere and at any time, whether he be young or more elderly. Yet then again, not to receive others, or go abroad elsewhere themselves, is at

950b once not entirely possible and in addition, would appear savage and hard to the other human beings, to whom they would seem to be adopting the harsh words of what are called "the expulsions of strangers,"[10] as well as stubborn and harsh manners. But one ought never to belittle the reputation one has among others for being good or not. For the many happen not to be as deficient in their judgment of who among the rest are wicked and good, as they are deficient in the essence of

950c virtue; there is a certain divine shrewdness even in bad men, such that very many even of those who are especially bad can distinguish well, in their speeches and opinions, the better human beings and the worse. That is why the exhortation to give preeminence in honor to one's good reputation among the many is a noble exhortation for the many cities. But the most correct and greatest thing, at least for the man who is to be perfect, is to be truly good and thus to hunt for a life of good repute, but otherwise not to do so at all; and indeed, it would be fitting for the city being founded in Crete to obtain from the other human beings the noblest and best reputation

950d possible, with respect to virtue. And there is every reasonable hope that if it should come into being according to plan, the Sun and the other gods will look upon it and a few others as being among the cities and countries with good laws. So in regard to travel abroad into other lands and places, and the reception of strangers, it is necessary to do as follows:

First, it shall not be permissible for a man younger than forty to go abroad anywhere in any way; moreover, no one is to go abroad in a private capacity, but heralds, ambassadors, and certain observation missions may do so in a public capac-

ity. Military expeditions abroad in wartime aren't worth in- 950e
cluding among these political trips. There should be persons
sent to the Pythian Apollo, the Olympian Zeus, to Nemea, and
to the Isthmus,[11] to take part in the sacrifices and contests dedicated to these gods; and they should do what they can to send
the most numerous, beautiful, and best men possible, who
will give the city a good reputation in the sacred and peaceful
gatherings, and provide a supply of reputation that is the 951a
counterpart to what is gained in war. When they return home
they will teach the young that the legal customs, pertaining to
the regimes, of the others are in second place. There are also
certain other observation missions they ought, with the permission of the Guardians of the Laws, to send out, such as the
following. If certain citizens desire to observe the affairs of the
other human beings at greater leisure, no law is to prevent
them. For a city without experience of bad as well as good 951b
human beings would never be able, because of its isolation, to
be sufficiently tame and perfect; nor, again, would it be able to
guard its laws, unless it accepts them by knowledge and not
solely by habits. The fact is, there are always among the many
certain divine human beings—not many—whose intercourse
is altogether worthwhile, and who do not by nature grow any
more frequently in cities with good laws than in cities without. These the inhabitant of cities with good laws, if he's un- 951c
corruptible, must always seek and track down, by going out
over sea and land, in order to place on a firmer footing those
legal customs that are nobly laid down, and correct others, if
they are lacking something. For without this observation and
search a city will never remain perfect—nor will it do so if they
should carry out the observational mission badly.

Kl. How then would both these things be accomplished?

Ath. As follows. First, our observer of this kind must be more than
fifty years of age; then he should have become one of those
with a good reputation in other respects and in war, if the 951d
Guardians of the Laws are to allow him to go to other cities as
an exemplar. After he gets to be over sixty years of age he is no
longer to go on observational missions. When he's spent as
many of the ten years as he may wish observing, and has arrived back home, he's to go to the council of those who keep
watch over the laws.

This council is to be composed of a mixture of young and el-

951e

derly men, and shall be compelled to meet each day, from dawn until the sun has risen. It shall be composed, first, of the priests who have obtained the prizes for excellence, and then of the ten Guardians of the Laws who are eldest at any time, and then there will be the Supervisor of Education as a whole—the new one and those who have stepped down from this office. Each of these is not to attend alone, but with a young man between the ages of thirty and forty, having chosen the man who pleases him. The intercourse and speeches of

952a

these men are always to be about laws and their own city, and anything they may have learned elsewhere that is different and pertains to such matters, as well as whatever branches of learning might seem to contribute to this inquiry by making things clearer for the learners, while, for those who don't learn these, things pertaining to laws appear darker and unclear. Among these, the matters the older men judge approvingly, the younger are to learn with complete seriousness, and if one of those invited should seem to be unworthy, the whole coun-

952b

cil is to blame the man who did the inviting. But those who are of good repute among these young men the rest of the city shall guard, watching over and taking care of them in a special way, honoring them when they do what is correct but dishonoring them more than the others, if they should turn out worse than the many.

It is to this council, then, that the man who has been observing the legal customs among the rest of humanity is to go immediately after he has arrived, and if he's found some persons capable of explaining some utterance concerning the laying down of laws, or education, or upbringing, or if he himself should return having thought some things up, let him share this with the entire council. If he should seem to have re-

952c

turned no whit worse or better, let him be praised for the sake of his great eagerness of spirit, at ány rate; but if he should seem much better, let him receive much more praise while he lives, and when he has died let him be honored with appropriate honors by the power of those in the council. If, however, he should seem to come back corrupted, he is not to associate with any young or elder man, making a claim to be wise. If he should obey the magistrates, he may live, as a

952d

private man, but if not, he is to die—if, that is, he should be convicted in court for being a busybody in some way concerning the education and the laws. And if he should deserve to be brought into court but none of the magistrates brings him, blame is to accrue to the magistrates on the occasion of the judging concerning prizes for excellence.

The man who goes abroad should go abroad in this way and be this sort of person; next, after this man has been dealt with, a friendly reception must be provided for the man who visits from abroad. There are four strangers whom it is necessary to discuss. The first, and perpetual, visitor mostly completes his 952e visits in summer, like the migratory birds; the bulk of these simply carry on their traffic across the sea for the sake of money, flying as if they had wings, to other cities in the summer of the year. The magistrates assigned to these fellows must receive the man at the marketplaces, harbors, and public buildings outside the city but near the city, keeping guard lest any of such strangers introduce some innovation, and appor- 953a tioning judicial matters to them in the correct way—having dealings with them as is necessary, but as little as possible.

The second is a real observer, with his eyes—and also with his ears, when it comes to the spectacles of the Muses. For every such person there must be lodgings prepared near the temples, with marks of humane hospitality, and the priests and temple custodians must look after and care for such persons until they have stayed a measured time; then, having seen and heard what they came for, they are to depart, having done 953b and suffered no injury. And the priests are to be judges for them, if someone should do an injustice to one of them or if one of these should do an injustice to someone else of less than fifty drachmas' worth; but if some greater charge should be made concerning them, the trials for such persons must be held before the Market Regulators.

The third stranger, who arrives on some public business from another country, must be received publicly. He ought to be received only by Generals, Cavalry Commanders, and Rank Commanders, and such persons should be taken care of 953c only by that man with whom one of them might be lodged and entertained as a guest, in conjunction with the Presidents.

The fourth, if ever one should arrive, is rare; but if ever someone should come who is the counterpart, from another country, of our observers, he must first be no less than fifty years of age, and in addition to this must ask either to see

953d something beautiful which is different from the beautiful things in the other cities, or to reveal some such thing to another city. Now every such man may go uninvited to the doors of the rich and wise, he being another such himself. Indeed, let him go to the house of the Supervisor of Education as a whole, trusting that he is a suitable guest for such a host,[12] or to the house of one of those who has won the victory in virtue; when he has kept company with some of these, teaching and learning, let him depart as a friend leaving friends, honored with gifts and fitting honors.

953e These are the laws that should regulate the reception of all male and female strangers from another country and their sending out of their own—honoring Zeus the god of strangers, and not using meats and sacrifices as a way of expelling strangers (as the nurslings of the Nile do now), nor savage proclamations.[13]

Any security that someone may pledge is to be pledged explicitly, with the entire affair agreed upon in writing and in the presence of not less than three witnesses, if the amount is under a thousand drachmas, and not less than five if it's over a

954a thousand. The previous seller is to stand as security for any seller who is not suable or is not at all solvent, and is to be liable to be sued to the same degree as the seller.

If someone should wish to conduct a search on anyone's premises, he is to conduct the search naked except for an ungirded undershirt,[14] and after having sworn an oath to the conventional gods that he does indeed expect he will find the thing. And this other shall hand over the household, the things that have been sealed as well as the unsealed things, to be searched. If someone should fail to give leave to somebody who wishes to search, the one who's prevented is to go to

954b court after having assessed the value of the thing he's looking for; if there should be a conviction, double the assessed value is to be paid in damages. If a master should happen to be away from home, the inhabitants of the house must allow the unsealed things to be searched, but the sealed things the searcher is to counterseal and put under the guard of whomever he may wish, for five days. If the master should be away a longer time, he is to call in the City Regulators and

thus conduct the search, opening the sealed things as well and   954c
then sealing them again in the same way in the presence of the
household members and the City Regulators.

The following is to be the time limit for disputed claims,
after which it shall no longer be possible to dispute the possessor's claim: There is to be no dispute as regards lands and
houses in this country; as regards the other things which
someone may possess, if someone should openly make use of
a thing in the city and in the marketplace and temples, and no
one seizes it, but then somebody claims they've been looking
for it during this time, while the man clearly wasn't hiding
it—if they spend a year this way, with the one in possession of   954d
something, and the other searching, then after the passage of a
year no one is to be permitted to seize such a possession. If
someone should make use of a thing not in the city or the
marketplace, but in the fields, openly, and someone doesn't
confront him within five years, then when the five years have
expired this person is no longer to be permitted to seize such a
thing. If someone should make use of something in the houses
in the city, the time limit is to be three years; if he should   954e
possess it in the fields in a way that isn't evident, ten years; if
in another country, there is to be no time limit on the seizure,
however long a time before it may be discovered somewhere.

If someone should forcibly prevent somebody from appearing at a trial, whether it be the party or the witnesses, then, if
it's a slave—his own or someone else's—the trial is to be nulli-
fied and invalid; if it's a free man, in addition to the nullifica-   955a
tion the one who does this is to be imprisoned for a year and
liable to prosecution for kidnapping by anyone who wishes.
And if someone should forcibly prevent a rival competitor
from appearing at some contest in gymnastic, in music, or in
something else, anyone who wishes should report it to those
who preside at the contest, and they shall allow the one who is
willing to compete to enter the contest freely. If they're unable
to do so, and the one who did the preventing should win the
contest, they're to give the victory prizes to the man who was   955b
prevented, and inscribe his name as the victor in whatever
temples he may wish; for the man who did the preventing
there is never to be any votive offering or inscription concern-

ing such a contest, and he is to be liable for the damages, whether he is defeated or is victorious in the contest.

If someone should knowingly receive anything stolen, he is to be liable to the same judicial penalty as the thief. The penalty for harboring a fugitive is to be death.

955c Everyone is to consider the same person a friend or enemy as the city does, and if someone should make peace or war with certain parties in private, apart from the community, the penalty is to be death in this case too. If some part of the city should by itself make peace or war with certain parties, the Generals are to bring those responsible for this action into court, and the judicial penalty for someone who is convicted shall be death.

Those who do some service to the fatherland ought to do the service without gifts, and it is no excuse, nor is it a praiseworthy saying, to aver that "for good deeds gifts should be re-
955d ceived, but not for petty deeds." Now it isn't easy to know and, having knowledge, to be firm; the safest course is to pay heed and obey the law, and do no service for gifts. He who disobeys is simply to die, if he's convicted in a trial.

As regards communal money revenues, each man's property is to be evaluated (for many purposes), and in addition the tribes are to report the yearly harvest in writing to the
955e Field Regulators; this way, the public treasury may deliberate and decide each year to use whichever of the two existing modes of revenue it might wish to use—either a portion of the whole assessed evaluation, or of the current annual income, apart from the contributions to the common meals.

As regards votive offerings to the gods, the well-measured man ought to bestow well-measured votive offerings. Now the earth and the household hearth are held sacred to all the gods by everyone. So no one should consecrate them a second time as sacred to the gods. In other cities, in private and in the
956a temples, gold and silver are possessions that arouse envy; yet ivory, being from a body that has lost its soul, is not a pure votive offering, while iron and bronze are tools of war. Let a person dedicate any wooden thing made of one piece that he may

wish, and likewise anything of stone for the common temples, or something woven that doesn't entail more than a month's work for one woman. The color white would befit gods, in something woven as well as in other things, and dyes are not to be added except in the case of the adornments for war. But the most divine gifts are birds, and figures that a single artist might complete in one day. The other votive offerings are to imitate such things.

956b

When there has been a thorough discussion of the parts of the entire city—how many and what they should be—and the laws concerning all the greatest business transactions have been discussed as best they can be, what ought to remain is judicial procedure. The first of the judicial courts would be those of the chosen judges, whom the defendant and the prosecutor should choose in common, and for whom the name "arbitrators" is more fitting than "judges." The second would be those composed of villagers and tribesmen, divided into twelve parts, before whom they should contest the case if they haven't arrived at a judgment before the first judges—but with a greater penalty at stake. The defendant, if he should lose the second time, must pay another fifth part of the value of the written judicial penalty. If someone should complain of the judges and wish a third contest, he is to take the case before the select judges; if he should lose again, he must pay one and a half the assessed penalty. Where the prosecutor is dissatisfied after losing before the first judges and goes before the second, he shall take away another fifth part, if he wins; but if he's defeated he must pay the same portion of the judicial penalty. If they should go to the third court and not abide by the earlier trials, and the defendant is defeated, he is to pay one and a half times the penalty, as was said, while the prosecutor is to pay half the assessed penalty.

956c

956d

The drawing of lots for and the filling of the courts, the appointments of assistants for each of the offices, the times at which each of these things ought to be done, what pertains to the recording of votes and adjournments, and all such necessary details concerning judicial actions—earlier and later written complaints, requirements for answers and attendance, and everything akin to these things—have been discussed by us earlier, but it is noble to repeat what is correct, at least, twice

956e

957a

or even thrice. Yet an elderly lawgiver may leave out all the legal customs that are minor and easily discovered, and the young lawgiver should fill them in. Indeed, the private courts would attain due measure if they were instituted in something like that way. But as for the public and common courts, and whatever courts magistrates must use in order to manage the tasks appropriate to each of the magistracies, there exist in many cities a number of pieces of legislation by decent men, which are not unseemly, from which the Guardians of the

957b Laws ought to select what is fitting and equip the regime that is now being brought forth. They should consider these pieces of legislation, correct them, and test them by experience, until each of them should seem adequately established; then they should set them up as final, seal them as simply unchangeable, and employ them for the whole of the city's life. Whatever pertains to the silence and auspicious speech of the judges, and the opposite, and whatever matters differ from the many just, good, and noble things in the other cities,

957c have in part been discussed and will in part be discussed later, near the end. He who is going to be a judge who is even handed, in accordance with justice, must look to all such things and learn the writings about them that he has acquired. For of all branches of learning, those which have the most sovereign influence in making the learner become better are the ones that pertain to the laws—if, that is, they should be correctly set up; and they would be, or else our divine and marvelous law [nomos] would in vain possess a name akin to intelligence [nous]. Moreover, as regards the other speeches, whatever praise or blame about certain men is uttered in

957d poems, and whatever is uttered in prose—whether in writings or in all the other kinds of daily intercourse (where they dispute, out of fondness for victory, and agree, sometimes in very empty ways)—of all these, the clear test would be the writings of the lawgiver. These latter writings the good judge must have acquired within himself, as antidotes to the other speeches, and must use to correct both himself and the city:

957e making the just things abide and grow in the good men, and effecting the greatest transformation he can in the bad men, away from lack of learning, lack of restraint, cowardice, and all injustice generally—that is, for whoever among the bad men seem to have curable opinions. As to those whose opinions

have really been fixed by fate, if to souls thus disposed they 958a
assigned death as the cure (a remark that it would be just to
make often), such judges and leaders of judges would become
worthy of the entire city's praise.

When the judicial trials for a year have proceeded to a conclusion, the following laws ought to govern the execution of
the verdicts:

First, immediately after the vote in each case has been announced by the herald, with the judges listening, the judicial
magistracy shall assign to the victor all the goods of the convicted party, except for the goods that must necessarily be re- 958b
tained. When the month after the months during which trials
are held has elapsed, if someone hasn't voluntarily received a
voluntary discharge from the victor, the magistracy that has
tried the case shall, in accordance with the request of the victor, hand over the goods of the convicted party. If the goods
should be insufficient, and there should be lacking no less
than a drachma, this man is not to be able to undertake any
judicial action against anyone else until he has paid in full ev- 958c
erything owed to the victor. But judicial actions undertaken
by others against this man are to have authoritative force. If
someone who has been judicially condemned should obstruct
the magistracy that did the condemning, those who have been
unjustly obstructed should bring the man before the court of
the Guardians of the Laws, and if someone should be convicted in such a trial he is to be punished with death, on the
grounds that he was subverting the whole city and the laws.

After this, for a man who has been born and brought up,
and has begotten and brought up children, and has mingled
in business transactions with due measure—paying judicial 958d
penalties if he has done someone an injustice and receiving
the same from another—for a man who has aged according to
destiny in the company of the laws, the end would come, according to nature. Now as regards those who have died,
whether it be a male or a female, the legal customs concerning
the divine things that belong to the gods beneath the earth
and here—concerning whatever rites are appropriately celebrated—are to be authoritatively explained by the Interpreters. Graves, however, are not to be located on any land that is
cultivable, whether the monument be great or small, but only

958e where the nature of the land is suitable for this alone: to receive and hide, in a way that is the most painless to the living, the bodies of those who have died—these are the areas that should be filled. But with respect to those areas which Mother Earth by nature intends to produce food for human beings, no one either living or dead is to deprive those among us who are living of them. And they shall not heap up a mound higher than what can be completed by the work of five men in five days; nor shall they make stone markers larger than are

959a required to contain at most four heroic lines of encomia on the life of the deceased. As for the laying out, first, it is not to be for a longer time than that which shows whether a man has fallen into a death-like swoon or has really died, and in dealing with human beings, the third day would be just about a well-measured time to carry the body out to the monument. One should be persuaded by the lawgiver in other respects, and also when he says that soul is altogether different from body; that in life itself, what constitutes each of us is nothing other than the soul, the body following each of us as a sem-

959b blance; and that it is a noble saying that the bodies of the corpses are images [15] of the dead, while the being that is really each of us—named "the immortal soul"—goes off to other [16] gods to give an account, as the ancestral law says. To the good man this is heartening, but to the bad man very frightening. Furthermore, there is no great help available for the man who has died. All his relatives should have helped him while he

959c was alive, so that he might have lived as justly and piously as possible while he was alive, and might have died without incurring retribution for evil faults, in the life after this one. Since this is the way things are, one ought never to squander one's substance, in the belief that this lump of flesh being buried especially belongs to one; instead, one should believe that that son or brother, or whoever it is one misses and strongly believes one has buried, has gone away to complete and fulfill his own destiny, and that one should make the best

959d of the present circumstances, spending a measured amount, as if one were spending money on a soulless altar of the infernal ones. And it wouldn't be very unseemly if the lawgiver were to divine what is a measured amount. So let this be the law:

The expenditures would be measured if not more than five

minas were spent on the whole funeral by a man of the highest class, three minas by a man of the second, two by a man of the third, and a mina by a man of the fourth.

The Guardians of the Laws must necessarily do many other things and supervise many matters, but not the least of these is that they should live supervising children and men and every age; and moreover at the end of everyone's life supervision should be exercised by some one Guardian of the Laws, whom the household of the deceased should take on as an overseer: let it be a noble thing to his credit if what pertains to the deceased proceeds nobly and with due measure, but a shameful thing if it proceeds ignobly. The laying out and the rest shall proceed in accordance with the convention concerning such matters, but something like the following measures must be conceded to the statesman-legislator: 959e

To command that there be crying for the deceased, or that there not be, is unseemly, but the singing of dirges and the raising of the voice outside the house are forbidden. Carrying the corpse in the open on the roads is to be prevented, as is crying aloud while it proceeds along the roads, and the procession is to be outside the city before daybreak. These are to be the legal customs in regard to such matters, and he who obeys shall avoid penalty, but he who disobeys one of the Guardians of the Laws shall be punished by all, with a penalty that is approved by all in common. Whatever other actions take place concerning the dead, whether they have tombs or are without tombs (as in the case of parricides and temple robbers and all such), have been discussed earlier and set down in laws, so that our legislation would be just about at an end. 960a 960b

But in every case, the end each time is not quite the doing of something, nor the acquiring and settling; it's rather when one has discovered a perfect and permanent safeguard for what has been begotten that one should believe that whatever needs to be done has been done, and prior to that one must believe the whole is unfinished. 960c

Kl. Nobly spoken, stranger. But explain more clearly what was aimed at in what was just now said.

Ath. Kleinias, many of the earlier things were sung beautifully, and it's likely that this applies not least to the designations given to the Fates.

Kl. Which designations?

Ath.   That "Lachesis" is the first, "Clotho" the second, and "Atropos" the third savior [17] of things fated, being likened to a
960d   woman who uses the third twist to give spun threads their capacity of irreversibility. [18] And indeed, for a city and for citizens provision must be made in these respects not only for the
health and safeguarding of the bodies, but also for a state of
good lawfulness in the souls, or rather, for a safeguard of the
laws. To me it seems evident that this is still lacking in our
laws—the way in which the capacity of irreversibility ought
naturally to be implanted in them.

Kl.   You're not speaking of a minor matter, if it proves impossible to discover how everything would acquire some such
thing.

960e   Ath.   But to me at least it appears altogether possible, from everything present.

Kl.   Then let's in no way desist, until we've provided this very
thing for the laws that have been discussed. For it's ridiculous
to have labored in vain, by building on a foundation that's not
at all firm!

Ath.   What you urge is correct, and you'll find me to be another
who's similarly disposed.

Kl.   Nobly spoken. So then what, do you claim, would be the safeguard for our regime and laws, and how would it operate?

961a   Ath.   Well, didn't we say that in our city there should be some such
council as the following? The ten Guardians of the Laws who
are the eldest at any time, and, together with these, all those
who have won prizes for virtue, are to meet together in the
same place. Moreover, those who have gone abroad seeking to
hear something, somewhere, that would perhaps be pertinent
to the guarding of the laws, when they've returned home safe,
are to be considered worthy attendants at the council, after
they've been tested by those same men. In addition to these,
961b   each man is to select one of the young men not less than thirty
years of age, after having first judged him to be worthy in nature and in upbringing, and is to introduce the young man
thus selected to the others; if the candidate should meet with
the approval of the others as well, he is to select him, but if
not, the judgment that has taken place is to be kept secret from
the rest, and especially from the man who was judged unacceptable. And the meeting should be at dawn, when everyone
would have the most leisure from the rest of their private and

common activities. Presumably some such thing was discussed by us in the earlier discussions?   961c

Kl.   Indeed it was.

Ath. Well, going back again to this council, I would say something
like the following: I assert that if someone were to cast this like
an anchor for the entire city, and it were equipped with everything that befits it, it would save all the things we wish for.

Kl.   But how?

Ath. The moment is ripe for us to explain correctly what comes after
this, without any abatement of spirited zeal.

Kl.   Very nobly spoken: do as you think.

Ath. Now, in the case of everything, Kleinias, it is necessary to un-   961d
derstand what is its appropriate savior in each of its activities—just as, in an animal, it is the soul and the head that are
by nature such, to the greatest degree at least.

Kl.   How do you mean, again?

Ath. Doubtless the virtue of these two provides every animal with
safety?

Kl.   How?

Ath. By the presence of intelligence in the soul, in addition to the
other things, and by the presence of sight and hearing in the
head, in addition to the other things. In short, when intelligence is mixed with the noblest senses and has become
one, it would most justly be called the salvation of each.

Kl.   That's likely, anyway.

Ath. That's likely, indeed. But what sort of intelligence, when   961e
mixed with senses, would become the salvation of ships in
storms, at least, and in fair weather? Isn't it the case on a ship
that the pilot and the sailors mix the senses with the intelligence of the piloting art to save themselves and what pertains to the ship?

Kl.   But of course.

Ath. There's no need for many examples of such things. But let's
consider,[19] in the case of armies, for instance, what goal generals—and the whole ministerial art of medicine as well—
would set up, if they were to aim in the correct way at salva-   962a
tion. In the former case, wouldn't it be victory and superiority
over enemies, and in the case of doctors and their assistants
wouldn't it be the provision of health for the body?

Kl.   What else?

Ath. Now would a doctor be ignorant[20] about what pertains to body, which we just now said was health, or would a general be ignorant of victory, or any of the other matters we've gone through, and still appear to have intelligence about some of these things?

Kl. How could he?

Ath. Then what about a city? If someone should be evidently ignorant of the goal at which the statesman should aim, would he,

962b in the first place, be justly called a ruler, and then, would he be able to save this thing—whose goal he didn't know at all?

Kl. How could he?

Ath. Then it's likely that in the present case, if our founding of the country is to have an end, there must be something in it that knows, in the first place, this goal we're speaking of (whatever our political goal might happen to be), and then in what way it ought to attain this, and who—first among the laws themselves, and then among human beings—gives it advice in a

962c noble or ignoble way. But if some city is devoid of such a thing, it won't be surprising if, lacking intelligence and senses, it acts haphazardly each time in each of its actions.

Kl. What you say is true.

Ath. Now then in which of the parts or practices of our city is there ever such a guard adequately prepared in any way? Can we explain?

Kl. Surely not in a clear way, at least, stranger. But if it's necessary to guess, this argument seems to me to be leading toward the council which you just now said had to get together at night.

962d Ath. You've caught on in a very fine way, Kleinias, and it is indeed necessary, as the argument that is with us now indicates, for this council to possess every virtue, the ruling principle of which is not to wander and have many aims, but to look to one aim, and always shoot all things, like shafts, at this.

Kl. By all means.

Ath. Now of course we'll understand that there's nothing surprising in the fact that the legal customs of the cities wander, since different parts of the legislated codes in each city look to different aims. And in most cases there's nothing surprising in the fact that for some, the definition of the just things is what

962e allows some to rule in the city, whether they happen to be better or worse, while for others it's what allows them to become wealthy, whether they're slaves of certain people or not, and that others are set in motion by the spirited zeal for the free way of life. Others, again, have a twofold legislation that looks to both—that they may be free and may also be despots over other cities; then the wisest, as they suppose, look to these and all such aims, but not to any one, being unable to give an account of anything that is honored preeminently and toward which their other affairs should look.

Kl. So then wouldn't our principle, at any rate, have been set down in the correct way a long while ago, stranger? For we declared that everything pertaining to our laws ought always to be looking to one thing, and this, we presumably agreed, was very correctly said to be virtue. 963a

Ath. Yes.

Kl. And virtue, now, we presumably set down as being four.

Ath. Indeed so.

Kl. And intelligence, now, as being the leader of all these, to which, indeed, everything else as well as the three of these ought to look.

Ath. You follow in a very fine way, Kleinias. Now follow the rest. For we said that intelligence in the piloting art, in the medical art, and in the art of generalship, looks to that one thing toward which it ought, and we're now examining here the intelligence that's in the political art; and let's ask just as if it were a human being, in which case we'd say: "Amazing one! Where do you aim? Whatever is that one thing, which intelligence in the case of the medical art can explain clearly, but which you, being indeed distinguished, as you claim, among all the prudent ones, are unable to describe?"—Or you, at least, Megillus and Kleinias, can you two articulate and explain for me, on its behalf, whatever you claim this thing is, just as I gave definitions on behalf of many others for you? 963b

963c

Kl. Not at all, stranger.

Ath. What then? Can you say that it's necessary to be zealous in spirit to know the thing itself and the things it's in?

Kl. Such as which things do you mean?

Ath. Such as when we claimed that there had come to be four forms of virtue: obviously, it's necessary to claim that each of them is one, since they're four.

Kl. But of course.

Ath. And yet we call all these one. For we claim that courage is virtue, and prudence is virtue, and also the two others, as if they're really not many but only this one, virtue. 963d

Kl. Certainly.

Ath. Now it's not difficult to say how it is that these two (and the others) differ from each other, and take two names; but how it is that we give to both the same name, virtue, and also give it to the others, this is no longer easy.

Kl. How do you mean?

Ath. There's no difficulty in clarifying what I'm saying. Let's just divide between ourselves the questioning and answering.

Kl. What is it, again, that you're explaining?

963e Ath. Ask me why, when we assert both to be the one, virtue, we then refer to them again as two, as courage and as prudence. For I'll tell you the reason: it's because the one—courage—is concerned with fear, and even the beasts share in it, as do the dispositions, at least, of the very young children. For soul becomes courageous without reason and by nature, but, on the other hand, without reason soul never has, does not, and never will become prudent and possessed of intelligence—for that is a different entity.

Kl. What you're saying is true.

964a Ath. Now you've received from me a reasoned account of how they're different and two; you give back to me in return how they're one and the same. And consider that you are going to tell how they're one when they're four, and then ask me—once you've demonstrated how they're one—to tell again how they're four. Moreover, after this let's investigate whether, for one who knows adequately any of the things for which there is both a name and a definition, it's sufficient to know only the name, and to be ignorant of the definition, or whether, for one who is anything, it isn't shameful to be ignorant of all such points in regard to things which are distinguished by their greatness and nobility.

964b Kl. That is likely, at any rate.

Ath. Now for a lawgiver and a Guardian of the Laws, and one who thinks he is distinguished from everyone in virtue, and who has received victory prizes in these very things, is there anything that is more important than these very matters about which we are now talking—courage, moderation, prudence, and justice?[21]

Kl. How could there be?

Ath. Now in regard to these matters, are the interpreters,[22] the teachers, the lawgivers, the guardians of the others—is the

one who deals with the man who needs to know and under-   964c
stand, or with the man who needs to be punished and re-
proved, when he has committed a fault, not to be superior to
the others in teaching and making entirely clear what power
vice and virtue have? Is some poet who comes into the city, or
somebody who claims to be an educator of the young, to appear better than the man who has won the victory in every virtue? In such a city, where there would be neither in word nor
in deed adequate guardians, who had adequate knowledge
about virtue, would it be surprising if this city, lacking a   964d
guardian, were to suffer what many of the present day cities
suffer?

Kl.   Not at all, it's likely.

Ath.   What then? Should we create what we're now talking about,
or what? Should the guardians be prepared so as to be more
precisely accurate than the many, in deed and word, concerning virtue? Or in what way will our city be made similar to the
head and senses of prudent men, by possessing within itself
some such guard?

Kl.   But how, and in what way, stranger, can we compare it to
such a man when we speak of it?

Ath.   Obviously, the city itself is the trunk, and the young among   964e
the guardians, who have been chosen as the ones who have
the best natures, and who are the sharpest in every part of the
soul, are, as it were, at the very top; they survey the whole city
in a circle, and as they keep watch they hand over perceptions
to the memories, and report everything in the city to the elders; the old men, who are an image of intelligence because   965a
they are distinguished by their prudent thinking about many
matters worthy of discussion, deliberate, using the young as
assistants in their collective deliberation. Thus both of them in
common really save the whole city. Shall we say that this is the
way we ought to arrange things, or some other way? Are we to
have them all the same and not have some who are brought up
and educated with greater precision? [23]

Kl.   But that's impossible, you amazing man!

Ath.   Then it's necessary to proceed to some more precise education   965b
than before.

Kl.   Probably.

Ath.   Wouldn't that which we just now almost touched on happen
to be the one which we need?

Kl. By all means.

Ath. Didn't we say that the man who was at any rate the top crafts-man and guardian in each thing must be able not only to look to the many, but also to pursue and know the one, and, know-ing it, to order everything with a synoptic view to that?

Kl. Correctly spoken.

965c Ath. Is there any way in which there would be a more precise vi-sion and seeing of anything than that which is the capacity to look to one *idea* from the many and dissimilar things?

Kl. Perhaps.

Ath. Not perhaps, but really, you demonic man! There is not a clearer way to proceed than this for any human being.

Kl. Trusting in you, stranger, I do indeed agree, and let's proceed in this way in our discussion.

Ath. Then it's necessary to compel, as is likely, even the guardians of our divine regime to see with precision, first, whatever is

965d the same in all the four: what it is that we assert is one in courage, moderation, justice, and prudence, and is justly called by one name, virtue. This, friends—if we wish—let's not let up on now, but let's bear down hard on it, as it were, until we may express in an adequate way whatever it is that ought to be looked to—whether it be one, or a whole, or both of these, or however it is by nature. Or do we suppose that if this eludes us, we'll ever be in a satisfactory situation as

965e regards virtue, when we won't be able to explain whether it's many, or four, or one? No. In that case (if, at any rate, we would obey our own advice), we will contrive some other way by which this will come into being in our city.[24] If, however, it seems that the topic should be completely abandoned, then it must be abandoned.[25]

Kl. By the god of strangers, stranger! Surely such a topic ought least to be abandoned, since what you're saying seems to us to be very correct. But now how would someone contrive this?

966a Ath. Let's not discuss yet how we might contrive it. First let's make sure, by agreeing among ourselves, if it's necessary or not.

Kl. But surely it's necessary—if, that is, it's possible.

Ath. But what then? Do we think this same thing in regard to the beautiful and the good? Should our guardians know only that each of these is many, or also how and in what sense it is one?

Kl. It's pretty likely that they must necessarily understand how it's one.

Ath. But what? Must they understand it, while being unable to give   966b
a demonstration of it through argument?

Kl. What? Now you're describing some habit that befits a slave!

Ath. What then? Is this not our argument concerning all the serious
things, that those who are really to be the Guardians of the
Laws must really know what pertains to the truth about them,
and must be capable of interpreting it in speech and following
it in deed, judging by the standard of nature what things come
into being in a noble fashion and what things do not?

Kl. How could they be otherwise?

Ath. Now isn't one of the noblest things that which pertains to the   966c
gods (which, we, indeed, went through in a serious way)—to
know, insofar as human power is capable of knowing these
matters, that they exist, and how much power they are evidently masters of, and to make allowance for most of those in
the city who only go along with what the laws proclaim; but,
in the case of those who belong to the guardianship, refusing
to admit anyone unless he has labored to grasp every proof[26]
that exists concerning gods? And isn't the import of this refusal to be that a man is never to be chosen as one of the   966d
Guardians of the Laws, nor again as one of those judged approvingly in regard to virtue, unless he is divine and has labored over these things?

Kl. It's just, at any rate, that—as you say—the man who is idle or
lacks capacity in such matters is to be kept widely separated
from the noble men.

Ath. Now don't we know that there are two things that lead to
belief concerning the gods, which we went through in the discussions earlier?

Kl. Which two?

Ath. One is what we said about the soul, how it is the eldest and   966e
most divine of all the things which are provided with ever-
flowing existence by a motion that receives its coming-into-
being. And one is the point about the orderly motion of stars
and of the other things which intelligence is master of, having
arranged the whole in an order. For no human being who has
looked at these things in a way that is not low or amateurish
has ever been by nature so atheistic that he has not experienced the opposite of what the many expect. For they think   967a
that those who busy themselves with such matters, through
astronomy and the other arts that necessarily go with it, be-

come atheists, having seen that, as much as possible,[27] actions come into being by necessities and not by the thoughts of an intention concerned with fulfillments of good things.

Kl. But then how would it be?

Ath. As I said, the situation now is entirely the opposite of what it was when those who think about such things thought they were without soul. Even at that time a sense of wonder crept in about them, and those who studied them with precision suspected what is now really believed: that if the beings were without soul, they would never have used on them wonderful calculations of such precision—if the beings didn't possess intelligence. Indeed, there were some even then who dared to hazard this very claim, saying that it was intelligence that had ordered all of the things in heaven.[28] But these same men erred again about the nature of soul, and how it is elder than bodies; by thinking that it was younger, they overturned everything again, so to speak, and themselves especially. For everything that moves in heaven and that appears to the eyes appeared to them to be full of stones and earth and many other soulless bodies, which provided the causes of the entire cosmos. These were the things which at that time caused many varieties of atheism and other disgusting views to infect such men; and indeed the poets took to reviling, and compared those who philosophize to dogs using vain howlings, and said other mindless things.[29] But now, as was said, the situation is entirely the opposite.

Kl. How's that?

Ath. No mortal human being can ever become firmly pious towards gods unless he has grasped these two things that are now being mentioned: that soul is the eldest of all the things that have partaken of coming into being, and is immortal, and rules all bodies; and, in addition to these things, he should grasp that which has now been discussed often—that intelligence of the beings, which has been said to be in the stars[30]—as well as the subjects of learning that necessarily precede these matters. He should see what is common to these things and the things that concern the Muse, and should apply this understanding, in a harmonious way, to the practices and customs that pertain to the habitual dispositions; and he should be able to give the reason for as many of these as have a reason. He who is incapable of acquiring these attributes in

967b

967c

967d

967e

968a

addition to the popular virtues would almost never become an adequate ruler of the city as a whole, but would be an assistant for the other rulers.

So now at this point, Kleinias and Megillus, it must be seen whether we shall add this to all the laws mentioned, which we've gone through: that the Nocturnal Council of Rulers, which will have shared an education such as we've discussed, is lawfully to become a guard, for the sake of security. Or what shall we do?   968b

Kl.   But best of men, how will we not add this, if we can do so to even a small extent?

Ath.   And let's all strive, at any rate, for such a thing. In this, at least, even I would with an eager spirit become your helper, making use of my very extensive experience and inquiry concerning such matters. And I will perhaps find others besides myself.

Kl.   But stranger, we must above all proceed in this direction, in which the god is virtually leading us! And what we should do   968c now is discuss and look for the way in which this might correctly come into being for us.

Ath.   It's not possible at this stage to legislate laws about such men, Megillus and Kleinias, until the council has been arranged in order—and then they themselves should have the sovereign authority to legislate what is necessary. But the present preparation for such things would take place through teaching and much intercourse, if it were to proceed correctly.

Kl.   How so? What is this, again, that we must claim has been said?

Ath.   Doubtless there should first be a list compiled of those who fit   968d the nature of the guardianship in age, capacity for learning, and characteristic dispositions and habits. But after this, it isn't easy either to discover what things should be learned, or to become the student of someone else who has made the discovery. Then in addition to these things there is the question of the times—at what times and for how much time each subject should be taken up; it is vain to discuss these matters in writings, for it wouldn't be clear to the learners themselves   968e whether the subject were being learned at the right time, until knowledge of the subject had, presumably, come into being within the soul of each. Thus, while it would be incorrect to speak of all that pertains to these matters as indescribable secrets, they are incapable of being described beforehand, because describing them beforehand would clarify nothing of what is being discussed.[31]

Kl. If this is the way things are, stranger, what then ought to be done?

Ath. It's likely, friends, that as the saying goes, "it lies in common and in the middle"[32] for us, and if we're willing to risk the entire regime and throw either three sixes, as they say, or three aces,[33] then that's what must be done; and I'll share the risk with you, by explaining and giving an account of my opinions, at least, concerning the education and upbringing that have now again become the topic of the discussion. The risk would indeed not be small, nor even comparable to certain others. And I call on you, Kleinias, to take charge of this. For with respect to the city of the Magnesians—or after whomever else the god has it named—it is you who will achieve the greatest fame by setting it up correctly, or who will never avoid the reputation of being the most courageous, at least, in comparison to all later successors. Now if, indeed, this divine council should come into being for us, dear comrades, the city ought to be handed over to it; of the present day lawgivers, none, so to speak, have any quarrel with this. And what we touched on in speech a little while ago as a dream, when we somehow mixed together a certain image of a community of head and intelligence, will really be almost a perfected waking vision—if, that is, our men have been mixed[34] with precision, fittingly educated, and, once educated, dwell in the country's acropolis as perfected guardians whose like, with regard to the virtue of safeguarding, we have not seen come into being in our lives previously.

Meg. Dear Kleinias, from all that has now been said by us, either the city's founding must be abandoned, or this stranger here must not be allowed to go, and by entreaties and every contrivance he must be made to share in the city's founding.

Kl. What you say is very true, Megillus, and I will do just these things, and you must help.

Meg. I'll help.

969a

969b

969c

969d

Interpretive Essay

Introduction

This essay is intended as a guide to Plato's presentation of "the art whose business it is to care for souls—the art of politics." On first perusing this longest Platonic dialogue, the reader will almost inevitably be filled with a mixture of wonder and repugnance; if he has imagination, he may feel as one cast upon a strange land, of alien language, foreign categories of thought, and sometimes distasteful criteria of moral judgment. This feeling should be the continuing focus of our attention, because it is the symptom of liberation. It is the first blaze on a trail that may lead us out of the cave of our contemporary culture to a vantage point from which we might begin freely to understand and judge the profound and hidden presuppositions of our age. For I do not know of any important contemporary political or moral principle that is not subjected, in this work, to implicit questions and doubts. By taking seriously the challenge posed by Plato's radically different conception of politics, we are led into an invigorating dialogue with the text, a dialogue that forces us to rethink our basic political beliefs.

We set out upon this inquiry animated partly by the longing men have always had to pierce the conventional delusions that trammel their minds. But this desire is given a special urgency in our time, by the awareness that our culture—a liberal republicanism fueled by the forces of modern technology—has come to be riddled with self-doubt, and is under attack from vigorous and influential thinkers of both the Left (e.g., Marx and the range of Marxisms) and the Right (e.g., Nietzsche, Heideggerian Existentialism, and Solzhenitsyn). No adequate defense of liberal democracy will be available, no complete evaluation of the attacks upon it will be possible, until we grasp its specific character in detail, by comparing it with the ancient Socratic tradition which the philosophic founders of liberalism in large part rejected and overthrew.

But why is it that this task requires a *commentary* on Plato's writing? Why cannot each of us simply confront the text by himself? This is of course the goal which a commentary should aim to promote. But the very distance we sense between Plato's outlook and our starting point implies that the meaning of his writing is not easily accessible. Our intellectual horizon has been so thoroughly shaped by modern ways of thinking and writing, alien to Plato, that most of us have been rendered largely unaware of the modes of reading, writing, and thinking that Plato could presume some among his contemporaries to be familiar with. What must be recovered is not only an appreciation of Plato's sense of the dangers involved in the publicizing of scientific inquiry, but also an awareness of his special notion of the difficulty of conveying or teaching genuine understanding. The *dialogue* form testifies to Plato's distrust of abstract propositions or models. He apparently holds that the truth about a human subject matter can be adequately understood and communicated only through a discourse that stays continually in touch with specific examples of human character types and their speeches and interactions. Works which convey the truth in an appropriate way are dramas, carefully chosen and designed down to the most minute detail, so as to require an interpretation through which the reader reenacts for himself the process of observation, questioning, and analysis that the author has previously undertaken. No statement in a dialogue can be understood except in the light of its full dramatic context. Of course, every Platonic dialogue has a philosophic character who is in some sense Plato's spokesman, and in this respect the dialogues are obviously different from, say, Shakespearean plays. But in Plato the "spokesman" *never* soliloquizes: every one of his utterances is directed primarily toward other unphilosophic or prephilosophic characters, and Plato's intended message can only be understood through an interpretation of all the characters and their changing situations. The present essay is meant to illustrate how one might begin reading and conversing with Plato in the light of these hermeneutic principles.

What has been said thus far limns the reasons for a commentary on Plato's political writings. But why should we focus upon the *Laws?* Surely there is a more famous and resplendent dialogue, the *Republic,* which is often claimed to embody Plato's political philosophy. A full discussion of the relation between the *Republic* and the *Laws* is beyond the scope of this essay. But even a superficial reading reveals that the *Republic* does not deal much with political *practice.* Socrates never suggests that the regime articulated in speech be tested in deed, or that it be the direct guide for any program of political action. Near the end of the conversation he says that "it makes no difference" whether the regime in speech exists or ever will exist (*Republic*, 592a–b). The *Republic* teaches about politics by examining the nature of justice, which appears to be the goal of political life, and by showing that the full realization of justice is impossible in politics. In this way the *Republic* circumscribes and defines the limitations of politics. Thus the central discussion in the *Republic* is the essential prelude, but only the prelude, to a study of what *can* be achieved through political action in the best circumstances. Plato elaborates that study in the *Laws,* where he presents a philosopher engaged in giving direct advice to the founder of an actual political community. The *Laws* shows how the man of reason, the philosopher, can work with and within the pious traditionalism that dominates most political life.

The relation between the *Laws* and Plato's other dialogues becomes clearer when we consider one striking fact: the *Laws* is the only Platonic dialogue (except for the sequel to the *Laws,* the *Epinomis*) in which Socrates is absent. What is the significance of this? Let us consider the dialogue in which Socrates is most emphatically present, the sole dialogue in which he figures even in the title. The *Apology of Socrates* is Socrates' only complete and public account of who he was and what he stood for. Socrates' account of his life is necessarily a *defense* of that life, for he is accused of "corrupting the young and not believing in the gods of Athens but introducing other, strange, demonic things." There is considerable evidence, even in the defense speech itself, that Socrates is indeed guilty of impiety as defined in this legal indictment. But Socrates utterly denies the imputation. He does admit that he leads a strange life, which requires some explanation. The first version of that explanation is contained in his story of how he reacted to a pronouncement of the Delphic Oracle. In that story he portrays himself as a rather extreme skeptic. He knows only that he knows nothing, certainly "nothing noble and good." In order to "refute" the oracle he goes about in public, before crowds that include young people, cross-examining the recognized authorities. He discovers and shows everyone that the authorities also know nothing, but are unaware of it; they are therefore inferior to him in wisdom. Because of this project of self-discovery and criticism, which he somehow comes to interpret as obedience to the oracle, Socrates admits that he never had time to do much of anything in the way of civic or family business.

This explanation is followed by Socrates' cross-examination of his chief official accuser, after which Socrates launches into another monologue, in which he gives a new and rather different account of his life through the famous "gadfly" image. He now makes himself seem considerably less skeptical than in his first portrayal. He knows the soul exists, and that its excellence is more important than money or honor; he knows that virtue exists, and that "from virtue comes money and all the other good things." Socrates even claims that he can recognize which people have virtue and which people do not. On the basis of this extensive knowledge, Socrates acts as a kind of soul doctor to his fellow men, approaching "each in *private*" and urging him to care for virtue. Socrates now claims that the reason he never accepted much civic responsibility, and never attempted or advocated any political reforms whatsoever, was because a demonic voice kept him from endangering his self-preservation.

It is very difficult to see how these two descriptions of Socrates' life fit together, and perhaps even more difficult to understand how either description is consistent with the picture Plato presents of Socrates in the other dialogues. One can surmise, however, that the twofold description in the *Apology* is a suitably rhetorical representation of the two sides of Socrates—the skeptical seeker after knowledge, and the private friend or benefactor.

This much, at least, is clear: the other dialogues as well as the *Apology* reveal Socrates as an essentially apolitical man, who rarely gives political advice to cities or statesmen, in public or in private. Nevertheless, there is one prominent occasion when Socrates does discuss the Athenian regime in public, and does imply constructive criticism of it. In the cross-examination of Meletus, Socrates for once confronts, in a solemn dialogue, a legal representative of the city of Athens. In that dialogue Socrates challenges the city on three grounds: first, he suggests there is something absurd in the system of moral education, which presumes the equality of the male citizens, and is not directed by one or a few experts (in this context he swears by Hera, a woman's oath); second, he contemns the penal code, which assumes men can do wrong voluntarily and therefore punishes rather than educates the criminal; and, finally, he indicates that the Athenian theology is so confused as to the relation between the gods, the demons, and the astral gods ("which the rest of mankind believes in"), that it renders impossible a clear distinction between those who are pious and those who are impious.

Now in the *Laws*, Plato presents a nameless old Athenian philosopher who acts and talks in a manner reminiscent of Socrates, and who advises statesmen as they elaborate a new code of laws. The salient innovations of that legislation are: an extensive new educational system for women as well as men, presided over by one magistrate who holds the highest administrative office in the regime; an unprecedented penal code based on the premise that no one ever voluntarily does wrong; and a new civil theology grounded on astral gods and elaborated through evident demonstrative reasoning. The *Apology* thus proves to reveal with some precision the basis for the dichotomy within Plato's dialogues, between the Socratic and the non-Socratic. In the *Laws* we learn what Socrates *would* have said and done if his quest for self-knowledge, and his friendships, had ever allowed him the leisure to engage in giving advice to political reformers—and if he had ever found himself in the appropriate circumstances.

PART ONE: *Drunkenness, Virtue, and Music*

624a–632d: From the Most Venerable Laws to the Question of Virtue

The *Laws* is a dialogue between a nameless old Athenian and two other old men, each of whom is a citizen of one of the two political orders widely believed to be the oldest and finest in Greece (see *Republic* 544c and Aristotle *Politics* 1273b25–27). Unlike the reluctant Socrates at the beginning of the *Republic*, the Athenian stranger in the *Laws* initiates and is eager to promote the discussion of politics. Our primary question must be: what motivates this philosophic character to begin such a conversation? Let us begin at the beginning and examine the evidence.

The conversation opens abruptly, with the Athenian asking whether the Dorian laws are reputed to derive from a god or a human. It is most unlikely that this question is prompted by simple ignorance, for Plato immediately shows us that the Athenian already knew the answer which the Homeric tradition, at least, provides. Besides, how could the Athenian be ignorant of the significance of the cave-sanctuary toward which he and the others are walking? What the Athenian can and does begin to learn by posing such a question is what sort of man Kleinias is, and what his posture is toward his tradition.

Kleinias begins to reveal himself by giving what he characterizes as "at any rate the most just answer." One way in which his "most just" answer is not most true is that it omits any reference to Minos, the human legislator. Some reflection on the tradition the Athenian insists on introducing helps us understand why a shrewd Cretan might be a bit reluctant to plunge into the whole story of his nation's origins. For that story dilutes the claim of the Cretan laws to direct divine inspiration: it indicates that between Zeus and the laws said to come from Zeus there was a semi-divine intermediary, who (like Numa and Moses and Christ and Mohammed) received the crucial oracles without any witnesses present. The claim to divinity of the Cretan laws thus comes to depend on the trustworthiness of Minos. Kleinias—who is slyer than most of the commentators who discuss him—at once shrouds the potential difficulty by introducing Rhadamanthus: surely a man whose brother was so just is a man whose words can be believed. There are probably two reasons why Kleinias does not say a word about the justice of Minos himself. For one thing, he knows that the founder "had war in view in everything he did" (625e); in war there are few "judicial affairs" such as Rhadamanthus won fame by arranging, and the status of justice itself is unclear. It is well known, for instance, that Minos was cruel and tyrannical towards Athens (706a). This points to the second consideration: Kleinias may very well think it would be going too far to try to praise the justice of Minos in a polite conversation with an Athenian. Indeed, in his urbanity Kleinias never so much as mentions the name "Minos"; it is the Athenian who brings out the ugly fact that in paying respect to Cretan law and its origins he is honoring the worst enemy of his own people (cf. the *Minos*).

The Athenian does not raise a single question about either the ancient tyrant's virtue or his claim to have talked with Zeus. He in fact reinforces Minos's claim, by bringing to its support the authority of Homer, whom it is doubtful Kleinias himself would ever have mentioned (cf. 680c). It is of course true that the reinforcement Homer provides for Cretan tradition is purchased at the price of entangling that tradition in the hermeneutic problems surrounding the sacred text. If we examine the poetic passage to which the Athenian alludes, we see that only with some stretching will the lines yield the interpretation the Athenian follows. Even then, the speaker is not Homer himself, but his Odysseus, who is not always veracious and who is at that point engaged in telling an elaborate lie. Plato thus quietly illustrates the extent to which the ambiguities of sacred texts need authoritative human interpretation.

Yet the greatest difficulty in the Dorian claim to divine sanction is one that does not stem directly from the Homeric passage but is implicit even in Kleinias's original, austere reply: "a god, a god." Kleinias must go on to reveal that there are in fact at least two gods, and at least a dual tradition. Are the many gods in agreement, or is the diversity of divine sources a sign of contradiction in the divine laws (cf. Farabi I 2)? This is a problem that will soon come dramatically to the fore.

Through this initial presentation of Cretan tradition Plato has led us to see the major questions that bedevil every sacred legal tradition. He does not, however, show the philosopher making explicit any of these doubts; instead he has him respond by giving an impression of reverent docility, in deed as well as in word. As the curtain rises, we find the old philosopher embarked on a rather arduous pilgrimage to the shrine that commemorates the divine origin of Cretan law. At the first opportunity, he contributes to a full articulation of the poetic support for Cretan tradition. Crete is venerable not only because it is widely respected; on the authority of the greatest of the divinely inspired poets it was Zeus, father of gods and men, who originated the Cretan laws. Through the opening scene Plato teaches that to understand the full potential of politics one must imagine what would happen if a philosopher respectfully encountered the phenomenon of law in its fullest and most awesome expression—in a regime admired by mankind at large and endowed, by the chief among poets, with the timeless authority of the highest god.

As the Athenian and Kleinias proceed to describe the visual setting of the speeches and events that are to follow, we are given our first vivid indication of the relation between this dialogue and the *Republic*. In the *Republic* the philosopher descends from the city to the licentious and "modern" seaport, where he discusses politics with young men restless and hardy enough to stay up all night without any supper. Only after the pious old father Cephalus has gone to his sacrifices and his supper does the discussion get underway. In the darkness of the night the interlocutors seek light, and catch a glimpse of the light beyond the cave by means of the metaphor of the sun. In the *Laws* the philosopher ascends from the city toward the cave of Zeus that is its ancient source, and on the way discusses politics with old statesmen who need to rest often as they make their way to the divine sanctuary. In the heat of a midsummer day they flee the light of the sun and seek the dark shade of old, sacred cypresses. (Compare the difference in the settings of Cicero's *Republic* and *Laws*.) In the *Laws* Plato truly compels philosophy to occupy itself with the darkness of the cave, to deal with politics as it is and not to speculate, in the company of irresponsible sophists and inexperienced youths, on how politics might be.

Continuing to take the initiative, the Athenian apparently begins his own education in the divine laws by asking the reason for three important Cretan customs. Kleinias's response explains not only these three customs but the legal system as a whole; he is eager to give an account of the general intention of the lawgiver. But he does not pretend that his personal view is what the Cretans usually say (cf. 625c–e with 624b–625a). Indeed, he shares what he interprets to be his lawgiver's contempt for the many and what they call things; he takes his bearings by "the deed" rather than "the word." In his account, the reason for Cretan Law is to be found in "nature" (625c, 626a: because Kleinias is what he is, nature is introduced much earlier in the *Laws* than it is in the *Republic*). The gods need never be mentioned. In short, Kleinias's words confirm our initial suspicion that he is a somewhat sophisticated old Cretan, and the dramatic setting is therefore not quite as bounded by tradition as it at first appeared. To grasp the essence and potential of the most august tradition Plato does not have us watch a philosopher encounter its purest representatives.

Kleinias's remarks, which are not so far from what is usually said by Dorians but what Megillus can approve, have, however, the following difficulty: everything is said to be arranged with a view to war, but war is also said to be for the sake of protecting or acquiring "the good things." Doesn't the latter statement imply that everything, including war, is for the sake of something else enjoyed by the citizens during peacetime? Or does Kleinias mean that "the good things" boil down to selfish security and glory, achieved through collective alliances and permanent belligerence? Is something like the Machiavellian conception of the human situation at the core of the tradition as articulated by Kleinias? It is to resolve this ambiguity that the Athenian asks his next questions. At first, Kleinias resolutely maintains that a state of war exists at every level, in domestic as well as international politics, between neighborhoods and households and even individual citizens. In this Platonic presentation of a representative of traditional civic virtue, we witness the considerable justification for Machiavelli's and Hobbes's starting point: this citizen, at least, claims that every social whole can be seen on analysis to be no more than a stabilized system of competing parts. But at some point the fragmentation must end; some specifiable unit must be atomic, a whole which is not constructed for the sake of something else. (I cannot discuss here the alternative posed by the Will to Power.) For Machiavelli and Hobbes, the natural unit is the individual motivated by the desire for security and glory. But the "amazing" Kleinias's understanding of the status of the individual is ambiguous, for what I call his Machiavellianism exists in uneasy combination with a sense of shame (a not unusual combination, even today). Kleinias vivifies the latent contradiction in traditional civic virtue, a contradiction crystallized in the very word "superior." On the one hand everything should be arranged with a view to "superiority," to triumph and survival; but on the other hand many triumphs are "shameful" and "inferior." When Kleinias focuses on external war he tends to see victory as the unambiguous goal, but when he considers the competition within the city and within himself he is aware that what is most important is the character of those who win the victory. He could harmonize his opinions, in a Machiavellian way, if he went on to say that what is better internally is what allows the city or individual to triumph over others. But guided by the Athenian (627a–b), Kleinias recognizes that in the case of individuals and domestic politics, at least, the "better" are the "just" and to be in the "just minority" is by no means necessarily to be stronger.

In an attempt to resolve the contradiction, and show Kleinias how much he errs in his understanding of the goal of politics, the Athenian invokes the analogy of the family. At this point he ceases to play the role of simple student and transforms the conversation into a common "hunt" (627c) or investigation. This is the first step in what gradually unfolds as his conspiracy to become the molder of a new regime with new laws and new gods, and in his analogy he foreshadows the character of his political project in the *Laws* as a whole. The quarreling brothers within one family are analogous to the warring factions within one city. When the Athenian proposes that for quarreling brothers there is "presumably" a judge, we, with Kleinias, must presumably agree: doesn't the father or the mother judge the quarrels of brothers (cf. 627c with 690a)? Not if we follow the Athenian. In asking Kleinias to choose between only three judges the Athenian ignores the claim to authority based on the parental, the ancestral. Platonic political science adopts the perspective of a founder, who in laying down the fundamental political rules attempts to escape from the authority of tradition and precedent as much as circumstances allow. The Athenian is certainly not a Burkean conservative (cf. also 630e–631a).

Kleinias chooses the judge who institutes the rule of law and who thus brings about reconciliation and friendship, even though the Athenian clearly characterizes the "lawgiver" as third among the judges with respect to virtue. Virtue and law (and virtue and civic friendship) are not the same. It is easy to see why Plato's Athenian ranks the second and central judge higher with respect to virtue; this is the judge who establishes a regime like that of Plato's *Republic*. But how can the Athenian believe that the first, harsh judge is superior in virtue to the lawgiver? There are at least two reasons. First, the rule of law is inferior to both the other arrangements insofar as it fails to provide the city with a complete "victory over itself," and allows wicked men to share rule with good men: it remains to be seen whether law is a sufficient safeguard against the dangers this implies. Second, if politics is analogous to medicine (628d), then keeping evil men alive in the city is like avoiding necessary purgations of disease from the body (cf. 735d–e). Even the *Republic* may fail to live up to the analogy with medicine. Perhaps, however, the analogy with medicine is not intended to be strict but merely provocative, revealing the limits of politics. Reflection on the medical analogy forces us to wonder if the body politic can ever be as naturally whole as the human body, and if virtue can be as unambiguously the standard for politics as health is the standard for medicine. In particular, the elimination of the wicked seems less viable if we remember that the city must concern itself with external enemies (628b). Plato teaches that despite our desire for what is best, we must begin with "what is most needed, that is, the lowest" (Farabi I 6). Although Kleinias fails to establish that victory in foreign war is the supreme goal, the Athenian surely does not argue that such victory is unimportant. Yet these reflections do not suffice to explain the Athenian's acquiescence in Kleinias's choice of the rule of law over the second alternative, and it is only later, in Book Five, that we will learn the full grounds for that acquiescence.

Through his analogy the Athenian has compelled Kleinias to agree that within the city the goal is not war, or even peace achieved through the victory of the just, but lawful peace brought about through friendship between the just and the unjust. The fundamental issue, however, remains unresolved: is this domestic concord good for any reason other than as a means to external conquest? The Athenian proceeds to assert that peace and goodwill are the "best" and that the lawgiver must see war as a means to peace. To justify this assertion, he will have to specify the activities of peace and demonstrate their excellence. Such clarification has become especially necessary now that he has indicated that the lawgiver's pursuit of concord attenuates his pursuit of virtue.

Before he can begin this exploration, however, the Athenian must confront a practical difficulty. Kleinias realizes that what has been said by the "stranger" is not in accord with the venerable Dorian laws. The Athenian avoids a fight by ceasing to examine Kleinias, or Minos, or Lycurgus, and turning instead to a poet, a poet who lived and flourished among the Spartans but who was, after all, an Athenian by birth. He asks Kleinias and Megillus to help him interrogate the poet. The potential dispute between an Athenian and the Dorian lawgivers is transformed into a muted dispute between two Athenians, one of whom was a turncoat poet. It is almost the Athenian stranger's patriotic duty to interrogate Tyrtaeus. Plato begins to teach us the crafty rhetoric employed by a philosopher who wishes to bring about fundamental political change.

In criticizing Tyrtaeus, the Athenian relies on the authority of another poet of equal fame. Only under Theognis's auspices does he dare to introduce the idea that virtue is the goal, and dare to assert that courage in foreign war is neither the whole of virtue nor its highest part. However, the turn to Theognis does entail a partial concession to Kleinias's original thesis: the Athenian ceases to speak of friendship and goodwill, and accepts an understanding of virtue according to which virtue is fully exhibited not in peaceful activity but in the midst of civil war. The Athenian's obvious difficulty in reconciling the goal of concord with the goal of virtue reflects the fact that the reconciliation of true concord and true virtue—the unqualified pursuit of the virtues that are exhibited in peaceful friendship— would be possible only in a community where virtuous men ruled alone and did not have to compete with and keep an eye on men who are not virtuous. In a city where good and bad share power under law, both concord and virtue can be pursued only in inferior versions that remain at a tension with one another.

Despite the Athenian's concession, and his reference to Zeus, Kleinias insists that what has been said constitutes a downright dismissal of the Cretan lawgiver. But the slippery Athenian totally disarms Kleinias by himself coming to the defense of Minos and Lycurgus. What the discussion has shown, he says, is not that the lawgivers were mistaken but that Kleinias underestimated them. Naturally, the guilty Kleinias has no choice but to accept the Athenian's offer to repair the damage, by showing what Kleinias should have said in praise of the finest lawgivers and of their superiority over all lawgivers "nowadays." The Athenian is thus enabled to outline the standard by which the Dorian legal systems will be judged, and it becomes clear that he has come to Crete not to seek the standard of good laws but to reform Crete in the light of it.

As we have come to expect, the criterion of "correct laws" is not that they promote virtue. It is rather that they bring about happiness. Virtue is not identical to happiness, because happiness requires "human goods" in addition to the virtues. This might imply that the city ruled by good laws may sometimes secure more happiness at the price of less virtue, in circumstances where much-needed "human goods" like wealth and strength can be secured only by relaxing the demands of certain virtues (cf. e.g., 706a ff.). The Athenian hastily tries to obviate this ugly possibility by affirming that for a city virtue is the necessary and sufficient condition for health, beauty, strength, and wealth (cf. Apology 30b 2–4). However noble the affirmation, it is a direct contradiction of facts the Athenian has previously described and will soon describe even more vividly (627a–d, 638a–b; cf. 706a, 707d, 770e, 936b). The Athenian, one is tempted to say, is carried away by the need to praise law and the lawgivers. But of course the Athenian is speaking not strictly in his own name, but on behalf of Kleinias, and hence finds himself compelled to obscure the fact that Kleinias's choice is "third in respect to virtue."

The happiness the laws are said to bring about is the happiness not of the gods but of "those who live under" the laws. Is it safe to assume that what makes the human inhabitants happy is the same as what makes the gods happy? At the founding of a new city may not the lawgiver displace and displease some old gods? This danger is perhaps mitigated by identifying the four human virtues as "the divine goods," the "leader" of which is intellect (nous); still, we will have to learn more about the relation between these divine goods and divinity itself (cf. Farabi I 7). For now we should note that piety is not one of the virtues named. In this connection we recall that the Athenian ignored the father's claim to be the authoritative judge of his sons. Piety is in fact never mentioned in Book One: the opposite of hubris is moderation (630b), and the only thing called "sacred" is calculation (645a). (On the other hand there are no oaths in Book One.) As we refine our impressions and become more familiar with the first book of the Laws, we begin to realize how substantial, if quiet, a break with tradition it represents.

Having stated the ranking of the virtues, the ranking the lawgiver should follow and communicate to the citizens, the Athenian turns to an elaboration of the lawgiver's task. He speaks first of what appears to be moderation: the lawgiver should use the laws themselves to apportion honor and dishonor in regard to the appetites. Then he speaks of what sounds like courage: the lawgiver should teach what is noble in regard to fear and anger, the passions that are aroused by opposition. Here he mentions the soul. Then, evidently descending from the sphere of noble challenges to the sphere which includes involuntary and voluntary calculation concerning money and property, he explicitly speaks of justice. He says nothing else about the promotion of prudence, let alone intelligence, among the general citizenry. The centrality and prominence of what sounds most like courage show us how large an ingredient courage is to be in the mixed version of "justice" aimed at by the lawgiver.

In addition to giving us a more detailed picture of what the lawgiver's ranking of virtue implies, the Athenian has indicated the complexity of the relation between virtue and happiness in the city. For on the whole the evils to be nobly endured are emphasized more than the goods to be happily enjoyed. Indeed, the question of the relation between virtue and happiness is put in a new light when the Athenian concludes by saying that the lawgiver is to set up "guards," only "some" of whom are to be "grounded in prudence"; with these guards the city is "knit together" by intelligence (*nous*) so as to "follow" moderation and justice. Even if for a moment we make the questionable assumption that prudence is the same as *nous*, and that therefore at least some of the guards (and not the legislator alone) will possess *nous*, we are left wondering whether anyone except these guards will possess all three of the higher virtues, and therefore be completely happy. As for the "whole political regime," its "end" (*telos*) is death, burial, and the honors paid to each of the dead. In a properly subdued manner, the Athenian has hinted that it will not be easy to find an answer to the question Kleinias failed to answer—what the "good things" are, for the sake of which the finest laws command all the citizens to endure nobly many evils, including death.

The Athenian's summary, while sketching the goals of good laws, foreshadows the problems which this dialogue articulates and begins to solve: the relation of virtue to happiness, to god, to the passions, and to economics; the nature, the ranking, and the interrelations of the various parts of virtue; the way in which good laws can bring happiness and virtue into being.

[387]

632e–641a: The Problematic Multiplicity of Virtue

The purpose of good laws is the fostering of the virtue that brings happiness. In the light of this standard it is necessary to start over again from the beginning. The Athenian starts off as if he meant to show how the Dorian laws follow the standard and promote virtue, but the initial intention is soon transformed into two rather different and deeper intentions. On a more theoretical level the Athenian inquires further into the nature of "virtue." On a more practical level he continues and extends his cautious assault on the Dorian laws in the name of virtue. One could also characterize the more practical intention as the attempt to bring together the virtue of the philosophic Athenian and the incomplete virtue of Kleinias and Megillus. Thus at every step the two levels are interwoven, for on both levels the problem is the unity or coherence of virtue. Virtue comes to sight as a plurality, as existing in at least four "forms." Do the many "forms" cohere—are they really "parts" of one form or *idea?* The interlocutors will go through each of the virtues, and, "later," they will perhaps see how the many virtues fit together in virtue "as a whole." Somehow some god will be involved with them in this latter task. From the beginning to the end of the *Laws* we will never lose sight of the problem of the unity of virtue, or more generally of the problem of the *ideas,* of the one and the many, as exemplified in the preeminent *idea* of virtue (cf. 963a–966b).

In his summary the Athenian has already presented us with enough information to allow us to reason about the virtues—to count, collect, and divide them. The four virtues fall into three groups. Courage is separated from the others by its lowness and equivocal nobility. Courage seems least eligible as an end in itself and most clearly a means to some other "good things." Prudence or intelligence is separated from the others by its rank as leader: according to the Athenian's second and central characterization, *nous* is closest to the goal and partakes least of the nature of a means to other things (cf. 631d with 631c; see Farabi I 7). Yet in the third reference to *nous* we hear that the lawgiver's city does not "follow" *nous,* that *nous* only "knits together" the city (632c 6–7): in the city under law *nous* appears as a means to something else, above all to moderation and justice, which the city does "follow." (Of course, since intelligence or prudence is one ingredient of the mixture that is justice, the city does follow an alloy of intelligence.) Moderation and justice belong together. The former refers primarily to the healthy inner ordering of an individual's appetites, for his own good, while justice refers primarily to the proper ordering of men's relations with one another, for the common good. Now since the city's justice is a mixture of moderation and the other two virtues, it must be understood in terms of its elements; hence, of the two principal civic virtues, moderation seems to call for the most attention at the outset.

But, continuing to humor the proclivities of his companions, the Athenian inquires first into the practices that promote not moderation but courage. At first he continues to associate courage with prowess in foreign war (633a), but when Megillus ventures beyond what "any Lacedaimonian would say" to speak of courage as including endurance of suffering, the Athenian seizes the opportunity to transform radically the ordinarily accepted definition of courage. According to his new definition, Sparta and Crete are seen to promote only a mutilated kind of courage. But the new definition seems wrong, since it reduces moderation to being a part of courage. The Athenian's curious procedure stems partly from a wish to embarrass the Dorians even on their strongest front; he is growing more aggressive. But the new definition of courage is not as strange as it first seems. In fact, the definition follows and illuminates the premise of the whole preceding discussion with Kleinias. In that discussion (although not in his own summary of the finest lawgiver's intention), "courage" was subordinated to the other virtues not so much because there was something clearly more important than war but because civil or internal war seemed "harsher" and more serious than foreign war (628a–b, 629e–630c; cf. 634b). All virtue was said to be good because it was good in some sort of war: Kleinias's original assertion about the omnipresence of war was not rejected, it was only refined. It follows that *all* virtue can be understood as prowess in war, as "courage" in a broader sense than is usually meant. The different "forms" of virtue can be distinguished according to the different "forms" of war (629c 6 ff.) to which they are directed. In particular, we are now reminded (633d) that a little earlier in this conversation the virtue usually called moderation—the control of oneself in the face of tempting pleasures—was understood to be a "combat" within the soul.

What the Athenian has done here is to adumbrate one possible solution to the problem of the unity of virtue. Virtue can be understood as the unending, courageous fight against evil, the greatest virtue being the "perfect justice" which is "trustworthiness in the midst of evils" (630c). In this context the Athenian introduces "freedom" for the first time (635d): virtue is the manly struggle to be free. Allied with fellow citizens one struggles against foreign oppression; allied with some fellow citizens one struggles against oppression by other citizens; within oneself one struggles against the passions that would render one easily enslaved by other men. According to this refined, Theognian or poetic, version of Kleinias's view, virtue is grounded in a human situation of permanent discord. Harmony is not to be expected, either among the passions or among men.

This whole interpretation of virtue sets a standard considerably above what is actually pursued in the venerable Dorian regimes, but it nevertheless has several grave problems. The first is the status of theoretical reason, which is difficult to understand as a form of courage, or internal war (though dialectic is often referred to in the *Laws* as a form of hunting: cf. 633b with 627c and 822d ff.). In the reduction of the virtues to forms of courageous warfare, reason seems to become merely prudence (cf. 630b with 631c–d). The second difficulty is the one we have seen before, the obscurity of the goal, or of the reason for the hierarchies (of passions, men, and cities) which virtue strives to uphold. Can virtue be defined sufficiently as the active resistance against slavery, or does such a definition not prove vacuous without a clear account of the "good things" pursued by freedom?

To understand all that is at stake here it is helpful to go beyond Plato to Kant, who provides an even more refined version of the Theognian position. Theognis and Kleinias do not, of course, have in mind the precise formula of the "categorical imperative." But Kant means by that formula no more than a systematic expression of the experience that is at the heart of virtue, and that men have known since the dawn of humanity. For Kant, just as for Kleinias, there is no natural harmony in the soul or in society, and all virtue is therefore courage and struggle: "Fortitude (*fortitudo*) is the capacity and resolved purpose to resist a strong but unjust opponent; and with regard to the opponent of the moral disposition within us, such fortitude is *virtue (virtus, fortitudo moralis)*" (*Metaphysics of Morals*, Part II, Preussische Akademie ed., p. 380; cf. pp. 406, 425, 483). In this life at least, the victory of good over evil must be fought out anew at every turn; in Aristotelian terms, there is no such thing as "moderation," there is only "self-restraint" (see Ibid., pp. 379–80, 386, 394). Kant of course gives a vastly more detailed explanation of theoretical reason, which is demoted to the rank of a servant, defending the autonomy of virtue against the false pretensions of science. Human reason at its highest is identical with the moral will and comes to know itself as such through the teaching of Rousseau, brought to full maturity by Kant himself. Virtue, which is the same as true freedom, has no justification beyond itself and needs none; to seek such justification is to misunderstand the fundamental experience of freedom. Kant resolutely resists any attempt to make virtue a means to or the embodiment of happiness, because doing so would demean the nobility of freedom and because he denies that the human mind can have an objective account of happiness.

The Athenian stranger, in contrast, insists on an objective account of happiness and on an account of the virtues which shows not only how they procure freedom but also how they embody or obtain happiness (cf. 663b). When the Athenian finally turns from "courage," including the "courageous" struggle against tempting pleasures, to "moderation," he indicates that he does not completely follow the "courageous" account of the unity of virtue. Like Socrates, the Athenian knows a higher moderation that is different from self-restraint (cf. 710a, 734b). The truly moderate man is no longer at war with himself, because he has gradually purged or suppressed the evil passions and established a pleasant harmony. A close approximation to such a man is extremely rare but probably not impossible. Similarly, the truly just city would be harmonious rather than an uneasy tension between good men and bad. But is even an approximation to the truly just city possible? In this dialogue at any rate, we have followed Kleinias in choosing the rule of law and hence avoiding the attempt to purge or strictly subordinate bad men. This implies that the virtue, or common good, pursued by the best laws is a mixture of the defective version rooted in Kleinias's or Theognis's outlook and the true version. These reflections should make it clearer why, in his summary of the purpose of the best laws, the Athenian characterized "justice" as a mixture of the higher virtues, and courage, the lower. Yet the Athenian did not say that the city's moderation would have an admixture of courage.

Let us now focus again on the dramatic action. When he hears what is going to be involved in the new beginning, Megillus speaks up—not to engage in but to ward off the onerous task. Megillus has been reserved and cautious in his reactions to everything the Athenian has said (cf. 627d). Though we cannot yet form much of a judgment about his character and role, we can be sure that he knows full well that there is more danger of friction between a Spartan and an Athenian than between a Cretan and an Athenian. The Athenian stranger is surely aware of the danger too, yet he now politely but firmly directs the conversation to Megillus. After Megillus has spoken well about the Spartan practices that promote what is ordinarily called courage, he is embarrassed by the demand that he speak about the Spartan practices that provide experience in pleasure and thereby promote the other side of "courage." The Athenian softens but does not remove the embarrassment by compelling the "Knossian" as well as the "Lacedaimonian" to share it (633d, 634b–c). This time, far from offering to give the proper defense of the lawgivers (who, he repeats, are divinely inspired: 634a), the Athenian gingerly introduces the possibility that somebody might have to blame somebody else's laws. He appeals for a gentle rather than a harsh reception of such blame. When Kleinias emphatically accedes, the Athenian addresses him by name for the first time. Megillus is silent, even though he was just addressed as one of the "best of strangers" (634c).

In the face of this stony silence, the Athenian takes a step back and says they will not have to get into the question of whether or not someone could justifiably blame the Dorian regimes. Still, for some reason or other, it is worthwhile to hear what "the many" say against these regimes. What "the many" say is not so well known by the two old Dorians because one of their finest laws forbids the young to question the laws, and commands all to say in unison that the laws are fine because made by gods. Almost as an afterthought, the Athenian adds that this fine law includes a provision which outlines a procedure for questioning the laws. In other words, the Athenian will question the laws only after he has reminded them of the legal basis for doing so. Nor is the legal basis a mere technicality or "loophole": according to Kleinias, at least, the Athenian has "divined" correctly the intention of the lawgiver. We and Megillus, as foreigners, are certainly in no position to dispute this. We may silently wonder, though, whether the ancient enemy of Athens, Minos, really intended to allow noncitizens, above all Athenians (who heed what "the many" say), to come to Crete and raise questions about his laws. And did he intend to allow a critique as radical as the one the Athenian has begun (contrast Farabi I 11)? If Kleinias is not naive, his enthusiastic delight at the Athenian's reading of the law betrays an untoward eagerness to hear a full critique of his lawgiver. Perhaps the remarks about the need for training in pleasure "ring a bell" with this old Cretan who has given thought to the general intention of the Cretan laws.

The most important point made by this turn in the drama is the emphatic and essential absence of the young from the discussion. The exclusion of the young at the beginning of the *Laws* is a mirror image of the exit of Cephalus at the beginning of the *Republic*. A central purpose of Plato in the *Laws* is to investigate how a philosopher may intervene directly in the most momentous political action, founding or refounding. We begin now to learn the first massive lesson: to understand political action is to try to understand, to write and speak primarily for, the *old*. The powers that be are characteristically the old men, because they, as fathers, control the families and property and, what is more, are the custodians of the all-powerful traditions and religious beliefs. The drama in the *Laws* is the greatest psychological-political study of old age that has ever been undertaken. The nonphilosophic characters explored in the *Laws* are the old *par excellence*, old citizens from the oldest and most traditional regimes, which give even more power to the old than do most regimes. Only a few of the old men in such regimes are open to being influenced, and then only under very special circumstances and by a very special rhetoric. First and foremost, the philosopher must do everything he can to avoid the suspicion that he is a corrupter of the young, a subverter of the moral authority of the old. He must not appear even to wish to talk to the young; initially at least, he must applaud the *nomos* that forbids the young to ask questions (contrast 888c). He must himself appear old, and, if he is generally known to have once embraced anti-gerontocratic leanings he must appear to have "changed his mind." Both the Athenian stranger, in the dialogue, and the author Plato, down through the ages, are totally successful in creating this impression. This is one reason why Plato sets the dialogue far away from the home of the "stranger": if a philosopher claimed among his own people to prefer to speak with the old, he would have trouble being believed.

This does not, indeed, suffice to justify the Platonic philosopher's refusal to mount an open attack on the power of the old, through the mobilization of a youth movement—a project executed by Machiavelli as well as some of his successors, like Marx. After all, Plato makes it unmistakably evident that he can conceive of the young becoming successful revolutionaries (*Apology* 39c–d; *Republic* 549c–563a). As the dialogue unfolds, we shall see that Plato rejects a direct attack on the political authority of the old because he doubts that a republican regime can endure in the absence of strong traditions (cf. *Republic* 557 ff.), and because he thinks that traditional, "conservative" virtue, despite its narrowness, provides the best moral upbringing (cf. *Apology* 41d–e and *Republic* 492–493).

Another important question about the setting remains. Granted that Plato could not easily depict a philosopher assisting in a re-founding in his own city; why must he also refrain from depicting a philosophic stranger who arrives from a regime far away but similar in character to Crete or Sparta? Why make the philosopher bow to the authority of regimes and founders who are so alien to his own city? One reason, as we shall see presently, is that the tensions between the interlocutors turn out to be very fruitful. But one must also wonder to what extent a philosopher *must* come from a regime like the Athenian (a rather progressive democracy). According to Plato's Socrates, the philosopher is more at home and safer in a democracy than in other regimes (*Republic* 557b–c, 561d; *Crito* 52b). This leads us to the question of why a philosopher would take the trouble to travel far away to alien regimes, to engage in political projects whose success is uncertain and which require him to avoid the young and talk exclusively with old men. Certainly the Athenian stranger has waited until very, very late in life to perform this duty. From reflection on all these questions concerning the setting we begin to understand the rarity of a revolution or refounding advised by a genuine Platonic philosopher.

Armed now with legal authority, the Athenian proceeds not to report what "the many" say, and not to blame the laws in his own name, but to express his "perplexity." Megillus's continued silence is not completely covered over by Kleinias's claim to be speaking for both, and the Athenian here shows that he is not yet in a position to address Megillus by name (635e). But when Megillus ventures a response to the next question, about moderation, the Athenian seems to throw caution to the winds and deliberately provokes a fight with the "Lacedaimonian stranger." His treatment of Megillus is very different from his treatment of Kleinias. The common meals and gymnastic training which, since their introduction by Kleinias, had been spoken of only in approving terms are subjected now to a harsh attack. These practices weaken the rule of justice by promoting civil strife and, more important, weaken moderation by encouraging homosexuality. Far from being practices "according to nature" as Kleinias had claimed, these practices lead to the violation of an "ancient law" that is somehow in nature. The Athenian seems sure that Zeus would not violate the natural law, and therefore that the famous myth about Ganymede is a Cretan lie. He provokes one to wonder, did the Cretans invent any other lies about Zeus? As is well known, this false myth is supported by Homer (*Iliad* XX 231 ff.), who apparently was too credulous about what Cretans say. The Athenian has thus raised some very sharp questions about both Crete and Sparta.

Megillus is not about to take all this lying down, although he knows he is not as good as the loquacious Athenian in "finding words to respond with." Gathering steam as he goes, Megillus asserts the absolute superiority of the Spartan lawgiver's injunction to "flee pleasures." The argument he gives is objectively rather weak but has a crude rhetorical effectiveness. Megillus defends by taking the offensive, *ad hominem*. Homosexual indiscretions pale in comparison with the effects of the drunkenness brought about by drinking parties, a practice proscribed in Sparta but encouraged at Athens, especially by the festivals in honor of the god of wine. It turns out that the many gods certainly do not agree, or at least that their human interpreters do not agree.

The Athenian threatens to respond in kind by relentlessly pursuing the very touchy subject of sexual misconduct, and even escalates the attack by passing from the Spartan men to their women. The Athenian has provoked what appears to be the start of a rather nasty quarrel. Why?

Let us consider what results from this incipient quarrel. Instead of carrying out his threatened counterattack the Athenian pauses, offers some conciliation, and stakes out a defense—which proves to be a very lengthy defense—of drunkenness and drinking parties. In defending drunkenness he creates a spirit and tone that will infuse the entire dialogue (cf. e.g., 890e), and almost from the very outset of his defense he quite transforms the subject matter. The discussion soon focuses on education, and then education in music and poetry. As Megillus's reference to the Dionysian festivals indicated, any talk of Athenian immoderation goes naturally with talk about what happens at those Athenian festivals honoring the god of wine, the festivals in which the most famous musical and poetic contests are held. Music has not been a theme hitherto because it is not a very important part of the Dorian regimes or the Dorian virtues.

By provoking Megillus's attack on Athens, the Athenian makes himself appear to be forced to come to the defense of his fatherland and of the gods and peculiar religious customs of his people. He is thereby allowed to introduce and defend alien Athenian ways before old Dorians, in a manner which frees him from all suspicion and even disposes his audience somewhat in his favor. For every old patriot honors patriotism, even in his enemies. Every decent old patriot at once understands and sympathizes with the situation of a solitary old foreigner who finds himself compelled to speak out in defense of his native religious customs.

Henceforward the Athenian stranger is enabled to speak as an advocate of foreign ways instead of as a docile student of Dorian ways or as a critic whose motives are unclear (and therefore suspicious). But this is not his sole rhetorical intention here. The defense of things Athenian proves to be a patriotic cover for the defense of laws and a regime which are unprecedented because they are according to nature. The stranger has succeeded in giving legitimacy to his project of creating what may be called a synthesis of Dorian virtue and Athenian music, or of the Dorian gods and the Athenian gods. A true synthesis is not a mere combination but a reconstruction in which the elements are in a sense destroyed.

What Plato teaches here may be stated in general terms as follows. A political philosopher who wishes to bring about fundamental changes is more likely to succeed if he appears to be not merely an old conservative, but a "foreigner" in some sense, whose circumstances compel him to defend the ways of "his people" against the implicit and explicit criticisms of his "hosts" (the persons he wishes to change or to be the agents of change). Only thus can he openly introduce and defend alien ways and yet appear to be neither a traitor nor a man without loyalty. Of course, this principle as well as the others Plato teaches in the *Laws* must be adapted to circumstances. It will perhaps be helpful to give some illustrations of such adaptation. In relatively modern times there is, for instance, Tocqueville's *Democracy in America,* a study of democracy which could never have been written by an American, as Tocqueville makes clear. One should also recall Rousseau's use of "Genevan patriotism" in speaking to the French, and Spinoza's use of "loyalty to the true Israel" in speaking to the Christians. In other times a more complex adaptation is found. Political philosophers like Marsilius, Maimonides, and Farabi (and lesser thinkers as well) write commentaries by which they introduce and loyally defend the challenging questions of alien, pagan Greeks. This adaptation, like the writings of Plato himself, in defense of Socrates, seemed aimed more at changing a few individual souls than at effecting great changes in society.

638c–650b: Education, in Citizenship and in Shame

The stranger begins his defense by saying that he wants it to be a model of the method they should follow in examining *all* institutions: the analysis of drinking parties will shed light on much besides drinking parties *per se*. The model method tries to discover how an institution should be administered and what its effect is (638c–d). One proceeds by considering the institution under question in the light of other examples of a class to which it belongs, in order to see certain general characteristics in which it shares. (Naturally, one will also learn about other members of the class.) The drinking party, the Athenian says, belongs to the class of communal associations aimed at action, and all such institutions should be administered by rulers. More precisely, the parallel examples reveal, the Athenian is considering the drinking party as an example of that sub-class of such institutions which requires an unlimited ruler—a "despot" (640e). As Farabi stresses (I 14–15), the political community as a whole belongs to the same sub-class, insofar as its true ruler is the lawgiver, whose authority is obviously not limited by law (cf. 709e ff., 735b–736c). Yet politics includes war as well as peace, while the drinking party aims only at peaceful and friendly action (640b); strictly speaking, then, the drinking party is an analogy of the city only in its peaceful pursuits.

The Athenian investigates the necessary qualifications or virtues of those who rule these associations. What is needed above all is knowledge, but, in addition, the ruler's body and passions must be able to resist the particular perturbations associated with the action of the institution he rules. In the case of an absolute ruler, the virtues other than knowledge have a status like that of the pilot's resistance to seasickness (absolutely essential but not very elevated and pertaining mainly to the body).

Kleinias is dissatisfied with the defense so far because he wonders what good would come from correctly ruled drinking parties, analogous to the good that comes from correctly led armies. Following the example the stranger has given, we should go further and extend the question to "despotic" associations in general, and especially the association of lawgiver and city. And we must wonder what the good is for the *ruler* as well as the ruled. In the case of the drinking party, the good seems entirely the followers': why would a knower become leader of a drinking party—or lawgiver for a city? In a "drinking party" the good is peace, goodwill, and friendship—among the ruled. To Kleinias these goods continue to seem pale compared with victory in war. And is this so unreasonable? Do the warm words goodwill and friendship have much meaning before their content is specified?

In his reply, the stranger indicates that within the city and within what has now become its analogy, the drinking party, the answer to the content of "peace" lies in education. Only at this point do they truly "embark on the discussion of law and regimes" (641d). The stranger is at last ready to consider what for him is *the* business of politics. Yet the "noble"—the goal of education which lies beyond victory in war—remains tantalizingly vague (641b–c).

Having barely introduced the amazing thesis that drinking together is a great contribution to education, the stranger proposes to abandon the defense. He cannot defend "his own view" except in an Athenian manner and he knows that Athenian manners are probably more irritating to Dorians than the substantive Athenian beliefs (cf. Montesquieu, *Spirit of the Laws* XIX 2–3, 7). He thereby creates a situation in which Megillus and Kleinias must commit themselves to hearing long Athenian speeches or else leave their curiosity unsatisfied. In committing themselves they also reveal themselves yet more, as quite untypical citizens of their respective cities. Plato thus indicates still another condition for the success of the project we see the philosopher here embarked upon: he must also have an audience that will listen to lengthy talk. Over this he has very little control.

In the Spartan's speech Plato puts perhaps the most beautiful and truest compliment he ever paid to Athens. The Athenian stranger is surely an example of what Megillus calls a "good Athenian," a man whose goodness is due not to Athenian education but to his inner nature, to a divine dispensation. Democratic Athens contributed to that natural goodness mainly by leaving it alone, by carelessly letting it flower without "compelling" it to become "educated." The Athenian stranger's patriotism is not then entirely feigned or simply inherited: a philosopher cannot help but have affection for permissive democracy. At the very beginning of the thematic treatment of education Plato incites us to ask what the relation is between civic education and this kind of goodness (cf. the *Meno*). Doesn't institutional education hinder a man gifted with a "divine dispensation"? If so, why should such a man endanger his own kind of human being in order to help educate the vast majority who lack a good inner nature?

Megillus's encouragement precedes that of Kleinias, who perhaps needed a moment to think. His inventive powers are displayed in a delightful "tall tale" that mixes just the right amount of judicious fantasy with truth or authoritative opinion. The cautious and sly Kleinias is not yet prepared to divulge the true circumstances that fire his curiosity.

By getting permission to speak in an "Athenian" manner, the Athenian stranger has alerted his interlocutors—and us—to the fact that henceforward he will employ a wider range of speech. What immediately follows demonstrates the new range of rhetoric. First we hear the Athenian ask for and give a scientific "definition"; then we hear him "clarify" something by means of an "image." We must watch to see what these two paramount examples teach about the nature and use of definitions and images.

The definition is dialectical to this extent: it forces the interlocutor to participate and thus tests the interlocutor. The Athenian first presents a *universal* definition which states what is *common* to *all* or *most* education. Before giving this definition, and after summing it up, the Athenian emphatically asks Kleinias to "think over whether it is acceptable." Kleinias wonders why it should not be acceptable. He is thereby revealed as a man whose education has not taught him the difference between a liberal and an "illiberal" education, or between what is truly education and what is "wholly unworthy" of the name. This is a very severe Platonic indictment of the most venerable laws. The Athenian has a long way to go in educating Kleinias.

An adequate definition of education is one that distinguishes "liberal education," the rare or *un*common education that makes a man "free." In rereading the Athenian's terse statement we can recapture some of the original meaning and vibrance of an idea which we now know only as a senescent platitude. Liberal education is education in politics, in becoming a perfect citizen of a republic where the citizen desires and loves to rule and be ruled in turn. Such education embodies both contempt and aspiration—contempt for money-making, merchant trade, and labor or artisanship in general; aspiration to the use of reason (*nous*) in shared activities of planning and shaping the collective life of a community. The aspiration gives us the first great answer to the question, "What is noble in peace?" What is noble is political participation in republican government, not merely as a means to security or profit or any sort of strength but as the erotically desirable (643e) field of activity on which man exercises his human intelligence in the company of friendly equals.

As usual we have to reflect on what is left unsaid or only implied as well as on the wonderful things that are said. For instance, the contempt for money-making and the crafts is surely noble—but it raises some difficult economic questions. For the moment it is more important to observe the specification of the virtues which are the goals of liberal education: justice and intelligence. By now we are not so surprised to find that courage is not mentioned; but what about moderation? Moderation is primarily a virtue of one's relation to oneself: does the silence about moderation not point to the fact that the individual and personal is neglected in this definition of education?

As if to highlight this silence about moderation, the Athenian turns abruptly from the definition of education to a new inquiry into self-mastery. "Long ago we agreed that the good are those able to rule themselves." Just now it was agreed that the good are those educated to rule others and be ruled by others. Precisely how do these two statements harmonize? What inner disposition of the soul makes men "lovers" of perfect citizenship? Since they are not yet in a position to give a scientific definition of the soul, they must speak about it in an "image." The image is also "the myth about virtue": it gives a mythical picture of how the soul and the city would have to resemble one another if the right order in the soul (moderation) were to harmonize with the right order in the city and the perfect citizen (justice). Thus through it we begin to learn the psychological obstacles to the unity of virtue.

Underlying the image is a premise that all but removes the possibility of an intrinsic tension between what is good for the soul and what is good for the city or for citizenship. The soul and the city are said to be almost identical, in the most important respect: the law *is* reason ("calculation" or *logismos*—the Athenian never mentions *nous* in this context). Kleinias and Megillus find this amazingly brief definition of law almost incomprehensible. Doubtless they are used to thinking of law as force more than as "calculation" (cf. 723a). Even if it transpires that "true law" includes more calculation than most actual laws possess, the Athenian's definition seems to obscure the bullheadedness of law.

According to the image, "to be stronger than oneself," both in the individual and in the city, now seems to mean the predominance of calculation over all the passions, which pull "against" calculation. No passion, only calculation, is "noble"—in the soul there is no "passion for justice," no "will," and, apparently, no "conscience" (cf. Farabi I 20). Yet, since calculation, though noble and even sacred, is very weak, the "argument" (*logos*) appeals to us to go to the aid of "calculation" (*logismos*) and pull with it "against the others." But what is it that the argument is appealing to within us? The image also leaves unclear how calculation gets its goal or direction. Does the image mean to say that calculation simply figures out its goal for itself? In the preface to the image, the passions are presented in a very simple scheme—pleasure and pain, hope and fear. Immediately after, *eros* and *thumos* are mentioned prominently (645d). Has the image abstracted from the complex natural order within the passions so as to put in relief the difficulties involved in the rule of reason in the city and in the citizen? Yet even if there is such an order of the passions, does that natural order coincide with the order required by perfect citizenship?

The image is followed by remarks which help make its import somewhat clearer. The rule of calculation in a "private individual" means "acquiring within oneself true reasoning about the cords and living according to it." This seems to imply that a true reasoning about the passions gives one both guidance as to the goal of life and the capacity to follow that goal—perhaps by somehow manipulating the opposing passions within oneself. In the image, the Athenian gave the impression that the rule of calculation was the same in the city and the individual. Now he corrects or refines that impression. The city and its citizens "take over a reasoning" from someone else, the city does not "acquire true reasoning within itself" (cf. Farabi I 20). The city cannot really think, for thought is a private activity rather than a political activity, and law, in the final analysis, is at best second-hand calculation. The city is said to take its reasoning either from "a private individual who is a knower" or from "one of the gods." The god is not said to be a knower and the city is not said to have "*true* reasoning"; the implication is that only in some cases will the city have law that is even second-hand truth.

We now understand that the image is intended to help us begin to grasp the distinction between the psychology of the perfect citizen and the psychology of the private individual who is a knower. The obvious next question is, in the case of a city that takes its reasoning about the passions from a knower, what is used to ensure the predominance of calculation in the city and in the souls of its citizens? In the light of the puppet image (645d), the Athenian proceeds to give the first answer to this question and at the same time to demonstrate, finally, the first benefit of drinking parties.

To show how drunkenness helps the soul, the Athenian introduces a thematic consideration of shame, which appears to be the principal iron cord the legislator (647a) should manipulate so as to assist the golden cord within his citizens. The sense of shame can be the source of the citizen's "moderation" and, to a considerable extent, his courage and even justice (647a–b, d, 648c–e). In other words, shame emerges as another conceivable basis for the unity of the virtues; moderation and courage, at any rate, again appear as the same virtue or passion, manifesting itself in two different spheres of life. Yet, just as the attempt to explain moderation as a version of the longing for victory and freedom seems to obscure the obedience and orderliness involved in the virtue, so shame does not quite do justice to the spirited, masterful aspects of courage.

Even as an interpretation of moderation, shame is problematic. Shame is a passion, a fear of the opinions of others. For this reason Aristotle denies that virtue based on shame is true virtue (see the discussion at *Ethics* 1128b 10 ff., and cf. *Charmides* 160e ff.). The puppet image itself implied that the Athenian stranger is here aiming at a form of self-mastery in the citizens that is inferior to what Aristotle calls "ethical virtue." Nevertheless, we should not overlook the fact that in making the citizens "puppets" controlled mainly by fear of the opinion of other citizens and of the legislator, the Athenian has eschewed reliance on the fear of the gods. "Awe" (*aidōs*) is not here called "divine" (contrast 671d), and its usual connotation of awe before gods as well as before men is ignored. The Athenian is not yet ready to invoke the aid of piety, and when he does so it will be less to instill fear than to instill graceful joy (*charis*), to transform traditional piety and to change its psychological emphasis (this is the point of what he says in conclusion: 672a–d).

After introducing shame, the Athenian again recalls the earlier identity of courage and moderation, and asks whether the lawgiver would not wish to make his education in moderation analogous to his education in courage, by exposing his students to the evils against which they must "fight triumphantly" (cf. 647d with 635b–d). If there were a fear-producing drug miraculously analogous to wine, wouldn't the legislator use it? Here the "dialogue" (648a) with the "lawgiver" immediately becomes a dialogue with Kleinias speaking for the lawgiver. We see that the Athenian has already "divined" that Kleinias is in fact about to become a lawgiver (702b–d). Indeed, we can suspect that Kleinias has undertaken the pilgrimage to the cave of Minos and Zeus in order to get some inspiration for the awesome task that lies before him. Didn't the Athenian join the two old men because he had heard of the political project that was afoot and decided to intervene?

The idea of the "drug" is presented mainly as good for testing purposes; the object we thought was in view, the use of the drug for education, comes in only secondarily, in the course of the test. One reason the Athenian thus redirects his argument is that in this way he can avoid having to deal explicitly with the touchy question of drinking parties for the adolescents.

This is not the only slippery feature of the Athenian's argument. When Kleinias is asked if the legislator might not refuse to use the fear-producing drug for some reason, he can see no reason why the legislator would refuse (648c). It is much easier for us than for Kleinias to perceive the dangerous "invasion of privacy" such testing by drugs could imply. The Athenian gives a partial remedy by going on to "add" that everyone must be allowed to practice alone for an indefinite period of time until he feels ready to undertake the public testing. The Athenian thus slips in a provision which implies that much of the "training" by means of drink will be carried out in private, with the publicly supervised drinking parties being like the examinations at the end of the course. Who is to administer these tests and lead the drinking parties? The answer seems to be the legislator himself (648b–c). But the legislator cannot rule in person forever. A more general answer is implied in the Athenian's final remark in Book One. The tests help provide the knowledge of souls; this knowledge is to be used by the art whose business it is to care for souls, politics. Somehow, for the education and testing based on drunkenness to work, the art of politics possessed by the knower-legislator must be preserved. We wonder if it can be preserved in laws and institutions. On the whole, the administrative details of the education and testing through drunkenness remain extraordinarily nebulous. The proposal has not yet been shown to be practical. But has the Athenian been defending the drinking parties as a practical proposal, or has he used the discussion of drinking as a vehicle for introducing the themes he wants to discuss and the mood he wants to discuss them in? The drinking party is either a model or a metaphor for an education that proceeds through the inculcation of shame and the exposure to heady pleasures; we certainly do not yet know the full content of that education.

To understand fully the dramatic reason for the surprising emphasis on drunkenness at the commencement of Plato's most sober dialogue we need to consider not only the subject matter itself and all it may imply for a future civic education, but also the dramatic impact of this topic on the Athenian's two old fellow discussants. Our attention is arrested when the Athenian here characterizes the conversation as a "banquet" (649a; cf. 671b, where he says drinking "is *now* taking place"). The lengthy private discussion of the forbidden plea-

sure of drunkenness and drinking parties has something like the effect of a lengthy private discussion of forbidden sexual pleasures—
the imagination is awakened, the memory and passions are aroused.
The old men become vicariously a bit drunk, or experience in very
mild, imagined and remembered form the effects of drinking
together at a banquet. To a slight extent, they become more youthful
in spirit: less prudent and careful (645e–646a), more cheerful, more
filled with a sense of their power and liberty, freer in speech, and less
hesitant to speak and act (649a–b). In short, by way of the subject
matter the Athenian creates a mood that opens the two old Dorians to
experimentation in speech and deed. Drinking will be like gymnastics for the future citizens and is like medicine for the two old men
(cf. 646c). The Athenian, we can say, becomes the leader of a *symposium* in speech. But does the philosopher follow his own rule and
remain sober? Or must he not become a bit intoxicated himself in
order to forget eternity and take seriously these two old men and
their dedication to the founding of a just regime that will last, at the
very best, only a thousand years or so (cf. 676b–c)?

652a–660a: Education in Music (The Apollonian Regime)

The Athenian has taught that the aim of good laws is to render the
citizens happy and free by making them dedicated to participation in
republican politics. Yet both the satisfaction and the freedom the citizens derive from their political participation seem qualified by the
fact that their political virtue is rooted in shame. Shame is a kind of
fear: that is to say, it is painful and it is not rational (though it can
obey reason). The limitations of the life of the citizen are highlighted
by the subdued contrast the Athenian has drawn with the life of the
"private individual" who is guided not so much by shame or law as
by his own reason. Moreover, though the Athenian implied that
good laws require the assistance of some private individual who is a
knower, he has led us to wonder why a knower would devote himself to a political vocation. In short, the civic way of life the Athenian
has outlined thus far does not yet fully justify the good city's claim to
be the source of happiness—either for the citizens or for a wise
founder. On the other hand, the Athenian has not yet discussed
"music," even though he seemed to say that the discussion of education was for the sake of the discussion of music (642a). In the second
book the Athenian attempts to make more satisfactory his understanding of the goal of politics by using music to enrich civic life and

to reconcile the philosopher and the nonphilosophers. The search for the underlying unity of virtue—the quest for the common good or goal that is shared by political virtue based on passion and philosophic virtue based on reason—continues.

The Athenian begins by asserting that wine parties have a benefit still greater than any mentioned hitherto: they contain a safeguard for education. To understand how this is so, it is first necessary that the Athenian "recollect," in the light of what was learned through the image of the soul, the earlier definition of education. That definition was given "for the purposes of the argument" (643a; cf. 641d, 643e, 644a, e, 646a, 652b), and while the Athenian took more personal responsibility for the first part of it (643b), he ascribed the second part—which so elevated citizenship—to the "wish" of "the moment" (643e–644a). His recollection is, in contrast, emphatically his own statement (653a–c). Accordingly, the recollection makes clear the great difference between virtue proper and the partial, subrational virtue that is education. The new version of the definition is completely silent about citizenship (the words "citizen" and "citizenship" are used only once in Book Two; they appeared eight times in Book One). Hence the goal of education as here defined is no longer so clear. The place taken by the "perfect citizen" in the earlier definition seems to be taken by the "perfect human being": is the perfect human being the goal? Yet according to the new definition, the perfect human being, who possesses prudence, true opinions firmly held, and all the good things that go with these, is not produced by education. The most education can do is habituate the passions in preparation for a consonance with reason that may occur at some later time.

Plato's Athenian thus advances the disturbing thesis that education can appear to be a grand thing, and perfect citizenship can seem to be its goal, only so long as true humanity is kept in the background. For the first time, the Athenian has broken through the barriers the "argument" imposed upon him (cf. 641d, 643a, e, 644a, e, 646a, 652b), and seems to be demanding that the city set itself a suprapolitical goal that eclipses citizenship. Can the city meet such a demand? Kleinias, at any rate, seems oblivious to the implicit challenge.

In response to Kleinias's bland response the Athenian turns back to presenting the "argument," which he now says is "singing," or is a kind of music. The argument's song is concerned not with perfect human beings but with the vast majority of adult humans, who by "nature" tend to become inferior to well-educated children, and who for this reason need the remedial aid given by the gods. For the first time the argument in defense of drunkenness suggests that the gods help men (contrast 644d): the gods are needed primarily to restore subrational virtue to adults.

The Athenian insists that they look to see whether the "argument" holds true in the light of nature. In answer to this demand, the argument reveals that the gods help men by means of music, which brings order to certain motions men share with lower animals. Furthermore, the argument now implies that this music is the same for adults and children, or that the same music provides both education and the safeguard for education. The Athenian's concluding question (654a) suggests that this explanation is incomplete, for he speaks as if the argument had been talking only about the help given by the Muses and Apollo, not that provided by Dionysus (the god of wine and wine parties). The slighting of Dionysian music, and of the safeguard wine parties supply, is apparently what allows the "argument" to leave the false impression that perception of rhythm and harmony is given by the gods, rather than being intrinsic to human nature (cf. 654a with 664e–665b, 672c–d, 673d). There is a higher part of man's musical nature that is only dimly visible in the argument thus far.

Education through shame is now seen to be insufficient. The first education should be through music, because music is the orderly channelling of passions man shares with beasts. Unlike the musical passions, shame is purely human: no part of it is shared with animals. Shame is therefore less capable of bringing order to man's animal passions. Yet music also has a clearer link to the superhuman than does shame. The Athenian is evidently expanding his discussion of education to consider the full range of man's divinity and animality, but is focusing first on the animality.

Kleinias agrees to the new definition, and then to the musical transformation of education, not because he cares for music but because, as we have already seen, he is so careless about education.

Having secured agreement to the proposition that "the first education" should come through music, the Athenian shifts (with breathless speed) to saying that to be educated is the same as to be able to give fine choral performances. When he proceeds to clarify the meaning of "fine performances" he reveals two difficulties in his nascent attempt to assimilate education in virtue to education in music. First, the performer may be educated to sing and dance "finely" (in a technical sense) while the content or message of his songs and dances is not noble. Second, the performance may be technically fine, and in addition the overall message may be edifying, but the performer may dislike the noble parts and take pleasure in the ignoble parts of his performance. By promoting education in music the Athenian may be strengthening the appeal of virtue in some cases but he is also running the risk of diverting education away from the goal of virtue toward other, "purely musical" goals like technique and pleasure. To overcome these dangers, "musical excellence" must be defined much more strictly and narrowly.

I must digress for a moment because in our time it is all too easy for us to fail to see what is at stake, what the problem is with which the Athenian is wrestling. Why should the arts be truncated and censored in the name of civic virtue? Are not the arts choiceworthy for their own sakes, regardless of their effects on "virtue"? Is not freedom the essence of art? When we ask these questions we are thinking of life in a political system which demands almost nothing in the way of political duties from the vast majority of citizens. Plato has insisted on approaching the question of the place of art in life within the context of a small republic which allows and compels every citizen to play a direct, meaningful role in the sovereign governmental decisions that shape his destiny. Such self-government carries with it enormous responsibilities, and hence requires what the Athenian calls virtue—whose delicate and rare preconditions we have been exploring. Now, in addition, the Athenian has undertaken the historically unprecedented task of combining this sort of civic virtue and self-government with artistic excellence. He is seeking to show the possibility of a city that would possess something like the political strength of Sparta but without Spartan philistinism, and something like the artistic splendor of Athens but without Athenian imperialism and civil strife. We have been made less alert to the problem because we have grown used to less careful thinkers, Marx above all perhaps, who praise and exhort to political action in the name of both more direct self-rule and more public dedication to the arts without awareness of the complex tensions and contradictions between the various good things they wish to promote.

In response to the first difficulty he has described, the Athenian suggests that music should be considered "fine" solely when it portrays the postures and sounds of virtue or its image. In this context the only virtue that he mentions is the lowest, courage: why? For one thing, it is easier to imagine the specific postures and tones of courage and cowardice (e.g., in a battle scene) than the ones that would unambiguously represent the other virtues. Courage is, more than the others, a virtue of action, "of the body" (655b), and less dependent on explanatory speech for its expression. If the Athenian's criterion is to be fulfilled for the higher virtues, the performance must rely more on the speeches and the narrative: the city's music will be further from the simple songs and dances of children, or from the animal motions, than Kleinias yet realizes. We must use our imaginations a bit to depict for ourselves just what sorts of music the Athenian means to encourage and discourage. As even the reference to courage shows (654e–655a), the virtues cannot be accurately portrayed except in contrast to the vices. Especially in the cases of the higher virtues, it is doubtful whether their splendor can be displayed without showing them in confrontation with perplexing situations and agonizing choices. We know from what has been stressed before that, on the model of drinking, citizens are to learn self-mastery by being exposed, in controlled and vicarious situations, to ever graver temptations. The intoxicating enhantment of musical poetry and drama is perhaps the most powerful form of such temptation. Does the Athenian not have in mind here an education in poetry that would move from simple tales of heroism to more intricate explorations of the dilemmas of family and city (e.g., *The Odyssey*— cf. 658d)? Would not the audience for each level of temptation or performance have to be carefully tested and selected, and, on the model of drinking parties, would it not be necessary for some poems or plays to be practiced, argued over, and "mastered" in private before the individuals came together to perform them in "public"?

Since the Athenian's first criterion for fine music is so much broader than it originally seems (or than it appears when taken out of the context, the defense of drinking parties), we see that in the city whose education comes through music there will be many temptations. Hence the Athenian must now devote even more attention to the second difficulty, the possible disproportion between the music that is edifying and the music that delights the performers.

We might at first suppose, on the basis of the discussion in Book One, that we could for the most part count on shame to control the danger. This approach to the problem would not require us to force a complete assimilation of education in music and education in virtue: in music education we could focus more on good technique and less on developing the proper inner experience of pleasure in the performer. Music education would merely accompany, and be one of the vehicles for, education in virtue based on shame. This in fact seems to be Kleinias's initial approach, as is indicated by his response (656a; cf. 654d). But the Athenian dislikes the response: he vigorously chides Kleinias's hesitation, and for the first time expresses grave doubts about the strength of virtue based on shame (656b). We gather now that the Athenian proposes to use music not merely to supplement shame but to foster a new kind of virtue rooted in a habituation that gradually establishes a pleasant harmony among the passions. It seems that citizens are to be educated so that they will not feel a competition within themselves between what they enjoy and what they must praise. At the same time, however, we see that the Athenian traces the inner competition to a tension, not between good and bad habits, but between "habit" and "nature" (655e–656a). Can any education, any habituation, correct a "bad nature"? Must the city not continue to rely on shame, at least to control those with bad natures (and perhaps those with superlatively good natures as well)? But will not the power of shame be undermined by the new commitment to pleasure?

Shame is not sufficient to control the pleasures that may be awakened by the civic commitment to music. To bring about the proper habituation of the children, the city will require a much more careful censorship of the poets. Kleinias's reliance on shame allowed a milder censorship than the Athenian will now propose, because he drastically underestimated the seductive power of artistic pleasure. He still has in mind a situation like that of the Dorian cities, where the theater is of minor significance, where there are no Dionysia, and where even Homer is barely familiar (cf. 666d–e, 680c, 886b). The outlook Kleinias begins with is in one respect curiously similar to our contemporary outlook. Part of the reason why we are shocked by the idea of artistic censorship is that we cannot imagine how the artist could be dangerous, except to despotic regimes. We are accustomed to regimes where the artist is left almost completely unhindered but where the artist has no responsibility—because our politics are in no direct way dedicated to, or informed by, the arts. This situation, almost without precedent in the history of the West, is at the heart of the most persistent theme of modern art: the "alienation" of the artist confronted by a social world which neither reflects nor invokes the need for artistic creation. The Athenian, in contrast, is now insisting on a public life that will be preoccupied with creating, performing, and attending musical performances. When the arts, instead of being a superficial adornment for a few, become a serious and central part of a whole society's life, their influence on the character of adults as well as children grows in proportion. We begin to realize how much the Athenian is willing to risk in order to bring about a "musical" city.

The music which was introduced as a great aid to virtue now seems to threaten virtue. The Athenian at once tries to allay the misgivings his elderly interlocutors may feel by returning (for the first time in his discussion of music) to the discussion of "law" (656c) and by praising the "extreme" Egyptian law of censorship. Essential to such law is the ascription of the poetic models to divine authors (the gods provide the occasion for music and also insure its stability). The implicit criticism of all Greek legal systems (cf. 654e) and the superiority of a barbarian female deity (Isis) are perhaps made palatable to Kleinias by the appeal to the old: Egypt is much older than anything Greek, and Isis is older than Apollo. Besides, the Athenian at this point seems willing to sacrifice beauty for stability. For is not experimentation and innovation essential to continued artistic excellence and pleasure? To say the least, the Athenian leaves it unclear whether the Egyptian art that is "in no way more beautiful" than it was at the beginning is "by nature correct." The Egyptian "beginning" was far from perfection in general (657a; cf. 747c). Kleinias is pleasantly "amazed."

Having laid down the criteria and reassured Kleinias (if not Megillus), the Athenian says they can "take heart and elaborate the correct use of music" (657c). In the afterglow of the Egyptian story the Athenian can begin to try to persuade Kleinias to side with "the many" and insist on youthful pleasure as the proper goal for a city's music. To be precise, music is now said to be established by the old so that they may vicariously recapture the joyful motion of youth. It now appears that the best music presents the virtues of action in a way that pleases spectators who are no longer very active themselves. Memory and "recollection" or thought are not the same, but they are akin (cf. 672c).

The music old men like best and which therefore turns out to be best is Apollonian epic poetry; its closest competitor and rival is Dionysian tragedy. It is not difficult to see why these two rank higher than puppet shows and comedy: both tragedy and epic treat seriously the gods, the heroes, and the tradition. The following may be among the reasons why the old men prefer epic, while the majority prefers tragedy: epic is older; epic is more austere while tragedy is more gripping; the gods are more visible in epic; epic requires less deceit in the performance; epic speaks more affirmatively about the divine orderliness of things while tragedy raises dubious or insoluble questions.

A very important question remains. Exactly how is this model music to be used in the education of the young? On a superficial reading, the Athenian may be taken to mean that they are to imitate the Egyptian model; that is to say, only the three poems named, and epics closely imitating them, would be allowed in the city. But this is not what is suggested by what the "argument" says in conclusion, where education is once again redefined. The "argument" here returns to a much more civic perspective on education. For the first time, education is defined in terms of law. Education is now said to aim at the consonance of the passions and the *logos* said to be correct by law and believed to be correct by the oldest and most decent men—the consonance of the passions and reason (*logos* simply), or prudence, or even true opinions, is no longer even mentioned. The aim is to "make the child's soul follow and feel the same joys and pains as an old man." To achieve this very conservative aim, however, the poetic music must consist of "incantations" aimed at the tastes of the *young*.

A more elaborate version of this picture emerges if we look closely at what the Athenian says and does just before he concludes with the new definition (cf. Farabi II 1). In order to choose the proper music for the city as a whole, the Athenian does not simply find out what the old men prefer. He asks Kleinias to consider the preference of the old men in the light of the tastes of the other kinds of people in the city, the others who are to be educated, step by step, to the point where they share the old men's tastes. The choice of the music that pleases the old men is the choice that must "necessarily" be made when the Athenian associates himself with his two interlocutors and their "habituation" (658e). But, the Athenian goes on to add, "for his own part," he conceives of two finer kinds of music, neither of which need be determined by consulting the old. "Almost the finest" is that which pleases the best and the adequately educated; "especially finest" is that which pleases the one man who is distinguished, or different, in his virtue and his education. This latter is the "true judge," and in describing his function the Athenian for the first time refers to a kind of virtue in which all the parts, even courage, are prudence (cf. also 710a). For the "true judge" such courage would be the key political virtue, because he would need it in order to apply his "prudence" in the public "theater" where he would often be in direct opposition to the loudly expressed demands of the vast majority. The Athenian claims to derive his model of such judging from "the ancient Greek law": in some sense, the oldest is still the wisest. The picture that emerges here is of music festivals where a variety of individual compositions are experimented with and then, after a showing, are either encouraged or excluded. Far from preserving the same models and making the audience always feel the same pleasures, the "true judge" is guided by the following principle: "an audience should be continually hearing about characters better than their own, and hence continually experiencing better pleasure" (659c); the theater would be more devoted to progress and innovation than the most democratic theater, precisely because it would be subject to a courageous, prudent judge rather than popular opinion.

What does this latter picture imply about the organization of the civic musical education? The judges or judge would employ a political science of pleasure like the one the Athenian sketches here for Kleinias: knowing the characteristic tastes and temptations of the various key social groups in the society, the judge would know which inclinations to combat in educating each group. In addition, he could use the form of music each group is inclined to enjoy as a device for leading that group toward delighting in a higher form. For example, puppet shows might be arranged in a sequence that would lead toward themes that make clear the limitations of puppet shows and whet the appetite for comedies.

The difficulty of imagining cooperation between the "true judge" and the old men is reflected in the yet unresolved tension, within the dialogue, between the Athenian and his old comrades. After making his most radical remark yet about the need for innovation in music (659c), the Athenian concludes by letting "the argument" present the most conservative definition yet of education.

Even supposing Kleinias accepts only the most restricted interpretation of the Athenian's proposal, he will be accepting a city much more preoccupied with music than any extant Dorian city (or, for that matter, any regime in the twentieth century). Moreover, the city will have not one but three very diverse epic models, the central one being the strange saga of the questionable and wily Odysseus.

Let us sum up what music achieves in what we may call the Athenian's Apollonian regime. Music brings civic virtue closer to happiness by mixing virtue with the physical pleasure of rhythmic motion and the visual pleasure of fascinating images; it thus makes possible an education by habituation that is stronger than the education by shame; music elevates the meaning of virtue by making it an object of the citizen's observation and thought or at least memory (a kind of *theoria*); music gives the poets an important role in civic life; and finally, music attempts to reconcile the philosopher to the city in two ways, by moving the goal of the city a little closer to intellectual virtue and by providing him a possible place, however tenuous, as judge of music alongside the old men.

660b–664a: The Ensnaring of Kleinias

Kleinias is understandably rather uncertain as to just what the Athenian has meant to endorse. His confusion does not, however, prevent him from expressing a strongly negative reaction (the depth of his feeling is revealed by his oath, the first we have heard in the conversation). Kleinias has gathered this much at least: there is something too favorable to innovation, and modern, if not Athenian, ways in what the "stranger" has said (cf. especially 656c, 658e–659a). Refusing to enter into the pros and cons of whatever innovations the Athenian may have intended to propose, Kleinias insists on reaffirming the continuing validity of the Cretan and Spartan system (together with the Egyptian—Kleinias blurs the differences) as the standard for any musical legislation.

The Athenian praises Kleinias for his frank remonstrance, which brings into the open the failure of the Athenian's first cautious attempt to secure agreement on a drastically revised, "musical," Dorian regime. In order to get Kleinias's agreement to such drastic reform, the Athenian will now have to enter more profoundly into the question of the content, or the "arguments" (661c, 664a), of poetic music.

The Athenian's failure at this juncture is twofold, revealing two serious problems. First, he has failed to persuade the future legislator. Through the character Kleinias, Plato reminds us that we cannot realistically expect the legislator to be himself a lover of music and the arts; we cannot therefore expect him to see great immediate attractions in the arts. Second, the Athenian has failed in his attempt to make the future citizens happy by supplementing virtue with music. For in addition to being a prospective legislator, Kleinias—not to speak of the silent Megillus (who is pointedly referred to six times here)—typifies the unmusical character that will be present in many of the citizens even in an Apollonian city. As the drama soon after brings into the open (661d–662a), Kleinias's virtue is grounded in shame, a shame riddled with suppressed longings for pleasure, wealth, and tyranny. Plato implies that this is the sort of inner makeup that is likely to characterize a man of great ambition, willing to undertake the founding of a new regime; but some lesser version of such a makeup is also likely to characterize many citizens whose hearts remain unsatisfied with republican politics, and whose half-conscious longings for tyrannical power will be restrained, if they are restrained, only by shame and fear. On the basis of his own experience of these passions, Kleinias senses grave dangers in the switch to education and virtue based on innovative musical pleasures.

Through the drama here, Plato raises in stark form the question that gnaws at such men, the question of the relation between justice and happiness. Why should politically talented men be just? Why should they share their pleasures and honors with more than a few friends? Do the opportunities of citizenship, the participation in the engrossing challenges of government, justify the self-restraint the city demands? But as a tyrant or member of a ruling clique a man can vastly expand his opportunities to exercise his capacities: the Athenian himself dares to declare here that becoming a tyrant is good for a good man (661b; cf. *Politics* 1325a 34 ff.). Does the civic dedication to the arts justify the self-restraint demanded? It is true, the good the arts provide is of a character very different from the goods money or rule provide. However great a role vanity may play in the artist's soul, neither artist nor audience can enjoy "more" poetry and music by "taking some away" from fellow citizens; on the contrary, the pleasures of the arts—both in performing and in witnessing them—seem enhanced by sharing, even with "competitors." But the question returns: how many citizens will have natures that enjoy music more than rule? Even for those citizens who are naturally "musical," will there not be a part of the soul that longs for tyrannical power? After all, the very themes of the music celebrate not musical performance itself but rather the employment of the active political virtues. How can men like Kleinias be made to agree that the unjust life is necessarily unhappy?

This is the Athenian's reply: "If some god were to give us consonance" (662b). Addressing Kleinias alone as his "friend," the Athenian tells what he would do "if I were a legislator." Then, swearing himself for the first time, swearing in the name of the musical Apollo as well as Zeus, the Athenian commands Kleinias to think about what the gods who are lawgivers, or a man who was a lawgiver and father, would say if he were questioned by one of his citizens or sons.

By bringing Kleinias's corrupt longings to the surface the Athenian shows Kleinias the enormity of the problem: looking within his own soul, Kleinias sees that shame would not be sufficient to restrain the appetites of citizens like himself, if they were given an opportunity for tyranny. Then, by reminding Kleinias of his responsibilities as a father and as future legislator for the new Cretan city, the Athenian leads him to think through for himself the response, the solution to the problem.

What is needed is a "consonance," a music, that sings passionately and convincingly of gods who sanction justice. Only if the legislator "compelled the poets to speak" would there be a chance of creating citizens whose hearts were purer than Kleinias's own, purer than the hearts of the present day Cretans. The legislator needs the poets with their powers of persuasion to create a theology whose "lies," and "myths" (663e–664a), can convince all the citizens, even the un-musical, that the just and the pleasant coincide. In short, piety now takes the place of moderation as the virtue that accompanies and un-derlies justice (cf. 660e with 661b and 661e, 662a, 663b). Piety re-places "the whole of virtue," including prudence (661c). But the po-etic theology must be new, better than any that now exists. The poetry must be superior to that of Tyrtaeus, who failed to support justice adequately, and the theology must be more convincing than that of Homer, Hesiod, Lycurgus, and Minos, whose gods have failed to convince a man like Kleinias (the one myth referred to as a "great example" is non-Greek: 663e). The lawgiver Kleinias is won over to the idea of a musical city with new and more captivating po-etry not because poetry delights him but because he is led to see that poetry is preeminently useful to him. "What follows after this," says the Athenian in conclusion, "would belong to me" (664b): the Athenian has at last secured almost a free hand to give *his* argument, the argument he thinks best.

Yet at the same time the Athenian has indicated that persuasive poetry and the piety founded on such poetry will not be enough. In the present context we hear more distinctly than ever before about the need for compulsion and penalties, especially for the poets, who are less likely to be persuaded by their own inventions (660e, 661c, 662b–c). It is at this point certainly no longer clear that the education and virtue rooted in music is more rational than that rooted in shame. Very much will depend on how much truth is mixed with fic-tion in the new official poetic theology, and how much questioning of that theology is permitted.

What does this remarkable dramatic interlude mean to tell us about the relation of justice and happiness? Does Plato teach here that it is only the belief in myths that can make the noble life identical with the good life, the just with the pleasant? But what then explains the fact that Plato has Kleinias spontaneously agree with the Athenian here? Kleinias agrees because of his devotion to the future city. But why is Kleinias so devoted to the future city? What motivates this unusual Cretan, who no longer believes whole-heartedly in his city's myths, and who was inclined to the view that by nature a state of war exists among all men, even fellow citizens? The Athenian has brought Kleinias's darkest political doubts and longings to the surface and given him a vivid reminder of the shakiness of the grounds for the assertion that injustice necessarily leads to unhappiness. Why has he risked the further corruption of Kleinias? And in doing so, how has he avoided sapping the public spirit of his founder-advisee?

Consider "fame, and the praise that comes from human beings and gods." Is that something unpleasant? "Far from it, friend lawgiver!"

For a man devoted to political action the greatest temptation is tyranny, but the greatest pleasure is fame, and the quasi-immortality that fame can bring. Compared to the gratitude and love that generation after generation of citizens will give to the founder of a strong and free republic, the successes and gratifications of a tyrant seem petty indeed. If the poets, the arbiters of fame, are friendly to him, the founder may eventually be honored as semi-divine. The Athenian risks the further corruption of Kleinias's flagging citizen-virtue in order to replace it with a new form of justice grounded in a sublime selfishness.

Plato teaches that, in the case of the founder, the love of fame is the iron cord that binds pleasure and justice together. Yet it can be doubted whether this solution is altogether satisfactory for anyone except the founder himself. It is true, the pleasure of honor, of public and mutual recognition from uncoerced fellow citizens, is a powerful weight to be added to the scales on the side of the just citizen's life. And, especially in a republic dedicated to music, every citizen will be able to see the fame that might be his. The poets are needed, then, not only for the sake of piety but also to adorn justice and promise fame to the just. In this light, we can understand better why the "end of the whole regime" was said to be "how each of those who has died should be buried and what honors should be allocated to them" (632c; cf. 707b).

Still, granting all this, must we not go on to admit that (as the present drama itself shows) the noble love of fame may lead, when fully developed, beyond the role of law-abiding citizen to the role of the "refounder," whose revolution destroys or eclipses the original founding? If neither political participation by itself, nor civic music by itself, nor lawful recognition by itself, can justify the city's claim to be the source of human happiness, then can all three added together be said to provide a satisfactory and coherent civic goal? Or must we recognize that the Athenian has not yet fully established the city's claim?

664b–674c: Education in Music (The Dionysian Regime)

In the last part of Book Two the Athenian outlines another and higher answer to the question of what the city, at its best, stands for. To our amazement, he begins by saying that the "incantations" for the young will present the gods as saying that the "best" life is the most pleasant life, not that it is the most just life. Apparently the "incantations" will preserve some of the ambiguity of the Athenian's own discussion of the relation between the just, the good, and the pleasant (cf. especially 663c). In the present section, as in the section prior to the interlude that converted Kleinias, the Athenian rarely mentions justice or the "community" (this goes with the complete silence about citizenship in these sections). Devotion to music and devotion to the community (to justice and to citizenship), are still not identical.

The Athenian begins to make the musical organization of the city clearer by introducing the choruses, which are "three in number." An important ambiguity emerges, however: are the men over sixty to be an appendage to the third chorus, or are they to form what is in effect a fourth, prosaic chorus? The place of the old has suddenly become uncertain. The alert old Kleinias is of course uneasy. It is good that he expresses his perplexity, for we now learn that "most of the arguments" have been for the sake of the third, Dionysian chorus. But before the Athenian will consent to clarify what he means by this chorus, before the city can come to be dominated by the highest sort of music, Kleinias must agree that education in music is to be extended to women and slaves as well as free males, that the city must continually be performing music, and that there must be "continual change, presenting variety in every way, so that the singers will take unsatiated pleasure." The Dorian standards, not to speak of the

Egyptian, have been left far behind. No wonder the place of the old men has become uncertain.

At first the Athenian starts to explain that the Dionysian chorus of the aged and prudent is the most important element in the city because of the educational service it performs for the rest, singing in public at the theater (665d–e). But after asking how they might encourage the *older* men to sing in public, the Athenian shifts to a very different description of the membership and activity of this "chorus." The new description centers on a new use of drinking parties. The drunkenness which in Book One was defended as a means of education and testing the younger men is said here to be for the sake of rejuvenating the men over thirty. Drunkenness is now forbidden to men under thirty. The rejuvenation of the middle-aged, as well as old, men, and their subsequent musical performances together, are now said to take place not in public but in private, at "enjoyable common meals" where the middle-aged and old gather in small groups of intimates. Before, the lives of the mature men seemed wholly serious; their music is now said to be play, and under the aegis of Dionysus their piety goes with their play (rather than with their justice or shame).

After reflecting on this description we begin to suspect that the Athenian meant that most of the arguments were "for the sake of" this chorus in the sense that the activity of this chorus is itself the purpose and goal of the city. Certainly the chorus's role as a means to something else—above all to educating the young—has suddenly become obscure. How will any of the young even get to hear the "most beautiful songs" (665d, 666e)? At this juncture, the Athenian provides a kind of answer in the form of an attack, his strongest attack yet, on the Dorian cities and especially on the collectivist and militarist educational institutions they provide for their young. The Dorians "have really never attained to the most beautiful song," because education in the most beautiful music is impossible as long as the young people remain together in a "herd." In language reminiscent of Socrates on trial, the Athenian asserts that the highest musical education can take place only when one drags a youngster apart and gives him a "private groom," a single teacher who will converse with him alone and in private (cf. *Apology* 20a–b). Kleinias's protest makes the Athenian realize that he perhaps went too far; he again disavows full responsibility for the argument; but whereas before "the argument" seemed to express views that were more civic and less suprapolitical than the Athenian's, the situation now is no longer so clear (667a, 670a, 671a).

Who is this "most beautiful Muse" whose epiphany has over-shadowed both of the traditional male gods, and who calls for such an extraordinary private education? In order to make Kleinias understand and accept a "chorus" devoted to the new Muse, the Athenian asks him to consider closely a threefold distinction between the charming or pleasant, the correct, and the beneficial. He illustrates this distinction with two very diverse sorts of pursuit—eating food and learning the truth. These two can be said to represent roughly the lowest and highest points in the spectrum of human pursuits, and we surmise that the most beautiful music falls between them. Even the highest part of the best practicable city cannot simply pursue the truth, because it must spend too much of its energies thinking about how to obtain "nourishment in general" for the city. The city can pursue only "images of virtue" (655b; cf. 668b). The city can know philosophy only dimly, in the guise of a "Muse"—though it can accord to this Muse image very great honor. To learn what sort of musical or artistic activity this is, we must try to grasp just what the Athenian intends by his discussion of the three possible sources of "seriousness" in art. On a first reading, the general impression conveyed is that "charm" means the pleasure art affords, "correctness" the accuracy of its imitations, and "benefit" ("the third thing"—670e) the moral edification it provides. Yet as one inspects the discussion, the threefold distinction, as applied to art, becomes more problematic.

The first difficulty is the ambiguity of "correctness" in art. Correctness is itself twofold, involving: a) knowing and being able to present the truth, or "the being that is intended" by the image, and b) knowing the proper artistic techniques by which harmonious and rhythmic (and not merely exact) images of the "being" are created. Initially the Athenian focuses on the first of these two aspects (667d ff.). But in doing so, he is drawn into what he explicitly admits is "not a very clear" (668d) account of artistic activity. By stressing the need for exact accuracy of correspondence between the truth about the being and the representation of it, the Athenian winds up characterizing "correctness" as if it were mathematical or scientific representation (667d, 668a, b). As a result, in order to characterize art properly he is compelled to do one of two things: either to create what is in fact a fourth element of art—aesthetic expertise—which he calls production of "similarity" or "resemblance" (667d, 668b), or to speak as if the "third" element were not moral "benefit" (nobility), but knowledge of "beauty" in an aesthetic sense—knowledge of "how well" the "correctly" apprehended being is translated into harmonious musical images (668d, 669b, and especially 669a: to know the "truth" about an image is not necessarily to know its "beauty"). Now instead of dealing with this difficulty in a straightforward way, explaining that art in fact has four and not just three elements, the Athenian slips into speaking as if "correctness" meant just aesthetic expertise, the tasteful and appropriate matching of words to tune, key, and rhythm (670b–c).

There is an undeniable link between "correct" knowledge of a being and "correct" knowledge of how to present that being in a harmonious artistic way; but it is also undeniable that these two sorts of knowledge are not the same. The Athenian does in fact give one succinct and precise formulation of the true nature of artistic representation: music "contains a resemblance to the imitation of the beautiful" (668b). Music presents its objects at two removes from being; in the best case, it receives its raw material from scientific representations, which are accounts that are only one remove from being. But why then does the Athenian leave his general discussion of "correctness" in such ambiguity?

The reason is this: his discussion reflects perfectly the ambiguous character of the proposed highest chorus's preoccupation with knowledge. The chorus's quest for truth will not be purely philosophic or scientific, but will be instead mingled with, and diluted by, its concern for artistic technique and tasteful harmony. The highest chorus, we may say, will be closer to being artists and art critics than to being philosophers. Its best members might remind one of Lessing. Nevertheless, we must not underestimate how much knowledge these strange new Platonic statesmen-musicians are supposed to possess. The Athenian uses the example of the knowledge of bodies and especially the human body (668d–669a). Clearly, this will be only the beginning. The music of the city will portray the soul animated by the virtues; it will portray the gods. The highest chorus must therefore have knowledge of the being that is the soul and the being that is god.

Once we have understood better what the Athenian intends by "correctness," we are in a position to grapple with the second difficulty, the status of "pleasure." Initially, the Athenian seems to denigrate pleasure while elevating correctness; he leaves the relative rank of the "beneficial" unclear (667d ff.). But in the midst of his demotion of pleasure the Athenian pauses to define "play." Play is pleasure that produces no "serious" harm or benefit (667e: the definition itself leaves unspecified the relation of play to correctness).

Now the supreme chorus is repeatedly said to be preoccupied with play and harmless pleasure (666b, 670d, 671e), and the chorus members are said to be "at the age when pleasure blooms" (669d). How can this emphasis on play be consistent with the devaluation of pleasure? What the Athenian says is consistent only if we take him very literally. Pleasure alone and "pleasure with untrue opinion" are indeed not appropriate criteria for the most beautiful music (667d–e, 668b); but pleasure or play put together with a concern for truth and true opinion is an appropriate criterion for some of the most beautiful music. The highest chorus, insofar as its activity can be called "play," is more concerned with its own pure pleasure, and less concerned with "benefiting" itself and others, than at first may appear.

Just as the Athenian must obscure somewhat the importance of pleasure and play in the highest chorus's activity, so the third chorus cannot be allowed to abandon itself to the pleasure of the highest Muse; for She must share her power with Dionysus and the other traditional gods (671a, e). The "most beautiful" Muse must be most beautiful in a morally beneficial sense (most "noble") as well as most beautiful in an aesthetic or theoretic sense (recall again the ambiguous use of the term "beauty" at 668d, 669a–b). The singing of the chorus is partly voluntary but partly "compelled," we are reminded (670d), and at some point the members must leave off their private carousing and assume public responsibilities, supervising the music and education of the city as a whole. In order to have "adequate incantations for the young," in order to make all the citizens "noble," the Dionysian chorus members must surpass the poets; they must rule over the poets and not merely drink and sing with them as equals. In the light of their supervisory responsibilities they are themselves in need of being supervised. That supervision will come about through their bowing to the laws, which restrain through "justice" based on shame. To insure that the chorus will remember all this, sober old men are to be made "Dionysian leaders" of the drinking parties, and share command with the "generals," who are not necessarily old (671d–e).

The program for the Dionysian chorus meetings is therefore not clear-cut. Within the chorus there will be a delicate, complex, and never resolved competition between the pleasurable pursuit of truth through artistic criticism and the beneficial pursuit of improved citizenship education. Plato compels us to use our own imaginations in pondering what the meetings will look like; yet he also assists us, with his superior imagination. For one can say that at every meeting some version of the drama presented in this dialogue—the eternal confrontation between the philosopher and the old citizen—will be reenacted. The drama in the *Laws* is Plato's concrete presentation of the highest activity possible within the official life of the city. To understand the Dionysian chorus, we must understand the drama in the *Laws* and then envision for ourselves the various adaptations it must undergo in the variety of historical times and places where it is conceivable. Plato does not set easy tasks.

If we turn back to the dramatic action at the end of Book Two to seek further guidance as to the character of the chorus meetings, we find the comparatively younger (cf. 892d) Athenian providing an example of bold insubordination to his elder's command (673c ff.). After tantalizing Megillus and Kleinias with the promise of a long chat about gymnastics, he refuses to deliver. Of course, unlike Megillus and Kleinias, who are vicariously a bit drunk (671b), the old leaders of the proposed Dionysian chorus are enjoined to remain sober—unless they too can be made vicariously drunk by their younger subordinates. I conclude that it is difficult to predict exactly what the Dionysian banquet will be like from day to day.

The third chorus justifies the city because through it the city can claim to come close to providing, for some of its citizens, rational self-consciousness and an opportunity to exercise not only the active, political virtues but also the intellectual and artistic virtues, in the pleasing and inspiring company of friends. Of course, if the city is to be truly just, it must create institutions which allow every citizen whose nature qualifies him for such happiness the opportunity to try to attain it. For the many citizens whose natures do not so qualify them, the city claims to provide the less perfect version of happiness to be found in the public cultivation of music, political participation and fame, family life, and private property. We will not be allowed to forget that it also includes dangerous military service and a very strict penal code.

Thus far, only the higher aspects of the Athenian's political program have been presented, and even those only in outline. We should not be too surprised to discover that, as the Athenian fills in his canvas, some of the original outline must be altered. In fact, we learn immediately that the whole discussion thus far must be qualified, or even rethought, because it has proceeded on a certain level of abstraction. In focusing on the "vocal aspect, reaching to the soul," the Athenian has slighted gymnastics, the "bodily aspect" of poli-

tics. In attending to the high goal or end, the Athenian has had to neglect the beginning—the original, primitive needs from which civic
life first springs and which the city never leaves behind. Book Three
will have as its theme "gymnastics" in this broad sense; expressed
dramatically, the time is rapidly approaching when Megillus, and all
that he represents, will take a more active role.

PART TWO: *Gymnastics*

676a–683b: The Pre-Dorian Origins

The third book of the *Laws*, like the first book of Aristotle's *Politics*,
testifies to Rousseau's claim that all political philosophers feel
required to return to a study of man's prepolitical condition. In striving for knowledge of those fundamental needs whose satisfaction is
the purpose of political life and which therefore provide the objective
norms for political deliberation, the philosophers must sooner or
later come to terms with the fact that developed political life emerges
late, after eons of precivic existence; moreover, when it does emerge
it seems to be remarkably fragile (676b–c). Does this not suggest that
civic life is artificial, or the result of divine intervention, or a product
of accident, rather than the response to permanent human needs? Although the classical political theorists deny these inferences, and all
their momentous consequences, they feel compelled to give an account of the massive difficulty from which Rousseau starts: the natural necessity of man's historical evolution from precivil to civil life
must be made plausible.

But the attempt to give such an explanation poses grave political
risks. Political society urges us to believe that man is so situated, in
relation to nature or god, that he is better off in a life of peaceful cooperation than in a life of radical independence, conspiring exploita-
tion, or marauding; an investigation into man's origins that cuts beneath the veneer of contemporary convention may not give
unambiguous support to this belief. Even Plato and Aristotle indicate that their inquiries lead to the conclusion that man is not *simply* a political animal by nature. That is to say, the permanent needs
and impulses that become fully visible only in developed urban life
are qualified and sometimes even contradicted by equally permanent
needs and impulses that are more visible in preurban society. The
philosopher with a sense of political responsibility therefore feels

constrained to mitigate the dangerous conclusions that may be drawn from his archaeological inquiries: this is the most important reason why both Plato and Aristotle present their accounts of man's prepolitical past in terms of selective appeals to "myth," ambiguous poetic quotations, and quasi-religious demands that we "believe" (cf. *Politics* 1256b 10 ff.). Still, it is the case, of course, that in the *Laws* the investigation of man's precivil past takes place in the context of the education of a future founder. The founder's project requires him to learn more than the ordinary statesman need learn about the root causes of political disruption and radical change; the dangerous tensions and prejudices inherited from the distant past may and must be spoken of more freely, because the founder will have to decide how to deal with them, and because there is some hope that his new beginning may be able to mitigate them.

The Athenian begins by leading the future founder to a height from which he can see his own project in the perspective of the perishability, the evanescence, of every regime and city. He must pay heed to the "ancient sayings" that tell of periodic cataclysms that have destroyed, and will destroy again, almost every trace of civilization. Unlike the versions Kleinias has probably heard before (cf. 713b–c), as the Athenian tells it the brutal ugliness of what has been is not softened by any indication that the catastrophes are meaningful acts—the just punishment wrought by solicitous gods in response to avoidable human sin. There is no indication that what we do, or what a god might do or promise, can avert the next catastrophe (contrast *Genesis* 9:8–17). There is not even clear grounds for the hope that a remnant of humanity will survive the next disaster. In short, Kleinias and Megillus must recall what men in general had to forget or reinterpret before they were able to dwell in cities (682b–c). The vision the Athenian gives his students reminds one of the kind of vision Machiavelli wants his students to have (*Discourses* II 5). Although he does not go so far as Machiavelli, the Athenian must to some extent liberate his student-founders from certain delusions— from too-great hopes for nonhuman assistance and from overconfident belief in the stability of man's present, civilized, condition (cf. Farabi III 1). Yet for Machiavelli, the frightening knowledge about man's nakedness before nonhuman nature merely enlarges and completes the frightening knowledge about man's original, natural treatment at the hands of his fellow man. The Athenian, in contrast, blunts the impact of the vision of the cataclysm by turning immediately to a comforting description of man's original relation to his fellow man.

The Athenian argues that the pervasive fear in which prepolitical man lived (677e, 678c, 682c) did not reduce him to a condition of wolfishness, but instead rendered him gentle and peaceful. The loss of the arts would have left men unaware of the luxuries which promote inequalities and competition, and ignorant of the major means for injuring and dominating one another. Human encounters would have been joyful, because when men are scarce they take a natural delight in one another's company (678c,e).

This does not mean to say that primitive men dwelled in a state of instinctual harmony, nor in the sort of cooperation Socrates describes in the "city of pigs" (*Republic* 369d ff.). Unlike Socrates, the Athenian describes men who are aware of a latitude in their behavior and who possess a sense of the "shameful" and the "noble" (679c). Ruling over this sense of shame is their powerful belief in the gods, with regard to whom their ignorance makes them extremely credulous (679c, 681b): the gods are more numerous and wield their greatest and most direct influence after each catastrophe. Does this help explain why they fail to prevent the disasters? Certainly, we now learn, the gods can and do intervene to some extent in the process: a god has given human beings the molding and weaving arts, so that the human race may grow and progress after each disaster (679b). But no god encourages men to go down in the valley and practice farming, not to speak of the other arts (682c): however much they care for men, the gods are reluctant to favor men who leave behind the life of herding (cf. *Genesis* 4:2–7). The Athenian's implication is this: if it is true that simple, unquestioning, faith is to some degree necessary for man's happiness, and if the establishment of cities tends over time to develop a level of sophistication that makes such belief more and more impossible, then perhaps the periodic cataclysms are not entirely bad for man. This possibility has as much bearing on our reflections about the fate of man in the twenty-first century as it has on our reflections about man in the distant past.

Early men were not only more peaceful and trusting than civilized men; the Athenian goes on to ask Kleinias to agree that they were "simpler and more courageous and also more moderate and in every way more just" (679e; cf. 680e). He thus compels us to wonder again about the unity of virtue. By now we have come to understand that the coherence of virtue is problematic not only because virtue comes to sight as a plurality of four cardinal "parts" but also because each of those parts can exist in more than one version. Moderation, for instance, can be rooted in self-restraint, or shame, or habituation, or calculation, or obedience to superiors (including gods). The behavior dictated for each virtue varies somewhat according to which psychological version of the virtue one focuses upon. What is more, the variety of psychological versions of each virtue implies a number of permutations and combinations of the cardinal parts of virtue; and the ranking of the parts in relation to one another differs from one such combination to another. For example, we have learned that when the virtues are rooted in self-restraint, then courage seems fundamental and the other virtues seem derivative; when the virtues are rooted in a sense of shame, then moderation and justice are preeminent; when the virtues are rooted in pleasant habituation, moderation and wisdom seem fundamental. A full grasp of the unity or *idea* of virtue entails understanding all the various psychological versions of each of the cardinal virtues, then knowing the extent to which each version may be combined with versions of each other cardinal virtue, and finally, knowing what the rank of the various combinations is and which is appropriate to each sort of political group and each sort of private person.

Thus far in the *Laws,* the Athenian has explained how several psychological versions of the cardinal virtues may fit together in a rather tense and complex harmony, each version of each virtue playing a role in the education and fulfillment of a section of the citizenry of a city openly dedicated to virtue. Now he presents us with a very different version of the virtues, a version based on the lack of education and on the utter absence of city life. He seems to suggest that this version is superior to any civic virtue; yet in practically the same breath he insists that primitive man, who possessed this sort of virtue, lacked "much virtue" (678a–b). More precisely, while the Athenian suggests that primitive man might have been superior as regards courage, moderation, and justice, he does not begin to ask whether primitive man was superior in wisdom; primitive man had no wisdom of any kind (cf. 679c). His simplicity, piety, and credulity took the place of wisdom.

What does this praise for a version of virtue the city can never possess imply about the virtue the city will possess? Plato's Athenian challenges, here, all civic excellence in the name of primitive innocence. He thus indicates that if one sets aside wisdom, if one conceives of virtue insofar as it does not depend upon or promote knowledge (and virtue can be so conceived), then the city's virtue becomes questionable. Confirming the impression we received from the last part of Book Two, the Athenian implies that the city's claim to be the locus of human excellence can in the final analysis be vindicated only on the basis of the hypothesis that man is mutilated without the pursuit of wisdom. The fullest *raison d'etre* of the city is then to awaken and satisfy the natural human desire to know. Yet very few men live mainly for the sake of knowledge; most are tempted to use knowledge as a means to other desires. In giving men the power that goes with knowledge of the arts and of nature, the city makes it possible for human behavior to become much less decent than it was prior to the emergence of cities. As a consequence, political virtue must be directed at controlling and repressing the potential for evil that knowledge brings, and it becomes doubtful whether civic virtue can actively and strongly promote the increase of knowledge. This is the root of the insuperable ambivalence of political virtue.

By the time the Athenian has finished his description, it has become difficult to discern any reason why primitive men would have left their peaceful and plentiful situation to form cities under laws (680a). On this all-important point the Athenian remains strangely reticent, unless his passing reference to population growth can be considered an explanation (678b, 682c; cf. 680e). The first walls were created by farming peoples "on account of wild beasts" (681a). The farming people's need for city walls becomes more intelligible on the basis of what is embedded in the Athenian's quotation from Homer in this context. Like Aristotle in the *Politics* (1252b 23 ff., 1253a 7), the Athenian forces his listeners to reconsider and question his explicit description of early man by using the cruel, impious, and cannibalistic Cyclops as his one and only example of prepolitical man. In the *Laws*, this use of the Cyclops passage is consistent with the later reference to the impiety and "harshness" of man's "ancient Titanic nature" (701c), and accords perfectly with the Athenian's assertion in Book Two that man at the beginning is "completely mad" and remains so until he possesses "prudence" (672c). The arts, after all, are "gentle" (709c); they soften man by bringing comfort and security (as Kleinias notes here, Homer belongs to "urban" life). Innocence, credulity, and lack of sophistication can go hand in hand with brutality and cruelty. Men were glad to see one another, the Athenian has said, because of "scarcity of numbers" (678c,e): but what happened in those places, like islands and rich pasture lands, where men ceased to be scarce (cf. Farabi III 2)? Exactly what meats were eaten during and just after the cataclysm (cf. 677e–678a with 679a and 782b)? In the light of the terrifying memory of the cataclysm, what sorts of gods might men have believed in, and what sorts of sacrifices

[427]

might those beliefs have demanded (782c; cf. 672c and *Minos* 315b–c)? In his description of early times, the Athenian never used the term "man" (*anēr*) but only the term "human being" (*anthrōpos*). After the Cyclops is introduced, we learn that there were two sorts of clans, the "more orderly" and the "manly" (681b; cf. 831e–832a). We conclude that the Athenian's description has focused exclusively on the more orderly clans, even though he indicates that the predations of the "manly" clans may have played a key role in urging mankind along the path to urban existence. It is in principle possible that the process was peaceful, the Athenian suggests, but the primary reason for the coming into being of walls and cities probably had a great deal to do with the need for security against other *humans*. The Athenian has played down these facts because he wished to confront squarely the challenge posed to civic virtue by the possibility, however slight, of primitive "goodness," and because he needed to counteract Kleinias's original tendency (cf. 702d) to see the city as exclusively an armed alliance among families enmeshed in permanent war. (Kleinias's ignorance of Homer probably leaves him in the dark as to the Athenian's real teaching about the beginnings; here and in much of Book Three, Megillus is clearly the more knowledgeable interlocutor.) Henceforward, however, the "facts" will compel the Athenian to concede more and more to the original Kleinian outlook.

Apparently guided by Homer, the Athenian now focuses on the patriarchal family as the unit of society in primitive times. The city comes into being out of the union of clans, each of which enters the civic association with its own peculiar gods and exclusive customs. Legislation, at the dawn of political life, was the process of selecting among the diverse gods and clan-customs those that were to be preserved—and casting all the rest into oblivion (681c–d). At least at the beginning, then, civic legislation involves the outright rejection of many gods and of customs held sacred by most of the families within the city. How confident can we be that the suppression of the family's independence is permanent (cf. 708d)? May not human nature remain, at its core, more familial than political (cf. *Ethics* 1162a 15 ff.)? The tension whose rudiments the Athenian exposes here will reemerge.

Only after the families had been integrated into the civic whole, only after many gods had been forgotten, can man be conceived of as having forgotten the primeval terror and as having finally reestablished true cities in the rich lands of the plain. In describing this "third pattern of regime" the Athenian returns again to his "divine" authority, Homer. But like the original legislators who picked and chose the gods they would make authoritative, so the Athenian picks and chooses from the divinely inspired texts those he wishes to make authoritative. In particular, the Athenian's version of Homer, which he says follows "nature" as well as "god," omits entirely Homer's emphatic reference to the essential role Zeus played in "begetting" the founder of the second pattern of regime: in the new version it is suggested, in suitably muted fashion, that the founders chose and therefore "begat" Zeus, not vice versa. In the reworking of Homer, the role played by Zeus—the first stage—is played by Cyclops.

Having reached the point where the complete city has emerged, the Athenian no longer suppresses mention of war. Once the city is fully grown it is no longer possible, even in mythic history, to conceive of a world at peace. The complete absence of any reason for the war among the cities points to the likelihood that the wars among cities are merely continuations of lesser wars among clans. This likelihood is also hinted at by the fact that, unlike Homer, the Athenian devotes more attention to the familial and civil wars that accompanied the first great international war than he does to that war itself. The process of resolving these troubles leads to a new, fourth, and final stage of civic evolution: somehow the third was not as complete as we supposed. The absent warrior-rulers of the "third" city were betrayed within their own "cities and homes" (682d). Was this betrayal not the counterrevolution of the family, of the old matriarchy and patriarchy (cf. Aeschylus's *Oresteia*)? This much is clear: according to the Athenian's myth, it was the warriors' reorganization and reconquest of their homes and cities that brought into being the Dorian way of life, with its stringent subordination of the family and the women, its all-male common meals, and its preoccupation with war and gymnastics. The "deeds" of history thus seem to justify at least the Spartan branch of the Dorians in a way Kleinias was unable to do in "speeches" for the Cretan branch. The Spartan-Dorian laws seem to be the necessary historical culmination of the process which brings political life to its maturity.

"As if according to god" they have returned to the beginning, to the praise of the Dorian laws. Suddenly, in the light of the reflections on history, all the talk about music and drunkenness appears as a "digression." Their return to the beginning, however, focuses on the more modern Sparta, not the more ancient Crete. In neglecting Sparta the conversation was surely unfair to the Dorians. For the

Spartans are in a sense the greater Dorians; they express themselves more in deed, and less in boastful speech (cf. 641e), and it is the Spartans far more than the Cretans who have filled the stage of Greek history with noble and unforgettable exploits (683e–684a). But what will be learned by doing full justice to the Spartans?

683b–702a: The Drama of Megillus

Megillus's response to the Athenian's proposal that they begin anew is the most enthusiastic he will be heard to utter. And it is not difficult to see why. The Athenian has not only proposed a new beginning that promises to do justice to Sparta; in addition, he has woven together a new version of Homeric history that obscures the role of that embarrassing Spartan, Helen, and that transforms the Dorian invaders into the direct descendants of the heroes who triumphed at Troy. He has made Homer no longer "alien" to Dorian culture (cf. 680c–d). For the first time, Megillus is in a position to see solid advantages in the idea of a city founded on a new poetry that blends and reworks the traditional epic models. Throughout the earlier discussion of music Megillus preserved an unaccommodating silence; now, in Book Three, the Athenian begins to win Megillus's support for a reform of poetry and a new Dorian regime based on that reform.

What we must wonder, of course, is what reason Plato has for placing this dramatic obstacle in the way of the conversation: what makes the presence and persuasion of a man like Megillus necessary to *the* Platonic conversation about law and the founding of the best practical regime? After reflecting on Megillus's role in the dialogue as a whole, I am inclined to think that he has an importance that is out of all proportion to the brevity of his utterances and the simplicity of their content. For Megillus resembles, much more than does Kleinias, a typical citizen of the future regime that is to be founded (cf. *Republic* 545a, 547e–548a).

Kleinias is more intelligent, imaginative, and ambitious than is Megillus or the bulk of the future citizens. We have by now gotten to know him well enough to understand that despite his age and training, he is a somewhat restless and even morally questionable old man. It is almost inevitable that a founder capable of being influenced by a philosopher should have such a character. These same qualities that open Kleinias to the charm of the innovative Athenian can make him somewhat impatient with the restrictions imposed by the necessity of creating a city for men who will be, for the most part, inferior to both the Athenian and himself. At the crucial moment in the dialogue when the Athenian starts to neglect the task at hand and drift into reflections on god and man that are unsuited to a conversation about a founding, it is Megillus, not Kleinias, who calls him back to earth (804b; cf. 716a–b: Kleinias is more ready to follow God than Justice; but cf. 769a). At the end of the day it is the firm and phlegmatic Megillus who insists that Kleinias and he must use any means necessary to make the Athenian stay and take an active part in the founding (969c–d). To an even greater degree than Kleinias, Megillus insists that the Athenian's speech be a program for action.

By including Megillus in the conversation, then, Plato establishes a pedestrian check on both the philosopher and the founder who is open to philosophy. Moreover, by including in the conversation a character who approximates the future citizens, Plato insures that everything said will be acceptable—even if not always fully comprehensible to them (cf. 891a).

Here in Book Three, we see that what the conversation with Megillus introduces is an attitude of dogged reservation as regards the high-flown domestic or musical goals the Athenian has proposed and a sober concern for foreign policy, for political offices and institutions, and for the creation of a respectable, patriotic, historical tradition (cf. *Hippias Major* 285d). By being forced to win over Megillus the Athenian is forced to make his political science and political poetry respond to these very legitimate demands.

The explicitly "mythical" history of Greece that the Athenian proceeds to unfold is intended to elaborate and make firmer the "argument" that the downfall of a regime is due to the rulers themselves and not to outside forces, or chance (683e, 685d–e, 688c–d, e, 695e). As the Athenian repeatedly reminds us (683e, 688b–c), a version of this "same argument" was presented in the summary of the finest lawgiver's intention (631b–c). The argument is certainly in need of being substantiated: to say nothing of its inherent dubiousness, the Athenian himself attacked Megillus's subsequent appeal to it (638a–b). In its original version, the argument stated that a city's possession of the four virtues guaranteed its prosperity; the more modest version presented now speaks only of a guarantee against dissolution of rule, and does not yet specify what qualities the city or its rulers must possess. In Book One the argument formed part of a speech that made no reference to piety or the gods; now the Athenian reintroduces the argument with one of his rare oaths. This passionate appeal to Zeus reminds us that pious belief in the assistance of a god would make the guarantee much more plausible (cf. 686a, 690c, 699c).

As the Athenian launches into his account of the qualities that seemed to promise success for the Spartan system, we see that the excellences he is appealing to and investigating are no longer the four virtues, but instead certain more narrowly political policies. Spartan tradition apparently teaches that in order to achieve stability and security from barbarians what is needed is not education in virtue, based on three republican choruses, but a foreign policy of confederacy, based on three monarchies and three populaces. This mutual checking mechanism needs to be cemented by pious oaths and rooted in a degree of economic equality.

Awakening Megillus's nostalgic regret, the Athenian dwells on the beauties of the ancient confederation and the enticing possibility of universal Dorian hegemony that it seemed to insure. Yet the Athenian will not let Megillus forget that somehow things just didn't work out as one might have hoped. "What sort of chance was it that ever destroyed so great a system?"—especially when its solid policies were rooted in intimate family kinship among the rulers, and informed by the voice of the Delphic Apollo (686a–b). The reminder that things went wrong, and that they must investigate why, goes together with a reminder that what they are doing is mere unserious play. The Athenian thus removes the sting from his suggestion that the cause of failure may lie in precisely the sort of experience this Athenian and this Spartan have been having together: the thoughtless admiration for everything big and strong. By pretending to stumble into the error along with Megillus, and by using Theseus (the founder of Athens) as the chief historical example for the error, the Athenian allows Megillus to admit the error without losing his dignity. He prompts Megillus to recognize for himself that the one thing most needed is not freedom or empire (687a), or even the Delphic Oracle, but "intelligence" (*nous*, 687e). Nor is this all. By laughing at himself, by evincing a posture of Socratic, "human," humility (686c–d), the philosopher leads the citizen to entertain—even if only half seriously—a profound theological innovation: "it is dangerous for one who lacks intelligence to pray" (688c). The Athenian's thesis here is this: the insistence that virtue imply power and happiness, that at the least it be a guarantee against political failure and unhappiness, necessarily leads men to "pray," because concerned gods must exist if the link between virtue and happiness is to hold. But the very awareness of our inadequacy that compels us to pray also leads us to admit that we do not yet know what is best, and do not know how to use what is "fine"; we therefore do not yet know what to pray for. Even worse, we must confess that we do not know god well enough to be certain he will correct our mistaken prayers. The only thing we know, therefore, is that we need intelligence. For that, and its preconditions, we can consistently strive and pray. Only by confronting and accepting this situation do men become prudent: power does follow virtue in the limited sense that the prudent tend to be less dissatisfied than others with the amount of power they already have. Virtue so understood does include a kind of piety, if only because the virtuous are led away from the ordinary form of *hubris*, the lust for power (cf. 691c–d).

In denying the gods' comprehensibility the Athenian does not deny here either their existence or their concern with men. In the case of the city at least, evidence of the inscrutable gods' special favor can and should figure in the city's interpretation of its own past (691d; cf. 681b, 691b,e, 692b, 699c). But neither the city nor the individual can leave it at simple obedience—to the elderly, to one's father, or to the god. Neither Sparta nor Plato's Socrates can blindly follow the Delphic Oracle, for they cannot be sure they understand the oracle. Throughout Book Three, the Athenian points the way to an epic tradition in which the role of the gods would be more distant and less graphic, and hence more in accord with the austere truth about man's relation to god.

Of course, by now we are hardly surprised to find that intelligence must be much diluted in order to become an object of the laws' or the city's striving. Following the lead of Megillus, the Athenian here treats intelligence, prudence, and opinion as if they were identical (687e; 688b,e, 689a,b). Thus, in his own manner, the citizen Megillus is won over to wholehearted agreement with the view that "intelligence" is the preeminent political good. On the other side, the philosopher has had to concede that in its political manifestation intelligence must concern itself with power, and attend to confederacies, property distribution, and other such stuff. As for the lawgiver Kleinias, he now for the first time in the dialogue spontaneously refers to the need for divine cooperation (688e; cf. 625c and 702c): could it be that the Athenian's strange new suggestions concerning prayer have made god seem more plausible and important again to this old Cretan?

When the conversation turns to an inquiry into what the political equivalent of intelligence might be, Kleinias naturally comes to the fore again as interlocutor. The Athenian focuses on what is needed to prevent the greatest lack of intelligence, or, in other words, what is needed to provide "even the smallest form of prudence" (689d). This minimal intelligence that is needed to prevent a city's downfall turns out to be self-restraint. Self-restraint is the "harmony" created by the obedience of the passions to "opinion" in the individual citizens, and by the obedience of the populace to the rulers and laws in the city. At first, it sounds as if Kleinias and his "friend" (689c) are about to resume the conversation in Book Two: the city will prosper if the souls of the citizens are consonant, i.e., moderate, and "consonance" is created by the pleasing habituation of music (cf. 691a), supervised by a wise Dionysian chorus. But because the conversation is now aimed at the more sober Megillus it can only point, it can no longer move, in such a direction. Instead of focusing on the formation of the soul through music education, and assuming that well-formed souls will cooperate to make a harmonious city, the Athenian feels constrained to deal with the problem of civic "harmony" through the construction of constitutional arrangements (a mixed regime) that will allow citizens to restrain and direct one another toward moderate behavior even if the harmony within each citizen's soul is very imperfect. "Education" has not yet been mentioned in the third book, and will not be for some little while. The supervisory wisdom of the highest chorus is absent here; what is now called "wisdom" is the harmony of opinion with passion, and rulers with ruled, that was only moderation and justice in Book Two. "Moderation" is relegated to an almost shockingly low status: it is now understood as the kind of self-control men share with beasts and children (696b–e; cf. 710a–b). As a result of this debasing of the word moderation, freedom substitutes for moderation in the list of the city's goals (693b–c, 694b, 701d; cf. 687a). The two higher virtues have been demoted, the goals of the city have been lowered, because the project of creating healthy souls has had to be adulterated for the sake of attaining the "gymnastic" goals of security and liberty.

The Athenian initiates the discussion of constitutional arrangements rather abruptly, by listing the seven "worthy titles" to rule. These seven are unequal in rank and are "by nature opposed to one another," yet none of them is "illegitimate." If reason is to have a place in government it cannot simply cut through and cast aside this web of irrational claims rooted in human nature, habit, and history. The claim of reason must be woven together with the other six claims.

The only two titles that are said to be by nature—that is, whose claims do not rest merely on what men believe—are the titles of the stronger and the more prudent. Only rulers who base their rule on these two titles base their authority on what they can really do to rule well; if the claims of fathers, mothers, the well born, the older, despots, and the lucky are to have intrinsic merit they must be advanced by persons who are also either stronger or more prudent. In the light of all we have seen so far in Book Three, we should not be surprised to find that the Athenian does not disagree with the "most wise" Pindar's assertion that the stronger have a natural right to rule. Yet the Athenian goes on to speak of the "likelihood" that the greatest title, to lead as well as to rule, belongs to prudence. Whether Pindar would agree or disagree is not clear. The clear difference with Pindar emerges when the Athenian immediately adds the assertion that "this title," being the same as the "rule of law over willing subjects without violence," is also sanctioned by nature. According to the fragment we possess of the famous poem referred to here, Pindar seems to have doubted that law could be identified with gentle prudence: for Pindar, the universal power of law or convention (*nomos*) testifies to the natural power of irrational, brute force, not to the power of prudence. To what extent is the Athenian's opposition to Pindar grounded in knowledge of laws that exist somewhere, laws the "wise" Pindar failed to observe or understand, and to what extent does he have in mind the unprecedented laws, with their unprecedented "preludes," that he will himself propose later in the dialogue?

In what immediately follows, at any rate, the Athenian seems to suggest that they will find the proper blending of the seven titles, including prudence or rational law, in Sparta—as opposed to Argos and Messene and countless other cities. At the beginning, and for a long time, Sparta was defective. Confederacy, economic equality, favorable prophecies, pious oaths, and a strong foreign policy proved to be inadequate. But it seems the Spartan regime did eventually become a model of excellence by coordinating, not three choruses, or three cities, but three institutions—which embody the titles of birth and strength (monarchy), old age (aristocracy), and chance (democracy). It is difficult to see how the other three titles, above all prudence, fit into the Spartan scheme. One might say that prudence *must* be lurking there somewhere—for otherwise how could the Spartans have devised the strategy that led to the victory over Persia?—except that in that war they were aided by Athens (692e–693a; cf. Thucydides VI 93). Certainly Kleinias, at least, is sure that the description of the old Spartan constitution and the Spartan victory cannot be the whole of what the Athenian wishes to teach about "what a lawgiver should aim at with regard to friendship and prudence and freedom" (693c).

The ostensible reason for considering Persia and Athens is to arrive at a better understanding of the mixed regime, supposedly perfected in Sparta. The mixing of the seven titles to rule is achieved by mixing the two mother regimes, monarchy and democracy. By examining the two fundamental ingredient regimes in their extreme or pure form (slavery and absolute freedom), they will better understand the nature of the proper synthesis. The obvious problem with this procedure is that it leaves unexamined the crucial third, catalytic ingredient that makes possible a proper synthesis, as opposed to a crude compromise: the Athenian apparently fails to examine the Council of Elders, which contributes the *"moderate* power of old age." But in fact, the Athenian does return to an inquiry into Sparta, after his analysis of Persian monarchy and before his analysis of Athenian democracy (696a ff.). In that inquiry he declares that "moderation," as it is understood by the Spartans and by the present discussion, is in itself quite unworthy of honor. He thus implicitly repudiates the Spartan version of the mixed regime.

It transpires that a regime like Persia's is the kind of regime where reason can play its greatest political role: the rule of intelligence in politics goes together with the absence of law, and with liberation from the charms of republicanism and Greek ethno-centrism (cf. Farabi III 13). Two of the seven titles seem entirely unrecognized in such a regime: luck and old age. The failure to honor old age goes with the neglect of the Spartan type of moderation. The "despotism" of the herdsman Cyrus filled Persia with friendship, based on equality, and freedom. As for Cyrus's foreign policy, it was an unqualified success. Most remarkable of all is the fact that Cyrus's Persia is the only regime considered in the *Laws* that is said to possess "freedom of speech," and thereby to achieve a "common sharing in intelligence." Yet the regime collapsed in a short time, because its excellence was wholly dependent on "education," which now is mentioned and becomes a theme for the first time in Book Three. (The Athenian's use of "divination" here highlights the silence about piety in Cyrus's Persia; civic education and musical piety go together: cf. also 697c.) The regime which gives the greatest freedom and power to intelligence necessarily has the frailest protection against misuse of power by the unintelligent. From the discussion of Persia, one may conclude that a stable best regime would avoid hereditary offices, would promote "moderation" and piety, and would exercise more supervision over luxury, women, education, and private households than did Persia. In some of these respects, and in regard to males at any rate, the mixed regime epitomized by Sparta may be superior. But the Athenian immediately indicates that whatever he may wish to say in her favor, he cannot bring himself to credit Sparta with promoting education or prudence (696a–b).

Having shown the advantages and disadvantages of absolute monarchy, the Athenian turns, after his digression on Sparta and "moderation," to a discussion of Athenian history. Once again, the early version of the supposedly defective regime proves to be at least as excellent as the Spartan paragon. In his first description of ancient Athens the Athenian lays stress on the despotic awe that pervaded the city, and explicitly harks back to earlier parts of the dialogue (cf. 699c); in his second description he emphasizes the laws promoting and regulating music. The only god mentioned by name is Dionysus (and the female Awe, replacing Athena or Wisdom). The description of ancient Athens makes it sound like a very pale reflection of the regime elaborated in the first two books. In foreign policy, as Megillus readily admits, this old Athenian regime performed splendidly (699b–d). It is true, Athenian education in pious awe and music was not the sole source of the regime's excellence. Virtue was supplemented by fear of the enemy. Ironically enough, the Athenian concludes Book Three by suggesting that what is needed is not so much a foreign policy that insures security and triumph as a foreign situation that induces invigorating anxiety.

Old Athens was far more stable and pious, but considerably less pervaded by intelligence, than Cyrus's Persia, while it was considerably less stable and far more prudent than Sparta. Institutions, save for the inegalitarian class structure, played very little role in the success or corruption of the regime. Old Athens declined because her poets got out of control. Her history thus seems to confirm the fears the Dorians have about attempting to base civic virtue on music— unless the Athenian means to imply that his proposal for a Dionysian chorus provides for a workable check on the poets. But Book Three as a whole has led us to see that the first two books were somewhat utopian. Only the rest of the dialogue will show to what extent the best regime will follow the safer and more stable Spartan model and to what extent it will follow the more splendid and fragile Athenian

[437]

and Persian models. The Cretan regime, the most ancient and venerable regime, has almost dropped out of sight.

Although Book Three reveals some merit in the Spartan argument for constitutional checks and balances, the conversation by no means leads to the conclusion that this famous version of the "mixed regime" is an adequate solution to the problem of rule and civic harmony. The Athenian has taken seriously the reservations Megillus feels, has given them their due, and has shown that they have a place in his political science. Certainly the teaching of Book Two has been supplemented, if not revised. But in the final analysis the Athenian has held his ground, and indicated (with the utmost delicacy) that the concerns and attachments the Spartan represents belong to a man whose sights are set too low and whose vision is too narrow to guide the founding of a truly excellent regime. Both by the manner and the content of his response to Megillus, the Athenian has at last passed the test and won the confidence of the circumspect Kleinias. Taking advantage of a divine or lucky coincidence, the philosopher has gradually insinuated himself into the position of trusted advisor to a geniune lawgiver.

704a–712b: The Preconditions and Origins of the Best Regime

As the interlocutors turn from their general discussion to the founding of an actual city, we might expect the mood of the dialogue to become more energetic and hopeful; yet the initial enthusiasm (702d–e) is immediately tempered by a series of disappointments (704c–d). Thus it will be with every founding: every particular place and people will exhibit certain unique and unforeseeable deficiencies. In the *Laws* Plato departs from the "average" only to the extent that he portrays a location "that is not incurable, at least."

Given such a location, Plato's Athenian departs markedly, however, from the usual first concerns of a lawgiver. When a founder surveys the geographical environment, he might be expected to direct his attention first at providing for economic and military security (cf. *Politics* 1265a 21 ff.). Unfortunately, this preliminary preoccupation can easily come to eclipse all further concerns—especially for a founder in a place as strategically situated as Crete (cf. *Politics* 1271b 33–40). This indeed is a chief reason why Machiavelli induces his readers to take their bearings by the founding situation. To counteract this tendency, the Athenian veers toward the other extreme, insisting more adamantly than ever before on the precedence of virtue over security (even though he now admits that virtue by no means guarantees security: 706a,c, 707d). He especially stresses the evils of reliance on navies, which he illustrates by going back to the original discussion of the Cretan lawgiver. Minos's use of this ignoble (but enormously successful) form of warfare almost corrupted the venerable old Athenian regime, not to speak of what it must have done to Crete itself. At all costs, it seems, there must be moral progress beyond the Minoan regime: the new Cretan city must differ from other Cretan cities past and present, and rely chiefly on its noble and plodding heavy infantry—despite the unsuitable terrain and the proximity of the sea (cf. 753b, 755e–756a). The Athenian silences but surely does not begin to answer the "demonic" (705d) Kleinias's trenchant objections, and interest in shipbuilding, by awakening Megillus's prejudices and forming a common front with him (707b–d). In military affairs stolid courage is to outweigh shrewdness and flexibility because of the dangers posed by Crete's being an island (cf. 662b): naval habits of deviousness and anonymity, and, perhaps worse, temptation to competitive commerce and Mediterranean empire (Cf. also *Politics* 1274a 13–16). One has to wonder how confident the Athenian is that Megillus-like prejudices can forestall the insidious effects of innovation in military technology (cf. *Politics* 1265a, 1330b–1331a).

The disappointment provoked by the natural environment pales in comparison to the disappointment verging on despair that arises from consideration of the human material. Either we find the population unified by a common heritage and therefore resistant to new ways, or we find a motley mix of divergent customs, implying less recalcitrance but much greater disunity and distrust (cf. Rousseau, *Social Contract* II 8–10). In both cases old and sacred habits must be uprooted and mere knowledge is therefore insufficient: "manly virtue" is equally important.

The "good" Kleinias's inability to divine here what is meant leads the Athenian into a general reflection on the inadequacies of all lawgivers, and of human art as a whole, when confronted with the overwhelming and capricious power of chance. Yet, he immediately adds, it seems equally good (he does not say it is or seems better or more true) to speak of the power of god together with the power of fortune. Unlike Machiavelli, the Athenian continues to distinguish god from Fortuna, and continues to refer to the need for prayer; not for a moment does he suggest that human art or virtue could ever predict and control fortune. Nevertheless, the introduction of god and prayer does not lead to anything resembling the Christian virtue of hope. According to the Athenian, the relation between "gentle" human art and the "piloting of the human things" by chance and god is illustrated by the relation between a human pilot's knowledge and the wild tempest that threatens his ship. Encapsulated in this illustration, I believe, is an unusually bold statement of Plato's understanding of man's place in the universe. Since it is dangerous for the ignorant to pray, the city needs to be lucky enough to have a wise lawgiver happen along who can "pray in the correct way" for that which must be "available to him through chance" (709d; cf. 710d). Though god and chance may not be identical, it seems impossible for men to distinguish divine providence from chance.

The doubt raised about divine providence (and, by implication, about divine retribution) is a kind of justification for the "oracular myth" (712a) that recommends tyranny. Refusing to take personal responsibility for this shocking "prayer," the philosopher puts it in the mouth of a nameless, wise lawgiver (709e). The tyrant who is the answer to the wise lawgiver's prayer need have very little education but must possess some extraordinary "natural" qualities, including a certain grandeur of ambition that would make him capable of becoming captivated by the glory and grandeur of the task a wise lawgiver might propose. Yet he must also be a man who will not refrain from using his youthful courage and self-control to do unjust, ugly, and dishonest deeds: his seven qualities do not include justice, grace, or love of truth (cf. 710c with *Republic* 486–487a).

Kleinias remains understandably reluctant to endorse—at least in speech—the unexpected proposal (710c). How would a young tyrant fit into Kleinias's situation, as one of ten republican lawgivers? When the Athenian generalizes and weakens the proposal by showing that tyranny itself is not absolutely necessary but may be approximated by less stringent forms of authoritarian rule, Kleinias seizes upon the idea that his present, oligarchic situation is at least second-best (710d–e). But the Athenian immediately dashes this hope by explaining that oligarchy is the most stable form of rule and therefore least advantageous for a founder. So Kleinias balks (711a). And we cannot help but sympathize. After all, where could he find a young tyrant? If he could find one, why should he risk a terrible struggle with his nine co-founders and all their supporters (711c)? If that succeeded, how could he be sure the tyrant would remain subservient to him?

The Athenian does not attempt to answer such questions. Rather, he shifts to describing a nontyrannical solution. He begins by pointing out that it is not impossible or even difficult for them to change the city's laws by a hegemony of all-powerful rulers (after all, Kleinias and his co-legislators seem already to have such power). What then is the difficulty? From what the Athenian has been saying up until now, we would expect him to say that the difficulty lies in uniting this power under prudence. But instead he proceeds to speak of the difficulty of subordinating such power to someone who has "a divine *eros* for moderate and just practices." The only example he gives is Homer's Nestor, an old man who relied on the power of speech. Nestor is perhaps a model Kleinias can follow; but how prudent was Nestor? How effective was he in bringing about fundamental legal reforms? Can Kleinias's rhetoric, or the rhetoric the Athenian teaches him, persuade the other nine co-founders, and obviate the need for violent compulsion? It is more likely that in "harmonizing" the "oracular myth" with his present situation (712b) Kleinias will have to give up some of the radical proposals the Athenian has and will set forth. In his conclusion, the Athenian makes it clear that the "natural" (as opposed to divine or lucky) genesis of the "best regime" can occur only where the *greatest* power coincides with prudence (not justice) and moderation. The Athenian still regards the present conversation as the unserious play of "elderly children" (712b).

Through the drama Plato shows that the tyrannical founder is less a practical solution than a full elaboration of the insurmountable practical problem: in those places where tyrants or demagogues abound, the citizenry is corrupt and potential lawgivers like Kleinias are very rare; where one finds lawgivers and citizens who are decent material for a new beginning, one is not apt to find the unchecked authority that is necessary to effect the change. We thus learn that the practical difficulty in founding a regime even approaching the best goes well beyond what the *Republic* teaches regarding the unlikely coincidence of philosophy and political power. From what I have said, the reader familiar with Machiavelli can now deduce for himself the numerous differences between the Machiavellian and the Platonic teaching regarding the necessity for tyranny.

712c–718a: The Despotism, and the Problem, of God

In accordance with what he suggested by his reference to Nestor's "divine passion," the Athenian invokes the aid of a god instead of a tyrant in the setting up of the city, and proceeds to raise the question of who is to rule *after* the founding. Kleinias's response shows how uneasy he has become as a result of the Athenian's praise of tyranny; so the Athenian asks for a description of the Dorian regimes as possible models, and thus encourages the older, solid citizen Megillus to bring forward again the newer Spartan regime. Apparently answering here the question that we saw was left open at the end of Book Three, the Athenian at first seems to advocate the adoption of this mixed regime for the new city. But he insists it be reinterpreted, and in fact quite transformed in meaning, so as to be understood as the "despotism" of the god who rules over "intellect": the only alternative to the human despotism underlying all unmixed regimes is a divine despotism underlying a mixed regime (713a). We may say that the answer to the "gymnastic" question of how to arrange a regime so as to provide security and freedom proves to be not exactly the Spartan mixed regime, or the old Athenian musical regime, but a new theocratic regime.

Kleinias's discomfort at the continuing drift toward tyranny or despotism (cf. Farabi IV 7, 9) is not alleviated when he hears that the nature of the unnamed despotic god can be clarified only by "a little more use of myth" (713a; cf. 712a); the Athenian's "myths" are becoming unrepublican and hence unsettling. Kleinias's subsequent relief at hearing the familiar name of Kronos prevents him from wondering about the absence of Zeus (who is supposed to have overthrown Kronos and inspired Minos, and to whose cave they were going to walk, at least until they paused—722c; see Book One, note 10).

This is our first glimpse of the theology that is to inspire the best regime and help prevent one part of it from exploiting another. We hear of a single deity, non-Olympian and pre-Homeric. By virtue of its age, the name the Athenian gives to this deity is eminently respectable; moreover, belief in the "philanthropic" Kronos could bring about the necessary obfuscation of the harsh truth about man's Cyclopian origins and the recurring catastrophes (cf. 682b–c; the Athenian is now silent about the ugly mythic tradition concerning the Titans: cf. 701b and 886c with Book Four, note 13). The Kronos myth that is to inform the city suggests that it is human nature, rather than the hostility and scarcity of nature, which is the source of man's original wickedness and unhappiness (713c); if the catastrophes are not denied, they are situated in a larger, comforting context (713b). According to the Athenian's version of the myth, the god's caring for mankind has always been indirect, but there was a time when the god decided to institute a universal regime of demons. For some unspecified reason—perhaps the catastrophe, or perhaps a revolt by other, less philanthropic gods—this happy epoch terminated. The Athenian surely does not claim that Kronos is omnipotent. Although the god no longer exercises any supervision through demons or other forms of providence, we can at least imitate the demonic rule by striving to discover and put into law the distribution ordained by the immortal intelligence within us. To profit in this way from the god's goodness, we must make great efforts on our own; our only access to god is through our own intelligence and the laws it ordains.

In worshipping this new version of god, the citizens would be revering the reason found within man, but they would revere it and its laws as something inferior to the demonic and the divine. There was apparently no need for human intelligence in the demonic age. Except for a possible hope for the return of the demonic age (a hope in which there need be no trace of messianism, since no human or semi-human savior is indicated), the worship of this Kronos would seem to be remarkably free of hopes or fears concerning divine intervention. Can belief in such a god, who does not punish the unjust, provide an adequate safeguard against political usurpation?

In the immediate context, the most pressing unanswered question is what distinguishes the content of laws which enforce the despotism of intellect from laws which enforce the various despotisms of men. The Athenian underlines and deepens this question by presenting, far more lucidly than ever before, the arguments of those who say that every law is in the interest of the part that rules the city, and that no law can be in the interest of all. It now appears more likely than ever that Pindar was correct about all regimes except perhaps theocracy. Yet the Athenian's "theocracy" will have laws made by men, rather than by gods or demons: even if we are eventually persuaded that these laws are ordained by intellect, and based on a rational understanding of man's natural needs, what guarantees that they are in the interest of all, and not merely of those few who possess the most intelligence? In what sense is intellect to be equated with the common good?

Since the regime is to be constituted above all by the religious beliefs the citizens actually hold, the Athenian begins to elaborate on the nature of the divine in a speech addressed directly to the future citizens. But these "colonists" are not yet citizens, and are therefore not yet adequately prepared to hear the full civil theology: accordingly, the Athenian's oration never mentions intellect, and presents divinity as dual in nature. There is in the first place "god," the original cause and support of all the beings, who moves according to an undeviating, paradoxical, and natural pattern. God is now nameless: the name "Kronos" has been dropped and "Zeus" does not take his place. The silence about Zeus is highlighted by the crude use of his name in an oath (715d; cf. the scholiast on 715e; in the Prelude as a whole, Zeus appears only as the god of strangers—730a). Accompanying god is the subordinate goddess "Justice" who, unlike god, moves in a changeable way, directly intervening in men's lives to bring punishment to those who forsake divine law, and especially to those who believe they should rule without also being ruled by others. The Athenian thus remedies the major political difficulty in his earlier discussion of Kronos. He who is going to become happy must humbly follow Justice. But when the Athenian gives Kleinias an opportunity to contribute to the homily, Kleinias shifts the emphasis from Justice back to god. As a result of Kleinias's intervention, the philosopher is induced to tell the colonists more about the nature of god. The chief characteristic of god is not justice (or courage) but moderation and inner measure. God does not actively benefit men, he does not even reveal a law; he does men good only by providing a model for them to imitate.

The Athenian claims that from his description of the dual godhead there somehow follows a principle that governs the prayers men address to the many "gods": it is dangerous for the bad, and advantageous for the good, to pray (no mention is made, in this speech to the colonists, of the need for intelligence in prayer). No explanation is offered of what the relation might be between the godhead and the many gods, who expect sacrificial offerings and who apparently intervene to reward good men (the oration ends with "good hopes"). As the Athenian enlarges upon the appropriate ways to honor the many gods, the first and higher part of the dual godhead is almost lost sight of among the other objects of worship. There are seven ranks of these objects, enumerated in descending order. The demons—whom "the prudent man worships"—are at the center. It is left ambiguous whether the highest rank belongs to the Olympians or to "the gods who possess the city"; this perhaps depends on whether or not the highest god is, for now, willing to be called "Zeus" (cf. Heraclitus, frag. #32). The gods who rule over the dead are ranked third, and ancestors and parents sixth and seventh, yet by far the lengthiest and most moving remarks are devoted to this lowest rank, comprising the living parents who are the divine things that are unmistakably one's own. It is in regard to this aspect of the divine that justice, righteous indignation, pity, and "spiritedness" (*thumos*) play a preeminent role.

On the basis of these observations, we see that the oration appeals to, and thus delineates, the two fundamental and contradictory roots of man's religious impulse: on the one hand, our admiration for, our desire to meditate upon and imitate, a Being that exists in harmonious, undisturbed fulfillment, who is somehow the source and explanation of all being, and especially conscious being, but who cannot be understood as directly involved in our daily lives and whose splendor dwarfs our significance as individuals; on the other hand, our "hope" for beings whose direct care affirms the eternal significance of ourselves and our families, insuring that any undeserved affronts to our dignity will be visited by retribution. At this point we are left wondering whether a coherent, and politically efficacious, religion can be derived from these complex, deepest, and most comprehensive of all human longings.

PART THREE: *The Preludes*

718b–724a: The Reasons for Having "Preludes"

After completing his oration about "the gods and those who are stronger," the Athenian does not proceed directly to the laying down of laws. For something else is required, which cannot be presented in the shape of laws: something is needed to make the people "as persuadable as possible with regard to virtue." But is this not precisely the function of the civil religion and the theological oration? The Athenian goes on to speak as if his oration were, and yet were not quite, what he has in mind (718d). The oration seemed to him to have the power to make the listeners "more tame and agreeable"; but, he adds, it would be "wholly desirable" only insofar as it made the listener "more agreeable and a better *learner*." At the end of Book Four, we learn more specifically what the oration failed to do: it did not *educate* the hearers by discussing the individuals themselves, their *own* souls, bodies, and property (724a–b; in the oration, property, body, and soul were strictly subordinated to ancestral piety: 717c).

What the Athenian is getting at becomes somewhat clearer

through his reference to Hesiod, who teaches that the gods make progress toward virtue difficult. The Athenian says that most men's lives bear out the wisdom of this poetic teaching. He thus seems to indicate that virtue is hard to attain for most men not only because of its intrinsic difficulty, but also because the gods' posture toward virtue suggests that virtue as it is ordinarily understood is not choice-worthy for its own sake but only for its ultimate rewards (cf. *Republic* 363e ff.). This suggestion was in fact present even in the Athenian's own oration on the gods, especially in the way it spoke of justice and obedience to law. Hesiod himself, in the lines immediately following those that are quoted, seems to assert that knowledge, discovered firsthand or learned from "one who speaks well," is the *only* authentic source of excellence.

From all this we can gather that the additional persuasion the Athenian now calls for is intended to teach the citizens that legal virtue is choiceworthy not only because of divine sanctions but also because it is in accordance with what is by nature good for the individual. ("Nature" was mentioned just twice in the entire theological oration; in the discussion of the "preludes" nature is mentioned eight times, and the gods are mentioned just twice, once in an oath.) This implies that the theological oration delivered to the colonists is an inadequate prelude for citizens, insofar as it fails to give an argument showing that the natural situation and needs of man's soul require worship of the ancestors and the gods that are described.

It is partly from a poet that one learns of the need for something beyond the theology, as heretofore presented, and the laws; could it not be that the poets also have something to teach the lawgiver in regard to the form and content of the additional persuasion? Apparently moved by this thought, the Athenian reopens a fundamental issue which we thought had been settled: the subordination of the poets to the lawgiver. He creates a dialogue, in which he himself speaks as a poet, on behalf of the poets: both in deed and in word the Athenian becomes a poet. He argues that the lawgiver is wrong in commanding the poets never to compose speeches that are opposed to the laws. One simply cannot demand this, because it is of the essence of poetry to present a variety of diverse characters who contradict one another, and the inspired poet doesn't know which character is speaking the truth. The Athenian goes further. Criticizing the oration on ancestral piety, he argues that the contradictoriness of poetry is not really a defect, for it allows the poet to specify crucial human qualities, like moderation, by contrasting them with particular examples of antagonistic qualities, like excess and deficiency. In addition, the speeches of contradictory characters can show how different sorts of behavior are appropriate to different persons in different circumstances. By his deed as well as his speech the Athenian implies that the good lawgiver too must in some sense go over to the side of the poets and supplement legal speech with musical poetry.

When the Athenian proceeds to the "image" of the doctors, he shows that the notion of poetic "preludes" involves even more than all this. The true lawgiver aims at healing or perfecting souls, just as the doctor heals bodies and the gymnast perfects bodies (cf. 720e with 650b). With regard to both body and soul there are two modes of ministering. One is through naked command—a mode that is "despotic" and fit for slaves; the other is through gentle, rational persuasion based on scientific inquiry into the nature of the body or soul. Carrying on a dialogue with the patient and his friends the doctor teaches and himself learns something in the process. This is the mode fit for men who are free. A perfect prelude, then, would seem to be a kind of poetry in which diverse characters argued with one another, but were presented in such a way that the composition as a whole involved the reader or listener in a dialogue with the author, by means of which the reader was led to the healing truth about his soul as it is by nature. We are given three examples of preludes: the first is the speech about marriage, the third is the theological oration (cf. 724a), and the central is the "dialogue" which they have been having and which Plato has created for us to read (722c–d).

Nevertheless, Plato does not for a moment let us forget that in politics the despotic mode cannot be dispensed with. The Athenian does not advocate using the "single" method of rational persuasion; the only choice is between the single despotic method and the "double" method of despotic command mixed with rational persuasion (720e; cf. Farabi IV 14–15). In the light of true, rational freedom all rule of law is revealed to be a kind of slavish tyranny (723a). The laws of the best city will transcend this tyranny, will enforce a "despotism of intellect," to the extent that they are supplemented by the preludes, which give all citizens access to self-understanding. Thus we learn how intellect can become, in some sense, a "common interest" (724b) shared by citizens and founder.

Very much now depends on exactly what the preludes will consist of. Two practical difficulties are evident. How many citizens can understand or profit from a full explanation of the nature of the soul, even one presented through the supreme didactic rhetoric of a Platonic dialogue, and how realistic is it to expect lawgivers to compose Platonic dialogues? In speaking of the "prelude" to the laws as a whole, the Athenian first says that the "dialogue" they have had together all morning is the prelude (722c–d), but then retreats to speaking as if only the theological oration presented a few moments earlier were the prelude (723a). Does the Athenian not mean to indicate that the relation between the dialogic prelude and the oratorical prelude exemplifies the difference between a perfect legal prelude and the sort of prelude one must usually settle for in practice (consider here 742c–743c)? At any rate, the first and paramount political example, the prelude to the marriage law, is surely not a dialogue, but resembles more a brief poetic oration.

According to the Athenian (721d–e), consideration of this leading example will help us understand better the nature of all the preludes. The prelude does not justify the command to marry on the grounds of utility to the city (population growth), or on moralistic grounds (avoidance of sexual promiscuity), or on the basis of obedience to gods and parents (impiety is here identified with self-deprivation, not disobedience to god; contrast 774a). Instead, it evokes the sublimely selfish, natural longing for immortality and invites individual citizens to satisfy that longing. Rather than asking the citizen to devote his soul to his family (717c), the prelude encourages him to use his family as the instrument for his own fulfillment. Through its unprecedented "preludes," the regime as a whole claims to be the vehicle through which individuals realize their natural potentials to become in some sense partakers of eternity. By urgings and sanctions the city directs men to fulfill the longing for eternity through children—which are, incidentally, essential to the city's survival. Yet at the same time the city quietly but clearly indicates that there is another route to immortality. For it presents the following evidence to support the assertion that *everyone* by nature desires immortality: "the desire to become famous and not to lie nameless after one has died is a desire for such a thing." The prelude is silent on the relation between marriage and fame. Nor does it say whether there may not be additional "desires for such a thing." It allows, and even prompts, the intelligent and passionate to raise these questions for themselves. Surely in the case of the author, Plato, the family was not the way he chose to express the desire for immortality. Marriage and fame, marriage and philosophy, are not completely compatible (cf. Bacon, *Essays* viii; Nietzsche, *Genealogy of Morals*, III 7). Even the nondialogic prelude can, then, stir up questioning of the ordinary citizen's life and duties, and open the way to a life with trans-familial and even trans-civic concerns. Through the preludes at their best the city transcends itself, in the direction of eternity, without sacrificing the sober persuasion and sanctions that are politically necessary and that make possible the greatest happiness for the citizenry as a whole.

The enchanting power, for ordinary citizens, of the Athenian's brief example is proven by its effect on Megillus. Kleinias too is satisfied, although more because of fame and the city that will belong to him than because of any children that may already belong to him (722a). He is therefore anxious to procreate these laws before more time slips away. His insistent haste compels or allows the Athenian to leave unrevised the theological oration. From this we understand why it is that of the seven topics the Athenian says are dealt with in the Prelude to all the laws, the central is "dead ancestors" (724a). It is now midday, and the three old men have therefore paused (722c); this is the time when they are most anxious to seek shade, and the theological oration and defense of the poets is the most "traditionalist" moment in the dialogue. Later, as dusk approaches, the interlocutors will welcome the sun, and Kleinias will be prepared to help the Athenian truly fulfill the promise of the "preludes."

726a–734e: The Public Teaching About the Soul

The rest of the prelude, exemplifying what we have just learned about the nature of preludes in general, is on the surface a sermon full of earnest exhortation, and between the lines a thought-provoking description of the good citizen's soul. At the outset, the sermon quietly highlights the key problem, the uncertain rank of the soul in relation to the ancestors and the gods. With some ambivalence, the soul now replaces the ancestors in the second rank of honor (cf. 726a–727b, 728d, 730b, 731c, 743e, and Farabi V 1). This accords with the fact that humility was considered a virtue in the theological oration and is now treated as a vice (cf. 728e with 716a).

When we hear the "despotism" of the gods being strongly reaffirmed, we are inclined to conclude that the soul, though second in rank, belongs among the slaves, as the highest ranking slavish thing. Yet the soul is soon said to be more honorable than everything "earthborn," to be "truly the most honorable"—to be, when linked with virtue, somehow "Olympian" (727e, 731c; cf. 732d–e). How is the soul's Olympian status consistent with the necessity that it eventually leave the light of day and enter Hades (727d)?

These paradoxes suggest that the soul is not indivisible, but comprises parts which may, by themselves or in their various combinations, have dissimilar destinies (cf. *Timaeus* 90a–d). The partition of the soul is in fact implied in all the Athenian says. For he proceeds to instruct the citizens to adopt a posture in which they step outside, as it were, and look back upon their souls or parts of their souls—opposing certain desires and fears, and even arguing with the soul, trying to "refute" it. To "honor" the soul is to try to improve it through an inner struggle among the parts. In guiding this struggle the prelude provides insight into the nature and relation of the parts.

The prelude begins its advice in a curiously negative fashion, by listing seven ways the soul is wrongly honored. Does avoiding the seven errors constitute correct honoring of the soul? From this it would follow that obedience, a hard-won self-restraint, and a keen sense of responsibility and honor are the chief attributes of the good citizen's soul. Yet the idea of moral responsibility and the exhortation to self-restraint seem undermined when the prelude sums up by saying that moral failing is due to ignorance (728b). Moreover, if it is only the "ignorant" who "refuse" to follow the lawgiver's guidance, it is difficult to see why any citizen, once he has heard and grasped the prelude, should ever incur guilt, or need to struggle within himself to do what is right. If we reconsider what the prelude has said thus far, we see that at least part of the reason why the citizens may be led to defy the lawgiver is that they have not yet really been told how to honor their souls, but only how to avoid dishonoring them. Except for a passing reference to good conversation (728b), the sermon has failed to give any indication of what might be "the better things" (728c), "the greatest goods of all by nature" (727d). The citizens remain exposed to the dangerous temptations such ignorance implies; they are commanded to take responsibility before they have acquired sufficient knowledge. The difficulty becomes glaring when the prelude finally gives the grounds for the soul's high rank; not merely its capacity to flee the bad, but also its natural suitability for *hunting* and *capturing* what is *best of all* and dwelling with it for the rest of life (728d). Once again the Athenian has implicitly raised the question: what is the goal; why is citizen-virtue good? But this time he does so in an oration that every citizen will study—and in the context of a thematic treatment of psychology.

Leaving his attentive listeners in some temporary wonderment as to what is good for the soul, the Athenian turns to the body, and asserts that "by nature" the body deserves the third rank in honor. So long as this means no more than that the body ranks after one's soul and before one's property, it is uncontroversial. But when, contrary to what we were led to expect (cf. 718a–b, 724a), the prelude goes on to deal also with family, friends, city and citizens, strangers and natives, the Athenian implies that the body ranks above all these as well (cf. 734d, 743d–e). This shocking suggestion is softened only by the concomitant subordination of body to soul: if, and insofar as, one's soul needs family, friends, and city more than it needs the body, those noble possessions become more honorable than the body. Nevertheless, it remains true that the Athenian indicates in a public address to the citizenry that the city is subordinate in value to the individual, body and soul. He also implies that each citizen should care for family and friends with an eye to his own advantage; this explains the rather calculating tone of his advice in these respects (729c–d; cf. above, pp. 446, 448). When he comes to advice regarding strangers, the Athenian appeals, for the first time in this sermon, to divine anger and retribution—perhaps because it is not easy to show what other disadvantages a man necessarily suffers if he treats strangers badly. We see again how the sermon strives to give sober, prudential reasons for good behavior; the question of the overall good reaped by a life of obedience to the law remains pressing. In speaking about the proper attitude toward the city (729d–e), the Athenian does remind us of one great reward that awaits the most diligent citizens: the "victory prize" (cf. 715c) of political fame. Is this not the goal of the type of soul the city aims at nurturing?

Responding somewhat to the questions his hearers may have, the Athenian admits that what he has said so far does not explain "what sort of person one should be"—and in the second and central part of his homily he finally turns to this theme (730b–c). He stresses that this positive goal, unlike the negative prohibitions that showed what one should *not* be, cannot be brought about by the law itself: the prelude at this point becomes truly superlegal, or truly educative. Two objects of psychic aspiration stand out: truth and justice.

The concern for truth comes first and appears to rank above all other virtues, including justice. In speaking of the preeminence of truth, the prelude mentions blessedness and happiness for the first time. Gods as well as men follow truth, and hence the hunting for truth would seem to be a key part of the "moderation" by which a man can resemble and become a "friend" of god (cf. 716c–d and 728d). Yet the Athenian says truth leads all *good* things for gods and all things for men: not everything that follows truth is necessarily good for men. Certainly the "partaking of truth" he praises is not the passionate pursuit of wisdom. The Athenian identifies "truthfulness" with "trustworthiness": his praise is focused on that virtue of gentlemanly honesty or candor which is opposed to the vices of deliberate lying, boastfulness, and irony (cf. *Ethics* 1127a 13 ff.; *Republic* 547e; *Iliad* IX 312–13). The prelude does take note of the fact that there are *two* vices opposed to "truthfulness": in addition to untrustworthiness, there is lack of intelligence. Only in this oblique manner does the prelude remind the hearer of the second and higher virtue of truthfulness—intelligence or wisdom. The Athenian dwells on the pitiful fate of the man who is both untrustworthy and ignorant, but he leaves the hearer to figure out for himself whether the two vices must necessarily go together, or whether there may not be men who are somewhat untrustworthy but wise, whose fate may not be so pitiful (among other versions of such men, there would be the wise boaster, like the comic poet, and the wise ironist, like Socrates). Thus in the public oration about the soul and its excellences, the concern for the truth comes to sight in a most incomplete and ambiguous version. It is indeed remarkable how little the prelude refers to music (cf. 729a), or to preoccupations resembling those we heard of in the discussion of the Dionysian chorus. The discussion of justice that comes next sheds some light on the psychological reasons why the public life of the city may have to be even less open to the pursuit of truth than we may have come to expect from Books One through Four.

The justice praised in the prelude is punitive justice: the winner of the prize for civic virtue turns out to be the executioner (730d). At the cost of a slight exaggeration, the sermon thus startles some of its hearers into a train of thought that leads to a deeper understanding of the psychology—and limitations—of civic virtue. For, the sermon adds (731b), the man who "in no way eases up on punishment" belongs to the "spirited form" (*thumoeidetic*).

In order to sense the full potential impact of this part of the prelude on the citizens who will hear it, we need to range beyond the prelude itself and compare what it says about "spiritedness" (*thumos*) with what is said elsewhere in the *Laws*, especially in Book Nine. Moreover, to grasp for ourselves the full significance of *thumos*, we need to bear in mind what Plato's Socrates teaches about the tripartite division of the soul. The soul comprises three "forms"—desire, reason, and spiritedness. One can even speak of "forms" of men, whose characters reflect the predominance of one or another of the forms within the soul (cf. 731b, 863b, with *Timaeus* 89e and *Republic* 434b,

435b ff., 580d). As the present passage indicates, we can best understand the part of the soul called *thumos* if we begin by reflecting on its manifestations in the phenomenon of angry indignation (cf. 717d and *Republic* 441a–b, 572a). In its most elementary form, shared with many animals, anger is the courageous reaction to frustrated desire or to injury: it is an immediate, fear-suppressing, and uncalculating impulse to overcome the obstacle or source of hurt (cf. 791d–792b, 863b, 866d, 963e). However, while it usually arises in service to desire or aversion, anger can rapidly take on a momentum of its own. This independence of anger is especially visible in man; indeed, the spectacular, even awesome, independence of *thumos* in its various aspects (some of which are barely nascent in the primitive version of anger) constitutes a great part of what we mean by "humanity."

If we attempt to distinguish those aspects, beginning from the simple case of anger, we see in the first place that the drive to overcome and destroy is accompanied by a vivid sense of one's own affronted dignity. In desiring, or in reasoning, we tend to forget ourselves as we attend to the object, but when an interruption evokes anger, the original object can be lost sight of, as we focus on our position relative to others, and above all to the one who is the source of the frustration. In human beings, anger proves to be merely the crudest manifestation of pride, the passionate concern for one's individual rank (cf. 866e–867b with *Republic* 581a–c, 586c–d). This insistence that one be treated with respect is the germ from which grows the moral sense that reaches sublime heights in the passionate demand that one be treated not as one wishes, or even as an equal, but as one has *deserved*—and that all others with whom one feels kinship be treated as they have deserved. If it is to develop in this way, *thumos* needs to acquire the habit of repressing its primary urge and submitting to the guidance of judicial reason (cf. 867b–c; *Republic* 409a–410b, 440c–d; *Timaeus* 70b).

Thumos is thus the source of a self-love that is different from the kind that consists in the desire for self-preservation, riches, and sensual pleasure. To be sure, a man of the "thumotic type" can love money and pleasure; yet he subordinates these things, or sees them as means, to the prize he "desires" above all: victory, independence, and honor (731a–b). "In a regime dominated by *thumos*, one thing alone stands out—love of victories and of honors" (*Republic* 548c; cf. 550b–d). One must immediately add that thumotic self-esteem can rise above even honor, or at least above vulgar honor. *Thumos* is what animates all self-restraint, insofar as the repression—of desire

and even of anger itself—is moralistic and not a prudential calculation that looks to later gratification (633d, 635c, 866e; *Republic* 440a–b,
442a; *Timaeus* 70a; Farabi V 7). Just as one desire can combat another,
and reason or *thumos* can enter the contest on one side or another, so
the various thumotic passions can struggle and invite the intervention of reason or desire (644e–645a, 645d; *Republic* 441b–c, 442b–c,
586d–e). But in the case of the man in whom *thumos* predominates,
reason or desire exerts influence by showing the way to a greater
self-exaltation and sense of independence, not to more security, possessions, or pleasure (cf. *Republic* 553d).

Still, it would be oversimplifying to divorce *thumos* completely
from the desire for security. For according to the Athenian, the *eidos*
that comprises *thumos* also comprises fear (864b; cf. 863e). We observe that anger and fear arise on similar occasions, but when one of
the two is strong the other is weak. Both tend to make one forget the
objects of one's desire, and lead one to focus on one's self. Could
anger (*thumos*) and fear be alternative expressions of the same fundamental psychic motion, which arises from a sense of one's threatened particularity?

The self-esteem of *thumos* readily extends beyond the individual
himself. Indeed, *thumos* makes a man seek something beyond himself with which he can identify and whose defense will lend a more
lasting significance to his sacrifices. The thumotic man is the partisan
defender not only of those he pities (729e) but of friends, family, and
city (cf. *Republic* 375d, 536c). He defends these things against harm
and against their being taken from him (717d), and also in the role of
moral reformer—defending family and city as he defends himself,
not merely to preserve but to make them "strong competitors in the
contest for virtue and fame" (731a–b). This aspect of *thumos* combines with the *eros* for what is eternal: it underlies the desire for personal immortality through children (cf. 717d) and through fame. In
short, "*thumos* is the power by which we care for things" (Aristotle
Politics 1327b 28–1328a 17; cf. 773c), insofar as we care for them *as our
own*. There is a wide and complex sphere of human caring where
thumos and *eros* reinforce one another even as they struggle for su-
premacy; the jealous friend, and the artists (of every rank except
perhaps the highest) are striking examples of this drama. In the manifold mystery that is the soul, the "parts" are not distinguished by
sharp boundary lines, any more than are the four forms of virtue or
the forms of the various regimes (cf. 878b with 681d and 714b). We
may say, however, that to the extent love is dominated by *thumos* it

cannot be self-forgetting devotion to a being which is not one's own and does not reflect one's uniqueness and self-importance. For Plato, therefore, *thumos* cannot be the source of the love of the truth, the love of the *ideas*. Philosophy qua philosophy has no indignation (*Republic* 536c; *Gorgias* 485a–486c). Megillus and Kleinias belong to the "thumotic type." The Athenian stranger does not; as a human being, he is not a "real man" (*anēr*, 731b) because he transcends "manliness." Not only is *thumos* to be distinguished from desire; in the final analysis it is profoundly anti-erotic because it always elevates and exaggerates the value of the "subjective" at the expense of the "objective." This is the reason for the paradox which haunts the existence that remains within the moral horizon of spiritedness: the proud assertion of self, or defense of one's own, has difficulty in finding a clear object of aspiration which would give its energetic strivings rational purpose and a coherent direction. And this is also the reason for the deep antagonism that is the dramatic theme of this whole dialogue.

One of the sharpest contradictions between moral indignation and the truth comes to sight in the Athenian's repeated references here to the question of responsibility (727b, 728b–c, 731c–d). It is peculiar to *thumos* to assign complete responsibility to whatever opposes it. *Thumos* personifies what is lifeless: we feel an urge to strike back at stones and branches that impede or hurt us (cf. 873–874a). Even when softened by reason into making allowances for uncontrollable external circumstances, moral indignation sternly insists that human dignity consists in a sane adult's capacity to take responsibility for his good and evil actions. *Thumos* endows men with a sense of independence and dignity based not on their knowledge, but on their freedom to choose and act. In direct opposition to all this, Plato's Athenian—like his Socrates—contends that crime is due to ignorance rather than willful choice. Men's actions are always guided by what they know or believe to be good for them, and since justice is good for men, "no unjust man is ever willingly unjust." The unjust man is not responsible, but "sick" (731d). He deserves not hurtful retribution but "pity," and "corrective" education that shows him how he has miscalculated his own interest by overlooking what sort of companions and conversation he will have to endure as a result of his life of crime (cf. 728b–c with *Apology* 25c ff. and *Timaeus* 86e, *Republic* 589c, *Gorgias* 509e, *Meno* 77c–78a). In questioning the moral responsibility of most men, philosophy threatens to subvert not only penal law but virtue and human dignity itself; this is a principal reason why the scientific knowledge of the soul must, in public life, be kept in a kind of twilight of ambiguity.

In view of the preceding reflections many of the ambiguities that pervade the public teaching about the soul become intelligible. In exhorting men to become "spirited," and indulge the pleasures of anger and pride, the sermon also begins to teach what spiritedness is and what its limitations are; what is more, the sermon qualifies or moderates the predominance of spiritedness in city and citizen. On a deeper and less obtrusive level the Athenian raises questions about the ultimate coherence and reasonableness of the thumotic outlook, and points toward another kind of life and outlook based on the uncompromising preoccupation with truth. Closer to the surface, and remaining within the moral horizon of *thumos*, he insists on identifying and preaching against certain bad extremes to which *thumos* is prone. Almost his first words of advice are directed against the overweening pride that makes men think they understand everything and need look to no superiors (727a–b; cf. 716a). Future citizens will be constitutionally inclined to "honor their own more than the truth" (732a); their competitiveness will make them prey to the vice of envy (731a). The remedy is to induce them to honor and "pursue," if not the truth, then "trustworthiness," and justice as embodied in various outstanding men who adorn the whole city to which all belong. The excesses of the proud man are to be controlled by evoking his capacity for reverent emulation and contempt; as we saw in the conversation with Megillus, history and poetry have an important role to play in this regard.

In addition, the Athenian attempts to soften the harsh thumotic conception of criminal responsibility. Not until Book Nine will we be in a position to discern how the two apparently contradictory approaches (the "spirited" and the "gentle," 731b–d) might be woven together in a coherent theory of penal law. The only hint given here is in the distinction between the "curable" and the "incurable" (731d; cf. 738e): against criminals who cannot be educated or restrained, "bitter *thumos*" is to be unleashed, and the criminal "destroyed so that many others may be saved" (728c).

The exhortation to and subtle questioning of thumotic citizenship continues as the prelude concludes with a proof of the superior *pleasure* of the "noblest" life (732d ff.; cf. 660e ff.). The philosopher prefaces this last part of the prelude with a remark to the effect that what the prelude is about to discuss, unlike what it has discussed previously, belongs to the realm of the merely human. It will apparently not be as obvious to the citizen-audience as it is to us and Kleinias that the prelude's treatment of pleasure excludes from consideration divine pleasures. The prelude presents, as the basis for a judgment of the degree of pleasure various lives attain, the outline of a rather complex scheme of calculations. But there is a strange disproportion between the subtlety of the pleasure calculus which is suggested, and the simplicity, not to say crudeness, of the actual argument for the greater pleasure of the virtuous life. The argument focuses on the advantages of the moderate life over the unrestrained life. In order to argue for the superior pleasure of the prudent and courageous lives, the prelude has to assume that in each case virtue leads to victory, and that in addition virtue is accompanied by health. In this section of the prelude, not a word is said about justice. The prelude thus leaves open the question whether a hedonistic calculation, guided by a "law that one gives to oneself" (733e), dictates that one should obey the city's law. Some citizens are thereby allowed to guess that once one takes away reputation, it is no longer easy to argue that civic justice is pleasant for men by nature (cf. 733a with *Republic* 361b).

Part Four: *The Rulers*

734e–747e: The Economic Basis

The stranger now turns to the law—or rather (he corrects himself) to the outline of the laws that constitute the *"regime."* The regime comprises two "forms," the appointment of rulers and the giving of laws to be administered by those rulers. The former is more important than the latter: the Athenian says a little later that if the rulers are unfit, even good laws will probably cause harm (751b), but he never says that good rulers might cause harm. Yet there is one obscurity in the definition of regime proposed here and repeated later: into which of the two forms does the prelude to all the laws fit? The preludes came to light in a discussion which began when the stranger asked what the city's regime was to be (712c). The Athenian claimed to reject the notion that a "regime" meant the men who rule, whose way of life authoritatively sets the tone for the whole society and whose purposes become the society's chief purposes (cf. also *Republic* 544d–e, 545c–d); he substituted for this rule of men an admittedly almost unprecedented rule of god. This true regime was elaborated in his own, human, account of god, which came to be called the first part of the prelude. Now, as the Athenian returns to a more commonsense definition of "regime," we see that the rule of god—even when supplemented by the human legislator's preludes and laws—is not by itself sufficient. Human rulers are also required, mortals whose predominance gives forceful effectiveness to the precepts of the preludes (cf. 729c). Only when we have discerned to what extent these rulers are appliers of the law and preludes, and to what extent reshapers, will we be in a position to understand completely what the Athenian means by "regime" in the best practical sense.

The first step in selecting rulers is to devise criteria by which they may be distinguished from the rest of the citizens on the basis of their "difference in regard to virtue" and their greater education. For, we may be surprised to learn, the bulk of the citizens will possess only a "small education." In these remarks the Athenian foreshadows a society in which the rulers form a separate class, differentiated on the grounds of superior merit and education—but surely not wealth or family ties (recall the promise given at 715b).

But, as Aristotle justly complains (*Politics* 1265b18–22), the Athenian does not proceed to describe such a ruling class or the criteria that would distinguish it. Instead, a long and apparently somewhat rambling monologue ensues, during which the actual lawgiver Kleinias is not given an opportunity to ask any questions (note especially 746b). At the end of this interlude the Athenian restates the distinction between the two "forms" that make up every regime, and then goes on to select rulers without referring to the qualitative difference between rulers and ruled (cf. 734e–735a with 751a–b). Somehow, the considerations raised in the digression render unnecessary or inadvisable the special virtue and training of rulers that was first envisaged.

The curious monologue begins when the Athenian says that before they think about separating out the rulers, they must think about how they will separate out those who are too corrupt even to be citizens. The need for a purge illustrates more clearly why, in the "best" case, the founder is tyrannical. When the legislator's authority is limited, as in Kleinias's case, he will not be able to investigate everyone, rich as well as poor, to discover the individuals who are "incurable." To avoid antagonizing the property-holding majority, he will have to settle for a crude purge which involves gently sending away those whose poverty has so degraded them that they are ready to follow any leader who attacks what belongs to the rest (735e–736a; Marx calls this class the *lumpenproletariat*, and suggests dealing with it more brutally).

The suggestion that circumstances compel the legislator to identify vice with poverty marks the resurgence of the economic question, which dominates the rest of the monologue. Explicitly reverting to the gymnastic discussion in Book Three, the Athenian reminds them that they are lucky, not only because they have no indigenous class of poor to deal with, but also because they, like Sparta, can avoid the strife brought about by redivision of lands and cancellation of debts (736c ff.). He does not add that the Spartans' "good fortune" was due to their use of tyrannical violence in enslaving the original inhabitants (682e, 684d–e, 702a). For a legislator who aims at preserving and refounding an existing city with many debtors and a lopsided distribution of land and wealth there seems to be small hope of success. Sound economics is the necessary (but not sufficient) precondition for sound politics. Little in the way of political reform is possible until numerous enlightened reformers have arisen among the rich and have, by example and maneuver, led their class to restore a more balanced distribution of wealth (736d–e). By stating the problem thus, the Athenian circumscribes but passes over in silence the obvious alternative: a legislator could lead the poor in an attack on the rich. With the greatest possible caution, he points to another major reason why a legislator might have to act with tyrannical force, and indicates which political class is most likely to be the enemy target. The Athenian refrains from giving any explicit encouragement to revolution against the rich because, as we have already learned, and as we hear emphatically reasserted in this book (742d), he believes it to be most improbable that a democratic movement could be influenced by a philosopher whose political programs rank the austere pursuit of true virtue far above the pursuit of prosperity. It is more likely that philosophy might influence a few of the old, or young, rich, whose lives are not dominated by the degrading sting of economic necessity.

Leaving behind these sad and turbulent exigencies, the Athenian addresses himself to the question of the proper economic distribution in fortunate circumstances. The reason why the city cannot expect to have rulers of truly superior ability and training starts to emerge when the Athenian announces that they will not be able to construct, even in speech, anything better than a second-best regime. In the closest thing to a direct comparison with the *Republic* that occurs in the *Laws*, the Athenian says that their regime cannot be best because it is not based on communism. Here he repeats and makes more emphatic what Socrates teaches in the *Republic:* Plato's best regime is, and is intended to be, impossible. It is impossible because complete communism is against nature. It would be possible only for "gods or the children of gods," who lack bodies and do not confront individual death. But since men have mortal bodies they cannot ever become totally devoted to a city, or share completely their existence with others. Men's eyes, ears, and hands remain individuated, and what they perceive and experience always remains to a degree incapable of becoming common. Citizens cannot overcome the privacy and competitiveness of physical eroticism and the family that results, with all the private joys and sorrows it entails. Yet if such total community is impossible, why be seriously concerned with it? Why look to it as the standard? To answer this question one must undertake a long and careful study of the *Republic,* and above all of the drama of Glaucon and Adeimantus. At the cost of great oversimplification, this can be said: the city, man's political existence, his longing for justice and political nobility and civic friendship, necessarily point beyond what is possible in civic life. Politics is animated by longings it can never satisfy, and these longings too are natural to man. Man's nature is not harmonious in any straightforward way; the body and the soul, the parts of the soul, exist in a complex tension. As the Athenian expresses it a little later, "our whole regime has been put together as an imitation of the noblest and best life, which we indeed assert is really the truest tragedy" (817b).

The clear reference to the *Republic* prompts comparisons which illuminate the strange course of the argument in Book Five. For the regime of the *Republic* devotes a massive part of its energies to educating a superior "guardian" class (cf. 745a) devoted to the good of the city as a whole (*Republic* 420b–421c). Essential to the training and way of life of those guardians is a total communism of property that removes all temptations rooted in private economic interest (416b–417b). This requires the abolition of the private home (416d) and eventually the private family (423e, 449c ff.). In other words, the demand that rulers be of a moral and intellectual superiority consonant with their responsibilities leads necessarily to the demand that they form a separate, communistic class. Plato thus indicates that in settling for what is feasible, in abandoning communism, they must also abandon the likelihood of having rulers who are educated in a manner that makes them wholeheartedly devoted to the public good.

That is why it is so important that the rulers be kept "enslaved to the laws" (715d). In the rest of Book Five the Athenian makes more concrete what the compromise with private property involves, and attempts to mitigate the consequences.

Perhaps the most disturbing consequence is the need to create a hierarchy based on wealth. Without giving Kleinias an opportunity to concur or demur (see especially 744d), the Athenian calls for a social structure resembling Solon's Athens (cf. 696a–b with 698b), rather than the officially classless Sparta and Crete. (At the end of Book Five Athena has found her way into the most important civic sanctuary, along with Zeus and Hestia, and the rather bemused Kleinias addresses the Athenian as "*Athenian* stranger" for the first time since almost the beginning of the conversation: 745b, 747e.) Once a special guardian class based on communism has been abandoned, the city's political life cannot avoid being deeply influenced by inequalities of wealth, and it is better that the city confront the situation openly rather than try to hide it or ignore it (cf. *Republic* 548a–b). The Athenian breaks his promise (715b–d; cf. 697b–c): if rulers are selected by popular election, then handsomeness, strength of voice, and gracefulness of carriage, as well as who one's relatives are and how one uses one's money, are all bound to have an impact (744b–d). Nor is this so evil: where no specially trained guardians are available, all these advantages can indeed make one better fitted to lead the city, and the voters know this. Wealth, especially, brings with it greater leisure and independence, and thereby more time for reading, reflection, and education, as well as for obtaining a wide experience by traveling around the country and serving in a variety of lesser, time-consuming posts that prepare one for greater responsibilities. The more wealthy men are, the less time and attention they need devote to their property, especially in an economy such as the Athenian has insisted on (741a–744a)—where there is almost no liquidity of capital and where, as a consequence, fortunes usually grow or decrease slowly. None of this is to deny that wealth also brings the opportunity for all sorts of corruption (cf. 687b ff., 691a, 694e–696b, 698a). What is needed is a careful policing of wealth: not only the drastic discouragement of capital investment, but complete and continuous disclosure of almost every bit of property, and narrow upper and lower limits on the total property held by each family. The division into four classes makes it easier to disperse the rich geographically (745d) and allows the legislator to arrange systematically the representation of rich and poor in the government.

It seems at first somewhat paradoxical to justify permanent, unequal classes on the grounds of "equality of opportunities" (744b). What the Athenian means, in the first place, is that once one allows private property to exist it is only fair that, within reasonable limits, one allow every citizen an equal freedom to benefit from his property and talents. Some will be more thrifty than others and some will turn out to be shrewder or more hard-working farmers. Yet granted that it would be unfair to force all men to benefit from their property only as much as the less diligent and less talented, why should these benefits be passed on to descendants? Why should the classes be hereditary? To understand the justification for the dilution of equality of opportunity that underlies the *Laws,* we need to turn again to the *Republic,* which elaborates a society with strict equality of opportunity. There, in principle, every child has access to every rank in society, depending on the virtue and zeal he or she has displayed by a certain age (415b). Yet to achieve this, the family must be obliterated. Every child is to be taken away from his mother at birth, and no one is to know who procreated whom. Only then will the otherwise inevitable favoritism be avoided and only thus will children not be "deprived" or "specially advantaged" because of their home surroundings. The *Republic* shows that if one insists that the family is essential to men's happiness, one must face up to the fact that man's nature will not tolerate true equality of opportunity. Once a city allows and encourages family affection, once it asks parents to cherish their own children and children to cherish their own parents, it would be outrageous tyranny, a mad contradiction, if the city then demanded that parents not look upon the advancement of their own children as one of their deepest gratifications and incentives. The Athenian does away with primogeniture and, as we shall see, seeks to dilute inherited privilege (773a ff.); but he knows that such privilege cannot be abolished without doing violence to man.

The abandonment of the attempt to provide rulers who are equipped with a superior education should not be taken to imply that the "small education" of the citizens is insignificant or paltry. To make this clear, the Athenian in his conclusion stresses again (cf. 738b ff.) the need for extensive training in mathematics. Every facet of life and every aspect of nature that is susceptible of quantification should be quantified, coherently and precisely. The Athenian does voice one reservation against the popularization of mathematics: a legislator must guard against the dangerous affinity that exists between applied mathematics and the cultivation of economics, rooted in the love of money (cf. *Spirit of the Laws* XVIII 15 and IV 6). This danger is illustrated by the debased regimes of Egypt and Phoenicia.

The reference to these faraway, non-Hellenic lands leads the Athenian, for a reason not at first apparent, to a further reflection on the relation between the knowledge of *nature* and the task of the legislator. The natural environment, especially the climate, may have a decisive influence on the political alternatives available to a legislator in any given spot on earth—or, we might add, on any given planet in the cosmos. Almost insensibly, we have shifted from the mathematical education of the citizens to the education in nature needed by the legislator; and it is likely that the Athenian has in mind more than just this legislator (Kleinias) in this place (Magnesia). The four natural things the legislator should inquire into (wind, sun, water, earth) are reminiscent of the four elements the Athenian later describes as the foundations of his predecessors' theories of nature (889b, 891c, 895c; cf. 903e and 845d). He thus indicates that the inquiry into physical nature which one might wrongly suppose to be a theme restricted to "pre-Socratic" philosophy is a necessary part of the education of the "intelligent legislator" (747e). For most political men, and for the Athenian insofar as he philosophizes "politically," what the pre-Socratics ascribe to the eternal elements is ascribed to the eternal gods. So, bowing to Kleinias's level of education, the Athenian goes on to say that the influence of the divine or demonic overshadows all else. The disproportion between Kleinias's education and the "intelligent lawgiver's" is as great as the disproportion between the education possessed by the future rulers of his city and the education possessed by truly "intelligent rulers." Fortunately, of course, Kleinias has a philosophic advisor. But does even the Athenian possess adequate knowledge of the nature of wind, sun, water, and earth—in Crete or in general? Perhaps the science of lawgiving is, in the final analysis, as elusive as the science of the whole. In that case, perhaps the Athenian's respect for the demonic or divine is not purely ironic. His respect, however serious it may be, does not in any way discourage the closest possible inquiry into the divine.

751a–771a: The Rulers Who Are to Bridge the Gap between Thought and Action, Beginning and End

Near the end of Book Five, the Athenian raised doubts about whether his thoughts concerning even the second-best regime could be translated into action (745e ff.). He now stresses the responsibility *Kleinias* has for actualizing the new political order; in contrast to the future deeds of Kleinias and his nine co-founders, what the Athenian is doing resembles the mere telling of a myth (751e–752a). The Athenian must begin his discussion of the rulers by addressing once again the grave practical problem of the founding, because each successive generation of future rulers, and citizen-electors, must be educated in the spirit of the laws by the previous generation, and this means that a great deal depends on the education of the first generation. The quality of rule (*archē*) depends on the quality of the beginning (*archē*).

In taking up again the problem of the founding, the Athenian adopts a surprisingly "sporting" and even light-hearted tone, seemingly out of keeping with what he himself characterizes as the "seriousness" of the task (751d–752a, 769a; cf. 752e). Perhaps this is due to his being struck by the almost comic disproportion between the youthful courage the task demands and the advanced age of Kleinias and himself (712b, 752a, 770a). Carrying further the "realistic" tendencies of Book Five, he no longer even mentions the theoretically illuminating but impractical suggestion of a young tyrant. The philosopher now characterizes the job of founding in the following way: after having somehow won over nine co-founders, who will presumably never have heard the philosopher, the student Kleinias must join seventeen compatriots (also unfamiliar with the Athenian) in trying to dominate a committee of thirty-seven, the majority of whom are chosen from colonists who "won't easily accept any of the laws" (752c). Despite all the compromises this arrangement may require, it at least insures that almost half the first rulers have a Cretan education, that they bring to the regime the direct support of Knossos, and that they have the power implied in the fact that some of them (except for Kleinias) may be young, and hence able to rule for three or four decades. The stranger seems to doubt whether Kleinias will voluntarily accept the responsibilities and difficulties this arrangement implies (753a). Kleinias does not, however, reject the arrangement; he merely wonders why his Athenian advisor, and Megillus (who is the only other witness of what the Athenian lawgiver has said), should not share the responsibility for founding "our" regime. The advantages are obvious. Giving Megillus no opportunity to reply, the Athenian disingenuously advances his and Megillus's ties to their respective fatherlands to try to justify his refusal to assume any practical responsibility. The philosopher's wish to maintain his independence leaves him strongly disinclined to help translate his ideas into practice; and it is partly because of a certain alarm he feels at Kleinias's eagerness to corral him into the city that the Athenian proceeds to obfuscate and transform his first and best suggestion for the founding. He starts by describing how the Guardians might later be elected all at one time, and exclusively from the citizenry of the new city (he never suggests that the original thirty-seven, including Kleinias, be replaced one by one as they grow old or die: he blurs the transition to a radically different set of Guardians by preserving the number thirty-seven, which seems to have no merit except as a way of balancing the two constituencies of the original committee of guardians). The Athenian then insists that the problem of instituting the rulers remains unsolved and that he, moreover, can see no solution (753e–754a). Claiming to "repeat" his first suggestion, he in fact quite transforms it. In the new version, Kleinias (not to mention Megillus and the Athenian) need play no role as ruler, and greater reliance is placed on old age (754c). Neither Kleinias nor Megillus is given a chance to respond.

Insofar as an answer has been given to the problem of translating the lawgiver's intentions into the daily life of an actual city, it lies with the "Guardians of the Laws." The description of these magistrates is set off from, and literally surrounds, the description of all the other magistrates (755b, 769a–771a). In what the Athenian says and in their proposed role, the Guardians are intermingled with the founders; their very number, the prime thirty-seven, is related not to 5040 or any of its factors, but to the ambiguous account of the founding. They embody the unfinished and unfinishable character of the founding, which requires that something like the human lawgiver must be present in the regime always.

These future lawgivers are given their charge through a speech addressed directly to them (770b ff.), in which the Athenian speaks in the first person and refers emphatically to the fact that the regime was devised by *three* men (i.e., by a diverse and possibly disharmonious triumvirate). Their goal, the Athenian informs them, is to make the members of the community—whether their nature be male or female—good men (*andres*). Once again, the importance of manliness or courage in the best regime is stressed. But in the same breath the Athenian indicates to the Guardians that the city aims at something beyond itself. The goal is not good citizens, or law-abiding men, but rather men (*andres*) who have the virtue of soul befitting a human being (cf. 765e–766a). For the first time the Athenian goes so far as to say that the Guardians should be ready, in extreme circumstances, to sacrifice the city for the sake of virtue. Since the Guardians are to apply the standard of virtue in judging the laws, it would seem that their knowledge of virtue must be to some extent independent of those laws: they cannot be simply "slaves of the laws" (cf. 762e).

Rulers who are supposed to thus preserve, supplement, and review all the laws cannot have their official powers very strictly defined beforehand, and this indeterminateness naturally leads to some imprecision in the definition of the duties of all the other magistrates. Indeed, the constitutional account of offices and powers is surprisingly unlegalistic, and lacking in strict rules or boundaries of authority; it therefore leaves many questions to be settled in the flux of political maneuver and struggle that will be natural to a self-governing republic (cf. *Politics* 1265a 1-2: "most of *The Laws* is laws, although he has said a few things about the regime"). There is of course no separation or even distinction between "legislative" and "executive" branches of government, and hence the rule of law appears very imperfect when viewed through the "Montesquieuian" optic that is almost second nature to us (cf. my *Montesquieu's Philosophy of Liberalism*, pp. 109-12, 118-38). More surprising is the Athenian's failure to make the distinction Aristotle makes between the deliberative and magisterial functions of government (cf. *Politics* 1297b 35 ff.). By neglecting to make this distinction, the Athenian leaves unspecified the locus of sovereign power (*to kurion:* see *Politics* 1298a 5). This has the effect of strengthening the authority of the laws and diminishing the pretensions of even the highest rulers.

It is true, the description implicitly points out the deliberative function by making clear which magistrates have the most responsibility for comprehensive deliberation (Guardians, Generals, Presidents), and setting them off from the others (758e). Among these magistracies, the politically most active is the Presidential Committee, which in constant session supervises the city and conducts foreign policy. The Presidents change every month. The inconstancy, inexperience, and lack of authority before the populace, which might initially seem to be the consequences of such frequent turnover, can be ameliorated by the following constitutional features. In the first place, the Athenian leaves open the extent to which he expects the Presidents to consult with, and be guided by, the Guardians and the Generals—both of whom have much longer terms of office (no term is specified for the Generals, whose nomination is in the hands of the Guardians; at the very least, the Generals must be consulted on foreign policy—847d, 953b). Secondly, the Presidents are member-delegates of a Council which represents all four classes equally and thereby gives a disproportionate opportunity for holding office to the more leisured men of the much smaller upper classes: there is no bar to being repeatedly elected, and no pay to recompense a poorer man for his time. Besides, the Council rarely meets as a whole (cf. 768a, 850b). All this implies that at any given time the Presidency is likely to be dominated by the few upper-class men who get repeatedly elected to the Council and who "know the ropes." Thirdly, the Presidents have the power to convene, and, what is more, dissolve the Assembly. The only regularly scheduled meetings of the Assembly—which receives amazingly short shrift—seem to be for purposes of election (cf. 772d, 850b). Attendance at the few public meetings that do occur is weighted in favor of the upper classes. I conclude that, without at all removing the need for prudence, the Athenian's proposed Presidency strikes a nice balance between unrepublican centralization and unwieldly diffusion of authority.

The more one attempts to envisage the workings of the Presidency, and its relation to the other institutions, the more aware one becomes of the leeway the Athenian gives the citizens to work out their own political life—perhaps in rather diverse ways from one generation to the next. In this connection it is noteworthy that, in accordance with his silence about the sovereign power, the Athenian gives no strict constitutional answer to the question of who manages the budget, treasury, and tax policy (cf. 759e–760a and Morrow, pp. 191–94), and who has authority to make war and peace. Generally speaking, the regime as a whole leans toward rule by the few, though there is plenty of opportunity for the many to begin political agitation that can force changes in public policy. The almost complete lack of Assembly meetings does forestall the development of democratic politics. Nevertheless, the many have a decisive voice in selecting Generals from the nominees proposed by the Guardians, every citizen has a veto over nominees for the Guardianship, every citizen is eligible to be elected General or Guardian, and, above all, the lowest classes are insured of equal representation on the Council, if not in the Presidency.

In describing the election to the Council, the Athenian brings to light the fundamental principles that guide him throughout. True or natural "political justice" is the equality that consists in distributing

honor and responsibility, or dishonor and correction, in direct proportion to each person's education, merit, and potential for meri-
torious service. But because of the powerful discontent of the
many—which the Athenian associates here with equity, and not
with brute force—natural right must of necessity be alloyed with the
vulgar arithmetical equality that distributes honor and office equally
to every citizen. Both the unqualified honoring of virtue and a too
great pursuit of democratic equality lead to civil war (cf. 757a,e with
627e–628a).

The difficulty in the Athenian's appeal to these principles is un-
derlined by Aristotle (*Politics* 1266a 6–8): the true or naturally just
equality is here characterized as "monarchic," and yet there seems to
be no element of monarchy, strictly speaking (cf. 693d ff. and 761e),
in the constitution. The Athenian admits here, in fact, that the
"monarchic" principle of justice belongs to god, to Zeus, and "assists humans only to a small degree" (757b; cf. above, pp. 436–37); he
thus reminds us of the distinction he is now muting, but which he
earlier stressed, between true merit and merit crudely ascribed on
the basis of greater wealth, better looks, better birth, etc. This
regime, and in particular its governing Council, mixes the democratic equality not with an aristocratic or monarchic principle, but
rather with a distribution on the grounds of wealth, and popularity
expressed by voting (cf. above, pp. 461–62). The appeal to a "monarchic" principle in the absence of a real monarchic element clarifies
the reason why the Athenian fails to clarify the "regime," and specify which offices hold the sovereign deliberative power: no element
in the constitution, not even the Council, deserves to be given monarchic or sovereign authority because no element really embodies the
pure principle of natural justice. The mixed regime of oligarchy and
democracy may be said to be channelled and elevated toward the
true, "monarchic" principle by the rule of the laws; but law, even the
Athenian's divine law combined with the educative preludes, was
found to have an inexpugnable element of tyranny (cf. *Politics*
1266a 3).

To check tyrannical acts by the magistrates, who are more likely to
be undeniably prosperous, leisured, and educated than undeniably
virtuous, the law provides for judicial appeal from the decisions of
most magistrates, and almost never empowers a magistrate to act
singly (with the notable exception of the officials in charge of education and contests). Still, in contrast to Sparta, this regime relies less
on the competition of distinct institutions and more on mixing dif-

ferent constituencies and qualifications for rule in each of the various
deliberative institutions. A mixed regime of this sort functions less
automatically than the Spartan type and rests more on the cooperation and virtue of the rulers (cf. pp. 431–38 above and Polybius VI xiii–
xiv, xviii 5–8). The system's stability is surely not guaranteed by the
Guardians of the Laws, since they are given rather restricted disci-
plinary powers (cf. Morrow, pp. 198, 249).

The sequence of the discussion of the rest of the magistrates is
perplexing. The source of the difficulty seems to be a kind of competition for first place between the sacred officials and the rather Spartan institution of the Field Regulators. The Athenian is eager to turn
to the supervisors and guards of what lies *beyond* the city (758e,
760a–b), but he recalls that he has not finished with the supervisors
of what lies within the city, "including the sanctuaries and temples."
So he moves, reluctantly it seems, to the sacred officials (see at 763c
the reference to the order he originally wanted to follow).

The sacred officials and the Field Regulators are the only major
magistrates who are not selected by either the whole citizenry or by
representatives of the whole, and who therefore have somewhat independent bases of power. The Priests and Interpreters "administer,
in accordance with the sacred laws, the divine things" (759c–d). But
these "divine things" do not include the sacred funds in each temple, or the sanctuaries with their harvests and revenues: for sensible,
if not perfectly pious, reasons these important financial matters are
not entrusted to the men the god chooses. Similarly, the "sacred
laws" are not the same as the "divine laws" which govern the city as
a whole. These paradoxes reflect the tensions we discerned in the
theological oration of Book Four. The Field Regulators are also somewhat involved in caring for the divine things. In the course of fortify-
ing the countryside against *enemies*, they defend it against "the water
Zeus sends"; having subdued this water, they use it to adorn the
temples and sanctuaries.

But unlike the Priests, and most of the other magistrates, the
Officers of the "Secret Service" have a great deal to do with educating
the younger men. They control recruitment to, and the substance of,
what will doubtless be a very important step in the career of a young
man whose family can afford to give him leisure and equip him with
heavy armor (763a). The Officers of the Secret Service are in charge of
the hunting which proves to be the culmination of this regime's education (cf. 763b with 822d and 824). Their age and the precise mode of
their selection are left somewhat indeterminate (cf. 763d–e), as is their

relation to the Guardians (cf. 762d–e). Their duties seem rather on-erous, and only a man of leisure and avid civic spirit, or great attach-ment to young men, would be likely to volunteer for more than one two-year stint. The office might well be attractive to two sorts of men: those who enjoy police work and a military life, and those who, untroubled by poverty and an outdoor life, enjoy secrecy and gymnasia, and wish to get away from family and other civic responsibilities.

Of the remaining magistrates, the one who is indisputably more important than the Officers of the Secret Service is the Supervisor of Education. The majesty accorded this office testifies vividly to the difference between Platonic politics and what we moderns know as politics. The sixty Officers of the Secret Service constitute a clear ma-jority of the officials who gather to elect the Supervisor of Education; in other respects, the relations between those two magistracies are not spelled out.

With the discussion of the Supervisor of Education, the Athenian seems at first to have brought his discussion of the rulers to a close (766c–d). But he proceeds—or returns (cf. 761e–762b)—to the judi-ciary, after confessing some doubt as to whether the judiciary is part of the ruling offices. We should hesitate to read into this doubt the now prevalent notion of the separation of powers, because the Athe-nian has evinced not the slightest compunction in assigning to most of the magistrates powers which Montesquieu and the authors of *The Federalist* would call judicial, and whose amalgamation with ad-ministrative powers would in some cases cause them unease (see 761e ff., 764b–c, 765a). The reason the Athenian distinguishes the courts from the other rulers does not seem to be that he descries a general distinction between the powers of ruling and judging, but rather because some kinds of judging deal with disputes and infrac-tions of an especially grave character. The daily judicial activities of the magistrates provide adequate adjudication of many controversies and of minor lapses; but there arise irregular occasions when the fab-ric of society threatens to be torn by individuals who are involved in severe, lasting disputes, or who find the judgments of a magistrate intolerable, or who have committed grave crimes, including official malfeasance. In these cases the society at large must become involved in a much more searching inquiry into the particular circumstances and the proper application of the spirit of the law to those circum-stances. The Athenian says of the courts, and only of the courts, that without them "every city would cease to exist as a city," and he remarks that "anyone who does not share in the right of judging considers himself not at all a sharer in the city itself." He thus indicates that the courts are needed to deal with those crimes and controversies in which individuals threaten to revert to a prepolitical discord, and that the courts assure to each citizen that minimal equal protection and fair resolution of disputes which is the elemental reason for the existence of all civic law and order. The discussion of the courts is the point where the Athenian's republicanism comes closest to the modern, liberal republicanism which sees the protection of individual security as the chief purpose of government. But what the moderns see as the chief end, the Athenian sees as only an indispensable end. Even in his treatment of the courts, the Athenian erects fewer protective barriers around the "rights" of individuals than does modern republicanism.

PART FIVE: *The Way of Life of the Best Regime*

768e–785b: The Beginning of the Laws and the Beginning of Life

The beginning of the laws is somewhat murky, being neither a prelude (cf. 772e) nor a law. This murkiness is due to the still unresolved tensions among nature, law, and god. The Athenian had asserted, "in the name of the gods!," that according to *nature* the laws should begin with the original cause (*archē*) of childbirth in cities—that is, marriage (720e–721a). The *natural* order of laws follows the natural sequence of man's existence (cf. 631d). In this city, however, "god, not man, is the measure," so the laws begin with the sacred things. The Athenian is still not prepared to present a theological prelude that explains the relation between human nature and god, so he permits himself only an enigmatic reference to the natural impulsion every city feels to sanctify the numerical divisions that correspond to the "revolution of the whole." Then, without having named any gods in particular, he moves rapidly to a discussion of how the sacred festivals foster familiarity, especially between prospective spouses. In this roundabout way he introduces the marriage law, which appears as the first law enunciated in strictly legal language. The Athenian contrives a compromise: the laws do begin with the sacred things, but the sacred things are in large measure made to serve and support the human sociability that must precede marriage.

[471]

Yet why should the gods, or for that matter the laws, be needed to support marriage, if human life *naturally* begins from marriage? The laws claim that the marriage laws alone make babies possible (721a; *Crito* 50d), but the laws also know better: *eros*, not marriage, is the natural beginning (772e, 783a, 784e). Unless the marriage laws are preceded by other laws that provide for nude dancing and erotic "looking," they will lead to "mistakes." The laws that govern what precedes marriage cannot, however, be simply the "erotic laws," because *eros* is a lawless "illness" or "madness" (783a). The natural beginnings are in truth wild, erratic, and uncanny (775c–e, 782a). The problem of the origins, which in Book Three was considered in the context of the history of mankind, must now be considered in the context of the history of the individual human being. The origins may become more ordered if the citizens associate them with the gods or even worship them, in the right manner, as god (775e, 838b–c; cf. 780e with 780b). Sexual desire must be repressed by the institution of the pious family; but even then, sex remains a private pleasure that points toward the unpolitical and prepolitical. The Athenian's discussion is aimed at tempering the wild and naturally private bent of male and female sexuality. In this effort he can count on only mixed support from the traditional gods, who are too entangled in vestiges of the primitive (773d, 775b–e, 782b–d, 783d).

Once we have recognized the problem the Athenian is wrestling with, we are in a position to understand the striking differences between the actual marriage prelude and the marriage prelude proposed back in Book Four. The actual prelude focuses much more on how and whom, rather than why, one should marry. The young citizens are now told that in marriage they should oppose their self-interest, and even the preferences and pleasures that are "according to nature," for the sake of what is in the interest of the city. The earlier prelude is indeed incorporated into the new version, but with this change: the partaking in the eternity of nature is now understood as also a service to the god (774a, 776b). In the light of what has been learned since Book Four about the inegalitarian and disuniting effects of the passions that attach men to the family, the prelude must now go to admittedly almost laughable lengths in trying to check the *thumotic eros* which underlies marriage and the family (stopping short of Aristophanes' *Ecclesiazusae*, the Athenian's prelude makes no attempt to overcome inequalities in physical beauty). One might well wonder why the Athenian did not select some other prelude, less subject to subsequent revisions, in order to illustrate his proposal for preludes. I conclude that the marriage law was an apt choice because it reveals with great lucidity the degree to which even the oratorical prelude (as I have termed it) may have to be adulterated when incorporated in an actual law code. Very few of the so-called preludes will resemble exactly what we were led to expect in Book Four.

When he commences his discussion of the way of life of the newlyweds, the Athenian delivers what one may term his strongest antiliberal statement yet (780a), and the assault on the privacy of the family comes more to the fore. The husbands must participate in the common meals *"no differently and* no less" than before marriage. Does the Athenian mean that only some of the husbands—those who served as Field Regulators—will continue to take their meals in common? Or does he now assume that all husbands will have served as Field Regulators? But could fathers of the lower classes afford to equip their sons with heavy arms and allow them to leave the farm for two whole years, supporting them with food, even of a humble sort? Perhaps the Athenian means that all young men, whether or not they serve in the Field Regulators, will partake of common meals, and continue to do so throughout their lives. But in that case one must still wonder how the lower class fathers and sons can afford to spend the time, and perhaps the money, required for continuing to partake in the common meals (cf. 842b, 847e–848c). And if only some of the citizens can afford the common meals, won't the city in fact have two kinds of citizens pursuing two very different ways of life, one more private and one more communal? The problems involved here are reminiscent of the problems Aristotle so correctly discerns in the *Republic*'s attempt to secure equality of opportunity (cf. *Politics* 1262b 25 ff., 1264a 13 ff.) In the *Laws* the institution of slavery will perhaps provide the necessary leisure that will enable all citizens to partake of the common meals (806e); if so, many more slaves will be needed than might at first appear. These economic difficulties can only be aggravated by the proposal that follows next.

For the women too must partake of common meals, or else, left to retire into their private "nests," they will lack public spirit and sap the public spirit of the men (the Athenian does not need to mention again the most shameful consequence of all-male common meals). The danger of leaving the women out is especially grave because of their natural inferiority as regards virtue: somewhat paradoxically, it is the natural inequality, not the natural equality, of the sexes that dictates having women share every practice in common with men.

[473]

The major obstacle to women's common meals is the resistance of the women themselves. According to the Athenian's explicit statement, this resistance is the result of the conventional habituation women have "unfortunately" received, an habituation which is so universal and so powerful that one cannot seriously think of even speaking against it except in those rare regimes which already have common meals for men. The Athenian is willing to defend his innovation by showing how it is "good and fitting" (not how it is possible), but only if his interlocutors think it is not "unlucky" to do so. He does not ask them to agree that it is not impious to do so.

The Athenian embarks on his admittedly obscure explanation by "going back again" to the primeval origins—in order, he seems to say, to understand better man's threefold fundamental erotic need (782d). Evidently the proof of the goodness of women's common meals depends on a better understanding of *eros,* which in turn requires a renewed reflection on man's past. Since the Athenian is no longer under the constraints he was under in Book Three, he is now more frank about the strange and savage extremes that prevail among primitive men. He dwells on the wide spectrum of beliefs men have held concerning what foods and drinks are suitable or unsuitable for themselves and their gods. By showing the diversity of men's tastes in eating, and suggesting how long it took mankind to arrive at a sensible notion of what food is appropriate, the Athenian seems to suggest that, similarly, the way men *gather* to eat may be more flexible, and require a longer time to perfect, than people tend to suppose. The rarity of common meals is no proof that they are not by nature good and fitting, at least from the point of view of man's erotic needs for food and drink. Yet the common meals involve also an ordering of the sexual desire. After making it clear that what is at stake is a *threefold* erotic desire, and stressing the fact that the sexual desire is for humans the "greatest" and the "maddest," the Athenian breaks off his explanation of the goodness of common meals for women. That explanation, he says, will perhaps be completed after the discussion of the procreation, upbringing, and education of the children. In fact, it is never completed.

Thus, having led us into these deep waters, the Athenian compels us to swim by ourselves. Let us try to respond to his implicit invitation to think through the defense of common meals for men and women. That defense requires an analysis of man's threefold erotic desire. The Athenian showed the way by delineating, in the case of the desire for food, two primitive extremes—cannibalism and human sacrifice on the one hand, and total abstention from eating and sacrificing flesh on the other. He thus seemed to point to a civilized mean that would involve the eating and sacrificing of some animals but total abstention from human flesh. In the case of drink, we can fairly easily bring together the Athenian's several discussions of wine drinking and thus construct the parallel extremes and mean, as regards both drinking itself and the worship of the god of wine (cf. 637d–e, 673e ff., 775b–e, 782b). Now what is the parallel in the case of sex? The obvious extremes are promiscuity and strict chastity; the supposedly civilized Greeks believe that the mean is monogamy, presided over by Zeus and Hera (774d). But would not a more rational mean be a controlled sexual communism (presided over by more sober gods), which would harmonize with the institution of common meals much better than monogamy does? Is the Athenian not hinting that a full defense of common meals from the point of view of the sexual appetite would require the introduction and defense of sexual communism (cf. 807b and the *Republic*)?

We get some more specific indication of the reasons why the Athenian cannot defend fully the goodness of sexual communism, and common meals for women, if we give close attention and thought to what he does say as he abruptly terminates his defense. In describing the threefold erotic desire, he draws a distinction between man and the other animals in regard to sexual desire. While the desires for food and drink produce frenzy, and a refusal to listen, in "every animal," sexual desire "makes *human beings* burn with complete madness." The sexual desire is "most insolent" in humans because man is the animal in whom sexuality is not instinctually controlled by heat periods or mating seasons. The Athenian thus brings into view one important reason why there is not a real parallel between man's sexual *eros* and his erotic desires for food and drink. The human sexual desire is far less a simply physical, animal appetite than are the human desires for nourishment. Human sexuality, to a large degree liberated from rigid instinctual patterns, is intertwined at every level of expression with human imagination, reason, and self-awareness. For this reason, human beings cannot distance themselves from, and thereby manipulate, their sexual needs as readily as they can their needs for nourishment. In the Athenian's remarks on the history of man's appetite for food, he showed both the manifold manifestations of the appetite and the extent to which social convention can exaggerate or eradicate its various manifestations; if we proceed to follow through and consider the parallel history of human sexuality, we are likely to conclude that the diversity of manifestations is both wider and less easily dominated by convention.

Obviously central to the distinctive character of sexual *eros* is the fact that it splits the human race into two "kinds" (781a), whose desires and actions are profoundly differentiated. The degree of the difference is somewhat obscured so long as one puts in relief the desire itself, and keeps in the background the engendering of children: unlike the other two desires, the sexual need is procreative, and human sexual desire is never wholly forgetful of the offspring which are its consequences. By remarking that the discussion of common meals for women must be postponed until after the discussion of children, the Athenian implies that children are the decisive obstacle to the full defense of the common meals.

The import of the preceding observations may be summarized in the following way. In beginning to discuss the way of life of the citizen, the Athenian focuses on the mealtime because that is the part of daily life in which humans gratify two of their three basic desires, and hence where much of life's ordinary joy is found. He wants the private pleasures of eating and drinking to be as convivial as possible; he aims at elevating these animal functions by mingling them with friendly adult conversations that make meals something far more than occasions for gratifying the body or listening to the platitudes of one's narrow family circle and the babble of one's children. The human way of eating, by nature, is in common meals of adult fellow citizens. Yet the Athenian admits that almost no human societies have ever regularly eaten in this natural human way. In this case at any rate, it is not sufficient to remind ourselves that for Plato the fully natural rarely occurs; the universal habituation of women which opposes common meals for both sexes cannot be mere convention. The natural human way of eating is contradicted in the first place by the private exclusivity of natural human love, and in the second place by natural human reproduction, which dictates that women bear, and devote years to raising, a number of offspring. The latter lengthy and delicate process requires that women be protected, and excused from some public duties, and seems to demand that women's chastity be guarded so as to interest a male in providing such protection and assuming such duties. The Athenian could for a moment partially abstract from these natural constraints because he raised the question of common meals for women in the context of the first months of married life—that is, in the context of the brief time during which no adult woman is supposed to have children.

The practical outcome of this contradiction within human nature will be, in the best regime, an uneasy compromise. If the women attend the same common meals as the men, they must have less rigorous attendance requirements, and thereby risk becoming second-class participants; besides, if common meals for men prompt homosexual misconduct, the mixing of men and women threatens to prompt heterosexual misconduct to an even greater extent. So there must be separate tables, and if the women are to attend their own tables regularly, they must be allowed to bring little children, who make only more obvious the difference in the tone of the conversation at the segregated tables (806e). The problem of sexual promiscuity is perhaps alleviated by situating the tables for men and the tables for women near one another; that this is not a complete solution is shown by the rather surprising lightness of the penalties the pagan Athenian suggests here for adultery (784e–785a; contrast More's *Utopia*, Surtz ed., pp. 111–12). After all, men and women who are not spouses may often cooperate in their public duties.

788a–835b: The Education of the Children and the Serious Play of the Adults

The Athenian now applies the educational principles he elaborated in Books One and Two, and thus answers some of the questions we had about the practical import of that discussion. At the outset, and repeatedly in the course of his presentation, he teaches that education should be regulated by "a kind of instruction and admonition" rather than by law in the strict sense. The "nature" of this new legislative speech is somewhat obscure (788c, 822d); it appears to be something like a legislation through "preludes" alone (cf. 822d–e with 823d ff.). If we look back over the ground covered since the notion of "preludes" was introduced, we see that the distinction between law and explanatory or admonitory speech has been far from clear-cut: in this respect the marriage law is the exception rather than the rule. The legislation has been in large part an "interweaving" (823a) of command and exhortation, and the manner in which education is treated only carries this tendency further. There seem to be at least two reasons why law is mainly, though not entirely, inappropriate for dealing with education. On the one hand, much of education takes place in the private homes, where law is not easily enforced, and where the attempt to enforce it is likely to make the law and the magistrates appear ridiculous (cf. 790a). On the other hand, the public as well as the private aspects of moral education involve the handing down of opinions and tastes; these are often not exhibited in easily specified and policed actions, and much of the time opinion can be best directed by authoritative persuasion and example rather than by coercive sanction (cf. 822d–823a). The Athenian's sparse use of law here is not due, then, to a fear of trenching on a sacred sphere of privacy; his concern is with showing the most effective way to intervene in the private lives of citizens. Book Seven, especially, exemplifies that art of legislating morals which Rousseau praises in the Spartans and finds "entirely lost" among the "moderns": the "moderns" try to shape *moeurs* by laws, and when that fails know of no recourse except tyranny or the abandonment of public enforcement of morals (*Social Contract* IV 7; *Letter to D'Alembert*, Bloom ed., pp. 65 ff.).

The discussion of correct upbringing begins with the gymnastic that is appropriate for the bodies of fetuses and babies. (We are at once alerted to how much was omitted in the "ungymnastic" account of education in Books One and Two.) On the basis of what he has learned from Athenian males who raise birds for fighting, the stranger proposes that pregnant women should go for walks, and that when the baby is born it should be swaddled, carried about continually, and not allowed to move by itself much. He is sure that women will find his rather extreme admonitions ridiculous, and will not obey them unless compelled by the male heads of the households.

As he turns to advice about the training of the babies' souls, the Athenian characterizes his admonitions about the bodies as "myths," and indicates that his real concern is with the beneficial effect the gymnastic motion and protective care have on the *soul*. The baby should be constantly rocked to the accompaniment of music, not so much because its body needs stimulation but because its soul needs to be calmed and distracted from its own spontaneous motion. For the primary, self-moving motion of soul is a mad terror. Women who care for babies are aware of the need for rocking and lullabies, but they (and Kleinias) have not fully recognized the terror that is the root of this need because they, unlike the philosopher, have not linked their experience with that of other women who cure madness in adults. In the case of adults, the dance motion and musical motion are made effective by being combined with the invocation of gods.

In these remarks the Athenian brings to light the fundamental, sinister source of the human need for "music," the source he only alluded to in Book Two (653e, 664e, 672c–d). Whatever may be true of other animals, the human infant is possessed by terror, a terror that would seem to be the not unreasonable response of the baby to its helplessness, lack of sheltering instincts, and dim awareness of its own fragility. The sense of fragility and the terror recur with varying intensity in adults, and, unlike other fears and pains, it may not be reasonable to expect citizens to confront and master this elemental terror by being exposed to it more and more. The terror *can* be counteracted and overlaid—by faith in healing gods and by music. In this context the *alogon* (speechless) dimension of music is at least as beneficial as the *logos* that gives content to the songs. The Athenian quite underestimated this aspect of music in Book Two because his discussion there abstracted from gymnastics, or the body and its formative influence on the soul.

The existence of the primary and enduring terror within the soul makes courage an even more important part of virtue than we have hitherto supposed. Since Book Two, as the Athenian has steadily deepened our understanding of the psychology of citizenship, he has been preparing us for the elevated rank and enormous emphasis that will be bestowed on courage throughout the account of education: it turns out that Kleinias underestimated rather than overestimated the importance of education in courage, rightly understood (cf. pp. 389–91 above and *Republic* 429a–430c).

When the Athenian turns to the baby's training in pleasure and pain, he gives further proof of this centrality of courage. The training is not characterized as a training in "moderation" but instead as part of the training in "stoutness of soul," or courage. A gracious posture toward the appetites is achieved by turning the baby's *thumos* inward, and habituating it to endurance and self-control. This is somehow an imitation of god, whose austere existence is not filled with either complete pleasure or great suffering—and certainly not with angry complaints and grieving. Once again the Athenian fears the ridicule of the women, who tend to overindulge children's appetites and angers, and thus unwittingly prepare them for a life of disappointment and weak-spirited complaining. Kleinias again shares the women's ignorance, because he uncritically follows their say as regards babies, and because, like them, he has heretofore been ignorant of the example god provides (cf. 792d with 716c; as for woman's *thumos*, see 731d and 935a). The training of the infants in the twofold "stoutness of soul" constitutes the entire training during the years "when, through habituation, the most decisive growth in the entire character occurs for everyone" (792e). There is no third part to this crucial training: in fact, nowhere in Book Seven is there an education in justice *per se* (contrast Xenophon *Education of Cyrus* I ii 6–7). We were forewarned that in the city under law, justice would appear as a composite of the other virtues, or even as a means to moderation (cf. pp. 387, 391 above). But justice now seems to be replaced by the manly sense of "freedom," or "magnificence"—a virtue not incompatible with a desire for tyranny (cf. 795e, 802e, 808c, 829a, 837c with 709e).

The Athenian's unprecedented stress on training in manly courage is in danger of being frustrated by the women, who in the private homes wield such influence over the babies. Yet the Athenian had tentatively suggested that women be forced into public life. If "every practice were shared in common by women" (781b), especially military practice, wouldn't the women sympathize much more with the lawgiver's concerns? After showing that the training in stoutness of soul is to be continued during the ages of three to six, still under women's supervision, the Athenian turns to the "studies" of the children over six, and rather hesitantly calls for a military training of females as well as males, on the grounds that prevailing custom in this regard is based on prejudice. When Kleinias is unable or too stubborn to recognize the prejudice the Athenian has attacked earlier, the Athenian shifts abruptly from his incipient argument for an almost equal training of the sexes in war to a rather eccentric plea for an almost equal training of the left and right hands. The argument for ambidexterity is a stalking-horse for the sexual argument; by switching to this analogy the philosopher prompts thought and tries to defuse the passions that always surround the sexual issue.

The argument for ambidexterity contains a remarkable concentration of appeals to "nature," in opposition to the almost universal practice of mankind and especially the Greeks; it thereby exemplifies, and allows us to ponder, the philosopher's appeal to "nature" as a standard generally. The "natural," as conceived here, is not what obtains always or even usually, except perhaps in potential. The "natural" is rather the full development, in a harmonious and uncontradictory way, of all the observed human capacities—in an individual or in society at large. (This is not to deny that some capacities are fully developed only when subordinated to others, as dexterity is properly subordinate to prudence.) Now the partiality of this conception of nature is made manifest by the simple example of ambidexterity. In all but a few rare individuals, is it not impossible to cultivate ambidexterity without sacrificing true dexterity in the right or left hand? Is the universal convention favoring "righties" not a fairly reasonable, if crude, response to the unbalanced endowment most human bodies receive from nature and chance? Put more generally, is not the failure of society to strive for all-around natural perfection, and the consequent divisions of labor—especially the sexual division—a fairly reasonable, if crude, response to another aspect of nature? One might go so far as to say that the cultivation of ambidexterity is analogous to the best regime by nature, while the cultivation of right-handedness is analogous to "natural law" (cf. 636b and *Ethics* 1134b 30 ff.). We see that reflection on our commonsense doubts about the simpler project of making all citizens ambidextrous is meant to illuminate the grounds for resistance to the idea of making men and women share the same military training. The fact is, very few women are as strong as men, and in trying to give both sexes the same military training the regime risks winding up with a rather low general level of proficiency. For the present, the Athenian seems to sketch yet another compromise: the "virgins" are to receive a partial military and gymnastic training, segregated from the boys (794c–d): to compensate for the tendency to a slacker military tone caused by the girls' participation in the public gymnastic festivals, those festivals must have an extremely militaristic flavor, with the "virgin" warrior-goddess Athena as the model.

The threat woman's integration into public life poses, on account of her inferiority in strength, would be limited if the education and excellence of the body were separable from the education and excellence of the soul. So the Athenian now tries to revert to his position in Book Two, saying that gymnastics pertains to the body, while music is for the soul (795d; cf. 791c and 673a–b, d); he tries to "finish" with gymnastics, and move on to education in music. But he attempts this gambit only to reveal its unworkability. On the one hand, gymnastic includes choral dancing, which involves "imitating the speech of the Muse" and exhibiting the virtues of the soul, above all manly magnificence and freedom (795e, 796b). On the other hand, music is "for the sake of stoutness of soul": insofar as courage is the basis for civic virtue of soul, music and gymnastics overlap in the chorus and both have the same principal end. As we learned in the case of babies, a human being's strength of soul depends decisively on the condition of his body. A citizen's courage and sturdy spiritedness are rooted in the self-confidence and self-control he attains through his achievement of proficiency in the military and in manly dancing. At the end of his discussion of music, the Athenian must make it clear that women are "by nature" inferior as regards the musical expression of the soul's "magnificence, and whatever inclines to courage" (802e; cf. 917a and 944d). The equal participation of women therefore tends to drag down the level of the city's excellence of soul, as well as body.

Nonetheless, we should by no means suppose that there would not be even graver risks involved in returning to the system which leaves women in a private condition. To grasp the full import of the new stress on education in courage, and hence the magnitude of the risks, we need to reflect further on what is implied by the connection the Athenian drew between woman's misunderstanding of "stoutness of soul" and her misapprehension of the nature of god. In presenting the very first of the "laws" of music, the Athenian strongly attacks the musical practice of "almost every city in [his] part of the world" because the choruses present interpretations of human life and of the gods that are too tragic or mournful, thereby evoking fear and loss of spiritedness (800b–e). Later, in his concluding remarks on music education, the Athenian makes his meaning even clearer (817a ff.): the proposed education, the new regime as a whole, is intended to overthrow and replace the tragic conception of god and human existence that is instilled by almost all the "serious" poets—the "tragic sense of the Greeks" so admired by Nietzsche. Like the women who lead the Corybantic dances, the tragic poets help man deal with the elemental terror, but they do so in a way that is at once too fearful and too flattering. The poets dwell on man's mortality and the perishability of what he loves (recall 719d–e); the "children of the soft Muses" (817d) indulge human weakness, not through the promise of an unbelievable happy ending, but by assuring man that his fears and his sadness have cosmic significance. The tragic poets teach that, in the case of the hero at least, human suffering and need (including financial need: 801b–c) reflect divine suffering and need, and that human excellence arouses divine compassion or regret ("whoever can make the city weep the most . . . wins the victory"—800d). Tragic religiosity leads man to believe that the most authentic human experience is noble failure and consequent sadness, consoled and elevated by divine compassion and eternal divine recognition. This tragic religiosity, the Athenian seems to suggest, not only obscures the truth; it ultimately makes political life less confident and less independent, and renders men prey to fanatic hopes and fears.

Now tragedy, we recall, is the favorite music of educated women (658d); and the elemental terror has heretofore been understood best

by the Corybantic priestesses. We may surmise that the terror tends
to be felt more by women because their bodies are weaker. Women
are therefore more prone to piety: "it is a habit of all women especially . . . to sanctify whatever happens to be around. . . . Moreover,
having been stirred awake by fears they experience . . . , they make
remedies against each of them by filling every house and every district with altars and temples . . ." (909e–910b; cf. 814b). By failing to
bring the women into public life, the Athenian would leave them
free to undermine not only the infant's education in courage, but the
whole vast innovation in piety which we now begin to see is a central part of the stress on courage (cf. 887d). Yet if the women are introduced into the public life and festivals, it seems their presence
must be compensated for by making that life extremely militaristic in
tone. Is such a tone altogether compatible with the new view of god
and human existence the Athenian wishes to promote? What exactly
is this new, untragic outlook? Before we can learn more about it, we
must attend to still another difficulty.

The complex harmony that was forged in Book Two, between civic
virtue and a dimmed version of intellectual virtue, must now be
rethought in the light of the new psychological facts that have
emerged concerning civic virtue. In commencing his discussion of
music education, the Athenian says they were mistaken in supposing they had given a complete account of music education, for they
omitted "the first things one tells everyone" (796e). He proceeds to
show what those "first things" are, by delivering the sternest and
lengthiest warning we have yet heard concerning the evils of innovation and critical thought. What underlies this warning is the following consideration. Civic virtue is based almost exclusively on habituation rather than reasoning: the decisive formation of soul occurs in
early childhood, and is just like getting the body used to food and
drink (802d, 653b, 792e, 797a–798d). Now the education in virtue we
are considering, because it is according to nature, is characterized
by very radical innovations, especially as regards the children's attitudes toward courage, women, and the gods. The support for these
innovations is not coercion or reason or even written law, but the
force of habit and public opinion. Yet, because they are so unprecedented, the new attitudes are opposed by the almost universal opinions and habits of the rest of the human race. The regime whose virtue and education are most according to nature is the regime that is
most endangered by the powerful consensus of mankind, and must
therefore be the most fearful of change and the intrusion of foreign

ways. The citizens must be convinced that their newest ways are the oldest ways, or are even eternal, and that they are ratified by the authority of the eternal gods (798b; cf. 793b–c). Consequently, the Athenian now reverts to the Egyptian model of regulation for public music, and proposes a new and much more stringent enforcement of the sanctified canon of songs and dances (799a–c, 800a). Nevertheless, the all-out advocacy of the Egyptian system proves to be somewhat provisional (799c–e, 800b), and in the succeeding pages the Athenian goes on to construct a very conservative version of the musical regime he sketched in Book Two. Some poetic innovation, based on "intelligence," is allowed (801a, d). New poetry is to be judged by a select group of citizens, and another such group is to study and judge ancient foreign poetry; these two groups, whose memberships overlap, include the poetic men of all ages, the musical magistrates of various ages, and the Guardians. Taken together, they constitute a divided, sober, and subdued version of the much more remarkable "Dionysian chorus" of Book Two.

At the beginning of this discussion of music, the Athenian characterizes his subsequent attack on innovators as "somewhat frightening" (797a; cf. 799c–e). But we see presently that Kleinias and Megillus hardly find it so (797d); it is the Athenian himself who feels fear and reluctance, because the argument requires him to attack and proscribe men like himself, men who engage in the very sort of innovative activity he is at the moment engaged in. The elaboration of the musical education of the soul represents a definite retreat from the aspirations to education of the soul that we were witness to in Book Two. By remarking this we are somewhat prepared for the strange dramatic interlude that follows, an interlude that makes clearer the problematic character of the new civil religion the Athenian proposes.

As we have noted, the discussion of music concludes with a clear admission of the fact that men and women differ by nature as regards the virtues of the soul. The Athenian thus brings to the fore the still unresolved dilemma of how, in practice, women are to share in the education. He now speaks as though he had completed his account of the subjects in the curriculum, and were prepared to turn "next" to an explanation of how "these very things" should be taught—and therefore how the girls' education should be managed (cf. 803a with 804c–e). He interrupts this sequence of thought, however, with a reflection on his own doings, a reflection seemingly prompted by the insurmountability of the practical difficulties. Once again he compares political life to a ship at sea, and is led to a profound disparagement of legislative activity and of "the affairs of human beings" in general (cf. 708e ff.). Yet he immediately indicates that he does not voice this disparagement out of anything like a sense of sorrow or despair; for he knows of the existence of god, whose "complete, blessed seriousness" renders human joy and sorrow insignificant, and reveals man to be, at best, only "a certain plaything of god." In his two earlier, parallel remarks, he had been unwilling to speak so precisely about man's status in relation to god (644d), and had referred to a "piloting" god, whom he assimilated to chance (708e ff.). Now he does not refer to chance; the god he has in mind does not "pilot" or intervene much at all in human affairs, except to "suggest things," perhaps through a "demon" (cf. 804a with 713c ff.). The Athenian reveals that he possesses a strength of soul that is not rooted in manliness or in hopes for victory or success, but instead in a resigned joy that comes from his knowledge and his contemplation of eternity.

What is at least as remarkable as this self-revelation itself is the fact that the philosopher goes on to suggest that the citizens should share his perspective. The philosopher's reflection on his inability to achieve political success, and his refusal to take political success or failure very seriously, should be the source of the best city's new attitude toward god and human destiny. The Athenian seems to suggest that the courage rooted in manliness should be supplemented, or even overshadowed, by a pious version of the philosopher's courage.

The Athenian concludes his elusive utterance by saying that the young should not suppose that the musical regulations thus far elaborated represent the final word on these matters. The "demon and god" will suggest other things to them. At this point, the Athenian speaks not of "looking at god" but of "sharing in truth." To illustrate his advice to the young, he borrows the words the goddess of wisdom uses when, disguised as an old man, she urges young Telemachus to question boldly the authoritative old Nestor. The philosopher thus dares to hint that he is the avatar of divinity, which in its nature partakes at least as much of the rather rebellious female as it does of the old male.

The Athenian has tried to convey the peculiar mixture of openness and closedness to the truth that he hopes will characterize the city he is founding. The only direct link between philosophy and the citizens would be the trail the philosophic legislator blazes for a few of the young, who could discern between the lines of his legislation his invitation to question, in a suitably prudent way, all authority and law. The citizens in general could look up to the life which is the philosopher's goal, the life that partakes of the truth, but they could know of such a life only through the veil of a particular kind of religious belief. The belief would lead them to acknowledge that such a life's serious activity takes place beyond political life, and beyond intense care for the city. The citizens could visualize some aspects of the elusive god through myths and songs that centered on a female deity like Athena. In short, the Athenian suggests that the citizens could be brought up in a belief which denies to them and their city great significance or hope, and which consoles them by awakening and responding to their capacity for a very austere, imitative reverence.

Yet there is a tension between this view, and the kind of courage it inculcates, and manliness. The tension appears in the Athenian's explanation of the way "every man and woman should think about" the religious festivals and play. "Nowadays" people think that war, being serious, is for the sake of peace, which lacks seriousness. (The Athenian thus gives a one sentence synopsis of his critique, in Book One, of the most widely admired regimes.) Against this, the Athenian argues that war does not contain the worthy play and education that are for "us" humans the most serious things. He seems to imply that the new city will differ from all existing cities in that it will subordinate war—which he does not deny is serious—to a peaceful play and education which are understood to be more serious, because they are a devotion to and imitation of the divine, the truly serious. But he then adds that each person should play so as to make the gods propitious to oneself *and* so as to defeat one's enemies. War is not the most serious thing, but the play that is most serious is at least partly for the sake of victory in battle. The confusing circularity of the Athenian's pronouncement reflects the city's inability to pursue a fully coherent peaceful goal: insofar as civic virtue is based on spirited manliness, it necessarily includes a passionate commitment to the love and defense of one's own city, family, honor, and property. As the example of Achilles shows, manliness is more in accord with a tragic view than with the view the Athenian professes. Instead of simply supplementing manliness, the Athenian's new kind of piety must coexist uneasily with manliness, counterbalancing its tendency to slip into a traditional, tragic piety.

At this point, however, even this sort of coexistence is politically unviable. Its unviability is revealed in the drama by the reaction of the manly Megillus, who protests in amazement. Megillus claims that the Athenian is "belittling our human race in *every* respect." Megillus is not the sort of man who can find much, if any, comfort in the fact that mankind "shares in small portions of the truth." In response to this outburst, the philosopher asks Megillus's forgiveness; bowing to what Megillus cherishes, the Athenian agrees to "let our race be something that is not lowly." Megillus's remonstrance seems to bring the philosopher back down to a human level, forcing him to reckon with needs he had temporarily lost touch with. At any rate, after taking up again the broken thread of his account of how the previously specified subject matters are to be taught, the Athenian allows that account to broaden into a whole new elaboration of the subject matters themselves—which he appeared earlier to have finished enumerating (cf. 796d, 803a, 809b, 813b). The Athenian is led to revamp his educational scheme because Megillus's reaction makes him realize that the education as outlined thus far does not adequately prepare citizens to accept the religious outlook he proposes. Things cannot be left as they now stand—with such a chasm between the philosopher, on one side, and the ordinary citizen, on the other, who is supposed to bow to a distant and almost unrecognizable beacon of philosophy and, in the name of that beacon, subdue within himself many of the usual forms of pious fervor. There must be some version of philosophy active within the life of the city. Among the leaders who guide religious worship there must be some who are educated to a point where they at least believe they have substantial knowledge of god, and who therefore possess a courage that stems not only from manliness but also from the authority and consoling satisfaction of knowledge. Among the citizenry, there must be some more vivid and concrete model of a human life suffused with the serenity the Athenian praises and demands. Moreover, the citizens should believe they have been provided with an education that allows them to appreciate the knowledge of their religious leaders, and that gives them a plausible defense of their regime's claim to a knowledge of god superior to the knowledge possessed by the rest of mankind.

Yet as the Athenian has made perfectly clear, philosophy, with its innovative and critical spirit, is as such, inimical to the habituation which underlies manly civic virtue. Philosophy endangers manliness; but it is the only source of true human courage, without whose

[487]

protective influence manliness collapses into tragedy. In what guise
or version can philosophy be part of civic life without destroying it?
We now see more clearly why the problem of the coherence or *idea* of
virtue is primarily, and perhaps above all, the problem of the coherence of courage (cf. pp. 389–91 above; 963e–964a; *Republic* 428a–430c,
521d–522a, 525b, 543a).

The Athenian now begins the discussion of "what follows these
things," and moves rapidly to confront the question of women's education. He asserts, with a firmness he had not evinced before, that
"his" law would say "females should be trained on an equal basis,"
and he claims that women can achieve an equal proficiency in war.
When Kleinias politely indicates that he is not exactly bowled over
by the "evidence" the Athenian adduces to prove his claim, the
Athenian tendentiously insists that the claim has been "sufficiently
demonstrated by deeds" (805c). But he quickly shifts his argument to
a new footing: if he can't give very persuasive evidence for the possibility of sexual equality in training for war, at least he can demonstrate the military defectiveness of the major alternative regimens for
women, especially the Athenian and Spartan. He then proceeds to
describe the new, superior regimen he proposes—the regimen
which women share (almost) equally with men. In doing so he raises
again, but more starkly, the question he managed eventually to answer in the ungymnastic discussion of Book Two: what exactly is the
activity which justifies the best city's claim to have a truly complete
and happy human existence? It is from the new attempt to answer
this question that the new articulation of education emerges. The
Athenian's obstinate insistence that women can be equal to men in
gymnastics and war is the *necessary* prelude to his endeavor to elaborate an education that transcends manliness in the direction of philosophy. The reason is this: if, or to the extent that, the legislator
were confident that women's deficiency in strength and courage
could be overcome, he could allow himself to place less emphasis on
education in manliness. The model for his citizens would be the
goddess Athena, who combines womanliness, war, and wisdom
(796b–c, 804a, 806b).

But the fact is that Athena is a goddess, a poetic vision, possessing
a combination of qualities no human woman can imitate. Through
his unsuccessful attempt to argue that the women can become Amazons, the Athenian spotlights the most massive obstacle that will
always hamper the city's devotion to virtues beyond manliness. By

the same token, Athena is and remains eternally a virgin (cf. 794c with 796b–c), and this cannot be the destiny of human women: women's deficiency in war and courage springs from the same physiological facts which tie her, and through her, the male, to the defense of the private family and private interest. The Athenian now warns again that "these things we're seeking probably would never be realized with adequate precision so long as women and children and homes are private" (807b). Even the higher education is not an education in justice, or in a truly *common* good.

Having thus prepared the ground, the Athenian is ready to delineate more precisely the limited character of the best city's higher preoccupations. After the citizens have finished feeding in common, they turn to the real substance of life, "cultivating the body in all respects and the soul as regards virtue" (806d–807d). But what exactly do they *do* to cultivate virtue? Curiously, the Athenian dwells on how the citizens spend the night. The only public business he specifies is defending the city against enemies and bad citizens; the only virtue he says is instilled by the nighttime activity is courage. What is the noble activity the citizens share together in the daytime? The Athenian does not say. Instead, he shifts suddenly to a description of the daytime activity of the children who go to school and of the few adult citizens who supervise their education. The vast majority of citizens share in the task of educating only to the extent that they stand ready to *punish* the children and their tutors (808e–809a; cf. *Ethics* 1179b 5 ff., and especially 1180a 19–24). Accordingly, the Athenian now ceases to advise the citizens in general and directs his remarks exclusively to the Supervisor of Education and the other Guardians; this dialogue is also an "education" of the Guardians (809a ff.). The Athenian thus reveals that the truly noble civic activity, which requires a special education, is educating the young, and that it is a serious concern of only a tiny minority of the adult citizens.

The education of the Educator begins with a statement of the part of the curriculum that has not yet been described: the study of nonmetrical writing—and also the lyre, and arithmetic, and the astral gods (809b–c). With barely a pause to allow us to catch our breath, the Athenian expands the education almost beyond recognition. Still, the new subjects are to be studied by "everyone" only insofar "as is necessary for war, household management, and the management of the city" (809c). Accordingly, only a very few citizens— including those who supervise education and music, of course—will attain more than a rudimentary knowledge of "the written things" and the lyre (810a).

The Athenian expands "written things" to include writings which are merely read, and not sung at public festivals. Since the earlier criteria for censorship dealt only with the poetry that was to be sung in public, further criteria must now be considered. Once again the Athenian must confront the awesome popularity of the poets; so naturally he is reluctant to proceed until he has assured himself of the firm support of his powerful political allies (810c–811c). But why should he need to assure himself that the old Dorians will take his side against poets and *hoi polloi?* By arousing old Kleinias's manly pugnacity, the Athenian enlists his commitment *before* revealing to him that the battle is not only against poets, but on behalf of a new kind of poetry. The Athenian now makes totally explicit what he has frequently adumbrated: the true legislator must be a poet—or, in biblical language, a prophet—who not only creates a way of life but who leaves behind a comprehensive justification of that life, viewed in the context of the whole of human existence.

As the Athenian subsequently admits, his new poetry that is meant to replace all previous tragedy is itself a kind of tragedy (817b): the city cannot share the untragic perspective of the philosopher. But the new tragedy is more austere, more beautiful, and better than the traditional, because it is an imitation of "the *truest* tragedy"; the new "Bible" will be less mythic than any earlier regime's because it will be, to a degree, the unvarnished truth. In their childhood at least, all citizens will read Kleinias's written record of the conversation that was the actual source of the regime (cf. *Epinomis* 980d). If we try to imagine the impression the citizens will receive from reading the *Laws,* we will understand more concretely just what the new tragic sense is that the Athenian hopes will penetrate the regime. The citizens, through this dialogue, will have access to the perplexities the founders confronted, the aspirations they had to abandon or qualify, and the alternatives they rejected. They will understand the achievements and disappointments to be the result not of unfathomable divine will, but of human reason struggling with natural necessities. Although they will be told that the founders did not proceed "without some inspiration from gods" (811c; cf. 682e, 722c), they will not be led to believe that god's voice was heard in the conversation, or that the regime is the object of very special divine solicitude. They will be made aware of the diversity and tensions among the three founders: above all, the Athenian leaves behind, for the citizens to revere and meditate upon, the model of his own personality. To this extent the philosopher does become a model for the city.

The citizens are also to study any foreign poetry (including tragedy), whose message is in accordance with—or perhaps a superior version of—the present drama (811e, 817d). It remains true, however, that only a very few are expected to devote careful attention as adults to all this literature, and, even in their case, the study is not for its own sake but for the sake of educating children in preparation for "serious," and quite unintellectual, adult lives. Besides, one must wonder how literally to take the Athenian's suggestion that the *whole* of this sometimes shocking dialogue should be available to the ten-year-olds, or, for that matter, the adults. It is not surprising to hear Kleinias voicing a prudent doubt about the correctness of their discussion "as a whole" (812a).

The Athenian turns next to that part of music he has thus far not discussed, and which is not accompanied by dancing. In this context he reintroduces the "Dionysian singers," describing them in a way that emphasizes almost exclusively their public, educative function, and their concern with rhythm and harmony, as opposed to the words of the songs (812c). Since lyre-singing involves a public presentation, the words must be governed by the same strict censorship that governs the choruses (812e–813a). The Athenian does not outline any organizational principles that would provide for a separate "Dionysian chorus" such as he described in Book Two: in practice, it would seem, the "Dionysian singers" are the officials who govern education and music. The coordination of these officials, and of the strangers who are hired to do the actual teaching, is left to the Supervisor of Education, who may coopt into the intellectual elite any other citizens he wishes, young or old, male or female (813c).

The Athenian says he wants the training in the lyre to be as simple as possible, so that the students may proceed smoothly toward other, necessary subjects. He is curiously unwilling to specify these subjects, but leaves us inclined to assume he means the arithmetic and astronomy he mentioned earlier. Instead of turning to these studies, however, he suddenly announces that they must take up again the discussion of gymnastics. We have been told repeatedly that the account of gymnastics has been completed, but the Athenian's reference to the boys' and girls' nude exercising reminds us that the question of women's military training has yet to be definitively settled. The Athenian now gives his final advice in this respect, and indicates the extent to which the city must fall short of his hopes (cf. also 945a). If the women cannot be made to resemble Athena, or even the Amazons, at least they could resemble female birds, who fight for their nests when the males are absent. Certainly the women should not react to emergencies by fleeing to the protection of gods. Kleinias's oath (814b) prompts us to wonder whether the belief in a god like Zeus is compatible with the rejection of the piety that has now been rejected.

The final clarification of the women's military status does not bring the renewed discussion of gymnastics to an end. For gymnastics includes dancing in the choruses. As we saw earlier, it is very difficult to distinguish sharply the bodily aspects of choral art from the soul aspects (cf. pp. 481–82 above), and the discussion of dance soon expands into a discussion of choral art as a whole, including the tragic drama and comic drama that are its most complex expressions; it becomes evident that the Athenian is really completing his account of education in choral music, the principal form of adult religious "play," but is doing so under the rubric of gymnastics. It is in this context that he characterizes his own poetry, the Laws, as a form of tragedy: he thereby suggests that his whole account of the regime, and the regime itself, is part of gymnastics. But gymnastics is the training of the body, with a view to the virtue of the body (813b; cf. 673a).

This strange culmination of the account of music education is meant to point out the dubiousness of the city's claim that through its fostering of music it is devoted to the excellence of the soul. Repeatedly the Athenian has tried—and failed—to "finish" with gymnastics, to transcend devotion to the body. The civic virtues which music imitates and cultivates—the city's courage, moderation, justice, and prudence—are virtues in which the soul's reasoning is directed toward regulating and defending the body, the subrational passions, and the external property the body needs. This is not to deny that music allows the poet and some among his audience, especially the educators, to study and learn about the soul; but the activity of knowing remains subordinate to, and limited by, the endeavor to encourage or discourage noble and ignoble action (cf. Ethics 1102a7–1103a10).

The subjects which seem most likely to foster the use of the mind for its own sake, and which therefore seem capable of providing the city with a truly common pursuit that is not in the main, or ultimately, subordinate to some aspect of the body, are the mathematical and astronomical studies. These, and the even higher studies to which they lead (818d), provide knowledge of the "divine" or "natural" necessities that govern the cosmos; through these studies men learn that the gods are not ruled by "human necessities," by human needs and cares (818b). Thus such studies provide the required foundation for the new, austere piety. Yet only a "certain few" of the sixteen-year-olds will have the talent to progress beyond an elementary acquaintance with the "divine necessities." The Athenian dares now to suggest even more openly that the men who come to know the divine necessities may become gods or demons, and as such "capable of exercising serious supervision over humans" (818c). He seems to imply that these wise men should rule the city, if only invisibly, like demons, while the majority would accept on faith their guidance in the most important matters.

When Kleinias reveals his total lack of familiarity with what the Athenian is talking about, we are made to see the enormous practical difficulty: the old Dorian legislator is in some ways less capable of being guided by advice about the gods based on mathematics and astronomy than would be even the average citizen in the future city. So the Athenian tries to postpone the legislation of the highest education (818e). It would seem that in order to organize the complex education that would produce men who could promulgate the new piety, such men would already have to be present among the founding generation. Kleinias is understandably reluctant to leave these crucial matters so much up in the air. The Athenian partially obliges him, by providing a glimpse of the mathematics the average citizen will learn—for the purposes of war, household management, and the dispelling of a certain shameful ignorance about god which afflicts all other Greeks. Yet the Athenian characterizes even this elementary mathematics as something "outside the rest of the regime," borrowed from another regime or group to which he, but not the "stranger" Kleinias, belongs (820e): the elementary mathematics depends on a higher mathematical education, which at this point remains beyond the regime.

The Athenian had said that the major reason for his reluctance to elaborate the education in the divine necessities was not his "fear" of Kleinias's ignorance but his "fear" of those who have engaged in these studies in a bad way (819a). He sheds a bit more light on the source of this fear when he alludes to the generally held opinion which says that the inquiry into the cosmos as a whole and its "causes" is impious (821a; cf. *Apology* 18b–c, 19b–c). Only much later will the Athenian dare to confront openly the grounds for this opinion, but if we are to understand what is at stake here, we must now take into consideration those later remarks. The many think that those who busy themselves with astronomy, and the other arts that necessarily go with astronomy, "become atheists, having seen that, as much as possible, actions come into being by necessities and not by the thoughts of an intention concerned with fulfillments of good things" (967a). The Athenian admits that indeed "many varieties of atheism" have arisen among men who have studied the stars and the causes of the cosmos—even among those who have said that "intelligence has ordered all of the things in heaven" (967b–c). It must be noted that the Athenian himself, in his present remarks about the higher studies, refers repeatedly to "divine necessities" and not once to divine intention or will. By elaborating in public the higher education in mathematics and astronomy, the Athenian would have to expose the citizens to some of the evidence, and also some of the questions and arguments, that have led so many wise men to atheism. In what context could such questions ever be raised in public by the authorities without casting grave doubts upon the religious worship that is the "most serious thing" about the city? How could Kleinias ever be persuaded to allow such risks to be run within his city? Yet surely the major themes, at any rate, of the higher education cannot be kept secret, especially if the men who undergo the higher education are to inform and shape public belief.

At this point, the Athenian's attempt to introduce even a preliminary version of the philosophic study of nature remains tenuous, and hence his whole religious reform stands on very shaky footing. He allows himself to make only a tentative proposal for a study of the stars that would allow the new city to avoid certain blasphemies prevalent among the rest of the Greeks (821d, 822c). Kleinias, who is of course quite unfamiliar with the doings of men like Anaxagoras, Socrates, and Protagoras, is nonetheless rather wary in giving his assent.

The philosopher's inability to make philosophy a part of civic education is brought home by the fact that the education as a whole culminates in hunting. In the *Republic*, mathematics and astronomy are part of the "prelude" to the "law itself," the "song" that is dialectic or philosophy (531d–e). In the *Laws*, education must bow to the need to inculcate "the manliness that is divine" (824a); philosophy can enter only surreptitiously, or can only be pointed at, through the metaphor of hunting. After the best young men have completed their higher studies they become eligible, at the age of twenty-five, for the "secret service"—which might conceivably be a haven for philosophy, though hardly a cozy one (cf. pp. 469–70 above). It is more likely that the Athenian hopes some of these young men will mull over his lengthy appeal to them concerning hunting, and especially its strange emphasis on the importance of going beyond the laws and mere obedience to law (822d–823a,c,d). Hunting includes a "hunting of human beings which is worth reflection." A great deal of this hunting of humans occurs through friendship, some of which is praiseworthy. This praiseworthy hunting of humans through friendship is not the same as the hunting which is "best for everyone," which cultivates manliness, and which the law calls "sacred" (cf. 823b with 824a).

By concluding his discussion of education with hunting, the Athenian prepares us for the account of the festivals that immediately follows. That account makes abundantly clear how serious the Athenian was when he said that the city's pious play should strengthen its capacity to defend itself and defeat its enemies. To a massive extent, the festivals are to be devoted to contests that foster physical conditioning, courage, and the military arts. (In accordance with his resolve to reduce unmanly hopes for divine intervention, the Athenian does not suggest that prayers for help from the gods should play any great role in the festivals.) It now appears that, just as the first discussion of education failed to do justice to gymnastic education, so the first descriptions of the music festivals failed to do justice to their gymnastic aspects (cf. 834e). The Athenian reaffirms his commitment to musical and poetic contests, but he now describes them in such a way as to suggest that the music is to be dominated by praise and encouragement for military valor (see especially 829a, 830a ff., 832b,d,e; cf. 942d). At the same time, he insists that the military exercises be shared by all citizens and be undertaken with a view to defense rather than conquest: he thus tries to prevent the "warrior education and play" from becoming incompatible with republican freedom (832c–d).

The contrast between the picture we are now given of the festivals, and the picture we were given in Book Two, highlights the fundamental problem that has been coming into steadily sharper focus as the Athenian has elaborated the details of the noblest part of the city's way of life. How may philosophy, which alone can satisfy the high aspirations of civic virtue and provide a foundation for sober piety and steadfast courage, be introduced in a version or institutional context that will not run athwart civic virtue, ordinary piety, and spirited manliness? The Athenian's response to this dilemma emerges in the last part of the *Laws*, in the course of his explanation of the penal law that deals with the criminals and the dissidents.

PART SIX: *Crime and Philosophy*

Our initial and massive impression is that with Book Eight the conversation begins a definite descent. Having apparently completed his discussion of the noblest themes, the Athenian descends to the "necessary" sphere of justice—the regulation of business matters and the punishment of those who defy the laws (cf. 632b). The transition is effected by way of a discussion of how to prevent sexual promiscuity. In this context it appears that the Athenian feels a renewed need to have recourse to a version of traditional, tragic piety, with its belief in divine sanctions for morality (835c, 838a–d, 841c). As he goes on to elaborate the farming laws, the Athenian must rely even more directly on the fear of punitive gods. Not only does the subject matter of the last books seem lower in rank, but its proper political handling seems to require the Athenian to qualify yet further his hopes for a more impersonal and austere religious outlook.

It is not surprising, then, that the Athenian should seek to move with great haste through the "shameful" legislation pertaining to true criminality (853b, 855d, 856e–857b). Yet his haste, however noble, is extreme, and arouses a just protest from Kleinias: the punishments must be varied to fit the crimes, in all their varying circumstances. By provoking Kleinias in this way, the philosopher absolves himself of full responsibility for proposing that they undertake a study of the criminal mind—of the circumstances, and the reasons, that might lead men to defy the noblest laws. For the circumstances include, above all, the degree of the lawbreaker's responsibility, and to ascertain this the lawgiver must inquire into the nature of responsibility in general, and into the nature of the soul as the source of responsible action.

The Athenian prefaces his inquiry by remarking that the subject they must now attend to is one of those which reveals that "what pertains to the laying down of laws has never been worked out correctly in any way" (857c). He goes on to underline the importance of this juncture in the dialogue by reminding his hearers of the "preludes," which make the laws analogous to the cure effected by a free doctor on free patients. Yet now he characterizes this doctor as one who "uses arguments that come close to *philosophizing*" (857d). For the first time in this longest Platonic dialogue, the word "philosophy" occurs. In this way Plato's stranger prepares us for the discovery that among the preludes to the penal law are the preludes that come closest to fulfilling the highest and truest purpose of the "preludes." All the preludes have been a kind of "medicine" for "sick" or defective souls; but it now begins to appear that the best medicine, which effects the most complete cure, has been reserved for the penal law. Could it be that only some among the "sickest" citizen-souls can become fully healthy human souls? This much seems certain: prior to their discussion of the psychological roots of crime, the Athenian and his companions have not yet succeeded in becoming lawgivers (859c), and have not yet inquired fully into either the highest or the lowest—into "what is best" or "what is most necessary" as regards the laws (858a).

The Athenian begins his "precise inquiry" into "all injustices" by bringing to light a contradiction in the way men talk about "the just things." The just things are all said to be noble; yet suffering just punishment is held to be not only lacking in nobility but positively shameful. We have to wonder: if suffering just punishment is disgraceful, can the infliction of that suffering be counted among the purely noble things? After all, the Athenian has just admitted that to lay down penal laws is "in a certain way shameful" (853b,c). And yet "the great man in the city, the man who is to be proclaimed perfect . . . is the one who does what he can to assist the magistrates in inflicting punishment" (730d). By highlighting the way in which the phenomenon of punishment reveals the just and the noble to be at odds, the Athenian discloses once again a key source of the problematic status of justice in this dialogue. We recall how difficult it was to discern, in Book Seven, any thematic discussion of an education in justice; if the distinctive activity of justice, as the perfection of civic virtue, is punishing, then the education in justice would seem to be conveyed through the discussion of the penal laws. But if civic justice consists above all in punishing, or, more broadly, in the spirited defense of the city, the laws, and one's own property and family (cf. 829a), can the best regime be said to be aimed at a noble or full version of justice (cf. *Politics* 1332a 12–17)?

The contradiction that has appeared could be resolved, the Athenian suggests, if punishment were reinterpreted on the basis of the claim he advanced some time ago—that all evil is involuntary

(860c ff.; cf. 731c–d and p. 455 above). The reasonable aim of most penal law could then be understood to be not retribution or deterrence but the guiding of perplexed men back to the path that is good for them. Now such guiding is a form of education, and the process of education is noble, for both educator and educated. To the extent that the penal laws are educative, they would appear to be the "noblest laws" (862e; cf. 635a–b), and penal justice as remedial education would take its place as a supplement to the noble education outlined in Book Seven. It is true, as *remedial* education, justice would seem to remain subordinate to the moderation and courage that are instilled mainly by childhood education and civic music festivals. Yet if it should transpire that what is needed to rehabilitate some of those who have lost the virtues fostered in childhood is a more elaborate explanation of the *reasons why* obedience to the laws is good, then justice as remedial education would appear to be closer to intelligence, the leader of all the virtues.

The education in justice itself, or in that activity of justice which is most distinguished from the other virtues, would be an education in how to "punish," or reeducate. Insofar as the "punishment" of some dissidents required a fuller presentation of the compelling reasons why the laws are good, the education in justice would include an education in those reasons and also in how they should be presented, in a variety of didactic circumstances. In enunciating the penal preludes that conveyed such an education in educating, the legislator would be acting like a doctor of souls who not only cured the sick but used "arguments approaching philosophy" to form other doctors like himself. Thus the split we drew attention to in Book Five, between the characteristics of a philosophic man and the characteristics of the "perfect" citizen who assists the magistrates in punishing, would in a few cases almost disappear. A philosopher could conceivably be proclaimed "the bearer of victory in virtue," if it should prove to be the case that the punishment of the most serious crimes required quasi-philosophic argument and education.

But the thrust of the Athenian's suggestion, as I have now elaborated it, proves to be subject to three major qualifications. First, since crime involves not only injustice but also damage, the penal law must compel the perpetrator to provide compensation for the victim, in addition to undergoing a "cure" (862b–c, 933e). Second, some criminals are "incurable" or ineducable: indeed, some crimes—like temple robbing and treason—are to be considered in themselves sufficient evidence of a citizen's imperviousness to education. In these cases, the penalty must be death, which at least prevents the evildoer from harming himself and others any further, and also furnishes an instructive example to others (862e–863a). It seems doubtful that the suffering of either of these sorts of just penalties can be understood as "noble."

The third qualification is more complex. The Athenian's claim that vice is involuntary must not be supposed to rest on, or imply, the thesis that all vice is due simply to ignorance and all virtue is knowledge. On the contrary, throughout the *Laws* we have seen that civic virtue is based not so much on knowledge as on opinion, and, most of all, habituation. Through habituation, especially in early childhood, the "iron cords" of the passions are made to balance and control one another in obedience to the opinion enunciated in the law and preludes (644b–645c, 653a–c, 875a–d). The breakdown of virtue is then usually due to a failure of self-control rather than ignorance, or intellectual doubt, of the city's authoritative opinions as to what is good (863b–c, 863e–864a). To help a man reestablish control over his passions, education through argument is of minor value; what is needed much more is a "cure" by means of rewards and penalties, promises and threats, that compel and entice the passions to become obedient again to opinions already known to the miscreant but obscured or rendered impotent by the force of his anger or the wiles of his appetites (862d). Just as with children, so (one may hope) with adults, the inflicting of pain may not only put an end to evil behavior, but may be the decisive step in getting errant passions used to going without gratification and in reminding prudence of its ability to deny the passions their demands (854d; cf. *Ethics* 1104b 16–18, 1179b 16 ff., and Thomas Aquinas *Summa Theologica* I–II, ques. 92 and 95). It is also true that the suffering of pain at the hands of the city may serve as a vivid reminder of the correct opinions. In the light of these considerations, we should not be surprised to find that some of the specific penalties the Athenian legislates are much like the suffering inflicted by traditional penal systems.

Still, this hardly suffices to account for the glaring contradiction between the Athenian's initial explanation of crime and his subsequent delineation of the actual penalties. For he in fact returns to a more or less traditional distinction between voluntary and involuntary crime, with harsher penalties for the voluntary. Moreover, it is in many cases difficult to see how the proposed penalty could possibly contribute to rehabilitation, or even test a criminal's capacity for reform. The extreme is reached when the Athenian proposes to execute beasts and exile stones which are convicted of "murdering" a citizen (873e–874a). It appears that in practice the Athenian must abandon his theorizing and give in to the naive view of punishment rooted in human anger, which always tends to assign responsibility to the agent who inflicts hurt.

It is possible, however, to discover a partial reconciliation between the contradictory sections of Book Nine. As we have learned earlier, the legislator's attempt to bring the passions into harmonious subordination to the soul's reason finds a key ally in the spirited passions. The *thumotic* "cords" within the soul are a key source of the dedication to the noble as opposed to the pleasant. *Thumos* gives rise to the individual's honorable sense of dignity and independence—his belief in his own responsibility, or in a freedom derived not from rational calculation but from a self-originating motion akin to what later thinkers call "will-power." When in the education of the young the crucial age is reached at which the individual is considered an adult, the legislator is counting not only on a habit of obedience in the desires, and a habit of rule, together with a clear grasp of correct opinion, in the reason, but also on the belief in responsibility that has been cultivated in the spirited part of the passions. By promulgating penal laws that treat men as if they were responsible (to a much greater degree than they in truth are) the legislator continues or reinforces this *thumotic* sense of responsibility. This of course implies that the educative impact of many of the penal laws is aimed more at the general citizenry than at the criminal, and that the "education" in these cases is more a kind of deterrence than a rehabilitation. The Athenian's claim that these penal laws are the "noblest" would have to be qualified accordingly (cf. 853b–c with 880e ff. and 934a–b).

In addition, insofar as the penal law continues "education" in a kind of virtue based on moral passion rather than knowledge, the legislator finds himself compelled to make considerable concessions to the irrational demands of moral indignation and guilt-feeling (the sense of "pollution"). By the end of Book Nine a strong note of retribution has crept into the Athenian's laws and preludes. Especially for criminals who violently offend the sacred relation within the family, the lawgiver must invoke the threat of vengeful deities, led by Justice the Avenger (872e). Political justice continues to require gods, and not only to strike fear in the hearts of potential criminals. The gods reflect and gratify the indignation that cries out for punishment of the wrongdoers who are not caught or who cannot be sufficiently "paid back" by the execution of human penalties.

The fact that the penal legislation rests on a sense of responsibility that is really an expression of *thumotic* passion is what explains the part of the Athenian's penal law which departs most from ordinary practice: the surprisingly light penalties for first offenders who commit violent crimes out of anger. Even in the case of premeditated murder, if the motive is found to be "hoarded rage," the penalty is only three years' exile (867c ff.). Because a loss of control over anger does not necessarily signal a breakdown of the fundamental discipline that subordinates desire to spiritedness, the penal law can allow for a greater possibility of rehabilitation in these cases. At the same time, the Athenian reinforces in the spirited citizenry the commonsense notion that men cannot be expected to suppress a rebellion of the spirited passions to as great an extent as they can a rebellion of the appetites (cf. *Ethics* 1135b 20 ff.). This part of the penal law may provide some of the more thoughtful citizens with a hint as to the true root of their "responsibility."

But it would seem that the principal way in which the Athenian tries to enlighten the citizenry and check or weaken the excesses of indignation is through his prefatory remarks on the irresponsibility of all criminals (and through an occasional reminder of those remarks, in the course of the actual legislation: 870a–c, 873a, 875a ff., 934a–b, 941d–942a, 957e–958a). Just as in his oration to the citizens in Book Five, the Athenian tries to soften the punitive zeal that is an essential concomitant of civic virtue, by boldly stating the truth that contradicts all indignation. Still, it must be noted that the conversation which contains the most complete expression of the denial of criminal responsibility is not part of any prelude, and is in fact explicitly said to be only provisional material, which may or may not be used in the future code of laws (858b). Plato thus leaves open the extent to which any regime, even the best, could tolerate the public presentation of such a view of criminal responsibility (cf. 860e–861a). If the Athenian's remarks were to be made available—perhaps only in the dialogue children read in school—the lawgiver would have to feel confident that his citizens had been imbued with such a degree of spiritedness as not to have their moral fiber sapped by hearing the remarks.

By the end of Book Nine, the Athenian's penal law has proved to fall so far short of the educative rehabilitation suggested by his image of the doctor, and the inquiry into responsibility, that we begin to wonder why he ever indicated such a standard for penal justice. His initial remarks may have softened the punitive zeal of Kleinias and Megillus, and may have allowed for some softening of the later penal legislation, but on the whole the Athenian seems only to have given a more vivid demonstration of the incompatibility between civic justice and the pursuit of the truth about the soul.

Yet the Athenian did say that criminal faults could arise not only from a loss of self-control but also from ignorance (863c). The ignorance might be simple (a failure to grasp the circumstances of an action) or it might be "double," consisting in the children's inability to agree with the city's opinion as to what is best. Now the city's primary response to any citizen who begins to doubt the authoritative opinions conveyed by the laws, preludes, and music is the claim that the regime is guided by the example and wisdom of virtuous gods (713a ff., 727a, 762e, 771a, 799a, 803c–804b). Hence anyone who, out of ignorance and not out of incontinence, persists in questioning the lawful opinions must do so because he doubts the city's claim that its opinions are sanctioned by the gods. He must either doubt that gods exist or that the gods are such as the laws say they are. So it is in punishing impiety, impiety in thought and speech, that the penal law is truly called upon to deal with crimes arising from ignorance; and it is in Book Ten, in the confrontation with the impious, that the penal law finally realizes the high level of rehabilitative education that was foreshadowed in the Athenian's image of the philosophic soul doctor. As we reflect on Book Ten, we come to realize that the chief practical purpose of the Athenian's disquisition on criminal responsibility was to prepare the way for a drastic reform in the punishment of impiety—the crime for which Socrates was convicted and executed.

In characterizing the criminal whose faults are due to ignorance of the "double" sort, the Athenian indicates that such a man is not "unjust" in the most important sense. Legally, of course, any man who breaks the law is "unjust"; but the Athenian now insists on a deeper and more precise criterion for justice and injustice: the disposition of the criminal's soul. *Injustice* he defines as "the tyranny in the soul of spiritedness, fear, pleasure, pain, feelings of envy, and desires" (863e–864a). The criminal whose faults are a result of ignorance is not subject to such tyranny. He is animated by false "opinion that he is wise," or by "the striving for expectations and true opinion concerning what is best" (863c, 864b). But *justice* is defined as the predominance in the soul of "the opinion about what is best . . . , even if it is in some way mistaken" (864a). So, as the Athenian later avers, it is quite possible for a man who breaks the law against impiety to have a "naturally just disposition" (908b). One might at first wonder why the Athenian does not try to define justice as the predominance in the soul of knowledge, or at least of true opinion, thus enabling himself to maintain a clear distinction between the justice of the law-abiding, pious citizen and the defective "justice" of the dissident criminal. Yet as we have repeatedly observed, the citizens have up to this point not been provided with an explanation of the nature of the gods. The necessary prelude to all the laws, the prelude that justifies the city's claim to divine or cosmic support, on which all other civic claims and beliefs rest, has never been presented in anything like an adequate version. The citizens' opinions about the most important matters are therefore mere opinions, with no better support than those of the dissidents: nay, insofar as the dissidents are at least acutely aware of their own ignorance, and are "striving for true opinion," they would seem to be less under the sway of false opinion than most of the law-abiding citizens.

Only by "punishing" (i.e., rehabilitating) the unbelievers, only by inducing the leaders of the city to enter into a public debate with the serious religious dissidents, "using arguments that approach philosophizing," does the philosopher at last enable the city to achieve a more adequate intellectual justification of its basic beliefs, and hence to acquire a version of justice that is to some extent rooted in knowledge. I will not repeat here the detailed analysis I have presented elsewhere of the way the Athenian gains Kleinias's consent to such a debate, and of the civil theology that emerges as a result (see "The Political Psychology of Religion in Plato's *Laws*," *American Political Science Review* 70 [1976]:4.). It will suffice to sketch the most important political consequences.

The old Athenian creates a dialogue within the dialogue, conjuring up fictitious young men whose theoretical questions, based on the writings of pre-Socratic philosophers, expose the city's incapacity to give an argued defense of itself. Kleinias, tricked into fearing that young men with an Athenian education might spring up in his city, is led to plead with the old Athenian to go "outside the realm of legislation" in order to find arguments that would defend the city's beliefs (891d–e). Thus philosophic argument finds a respectable, official place in the best regime, as the theological defense of the faith. By suggesting that the defense should be adequate to meet the most radical versions of atheism, the Athenian contrives to insert the searing, thought-provoking challenges of pre-Socratic philosophy into the city's supreme legal prelude. He thereby plants lasting seeds of doubt, even as he enunciates a complex response that protects and supports the spirited commitment of most citizens. The true, rational justification of the best regime does not rest simply on his arguments, which are elusive and even contradictory, but rather on what the Athenian demonstrates in deed: he shows that the "punishment" of impiety can provide a setting in which the unphilosophic legislator and citizens can tolerate and even honor a somewhat disguised version of philosophic disputation. The city's piety is based on the truth inasmuch as its piety provides an avenue for philosophic pursuit of truth. Since the Athenian's theological arguments are admittedly quite incomplete (907b–d), and since they must be applied in lengthy discussions with the dissidents who are to be refuted and reeducated, the Athenian successfully proposes the creation of a special "Council of Elders" responsible for elaborating and arguing the theoretical defense in private consultations with the imprisoned unbelievers (899c, 905c, 908a, 909a; cf. 692a). Through this "nocturnal council," which guides the citizenry's opinions on the most important questions, men who "use arguments approaching philosophizing" exercise a powerful, if indirect influence over the city and become exemplary models of citizenship.

In Book Ten the Athenian says remarkably little about how this Nocturnal Council is to be organized. He is not yet ready to be more specific, because the Council he has succeeded in introducing in the context of apologetic theology is in fact only the embryonic version of an institution by which he seeks to transform the regime ruled by laws into a regime ruled by philosophers. In "bringing the regime around by degrees toward that of the *Republic*" Plato moves the conversation toward what is utopian (cf. *Politics* 1265a 4–5). But, in accordance with his self-imposed rule that the *Laws* remain within the bounds of the politically possible, Plato demonstrates that some such reaching toward the utopian is essential to practical politics: he shows that only the rule of philosophers will satisfy certain political needs that are inescapable, and that gradually become obvious to unphilosophic statesmen like Kleinias and Megillus.

The Athenian is ready to take the next step in this project only after a considerable time has passed. He leads into his discussion of the "Auditors" by describing, more stringently than ever before, the habits of strict obedience the citizens must possess if the city is to have a strong military organization (942a ff.). By stressing the awesome power the magistrates will possess, he brings into relief the need for some check on the magistrates, and is enabled to insist that the process of auditing the magistrates, to which he has alluded a couple of times, be of far greater significance than might previously have been supposed (cf. 774b, 881e, with Aristotle *Constitution of Athens* xlviii 4–5). The Auditor is to be a "ruler over rulers," armed with the power to punish any magistrate (including a Guardian of the Laws). Though the Auditors' decisions remain subject to judicial review, their emergence transforms the constitution as described in Book Six. The men who are assigned the immense responsibility of auditing must be "in every way amazing men with regard to the whole of virtue" (945e). The election of the Auditors is at the same time the awarding of the "prize for excellence," and the Athenian dwells on the supreme honors that are to be given the Auditors, in life and after death. They are to be the highest priests, and it should be no exaggeration to call them "divine" (945c). The political activities by which a man proves himself deserving of the prize for excellence are lower in rank than the tasks he engages in as Auditor: the most honorable political vocation involves thinking more than acting, and is hence altogether appropriate for elderly men.

Kleinias does not voice a single reservation or question concerning the Auditors. He and Megillus are naturally receptive to the notion that men of their age and experience should be given such authority, exercised in such a fitting way, and surrounded with such magnificent honors—they could not have imagined a more splendid funeral for themselves (consider here 719d–e)! So the poetic Athenian feels emboldened to make his next move, after allowing a suitable interval to pass. He suggests that if the city is to maintain its laws and correct them properly, it must have access to a wider experience than is available to men who remain within the horizon of the city and its good habits (951a ff.). The Guardians must send out selected individuals who will undertake a comparative study of other legal codes, and search out certain rare, divine human beings, who do not by nature grow any more frequently in good cities than in bad—human beings, that is to say, who resemble the Athenian stranger. Of course, the reception and implementation of the innovative, alien wisdom brought back by the travellers poses some ticklish problems. Kleinias's question makes manifest his unease (951c).

In the course of responding to this concern, the Athenian proposes the creation of a special council that will continually engage in comprehensive deliberations about the laws. Their deliberations will be stimulated by what they hear from the returning travellers, who must report to and be judged by this conclave. We are not surprised to hear that the Auditors make up the predominant part of the Council. Unlike the Guardians of the Laws (cf. 959d–e), the Council will confine itself to discussion and deliberation; but its discussions will surely influence the thoughts and actions of the Guardians, as well as the lesser magistrates. The most remarkable feature of the proposed Council is that it is to include as many young men as old. These young men are to learn "with complete seriousness" any subject matters that "might seem" to contribute to the inquiry into laws, after receiving the old men's approval. The old men need not pursue such learning; moreover, one wonders whether the debilities of age will not frequently prevent some of the old men from attending the daily meetings at dawn. The Athenian leaves rather vague the precise topics of the Council's discussions and researches. This goes with his failure to point out that the Council he has in mind is in fact identical to the Nocturnal Council, and that it will therefore hold its meetings at the prison where the atheists dwell. By leaving in obscurity this primary function of the Council, the Athenian temporarily masks from Kleinias the extent to which the Council's deliberations on law will take place in the context of extensive theoretical inquiries into astronomy, god, and the soul.

Having capitalized on the opportunities afforded by three rather diverse political needs, the Athenian has now put together an institution that comes close to being capable of performing the highest civic function. That function emerges only after the laws proper have been completed: the best city needs a "safeguard" that will implant a fate-like capacity of "irreversibility" in the laws (960b–d). The Athenian suggests that the Council described above (or in fact a considerably modified version of it) could provide such a safeguard. Kleinias remains understandably perplexed, until the stranger makes it clear that what he means is not quite what Kleinias (and we) first supposed. He doesn't want to make the laws unchangeable (962b), he rather wants to insure that the laws will always be guided, judged, and revised by men who have knowledge of the true political goal.

At first, Kleinias is inclined to suppose that this knowledge is not that hard to come by. Haven't the three of them long ago agreed that the goal is virtue, which is fourfold? And haven't they agreed that the leading virtue is intelligence, to which the other virtues ought to look? But the Athenian now raises a most perplexing question. What is the one aim or purpose of this leading virtue, in its political version? Kleinias and Megillus are left at a loss (963b–c). Their bafflement is surely pardonable. If they were to reply that the aim of intelligence is the fostering of courage, moderation, and justice, they would seem to speak in circles—for they have agreed that these virtues "look to" intelligence as their leader. Besides, can the higher, can that virtue which is shared with the supreme god (897b), have as its purpose the lower? With an eye to the Athenian's civil theology, one is tempted to say that the aim of intelligence is intelligence itself, or its active contemplation of its own nature and the eternal structure of the cosmos (898a–b). But can this description fit *political* intelligence, the intelligence that governs a human city? Moreover, could the three nonintellectual virtues be fully understood as mere means to contemplation? Would that do justice to their *nobility*, to the fact that they come to sight as ends, intrinsically worthy of honor?

The Athenian makes it clear that what he has stirred up is nothing less than the problem of the *idea* of virtue—the elusive question of how virtue, in all its diversity, is yet a unity. The enigma manifests itself most vividly in the case of courage: what can be shared between healthy animal spiritedness and the excellence of human reason (963e)? If one were to argue that true virtue is the habituation of the animal passions under the governance of calculation or prudence (644e, 653b), one would only move to a deeper level of the mystery: for what can be shared between such virtue and the virtue that is the exercise of contemplative intelligence? The core of the difficulty, we have learned throughout this dialogue, is the unity, or commonality in aim, of philosophic and political virtue. If the Nocturnal Council is to guide the city wisely, educating and punishing the citizens and defending the city's beliefs against the intrusions of foreign poets and educators (964b–d), it seems it must possess an answer to this question.

To this end, the Council members (whom the Athenian now begins to call "Guardians," and not "Guardians of the Laws") must be given a more precise and accurate education than the other citizens. Their education in the most important theme, the *idea* of virtue, should be supplemented by an education in the *ideas* of the noble (beautiful) and the good. Of one thing the Athenian seems sure: the noble (beautiful) and the good are *not* the same (this does not prevent some things from being both noble and good, and it may not prevent the noble from being an aspect of the good). Will not an understanding of the difference between the noble and the good provide a clue to the diversity and unity of virtue? Once the Guardians have grasped the distinction between the noble and the good, they will use this and their knowledge of all the other serious things to judge, according to nature, "what comes into being in a noble fashion and what does not" (966b): the noble or beautiful, rather than the good, is the main preoccupation of political intelligence or prudence.

The third subject the Guardians must understand is one that belongs within the sphere of the noble. "One of the noblest things" (not the noblest) is what pertains to the gods, as they have been explained in Book Ten. Yet in his final statement on the soul the Athenian conspicuously drops the claim that soul is divine; what is more, he fails to call intelligence "divine" and evinces a certain reluctance to claim that it is in fact "in the stars" (cf. 967d–e with 966e). He is altogether silent about the second and third demonstrations he presented in his civil theology. If it should prove to be the case that what the Athenian said about the gods in Book Ten was a partial lie, then one of the noblest things would be by nature a partial lie. This would not have surprised Socrates (*Republic* 377b–d, 414b–c). To become "firmly pious," it is not sufficient that one grasp the nature of soul and the intelligence "said to be" in the stars; in addition, one must understand the connection between these matters and the musical things, and must apply this understanding to "the practices and customs which pertain to the habitual dispositions," or the "popular virtues" (967e–968a). For is not the theology, as it was presented, in large part a kind of music aimed at forming the habits of the citizenry (cf. especially 897e, 903b, 966c)? This applied knowledge of the Guardians constitutes a "firm piety," which transcends the "popular virtues," including popular piety (968a, 966c).

We see that the ruling council the Athenian has now proposed goes beyond what he called the "Dionysian Chorus." Neither the poets nor the Supervisor of Education need be members (961a–b). The wisdom of the poets is replaced by the wisdom of philosophic men, who incorporate and transcend what the poets know. Yet the fundamental tension we discerned in the Dionysian chorus remains present in the Nocturnal Council: to what extent must true intelligence bow to old age, which is only an "image of intelligence" (965a)? The impossibility of overcoming this tension once and for all is a principal reason for the Athenian's doubt as to whether the highest education can be elaborated. Nevertheless, the Athenian is eager to assist in preparing the way for the Council, which must itself deal with the practical difficulty and set up its own education. The prudent Megillus sees the solution: the Athenian must be made to stay and share in the actual founding. Kleinias completely agrees. By this dramatic intervention, Plato seems at first to show that the fundamental tension can be overcome. The unphilosophic old men have been led to place themselves under the guidance of a philosopher, in deed as well as in speech. But the Athenian stranger remains silent (contrast the ending of the *Republic*). By this silence, I believe, Plato means to point to the reason why there cannot be a complete harmony among the virtues. The greatest obstacle, in the final analysis, is not the city's refusal to be ruled by philosophy, but the philosopher's reluctance to accept political responsibility. For the "philosopher" is not a wise man: he wishes to remain free in order to attend to his own unfinished business, including his unfinished search for the full meaning of "intelligence."

Conclusion

Whatever shape the Nocturnal Council may take, it seems certain that it will find the study of the *Laws* to be of great assistance in its quest for an understanding of the *idea*, i.e., the problem, of virtue. For one may say that this dialogue as a whole is devoted to that theme. In the *Republic*, Plato had his Socrates explore the nature of justice, or the aspiration to a true community devoted to a truly common good. In order to unravel all that is implied in the demand for justice, Socrates approached the question in the context of an attempt to respond to the extreme, idealistic longings of young men who lacked political experience and were revolted by the tawdriness of what they had observed in ordinary politics. The drama revealed that what they longed for could never be achieved in politics, but could be found only in the harmony of the philosophic soul and the community of philosophic friendship (*Republic* 592a–b). The conversation tempered and sublimated the young men's rebellion against politics, but it is doubtful whether it reconciled them, or the attentive reader, to political life. The *Republic*, taken by itself, threatens to produce a less passionate and dangerous, but ultimately more profound, contempt for politics. In the *Laws* we find the essential correction to this incomplete teaching conveyed by the *Republic*.

Through the drama of the *Laws*, Plato shows how experienced statesmen charged with the gravest responsibilities can be guided by a philosopher to see that their goal is virtue as a whole. Virtue is understood primarily as the rational ordering of the passions, especially the spirited passions for freedom and honor. Such virtue comes to sight as noble; that is to say, as an end in itself and not only as a means to security, prosperity, and prestige. Yet in the course of detailed analysis, and the attempt to implement this noble goal, it becomes evident that virtue so understood cannot stand by itself as the completion of man and the fulfillment of human happiness. If it is not to collapse into a means to the satisfaction of the lower needs, the sense of honor must find some higher existence to which it can look up and be dedicated—some existence which is more enduring, more independent, and more joyful. Virtue can find this object of reverence through a piety centered on a conception of god that does not simply mirror the political virtues but that provides a glimpse or image of the philosophic life, which is truly the noblest, freest, and most fulfilling existence man can know (cf. Aristotle *Eudemian Ethics* 1248b 8–end). The statesman can be brought to see the need for the presence of philosophic men who are able to articulate and defend the new gods and explain the relation between divine virtue and civic virtue. Needs that are intrinsic to politics lead, when fully elaborated, to a city which honors the philosopher and, to some extent, tolerates his "hunting" for kindred souls. For this reason, the city at its best, and every city insofar as it strives for such completeness, becomes an object of respect for the philosopher. Yet the city cannot philosophize; it can only look up to an incomplete and mutilated version of philosophy. Law only *"wishes* to be a discovery of Being" (*Minos* 315a). No law, no political order, deserves the complete respect or allegiance of the greatest human soul.

Notes

BOOK I

1. This dialogue is one of four Platonic dialogues whose titles reveal the subject matter (the others being the *Republic*, the *Statesman*, and the *Sophist*). The subtitle (literally: "Acts of Lawgiving") was probably added by a very early scribe or commentator, though an argument has been made for the authenticity of the Platonic subtitles: R. G. Hoerber, "Thrasylus' Platonic Canon and the Double Titles," *Phronesis* 2 (1957): 10–20. At any rate, here as in other dialogues the subtitle may be illuminating, especially when contrasted with the subtitle of the *Republic* ("On the Just"). The *Laws* will deal more with political action, above all the awesome act of founding, and the conversation is portrayed as a key part of an actual political founding.

The Greek word for "law" (*nomos*) has a more extended meaning than the English word. *Nomos* means primarily written and unwritten "law" but also "authoritative custom, way, tradition, or habit" and sometimes even includes "manners and morals" (cf. the French *moeurs*). Although, in Greek, custom and habit are often contrasted with law, the distinction between the legal and the conventional or customary is not nearly as sharp as in modern English: in particular, there is in Greek no clear sense of a "social" realm of custom that is quasi-independent of politics and legal authority (see below, note 5). The word *nomos* is closely connected with another word, *nomima*, which tends to connote less formal aspects of *nomos*, though the distinction between the two often melts away. I shall usually translate *nomos* by "law" and *nomima* by "customs," "ways," or "usages." See below, Book Four, note 26, and Emmanuel Laroche, *Historie de la racine NEM- en grec ancien* (Paris: Klincksieck, 1949), chap. 6.

The word *nomos* may also mean "convention," i.e., the realm of the conventional in general. In this more philosophic sense it is to be opposed to "nature" (*phusis*: see note 12).

The thematic investigation of the nature of *nomos*, directed by the Socratic form of questioning ("What is *nomos*?"), is to be found in the *Minos*, the dialogue which serves as an introduction to the *Laws*, and nowhere else in the Platonic corpus. In the *Laws* in particular, the question, "What is *nomos*?" is never raised—and *nomos* is defined only in a context of myths and images (644d ff.; contrast the treatment of education at 643a–644b).

2. Unlike the *Republic*, the *Laws* is a performed and not a narrated dialogue. The Athenian stranger, who in this dialogue takes the place usually assigned to Socrates (but also to others, like the Eleatic stranger), is never named. It is surely remarkable that Kleinias and Megillus never use the Athenian stranger's name; obviously (634d) Kleinias and the Athenian have been introduced (though barely) just prior to the opening of the dialogue. It seems that a sense of delicacy restrains Kleinias from addressing the Athenian by his name (or asking for his name if they have not been told it). Have they been informed that he wishes to travel incognito for some reason? According to Cicero (*Laws* I v 15), and the scholiast (in the *Hypothesis*), the Athenian stranger is meant to represent Plato himself. Aristotle (*Politics* 1265a 12) identifies him as Socrates. Leo Strauss has presented an argument that explains and justifies the Aristotelian identification: *What Is Political Philosophy?* (Glencoe, Ill.: The Free Press, 1959), pp. 31 ff.

The Greek for "stranger" is *xenos*, a word that may sometimes be used in a way that is less strong than the English "stranger." *Xenos* may mean "foreign guest," and sometimes "foreign host." But the connotation of being alien or foreign is almost never absent, especially in the present dialogue. So, with this note of caution, the word will always be rendered "stranger." Cf. Emil Benveniste, *Indo-European Language and Society* (London: Faber and Faber, 1973), pp. 71–83, 293–94.

3. The word is *anthrōpos*. Greek makes a distinction, difficult to render into English, between "man" in the sense of human beings generally (*anthrōpos*), and "man" the male (*anēr*: cf. Spanish *hombrē*). *Anēr* is the root of the word for "courage" (*andreia*); in Plato and Xenophon above all, its use always carries a more or less subtle reference to manliness, action outside the house, political rule, and self-assertion. In contrast, *anthrōpos* is used especially in two contexts: where the human is somehow contrasted with the divine, and where the distinction of being male is either missing or unimportant. In this translation, "human" or "human being" will always be used to render the Greek *anthrōpos*. *Anēr* will be translated "man" or occasionally "sir"; but it has of course not been possible to avoid using the English "man" and "men" at many points where neither *anthrōpos* nor *anēr* appear in the Greek, for English lacks the indication of genders found in Greek. In Greek, the first word of this first sentence is "god."

4. *Odyssey* XIX 178–9: Odysseus speaks, at the beginning of a long lie he tells his wife while pretending to be the grandson of Minos (among the Greeks, Cretans were apparently famous for being liars). Considerable stretching is needed to get from these lines the interpretation the Athenian gives them. In the *Minos* (319b ff.) Socrates gives a similar interpretation of these Homeric lines and adds the information that Minos and Zeus got together in the "cave of Zeus." In the *Apology of Socrates* (41a) Minos and Rhadamanthus are the first two names on the list of persons Socrates says he hopes to converse with after his death, in Hades (cf. *Gorgias* 523e ff.). Minos was perhaps the worst enemy of Athens in Greek mythology (see Plutarch *Theseus* xv).

The word used here for "getting together" is *sunousia*; it is also a word for sexual intercourse. Whenever the effect produced is not too jarring, I will translate it "intercourse," for a sexual overtone is frequently present.

5. The word is *polis*, and will always be rendered "city." The *polis* is not a city in our sense, for it is a self-sufficient and independent political community; but it is even less a state or a "city-state." The word "state" cannot be used in translating Greek, for in modern usage it presupposes a distinction between "state" and "society," as well as "country," distinctions which are wholly alien to Plato and to Greek thought in general. Our word "state" refers to the government, to the political authority which holds a monopoly on the use of legitimate violence. The state is opposed both to the web of free or uncoercive private associations which constitute "society" and to the traditions and the land we think of when we speak of "our country." "State" is therefore a cold word (Nietzsche said it was a name for the coldest of all cold monsters). *Polis* has none of these connotations, for in Greek life as well as in Plato's thought, politics is not thus separated from, and subordinated in value to, the rest of social life. A good equivalent for *polis* might be "country" if this term did not obscure the emphatically urban character of the polis. The reader must follow carefully the usage of "city," to discover for himself the full meaning of the word in the *Laws*. Cf. Allan Bloom, *The Republic of Plato* (New York: Basic Books, 1968), p. 439, n. 1; Leo Strauss, *The City and Man* (Chicago: Rand McNally, 1964), pp. 30–35.

6. Rhadamanthus, like Minos, was the son of Zeus by Europa. Homer places him in the Elysian Fields (*Odyssey* IV 564), and Pindar says he is there because of his prudence and uprightness (*Olympian Odes* ii 75; *Pythian Odes* ii 73).

7. The word is *kalon* and means "beautiful," "noble," or "fine." The frequency of its use and the range of its meaning require us to translate it variously; whether or not it is used in a passage may be ascertained by consulting the index under "fine." In Platonic usage the *kalon* overlaps with, but is distinguished from, the *agathon* (the good). Broadly speaking, the *kalon* is used to refer to those things which bring honor, which are splendid, difficult to obtain, and often, good as ends in themselves. The "good" (*agathon*) is used to refer to a much wider range of things, including, on the one hand, ugly necessities or things good only as means, and on the other hand, good things whose attainment is not rare. The good is not necessarily noble; e.g., a visit to the dentist, on the one hand, and physical pleasure on the other. The noble is not necessarily good; e.g., victory in battle. (Cf. 663b, 966a.)

The noble (*kalon*) is also to be distinguished from the "true," and the "correct" or "right" (cf. 667b). All these distinctions have significance even in the brief responses of the interlocutors. Subtle but most revealing differences in reactions to what has been said are conveyed in the variety of positive responses, and these differing reactions reveal both the nature of the argument and the characters of the participants. To say what is "good" or helpful may not be to say what is "fine" or beautiful. Seth Benardete's careful investigation of the use of the terms "correct" (or "right," *orthōs*), "true" (*alēthē*), and "fine" (*kalōs*) in responses given by Platonic characters has resulted in the following tentative conclusions:

1. *"kalōs:* a signal that a difficulty has been got around and that the way of the argument has now been made easier . . . often it implies that some simplification (warranted or not) has been made."

2. *"orthōs:* something is defined as a single whole and strictly separated and opposed to everything else; a statement involves a negation of what was previously claimed—a 'correction' . . . the central notion is discrimination and exclusion: nothing else but such and such is true. *Orthōs* is almost our 'you have hit the nail on the head.' "

3. *"alēthē:* a mistake, an inadvertance, or lack of understanding is pointed to and now corrected—here it partly coincides with *orthōs*—a mistake is made; or more generally a dispute, difference, contradiction is noted."

Especially clear examples from the first few pages of the *Laws:* for #1, 626b, 627d, 636e; for #2, 634e, 640b; for #3, 627d, 628a. Of course, as Benardete emphasizes, "every context would have to be thoroughly analyzed before we could decide on the scope and accuracy of these tentative definitions." See " The Right, the True, and the Beautiful," *Glotta* 41 (1963): 54–62. As nearly as possible, *orthōs* will always be translated by "correct" and *alēthē* by "true."

8. The phrase, "it would not be unpleasant to pass the time" reproduces a phrase which plays an important role in the *Apology of Socrates* (33c and 41b).

9. The word is *politeia*, the same word which stands as the title of the dialogue we call *Republic*. It is conventionally translated as "constitution," but has an even weightier significance than this English word. *Politeia* includes what we mean by "constitution"—the fundamental law and institutional ordering—but it also means, as the scholiast here notes, "the one way of life of a whole *polis*." Keeping in mind what has been said in note 1, we may say that the *politeia* is the unifying principle of the laws or that it is the spirit of the laws. It will always be translated as "regime" or "political regime." Cf. Aristotle *Politics* 1278b 6–15, 1295b 1–2; Leo Strauss, *Natural Right and History* (Chicago: University of Chicago Press, 1953), pp. 135–39.

10. The cave-sanctuary to which the three old men are headed (but which they never reach, at least in the dialogue) is apparently the same as the one where Minos met with Zeus (*Minos* 319e). It was among the oldest and most important of all Greek religious sites. In this cave, probably on Mt. Ida, Zeus himself was reared and perhaps even born (his mother Rhea had to hide him from his father Kronos). Each year an orgiastic rite, with Corybantic dancers (the *Kuretes,* cf. 796b), was held near the cave to commemorate the birth. Cf. W. K. C. Guthrie, *The Greeks and Their Gods* (London: Methuen, 1950), pp. 40–53. Glenn Morrow, *Plato's Cretan City* (Princeton: Princeton University Press, 1969), pp. 27–28, has more extensive geographical details and Saunders's translation, p. 15, has a map showing the location.

11. Cypresses are associated with death and graves in antiquity (cf. Horace *Epodes* V; *Odes* II xiv).

12. The word is *phusis*, perhaps the most important term in Greek philosophy. *Phusis* will always be translated "nature," unless otherwise noted, and as nearly as possible all words with the same root (*phu*) will be rendered by some phrase which includes reference to "nature." On no other occasions will the English words "nature" or "naturally" be employed. The idea of nature is a discovery of pre-Socratic philosophy, adapted and transformed by Socrates and Plato (see Book Two, note 17). The primary meaning and the bearing of the idea on politics are well illustrated in the present passage. "Nature" means that which does not owe its existence and force to human belief, making, or custom. The natural is thus understood in contradistinction to the "conventional" and to "art" (*nomos* and *technē*, see notes 1 and 29), as something more comprehensive, more lasting, and more powerful than convention and art. The natural is the inescapable environment within which convention and art exist.

The fundamental question of classical political philosophy is whether there are some conventions (*nomoi*) which are natural, i.e., whose force is not due simply to arbitrary human invention. In modern philosophy this question undergoes a considerable transformation but does not lose its urgency. The crucial thematic discussion by Platonic characters will be found in Book Ten of the *Laws*, where additional distinctions between nature and chance, necessity, and divinity are outlined or adumbrated. Cf. Aristotle *Physics* Bks. I–II, and *Nicomachean Ethics* 1134b 17 ff.; Strauss, *Natural Right and History*, chap. 3.

13. Kleinias speaks as if the Athenian were very familiar with Thessaly, or had just come from Thessaly (cf. *Crito* 53d–54a, and note 2 above).

14. The scholiast here comments: "He is apologizing for the use of archery. It was blamed, as in the phrase 'miserable bowman' (*Iliad* XI 385), because archers don't fight at close quarters but strike from far away." (Cf. 706c.)

15. "Gymnastic" refers to bodily exercise and training in the nude. As England here remarks, the word "gymnastic" is "used with a jocular reference to the above mentioned gymnasia." It should be added that this jocular misapplication of the word gymnastic to training of the understanding or the soul is also the first indication of a problem which pervades the whole dialogue: the uncertain status and place of gymnastic, or training of the body, in relation to "music" (training of the soul, see note 50). The Greek word will consistently be rendered by "gymnastic."

16. As the scholiast remarks at this point, "Divine (*theios*) was a favorite Spartan epithet of praise." Cf. 629b, 630e (and England ad loc.), 642d, 666a, as well as *Meno* 99d and Aristotle *Nicomachean Ethics* 1145a 28 ff.

17. The word rendered "neighborhood" (*komē*) is ambiguous in Greek: it may mean either "village" or "quarter of a city."

18. The word is *kreittōn*. Its precise original meaning (not exactly "stronger," but rather "authoritatively superior," though not necessarily in a moral sense) has been clarified only recently. See Benveniste, pp. 357–67. The ambiguity which the Athenian plays on here and elsewhere is even more marked in the Greek, since the root of the Greek word for "self-restraint" or "continence" is the same as the root of this adjective. Cf. 626c, 690b, 714c, and *Republic* 338c ff. I will usually translate the word as "stronger."

19. The word is *aretē*. "Excellence" is perhaps a more strictly literal rendering, but the weight of tradition and the need to keep the word's moral significance in the foreground have led me to translate the word always by "virtue."

20. Tyrtaeus lived in the late seventh century B.C. and composed war elegies and exhortations as well as songs for choruses. Among the scattered fragments of his which survive is, fortunately, the song from which the Athenian takes his quotation here and below. The Athenian accurately quotes the first line of the song but in summarizing the list of goods in lines 2–9, he puts the reference to wealth first, whereas in the original it has only the fourth place. The goods mentioned, in the original order, are: stature and strength, speed, beauty, wealth, monarchy, persuasive speech, and fame. See J. M. Edmonds, ed. and trans., *Elegy and Iambus*, 2 vols. (London: Heineman, Loeb Library, 1931) 1: 74–7: "Tyrtaeus," #12.

21. The Greek idiom is opposite to the English in its use of "nature": the Athenian literally says, ". . . who was by nature Athenian but became a citizen of this fellow's people."

22. This is the first use of the word *eidos*, one of the two names (the other being *idea*) for those "much babbled about things" (*Phaedo* 100b), the Platonic "forms" or "ideas." Following Bloom (pp. 446, n. 1 and 448, n. 24) I shall always translate *eidos* as "form" and *idea* as "idea," unless otherwise noted.

23. These are lines 11 and 12 from the same song quoted earlier (see note 20). The next two lines are: "This is virtue, this is the best prize among human things/and the finest for a young man to win."

24. Theognis lived in the late sixth century B.C. and was probably from Attic Megara, not Sicilian. According to the scholiast, Plato was attacked by an ancient critic (Didymus) for deliberately misrepresenting the well-known fact of Theognis's Attic origin. Theognis wrote *Elegies*, many of them in the form of private admonitions to his friend or beloved, Cyrnus. The lines quoted here are lines 77–78 of Book I of the *Elegies*. In the lines immediately preceding and following these, Theognis emphasizes

how few men are trustworthy and hence how important secrecy and deception are, even with some of one's friends. Lines 935–38 and 1003–6 of the *Elegies* are copied or paraphrased from lines 37–42 and 13–16, respectively, of the poem of Tyrtaeus under discussion.

25. There is a lacuna here in the manuscripts, which have only "divine . . ." without any substantive. We are thus forced back on conjecture. Following England, I have preferred the conjecture of Badham to that of Des Places. The scholiast (and Stephanus) conjecture "regime" in the place of "man."

26. The word is *plutos*; it means both "wealth" and the God of wealth, Pluto, who was often represented as being blind.

27. I depart from Des Places's text and follow the manuscripts and Stobaeus here. Des Places follows Eusebius and Theodoret, who, like Stobaeus, also had manuscripts much older than ours. The reading they quote would be rendered: "Second is a moderate disposition of the soul accompanied by intelligence. . . ."

28. The word is *telos* (end). As in English "end," it may mean either termination (finish) or purpose (goal).

29. The word is *technē*, meaning art or craft, and more generally any kind of knowledge that is reducible to a teachable system, with a clear end and clear principles that can be applied universally to a given subject matter. To what extent all genuine knowledge is *technē* is a question that pervades the Platonic dialogues.

30. The Greek is *diamuthologountes paramuthia*; both the verbal participle and the object have as their root *muthos*, which means myth, tale, or persuasive story. Originally (in Homer) *muthos* and *logos* (rational discourse, argument, reason) are not clearly distinguished: both may mean simply speech in general. But in Plato they are distinguished and often opposed (cf. England ad 645b1). I have usually translated *muthos* as "myth" and sometimes as "tale," depending on the context. See H. Fournier, *Les Verbes "dire" en grec ancien* (Paris: Klincksieck, 1946), pp. 211–20. (Cf. 625b above.)

31. This *krupteia* was a practice which seems to have involved a systematic terrorism exercised over the enslaved Helot population. The details were kept secret, partly out of a sense of shame, for the cruelty brought opprobrium from other Greeks. See Plutarch *Lycurgus* xxviii, and below, Book Six, note 30.

32. This was apparently a solemn all-day dance festival that took place in midsummer. Athenaeus says there were three choruses of men—boys, adults, and old—who danced naked (*Deipnosophistae* XIV 630, XV 678).

33. The word is *thumos*, one of the most important psychological terms in Plato. *Thumos* means primarily anger or a proud spiritedness, but it is applied to a wide range of phenomena all of which seem to be rooted in a specific part of the soul, a part which cannot be reduced either to desire or to reason. The principal thematic treatment of *thumos* is in the *Republic*, especially Book IV, but there is good reason to believe that the parallelism Socrates draws between the city and the soul leads to a distoriton of the soul in the account given in that dialogue. Hence the more unobtrusive but pervasive reference to *thumos* in the *Laws* should be followed carefully and without preconceptions. The word will always be translated "spirit," "spiritedness," or "spirited anger" except where otherwise noted, and the English "spirit" will be used on no other occasions. Cf. Bloom, pp. 353–58, 375–79, 436, 449, n. 33; Strauss, *The City and Man*, pp. 110–12, 129, 138.

34. Miletus was an Ionian city on the coast of Asia Minor, north of Rhodes: in 405 B.C. an oligarchic revolt took place, instigated by the Spartan admiral Lysander (Plutarch *Lysander* viii; Kathleen Freeman, *Greek City-States* [London: MacDonald, 1950], pp. 165–66). Boeotia is a region bordering on Attica to the north. Its principal city was Thebes where, in the years immediately following the Peloponnesian War, an oligarchic political faction opposed to Sparta was gradually gaining the upper hand over the pro-Spartan oligarchic faction which had dominated Boeotia for many years (Paul Cloché, *Thebes de Béotie* [Paris: Desclée de Brouwer, n.d.], pp. 95–112). Thurii was a city on the coast of southern Italy, founded as a pan-Hellenic colony by Pericles. It was plagued by civil strife. Especially after the Athenian defeat in Sicily, it adopted Spartan customs and a pro-Spartan policy (Aristotle *Politics* 1307a 27, 1307b 6 [see Newman ad loci]; Freeman, pp. 23–36).

35. Literally, "belonging to Aphrodite" (*ta Aphrodisia*). I reluctantly render this ex-

pression as "sexual," although there is in fact no Greek equivalent to our barren term "sex." This English word in its present usage emerged only in the late nineteenth century, out of clinical discourse. Greeks spoke of what we now call "sex" by referring to gods—Eros and Aphrodite. Because of the broad and manifold significance Eros takes on in Plato, I have decided to translate references to "the erotic things" as literally as possible on each occasion. However, in the case of "the things of Aphrodite" such a policy seemed too awkward and not as necessary, since in the *Laws* at any rate the expression almost always refers to what we call "the sexual." There exists a precise English equivalent for *ta Aphrodisia* in the archaic word "venereal," but its current usage has of course become so debased as to make it unsuitable.

36. With Burnet and Post I follow the original readings of the best manuscripts here, departing from the text of Des Places.

37. Cf. *Iliad* XX 231 ff. For the Cretans' reputation as pederasts (a reputation that rivalled if it did not surpass that of the Spartans), see Athenaeus XIII 602; Aristotle *Politics* 1272a 24–26; Sextus Empiricus *Pyrrhonism* III 199; and D. G. Maxwell-Street, "Antipater's Eupalamus," *American Journal of Philology* 96 (1975): 13–15.

38. "Lacedaimon" was the official name for the city and land; "Sparta" applies only to the city and has more patriotic and poetic connotations. "Laconia" is another name for the region or territory.

39. The word is *sumposium*. Descriptions of such parties are to be found in Plato's (and Xenophon's) *Symposium*. There is evidence suggesting that drinking parties were not as completely unknown in Sparta as Megillus claims (cf. 674a–c with Critias, fragment # 6, from *Constitution of Lacedaimon*, translated in Rosamond Sprague, *The Older Sophists* [Columbia, S.C.: U. of S. Carolina Press, 1972], pp. 251–52).

40. "The Dionysia" was a festival in honor of Dionysus. Dionysus, or "Bacchus," was a Minoan deity; in classical times he was the god of wine and the focus of a cult which seems to have reentered Greece from Thrace and Phrygia some time after the rest of the Pantheon had been established in Greek belief. The worship of Dionysus was characterized by orgiastic rites in which women played an important role and in which phalluses were very conspicuous. There was supposed to be a traditional disapproval of the worship of Dionysus among the Greek men who from the beginning, it seems, were leery of the new god and cult. But by classical times Dionysus was firmly established in Greek belief. See Guthrie, *The Greeks and Their Gods*. In Athens there were four Dionysia—the Greater, the Anthesterian, the Lenaean, and the Rural. It was at the Rural, the Lenaean, and above all at the Greater that the dramatic contests took place and tragedy and comedy were performed. As a foreigner, Megillus would almost certainly have been at the Greater. In all these festivals there was much drinking and carousing, slaves and women celebrating along with citizen men. A feature perhaps common to other festivals as well as the Dionysia was a procession of carts welcoming the god Dionysus during which obscenities were shouted from the carts. See Arthur Pickard-Cambridge, *The Dramatic Festivals of Athens*, 2nd. ed. (Oxford: Clarendon Press, 1968), especially chaps. 1 and 2.

41. With England I follow here the text as quoted by Athenaeus at IV 155–56 (incorrectly cited in England's commentary). Our manuscripts have a reading that would be rendered ". . . and we wouldn't let him off just because he had the Dionysia as an excuse."

42. Tarentum was a city on the site of modern Taranto, on the coast of the instep of Italy. It was founded by *Partheniae*, persons from Sparta who were the bastard offspring of the illicit relations between Spartan women and Helot men. The city had a democratic regime after 475 B.C.

43. In Sparta there was no adequate provision for the education and discipline of women, who lived at home and did not partake in the common meals. The problem was compounded by the fact that the Spartan women could hold landed property, and were accustomed to receive very large dowries and inheritances (cf. 630e, 774c–e, 780d–781a, 806a). Moreover, homosexuality was condoned among the men. As a result, the dissoluteness of Spartan women, first reflected in Helen (wife of Menelaus, king of Sparta) was proverbial. Cf. Aristotle *Politics* 1269b 13 ff., and Euripides *Andromache* 595 ff.

44. All the peoples named are non-Greek; except for Carthage and Persia they were rather uncivilized.

45. Locri was a Dorian city in the toe of Italy, famed for the excellence of its oligarchic political institutions (cf. *Timaeus* 20a; Pindar *Olympian Odes* ix, x, xi; Demosthenes *Against Timocrates* 139). It was almost always a close ally and follower of Syracuse, and was never literally enslaved. Des Places and some other editors see a reference here to an assault on the Locrian citadel by Dionysus the Younger about 352 B.C. From this they claim to deduce the date before which the *Laws* could not have been written, and assume that Plato has the Athenian Stranger referring to an event that took place long after the death of Socrates. But as L. A. Post rightly observes, "the passage simply affords no *terminus post quem* at all, and the supposition that it does will not bear scrutiny." See his "The Preludes to Plato's *Laws*," *Transactions of the American Philological Association* 60 (1929): 5–24; and his review of Des Places's edition in *American Journal of Philology* 75 (1954): 201–6. As Post again remarks, "Plato uses the present tense, and the Cean parallel illustrates his meaning": the Athenian stranger is not referring to any particular event in the case of either Locri or Ceos, but only to their general condition of figurative "enslavement," Locri to Syracusan hegemony and Ceos to the Athenian empire. The laws of Ceos were also apparently famous for their rectitude (cf., e.g., Athenaeus XIII 610).

46. Here I follow Cornarius against the manuscripts, which read "wheat" instead of "cheese." The reference to cheese is a reference to a typical medical diet, as prescribed by a doctor. See England ad loc. and T. J. Saunders, "Notes on the *Laws* of Plato," University of London, Institute of Classical Studies, *Bulletin Supplement* XXVIII (1972): ad loc.

47. The word here and in the Athenian's reply is *paidagogeō*, and refers primarily to the care and instruction of children.

48. A chorus is a performing group that sings, dances, and recites (cf. 654b). There were many types of choral performance, including Hymns, Dirges, Nomoi, Paeans, Dithyrambs, Tragedies, Comedies, and Satyr plays. The last four were performed in competitions at the Dionysiac festivals; Paeans were songs to Apollo. Cf. note 40 above, as well as Book Three, 700b, and the discussion of that passage in A. E. Harvey, "The Classification of Greek Lyric Poetry," *Classical Quarterly* N.S., 5 (1955): 165–75.

49. The Phoenician Cadmus was the mythological founder of Thebes. He sowed the teeth of a dragon he had killed and from the teeth sprang up armed men. To kill most of them off he set them fighting one another; hence, probably, the proverbial expression "Cadmean victory," roughly equivalent to our "Pyrrhic victory." Cf. Saunders, "Notes on the *Laws* of Plato," ad loc.; and see below, Book Two, note 16.

50. The word is *mousikē* and has a wider meaning than the English "music." Especially as used by Plato, it can refer to the fine arts generally and the cultivation of taste: it may even embrace philosophy in some contexts. But any general term, like the bloodless word "culture," would not convey the strong connotation of song, or poetry sung to music, which is the core of the Greek word. I have therefore decided to render the term always by the English "music," despite the slight inaccuracy. The word "music" is most important in the *Laws*, as in the *Republic;* in both dialogues "music" undergoes a very complex scrutiny, and a development or transformation in its usage results. A consistent translation will help the reader share some of the perplexity a Greek reader would feel, and will allow him to think through for himself the meaning of this thematic development. Cf. Bloom, p. 449, n. 36.

51. The word is *proxenus;* this was a local person or family who looked after the interests of a foreign city and aided its citizens when they visited.

52. Epimenides, a historical figure, was a seer and doctor closely associated with the Cretan worship of Zeus. Many stories compounded of fact and legend circulated around him. A good brief account and list of sources can be found in George Grote, *History of Greece,* 10 vols. (London: John Murray, 1888), 2:456–59. It seems that Epimenides did in fact visit and "purify" Athens (see esp. Aristotle *Constitution of Athens* I), but the time referred to by Kleinias is off by about a century—"a remarkable example of carelessness as to chronology," in the words of Grote (p. 458, n. 3). Cf. Book Three, note 4.

53. The word for "the argument" is *logos;* it may also mean here "reason." The word for "calculation" (*logismos*) is closely related.

54. The language used here is identical to that used at the end of the "Myth of Er" in the *Republic* (621b). Plato sometimes has his characters speak of "saving" an account

(*logos*) in the sense of establishing its full validity and of "saving" a myth (*muthos*) in the sense of giving it full persuasive power in our lives. Cf. England ad loc. and *Theaetetus* 164a, 167d.

55. The word is *aidōs*. It can be used synonymously with the other Greek word for shame, *aischunē*, which the Athenian has used heretofore. But it has a more august connotation perhaps best conveyed by the English "awe" (or "reverence"). It will usually be translated "awe." *Aidōs* can have overtones of piety (cf. 671d), but, to say the least, the Athenian does not here emphasize the divine sources or supports for the awesome sense of shame (cf. Jacqueline DeRomilly, *La Crainte et l'angoisse dans le théatre d'éschyle* [Paris: Assoc. Guillaume Budé, 1958] pp. 112–14). According to Plutarch (*Cleomenes* ix), the Spartans had a temple dedicated to Fear: "And they honor Fear not as one of those demonic things they wish to ward off as harmful, but rather because they believe that it is fear which especially holds their regime together . . . for it has been well said, 'where there is fear, there is awe.' " Cf. also Thucydides II 11 and *Euthyphro* 12.

BOOK II

1. The word is *sumphonia*. "Consonance" will be used to translate this word, and "harmony" will be reserved for *harmonia*—though it should be noted that Greek music almost certainly lacked what is now termed harmony, chords, or counterpoint in the precise sense. A good general introduction to what is known about the technicalities of Greek music is Isobel Henderson, "Ancient Greek Music," in *New Oxford History of Music*, 11 vols. (London: Oxford University Press, 1960), 1: 336–403.

2. The phrase could also mean, "This consonance is virtue as a whole."

3. I follow Ast and England in deleting *tois theois* ("for the gods"), which appears in all our manuscripts but not in the passage as quoted by Clement of Alexandria, who had access to much older manuscripts. The meaning of the sentence is hardly affected.

4. The authoritative account of the Muses is in the opening lines of Hesiod's *Theogony*, which should be consulted. The Muses were the nine lesser goddesses who presided over and inspired the realm of music (*mousikē*, see Book One, note 50).

5. I depart from the Greek text of Des Places, as he himself does in his facing French translation. Cf. Saunders, "Notes on the Laws of Plato," ad loc.

6. Here I follow, with England, the emendation of Badham. The manuscript reading, accepted by Des Places, would make this part of the sentence read: "or he who is not fully able *to express correctly or to understand with his voice and body*, but who (etc.)." The difference in Greek orthography is very small, and could easily result from a mistake in copying.

7. The word is *hosion*. I have not been able to follow Bloom in translating it as "holy," partly because I doubt whether the notion "holiness," as it has entered English from the Judaeo-Christian tradition, is applicable to Greek piety (cf. Rudolph Otto, *The Idea of the Holy*, trans. John Harvey [London: Oxford University Press, 1972]). In this translation, *hosion* will usually be rendered by the English "pious." The thematic treatment of piety is to be found in the *Euthyphro*. The "pious" (*hosion*) is to be distinguished from the "sacred" (*hieron*: also the word for temple or sanctuary). Neither term allows of a simple definition; the difficulty is most apparent when one learns that *hosion* (pious) can sometimes mean "profane" (e.g., 857b, 878a). At the cost of some oversimplification it can be said that the "sacred" (*hieron*) is what is filled with the divine presence, what the gods reserve to themselves; the "pious" (*hosion*) is what they allocate to, or require of, humans. Hence a temple and the space around it, the place of the god, is called "sacred" (*hieron*) rather than "pious" (*hosion*); the rest of the city is "pious" or "profane" (*hosion*), but not "sacred" (*hieron*). A priest is "sacred" (*hieron*); a layman who has fulfilled all his obligations to the gods is "pious" (*hosion*). Generally speaking, everything that exists is "sacred" (*hieron*) until the gods have indicated that it is "profane" (*hosion*), or for the (pious) use of men. Cf. 899b: "Everything is full of gods." See H. Jeanmaire, "Le substantif *Hosia*," *Revue des études*

grecques 58 (1945): 66–89, especially 72–73; Emil Benveniste, "Profanus et profanere," *Collection Latomus* 45 (1960): 46–53; and *Indo-European Language*, pp. 445–69.

There is another word, *eusebeia*, which is used somewhat less frequently in the *Laws*, but which approaches even more closely in meaning to the English "piety." In Plato *eusebeia* and the *hosion* are closely related (cf. *Definitions* 412d and 415a with the *Euthyphro*). *Eusebeia* will be translated "piety" and "reverence" or "pious reverence."

8. Egyptian customs were generally renowned and venerated for their antiquity, but there is no independent substantiation of the characterization of Egyptian law given here. The substance and tone of the passage, including the irony, is reminiscent of Herodotus's treatment of Egypt.

9. The text, from "it is possible . . ." is corrupt, and the original reading uncertain. With England I delete *tharrounta*, but I cannot follow the rest of his bold emendation. Des Places retains the manuscript reading without any explanation, and his facing translation bears but a tenuous relation to the Greek.

10. One of the manuscripts of Eusebius reads (in a correction by the original hand) "divine *man*" (*anēr*).

11. The most important Egyptian goddess; her worship was gradually spreading through the Hellenic world in the fourth century.

12. The *kithara* was a harp-like instrument, usually having eight to ten strings stretched on a u-shaped wooden frame with a tortoise-shell sounding board. It was plucked and strummed; its playing was restricted mainly to professionals (*kitharists*) who performed in public.

The lyre was a smaller instrument with fewer strings; it was played mainly by amateurs and poetic reciters, but to gain instruction in the lyre one would go to a kitharist (cf. 812).

13. The meaning of the Greek sentence is ambiguous. Saunders may be right when he translates "To us, from among all the customs followed in every city all over the world today, this looks like the best," explaining in a footnote that the custom referred to is that of deferring to age. The various proposed emendations seem unjustified and do not really clarify the ambiguity.

14. The Greek here is obscure: I depart from Des Places and with Burnet adopt Winkelmann's economical emendation. It is possible that the reference to the ancient Greek law is a marginal note by a scribe that came to be wrongly copied as a part of Plato's text (so England suggests).

15. Here the Athenian begins to quote and paraphrase sections of the song of Tyrtaeus he quoted in Book One (see Book One, note 20). Once again the Athenian rearranges the order of goods: this time size and strength are correctly placed first, though Tyrtaeus's allusion to the Cyclops is dropped; the Athenian now puts wealth in second place, pushing speed back to third. Tyrtaeus mentions two goods, fame and speech, which are not explicitly mentioned at any point in the Athenian's paraphrase of the poem. On the other hand, the Athenian emphatically mentions health, and also becoming tyrant and doing whatever one desires; none of these goods are spoken of by the poet (cf. 631c).

Midas was the legendary king of Phrygia whose touch turned everything to gold. He and Cinyrus are also mentioned by Tyrtaeus, though the Athenian transposes the order, putting Cinyrus first and substituting Attic forms for Doric. This "correction" would seem justified: Cinyrus, a legendary king of Cyprus, deserves to be named first because, according to an ancient saying that has come down to us, "Midas was blessed; thrice-blessed was Cinyrus." See D. L. Page, ed. and trans., *Select Papyrii*, 5 vols. (London: Heinemann, Loeb Library, 1950), 3: 512–13.

16. Sidonia is another name for Phoenicia. The myth referred to is the tale of Cadmus (see Book One, note 49 above: it turns out that a good education is "Cadmean" after all). Cf. the reference to Phoenicia in the context of the "noble lie" in the *Republic* 414c.

17. The verb "to grow" (*phuō*) has the same root as the word for "nature" (*phusis*), and the original meaning of "nature" was probably "that which grows, by itself." Cf. Book One, note 12.

18. An epithet of Apollo, "the deliverer" or "healer" (cf. *Critias* 108c).

19. The word is *teletē*, a term applied to rites employed in mystery cults. Generally speaking, they were "a form of ritual whose chief function was not worship of gods

but the direct benefit of the participant": Ivan Linforth, "The Corybantic Rites in Plato," *University of California Publications in Classical Philology* 13 (1946): 155. These rites often involved ecstasy, orgiastic dancing, and a sense of the purifying presence of a god. The *teletae* were closely associated with Orpheus. Cf. Aristophanes *Frogs*, 1030; W. K. C. Guthrie, *Orpheus and Greek Religion* (London: Methuen, 1935), pp. 201–3; and note 23 below.

20. Here I depart from Des Places and, following England, accept Burnet's emendation and punctuation.

21. The Athenian plays on the fact that the words for "grazing" and "fellow grazers" have the same root as the word for "law" (*nomos*).

22. The word rendered "charm" here and in the following lines is *charis*. It means primarily "grace" or "charm" and connotes a kind of enjoyment more refined and more akin to the divine than ordinary pleasure (*hēdonē*). It also can mean gratitude and generosity. The "Graces" (*charites*, cf. 682a) were goddesses personifying grace, beauty, and gratitude. They presided over spring flowers and were the handmaids of Aphrodite (Athenaeus, XV 682); they lived just next to the Muses (Hesiod *Theogony* 64–65).

23. This legendary pre-Homeric singer form Thrace played the kithara (cf. 658b) and was able to charm anyone and anything—including trees and stones. He was supposed to be the founder or the chief priest of important mystery cults centered around the worship of Dionysus and the belief in an afterlife; yet he was also closely associated with Apollo (cf. e.g., Pindar *Pythian Odes* iv 177), and later Orphic cult literature tended toward a syncretistic assimilation of the two gods. Much religious and theogonic literature attributed to Orpheus circulated in classical times, but it is unclear to what extent this literature contained a systematic body of doctrine. See W. K. C. Guthrie, *Orpheus and Greek Religion*, and *The Greeks and Their Gods*, chap. 11; Ivan Linforth, *The Arts of Orpheus* (Berkeley: University of California Press, 1971). Plato refers to Orpheus and "Orphic" beliefs more often in the *Laws* than in any other dialogue (cf. 677d, 701b–c, 715e–716a, 782c, 829d–e; Otto Kern, ed., *Orphicorum Fragmenta* [Berlin: Weidmann, 1922], frag. 12). In the *Republic* 363c–366b, Adeimantus attacks Orphic beliefs as epitomizing an outlook which treats the gods as if they were bribable.

We do not possess the context of the present line fragment, but it has been conjectured that Orpheus was referring to adolescents who have just reached puberty. Chr. Augustus Lobeck, *Aglaophamus*, 3 vols. (Regimentii Prussorum: Borntrager, 1829), II x 1. See also Paul Tannery, "Orphica Fr. 221, 227, 228 Abel," *Revue de Philologie* 25 (1901): 313–14 and Robert Boehme, *Orpheus: Der Sanger und Seine Zeit* (Bern: Franche Verlag, 1970), p. 81, n. 5.

24. The *aulos* was a double reeded wind instrument bearing some resemblance to our modern oboe. Although traditionally translated as "flute," the aulos was in fact altogether unlike our modern flute.

25. Here I have simply transliterated a technical term of Greek music. Greek music was divided into a number of harmoniae or scales, each of which seems to have conveyed a certain mood appropriate only for certain kinds of expression. The "Dorian" was one of the oldest and most sober, and was well suited to the kithara; "Lydian" and Mixolydian" were less restrained and were suited to the aulos, with its wider range of sounds. "Phrygian" was perhaps the most unrestrained, but there was dispute about this even in antiquity. Cf. *Republic* 398d–399a; *Laches* 188d; Aristotle *Politics* 1342a 28–end; *Problems* XIX; Isobel Henderson, pp. 376 ff.

26. Here, unlike Des Places, I follow the readings of the manuscripts.

27. Ares is the god of war.

28. This much of the story is alluded to at the beginning of Euripides' *Cyclops*, but the rest is otherwise unknown. Hera is the wife of Zeus, and mother of Ares.

29. The Greek for "to be born" is *phuō* (see note 17 above).

30. Here I depart from Des Places and adopt L. A. Post's minor emendation: "Some Emendations of Plato's *Laws*," *Transactions of the American Philological Association* 61 (1930): 37.

31. England remarks here: "Bruns finds in this a direct contradiction of what was said about Carthaginian drunkenness at 637d. But surely it is just the drunken nation which would find such a regulation imperative in war time." Aristotle mentions that the Carthaginians refrain from drinking while on campaign (*Oeconomicus* 1344a 33).

BOOK III

1. The major manuscripts attribute this sentence to Kleinias. I adopt Immisch's attribution, accepted by most scholars (though not by Post); Burnet pointed out that this alteration solves a syntactical problem noted by the scholiast.

2. *Daedalus*, an Athenian, was the most famous inventor in Greek mythology: he is said to have invented carpentry and many tools, statues that walked (cf. *Meno* 97d), and wings for men. After being exiled from Athens he went to Crete and worked for Minos, creating the Labyrinth where the Minotaur lived and where the Athenian youths were sacrificed. But he also gave Ariadne the thread by which Theseus found his way through the Labyrinth and escaped, after slaying the Minotaur. As a result he was persecuted by Minos and eventually retaliated by bringing about the death of Minos. In *Alcibiades* I (121a) and *Euthyphro* (11c), Socrates claims to be descended from Daedalus. For *Orpheus*, see Book Two, note 23. *Palamedes* invented the alphabet (cf. *Apology* 41b; *Phaedrus* 261d). *Marsyas*, the fourth and central in the list of seven inventors, was a satyr who invented the first music for the aulos; he challenged Apollo to a musical duel, claiming that his new music was superior to the Apollonian. He lost and was flayed alive for his impudence (cf. *Minos* 318b and context; *Symposium* 215c). *Olympos* was the lover of Marsyas and invented certain melodies (cf. *Minos* 318b). *Amphion* was a son of Zeus by Antiope; he invented some music for the aulos and constructed the walls of Thebes, moving the stones by music.

3. This sentence as it stands in the manuscript is hardly intelligible. I accept Post's emendation ("Some Emendations of Plato's *Laws*," ad loc.). Des Places and England accept Burnet's, which is supported by a marginal note in one manuscript: "You do very well, Kleinias, to omit etc."

4. For Epimenides, the seventh inventor, see Book One, note 52. Hesiod (*Works and Days* 41) praises a diet of mallow and asphodel, saying that its advantages are unknown to corrupt kings and judges who take bribes. Epimenides apparently interpreted this as a covert indication of the ingredients for a drug that would abolish hunger, or the need to eat. He is said to have proceeded to invent and use such a drug. Cf. Plutarch *Banquet of the Seven Wise Men* 157d–158c.

5. The word is *dunasteia*, meaning arbitrary rule. Cf. 711c and *Republic* 473d, 499c (and Bloom ad loc.), 540d, 544d; Aristotle *Politics* 1292b; Raymond Weil, *L'Archéologie de Platon* (Paris: Klincksieck, 1959), pp. 68–69.

6. *Odyssey* IX 112–15; the speaker is Odysseus, who is telling the story of his encounter with the Cyclops. As Megillus's reply makes clear, the context in the *Odyssey* should be studied. Compare also Aristotle's use of the same passage in *Politics* 1252b–1253a, and Strabo's illuminating discussion of this section of the *Laws* (*Geography* XIII i 24–25).

7. The words translated "clan-rules" and "rule" are from *themis*, an early word for "justice" and "law." *Themis* was the law regulating a family-clan society, and was understood to be laid down by the gods themselves. *Dikē*, the more common term for "justice" in classical times, referred originally to the law regulating relations with those who do not belong to the clan. Both *Themis* and *Dikē* are sometimes personified as goddesses (e.g., below, 936e; cf. Hesiod *Theogony* 901–2). Cf. Benveniste, *Indo-European Language*, pp. 379–88.

8. The bird simile seems to be an echo of Homer. See Weil, p. 72.

9. *Iliad* XX 216–18; the speaker is Aeneas. The Athenian omits the first part of the sentence: "Zeus the cloud-gatherer first begat Dardanus . . . ." Homer makes no reference to a "first city," and does not call Ilium the "third city." "Ilium" is another name for Troy, and refers primarily to the citadel while "Troy" refers to the land of the Trojans as a whole. Dardania was a country north of Troy ruled by Anchises, the father of Aeneas.

10. This is one of the Homeric names for the Greeks.

11. Homer's *Odyssey* and Aeschylus's *Agamemnon* portray revolts against the authority of the absent warriors but do not indicate that the revolts were widespread. Thucydides (I xii 2) makes a vague reference to civil strife after the fall of Troy. Cf. Weil, pp. 82–83.

12. According to everything in history and legend that has come down to us, the Dorians were not said to be descended from the Achaeans. They were believed to have overrun Greece about eighty years after the Trojan War, plunging Greece into a kind of dark age that lasted for a number of generations. Cf. Thucydides I xii; Herodotus I 56 (and How and Wells, *Commentary*, ad loc.), VIII 73. The Athenian domesticates and legitimizes the Dorian invasions. Apart from the present passage, there seems to be no extant reference to the man named Dorieus (cf. Weil, pp. 84–85).

13. The phrase is from wrestling (cf. *Republic* 544b and the scholiast there).

14. The summer solstice; Megillus apparently refers to Helios, the sun god.

15. Most of the account that follows of the original three Dorian cities is unsupported, even contradicted, by the other testimony that has come down to us (except perhaps for *Eighth Letter* 354b–c). As England remarks at this point, "Plato is here continuing to some extent the *invention* of history" (italics in original). The "invention" is in general very favorable to Sparta and to the idea of a unification of the Peloponnesus under Spartan hegemony. In tone and to some extent in substance the "history" resembles that in Isocrates' *Archidamus* (17 ff.). A detailed historical commentary with numerous cross-references can be found in Weil, pp. 90 ff.

16. According to the scholiast on *Theaetetus* 181b, this was a proverbial expression referring to statues, altars, graves, and boundary stones. Cf. 843a, 913b.

17. The word is the privative of *nemesis*. See Book Four, note 20.

18. There is no indication in Homer that Troy relied on an Oriental empire (although cf. Diodorus Siculus II ii). The Athenian is silent about the kidnapping of Helen, the Homeric reason for the war.

19. This was the official title for the Persian emperor (cf. Weil, p. 100).

20. According to the *Iliad* (V 640–51), Heracles sacked Troy a generation prior to the Trojan War.

21. The Athenian now shifts from his initial account of the Dorian origins to another version more in line with the mythological tradition of the Dorians themselves. According to this tradition, the Dorians either allied themselves with or actually were the descendants of the hero Heracles. Heracles' line was descended from Perseus, who had originally controlled the Peloponnesus. Pelops, the grandfather of Agamemnon and Menelaus, had taken control of the Peloponnesus away from the descendants of Perseus sometime before the Trojan War. After the war, the descendants of Heracles returned and regained the hegemony of their ancestor Perseus. Cf. Thucydides I ix, xii; Herodotus VI 52, VII 204, VIII 131, IX 26; Weil, pp. 84, 101. As is indicated by what the Athenian says next, the tradition according to which the Dorians were the descendants of Heracles contradicts the story that the Dorians were the Achaeans who fought at Troy (cf. also *Menexenus* 239b).

22. Hippolytus was the son of Theseus by the Amazon Hippolyta. After Hippolyta died, Theseus married Phaedra, daughter of Minos. According to the myth as presented in Euripides' *Hippolytus* (q.v.), Aphrodite was angry at Hippolytus because he was unerotic and honored the chaste goddess Artemis. So she made Phaedra fall in love with her stepson while her husband was away from home. When Hippolytus repulsed her, Phaedra committed suicide and left behind a note accusing Hippolytus of having raped her. In angry revenge, Theseus drove his son into exile and laid upon him a curse that led Poseidon to bring about his painful death. Theseus learned the truth from Artemis eventually, but too late to undo the harm.

23. Here I follow Burnet instead of Des Places. See England ad loc.

24. Here, and again at 715a, the Athenian refers to a poem of which we possess only a fragment (#169, Snell ed.). What we have goes as follows:

Law [*nomos*] is king of all
Of mortals and immortals;
It pushes through and makes just the greatest violence,
With a high hand. I bring as evidence
The deeds of Heracles, when the cattle of Geryon
Into the Cyclopian courtyard of Eurystheus
Were driven by him, without permission or purchase.

The same passage is quoted approvingly by Callicles (*Gorgias* 484b) and the poem was famous in antiquity, especially among the sophists (cf. *Protagoras* 337d). The interpretation has long been disputed. The sophists, Plato's Callicles, the Athenian stranger, and Herodotus (III 38), all seem to take Pindar to be indicating the moral arbitrariness and brute force of law or convention as well as nature. Later, especially among the Stoics, it seems, Pindar was understood to be referring to a higher law which makes some violence legitimate. See Plutarch *To an Uneducated Prince* 780c (cf. Montesquieu, *Spirit of the Laws* I i note a). Modern scholars tend to doubt the older line of interpretation, even though it was based on familiarity with the complete poem and with all the other works of Pindar that have since disappeared, on the grounds that "we can hardly credit the pious Pindar with this shocking opinion": E. R. Dodds, *Plato's Gorgias* (Oxford: Clarendon Press, 1959) ad 484b1–3. A history of interpretations is to be found in Marcello Gigante, *Nomos Basileus* (Naples: Glaux, 1956), especially pp. 76–102, 146–57, 257–60.

25. *Works and Days* 40; in the context, Hesiod is attacking kings who are corrupted by gifts; the same sentence contains the remark about diet alluded to earlier (cf. note 4).

26. The evidence available to us in no way indicates that Argos and Messene underwent such a development; in fact, it suggests the problem was that the kings were too weak and unassertive (cf. Weil, pp. 111–12; but see *Eighth Letter* 354b).

27. The word used here has the same root as "nature."

28. Herodotus (VI 52) reports the Spartan tradition rather differently: nothing is said of a god bringing about the birth of twins; instead, when the Spartans were in a quandary as to which of the twins should inherit the throne they asked the Delphic Oracle for advice and were told by the Oracle to create a dual kingship. Herodotus adds that the two kings feuded constantly, as did all their descendants (cf. Aristotle *Politics* 1271a–b). Throughout, the Athenian diminishes the role of the Delphic Oracle (cf. 686a).

29. The Athenian makes no mention here of Lycurgus or of the help Lycurgus was supposed to have received from Apollo by way of the Delphic Oracle. Contrast 624a; *Eighth Letter* 354b; Plutarch *Lycurgus* v (commenting on the present passage); Herodotus I 65. Cf. 696b.

Contrary to what the Athenian suggests, the power of the kings seems to have been much less than that of either the elders or the Ephors (Herodotus VI 56–58; Thucydides I xx).

30. The phrase recalls the third libation always offered to Zeus the Savior at banquets (cf. England ad loc. and Weil, p. 115).

31. Lycurgus was often credited with creating the Ephorate as well as the Council of Elders (see the references in note 29). The Ephors were five officials chosen annually who exercised very wide powers, especially in domestic affairs (cf. Aristotle *Politics* 1270b ff.).

32. The father of Eurysthenes and Procles.

33. According to Herodotus (VI 106) the Spartans delayed not because of any war with Messene but because of pious scruples against marching on certain days of the month (cf. 698e).

34. According to Herodotus (VII 148) the Argives claimed that they had been advised by the Delphic Oracle to remain neutral.

35. This is an embellished portrait of Cyrus's Persia (cf. Weil, pp. 123–24). In general, the Athenian's presentation of Persia bears some resemblance to that of Xenophon in his fictional *Education of Cyrus*.

36. This depiction of the ruin of the empire through Cambyses' corruption is quite different from the picture given in Herodotus III. Cf. also *Menexenus* 239e and Weil, p. 134.

37. This noble protrayal of Darius resembles that in *Seventh Letter* 332b and *Phaedrus* 258b–c, but seems at a tension with 698e and *Menexenus* 239e–240a. See Herodotus III for a more mixed picture.

38. This discussion of Xerxes' education is supported by no other sources and seems to contradict 698e. Contrast Herodotus VII. The notion that the empire under Xerxes ceased to be strong seems contradicted by 685c.

39. This division into four classes was the work of Solon (cf. Aristotle *Constitution of Athens* VII). The Athenian ignores the changes and revolutions that had taken place

prior to the time of the Persian Wars and that continued during those wars (cf. Weil, pp. 144, 147).

40. The account of the Persian Wars given here corresponds fairly closely to the facts as they have come down to us. Cf. especially Herodotus VI 94 ff. and Weil, pp. 147 ff. The major differences are that the Athenian emphasizes much more the fear felt by the Athenians and omits to mention the assistance they received through the battles of Thermopylae and Artemisium (cf. 707c).

41. The Athenian ignores the substantial aid furnished by Plataea, partly at Spartan urging. Plataea was later brutally destroyed by Sparta, in the Peloponnesian War.

42. The Athenian does not make precise the fact that the Delphic Oracle is said to have helped the Athenians in deciding what to do (Herodotus VII 142), and he does not make it explicit that he is referring to the great naval battle of Salamis (cf. 707b–c).

43. The Greek here is obscure, and I follow Post ("Some Emendations of Plato's Laws," ad loc.) in supposing a lacuna. A variety of emendations have been proposed. Des Places and England accept the Greek as it stands, although Des Places does not translate it literally. The Greek as we have it would read "If fear had not seized the coward at that time he would never have banded together, etc."

44. According to Hesiod (Theogony 131 ff., 207–10, 450 ff., 629 ff.) the Titans were the gods who ruled before Zeus and the Olympians. They were the children of Heaven (Ouranos) and Earth (Gaia), and the Cyclopes were their brothers. They were called "Titans" because of the crime they committed against their father: led by Kronos, the youngest, they castrated and dethroned him. They were overthrown in the revolt of Kronos's children, the Olympians led by Zeus.

45. The phrase appears in comedy. See Aristophanes Clouds 1274.

46. This is perhaps a proverbial expression (cf. Phaedrus 242b).

BOOK IV

1. A little over nine miles. Plato leaves the exact location within Crete vague. Saunders's translation has a map (p. 15) showing the probable region, based on the speculations of Morrow (pp. 31, 95).

2. The phrase seems to be from a poem of Alcman's which has not survived. See Edmonds, Lyra Graeca 1: 108–9.

3. Here the Athenian may be alluding to or quoting phrases from poems no longer available to us.

4. Iliad XIV 96–102. The Athenian makes two significant changes in the Homeric text: in line 98 Homer wrote "even though they have already achieved a victory" instead of "even though they have long wished for this"; and at the end of the last line (102) Homer has "O leader of the hosts" instead of "you're proclaiming." For a discussion of the import of these changes, see Seth Benardete, "Some Misquotations of Homer in Plato," Phronesis 8 (1963), 175. One should also consider what Homer's Odyssey indicates about Odysseus's attitude toward the sea and marine fighting.

5. In the battle of Marathon (490 B.C.), the first great battle of the Persian Wars, the Athenians under Miltiades defeated the Persians under Datis. In the battle of Plataea (479 B.C.), the last great battle, an allied Greek army under the Spartan Pausanias defeated the Persians under Mardonius, and ended the Persian invasion of Greece. Near the promontory of Artemisium in August, 480 B.C., the Greek fleet, mainly Athenian, held the Persian fleet for three days while the Persian army was being held at nearby Thermopylae by a small number of Spartans. When the Spartans were outflanked and overrun, the Greek fleet retreated to the straits of Salamis. There, in September of the same year, they decisively defeated the Persian fleet and gained command of the sea.

By failing to mention the famous land battle of Thermopylae while he does mention and praise the related and simultaneous sea fight off Artemisium, the Athenian seems to indicate that he regards the sea battle as more important from the point of view of ultimate victory in the Persian Wars.

6. Gortyn was the second most important Cretan city after Knossos, and the two were frequent rivals. Gortyn was situated in the south-central part of the island, not far from the region where the city in the *Laws* would probably have been situated (see Note 1 above). The older, Peloponnesian, Gortyn was a city in Arcadia, not Argos: Kleinias falsely links the Cretan Gortyn to Argos.

7. The word translated "grow" here does *not* have the same root as the word for "nature."

8. The word translated as "all-powerful rulers" here and below is derived from the word "dynasty" (see Book Three, note 5).

9. For Nestor, see especially *Iliad* I 247 ff., IV 301 ff., IX 52 ff., 96 ff., 163 ff., XI 670 ff., XXIII 306 ff., 626 ff.; *Odyssey* III. Nestor is not remarkable for his effectiveness.

10. This sentence is like that of *Republic* 499b–c, though with fascinating differences.

11. Similarly, this phrase recalls ibid., 473c–d.

12. Here I follow England's punctuation and suggested rendering. On this rare occasion Des Places's apparatus is inadequate. He fails to indicate that all the manuscripts give Kleinias's line to the Athenian (in which case it might be translated, "Isn't that the way we must proceed?"), and give to Kleinias the words, "By all means." Des Places assigns the same words to each speaker as England, but unlike England he punctuates Kleinias's line as a declarative sentence ("This, then, is the way we must proceed."). Cf. England ad loc.

13. See Book Three, note 44, and Book One, note 10. The major myths regarding Kronos manifest a certain ambivalence. On the one hand Kronos came to power through a hideous crime, and attempted to devour all his own children because he feared the punishment that had been prophesied (namely, that he would be overthrown by a child of his, just as he had overthrown his father: Zeus lived to fulfill the prophecy). On the other hand, the age of Kronos was frequently held to have been a golden age for all except the children of Kronos.

14. See Book Three, note 24.

15. The scholiast says here: 'The ancient saying to which he refers is Orphic, and goes as follows: 'Zeus is the original cause, Zeus is the middle, from Zeus all things are created, Zeus is the foundation of earth and of the starry heaven.' " Cf. Des Places's note ad loc.

16. A version of this saying appears in the *Odyssey* (XVII 218), though, to say the least, without the qualification about "measure": the same line is quoted in *Lysis* 214a.

17. The Athenian refers here to the famous saying of Protagoras, "Man (*anthrōpos*) is the measure of all things, of the things that are, how they are, and of the things that are not, how they are not" (*Theaetetus* 152a; cf. *Cratylus* 385e–386a).

18. Here, unlike Des Places, I retain the reading of all the manuscripts and reject Ritter's emendation.

19. The Olympians were the twelve preeminent gods who dwelled on Mount Olympus and in the heavens: Zeus, Hera, Poseidon, Demeter, Apollo, Artemis, Ares, Aphrodite, Hermes, Athena, Hephaestus, and Hestia (or sometimes Dionysus, in place of Hestia).

The gods of the underworld dwelled beneath the earth, ruling over the spirits of the dead and insuring the fertility of the soil (and therefore wealth). Their names and worship were more closely tied to local traditions than was the case with the Olympians, and hence varied from one place to another. The chief of the infernal dieties was Pluto (also known as Hades or as the Underworld Zeus).

"Demon" was a rather loose term covering a variety of semi-divine or superhuman beings and forces, often worshipped only in a restricted locality; the original and primary meaning may have been the personified fate or allotment of each human (cf. 732c). Socrates calls his special sign a demon or a demonic thing.

Heroes were legendary individuals, women as well as men, thought to have been descended from the union of a god and a human or believed to have been elevated to semi-divine status as a reward for their exploits. Each one was usually worshipped only within a restricted local area.

The souls of dead ancestors were generally regarded as capable of exercising influence among the living, for good or for evil. A good introduction to Greek beliefs about the gods is W. K. C. Guthrie's *The Greeks and Their Gods*, though it should be supplemented by Fustel de Coulanges's *Ancient City*.

20. *Nemesis* is a word for anger and righteous indignation. Starting with Hesiod, *nemesis* is often personified as a goddess; she is frequently mentioned in conjunction with *Dikē*, retributive justice. Homer does not treat *nemesis* as personified or divine. See Laroche, *Histoire de la racine NEM- en grec ancien*, chap. 3.

21. Here I follow Ast and England. The manuscripts and the other editors, including Des Places, do not assign this question to Kleinias but include it as a rhetorical question in the uninterrupted speech of the Athenian.

22. *Works and Days* 287–92. In the last line, by changing one word, the Athenian introduces "to endure," which is not in Hesiod. The immediately preceding lines, which the Athenian paraphrases and alters, are:

Vice can be had in abundance and
Easily; the path is smooth and lies very near.

In the lines that immediately follow Hesiod says:

This man is wholly best: he who understands all things by himself,
By pondering what will be better later and in the end;
Good also is that man who hearkens to one who speaks well.
But the one who neither understands by himself nor listens to another,
And takes to heart what he hears, that man is utterly worthless.

The lines quoted here in the *Laws* are also quoted in *Republic* 364c and *Protagoras* 340d. Kleinias's reply here and again at 722a is in meter.

23. There seems to be no other extant reference to the "tripod of the Muses." Tripods were associated with the Delphic Oracle, whose priestesses delivered their oracles while seated on a tripod. Apparently the phrase "to speak from the tripod" was used proverbially to signify "to speak authoritatively." Cf. Euripides *Ion* 91, *Orestes* 164; Aristophanes *Knights* 1016; Athenaeus II 37 ff.

24. The word is *paramuthion*. See Book One, note 30.

25. In place of the word "compulsion" all the manuscripts read "battle." Almost every editor has found the manuscript reading unacceptable. With Des Places and England I adopt Ast's suggestion. England remarks, "the only defense of the ms. reading that seems possible is the assumption that [the phrase] is a poetical quotation."

26. The Greek word for law, *nomos*, was also the word for a form of poetry, a song sung by a chorus or by soloists to the accompaniment of the kithara. Cf. 700b.

27. Here I depart from Des Places's text and adopt Post's small but illuminating emendation ("Some Emendations of Plato's *Laws*," p. 40).

BOOK V

1. The word translated "scheme" is literally "rhythm" (*ruthmos*).

2. The word is *hagios*; its meaning is closely related to *hieros* (see Book Two, note 7). Both mean "sacred," but whereas *hieros* carries a positive connotation, referring to the divine presence or to man's dedication to the divine, *hagios* has a more negative connotation and indicates the forbidden character of the divine, the sanctioned limits with which man must not tamper. *Hagios* will be translated "hallowed." Cf. Benveniste, *Indo-European Language*, pp. 465–69.

3. Literally, "ungymnastic."

4. Literally, "form" (*eidos*).

5. Here I depart from Des Places and follow Ficinus. See Post, "Some Emendations of Plato's *Laws*," ad loc.

6. Most editors, except for Des Places and Burnet, emend this sentence. Saunders ("Notes on the *Laws* of Plato," ad loc.) explains why emendation is incorrect, and I have construed the Greek as he suggests.

7. Here the Athenian alludes again to the musical double-entendre in the Greek words for "prelude" and "law" (*nomos*). Cf. Book Four, note 26.

8. In weaving cloth on a loom, the "warp" is the set of threads extended lengthwise, and usually wound tighter; the "woof" is the set of threads that crosses the warp at right angles and is woven under and over the warp to create the web of cloth.

9. Literally, "two forms" (*eidē*).

10. The word for "growing" has the same root as the word for "nature."

11. Here I follow Saunders's punctuation ("Notes on the *Laws* of Plato," ad loc.).

12. Here I follow England, and what is implied in Des Places's translation, but not what is printed in his Greek text. (Is the accent on *posous* a misprint, perhaps?)

13. 5040 is seven factorial (i.e., $1 \times 2 \times 3 \times 4 \times 5 \times 6 \times 7 = 5040$). The forty-nine ($7 \times 7$) divisors in addition to the first ten numerals are: 12, 14, 15, 16, 18, 20, 21, 24, 28, 30, 35, 36, 40, 42, 45, 48, 56, 60, 63, 70, 72, 80, 84, 90, 105, 112, 120, 126, 140, 144, 168, 180, 210, 240, 252, 280, 315, 336, 360, 420, 504, 560, 630, 720, 840, 1008, 1260, 1680, 2520. Twenty-eight of these are multiples of seven; twenty-one are not. Cf. above, 711a ff.

14. These are the three most famous Greek oracles. Delphi was the oracle of Apollo on the slopes of Mount Parnassus; it was the most authoritative. Dodona, the most ancient, was an oracle of Zeus in Epirus; it was revered by Achilles and Odysseus (*Iliad* XVI 233 ff.; *Odyssey* XIV 327 ff., XIX 296 ff.). Ammon was an oracle of the Egyptian god Ammon, located at the oasis of Siwa. Dodona and Ammon are linked by Herodotus (II 55 ff.).

15. Etruria was the land of the Etruscans, in the area of modern Tuscany in Italy; the Etruscans were famed for their religiosity. Cyprus was the traditional birthplace of Aphrodite and was the home of an important cult in her name.

16. "Draughts" is the usual translation for the Greek word *petteia*, a generic name for several board games whose precise rules are unknown to us. Most of them were probably games of skill akin to checkers. One game was apparently called "cities" (cf. *Republic* 422e) and had as its object the isolation and capture of enemy pieces (cf. Aristotle *Politics* 1253a). Another game had something called a "sacred line" on the board, which each player apparently tried to keep his pieces next to. Cf. R. G. Austin, "Greek Board-Games," *Antiquity* 14 (1940):257–71. Plato's Socrates frequently uses *petteia* as a metaphor for dialectic. Cf. also *Minos* 316c.

17. The same proverb is cited by Socrates in the *Republic* (424a; cf. 449c and Euripides *Orestes* 725). Cf. 818b.

18. Here, unlike Des Places, I adhere to the major manuscripts and do not accept Apelt's emendation.

19. The saying is found in a poem by Simonides, quoted in *Protagoras* 345d. The same saying is referred to below, at 818d–e.

20. The last phrase is elliptical: it may be a colloquial reference to prostitution, or may refer to a variety of questionable sorts of business.

21. Hestia was the goddess of the hearth, the sacred fire in every family home (cf. 740d). Her name was the same as the word for "hearth." The worship of Hestia and of the family fire was closely linked with the worship of the ancestors; but there was also a hearth-fire shared by the whole city and housed in a building called the *Prytaneum*. The city hearth seems to have been a kind of symbol of the unity of the many families, their hearths, and their various ancestral deities. Cf. Fustel de Coulanges, *The Ancient City* I iii; III ii 2, vi, ix 1.

BOOK VI

1. The word is *archē*: it means "rule," "office," or "magistracy," but also "beginning," "source," and "first or fundamental cause." The frequency and variety of its use throughout the *Laws* precludes the attempt to render it always by the same English word.

2. Literally, "two forms" (*eidē*). Cf. Book Five, note 4.

3. The Greek here is corrupt; I do not follow Des Places's emendation but instead adopt the ones accepted by most previous editors. Des Places's emendation translates, "those who are to do the selecting should be *the first* to be well educated etc." (Des Places's apparatus is not very complete here.)

4. The Greek idiom the Athenian uses for "unfinished" is "headless."

5. See Book Seven, note 7.

6. The word (*dokimasia*) refers to an inquiry into whether a candidate had paid his taxes, had performed his military service, possessed proof of citizenship, and was in good standing with his parents. See 759c and Aristotle *Constitution of Athens* XLV 3, LV 2.

7. See note 1 above.

8. A mina was a standard Greek unit of money, equal to one hundred silver drachmas. Its equivalent in modern money cannot be stated with any precision, but we do know that one mina was considered a reasonable ransom for a prisoner of war (Aristotle *Ethics* 1134b 31), and that thirty minas was considered a handsome dowry (Lysias *Orations* xvi 10). Plato and others offered to put up thirty minas as a fine to be paid on behalf of Socrates (*Apology of Socrates* 38b). Apparently a trousseau could be put together for between fifty and two hundred drachmas (below, 774d).

9. The word for "grow" has the same root as the word for "nature."

10. The word for "sound" means literally "to be of a whole allotment," and thus contributes to the irony of this passage.

11. The election formula for the interpreters is compressed, and the closer one looks, the more ambiguous or inscrutable the formula gets, despite a superficial appearance of terse precision. It reminds one of a Delphic Oracle: it certainly needs an interpreter. For a summary of the widely varying interpretations scholars have earnestly advanced, see Saunders, "Notes on the *Laws* of Plato," ad loc., and Morrow, pp. 419, 496–99. Characteristically, none of the commentators is alive to the Athenian's irony or wit.

12. Here, and at 760e and 762e, the Athenian leaves the number of Field Regulators ambiguous. The Greek here may mean either "each group of five is to choose twelve young men," or "each one of the five is to choose twelve young men." In the former case, there will be seventeen (five officers and twelve young men) in each contingent, and 204 all together (sixty officers and 144 men); this seems supported by the reference to "seventeen" (761e) but hard to reconcile with the reference to "each group of sixty" (761d). In the latter case, there will be sixty-five (five officers and sixty men) in each contingent, and 780 all together (sixty officers and 720 men); this reading seems numerically impossible for a city with only 5,040 households, unless, perhaps, young women share the duties equally with young men and every young person serves. As usual, the reader should consider the significance of the numbers involved, especially insofar as they are related to twelve, as well as seven and seventeen (cf. *Apology of Socrates* 33d–34e with Maimonides, *Guide for the Perplexed*, Bk. I, chaps. 7 and 17). For further arithmetical details, see Morrow, pp. 128–29, 186n.; Morris Davis, "How Many Agronomoi Are There in Plato's Laws?," *Classical Philology* 60 (1965): 28–29; see also L. A. Post, "Notes on Plato's *Laws*," *American Journal of Philology* 60 (1939): 94.

13. The word for "shrubbery" has the same root as the word for "nature."

14. The word is *athlētēs*; as England remarks, ad loc., it is here "rather unusually applied to competitors in musical contests as well as to those in gymnastic contests."

15. Here and in the rest of this paragraph, the word for "grow" has the same root as the word for "nature."

16. The word for "writing" is the same as the word for "painting."

17. The phrase "twilight of life" is ascribed to Empedocles (Aristotle *Poetics* 1457b 25–6).

18. The word is *anēr*. See Book One, note 3.

19. The Greek here is probably corrupt, though Des Places prints it as it stands in the manuscripts, without comment. I have adopted the punctuation and two small emendations suggested by England, *faut de mieux*. His lengthy discussion ad loc. describes the major alternative editorial suggestions.

20. Here I follow England, rather than Des Places, and adopt Apelt's emendation; instead of "pass in review" the manuscripts (and Des Places) have "praise." In Greek, the spelling of the two readings is almost the same.

21. 5038 (which equals 5040 minus 2) and 418 (which equals 5040 divided by 12, minus 2) and 33 (which equals 420 divided by 12, minus 2) are all multiples of eleven. The "other way" the number becomes "whole" is by adding nine, which produces a total that is divisible by seventeen.

22. I construe the Greek here as suggested in Wesley Thompson, "The Demes in Plato's *Laws*," *Eranos* 63 (1965):133–36.

23. The word for "grow" has the same root as the word for "nature."

24. The word is *paramuthia*. See Book One, note 30.

25. Hera, the wife of Zeus, was the patron goddess of marriage and (with Artemis or Eileithuia) presided over childbirth.

26. Once again we have here a play on the word law (*nomos*): the phrase in the text may also mean "the *songs* of the Muses of marriage." Cf. Book Four, note 26.

27. The word for "grow" has the same root as the word for "nature."

28. Here I adopt Cornarius's conjecture; the manuscripts, which Des Places follows, have "in place" (*en moira*) instead of "in the mother" (*en mētra*).

29. In the *Republic* (548a) this word is used pejoratively to describe the domestic life of citizens in a timocracy, the second-best regime. In the best, communist, regime, children are raised in public "pens" (cf. 460a).

30. The "Helots" were the descendants of the original inhabitants of Laconia and Messene whom the Spartans had reduced to serfdom. A similar serf class of the original inhabitants existed in Heraclea (located on the southern shore of the Black Sea) and in Thessaly. In all these places revolts seem to have been quite frequent. The Athenian politely refrains from mentioning the serf class in Crete (the "Minoans" or "Mnoans")—revolts among them were nonexistent or rare. See Strabo *Geography* XII iii 4 (incorrectly cited by England); Aristotle *Politics* 1269a 34 ff., 1272a 1–4, 19; Henri Wallon, *Histoire de l'esclavage dans l'antiquité*, 3 vols. (Paris: Hachette, 1879): I iii 6.

31. *Odyssey* XVII 322–23: the slave Eumaeus is speaking to Odysseus. The original has "virtue" where the Athenian stranger has "intelligence" (*nous*), and the Athenian uses a different verb for "to take away," to bring the line back into meter after the first change. Finally, the Athenian uses the plural "men" where the original has the singular.

32. These "Peridinoi" are not otherwise known.

33. See Book Three, note 5.

34. The poem is not otherwise known. "Bronze and iron" refers to soldiers' armor.

35. *Demeter* was the Olympian earth goddess, the goddess of corn and fertility. Her daughter had two names: as *Korē* she assisted her mother in presiding over the young plants, and as Persephone she was the wife of her brother Pluto (son of Demeter by Iasion) and presided with him over the underworld. The daughter spent each winter with Pluto. Demeter had a very important mystery cult at Eleusis (the "Eleusinian Mysteries"), supposedly founded by *Triptolemus*, son of the king of Eleusis. She had given to Triptolemus the gifts of corn and agriculture.

36. The Greek throughout this paragraph is rather obscure, and the manuscripts diverge. I have not followed Des Places, who accepts England's emendation and Burnet's punctuation, but have instead agreed with Stallbaum and Hermann in accepting the reading of a lesser but reliable manuscript. See also L. A. Post, "Notes on Plato's *Laws*," ad loc.

37. An epithet of Artemis, in her role as goddess of childbirth.

BOOK VII

1. There is a play here on the word *orthon*, which means both "correct" and "straight."

2. The word for "grow" has the same root as the word for "nature."

3. The *Corybantes* were demons who presided over and participated in ecstatic mystery-rites performed in Crete and Athens, as well as elsewhere. Plato's allusions here, in the *Phaedrus* (228b, 234d), and in the *Ion* (533d ff.), indicate a kinship between the Corybantic rites and the ecstatic rites surrounding Dionysus (Bacchus), but the scanty evidence we have does not indicate clearly which god or gods the Corybantes were principally associated with. At any rate, both Bacchic and Corybantic rites seem to have involved attempts at curing manic-depressive conditions by means of frenzied

dance to aulos music, supervised by priestesses. For a fuller discussion see Ivan Linforth, "The Corybantic Rites." Against Linforth I have with Diès adopted Bury's emendation. The textual problem is discussed by Saunders ("Notes on the Laws of Plato," ad loc.).

4. The word for "stoutness of soul" (*eupsuchia*) means primarily "courage," but its literal meaning is "good condition of soul." Cf. 830e.

5. I adopt here the punctuation of Bury.

6. The word for "growth" has the same root as the word for "nature."

7. Bows and arrows, javelins, and slings were the weapons of the lightly-armed auxiliary forces and the cavalry. The heavily-armed infantry used full armor, large body-shields, swords, and long spears (cf. 625d and 795b).

8. A kind of fighting contest that combined wrestling, bare-fisted boxing, and kicking. Unlike ordinary Greek wrestling, the object was not to throw the opponent but to make him admit defeat. See H. A. Harris, *Greek Athletes and Athletics* (London: Indiana University Press, 1964), pp. 102–9.

9. The word for "grow" has the same root as the word for "nature."

10. Geryon and Briareus were famous monsters: Geryon had a body composed of three human bodies, while Briareus had a hundred arms. Briareus is sometimes described as one of the Cyclopes.

11. See note 4 above.

12. *Antaeus* was a son of Poseidon who forced all strangers to wrestle with him to the death; he could not be beaten so long as he touched the earth. (Heracles killed him by holding him aloft and squeezing him to death.) *Cercyon*, another son of Poseidon with an identical notion of hospitality, introduced the use of the feet in wrestling; he was defeated and killed by Theseus. *Epeius* built the wooden horse at Troy and won the boxing contest at the games held in honor of Patroclus. *Amycus*, still another son of Poseidon, forced all strangers to box with him; he was defeated and killed by the Argonaut Pollux. He introduced the art of boxing with leather thongs wrapped around the fists.

13. Literally, "community."

14. The *Kuretes* were armed demons who attended and guarded the infant Zeus while he was being raised in the cave that the three interlocutors are walking toward. By their loud dancing, to the clash of weapons and cymbals, they veiled the infant god's cries and thus hid him from his father. A dance festival imitating them was performed each year near the cave (see Book One, note 10).

The *Dioscuri* were the "twin" brothers Castor and Pollux, the sons of Leda by Tyndareus and Zeus, respectively. They performed many feats: Castor was a great charioteer, Pollux a great boxer (see note 12 above). They were born in Laconia and were in many respects patron deities of Sparta. Their cult there apparently included festivals with armed dancing.

15. Athena. The word for "mistress" (*despoina*) is the feminine of the word for "master," "despot," or "absolute ruler" (*despotēs*).

16. The phrase could also mean "as they honor what is pleasing to the goddess," or "as they strive for the favor of the goddess," or "as they honor the gift of the goddess."

17. Cf. 633b–c above.

18. The word is *eispherō*. According to Xenophon's *Memorabilia* (I i 1) this is a verb that was used in the indictment of Socrates. Cf. John Burnet, *Plato's Euthyphro, Apology of Socrates, and Crito* (Oxford: Clarendon Press, 1924), ad *Apology* 24b 8.

19. The word for "grow" has the same root as the word for "nature."

20. According to Hesiod, the Fates (Clotho, Lachesis, and Atropos) are the children of Zeus and Themis (*Theogony* 904–6). The Fates are represented as spinning or weaving the destinies of individuals (see especially *Republic* 617c ff.). Cf. 960c–d.

21. See Book Four, note 26.

22. The word (*athumia*) is the privative of *thumos*.

23. See Book Four, note 26.

24. According to the scholiast, these were days set aside for pouring libations at tombs and avoiding business affairs.

25. Carian music was mournful, and usually accompanied by the aulos (cf. the scholiast here and Aristophanes *Frogs* 1302). The Carians were a non-Greek people inhabiting Asia Minor in the area now known as Muntesha.

26. Pluto was god of wealth and of the underworld. Cf. Book Four, note 19.

27. The Athenian here plays on the Greek words "keel" (*tropideion*) and "character-istic" (*tropos*).

28. *Odyssey* III 26–28. Athena, disguised as an old man (Mentor), speaks to the young Telemachus, urging him to overcome his reluctance to question the authoritative old Nestor.

29. According to Herodotus (IV 110 ff.) the Sarmatians were a people dwelling east of the Scythians, and descended from intermarriage between some Scythian men and a band of marauding Amazons who had just massacred a number of Greeks. It was a custom among these Sarmatians that no virgin could marry until she had killed an enemy in battle.

30. Athena, who was almost always depicted in arms.

31. The Athenian at this point switches from the second person singular to the plural, or from addressing the Supervisor of Education to addressing all the Guardians of the Laws.

32. Athenaeus (XIV 629–30) reports that "the Pyrrhic dance received its name from Pyrrichus, a Spartan . . . the dance shows by its warlike character that it originates in Sparta."

33. Here, unlike Diès and England, I follow the suggestion of W. R. Paton: "Notes on Plato's *Laws*," *The Classical Quarterly* 3 (1909): 111. As England admits, the manuscript sentence he accepts is "confused."

34. Once again the Athenian plays on the word *orthon* (see note 1 above).

35. Cf. Book Five, note 17. As England remarks, the way the Athenian speaks here may imply that Simonides was quoting what was already a proverbial expression.

36. Benedict Einarson argues for a much more complex rendering of this passage, based on the threefold division of even numbers discussed by Nicomachus. See "A New Edition of the Epinomis," *Classical Philology* 53 (1958): 97–98. This passage is also discussed in Athenaeus XV 670 ff.

37. "Commensurable magnitudes have to one another the ratio which a number has to a number" (Euclid X, proposition 5). On the subject of commensurability and incommensurability (or irrational numbers) see Euclid X; Plato *Theaetetus* 147d–148b, *Hippias Major* 303b–c; Thomas L. Heath, *A Manual of Greek Mathematics* (New York: Dover, 1963), pp. 54–55, 105–6, 180–81. According to the scholiast on Book Ten of Euclid, the Pythagoreans who first discovered incommensurability regarded the discovery as a dangerous one, whose publication would be an impious act punishable by the gods.

38. "Planets," from the verb *planaomai*, "to wander."

39. I follow England in adopting a manuscript reading different from that adopted by Diès. The reading Diès uses would translate: ". . . and I've often seen the sun and moon doing these things we all know they do all the time," although Diès's own translation is not faithful.

40. The word is *telos* (cf. Book One, note 28).

41. See the preceding note.

BOOK VIII

1. The phrase translated "better and more agreeable" is a customary formula used in consulting oracles. See Lobeck, *Aglaophamus* III, p. 1094.

2. In the Greek calendar the twelfth month was *Scirophorion* and corresponded roughly to the latter part of June and beginning of July. The month was considered sacred to Pluto, apparently because it marked the end of the spring growing season.

3. Thamyrus was a Thracian singer who challenged the Muses to a contest, and was deprived of memory for his arrogance (*Iliad* II 594–600). For Orpheus, see Book Two, note 23.

4. See Book Seven, note 8.

5. The word for "grow" has the same root as the word for "nature."

NOTES

6. I follow the manuscripts in giving this and the next reply to Kleinias; Diès follows Apelt and Wilamowitz in assigning the two responses to Megillus. Cf. Saunders, "Notes on the Laws of Plato," ad loc.

7. A stade is equal to 606.75 English feet.

8. The length of this race seems to have varied, but not to have exceeded twenty-four stades. See H. A. Harris, *Greek Athletes*, p. 73.

9. See Book Seven, note 8.

10. The father of Oedipus. He was supposed to have begun the practice of homosexuality: in one version, an oracle warned him that he would be killed by his own son and he therefore had to refrain from intercourse with his wife; in another, he became enamored of Pelops's son while a guest in Pelops's house and stole the boy away to Thebes (cf. Athenaeus XIII 602).

11. The manuscripts read "persuasive" instead of "unpersuasive." I follow Diès and England in adopting Badham's emendation, but Hermann has an almost equally attractive suggestion: he would suppose an "if" has been omitted and read ". . . his argument would probably be persuasive, even if not at all in consonance with your cities."

12. This word has the same root as the word for "nature."

13. *Thyestes* raped his own daughter (Pelopia) in the dark, without knowing who she was; she bore a son from the union, Aegisthus. Thyestes never killed himself and was on good terms with the son, though Pelopia eventually did kill herself after Aegisthus had grown to manhood and discovered who his father was (see Hyginus 88). There are lost plays by Sophocles and Euripides about Thyestes.

Oedipus, in ignorance of who his parents were, killed his father and married his own mother, who bore him several children. When the truth was discovered his mother killed herself and Oedipus put out his own eyes (see the *Oedipus* trilogy of Sophocles). In another version, Oedipus went on to kill himself (Hyginus 242).

Macareus killed himself after committing incest with his sister Conace, and she either killed herself or was killed by their father, Aeolus (see Hyginus 238, 242, 243 and Ovid *Heroides* XI).

14. The word for "grow" has the same root as the word for "nature."

15. *Iccus* was a winner of the pentathalon and became a famous trainer (cf. *Protagoras* 316d). *Crison* was a famous runner from Himera who was at the Olympics in 447 B.C. (cf. *Protagoras* 335e). *Astylus* of Crotona won races in three successive Olympics around 480 B.C.: Simonides wrote a poem to him, and he was a friend of the tyrant Hiero. *Diopompus* seems otherwise unknown.

16. According to Aristotle (*Politics* 1271a 27 ff., 1272a 13ff.), the common meals at Crete were supported out of common funds, while at Sparta each citizen had to pay a head-tax. Any Spartan who couldn't pay was excluded from the meals and lost his rights of citizenship. Aristotle is severely critical of the anti-democratic effects of this Spartan system.

17. Cf. 684d–e and 913b.

18. The word for "plants" has the same root as the word for "nature."

19. There is a "gap" here—the sentence is inconclusive and the penalty for leaving insufficient gaps is never stated.

20. The goddess is *Opōra*, the Harvest. The two gifts are apparently table grapes and wine grapes respectively. In what follows, "field" fruits seem to be those that are used for wine or are dried and stored, while "well-born" fruits seem to be those eaten fresh.

21. The word for "plant" has the same root as the word for "nature."

22. The word for "grow" has the same root as the word for "nature."

23. Here I adopt Paton's minor emendation ("Notes on Plato's *Laws*," ad loc.); the manuscript, followed by Diès, has a reading that might mean "on the twentieth of every third month."

BOOK IX

1. The word for "grow up" has the same root as the word for "nature."
2. The word for "blame" is *nemesis*. See Book Four, note 20.
3. According to the scholiast, this was a term applied to beans which were so dried and hard that they wouldn't soften when boiled over the fire.
4. The word is *paramuthoumenos*. See Book One, note 30.
5. This is not the same word for "gadfly" that Socrates uses in the *Apology*; both words are sometimes used metaphorically to mean "goad," or "frenzied excitement."
6. Cf. 767d.
7. Kleinias is not necessarily referring here to temple robbery; there was a common distinction in Greek law between robbery from the temple sanctuary itself and robbery of sacred funds, or from sacred places located outside the temple sanctuary. See Louis Gernet, *Platon: Lois, livre IX, traduction et commentaire* (Paris: Ernest Leroux, 1917), pp. 66, 88–89.
8. The Greek could also mean "about every regime."
9. The word "ugly" (*aischron*) also means "shameful," and is the antonym of *kalon* (see Book One, note 7).
10. The word for "according to legal custom" (*nomimon*) is a correction found in the margins of the manuscripts, whose original hands read "my [way]" (*emon*).
11. The word is *dunasteuō*: see Book Three, note 5.
12. Here, unlike Diès, I follow the manuscripts. See Saunders, "The Socratic Paradoxes in Plato's *Laws*," *Hermes* 96 (1968): 425–26.
13. Unlike Diès, who adopts Bury's emendation, I stay closer to the manuscripts and adopt Hermann's minor emendation. The Greek as it stands seems unintelligible.
14. Unlike Diès, I follow the manuscripts. In a footnote Diès erroneously asserts, "no one accepts that Plato could have written that"; Burnet accepts it, without even noting a difficulty. Cf. Leo Strauss's discussion of the line in *The Argument and the Action of Plato's Laws*, pp. 132–33.
15. In paraphrasing the ancient myths here, the Athenian uses archaic and poetic language (cf. Gernet, pp. 125–27).
16. The word for "forgiving" is *aidōs*. See Book One, note 55.
17. The best manuscript has "law" instead of "argument," corrected by a later hand to "argument."
18. Once again the Athenian plays on the word *nomos*. See Book Four, note 26.
19. Here the Athenian speaks as if the citizens were all kinsmen (cf. Gernet, pp. 142–43).
20. See note 16 above.
21. Unlike Diès, I follow England in adopting Cornarius's minor emendation: the meaning is hardly affected.
22. The word is *themis*. See Book Three, note 7.
23. See note 2 above.
24. See note 16 above.
25. Unlike Diès, I follow the manuscripts. See Saunders, "Notes on the *Laws* of Plato," ad loc.
26. The word is *paramuthion*. See Book One, note 30.

BOOK X

1. The word is *paramuthion*. See Book One, note 30.
2. I have tried to preserve the ambiguity of the Greek, which may mean either "no one who believes the gods exist as the laws say they do," or "no one who believes the gods exist according to what the laws say." The admonition begins, in the original, with the word "gods."

3. The word for "easily persuaded" is *euparamuthētos*. See Book One, note 30.

4. The last part of this sentence is ambiguous. It may mean "believe that they [i.e., the heavenly phenomena just mentioned] are gods."

5. Here and in the following exchanges the Athenian uses the second person plural.

6. The word for "how the gods came into being" is *theogonia*, the title of Hesiod's poem.

7. The word for "pronounce a defense" is *apologeomai*, and is the verbal form of the word used in the title of Plato's *Apology of Socrates*.

8. The words "that gods exist" may also mean "as if gods exist," or "on the assumption that gods exist."

9. The word for "without spiritedness" (*athumos*) also means "without hope," or "resigned."

10. See note 3 above.

11. The scholiast on one of the major manuscripts says he knows of another manuscript that reads "by nature, by chance, and through art."

12. The word for "plant" has the same root as the word for "nature."

13. The word for "assumptions" could also mean "enactments."

14. Literally, "young human beings." The Athenian uses *anēr* for the "men considered wise" and *anthrōpos* for the "young." See Book One, note 3.

15. I have tried to preserve the ambiguity of the word *idiotēs*, which may mean either "private man" or "prose writer." Cf. *Phaedrus* 248d and *Symposium* 178b.

16. See note 14 above.

17. Diès deletes "law's"; I follow the manuscripts and Einarson, in *Classical Philology* 52 (1957): 272–73.

18. The word for "especially" may also mean "in a different way."

19. The word for "motion" here and throughout may also mean "change."

20. "They possess one axis of support"—that is to say, gliding motion.

21. In this and the four preceding speeches, I have followed the attribution of Stallbaum and Burnet, rather than Diès and England, who have Kleinias introduce the example of even numbers. This strikes me as dramatically implausible, and is suggested only by the fact that the manuscripts indicate a change of speakers here, instead of after the "Yes" that immediately precedes.

22. The words between dashes translate a much disputed line in the Greek. Unlike Diès, I follow the major manuscripts with Burnet. See England ad loc. for a list of proposed emendations. In construing the text I have been helped by Burnet's remark on *orthōs* in his *Plato's Phaedo* (Oxford: Clarendon Press, 1963), ad 67b 4.

23. The word is *paidagogeō*. See Book One, note 47.

24. The phrase for "it is very likely" could also mean "there is a great hope."

25. According to Aristotle (*On the Soul* 411a 8), "Thales thought that all things are full of gods."

26. The word is *paramuthetēon*. See note 1 above.

27. The phrase "but more" comes from the texts of Eusebius and Theodoretus; it exists in none of our manuscripts and may be suspect, given the Christian source (so England suggests).

28. Here the Athenian shifts from the singular to the plural, and in what follows there is a blurring of the difference between the second and third heretical positions (cf. 901c–d).

29. *Works and Days* 304. Since work, idleness, and the difference between man and god in relation to work are Hesiod's central themes, the poem in its entirety should be considered here. According to Hesiod, the gods hate idleness in men but are themselves idle, for work derives from a curse god has put upon man. Work implies mortality and neediness.

30. Against Diès, England, Burnet, and Bury, I return to the reading of the major manuscripts. The editors adopt the reading of one lesser manuscript: "Is this the way you say these things are, or what?" The editors' confidence in this reading overlooks the shiftiness of the Athenian's ascription of speakers in this section.

31. Here the Athenian shifts back to addressing a single interlocutor (Cf. notes 28 and 30 above).

32. For "draughts" see Book Five, note 16.

33. Unlike Diès, I adopt Stallbaum's emendation. For "cold" (*empsuchron*) the manuscripts read "ensouled" (*empsuchon*).

34. *Odyssey* XIX 43: Odysseus speaks to Telemachus, referring to the light Athena, goddess of wisdom, brings to help him as he hides all the weapons of the suitors in preparing their violent punishment. In the line immediately preceding, Odysseus, who is disguised as an old stranger, orders Telemachus not to voice any questions about the light.

35. Unlike Diès, I follow Einarson in maintaining the reading of the manuscripts: see *Classical Philology* 52 (1957): 273, and Saunders, "Notes on the *Laws* of Plato," ad loc.

36. The manuscripts have "still more hallowed" with two suggestions indicated in the margins: "still fiercer" and "still more remote." Unlike Diès, who chooses the latter, I choose the former, whose spelling is closer to the manuscript reading.

37. Literally, "with a bad demon"; the word for "happiness" in Greek (*eudaimonia*) means, literally, "having a good demon" (cf. Book Four, note 19).

38. The Council of Elders (*Gerousia*) was an important Spartan institution. See 692a above.

39. The reading "perpetually" we owe to Stobaeus; our manuscripts have "perfectly."

40. The word for "plants" has the same root as the word for "nature."

41. *Iliad* IX 500. The phrase occurs in a long speech by Phoenix, Achilles' teacher, in which Phoenix beseeches Achilles to allow his righteous wrath to be assuaged by gifts, in imitation of the gods. As an authoritative statement of traditional Homeric piety on the question under discussion, the speech should be considered in its entirety. Phoenix seems to make a distinction between the gods' willingness to be appeased when men have done wrong to them and their lesser willingness to be appeased when men have wronged other men (compare lines 453 ff. with 493). This phrase is also discussed by Adeimantus in the *Republic* (364d–e).

42. A comic word (*sōphronisterion*) coined here by Plato, in response to the word "Think-Tank" (*phrontisterion*) coined by Aristophanes as the name for the dwelling place of Socrates and his disciples (see *The Clouds*).

BOOK XI

1. This is apparently a quotation from the legislation of Solon, the Athenian lawgiver. See Diogenes Laertius I 57.

2. Artemis—or Hecate, her underworld counterpart.

3. Epilepsy.

4. To appreciate the overtone of the next sentence after this one, the reader should be aware that the word for "currency" (*nomisma*) also means "legal custom."

5. A similar, or perhaps the same, proverb is referred to at *Phaedo* 89c and *Euthydemus* 297c.

6. There are six *obols* in a *drachma*.

7. In Aristophanes' *Clouds*, the first line of Socrates' first speech (l. 223) has Socrates addressing Strepsiades as "creature of a day." The plot of that play concerns an old father who seeks a philosopher's aid in restoring his family finances: the results are disastrous.

8. Referring to the famous Delphic inscription, "Know thyself."

9. The word is *paramuthia*. See Book One, note 30.

10. The word is *themis*. See Book Three, note 7.

11. See 767d.

12. Unlike Diès, I have with Burnet retained the reading of the manuscripts (cf. England ad loc.).

13. The word for "indignant" is the verbal form of *nemesis*. See Book Four, note 20.

14. The word for "obey" also means "believe."

NOTES

15. See note 9 above.

16. This phrase seems to echo part of a line in the *Iliad* (VI 47).

17. After *Oedipus's* incest was discovered (see Book Eight, note 13), his two sons/brothers cast him into exile; in return, Oedipus laid upon them the curse that they would die fighting one another for his inheritance, and the curse was fulfilled. See Sophocles *Oedipus at Colonus* 1370 ff.; Aeschylus *Seven Against Thebes* 709 ff.

Phoenix tells of his father's curse near the beginning of his long speech to Achilles (*Iliad* IX 448 ff.; cf. above, Book Ten, note 41). Amyntor was enamored of a concubine and dishonored his wife, Phoenix's mother; in obedience to her entreaties, Phoenix had intercourse with the concubine in order to win her affections away before his father could sleep with her and further shame his mother. Amyntor then laid upon him the curse that he should never have children of his own, and the curse was fulfilled.

For *Hippolytus* see Book Three, note 22.

In all three of these examples, the cursing father's moral claim is rather ambiguous, to say the least.

18. The word for "godsend" means literally "gift of Hermes."

19. This phrase seems to echo Pindar (*Olympian Odes* VII 18).

20. Unlike Diès, I have with Burnet retained the reading of the manuscripts.

21. Unlike Diès, I have with Burnet retained the reading of the manuscripts.

22. Plato uses here an unusual Doric variant for "moderation."

23. Here I depart from the punctuation of Diès and follow that suggested by Saunders ("Notes on the *Laws* of Plato," ad loc.).

24. The word for "grow" has the same root as the word for "nature."

BOOK XII

1. Herrṣ was the messenger of the gods and the god of speech, including rhetoric and dishc. est speech of all kinds. He was also the god of thievery.

2. The word translated "growth" also means "nature."

3. Unlike Diès, I retain the reading of the manuscript (cf. England ad loc.).

4. There seems to be no other extant identification of Justice as the daughter of Awe.

5. The adjective is from *nemesis*. See Book Four, note 20.

6. The story of Patroclus who died wearing Achilles' armor (given to Achilles by his father, Peleus) is a key feature of the *Iliad* (Books XVI ff.).

7. According to Ovid (*Metamorphoses* XII 171 ff.). Caenis was a beautiful virgin who was raped by Poseidon, who then offered to grant any wish she had; in order never to be raped again, she asked to be made a man, and Poseidon proceeded to make her an invincible warrior. As a man (Caenus), she fought as one of the Lapithae in the battle against the Centaurs. See also the scholiast here.

8. The word for "Auditor" (*euthuntēs*) means, literally, "straightener," and the Athenian plays on this double sense.

9. Unlike Diès, I follow the manuscripts and the interpretation of England (which Diès himself seems to follow in his facing translation, although in his Greek text he adopts an emendation of Bury).

10. This was a Spartan practice, whereby strangers were forbidden from coming to stay in Sparta (cf. Thucydides II 39 and Xenophon *Constitution of the Lacedaimonians* XIV 4).

11. These are the sites of the four major Panhellenic festivals and games.

12. The word for "guest" and also for "host" is *xenos*. See Book One, note 2.

13. The Athenian seems to refer here to Egyptian customs that prohibit strangers from attending sacrifices, with an allusion to Spartan practices as well (see note 10 above).

14. Here I follow Hermann's emendation. Diès follows the manuscripts, which have "naked *or with* an ungirded undershirt." See England ad loc.

15. The word the Athenian uses here (*eidolon*) is frequently applied by Homer to the dead soul.

16. The underworld gods are sometimes called the "other" gods (cf. *Phaedo* 63b and Aeschylus *Suppliant Maidens* 230–31).

17. For the phrase "third savior" see 692a and the note there.

18. The last phrase of this sentence, beginning with "being likened," is corrupt and unintelligible in the manuscripts. Proposed emendations abound, none of them entirely satisfactory. I have rather arbitrarily adopted Diès's text, which contains three alterations of the manuscript and seems as persuasive as any of the other suggestions. For the "third twist" (referring to a third twist of thread on a spool) the manuscripts have "the fire." Cf. England ad loc. and Saunders, "Notes on the *Laws* of Plato," ad loc.

The Athenian is making an etymological point which cannot be easily rendered into English. "Lachesis" means "Distributor of Lots" and has the same root as the word for "things fated"; "Clotho" means "Spinner" and has the same root as the word for "spun threads"; "Atropos" means "Unturnable" and has a root that is similar to the root of the word for "irreversibility." The Fates allot and spin the destinies of men: for a fuller account, see *Republic* 617 ff., esp. 620e. Cf. Book Seven, note 20.

19. The word translated "consider" is the verbal form of the word for "intelligence."

20. The word translated "ignorant" here and in what follows has the same root as the word for "intelligence."

21. Unlike Diès, I retain the reading of the best manuscripts. Diès adopts a marginal correction in the manuscripts which gives the order as: courage, moderation, justice, prudence.

22. Since it is not clear whether or not the Athenian refers here to the officials who are Interpreters, I have not capitalized the word. Cf. 809b, 966b.

23. Here, unlike Diès, I retain the reading of the manuscripts (cf. England ad loc.).

24. This sentence as it stands in the major manuscripts is probably corrupt, and various alterations have been proposed by the scholiast and the editors. I have followed Diès's text, but I take the meaning of the Greek to be somewhat different from what I gather (from his translation) he understands it to be. As I understand it, the Athenian is saying that if the knowledge sought for eludes the three of them, they'll have to contrive some other way (e.g., the nocturnal council) by which the future city will obtain it.

25. The last few words of this sentence are mutilated in the manuscripts. With Diès I follow Baiter's reconstruction, but Burnet has an equally plausible one: for "then it must be abandoned," he has "then this must be faced up to."

26. The word for "proof" (*pistis*) also means "belief."

27. Here, unlike Diès, I retain the reading of the manuscripts (cf. England ad loc.).

28. This is an allusion to the doctrine of Anaxagoras (cf. *Phaedo* 97b ff.).

29. In the *Republic* (607b–c) Socrates refers to similar poetic reviling of the philosophers, though he is far less forthcoming there in explaining the reason for the reviling. The poetry seems by its tone to be comic (cf. above, 935d ff.). In translating this sentence I have followed Malcom Schofield, in *Museum Helveticum* 38 (1971): 9.

30. Here, unlike Diès, I follow Burnet and England in retaining the reading of the manuscripts; for the translation I have been helped by Jowett's suggestion.

31. The Athenian's remarks here are reminiscent of *Seventh Letter* 341c–d.

32. This apparently means, "the odds are fifty-fifty," or "we must take our chances with the rest."

33. According to the scholiast, the expression is from dice throwing: three sixes was a sure winner and three ones a sure loser.

34. Here, unlike Diès, I follow the major manuscripts (see Einarson in *Classical Philology* 53 [1958]: 98, n. 2). Diès adopts the marginal correction in one manuscript, which would read "chosen" instead of "mixed." Cf. above, 951d.

Index of Names

Achaeans, 682d,e, 685e, 706d,e
Aegina, 707e
Agamemnon, 706d
Amazons, 806b
Ammon, 738c
Amphion, 677d
Amycus, 796a
Amyntor, 931b
Antaeus, 796a
Aphrodite (cf. Sex), 840e
Apollo (cf. Pythian; Muses; Delphi), 624a,
    632d, 653d, 654a, 662c, 664c, 665a*,
    672d, 686a, 766b, 796e, 833b, 936e,
    946a,c,d, 947a, 950e
Arcturus, 844e
Ares, 671e, 833b, 920d
Argos, 683c,d*, 690d, 692e, 707e, 708a
Aristodemus, 692b
Assyria, 685c
Athena, 745b, 848d, 920d*, 921c
Athens (cf. Attica), 626d, 629a, 634c, 638b,
    642b,c,e, 692e, 693e, 698c,d, 699a,
    753a
Athos, 699a
Atropos, 960c
Attica (cf. Athens), 626d, 698a, 706a

Boeotia, 636b
Briareus, 795c

Cadmus, 641c
Caenus, 944d
Cambyses, 694c, 695b,e*
Carian, 800e
Carthage, 637d, 674a
Cea, 638b
Celts, 637d
Cercyon, 796a
Cinyrus, 660e
Clotho, 960c
Corybantes, 790d
Crete, 625a,c, 626a,b, 631b, 634c,d, 636c,
    641e, 642c, 648a, 650b, 662b,c, 673b,
    674a, 680c, 683a, 693e, 702c, 704d,

705d, 707b,e, 708a, 751e, 752d,
    834b,d, 836b, 842b
Crison, 840a
Cyclops, 680b, 682a
Cyrnus, 630a
Cyrus, 694a,c, 695b,d*,e

Daedalus, 677d
Dardanos, 702a
Dardania, 681e
Darius, 694c, 695c*,d, 698c,e
Datis, 698c*,d
Delphi, Delphic Oracle (cf. Apollo;
    Muses; Pythian), 686a, 738c, 759c,d,
    828a, 856e, 865b, 914a
Dikē, see Justice
Dionysus, Bacchus, 637b*, 653d, 665a,b*,
    666b, 671a,e, 672a,b,d, 700b,d, 790e,
    812b, 815c, 844d,e
Diopompus, 840a
Dioscuri, 796b
Dorian, 670b, 682e, 684e, 685e, 702a
Dorieus, 682e

Earth, Mother Earth, 741c, 958e
Egypt (cf. Nile), 656d*, 660c, 747c, 799a,
    819b
Eileithuia, 784a
Eretria, 698c*,d*, 699a
Epeius, 796a
Epimenides, 642d, 677d
Etruria, Etruscans, 738c
Europe, 698b
Eurusthenes, 683d

Fates, 799b, 960c

Ganymede, 636c
Geryon, 795c
Gortyn, 708a*

*The asterisk indicates that the term appears more than once in the passage.

[539]

Index of Oaths

Index of Familiar Address

Index of Subjects

INDEX OF SUBJECTS

DATE DUE

10-26-11		